Time Out

Rome

timeout.com/rome

Time Out Guides Ltd
Universal House
251 Tottenham Court Road
London W1T 7AB
United Kingdom
Tel: +44 (0)20 7813 3000
Fax: +44 (0)20 7813 6001
Email: guides@timeout.com
www.timeout.com

Published by Time Out Guides Ltd, a wholly owned subsidiary of Time Out Group Ltd.
Time Out and the Time Out logo are trademarks of Time Out Group Ltd.

© Time Out Group Ltd 2011
Previous editions 1991, 1996, 1998, 1999, 2001, 2003, 2005, 2007

10 9 8 7 6 5 4 3 2 1

This edition first published in Great Britain in 2011 by Ebury Publishing.
A Random House Group Company
20 Vauxhall Bridge Road, London SW1V 2SA

Random House Australia Pty Ltd 20 Alfred Street, Milsons Point, Sydney, New South Wales 2061, Australia

Random House New Zealand Ltd 18 Poland Road, Glenfield, Auckland 10, New Zealand

Random House South Africa (Pty) Ltd Isle of Houghton, Corner Boundary Road & Carse O'Gowrie, Houghton 2198, South Africa

Random House UK Limited Reg. No. 954009

Distributed in the US and Latin America by Publishers Group West (1-510-809-3700)
Distributed in Canada by Publishers Group Canada (1-800-747-8147)

For further distribution details, see www.timeout.com.

ISBN: 978-1-84670-181-8

A CIP catalogue record for this book is available from the British Library.

Printed and bound by Firmengruppe APPL, aprinta druck, Wemding, Germany.

The Random House Group Limited supports The Forest Stewardship Council (FSC), the leading international forest certification organisation. All our titles that are printed on Greenpeace approved FSC certified paper carry the FSC logo. Our paper procurement policy can be found at www.randomhouse.co.uk/environment.

Time Out carbon-offsets its flights with Trees for Cities (www.treesforcities.org).

Contents

Introduction

Stand on the pavement outside the Colosseo metro station, and you'll experience some of Rome's deep dichotomies. Looming before you is one of the chief marvels of the ancient world: the Colosseum (*see p60*) in all its towering glory – a fantastic feat of engineering, a thing of grace and beauty, and the blueprint to this day for sports stadium design. Between you and it, however, are an indeterminate number of lanes of unruly, smelly traffic. And around the monument itself, there are quite likely to be roped-off areas to protect you from showers of crumbling masonry. Outside, a horde of characters in pantomime gladiator outfits vie to relieve you of your holiday cash by charging for posing in your photographs, while inside very little indeed has been spent on informative panels or elucidation of any kind. Yet 3.2 million people survive their road-crossing experience and pay to get inside the Colosseum each year, so dazzled by the extraordinary sight that they are prepared to forgive – momentarily at least – the city's shortfalls.

This is Rome: unique in its marvels and in its deficiencies; its monuments immeasurably stately, its galleries immensely rich and its services hopelessly inadequate; a city with a cultural heritage second to none that can only scrape together an annual budget of €500,000 for regular upkeep on the Colosseum – a monument that brings in €32.5 million each year in ticket sales (2008 figures). Here – as in much of Italy – there has to be a disaster (and thus disaster funds) before anything much gets done.

Undeterred by much official foot-dragging and considerable incompetence, Rome and her citizens continue, however, to put on a good show for the visitor. The backdrop – the city itself – is incomparable of course, which helps. The cultural offerings are not only exquisite but also expanding, with the opening of new galleries such as MAXXI (*see p41* **Profile**) and the new-look MACRO (*see p157*). The gastronomic and shopping opportunities are – so far – keeping their heads above the tidal wave of international retail chains and style-over-substance eateries. And the Romans continue to provide the ebullient street-life spectacle that they have been perfecting for millennia: pushy they may be, and abrupt verging on the rude, but when the sun shines, the city beckons and there's always a handy café for knocking back a drink with friends. Focus on the show, forgive and forget the inconveniences, and Rome will win your heart. *Anne Hanley, Editor*

Rome in Brief

IN CONTEXT

With its three millennia of history – and fine architecture and art to show what its citizens were up to during that time – Rome is truly unique. We chart the city's rich culture, explain how it bounced down from *caput mundi* to strife-plagued backwater and back up again, and wonder what it did in the 21st century to deserve a finance minister who can state dismissively 'people can't eat culture'.

▶ *For more, see pp15-50.*

SIGHTS

Michelangelo – tick. Bernini – tick. Caravaggio – tick. Raphael – tick. From galleries to churches, towering ancient ruins to grand *palazzi*, you could spend weeks exploring Rome's wonders and barely scratch the surface. We point you in the direction of the most awe-inspiring and the rewardingly humble... and remind you that just soaking in the grand spectacle of everyday life is a key part of the experience.

▶ *For more, see pp52-161.*

CONSUME

From Michelin-starred chefs to *mamma* in the kitchen, Rome has cuisine on every gastronomic level and in every price range. There's also a range of bars and cafés (more or less interchangeable terms here) for your every mood: great pavement tables to catch morning rays while surveying the locals, and cool evening *aperitivo* haunts. When the sights get too much, try some very modern retail therapy.

▶ *For more, see pp164-238.*

ARTS & ENTERTAINMENT

A turn-of-the-millennium upsurge in Rome's entertainment and nightlife scene has levelled off somewhat, but there's still plenty going on: the Auditorium-Parco della Musica is the fulcrum of Rome's performing arts, but there's plenty more on offer in theatres around the city. For the brightest lights on the clubbing scene, the southern districts of Testaccio and Ostiense are the places to head for.

▶ *For more, see pp241-284.*

ESCAPES & EXCURSIONS

Beyond Rome's ancient walls lies the *campagna romana*, once fêted by poets – though now rather built-over. Our selection of easily reachable sights and attractions steers you through the suburbs to beaches, gardens, archaeological sites in gorgeous settings and some truly lovely bits of Lazio countryside: the perfect antidote to Rome's relentless urbanity.

▶ *For more, see pp286-304.*

Rome in 48 hours

Day 1 Ancient Sites, Great Views

10AM You might want to fill your pockets from the breakfast buffet to keep you going through this tough day's immersion in all things ancient: there's a lot of ground to cover. It may seem clichéd, but the **Colosseum** (*see p60*) is a very good place to start. The newly opened top level has breathtaking views.

11AM The **Roman Forum & Palatine** are the next logical step for covering Rome's ancient ground. Enter at the via di San Gregorio gate: our itinerary (*see p62*) should help you to understand these difficult-to-read ruins. In any case, its sheer scale can't fail to impress.

1.30PM Unless you're fainting with fatigue or hunger, it's worth making the dash across piazza Venezia to catch the 1.30pm English-language tour of the remarkable digs – complete with digital reconstructions – beneath **Palazzo Valentini** (*see p58*; book ahead). Having seen the public domain earlier, this unique peek into the private realm is fascinating. Alternatively, collapse at a table at the **Enoteca Provincia Romana** (*see p187*) and enjoy food and wine from around Rome.

3.30PM Another superlative view awaits you back across piazza Venezia. The **Vittoriano** monument (*see p59*) may be unsightly but, from the top, you can see the whole of Rome and far, far, beyond. For the lift, access is through the entrance to the right of the monument as you look at it, or from the top of the steps leading up to the **Ara Coeli** church (*see p59*).

4.30PM If you can take any more, exit through the Ara Coeli to piazza del Campidoglio where the **Musei Capitolini** (*see p53*) – the first ever public museum – contain a jaw-dropping collection, from the ancient to the Renaissance and beyond. But as the sun dips, perhaps the most satisfying sight is the view back down the Forum from the windows of the Tabularium, the ancient record-office, which links the two halves of the museums. By which time, you'll be ready to limp home for a shower before dinner.

NAVIGATING THE CITY

Much of Rome's *centro storico* can be easily explored on foot. For slightly more distant destinations – Galleria Borghese, the Vatican, the Colosseum – buses are cheap, frequent and simple to use. Purchase a three- (€11) or seven-day (€16) transport pass (www.atac.roma.it).

PACKAGE DEALS

The Roma Pass (€25, www.romapass.it) is a three-day pass including buses and metro, free entrance to two sites (choose the pricier ones to make it worthwhile) and reduced entrance to many more.

A combined ticket for the four Museo Nazionale Romano museums (Palazzo Altemps, Palazzo Massimo alle Terme, Crypta Balbi, Terme di Diocleziano) costs €7 (€3.50 reductions) and is valid for three days. A combined ticket for Musei Capitolini and Centrale Montemartini costs €13 (€11) and is valid for seven days. There are also two themed passes, both

Day 2 Superb Art and Retail Therapy

10AM Make sure you've pre-booked your slot at the **Galleria Borghese** (*see p78*), the receptable of a jaw-dropping art collection, from Bernini's *Apollo and Daphne* to an array of works by Caravaggio.

NOON If the weather's fine – as it so often is – wander through the surrounding **Villa Borghese** park (*see p74*). For the super-fit there's a seven-kilometre jogging course. For a more relaxing approach, stroll for hours beneath the trees, hire a rowing boat on the little lake and visit the **Pincio** (*see p74*) balcony for an impossibly romantic panorama across to the dome of St Peter's. Wiggle down the hill to piazza del Popolo and on to plenty of lunch options: try **Buccone** (*see p188*), or – for an Italian take on vegetarian – **RistorArte Il Margutta** (*see p191*).

2PM You're deep in shopping territory now: all you have to do is select your style (and budget). Take **via del Corso** for high-street favourites, or meander through the cross-streets between via del Corso and via del Babuino/piazza di Spagna for all the big fashion names. You might like to detour off to the left to join the crowds on the **Spanish Steps** (*see p89*). Or continue on via del Corso to the **Galleria Doria Pamphilj** (*see p100*), for more Caravaggios, Beninis and a glimpse inside Roman aristocratic magnificence... hurry: it closes at five.

5PM In nearby piazza di Pietra, **La Caffettiera** (*see p213*) is a very urbane place for a pick-me-up cup of tea. Depending on how much picking up you need, you may or may not make it across to the **Pantheon** (*see p100*) before it shuts at 6pm. But even without going inside, this is a superb piece of ancient architecture, as good from outside as in.

6PM Aperitivo time is drawing nigh, and you're no distance away from the trendy, buzzing **triangolo della Pace** (*see p269*). Cut across, through spectacular piazza Navona, to the warren of little streets beyond. **Bar del Fico** or **Etabli** (for both, *see p271*) will, in their different ways, revive your flagging spirits.

---

valid for seven days: Appia Antica Card (€6, €3 reductions) covers the Appian Way; Archeologia Card (€23, €13) covers sites along the Appian Way, the Roman Forum, Colosseum, Palatine and the four MNR museums. The passes are subject to extra charges if exhibitions are in progress. For details, see www.060608.it.

LOCKED SITES

Sites listed as locked in this guide can be visited either by requesting a guide well in advance at 06 3996 7700 or, sometimes, by booking through www.pierreci.com.

EXTRA CHARGES

Many museums and galleries increase ticket prices whenever they are hosting one-off exhibitions on the premises. In some cases (the Colosseum, for example) this is much of the time. Visitors cannot opt out of paying for the exhibition: the extra charge is automatic. In this guide we have given basic ticket prices throughout.

Rome in Profile

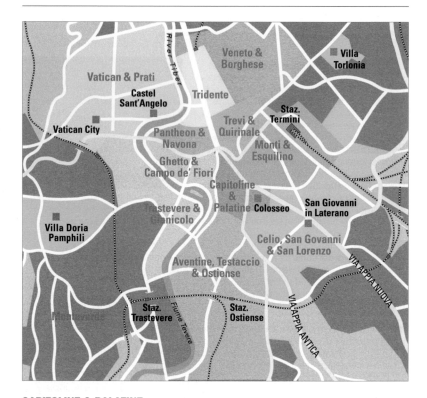

CAPITOLINE & PALATINE
Impressive Roman remains still dominate the ancient city's nerve centre: it was fun at the Colosseum, business in the Forum, power on the Capitoline and fine living on the Palatine.
► *For more, see pp52-66.*

TREVI & QUIRINALE
Aristocratic *palazzi* and the machinery of state surround the former papal (now presidential) Quirinale palace, with a watery soundtrack from one of the world's most famous fountains.
► *For more, see pp67-73.*

VENETO & BORGHESE
The *dolce vita* has given way to expense account lunches on the via Veneto but the art-packed Villa Borghese is great for culture and a stroll.
► *For more, see pp74-84.*

THE TRIDENTE
The Tridente has designer delights, elegant cafés and the Spanish Steps.
► *For more, see pp85-92.*

PANTHEON & NAVONA

A cool and stylish nightlife scene revolves around magnificent piazza Navona, but this area's museums and art-packed churches make it a daytime draw for culturally inclined visitors too.
► *For more, see pp93-101.*

GHETTO & CAMPO DE' FIORI

The city's medieval heart is a scenic warren around lively campo de' Fiori and stately piazza Farnese. In the Ghetto, quaint charm and a great street life conceal a history of suffering.
► *For more, see pp102-112.*

TRASTEVERE & GIANICOLO

The picturesque alleys on the Tiber's right bank in Trastevere buzz with *trattorie*, *pizzerie* and innumerable wine bars. Above, the residential Gianicolo hill offers spectacular views.
► *For more, see pp113-118.*

AVENTINE, TESTACCIO & OSTIENSE

The leafy, well-heeled Aventine looks down over workaday Testaccio, with its bustling market and a buzzing club scene that has extended down the via Ostiense into some hip new areas.
► *For more, see pp119-123.*

CELIO, SAN GIOVANNI & SAN LORENZO

Christianity's first great basilica still stands at San Giovanni, and the pretty Celio conceals more early churches. Students flock to radical-chic San Lorenzo for its nightlife scene.
► *For more, see pp124-132.*

MONTI & ESQUILINO

From the twisting medieval streets of Monti to the cold post-Unification *palazzi* of the Esquilino, this area has many hidden artistic gems – and some great retail opportunities.
► *For more, see pp133-141.*

VATICAN & PRATI

The nerve centre of Catholicism rubs shoulders with secular streets in this lively area on the Tiber's right bank. Great art, great shopping and some good eating options too.
► *For more, see pp142-150.*

THE APPIAN WAY & THE SUBURBS

The Appian Way, begun in 312 BC, was the first great consular road of ancient Rome. It remains the most impressive, with its scattered statuary, catacombs and stately Roman remains. The northern suburbs are filling up with media centres in stunning contemporary buildings, while the southern EUR business district is dramatic in its icy Fascist-era travertine.
► *For more, see pp151-161.*

Time Out Rome

Editorial
Editor Anne Hanley
Deputy Editor Patrick Welch
Copy Editor Simon Coppock
Listings Editor Fulvia Angelini
Proofreader Marion Moisy
Indexer Jess Fleming

Managing Director Peter Fiennes
Editorial Director Ruth Jarvis
Business Manager Dan Allen
Editorial Manager Holly Pick
Assistant Management Accountant Ija Krasnikova

Design
Art Director Scott Moore
Art Editor Pinelope Kourmouzoglou
Senior Designer Kei Ishimaru
Group Commercial Designer Jodi Sher

Picture Desk
Picture Editor Jael Marschner
Acting Deputy Picture Editor Liz Leahy
Picture Desk Assistant/Researcher Ben Rowe

Advertising
New Business & Commercial Director Mark Phillips
International Advertising Manager Kasimir Berger
International Sales Executive Charlie Sokol
Advertising Sales (Rome) Margherita Tedone,
  Julie Simonsen

Marketing
**Sales & Marketing Director, North America
  & Latin America** Lisa Levinson
Senior Publishing Brand Manager Luthfa Begum
Group Commercial Art Director Anthony Huggins
Marketing Co-ordinator Alana Benton

Production
Group Production Manager Brendan McKeown
Production Controller Katie Mulhern

Time Out Group
Director & Founder Tony Elliott
Chief Executive Officer David King
Group Financial Director Paul Rakkar
Group General Manager/Director Nichola Coulthard
Time Out Communications Ltd MD David Pepper
Time Out International Ltd MD Cathy Runciman
Time Out Magazine Ltd Publisher/MD Mark Elliott
Group Commercial Director Graeme Tottle
Group IT Director Simon Chappell

Contributors
Introduction Anne Hanley. **History** Anne Hanley (*Naming Baby* Clara Marshall). **Rome Today** Anne Hanley. **Architecture** Anne Hanley. **Art in Rome** Frederick Ilchman (*Walk: Caravaggio* Julia Crosse). **Sightseeing Introduction** Anne Hanley. **From the Capitoline to the Palatine** Agnes Crawford (*Keeping Cool* Clara Marshall). **The Trevi Fountain & the Quirinale** Agnes Crawford. **Via Veneto & Villa Borghese** Natasha Foges. **The Tridente** Agnes Crawford. **The Pantheon & Piazza Navona** Julia Crosse. **The Ghetto & Campo de' Fiori** Julia Crosse. **Trastevere & the Gianicolo** Sarah Delaney. **The Aventine, Testaccio & Ostiense** Anne Hanley. **Celio, San Giovanni & San Lorenzo** Sarah Delaney. **Monti & Esquilino** Agnes Crawford (*Profile* Julia Crosse). **The Vatican & Prati** Agnes Crawford. **The Appian Way** Agnes Crawford. **The Suburbs** Anne Hanley. **Hotels** Natasha Foges. **Eating Out** Lee Marshall. **Cafes, Bars & Gelaterie** Julia Crosse. **Shops & Services** Annie Shapero. **Festivals & Events** Natasha Foges. **Children** Philippa Hitchen. **Film** Lee Marshall. **Galleries** Cathryn Drake. **Gay & Lesbian** Peter Douglas. **Music: Classical & Opera** Linda Bordoni (*The Sound of Perfection* Julia Crosse). **Nightlife & Live Music** Raffaella Malaguti, Luciano Levrone. **Sport & Fitness** Natasha Foges. **Theatre & Dance** Linda Bordoni. **Escapes & Excursions** Nicky Swallow, Anne Hanley. **Directory** Richard McKenna.

Maps LS International Cartography, via Decemviri 8, 20138, Milan. www.geomaker.com. Rome Metro map John Oakey

Cover photograph: Getty Images
Back cover photography by Gianluca Moggi

Photography by Gianluca Moggi except pages 3, 285 ShopArtGallery; pages 4, 57, 131, 156, 159, 163, 171, 183 (bottom), 185, 195, 199, 201, 202, 213, 223, 233, 269, 272, 273, 275, 286, 287, 293, 323 (top) Alessandra Santorelli; page 5 (top right) Bartlomiej K. Kwieciszewski; page 5 (top left) Sailorr; page 5 (bottom right) Maurizio Farnetti; page 13 Demetrio Carrasco/Photolibrary.com; page 15 Luciano Mortula; page 27 Bridgeman Art Library/Getty Images; page 30 Nikonaft; pages 31, 139 Hulton Archive/Getty Images; page 32 Michael Juno/Alamy; pages 47, 97, 182, 207, 239, 268, 274 Agnese Sanvito; page 51 Circumnavigation; page 58 Julian Toledo; page 70 Ackab Photography; page 90 Konovalikov; page 95 Nadja1; page 101 Shutterstock; page 109 Roger Viollet/Getty Images; page 110 Alexey Biryukov; page 147 Selfiy; page 160 Alfredo Ragazzoni; pages 241, 279 Michele D'Annibale; page 249 Luca Dammico; page 251 AFP/Getty Images; page 256 photos courtesy Gagosian Gallery/Matteo Piazza; page 280 marcokenya; page 291 Angelo Giampiccolo; page 296 Bruno Pagnanelli; page 302 Lucarelli Temistocle.

The following images were provided by the featured establishments/artists:
pages 41, 129, 165, 172, 188, 242, 247, 250, 253, 255, 264, 277.

The Editor would like to thank Fulvio Marsigliani, Lee and Clara Marshall, and all contributors to previous editions of *Time Out Rome*, whose work forms the basis for parts of this book.

MAD & Co. Advertising & Marketing Director: Margherita Tedone. Tel: +39 06 3550 9145. Fax: +39 06 3550 1775. mad&co@alfanet.it

About the Guide

GETTING AROUND

The back of the book contains street maps of Rome, as well as an overview map of the city and its surroundings. The maps start on page 337; on them are marked the locations of hotels (**①**), restaurants (**①**), and cafés and bars (**①**). The majority of businesses listed in this guide are located in the areas we've mapped; the grid-square references in the listings refer to these maps.

THE ESSENTIALS

For practical information, including visas, disabled access, emergency numbers, lost property, useful websites and local transport, please see the Directory. It begins on page 307.

THE LISTINGS

Addresses, phone numbers, websites, transport information, hours and prices are all included in our listings, as are selected other facilities. All of these were checked and correct when this book went to press. However, business owners can alter their arrangements at any time, and fluctuating economic conditions may cause prices to change rapidly.

The very best venues in the city, the must-sees and must-dos in every category, have been marked with a red star (★). In the Sights chapters, we've also marked venues with free admission with a FREE symbol.

PHONE NUMBERS

The area code for Rome is 06. You must use the code, whether you're calling from inside or outside the city.

From outside Italy, dial your country's international access code (00 from the UK, 011 from the US), followed by the Italy country code (39), 06 for Rome (without dropping the initial zero) and the rest of the number as listed in the guide.

For more about phones, including information on calling abroad from Italy and details of local mobile phone access, *see p317*. Numbers that begin with a 3 are cellphones.

FEEDBACK

We welcome feedback on this guide, both on the venues we've included and on any other locations that you'd like to see featured in future editions. Please email us at guides@timeout.com.

Time Out Guides

Founded in 1968, Time Out has grown from humble beginnings into the leading resource for anyone wanting to know what's happening in the world's greatest cities. Alongside our influential weeklies in London, New York and Chicago, we publish more than 20 magazines in cities as varied as Beijing and Beirut; a range of travel books, with the City Guides now joined by the newer Shortlist series; and an information-packed website. The company remains proudly independent, still owned by Tony Elliott four decades after he launched *Time Out London*.

Written by local experts and illustrated with original photography, our books also retain their independence. No business has been featured because it has advertised, and all restaurants and bars are visited and reviewed anonymously.

ABOUT THE EDITOR

Anne Hanley has lived in Italy since 1984, first in Rome and now in rural Umbria. When she is not editing Italian titles for Time Out Guides – something she has been doing since 1997 – she designs gardens (www.laverzura.com).

A full list of the book's contributors can be found opposite. However, we've also included details of our writers in selected chapters through the guide.

WHENEVER, WHEREVER YOU NEED MONEY...

WE GET IT THERE IN 10 MINUTES*

CHOICE IS IN YOUR HANDS

1. Arrange for the person sending the money to visit a MoneyGram agent near them. After sending the money, they will give you a reference number.

2. Find your nearest MoneyGram agent at **www.moneygram.com** or visit any Poste Italiane branch.

3. Give the reference number and your ID** to the MoneyGram agent.

4. Fill out one simple form to receive your money.

Service available anywhere you see the MoneyGram sign and in over 10.000 Poste Italiane branches

Posteitaliane

Freephone: 800 088 256   www.moneygram.com

In Context

Via A Canova.

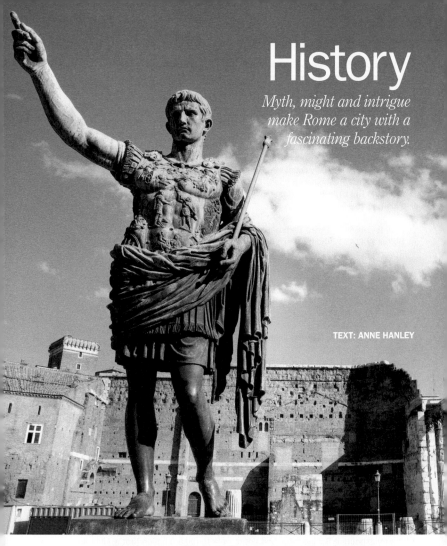

History

*Myth, might and intrigue
make Rome a city with a
fascinating backstory.*

TEXT: ANNE HANLEY

Each year on 21 April, Romans and visitors in their
thousands flock to the Campidoglio for extravagant
fireworks and illuminations marking the *Natale di Roma* –
Rome's birthday. On 21 April 2012 (allowing for some
tweaks in calendars over the ages) the Old Girl is set to
celebrate the 2,765th anniversary of her birth. How many
other cities boast such a precise foundation date (or as
impressive a tale to go with it, *see p16*)? Then again, how
many other cities manage to blend myth and history, fact
and fiction, past and present quite as seamlessly as Rome?
From Julius Caesar to the post-war boom, if you're looking
for history, you've come to the right place.

Popes of the Renaissance

Martin V (1417-31; Oddone Colonna) brought the papacy back to Rome at the end of the Great Schism.
Eugenius IV (1431-47; Gabriel Condulmer).
Nicholas V (1447-55; Tommaso Parentucelli), generally considered to be the first Renaissance pope.
Callixtus III (1455-8; Alfondo de Borja).
Pius II (1458-64; Enea Silvio Piccolomini).
Paul II (1464-71; Pietro Barbo).
Sixtus IV (1471-84; Francesco della Rovere).
Innocent VIII (1484-92; Giovanni Battista Cibò).
Alexander VI (1492-1503; Rodrigo Borgia).
Pius III (Oct 1503; Francesco Todeschini Piccolomini).
Julius II (1503-13; Giuliano della Rovere).
Leo X (1513-21; Giovanni de' Medici).
Adrian VI (1522-3; Adrian Florenz) the last non-Italian pope until Karol Wojtyla (John Paul II) was elected in 1978.
Clement VII (1523-34; Giulio de' Medici).

Paul III (1534-49; Alessandro Farnese) summoned the Council of Trent, which ushered in the Counter-Reformation.
Julius III (1550-55; Giovanni Maria Ciocci del Monte).
Marcellus II (Apr-May 1555; Marcello Cervini).
Paul IV (1555-9; Gian Pietro Carafa).
Pius IV (1559-65; Giovan Angelo de' Medici).
Pius V (1566-72; Antonio Ghislieri).
Gregory XIII (1572-85; Ugo Buoncampagni).
Sixtus V (1585-90; Felice Peretti).
Urban VII (Sept 1590; Giovanni Battista Castagna).
Gregory XIV (1590-91; Niccolò Sfondrati).
Innocent IX (Nov-Dec 1591; Giovan Antonio Facchinetti).
Clement VIII (1592-1605; Ippolito Aldobrandini).
Leo XI (Apr 1605; Alessandro de' Medici).
Paul V (1605-21; Camillo Borghese).
Gregory XV (1621-23; Alessandro Ludovisi).

IN CONTEXT

THE BEGINNING

The 'facts' behind the city's birth date tale: twins Romulus and Remus were the fruits of a rape by the god of war, Mars, of an Italian princess called Rhea Silvia. Cast adrift as babies and washed into the marshy area below the Palatine hill, the twins were suckled by a she-wolf until found by a shepherd. Romulus became leader of his tribe, quarrelled with and killed his brother, and – on 21 April 753 BC – founded the city of Rome. Then, because his community was short of females, he abducted the women of the neighbouring Sabine tribe, and got to work to raise a nation that would rule the known world.

Ninth-century BC huts have been excavated on the Palatine – proof there was a primitive village there. But the first historically documented king of Rome was an Etruscan, Tarquinius Priscus, who reigned from 616 BC. And it was probably Etruscans who drained the marshy area between the seven hills to create the Forum, hub of the city's political, economic and religious life.

THE ROMAN REPUBLIC TAKES OVER

According to Roman historians, in 509 BC the son of King Tarquinius Superbus raped Lucretia, the wife of Collatinus, a Roman. The next day, before killing herself, she told her husband and his friend Brutus what had happened, and in revenge they led a rebellion against the Tarquins. The Etruscan dynasty was expelled and the Roman Republic founded, with Brutus and Collatinus as its first consuls.

'By the end of the second century BC, the Romans were a race of soldiers, engineers, administrators and merchants.'

This account is doubtless as historically (in)accurate as the city's foundation yarn but, in time, Etruscan influence over the region did wane and authority passed to Rome's magistrates. Chief among these were the two annually elected consuls, who guided a council of elders called the Senate. Only the few ancient families or lclans who formed the patrician class could participate in the political life of the Republic. The lower classes, or *plebs*, struggled for a greater say in their own affairs. In 494 BC, the office of Tribune of the Plebeians was created to represent their interests, and by 367 BC a plebeian could hold the office of consul. To keep up standards, rich or successful plebeians were simply designated patricians.

Romans were united by a belief in their right to conquer other tribes. Their superb military organisation and an agile policy of 'divide and rule' allowed them to bring the peoples – including the Etruscans – under Roman control. New cities were established in conquered territories and an extensive infrastructure was created to support the many conquests. The first great consular road, the via Appia (*see p151*), was begun in 312 BC. Shortly afterwards, work started on the Acqua Appia, the first aqueduct to bring fresh water to the city. The port of Ostia (*see p287* **Ostia Antica**) – founded at the mouth of the Tiber in 380 BC – expanded rapidly. Barges plied the river, bringing corn, wine, oil and building materials into Rome.

IN CONTEXT

Romulus and Remus, the legendary founders of Rome.

Rome's expansion brought the Republic into conflict with two equally powerful peoples: the Carthaginians, who populated North Africa and Spain, and the Greeks, who had colonised southern Italy and Sicily. The latter had been expelled from mainland Italy by 272 BC, but the Punic Wars against the Carthaginians were to last for almost 120 years. In 218 BC Hannibal crossed the Alps, gaining control of much of the Italian peninsula, but was too cautious – and his supply lines were too stretched – to launch an assault on Rome. When Carthage was destroyed in 146 BC Rome held sway over the whole western Mediterranean.

In the early days of the Republic most Romans, whether rich or poor, had been farmers, tending their own land or raising livestock in the surrounding countryside. Wars like those against Carthage, however, required huge standing armies. At the same time, much of the agricultural land in Italy had been laid waste, either by Hannibal or by the Romans themselves as they attempted to starve the invading Carthaginians into defeat with a scorched-earth policy.

Wealthy Romans bought estates at knock-down prices, while landless peasants flocked to the capital. By the end of the second century BC, the Romans were a race of soldiers, engineers, administrators and merchants, supported by tribute from defeated enemies and the slave labour of prisoners taken in battle. Keeping the mass of the Roman poor content required the exaction of more tribute money from the conquered territories, creating a parasitic relationship in which all classes in Rome lived off conquered peoples.

The political situation in the first century BC became more and more anarchic. Enormous armies were required to fight wars on the distant boundaries of the Republic's empire; soldiers came to owe greater loyalty to their general than to the government back in Rome. The result was a succession of civil wars fought between rival generals.

HAIL CAESAR!

Julius Caesar and Pompey, the two greatest generals of the first century BC, tried to bury their differences in a triumvirate with Crassus, but in 49 BC Caesar, then governor of Gaul, defied the Senate by bringing his army into Italy ('crossing the Rubicon', the muddy stream that marked the border). All opposition was swept aside and for the last six years of his life Julius Caesar ruled Rome as a dictator. The Republican spirit was not quite dead, though: in 44 BC he was assassinated. His death did not lead to the restoration of the Republic: instead, there was a power struggle between Mark Anthony and Caesar's nephew Octavian, which escalated into a full-blown civil war. Octavian eventually defeated Mark Anthony and Cleopatra at the Battle of Actium in 31 BC. Rome's influence now stretched from Gaul and Spain in the west to Egypt and Asia Minor in the east. To hold it together a single central power was needed, and Octavian was that power. To drive the point home, he took the name of Augustus: 'favoured by the gods'.

To give himself greater authority, Augustus encouraged the cult of his uncle Julius Caesar as a god, building a temple to him in the Forum (the Temple of Divus Julius; *see p62*). The Ara Pacis (*see p92*) was a reminder that it was he who had brought peace to the Roman world. Statues of Augustus sprang up all over the Empire, and he was more than happy to be worshipped as a god himself.

Augustus lived on the Palatine hill in a relatively modest house. Later emperors built extravagant palaces. The last member of Augustus' family to inherit the Empire was the megalomaniac Nero, who built himself the biggest palace Rome had ever seen: the Domus Aurea (Golden House; *see p135*).

When Nero died in AD 68, he had not produced an heir. Suddenly, the Empire was up for grabs. Generals converged from right across the Empire to claim the throne, and the eventual winner was a bluff soldier called Vespasian, the founder of the Flavian dynasty.

IN CONTEXT

'The golden age of Rome ended in AD 180 with the death of Emperor Marcus Aurelius.'

THE GOLDEN AGE OF PAX ROMANA

Over the next 100 years Rome enjoyed an era of unparalleled stability. The Empire reached its greatest extent during the reign of Trajan (98-117). Thereafter it was a matter of protecting the existing boundaries and avoiding civil war.

Peace throughout the Mediterranean encouraged trade and brought even greater prosperity to Rome, but the power and influence of the capital and its inhabitants declined. Many talented Imperial officials, generals and even emperors were Greeks, north Africans or Spaniards: Trajan and Hadrian were both born in Spain.

To keep an increasingly disparate mass of people content, emperors relied on the policy of *panem et circenses* (bread and circuses). From the first century AD, grain was regularly handed out to the poor, ostensibly to maintain a supply of fit young men for the army, but also to ensure that unrest was kept to a minimum. Such generosity to Rome's poor necessitated further exploitation of the outlying provinces of the Empire.

The other means used to keep more than a million souls loyal to their emperor was the staging of lavish public entertainments. The most famous venue for such spectacles was the Colosseum, built by emperors Vespasian and Domitian and completed in AD 80.

In the time of Augustus, Rome was home to about one million people. By the reign of Trajan a century later this had risen to 1,500,000. No other city in the world would even approach this size until the 19th century.

A SLOW DECLINE

The golden age of Rome ended in AD 180 with the death of Emperor Marcus Aurelius. Defending the eastern provinces and fortifying the borders along the Danube and the Rhine placed a huge strain on the Imperial purse and legions. Moreover, the exploitative relationship between the Roman state and its distant provinces meant that the latter were unable – or unwilling – to defend themselves.

The threat from barbarian invaders and civil wars became so serious that in the third century Emperor Aurelian (270-75) was obliged to fortify the city of Rome with massive defences. The still-extant Aurelian Wall, which was later reinforced by medieval popes, is a splendid monument to the engineering skills of the ancient Romans. But in its heyday, the city needed no defences: its protection lay in the vastness of the Empire and the security of the *Pax romana*.

The end of the third century AD was a turning point in the history of Rome. Diocletian (284-305) established new capital cities at Mediolanum (Milan) and Nicomedia (now in Turkey). He divided the Empire into four sectors, sharing power with a second 'Augustus' – Maximian – and two 'Caesars', Constantius and Galerius. The priorities of the over-extended Empire were now to defend the Rhine and Danube borders against invading Germanic tribes and the eastern provinces from the Persians. Rome was, essentially, abandoned.

CHRISTIANITY AND CONSTANTINE

The reign of Diocletian is also remembered as one of the periods of most intense persecution of Christians in the Empire. Christian communities had been established in Rome very soon after the death of Jesus. Christianity, though, was just one of many cults that had spread from the Middle East. Its followers were probably fewer than the devotees of Mithraism, a Persian religion open only to men, but Christianity's promise of salvation in the afterlife had great appeal. Within two decades of Diocletian's

Statue of **Marcus Aurelius** on the Campidoglio.

IN CONTEXT

persecutions, Emperor Constantine (306-37) would first tolerate Christianity and then recognise it as the Empire's official religion.

The early part of Constantine's reign was largely taken up with campaigns against rival emperors, the most powerful being Maxentius, who commanded Italy and North Africa. The decisive battle was fought just to the north of Rome at the Milvian Bridge (Ponte Milvio) in 312. Before the battle a flaming cross is said to have appeared in the sky, bearing the words *in hoc signo vinces* (by this sign shall you conquer). As the legend goes, Constantine's cavalry then swept Maxentius' superior forces into the Tiber. The following year, in the Edict of Milan, Constantine decreed that Christianity be tolerated throughout the Empire. Later in his reign, when he had gained control of the Eastern Empire and started to build his new capital city at Byzantium/Constantinople (now Istanbul), it became the state religion.

Christianity's effect on Roman life was at first limited, the new faith simply co-existing with other religions. Constantine's reign saw the building of three great basilicas, all on the outskirts of the city. St Peter's and St Paul's Without the Walls (San Paolo fuori le Mura; *see p159*) were built over existing shrines, whereas Constantine donated land to build a basilica – San Giovanni in Laterano (*see p131*) – beside the Aurelian Wall. To give Rome credibility as a centre of its new religion, fragments of the 'True' cross were brought from the Holy Land by Constantine's mother, St Helena.

Meanwhile, life in fourth-century Rome went on much as before. The departure of part of the Imperial court to Constantinople was a heavy blow, but the old pagan holidays were still observed, games staged and bread doled out to the poor.

All around, however, the Roman world was falling apart. Constantine learned nothing from the conflicts created by Diocletian's division of power: on his death he left the Empire to be split between his three sons. From this point on, the Western Empire and the Byzantine Empire were two separate entities, united for the last time under Theodosius in the late fourth century. Byzantium would stand for another 1,000 years, while Rome's glories were destroyed by waves of invaders.

THE FALL OF THE WESTERN EMPIRE

The first great shock came in 410, when Alaric's Visigoths marched into Italy and sacked Rome. Even more significant was the conquest of north Africa by the Vandals in 435, which cut Rome off from its main grain supply. In 455 the Vandals sacked Rome, removing everything they could carry. After this the Western Empire survived in name only. The great aqueducts supplying water to Rome ceased to function. Emperors in Rome became nothing more than puppets of the assorted Germanic

Popes of the Baroque

Urban VIII (1623-44; Maffeo Barberini). Bernini's *baldacchino* in St Peter's, made in 1625 for Urban, is considered to be the first Baroque work of art.
Innocent X (1644-55; Giambattista Pamphili).
Alexander VII (1655-67; Fabio Chigi).
Clement IX (1667-69; Giulio Rospigliosi).
Clement X (1670-76; Emilio Altieri).
Innocent XI (1676-89; Benedetto Odescalchi).

Alexander VIII (1689-91; Pietro Ottoboni).
Innocent XII (1691-1700; Antonio Pignatelli).
Clement XI (1700-21; Giovanni Francesco Albani).
Innocent XIII (1721-24; Michelangelo de' Conti).
Benedict XIII (1724-30; Pietro Francesco Orsini).
Clement XII (1730-40; Lorenzo Corsini).

'The Western Empire survived in name only. Emperors in Rome became nothing more than puppets of the assorted Germanic invaders.'

invaders. The last emperor, Romulus, was given the nickname Augustulus, since he was such a feeble shadow of the Empire's founder. In 476 he was deposed by the German chieftain Odoacer, who styled himself King of Italy. Odoacer was in turn deposed by Theodoric the Ostrogoth, who invaded Italy with the support of Byzantium and established an urbane court in Ravenna, which was to provide stable government for the next 30 years.

In the sixth century much of Italy was reconquered by the Eastern Empire. Then, in around 567, yet another Germanic tribe swept in. The Lombards overran much of the centre of the peninsula, but when they threatened to besiege Rome they met their match in Pope Gregory the Great (590-604), who bought them off. Gregory was a tireless organiser, overseeing the running of the Church's estates around Europe, encouraging the establishment of new monasteries and sending missionaries as far afield as pagan Britain.

He also did a great deal to build up the prestige of the papacy. Rome had been merely one of the centres of the early Church, the others – Byzantium, Jerusalem, Antioch and Alexandria – all being in the East. Disputes were sometimes referred to the Bishop of Rome, but many Christians did not accord him overall primacy. The collapse of secular government in the West meant that the papacy emerged almost by default as the sole centre of authority, with the pope a political leader as well as head of the Roman Church.

IN CONTEXT

A SHADOW OF ITSELF

The Dark Ages must have been a particularly galling period for the inhabitants of Rome, living as they did among the magnificent ruins of a golden age that had now vanished. The population had no fresh water, and disease was rife. Formerly built-up areas reverted to grazing land, or were planted with vegetables by religious orders. Fear of attack meant that the countryside around the city was practically deserted. Having reached over a million at its zenith, Rome's population by the sixth century could be counted in hundreds. The city's ancient ruins became little more than convenient quarries: marble was burned to make cement, most of which was used to repair fortifications.

For several centuries the city still owed nominal allegiance to the emperor in Byzantium and his representative in Italy, the exarch, whose court was at Ravenna. However, the exarch's troops were normally too busy defending their own cities in north-east Italy to be of much help. The city had a military commander – a *dux* – and a *comune* (city council). But the papacy also had its courts and administration. In the end, the power of the Church prevailed; this would lead to a permanent rift with Byzantium and the Eastern Orthodox churches.

When the Lombards seized Ravenna in 751 and threatened to do the same to Rome, Pope Stephen II enlisted Pepin, King of the Franks, as defender of the Church. The papacy's alliance with the Franks grew with the victories of Pepin's son, Charlemagne, over the Lombards and was sealed on Christmas Day 800, when the pope caught Charlemagne unawares in St Peter's and crowned him Holy Roman Emperor.

HOLY ROMAN POLITICS

Now Rome had the protection of an emperor (with a power base comfortably far away in Aachen) anointed by the pope, who in return was rewarded with the gift of large areas of land in central Italy. As things turned out, this arrangement caused nothing but trouble for the next 500 years, as popes, emperors and other monarchs vied to determine whose power was greatest. Roman nobles took sides in the disputes, taking advantage to promote members of their own families to the papacy, frequently reducing the city to a state of anarchy.

Papal independence was reasserted in the second half of the 11th century by Pope Gregory VII (1073-85), who also established many of the distinctive institutions of the Church. It was Gregory who first made celibacy obligatory for priests; he set up the College of Cardinals, giving it sole authority to elect all future popes. He also insisted that no bishop or abbot could be invested by a lay ruler, which led to a cataclysmic struggle for power with the Holy Roman Emperor Henry IV.

When Henry marched on Rome in 1084, bringing with him a new papal candidate, Gregory demanded help from Robert Guiscard, leader of the Normans who had a strong power base in southern Italy. By the time Robert arrived, Rome had already capitulated to Henry's army; in protest, the Normans indulged in a three-day orgy of looting, then torched what was still standing. From the Palatine to San Giovanni in Laterano, little remained but smoking ruins. Gregory slunk out of his hiding place in Castel Sant'Angelo and left Rome a broken man; he died the following year.

Despite conflict between rival factions, the 12th and 13th centuries were times of great architectural innovation. The creative spirit of the Middle Ages is preserved in beautiful cloisters like those of San Giovanni and in Romanesque churches with graceful brick bell towers and floors of finely wrought mosaic.

Rome's prestige suffered a severe blow in 1309, when the French overruled the College of Cardinals and imposed their own candidate as pope, who promptly decamped to Avignon. A pope returned to Rome in 1378, but the situation became farcical, with three pontiffs laying claim to St Peter's throne. Stability was restored only in 1417, when Oddo Colonna was elected as Pope Martin V at the Council of Constance. He returned to Rome in 1420 to find the city and the surrounding Papal States in a ruinous condition.

With the reign of Martin V (1417-31), some semblance of dignity was restored to the papacy. City councillors were nominees of the pope, who made the Vatican his principal residence: it offered greater security than their traditional seat in the Lateran Palace. Successive popes took advantage of this new sense of authority; Rome became an international city once more.

The renewed prestige of the papacy enabled it to draw funds from all over Europe in the form of tithes and taxes. The papacy also developed the money-spinning idea of the Holy Year, first instituted in 1300. Such measures financed the lavish artistic patronage of Renaissance Rome.

THE RENAISSANCE IS BORN

Nicholas V (1447-55) is remembered as the pope who brought the Renaissance to Rome. A lover of philosophy, science and the arts, he founded the Vatican Library and had many ancient Greek texts translated. He also made plans to rebuild St Peter's, the structure of which was perilously unstable. The Venetian Pope Paul II (1464-71) built the city's first great Renaissance palazzo, the massive Palazzo Venezia (*see p57*), and his successor Sixtus IV (1471-84) invited leading artists from Tuscany and Umbria to fresco the walls of his new Sistine Chapel (*see p148*) in the Vatican.

Since the papacy had become such a fat prize, the great families of Italy redoubled their efforts to secure it. The French and Spanish kings usually had their own candidates too. Political clout, rather than spirituality, was the prime concern of Renaissance popes. Sixtus IV and his successors Innocent VIII (1484-92) and

IN CONTEXT

The Sack

Bloodshed and devastation as the 'imperial' army descends.

On 5 May 1527, an ill-disciplined force gathered beneath Rome's walls. Some 14,000 were Germans with Martin Luther's fulminations against Rome ringing in their ears; 6,000 were Spanish troops led by Constable Charles, Duke of Bourbon; the rest were a rabble of mainly Italian deserters and free-booters. All of them were angry: it was months since their nominal commander-in-chief, the Holy Roman Emperor Charles V (who was also King Charles I of Spain), had paid them. And all of them knew that wealthy Rome was bursting with treasure to be looted.

In many ways, Pope Clement VII had brought this situation on himself: he had gone against tradition and turned his back on the Holy Roman Emperor, allying himself instead with France, England and Venice in the League of Cognac. But with the Ottomans battering his eastern borders, Charles's attention was elsewhere as this 'imperial' army descended on *caput mundi*. A furious assault was launched on the Vatican on 6 May, during which the Duke of Bourbon was killed. And the Sack that followed was pure anarchy.

What the imperial army found as it piled over the walls must have seemed an El Dorado. This was the city of Michelangelo and Raphael, a city of stupendous villas and sumptuously appointed churches.

As Clement high-tailed it into Castel Sant'Angelo (*see p150*) protected by his Swiss Guard – only 42 of the original 189 survived – the attackers ran amok in an orgy of rape and pillage. Women were dragged into churches to be raped by Lutherans dressed in priests' robes; young children were hurled from high windows; priests suffered unspeakable tortures; the corpses piled up in the city's streets.

Clement was forced to capitulate on 6 June, and was fined 400,000 ducats. But it was months before any kind of order returned to the devastated city. In a 1526 census, Rome had 55,000 residents. By the end of 1527 there were no more than 10,000. Many had fled, but as many as 20,000 died – both in the Sack and in the plague that swept through the city towards the end of the year.

Not content with this bloodshed, Romans looked for a scapegoat for their misfortunes. They found it in the Jews, who were accused of saving their own skins and profiteering by buying up looted goods from the attackers. The accusations were probably false. But even if they weren't, there's a case to be made that the Jewish community was responsible for salvaging Roman treasures that would otherwise have been lost.

IN CONTEXT

Alexander VI (the infamous Rodrigo Borgia; 1492-1503) devoted far more of their energies to politics and war than to spiritual matters.

The epitome of the worldly Renaissance pope, Julius II (1503-13) made a strong papal state a reality. He began the magnificent collection of classical sculpture that formed the nucleus of today's Vatican Museums (*see p148*) and invited the greatest architects, sculptors and painters of the day to come to Rome, including Bramante, Michelangelo and Raphael.

Julius' successors accomplished far less than he did. Some were simply bon viveurs, like Giovanni de' Medici, who, on being made Pope Leo X in 1513, said to his brother, 'God has given us the papacy. Let us enjoy it.' Enjoy it, he did. A great patron of the arts, Leo's other passions were hunting, music, theatre and throwing

'Papal independence was reasserted in the second half of the 11th century by Pope Gregory VII.'

spectacular dinner parties. He plunged the papacy into debt, spending enormous sums on French hounds, Icelandic falcons and banquets of nightingale pies and dishes involving peacocks' tongues.

PROTESTANTS AND IMPERIALISM
Later popes had to face two great threats to the status quo of Catholic Europe: the protests of Martin Luther, and the growing rivalry between Francis I of France and Spanish King/Holy Roman Emperor Charles V.

The year 1523 saw the death of Pope Adrian VI, a Flemish protégé of Charles V. He was succeeded by Clement VII (1523-34), formerly Giulio de' Medici, who rather unwisely backed France against the all-powerful emperor. Charles took the Duchy of Milan in 1525 and threatened to annex all Italy in retaliation for the pope's disloyalty. In 1527 an ill-disciplined Imperial army, many of whom were Germans with Lutheran condemnations of Rome ringing in their ears, sacked the city. Chiefly interested in gold and ready money, the looters also destroyed churches and houses, burned or stole countless relics and works of art, looted tombs, and killed indiscriminately. The dead rotted in the streets for months.

Pope Clement held out for seven months in Castel Sant'Angelo, but eventually slunk away in disguise. He returned the following year, crowning Charles as Holy Roman Emperor in Bologna shortly afterwards. In return, Charles grudgingly confirmed Clement VII's sovereignty over the Papal States.

The Sack of Rome put an abrupt end to the Renaissance popes' dream of making Rome a formidable political power. The primary concerns now had to be the rebuilding of the city and pushing forward the Counter-Reformation, the Catholic Church's response to Protestantism.

THE COUNTER-REFORMATION
The first great Counter-Reformation pope was Alessandro Farnese, Paul III (1534-49). He summoned the Council of Trent to redefine Catholicism and encouraged new religious groups such as the Jesuits – founded by the Spaniard Ignatius of Loyola and approved in 1540 – over older, discredited orders. From their mother church in Rome, the Gesù (*see p105*), the Jesuits led the fight against heresy.

Pope Paul IV (1555-59), the next major reformer, was a firm believer in the Inquisition. He expelled Jews from the Papal States, except for those in Rome itself, whom he confined to the Ghetto in 1556.

By the end of the 16th century the authority of the papacy was on the wane, and the treasury was increasingly dependent on loans. But in the following century popes continued to spend money wildly, commissioning architects such as Bernini and Borromini to design the churches, *palazzi* and fountains that would transform the face of the Eternal City for ever. The economy of the Papal States became chronically depressed.

POOR LOCALS AND RICH TOURISTS
If two centuries of papal opulence had turned monumental Rome into a spectacular sight, squalor and poverty were still the norm for most of its people: the streets of Trastevere and the Suburra – ancient Rome's great slum – in the Monti district were

Profile Queen Christina

A controversial monarch.

In 1655, Queen Christina abdicated the Swedish throne and came to Rome, entering triumphantly through a gate in piazza del Popolo (*see p91*), designed for the event by Gian Lorenzo Bernini. She was to spend the next 34 years in the Eternal City, her intellect, culture, audacity and ambiguous sexuality making her an object of admiration and gossip – and an embarrassment to the Church.

Christina became queen at age six, but soon managed to alienate her people not only by her conversion to Catholicism in that rigidly Protestant country, but also because she dressed like a man, demanded to be the king rather than queen and plunged her exchequer into debt.

But such a high-class conversion to a Church in the throes of an ideological battle with the followers of Martin Luther made her a darling of the Catholic hierarchy. Once in Rome, however, Christina gave Pope Alexander VII nothing but grief.

Christina's devotion to Catholicism was questioned, but not her attachment to a Catholic priest, Decio Azzolino, to whom she left her entire patrimony. Her tastes (sexual and otherwise) were unshackled, and her manners offended and confounded the conventions of the day. During her three decades in Rome – mostly in the Palazzo Riario (now

Corsini; *see p115*) – she surrounded herself with the greatest philosophers and artists of the time, amassing a connoisseur's collection of art, despite shaky finances. Her parties were legendary. She studied alchemy and astrology. Her attachment to a series of women fuelled speculation about Sapphism.

Short, stout, pockmarked and with a hump on her shoulder, Christina – said contemporary sources – exerted an extraordinary degree of fascination, right up until her death in 1689 when she was buried, against her explicit wishes, in St Peter's.

filthy and dangerous. The city was, however, a more peaceful place to live. The rich no longer shut themselves up in fortress-like *palazzi*, but built delightful villas in landscaped parks, such as Villa Borghese. A Europe-wide resurgence of interest in the classical past was under way, and shortly the city would discover the joys – and earning power – of tourism.

By the 18th century a visit to Rome as part of a 'Grand Tour' was near obligatory for any European gentleman, and Romans responded eagerly to the influx. The city produced little great art or architecture at this time. The two great Roman sights that date from this period, the Spanish Steps and the Trevi Fountain, are a late flowering of Roman Baroque. The few big building projects undertaken were for the benefit of tourists, notably Giuseppe Valadier's splendid park on the Pincio (*see p74*) and the neo-classical facelift he gave to piazza del Popolo.

Although on the surface Rome was a cultured city, it remained a place where many customs reeked of medieval superstition. Executions were mostly staged in piazza del Popolo, and they were often timed to coincide with *carnevale*, a period of frantic merrymaking before Lent. For a few days, via del Corso was one long, masked ball. Here bands played and people would shower one another with confetti, flour, water and more dangerous missiles.

Indeed, Rome was a city of spectacle for much of the year. In summer, piazza Navona was flooded by blocking the outlets of the fountains, and the nobility sploshed

Naming Baby

The narrow world of Roman nomenclature.

The most ancient of Romans were limited in the extreme where names were concerned. Most only had one – later known as a *praenomen* – like Remus or Romulus. This was similar to a modern first name, but there were only about 18 of them to choose from: the scope for confusion was thus immense, a situation that wasn't helped by the fact that the eldest son was always named after his father. Clearly, some distinguishing nomenclature was called for.

To begin with, different generations adopted different formulas so they could be told apart. Then, as the city's population grew in the early Republic, Romans began using a binominal system, embellishing their *praenomen* with a *nomen gentile* name derived from the *gens* – or clan – they belonged to. Soon this clan nomen became more important than the *praenomen*.

Finally, around 100 BC, the Tria Nomina system became the norm, with the introduction of a *cognomen*, which often started off as a descriptive nickname (such as Cicero, meaning 'chickpea' – presumably referring to a wart on the great man's nose).

As for females – ever dependent on the male members of their household – they tended to take the feminine form of the name of their own clan, followed on occasion by the possessive form of their father's (and later, on occasion, husband's) *cognomen*. If there were several daughters in one family, they would share the same name: girls of the *gens* Julii, for example, were generally called Julia after which, as a concession to any possible individuality, they were given... a number. The third daughter who was a member of this family would be called Julia Tertia – Julia the third.

Foreigners wishing to reinvent themselves as Roman citizens – freed slaves often found themselves in this position – would chose their own *praenomen*, then model the *cognomen* on their previous name and their *nomen* usually on that of a patron to whom they were indebted.

'Looters destroyed churches and houses, burned works of art and killed indiscriminately.'

around in their carriages. The only time the city fell quiet was in late summer, when everyone who could left for their villas in the Alban hills to escape the stifling heat and the threat of malaria.

OCCUPATION, THEN UNIFICATION

In 1798 everything changed. French troops under Napoleon occupied the city and Rome became a republic once more. Pope Pius VI (1775-1799), a feeble old man, was exiled from the city and died in France. Like most attempts to restore the Roman Republic, this one was short-lived. The next pope, Pius VII (1800-1823), elected in Venice, signed a concordat with Napoleon in 1801, which allowed the pontiff to return to Rome. The papacy was expelled for a second time when French troops returned in 1808. Napoleon promised the city a modernising, reforming administration, but Romans were not keen to be conscripted into his armies. When the pope finally reclaimed Rome after the fall of Napoleon in 1814, its noble families and many of the people welcomed his return.

The Papal States were returned to Pius VII. But the brief taste of liberty under the French had helped to inspire a movement for unification, modernisation and independence from the domination of foreign rulers.

The Risorgimento was a movement for the unification of the country, but in itself it was very diverse. Its supporters ranged from liberals who believed in unification for economic reasons, to conservatives who looked to the papacy itself to unify Italy. Initially, the most prominent players were the idealistic republicans of the *Giovine Italia* (Young Italy) movement, headed by Giuseppe Mazzini. They were flanked by more extreme groups and secret societies, such as the Carbonari.

Two reactionary popes, Leo XII (1823-29) and Gregory XVI (1831-46), used a network of police spies and censorship to put down any opposition. Most of the unrest in the Papal States, though, was in the north; in Rome, life went on much as before. Travellers continued to visit: Shelley and Dickens expressed horror at the repressive regime.

The election of a new pope in 1846 aroused great optimism. Pius IX came to the throne with a liberal reputation and immediately announced an amnesty for over 400 political prisoners. But the spate of revolutions throughout Europe in 1848 radically altered his attitude. In November that year his chief minister was assassinated and Pius fled. In his absence, a popular assembly declared Rome a republic. Seizing the chance to make his dream reality, Mazzini rushed to the city, where he was chosen as one of a triumvirate of rulers. Meanwhile, another idealist arrived in Rome to defend the Republic, at the head of 500 armed followers. He was Giuseppe Garibaldi, a former sailor who had gained military experience fighting in wars of liberation in South America.

Ironically, it was Republican France, with Napoleon I's nephew Louis Napoleon as president, that decided it was duty-bound to restore papal rule to Rome. Louis Napoleon did so to stop Austrian power spreading further within Italy. A French force marched on Rome, but was repelled by the ragtag *garibaldini* (followers of Garibaldi). The French attacked again in greater numbers, mounting their assault from the gardens of Villa Pamphili. For the whole of June 1849 the defenders fought valiantly from their positions on the Gianicolo, but the end of the Republic was by now inevitable.

IN CONTEXT

The **Vittoriano** monument.

For the next 20 years, while the rest of Italy was being united under King Vittorio Emanuele II of Savoy, a garrison of French troops protected Pope Pius from invasion. Garibaldi protested vainly to the politicians of the new state – it was, he said, a question of *Roma o morte* ('Rome or death') – but the Kingdom of Italy, established in 1860, was not prepared to take on Napoleon III's France. Meanwhile, the former liberal Pius IX was becoming more and more reactionary. In 1869 he convened the first Vatican Council in order to set down the Catholic Church's response to the upheavals of the industrial age. It did so with intransigence, making the doctrine of papal infallibility an official dogma of the Church for the first time.

IN CONTEXT

A CAPITAL ONCE MORE
Though still under papal rule, Rome had been chosen as the capital of the newly unified kingdom. In 1870, with the defeat of Napoleon III in the Franco-Prussian War, the French withdrew from Rome and unification troops occupied the city.

There followed the most rapid period of change Rome had experienced since the fall of the Empire. The new capital needed government buildings and housing for the civil servants who worked in them. Church properties were confiscated and for a time government officials worked in converted monasteries and convents. Two aristocratic *palazzi* were adapted to house the Italian parliament: Palazzo di Montecitorio (*see p89*) became the Lower House, and Palazzo Madama (*see p97*) the Senate.

The city's great building boom lasted for over 30 years. New avenues appeared: via Nazionale and via Cavour linked the old city with the new Stazione Termini, and corso Vittorio Emanuele was driven through the historic centre. The new ministries were often massive piles quite out of keeping with their surroundings; still more extravagant was the monstrous Vittoriano (*see p59*), the marble monument to Vittorio Emanuele erected in piazza Venezia.

FASCISM AND THE POST-WAR ERA
Though Rome was little affected by World War I, social unrest broke out following the war, with the fear of Socialism encouraging the rise of Fascism. Benito Mussolini was a radical journalist who, having become alienated from the far left, shifted to the extreme right. He turned to ancient Rome to find an emblem to embody his idea of a totalitarian state: *fasces*, bundles of rods tied round an axe, were carried by the Roman *lictors* (marshals) as they walked in front of the city's consuls. In 1922 Mussolini sent his Blackshirt squads on their 'March on Rome', demanding – and winning – full power in government. Mussolini made the 'march' by train.

'While other Italian cities and towns were pounded by bombs, Rome suffered only one serious bombing raid during the whole war.'

Mussolini's ambition was to transform the country into a dynamic, aggressive society. His ideas for changing the face of Rome were far-fetched. He planned to rebuild the city in gleaming marble, with fora, obelisks and heroic statues proclaiming *il Duce* ('the Leader') as a modern Augustus at the head of a new Roman Empire. The most prominent surviving monuments to his megalomania are the suburb of EUR (*see p160*) and the Foro Italico sports complex (*see p156*).

When put to the test in World War II, Fascist Italy rapidly foundered. Mussolini was ousted from power in 1943 and Romans switched their allegiance. During the period of German occupation that followed, Italian partisans showed themselves capable of acts of great courage. Rome was declared an 'open city' meaning that the Germans agreed not to defend it, pitching their defence south of the city. While other Italian cities and towns were pounded by bombs, Rome suffered only one serious bombing raid during the whole war.

After the war Italy voted to become a republic and Rome quickly adapted to the new political structures. *Partitocrazia* – government by a group of political parties sharing power and dividing up lucrative government jobs and contracts between them – suited the Roman approach to life. The political unrest that hit Italy in the 1970s and '80s – a spate of right-wing bomb attacks, and kidnappings of key figures by the far-left Red Brigades – affected Rome less than it did Milan or Turin. Romans simply swam with the political tide: they voted in their first Communist mayor in 1976.

The city benefited greatly from Italy's post-war economic boom, spreading out along its major arterial roads. The problem for the post-war city authorities has been how to preserve the old city yet encourage development. Rome's main industry remains itself, whether capital of Italy or historical relic, and the city continues to thrive, trading – as it has done for the millennium and a half since the Empire fell – on its unforgettable past.

IN CONTEXT

Benito Mussolini.

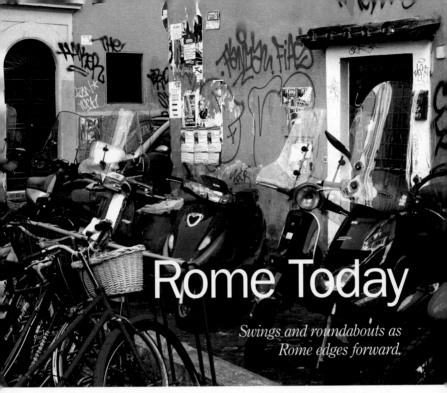

Rome Today

*Swings and roundabouts as
Rome edges forward.*

Perhaps it was inevitable after a rush of millennial activity; and of course the economic downturn hasn't helped; or perhaps the current centre-right incumbents of city hall simply aren't as adept at spinning their achievements as their centre-left predecessors. For one reason or another, as the Eternal City moved into the second decade of the 21st century the atmosphere was decidedly less buoyant.

Which is not to say that there aren't bright spots and exciting novelties. The inauguration in 2010 of Zaha Hadid's Stirling Prize-winning **MAXXI** (*see p41*) centre for contemporary art and architecture was a healthy shot in the arm for the city. Yet the project wasn't new: in fact, MAXXI opened 11 years after Hadid's project was selected – 11 years of interminable stop-go construction, political wrangling and financial bungling.

And the 2010 opening to the public, for the first time ever, of the **Colosseum**'s hypogeum (underground tunnels) and top floor complete with dramatic view over the city, and of the massive Temple of Venus in the **Roman Forum** gave the impression that the city's heritage was taking centre stage again. The effect was spoiled somewhat by sections of the **Domus Aurea** collapsing and chunks of plaster sheering off the Colosseum.

'2.8 million – that's 0.98 cars per inhabitant – in 2009, according to the Automobile Club d'Italia.'

UP AND DOWNS

Grand openings and archaelogical mishaps were set against a backdrop of a centre-left regional council president forced to resign in a squalid tale of transvestite prostitution (honeytrap or predeliction? – perhaps we'll never know); a centre-right mayor dogged by allegations that hundreds (literally) of friends, relations, political supporters and their offspring had been eased into plum council jobs in the first years of his administration; arson attacks on gay venues and racially motivated muggings in inner-suburb areas... all in all, not the brightest of pictures.

It should be said, of course, that even in those heady days around the turn of the millennium when successive centre-left administrations were working hard to inject a sense of self-worth into what had become a rather grimy, sadly resigned capital, Rome was never wholly a paragon of streamlined efficiency. Far from it. Then as now, you could ask any taxi driver what state he thought his city was in, and chances were that your trip wouldn't be long enough for his litany of woes: the relentless year-on-year increase in cars bumping over the city cobbles (2.8 million – that's 0.98 cars per inhabitant – in 2009, according to the Automobile Club d'Italia); skyrocketing pollution levels; the disruption caused when the pope or the president or some foreign VIP is whisked through the streets in high-speed, high-security dashes, or when demonstrators process through the city centre; the chaos – occasionally violence – when key football matches are played at the Stadio Olimpico; the transport strikes that bring the city to gridlock; the treacherous potholes; the unending road works; the never-ending works on never-ready new metro lines; the nose-to-tail tour buses disgorging ever more people into the narrow medieval streets.

All of which was – and is – true... to some extent. But Romans are inveterate moaners, with very short memories. They have to be forced to recall how it was back in the bad old days of the 1970s and '80s, when corruption paired with indifference and incompetence meant total stasis for the city. And many won't even admit that when large sums of money were funnelled towards the capital for the 2000 Holy Year, the city took on a new lease of life and began once again to look like a world capital – with all the morale-boosting side effects that can have. Parks were created and historic buildings received a fresh coat of paint. Long-closed museums were spruced up and opened with user-friendly visiting hours. Even then, critics moaned that the 'renaissance' was skin-deep, a PR exercise for out-of-towners visiting the *centro storico*. But wheels were put in motion, and Romans could once again expect pleasant surroundings as the norm.

In some areas, Rome even leap-frogged other cities to provide services that the most avant-garde simply didn't have: for years now anyone with a laptop or smartphone has been able to relax in city-sponsored hotspots in the city's main parks, including **Villa Borghese** (*see p74*), or switch on in much of the *centro storico* and find themselves online through www-romawireless.com.

The Renzo Piano-designed **Auditorium-Parco della Musica** (*see p265*), inaugurated in 2002, has continued to revolutionise cultural life in the city with an intelligent, all-embracing programming philosophy. And the **Teatro Palladium** (*see p283*) – like the Auditorium, located in a suburb with little or no arts 'tradition' – is equally lively, and the trickle-down effect on the whole cultural and entertainment scene can still be felt.

'Anyone who passed through the Eternal City 15 years ago will remember having to get up with the birds in order to see anything'

Moreover, while much of Italy has struggled through a rough economic patch, Rome and its surrounding province have done better than the national average in many areas. The city continues to produce the largest single share of the country's GDP, but tourism, on the other hand, was still feeling the effects of recession in 2009 with a 1.3 percent fall in the number of tourists staying in the city's hotels and other registered holiday accommodation, the *Ente Bilaterale per il Turismo* reported.

Compounding its problems, Rome is dogged by transport problems, due in large part to the fact that the mass-transit system – the *metropolitana* – is woefully inadequate: for decades, the city has limped on with two lines that skirt the city centre and head to outlying residential and business districts. This, in turn, is due to the fact that at the bottom of any hole dug anywhere remotely central is layer upon layer of history. In spring 2006, work began on Rome's new metro line C: this will slice north-west to south-east, right through the most visited areas – not, planners hope, ferrying tourists, so much as carrying rushing Romans, thus leaving visitors to enjoy extensive pedestrianised zones above. All this, authorities say, will have been achieved by 2013. We'll see.

Other headaches stem from the result of the economic boom of the 1960s and '70s. From 1.65 million in 1951, the city's population had risen to 2.78 million by 1971, a 68 per cent leap. To house the new residents, property speculators threw up jerry-built high-rises along the major arteries out of town. These developments were unplanned, sometimes unplumbed and largely unconnected with the centre... except for those people who were able to invest in a Fiat 500 and, for their entertainment, pile into a *centro* that was far too small and ill-equipped to accommodate them.

The urban development masterplan – the Piano Regolatore Generale (PRG) – approved in 1962 was a sorry case of shutting the stable door after the horse had bolted. Its good intentions were tardy and largely ignored thereafter. It wasn't until March 2006 that a replacement finally went into effect. The PRG lays down stringent rules on the percentage of territory given over to parks and gardens, and sets out high mandatory targets for energy production – each new building, depending on type and destination, must produce a certain percentage of its energy with solar or photovoltaic panels – and conservation. It remains to be seen how far this will be implemented.

WHAT'S IN IT FOR US?

So much for the Rome of the Romans. And the Rome of the visitor? As you hesitate on the kerb, aside life-threatening traffic, you might be forgiven for thinking that nothing much has changed in Rome since *Roman Holiday*. But it has.

Anyone who passed through the Eternal City 15 years ago will remember having to get up with the birds in order to see anything: museums – the ones that weren't *in restauro* – generally closed at 1pm. This happier state of affairs is sometimes threatened, in less-visited sites, by staff shortages forcing early closures, and poor maintenance creates inexcusable problems even in such Roman icons as the Colosseum. But the major attractions continue to extend opening hours, with online and phone booking becoming increasingly easier.

Besides, there's more to see. The **Ara Pacis** (*see p92*) is now encased in a museum that – love it or hate it – restores its sense of monumentality; the bronze statue of Marcus Aurelius has re-acquired grandeur in its airy new pavilion in the

IN CONTEXT

Musei Capitolini (*see p53*). The recently reopened **Museo dei Fori Imperiali** has given Trajan's remarkable markets a new lease of life. MACRO's new wing and MAXXI building site provide more room for contemporary art. And the latest technology is at least being used to good effect in the new-for-2010 digs beneath **Palazzo Valentini**.

The events on offer during the **Estate Romana** (Roman summer; *see p242*) are holding up fairly well in the face of budget cuts; the **Rome International Film Festival** (*see p244*) in October, while no rival for its Venice counterpart, is a glam attraction.

A few years ago, it looked like Rome was in danger of falling prey to its own success: in the *centro storico* international chains were driving the old one-off shops... at times cheered on by misguided younger Romans who equate international blandness with worldly sophistication. Charming, dependable neighbourhood trattorias were being superceded by sophisticated places with much style and little substance.

Now the question is whether the Eternal City might be back-sliding. Late in 2010, local problems were being exacerbated by the national mood. General disinterest in and disgust with politics at all levels meant that the usual democratic checks and balances were being eroded. In a country where tourism – much of it to historic, art-packed cities like Rome – accounts for some 11 percent of GDP and occupies over four percent of the national workforce, it is inconceivable a finance minister should justify budget restrictions saying dismissively and condescendingly 'you can't eat culture'. Yet that's how Minister Giulio Tremonti sees Italy's immense artistic and cultural heritage. Italy in general and Rome in particular seem to be in need of the kind of guidance that truly values what it has, and ensures that it isn't allowed to crumble.

Popes of the Modern Era

Deprived of their temporal clout when Rome fell to newly united Italy in 1871, the popes of the 20th and 21st century have still made their presence felt.

Pius X (Giuseppe Sarto, 1903-14) a virulent anti-modernist with a dim view of democratic institutions. Created a network of spies to keep priests in line.

Benedict XV (Giacomo della Chiesa, 1914-1922) earned equal measures of admiration and vilification when he remained neutral in World War I; he was described as a 'prophet of peace' by the current pope who took his name.

Pius XI (Achille Ratti, 1922-39) railed against totalitarianism, but then opted for Fascism over Communism. Signed an anti-Communist pact with Hitler and the Lateran Pacts with Mussolini.

Pius XII (Eugenio Pacelli, 1939-58) maintained close contacts with both sides in World War II; later accused of not protecting Italy's Jews. The first modern pope to invoke papal infallibility on his teaching on Mary's Assumption.

John XXIII (Angelo Roncalli, 1958-63) the 'Good Pope' and most beloved of modern times, convened the Second Vatican Council to bring the Church into the modern era.

Paul VI (Giovanni Battista Montini, 1963-78) wound up and instituted changes introduced by Second Vatican Council; Paul VI was the first pope in 150 years to travel outside Italy; author of controversial *Humanae Vitae* encyclical codifying Church's ban on contraception and abortion.

John Paul I (Albino Luciani, 1978) pope for just 33 days, remains the darling of conspiracy theorists: did his heart condition kill him, or was he murdered because he knew too much?

John Paul II (Karol Wojtya, 1978-2005) the first non-Italian pope in 455 years, jet-setting Pole JPII was intensely anti-Communist and traditionalist but a great media manipulator.

Benedict XVI (Joseph Ratzinger, 2005-) a scholarly pope with little media savvy and a long record as head of the orthodoxy-imposing Congregation for the Doctrine of the Faith (aka Inquisition).

Architecture

Classical ruins, futuristic modern design and everything in between.

TEXT:ANNE HANLEY

There has never been a time in Rome when architecture wasn't about making a statement – and the statement has always been, first and foremost, political. From the ancient fora with their marbled temples and towering statues, to the overwhelming churches of the Baroque and the gleaming white EUR district – a Fascist ideal city – the goal was always to awe. Still today, city councils of all political hues summon international archi-stars to show their clout. The long slump in new architecture between the late 1980s and 2000 is very much over, and talented and original architects have been – and continue to be – hard at work in the city. Packed as it is with significant buildings, Rome just keeps adding more.

THE ANCIENT CITY

The classical ruins we see today are, to an extent, misleading. What's missing (besides roofs and walls) is colour: there was nothing minimalist about ancient Rome. Statues were multi-hued: buildings and temples were a riot of variegated marbles; bas-reliefs were painted in garish shades. What they still give is an idea of size: major buildings were designed to express the might of Rome. Perhaps for this reason, it was a while before the Romans developed much in the way of architectural style.

The Romans had the Etruscans to thank for insights into hydraulics and town planning. The Greek system of orders was followed for important façades. The main Greek orders – with columns of different proportions based on their width – were Doric (plain and sturdy), Ionic (more slender and ornate) and Corinthian (the most delicate and ornate of all). The **Colosseum** (*see p60*) is a good example of how they were used: hefty Doric at the bottom to support the construction; lighter, more elegant Ionic in the middle; and the decorative Corinthian top layer. It wasn't only columns that were copied from Greece: whole genres of building were based on Greek models: temples were colonnaded and either rectangular or circular; theatres were derived from their Greek counterparts.

Eventually, however, the Romans came up with some ideas of their own: elliptical arenas – known as amphitheatres – designed for blood sports; rectangular meeting houses flanked by columns, known as basilicas; and efficient plumbing and heating systems, complete with hot running water. Perhaps most importantly, the Romans took the arch to unprecedented heights of perfection, giving the world its first large-scale, free-standing masonry.

The most common stone found around Rome was soft, volcanic tufa. This was not an ideal building material, and as early as the third century BC a form of concrete was developed, made of pozzolana (volcanic ash), lime and tufa rubble. Without concrete, constructing the **Pantheon** (*see p100*) would have been impossible: the huge hemispherical dome was the largest cast-concrete construction made before the 20th century. Other feats of cast-concrete engineering include the **Terme di Diocleziano** (*see p141*) and **Terme di Caracalla** (*see p120*). But concrete was not aesthetically pleasing, so buildings were faced with veneers of coloured marble or travertine. Brick, another fundamental Roman building material, was used to face buildings, to lend internal support to concrete walls and as a material in its own right. The most impressive example is the **Mercati di Traiano** (*see p65*).

EARLY CHRISTIAN ROME

Stylistically speaking, the transition from pagan to paleo-Christian was a smooth one, though this isn't always immediately apparent. The earliest Christian meeting places – known as *tituli* – were in very ordinary private houses. The first churches happily adopted the basilica form. Churches founded in the fourth and fifth centuries such as **San Giovanni in Laterano** (*see p131*), **Santi Quattro Coronati** (*see p127*) and **Santa Maria in Trastevere** (*see p115*) are the most tangible connection we have with the interiors of ancient civic Rome. Most are rectangular, with a flat roof and a colonnade separating a tall nave from lower aisles. Natural light enters the nave through high windows. Behind the altar, opposite the entrance, is an apse topped by a conch (domed roof). Perhaps the best example of all is **Santa Sabina** (*see p119*), which was shorn of later additions in a no-holds-barred restoration in the 1930s.

You can trace the fortunes of the Catholic church in Rome's architecture. When it was poor, as in the fifth century, buildings were plain and functional; when it was rich, in the eighth and 12th centuries, churches were adorned with brilliant mosaics. The most magnificent to have survived are in **Santa Maria Maggiore** (*see p140*), **Santa Prassede** (*see p134*) and Santa Maria in Trastevere. Many churches were decorated with cosmati-work: choirs, candlesticks and floors inlaid with dazzling patterns in chips of coloured marble and glass. Very occasionally, circular churches were built: **Santa**

Costanza (*see p157*) – with its swirling mosaics, which owe much to pagan symbolism – was probably built in the fourth century as a mausoleum for the daughters of Emperor Constantine; its contemporary, **Santo Stefano Rotondo** (*see p128*), may have been inspired by the church of the Holy Sepulchre in Jerusalem.

During the Middle Ages, Rome's influential families were engaged in an almost constant battle for power – something reflected in the city's architecture. Anyone who could, opted for a fortress-home with lookout towers like **Torre delle Milizie**, behind Trajan's market (*see p66*).

The quarrels between the families were to have long-lasting effects: with daggers constantly drawn, they failed to impose a Roman candidate on the throne of St Peter's. France stepped in, had Clement V elected, and helped him to shift the papacy to Avignon in 1309, where it remained until 1378. The international funds that had shored up the spendthrift papacy were diverted to the French city and Rome was left bankrupt. The Gothic period passed the city by (the one exception being the church of **Santa Maria sopra Minerva**, *see p101*). The early Renaissance, too, was lost on the shadow of its former self that Rome had become.

Museo dell'Ara Pacis. *See p42.*

'There was nothing minimalist about ancient Rome. Buildings and temples were a riot of variegated marbles.'

THE RENAISSANCE

In the late 14th century a revolution in art, architecture and thought was under way in Tuscany. In crumbling, medieval Rome it was not until the following century that the Renaissance began to gather momentum (the sole exception being the group of artists around genius Pietro Cavallini). In 1445 the Florentine architect Antonio Filarete created one of Rome's first significant Renaissance works: the magnificent central bronze doors of **St Peter's** (*see p144*).

It was Pope Nicholas V (1447-55) who realised that if Rome was to take on fully its role as the focus of Christianity, she had to look the part. As a first step, Nicholas commissioned extensive restoration work on the fourth-century basilica of St Peter, which was in imminent danger of collapse. Meanwhile, those with lucrative church connections built fabulous palaces: papal banker Agostino Chigi commissioned a lavish villa in 1508 (it's now the **Villa Farnesina,** *see p116*) and in 1515 work started on **Palazzo Farnese** (*see p106*) for Cardinal Alessandro Farnese.

Pope Pius II (1458-64), a cultured Tuscan, banned the quarrying of ancient buildings for construction materials for the new. Sixtus IV (1471-84) had roads paved and widened, churches such as **Santa Maria della Pace** (*see p95*) and **Santa Maria del Popolo** (*see p91*) rebuilt, and the **Sistine Chapel** (*see p148*) built and decorated by the foremost artists of the day.

Rome's Renaissance reached its peak with Julius II (1503-13), who made Donato Bramante (1444-1514) his chief architect. Bramante came to Rome from Milan in 1499, and in 1502 built the **Tempietto** (*see p118*). With its domed cylinder surrounded by a Tuscan Doric colonnade, the Tempietto came closer than any other building to the spirit of antiquity. Julius also commissioned Michelangelo (1475-1564) to sculpt his tomb and fresco the ceiling of the Sistine Chapel. Raphael (1483-1520) was called in to decorate the *stanze* (private apartments) in the Vatican palace.

Not satisfied with the restoration of St Peter's initiated by his predecessors, the supremely self-assured Julius decided to scrap the basilica that for 12 centuries had been one of the holiest sites in Christendom and start again. The job was given to Bramante, and in 1506 the foundation stone was laid. Work began on Bramante's Greek-cross design, but was halted after his death in 1514. In 1547 Michelangelo took over, increasing the scale tremendously. During the papacy of Sixtus V (1585-90) – an obsessive planner responsible for the layout of much of modern Rome – Giacomo della Porta (1533-1602) erected the dome to a design by Michelangelo. The second half of the 16th century in Rome was dominated by the austere reforms of the Council of Trent (1545-63), designed to counter the ideas of the Reformation, and by the establishment of heavy-handed new religious orders such as the Jesuits. With the dictates of the Counter-Reformation in mind, Paul V (1605-21) finally scuppered the original Greek-cross design for St Peter's and instead commissioned Carlo Maderno (1556-1629) to lengthen the nave to create a Latin cross.

The earliest churches of the period, such as the **Chiesa Nuova** (*see p94*), were plain and provided with long naves suitable for processions. The **Gesù** (*see p105*) was ideal for the purposes of the Jesuits, as no architectural obstacles came between the preacher and his flock.

As the Counter-Reformation gathered pace, great cycles of decoration teaching the mysteries of the faith or inspiring the onlooker to identify with the sufferings of martyrs (as in the bloodthirsty frescoes of Santo Stefano Rotondo) began to appear.

IN CONTEXT

'The Florentine architect Antonio Filarete created one of Rome's first significant Renaissance works: the magnificent central bronze doors of St Peter's.'

THE BAROQUE

This austerity gave way to an exuberant, theatrical Baroque. It is to a great extent the endlessly inventive confections of the Baroque that make Rome what it is today. Architects such as Giacomo della Porta and Domenico Fontana (1543-1607) set the scene for the real shapers of the Baroque: Gian Lorenzo Bernini, Francesco Borromini and Pietro da Cortona.

Bernini (1598-1680) virtually made the Baroque his own, with his imaginative use of marble, bronze and stucco. He was jealously guarded by his Barberini family patrons, carrying out much of the decoration of the interior of **St Peter's** for the Barberini Pope Urban VIII.

Bernini said that quarrelsome, neurotic Borromini (1559-1667) 'had been sent to destroy architecture', and for centuries Borromini was vilified; today he is recognised as one of the great masters of the period, perhaps the greatest in the inventive use of ground plan and spatial effects. The most startling examples of his work are **San Carlo alle Quattro Fontane** (*see p71*) and **Sant'Ivo alla Sapienza** (*see p99*).

Like Bernini, Pietro da Cortona (1597-1669) created some of his greatest works for the Barberini popes. At Santa Maria della Pace he combined opposing convex forms that, curving sharply at the ends, are nearly flat in the middle. The result is overwhelmingly theatrical.

Throughout the Baroque period the patronage of papal families and the religious orders sustained an explosion of architectural and artistic fervour. Several popes commissioned the decoration of St Peter's (Urban VIII, 1623-44); the colonnade in front of it (Alexander VII, 1655-67) and the layout of **piazza Navona** (*see p97*). Their cardinal nephews inspired many lesser building schemes: the redecoration or restoration of existing churches, and private villas, gardens and palaces. The Jesuit church of **Il Gesù**, though begun in the 1560s, was completed decades later with a façade by Giacomo della Porta.

NEO-CLASSICISM AND UNIFICATION

During the 18th century the Baroque gained a rococo gloss, as demonstrated by Nicola Salvi's **Fontana di Trevi** (*see p67*) and Francesco de Sanctis' **Spanish Steps** (*see p89*). Giovanni Battista Piranesi imposed his neo-classical theories on the city in the later part of the 18th century, creating a striking tableau in **piazza dei Cavalieri di Malta** (*see p119*).

The French occupation of the city (1809-14) brought a flurry of Gallic town planning. Some plans – such as Giuseppe Valadier's magnificent reorganisation of **piazza del Popolo** (*see p91*) and the **Pincio** (*see p74*) – were carried out under French rule. Others were adopted after 1815 by the restored papacy.

In 1870 the city became capital of a united Italy, ruled by the Savoy dynasty, which sought to impose order on the chaotic cityscape, providing it with a road system and structures to accommodate the burgeoning bureaucracy… even if this meant razing entire medieval and Renaissance quarters in the process. **Piazza Vittorio** (*see p59*), **Palazzo delle Esposizioni** and the jingoistic **Vittoriano** monument (*see p59*) in piazza Venezia are fine examples. Occasional relief from the pomposity comes in the shape of lovely Liberty (art nouveau) outcrops, such as the **Casina della civette** (*see p158* **Villa**

Profile MAXXI

Rome's award-winning 21st-century arts facility.

In 1999, a futuristic design by Anglo-Iraqi architect Zaha Hadid was selected to house Rome's answer to London's Tate Modern: **MAXXI** (Museo nazionale delle arti del secolo XXI – 21st-century Arts Museum; for listing, *see p156*). Eleven years later, after many hiccups, MAXXI exploded on to the city scene.

Occupying the site of a former army barracks in the northern Flaminio suburb, the new complex is a snaking structure that insinuates itself into and over the surrounding apartment blocks. It has a library, a resource centre, a café and a bookshop. From an original budget of around €57 million, the cost of building MAXXI shot up to some €150 million, providing ammunition for critics who argued the last thing glory-filled Rome needed to lavish funds on was a space to exhibit what it does least well: contemporary art.

The enthusiastic crowds that queue through MAXXI's outdoor spaces as they wait to get past the beetling grey-concrete lobby into the five interconnecting exhibition spaces don't seem to agree. Whatever the contents – and the complex opened with a winning array of shows, including an excellent retrospective on Rationalist architect Luigi Moretti – Hadid's building is a triumph in a city that tends to rest on its architectural laurels.

No one could have got away with this in the *centro*

storico: MAXXI follows Renzo Piano's striking but rather tamer Auditorium (2002) just down the road, in a district where the only real competition is Pierluigi Nervi's wonderful Palazzetto dello Sport (1956). On the outside, MAXXI's concrete walls unexpectedly lurch and lean; inside, sinuous black staircases criss-cross through the towering central spaces. Natural light floods in through huge glass walls: on the top floor, the whole roller-coaster comes to an abrupt halt at one of them – tilting outwards towards the top, it makes you feel you're teetering on the brink, about to take flight into the surrounding cityscape.

The project earned Hadid the Royal Institute of British Architects' (RIBA) Stirling Prize in 2010. And it gave Romans something to think about: a vibrant modern city can't simply cling to its architectural gems – it needs to continue its dialogue with the contemporary. MAXXI has set that conversation going.

IN CONTEXT

Torlonia), the palazzo housing **Museo Hendrik Christian Andersen** (*see p81*), and the whole, extraordinary **Coppedè district** around piazza Mincio in the northern suburbs.

20TH CENTURY AND CONTEMPORARY

During the Fascist period (1922-43) the expansion of Rome was given a push by several large-scale projects. One of the most impressive was Luigi Moretti's **Foro Italico** (*see p155*), a sports complex with two stadiums and an army of towering statues of naked athletes. To celebrate the 20th anniversary of the Fascist revolution construction began on a whole new district, initially called E42 but later renamed *Esposizione universale romana* (**EUR** for short; *see p160*). It is one of the most striking examples of town planning anywherein Europe.

With construction under way at EUR, Mussolini turned his attention to the *centro storico*: here, according to his Grand Plan, chunks of the medieval and Renaissance urban fabric would be destroyed, making room for a network of boulevards to improve sight lines between major monuments. Thankfully, the outbreak of war stopped *il Duce* wreaking too much havoc. He did, however, manage to bludgeon the **via dei Fori Imperiali** through the ruins of ancient Rome from the Colosseum to piazza Venezia.

During his rule, however, some of Rome's most interesting modern buildings were built, with a philosophy that was dubbed *razionalismo*, a blend of European functionalism with the elegance of Mediterranean/classical tradition. In the state-sponsored building spree of the 1920s and '30s, the architects working in this style contributed some gems: **post office buildings** in via Marmorata by Adalberto Libera and in piazza Bologna by Mario Ridolfi, and Moretti's **Casa della Gioventù** in largo Ascianghi (all 1933-35) are masterpieces of the modern movement. By the '30s, the *razionalisti* realised that they were propaganda pawns. Their last great works of the period were in the *Città universitaria* campus. Libera stayed on to design the **Palazzo dei Congressi** in EUR.

After the war, with Italians from all over the country drifting to the capital, a number of successful public-housing projects were developed. Economic prosperity in the 1950s allowed unfinished projects to be completed: **Termini railway station** was given a magnificent wave-like canopy, and building resumed in EUR. The prosperity fuelled many elegant modernist projects, including the sports venues built by Pier Luigi Nervi for the 1960 Olympics.

A growing population with money to spend was to have dire effects on the capital's outskirts, where property speculators had a zoning-free field day. From the 1960s to the '80s, high-rise blocks galloped across previously unspoilt countryside. Though the *centro storico* was spared atrocities, there was a distinct lack of anything new: work on the first major post-war building project within the Aurelian Walls (the **Ara Pacis** museum, *see p92; photo p38*), only began in 2000.

The decades-long slump in new architecture is over, with talented and original architects at work. Rome's **mosque** (*see p317*), one of the largest in Europe, was completed in 1995 to a design by postmodernist Paolo Portoghesi. In 2002 Renzo Piano's **Auditorium-Parco della Musica** (*see p266* **The Sound of Perfection**) went into operation and has been a resounding success. Richard Meier's slick container for the Ara Pacis was inaugurated in 2006 to much trumpetting and even more criticism.

In the **Mattatoio** (*see p121*), the former slaughterhouse in Testaccio, the old holding pens and fridge units have been transformed into a MACRO exhibition space, a branch of the Academy of Fine Arts and an organic outlet (*see p233* **Organic in the Abbatoir**).

The trend continues, and 2010 saw the inauguration (finally) of Odile Decq's new building for **MACRO** (*see p157*) and Zaha Hadid's Stirling prize-winning **MAXXI** (*see p41* **Profile**). Work is plodding on on Massimiliano Fuksas' 'Cloud' – the new **Centro Congressi Italia** in EUR – and Rem Koolhaas' **Città dei Giovani** (City of Youth) arts and retail development for the old wholesale vegetable *Mercati generali* on via Ostiense is slowly coming to life. For a **glossary** of architectural terms, *see p324*.

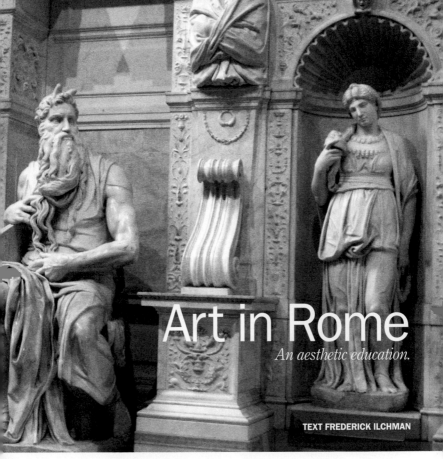

Art in Rome

An aesthetic education.

TEXT FREDERICK ILCHMAN

From the Renaissance through the 19th century, an artist's education was not complete without a journey to Rome. The whole city was seen as an overflowing 'studio' with classical ruins, ancient statues, and the newest works furnishing the models.

Few travellers today have such lofty artistic goals, but looking closely at the art of Rome still offers a stirring aesthetic experience – and a great education. Art in Rome embraces both quality and stunning chronological range. That the city displays art covering nearly 3,000 years is staggering; that almost all of it was produced right here even more so. Furthermore, many of the greatest works are still in their original settings, offering an authentic context that museums can never duplicate.

Yet today, as in the 16th century, visitors can find Rome overwhelming. With a little forward planning, however, you can experience Rome's unique continuum of past and present for yourself.

Frederick Ilchman spent five years in Italy researching 16th-century painting. He is now a curator at the Museum of Fine Arts in Boston.

Frescos in Santa Cecilia in Travestere by **Pietro Cavallini**.

'Two centuries ago the Vatican's Pio Clementino sculpture gallery was undoubtedly the most famous museum in the world.'

ART OF THE ANCIENTS

Although the art of Rome has furthered the needs of the Catholic church for nearly two millennia, the single strongest influence has always been the weighty legacy of the ancient world. Ancient Rome, as *caput mundi*, harvested or created much of the best art of antiquity. Those who successively sacked or occupied the city – from Alaric in 410 to Napoleon in 1808 – pillaged much of this patrimony, but the fraction that survives continues to amaze.

Egyptian obelisks transported across the Mediterranean still mark key squares in Rome and, despite a lack of Greek originals, the miracle of Greek art can be studied and appreciated in scores of important Roman copies. These marbles – often copies of bronzes that have long since been destroyed – display the Greek flair for endowing the body with beauty, purpose and a sense of movement. The classical ideal, combining striking naturalism with idealised body types, offered a standard of beauty that was hard to ignore.

Although the most famous Greek sculpture in Rome is the *Ludovisi Throne* – in the Ludovisi family collection housed in Palazzo Altemps – many works are transitional in nature, between Greek and Roman. An outstanding example in this category is the hulking *Belvedere Torso* – a superhuman physique from about 50 BC that inspired Michelangelo – now housed in the Vatican Museums.

The Etruscans, the pre-Roman peoples who dominated central Italy from the sixth to the third century BC, produced an exuberant, violent and sensuous art. Villa Giulia (*see p81*) offers an extraordinary selection, including life-size terracotta sculptures from Veio and a tender terracotta sarcophagus of a married couple. Equally important is the Etruscan bronze work known as the *Lupa Capitolina* (the 'Capitoline She-Wolf'), which is in the Musei Capitolini.

COME THE ROMANS

Beginning in the third century BC the Romans literally built upon this Greek and Etruscan legacy with an unprecedented construction boom. New structural techniques – notably the arch and poured-concrete technology – gave birth to daring and spacious buildings. The Romans were also responsible for monumental forms that blur the boundary between architecture and art, such as the triumphal arch ornamented with reliefs (those of Septimus Severus and Titus in the Forum, *see p62*; and Constantine's, *see p60*) and the independent column ornamented with a spiral band (Colonna di Traiano, *see p65*; Colonna di Marco Aurelio, *see p89*). A further Roman innovation on a smaller scale was the portrait bust, which recorded facial features of the great and the average with arresting honesty.

Much of the best classical art is now concentrated in a few major museums. The Palazzo Altemps, which contains the statue of the *Gaul's Suicide*, is an ideal first stop. The Palazzo Massimo alle Terme (*see p138*) houses important works of Roman painting and sculpture. The large collections of the Musei Capitolini feature the *Dying Gaul* and beautiful centaurs from Hadrian's Villa (*see p298*). Today the sheer size of the classical collection of the Vatican Museums can be demoralising, and the galleries may seem a distraction in one's march towards the Sistine Chapel, but two centuries ago the Vatican's Pio Clementino sculpture gallery was undoubtedly the most famous museum in the world. Even today one sculpture there gives modern tourists the same frisson that countless other classical works imparted to 18th-century visitors: this is the *Laocoön*, a Hellenistic sculpture showing a powerful man and his sons struggling for their lives against serpents. It remains perhaps the most dynamic statue in the whole history of art.

HOLY INSPIRATION

Christian art flourished in Rome after AD 313, when Emperor Constantine's Edict of Milan legitimised the new religion. Rome was transformed from a city of temples to one of churches. Little of the devotional apparatus of the newly recognised religion survives, but stunning mosaics decorate a number of venerable churches: including Santa Costanza (fourth century, *see p157*), Santa Maria Maggiore (fifth century, *see p140*), Santi Cosma e Damiano (sixth century, *see p66*), and Santa Prassede (ninth century, *see p134*). Two of the most atmospheric early churches are the austere, lovely Santa Sabina (*see p119*), and San Clemente (*see p125*), with its 12th-century mosaics.

Later medieval art can be enjoyed in Santa Cecilia in Trastevere (*see p117*), which contains a ciborium (1283) by **Arnolfo di Cambio** (best known as the architect of the Duomo in Florence) and a pioneering fresco of the *Last Judgment* (1293) by **Pietro Cavallini** above the nun's choir. The little-known Cavallini – who perhaps deserves to rank with Giotto as an early initiator of the Renaissance – also impresses with his narrative mosaics (1291) in nearby Santa Maria in Trastevere (*see p115*).

From 1309 to 1377 the papacy was based in Avignon; Rome withered, and only a fraction of the population remained. Thus the Gothic is largely absent in the Eternal City. The lack of late-medieval art, however, is compensated for by the wealth of Renaissance, and particularly High Renaissance, art of the 15th and 16th centuries.

THE RENAISSANCE BEGINS IN ROME

The definitive return of the papacy in 1420 permitted the Renaissance and its doctrine of humanism to take root and eventually flourish in the primary seat of classical glory.

Humanism was preoccupied with reviving the language and art of the ancient Greeks and Romans, and reconciling this pagan heritage with Christianity. Renaissance ideas began to leave their mark on the city with architecture based on ancient examples, and sculpture and painting that assimilated the grace and naturalism of the best classical

Filippino Lippi's Caraffa chapel frescoes.

Walk Caravaggio's Masterpieces

Explore the works of the Bad Boy of Baroque.

Michelangelo Merisi da Caravaggio (1571-1610) burned through the Roman art world like a dangerous, dazzling meteor. A hard-drinking rebel with an uncontrollable temper, he died, aged 39, on a Tuscan beach. Of the 50 or so of his paintings to have survived, 22 of the very best are in Rome.

In the late 16th century, **Palazzo Madama** (*see p97*) was the residence of cultured Cardinal Francesco del Monte; Caravaggio lived in a small room on an upper floor. Through Del Monte, Caravaggio was commissioned to decorate a chapel in the French church of **San Luigi dei Francesi** (*see p98*): three scenes from the life of St Matthew – *The Calling* (c1602), where rich tax collector Matthew is called by Jesus; and *The Martyrdom* (c1600) where the saint collapses, watched by a horrified crowd as an angel flies over the executioner's sword. In the central altarpiece is *The Inspiration* (c1602), in which another angel hovers above the head of the pensive saint.

Outside the church, turn left and left again into via delle Coppelle. In the church of **Sant'Agostino** (*see p99*; pictured), Caravaggio's shockingly realistic portrayal of the *Madonna of the Pilgrims* (c1604) caused a storm of controversy, not least because of the dirty feet of the impoverished pilgrims kneeling before the infant Jesus.

Heading north, via della Scrofa (which becomes via Ripetta) leads to piazza del Popolo where **Santa Maria del Popolo** (*see p91*) contains two of Caravaggio's most dramatic canvases: the *Crucifixion of St Peter* (1601) and the *Conversion of St Paul* (1601).

Climb the hill to the Pincio, and wander through Villa Borghese to the **Galleria Borghese** (*see p78*), which has six Caravaggio masterpieces: the dazzling *Boy with a Basket of Fruit* (c1593), bursting with good

health; the greenish *Sick Bacchus* (c1593); a shocking *David with the Head of Goliath* (c1610); an aged, wrinkled *St Jerome in his Study* (1605); a youthful, naked *St John the Baptist* (1606); and the breathtaking *Madonna and Child with St Anne* (1606).

Down via Veneto, **Palazzo Barberini** (*see p71*) houses the haunting *Narcissus* (c1599) and a *Decapitation of Holofernes* (c1599) in which Judith calmly saws off her rapist's head with a kitchen knife.

Continue on to via del Corso and the **Galleria Doria Pamphilj** (*see p100*), where there's a young *St John the Baptist* (c1602), but also a tender *Penitent Magdalene* (c1597) and one of the finest paintings of all: *The Rest on the Flight into Egypt* (c1595).

Proceed to the **Capitoline Museums** (*see p53*), home to the *Gypsy Fortune Tellers* (c1594) and another simpering *St John the Baptist* (c1602).

For yet more Caravaggio, the **Vatican Pinacoteca** (*see p149*) has a fine *Deposition of Christ* (c1604).

IN CONTEXT

'The cruelty often depicted in Caravaggio's paintings mirrored his violent life, and altercations with police and patrons marked his Roman years.'

statues. In 1455, on his deathbed, Pope Nicholas V informed his successors that 'noble edifices combining taste and beauty with imposing proportions would immensely conduce to the exaltation of the chair of St Peter'.

Nicholas' extant contribution to Vatican beautification – the little chapel of Nicholas V, frescoed by **Fra Angelico** and **Benozzo Gozzoli** (1447-79) – may be modest in the light of his ambitions, but it remains an extraordinary jewel of the early Renaissance. Later popes undertook grander campaigns: Sixtus IV (1471-84) engaged the greatest painters of the day – **Perugino**, **Botticelli**, **Ghirlandaio** and **Cosimo Rosselli** – to fresco the walls of his Sistine Chapel in 1481-82. And think what you may of the morals of the Borgia pope, Alexander VI, his taste in art was exquisite, as seen in the frescoes (1493-95) by **Pinturicchio** that perpetuate Perugino's sweet style throughout the many rooms of the Borgia Apartments.

Outside the Vatican the grace of 15th-century Florentine art can also be seen in the joyful and energetic frescoes (1489-93) of **Filippino Lippi** in the Caraffa chapel in the church of Santa Maria sopra Minerva (*see p101*).

THE HIGH RENAISSANCE

In the 16th century, art and architecture took a monumental turn. In painting, the human figure grew in relation to the pictorial field: the busy backgrounds of 15th-century art were eliminated. Sculptors took their cue from ancient statues, making the human body newly heroic. Florentine Michelangelo (1475-1564) first worked in Rome from 1496 to 1501 for clerics and businessmen. He carved his first *Pietà* (now in St Peter's) for a French cardinal. Michelangelo positioned the dead Christ gracefully in his mother's lap, creating an eternal meditation on death.

Under Julius II (1503-13) papal patronage called ever greater artists to work on ever larger projects at the Vatican, shifting the centre of the Renaissance from Florence to Rome. Julius summoned Michelangelo back from Florence to begin work on a monumental tomb, a work destined for the choir of the old St Peter's and crammed with larger-than-life statues. The headstrong Julius soon changed his mind, insisting that the young sculptor paint the ceiling of the Sistine Chapel instead. Complaining bitterly that he was 'no painter', Michelangelo rapidly frescoed the ceiling (1508-11), retelling the first nine chapters of Genesis with a grandeur and solidity previously associated with sculpture.

Although a later campaign to fresco the chapel's altar wall produced the awe-inspiring *Last Judgment* (1534-41), the tomb for Julius limped to an unsatisfactory conclusion in the early 1540s in San Pietro in Vincoli (*see p136*), employing the powerful *Moses* (c1515) as its centrepiece. Following restoration, however, the tomb looks brighter than it has for centuries.

Julius initiated his grandest plan of all when he called upon **Donato Bramante** (1444-1514) to design a new basilica of St Peter's. The stateliness of Bramante's style inspired painters as well as other architects. The most influential of the former was **Raphael** (1483-1520).

Julius would occupy the apartments of his dissolute Borgia predecessor; he insisted on a new suite of rooms – the so-called *Stanze*. These were decorated by Raphael starting in 1508. The presence of Michelangelo working next door on the Sistine ceiling

Hercules and Lichas (left) and *Venus Victrix* (right) by **Canova**.

was a spur to the young painter: the elegant *School of Athens* (1510-11) exemplifies the notion of the High Renaissance, with its re-creation of the philosophers of ancient Greece against a backdrop of imaginary architecture borrowed from Bramante.

If Michelangelo was unsurpassed in depicting the human body in complex poses, the *Stanze* show Raphael's superiority in arranging compositions. The latter's astonishingly swift development can be appreciated in a single room of the Vatican Pinacoteca. There, three masterful altarpieces – *The Coronation of the Virgin* (1505), *The Madonna of Foligno* (c1511) and *The Transfiguration* (c1518-20) – chart the amazing shift from a sweetness reminiscent of Perugino to a brooding, dramatic late style. In the same room, you can also take note of the lavish tapestries, designed by Raphael for the lower walls of the Sistine Chapel.

The Sack of Rome in 1527 halted the artistic boom of the High Renaissance, as frightened artists sought employment elsewhere. The spread of the Protestant Reformation prompted a more hardened, pessimistic spirit that gave preference to mannerist art, a style of exaggerated proportions and contorted poses that developed out of the mature work of Raphael and Michelangelo. Frescoes (c1545) by Raphael's assistant **Perino del Vaga** (1501-47) in the Castel Sant'Angelo (*see p150*) depict both hyper-elegant humans and statues, playing with the viewer's sense of what is real.

GOING FOR BAROQUE

By the second half of the 16th century, the mannerist style had lost its energy. Baroque rescue came through the works of **Annibale Carracci** (1560-1609) of Bologna and the shocking naturalism of Michelangelo Merisi, better known as **Caravaggio** (1571-1610; *see also p47* **Walk**). Carracci, who sought a buoyant version of High Renaissance harmony, is best experienced at the Galleria Doria Pamphili which has a lovely *Flight into Egypt*. Carracci's contemporary Caravaggio left paintings throughout the city during his stormy career. These works, with their extreme *chiaroscuro*, can be seen in the churches of Sant'Agostino (*see p99*) and Santa Maria del Popolo (*see p91*). His masterpiece may be the *Calling of St Matthew* (c1599-1602) in the church of San Luigi dei Francesi (*see p98*).

The Galleria Borghese houses a fine nucleus of Caravaggio paintings, from the coy secular works of his early years to the brooding religious canvases of his maturity, notably the powerful *David with the Head of Goliath* (c1609), in which the severed head is Caravaggio's self-portrait. The cruelty often depicted in Caravaggio's paintings mirrored his violent life, and altercations with police and patrons marked his Roman years. After losing a tennis match and killing his opponent, Caravaggio fled south. His bold style persisted for a generation, though, as witnessed in the Vatican Pinacoteca's extraordinary room of Baroque altarpieces by **Domenichino**, **Guido Reni** and **Nicolas Poussin**. Equally weighty Baroque altarpieces can be seen in the Pinacoteca of the Musei Capitolini, with **Guercino**'s *Burial of St Petronilla* (c1623) winning the prize.

The most faithful followers of Caravaggio's style were **Orazio Gentileschi** (1563-1639) and his daughter **Artemisia** (1593-1652). Artemisia had to endure male prejudice to pursue her career, and both artists left Rome, resurfacing together in London in the late 1630s to work for Charles I. Canvases by father and daughter can be seen in the Galleria Spada (*see p105*).

The consummate artist of the Roman Baroque, however, was primarily a sculptor: **Gian Lorenzo Bernini** (1598-1680). The confident energy inherent in Baroque art is revealed in Bernini's greatest religious sculpture: *The Ecstasy of St Theresa* (1647-52) in Santa Maria della Vittoria (*see p140*) brilliantly captures a split second of sensual rapture. The theatricality of such works as *Apollo and Daphne* (1622-25) in the Galleria Borghese pushed back the boundaries of sculpture, capturing whole narratives in a frozen instant, and describing textures more vividly than any previous carver.

Similarly, the Galleria Doria Pamphili evokes the epoch with outstanding pictures in a magnificent setting. One small room forces a comparison of two portraits of the Pamphili Pope Innocent X (1644-55): a bust by Bernini and a canvas by the Spaniard Diego Velázquez (the pope found the painting 'too truthful'). Both museums are awash in aristocratic atmosphere.

ART MOVES ON

Subsequent generations insisted further upon the artistic unity of architecture, sculpture and painting pioneered by Bernini. Illusionistic ceiling decoration became more and more elaborate. Ceiling paintings – like those in the Palazzo Barberini and the church of the Gesù (*see p105*) – depicted heavenly visions: assemblages of flying figures bathed in celestial light. Perhaps the most inventive practitioner of ceiling painting was **Andrea Pozzo** (1642-1709), a Jesuit painter, architect and stage designer. In **Sant'Ignazio di Loyola** (*see p101*), Pozzo painted both a fresco of the *Glory of St Ignatius Loyola* on the vault of the nave and a false dome on canvas. The latter fools the viewer only from the ideal viewing point, which is marked by a disc on the floor. The Baroque style and the interest in illusionism limped on well into the 18th century.

The final great artistic movement born in Rome was neo-classicism, a nostalgic celebration of ancient Greek art, expressed in stark white statues and reliefs. **Antonio Canova** (1757-1822) created enormous, muscular statues like *Hercules and Lichas*, which can be seen in the Galleria Nazionale d'Arte Moderna (*see p81*), dignified tombs in St Peter's, and plaster wall panels now on show at the Villa Torlonia (*see p158*).

Later movements of the 19th and 20th centuries can be seen at the Galleria Nazionale d'Arte Moderna. For contemporary art, the new **MAXXI** (*see p41* **Profile**) and **MACRO** (*see p157*) galleries show that – at least as far as exhibiting goes – the city isn't entirely trapped in its past.

Works mentioned in this chapter can be seen at the **Galleria Borghese** (*see p78*), **Palazzo Barberini** (*see p71*), **Musei Capitolini** (*see p53*), **Vatican Museums** (*see p148*) and **Palazzo Altemps** (*see p97*).

For a **glossary** of art terms, *see p324*.

Sights

Foro romano (Roman Forum). *See p62.*

From the Capitoline to the Palatine

Sights galore in the iconic heart of ancient Rome.

In the eighth century BC a collection of grass huts was built on a hill overlooking the marshy flood plain of a tributary of the river Tiber. The following century the land was drained, and the settlement expanded down the slopes into what would become the **Roman Forum**. A thousand years of expansion later this was the heart of the ancient world's most powerful city, the capital of an empire that stretched from Scotland to Tunisia. The long-forgotten grass huts were replaced with splendid Imperial palaces (the **Palatine**), great temples were constructed on the neighbouring hill (the **Capitoline**) and Emperors kept public discontent to a minimum with gory entertainment in the **Colosseum**.

| **Map** p344 | **Cafés, Bars &** |
| **Eating Out** p187 | **Gelaterie** p208 |

PIAZZA VENEZIA & THE CAPITOLINE

Heavily trafficked piazza Venezia is dominated by a brash monument to a dynasty that produced five kings. Il Vittoriano (*see p59*) – aka *l'altare della patria* – is a piece of nationalistic bombast made of unsuitably dazzling marble brought at vast expense from Brescia; totally out of proportion with everything around, it was constructed between 1885 and 1911 to honour the first king of united Italy, Vittorio Emanuele II of Savoy. Centred on a colossal equestrian statue of the king (before the statue was welded together, metalworkers held a dinner for 20 in the horse's belly), it's also Italy's memorial to the unknown soldier.

On the western side of piazza Venezia stands **Palazzo Venezia** (*see p57*). Constructed by the Venetian Pope Paul II in the 15th century, it was to become Mussolini's HQ: *il Duce* addressed the crowds from the central balcony. To the south of the palazzo is **San Marco** (*see p58*), a church

founded in the fourth century and remodelled in the 15th century for Pope Paul II.

Across the piazza, newly opened digs beneath the provincial HQ **Palazzo Valentini** (*see p58*) give a fascinating multi-media insight into life here in the late imperial era.

To the right as you face the Vittoriano are the remains of a Roman *insula* (apartment building) which managed to survive the bulldozers that devastated the area to make way for the Vittoriano. Further to the right, steep steps lead up to **Santa Maria in Aracoeli** (*see p59*), built on the spot where, legend says, a sybil prophesied the birth of Christ. Next to that, the ramped *cordonata* ascends to piazza del Campidoglio.

Il **Campidoglio** (the Capitoline) was, politically and religiously speaking, the most

About the author

***Agnes Crawford** came to Rome in 2000 intending to stay six months. She gives tailor-made tours of the city (www.understandingrome.com).*

Capitoline.

SIGHTS

important of ancient Rome's hills and was the site of the two major temples. Chunks of the one to Jupiter Capitolinus, symbolic father of the city – whose cult chambers also included shrines to Minerva, goddess of wisdom, and Juno, wife of Jupiter – can now be seen inside the Musei Capitolini. The other, to Juno Moneta ('giver of advice'), stood on the site of Santa Maria in Aracoeli. It housed the sacred Capitoline geese, whose honking raised the alarm when Gauls attacked Rome in 390 BC; so failsafe was this alarm system that Rome's first mint was built beside it – from *moneta* comes the word 'money'.

The piazza on the Campidoglio was designed in the 1530s by Michelangelo for Pope Paul III, a symbolic rebuilding of the heart of the city after centuries of degradation. It took about a hundred years to complete, and some of Michelangelo's ideas were modified along the way, but it is still very much as he envisaged it. At the top of Michelangelo's *cordonata* are two giant Roman statues of the mythical twins Castor and Pollux, found near piazza Cenci and placed here in 1583. Looking straight ahead from the top of the steps, you'll see Palazzo Senatorio, Rome's city hall, completed by Giacomo della Porta and Girolamo Rainaldi to Michelangelo's design. To the left is Palazzo Nuovo and to the right Palazzo dei Conservatori, both of which house the **Musei Capitolini** (Capitoline Museums; *see below*). For four centuries the piazza's central pedestal supported a magnificent second-century gilded bronze equestrian statue of Emperor Marcus Aurelius. The statue there now is a copy, with

the original inside the Palazzo dei Conservatori. From the top of the *cordonata*, take a right on the road which skirts this palazzo: it leads to a little park with a fantastic view. Beyond a gate, a series of pathways hugs the side of the hill (as dusk falls this is Rome's most central gay cruising area). The upper road continues to that part of the hill known as the Tarpeian Rock, where traitors and murderers were flung to their death. There's a great view of the Roman Forum (with the Colosseum in the distance) and, to your left, the back of the Palazzo dei Senatori, which incorporates the great stone blocks of the Tabularium, where the archives of the ancient city were once held.

★ Musei Capitolini

Piazza del Campidoglio 1 (06 06 0608/06 679 8708, www.museicapitolini.org). Buses to piazza Venezia. **Open** 9am-8pm Tue-Sun. **Admission** €6.50; €4.50 reductions. Extra charge for exhibitions. **Credit** AmEx, DC, MC, V. **Map** p342 E2.

Housed in the twin palaces of Palazzo Nuovo and Palazzo dei Conservatori standing on opposite sides of Michelangelo's piazza del Campidoglio, the Capitoline museums constitute the oldest public gallery in the world. Their collection was begun in 1471, when Pope Sixtus IV presented the Roman people with a group of classical sculptures. Sixtus' successors continued to enrich the collection with examples of ancient art (mostly sculptures) and, at a later date, some important Renaissance and post-Renaissance paintings. The entire collection was

The purchase of a mosaic picture is a nice choice and his value increase in time

Il Gruppo Savelli, unica impresa privata a Roma, unisce all'attività di esposizione e vendita di mosaici antichi e moderni anche quella di produzione di opere in mosaico. Gli ambienti in cui risiede, a fianco del colonnato di San Pietro, ospitano un vero e proprio atelier del mosaico nel quale si possono ammirare al lavoro sia mosaicisti esperti che giovani apprendisti.

Savelli Company, unique private enterprise in Rome with exposition and sales of antique and modern mosaics, unites to its activity the production of mosaic works of art. It is situated next to the colonnade of St. Peters, where they host a true mosaic Gallery and you can admire the work of expert and young apprentice of Mosaic.

Savelli, unica empresa privada a Roma en exposicion y ventas de mosaicos antiguos y modernos, une a la actividad la produccion de estas obras de arte. El lugar donde se encuentra, al lado del colonado de San Pedro, hospita una verdadera boutique del mosaico, donde se puede contemplar el trabajo de expertos y jovenes aprendistas del mosaico.

GALLERIA SAVELLI
Religious Articles
Piazza Pio XII, 1-2 - 00193 Roma
Tel. +39.06.68.80.63.83
Fax +39.06.68.80.44.41

TOLL FREE NUMBER from USA and Canada
(011)800.190.22004
From EUROPE (00)

SAVELLI Arte e Tradizione
Mosaic Art Gallery
Via Paolo VI, 27-29 - 00193 Roma
Tel. +39.06.68.30.70.17
Fax +39.06.68.80.44.39

http://www.savellireligious.com
e-mail: vatican@savellireligious.com

finally opened to the public in 1734, by Pope Clement XII. Many statues remain frustratingly label-less but there is a decent audioguide.

Entrance to the Musei Capitolini is by the **Palazzo dei Conservatori**, on the right as you come up Michelangelo's stairs. The courtyard contains what's left of the colossal statue of Constantine (the rest was made of wood) that originally stood in the Basilica of Maxentius in the Roman Forum.

Upstairs, the huge Sala degli Orazi e Curiazi (Room 1) is home to a statue (1635-40) by Bernini of his patron Urban VIII in which everything about the pope seems to be in motion. There's also a second-century BC gilded bronze statue of Hercules. Room 2 (Sala dei Capitani) has late 16th-century frescoes of great moments in ancient Roman history. In Room 3 (Sala dei Trionfi), the first-century BC bronze of a boy removing a thorn from his foot, known as the *Spinario*, is probably an original Greek work. There's also a rare bronze portrait bust from the fourth or third century BC, popularly believed to be of Rome's first consul, Brutus.

Room 4 (Sala della Lupa) is home to the much-reproduced She-Wolf (*lupa*). This statue is supposedly a fifth-century BC Etruscan bronze, though the suckling twins were added in the Renaissance (attributed to Antonio del Pollaiolo). In Room 5 (Sala delle Oche) is Bernini's pained-looking Medusa and an 18th-century bronze portrait of Michelangelo, believed to have been based on the great master's death mask. Room 6 (Sala delle Aquile) is frescoed with 16th-century Roman scenes amid faux-ancient 'grotesque' decorations. In Room 10 (Sala degli Arazzi) a marvellous marble group shows the Emperor Commodus dressing up as Hercules and being adored by two Tritons. Room 11 (Sala di Annibale) still has original early 16th-century frescoes that show Hannibal riding on an elephant of which Walt Disney would have been proud.

The second-century AD gilded bronze equestrian statue of Marcus Aurelius that for centuries stood in the centre of piazza del Campidoglio has now found a worthy home in an airy new wing of the museums which also contains large sections of a temple to Jupiter (Giove). Though the statue now on the plinth in the piazza outside is a 'perfect' computer-generated copy, it can't compare with the sheer delicacy and majesty of this original.

On the second floor, the **Pinacoteca Capitolina** (Capitoline art gallery) contains a number of significant works. The most striking is Caravaggio's *St John the Baptist* (1596; in the Sala di Santa Petronilla), who has nothing even remotely saintly about him. There's a weepy *Penitent Magdalene* (c1598) by Tintoretto, a *Rape of Europa* by Veronese, and an early *Baptism of Christ* (c1512) by Titian in Room 3. There are also some strangely impressionistic works by Guido Reni in Room 6, various busy scenes by Pietro da Cortona in the room named after him, and some luscious portraits by Van Dyck in the Galleria Cini, which also contains a self-portrait by Velázquez (1649-51) and some lovely early 18th-century scenes of Rome by Gaspare Vanvitelli. While you're up here, check out the café; the view from the terrace is spectacular.

To get to the other side of the Musei Capitolini, housed in the Palazzo Nuovo, visitors pass through the **Tabularium**, the ancient Roman archive building upon which the Palazzo Senatorio was built. The tufa vaults of the Tabularium date back to 78 BC,

Musei Capitolini. *See p53*.

SIGHTS

Roman Forum & the Palatine

and the view from here over the Forum is simply breathtaking. Also visible in this area are the ruins of the Temple of Veiovis ('underground Jupiter').

Palazzo Nuovo houses one of Europe's most significant collections of ancient sculpture. The three ground-floor rooms have portrait busts of Roman citizens, the endearing *Vecchio ubriacone* ('old drunk', part of Bacchus' entourage) and a huge sarcophagus with scenes from the life of Achilles, topped by two reclining second-century AD figures. Dominating the courtyard is the first-century AD river god known as Marforio, reclining above his little fountain.

Upstairs in the long gallery (Room 1), the wounded warrior falling to the ground with his shield is probably a third-century BC discus thrower's top half, turned on its side and given a new pair of legs in the 17th century. Room 2 (Sala delle Colombe) contains a statue of a little girl protecting a dove from a snake, a much-reworked drunken old woman clutching an urn of wine, and a dove mosaic from Hadrian's villa (Villa Adriana; *see p298*) at Tivoli. Room 3 (Gabinetto della Venere) is home to the coy first-century BC *Capitoline Venus*. This was probably based on Praxiteles' *Venus of Cnodis*, considered so erotic by the fourth-century BC inhabitants of Kos that one desperate citizen was caught *in flagrante* with it. In Room 4 (Sala degli Imperatori), portrait busts of emperors, their consorts and children are arranged chronologically, providing a good insight into changing fashions and hairstyles. Next door in Room 5 (Sala dei Filosofi) are ancient portraits of philosophers and poets. Larger statues of mythical figures grace the huge Salone (Room 6). Room 7 (Sala del Fauno) is named

after an inebriated faun carved from *rosso antico* marble in the late second century BC; the smirking, pointy-eared statue inspired Nathaniel Hawthorne's *The Marble Faun*. In Room 8 (Sala del Gladiatore) is the moving *Dying Gaul*, probably based on a third-century BC Greek original. *Photo p55*.

▶ *Many ancient sculptures long hidden in the storerooms of the Musei Capitolini can now be seen at the Centrale Montemartini; see p122.*

Museo di Palazzo Venezia

Via del Plebiscito 118 (06 678 0131). Buses to piazza Venezia. **Open** 8.30am-7.30pm Tue-Sun. **Admission** *Museum* €4; €2 reductions. Extra charge for exhibitions. **No credit cards. Map** p342 E1.

This collection contains a hotchpotch of everything from terracotta models by Bernini to medieval decorative art. In Room 1 are Venetian odds and ends, including a double portrait by Giorgione, while in Room 4 you'll find a glorious zodiac motif on the ceiling. Amid the early Renaissance canvases and

SIGHTS

Il Vittoriano. *See p59.*

Colosseum. *See p60.*

SIGHTS

triptychs in Room 6 is a breastfeeding Madonna dell'Umiltà – a racy show of anatomy for the 14th century, and quite a contrast to the pastel portraits of 18th-century aristocrats adorning Room 8. Collections of porcelain line the long corridor leading to Rooms 18-26, where you'll find Bernini's terracotta musings for the Fontana del Tritone (*see p70*) and the angels on Ponte Sant'Angelo. Six years in the planning, the Lapidarium opened in summer 2006. It occupies the upper level of the cloister of the 'secret garden of Paul II'. As the name suggests, it houses a collection of stone: ancient, medieval and Renaissance sarcophagi, coats of arms, funerary monuments and assorted fragments. The eastern half of the palazzo often hosts major-sounding exhibitions that are sometimes worth checking out but that don't always live up to expectations, but if you stump up the extra fee you at least get to see Mussolini's old office, the huge Sala del Mappamondo, so-called because of an early map of the world that was kept there in the 16th century.

Palazzo Valentini – Domus Romane

Via Quattro Novembre 19A (06 32 810, www. provincia.roma.it). Buses to piazza Venezia. **Open** *9am-5pm Mon, Wed-Sun.* **Admission** €6; €4 reductions. No credit cards. **Map** p342 E2.

INSIDE TRACK ALTA VISTA

Take a ride in the lift at the back of **Il Vittoriano**. From the terrace, there are marvellous views out over the countryside.

Excavated beneath the offices of the Province of Rome, this new-for-2010 attraction not only allows a glimpse into the richly decorated houses of well-heeled citizens of the Roman Empire, but uses ultra-modern technology to reconstruct the surroundings and lifestyles of the ancients. The hour-long visit is definitely the best that central Rome offers for putting the ancient world in context.
▶ *Visits in English leave at 1.30pm: they are always oversubscribed, so book well ahead.*

FREE San Marco

Piazza San Marco (06 679 5205). Buses to piazza Venezia. **Open** 4-7pm Mon; 8.30am-12.30pm, 4-7pm Tue-Sun. **Map** p342 E1.
There's a strong Venetian flavour to this church, which, according to local lore, was founded in 336 on the site of the house where St Mark the Evangelist – the patron saint of Venice – stayed. There are medieval lions, the symbol of St Mark, by the main entrance door; inside are graves of Venetians and paintings of Venetian saints. Rebuilt during the fifth century, the church was further reorganised by Pope Paul II in the 15th century when the neighbouring Palazzo Venezia was built. San Marco was given its Baroque look in the mid 18th century. Remaining from its earlier manifestations are the 11th-century bell tower, a portico attributed to Leon Battista Alberti, the 15th-century ceiling with Paul II's coat of arms, and the ninth-century mosaic of Christ in the apse. Among the figures below Christ is Gregory IV, who was pope when the mosaic was made: his square halo marks him out as bound for sainthood though still alive. In the portico is the gravestone of

Vannozza Catanei, mistress of Rodrigo Borgia – Pope Alexander VI – and mother of the notorious Cesare and Lucrezia. The chapel to the right at the end of the nave was designed by Pietro da Cortona and contains a funerary monument by neo-classical sculptor Antonio Canova.

FREE Santa Maria in Aracoeli

Piazza del Campidoglio 4 (06 6976 3839). Buses to piazza Venezia. **Open** *Apr-Oct* 9am-12.30pm, 3-6.30pm daily. *Nov-Mar* 9.30am-12.30pm, 2.30-5.30pm daily. **Map** p342 E2.

At the head of a daunting flight of 120 marble steps, the Romanesque Aracoeli ('altar of heaven') stands on the site of an ancient temple to Juno Moneta. It was here, legend has it, that a sybil whispered to the Emperor Augustus *haec est ara primogeniti Dei* ('this is the altar of God's first-born'). Though there is an altar purporting to be the one erected by Augustus in the chapel of St Helena (to the left of the high altar), there's no record of a Christian church here until the sixth century. The current basilica-form church was designed (and reoriented to face St Peter's) for the Franciscan order in the late 13th century, perhaps by Arnolfo di Cambio.

Dividing the church into a nave and two aisles are 22 columns purloined from Roman buildings. There's a cosmatesque floor punctuated by marble gravestones and a richly gilded ceiling commemorating the Christian victory over the Turks at the Battle of Lepanto in 1571. The two stone pulpits in front of the altar have intricate cosmatesque mosaic work – a rare case of work signed by Lorenzo Cosma and his son Jacopo, originators of this much-copied style. Just inside the main door, on a pilaster to the right, is the worn tombstone of a certain Giovanni Crivelli, carved and signed (c1432) by Donatello. The first chapel on the right contains enchanting scenes by Pinturicchio from the life of St Francis of Assisi's helpmate St Bernardino (1486).

On the main altar is a tenth-century image of Mary. To the left of the altar, eight *giallo antico* columns mark the round chapel of St Helen, where relics of this redoubtable lady – mother of the Emperor Constantine – are kept in a porphyry urn. An ancient stone altar, said to be that erected by Augustus, can be seen behind and beneath the altar. Beyond the chapel, at the back of the transept, is the Chapel of the Holy Child. It contains a much-venerated, disease-healing *bambinello*, which is often whisked to the bedside of moribund Romans. The original – carved, it is said, in the 15th century from the wood of an olive tree from the Garden of Gethsemane – was stolen in 1994 and replaced by a copy, just as holy as the other according to the custodian. The Gothic tomb opposite the Chapel of the Holy Child entrance is that of Matteo d'Acquasparta, who was mentioned by Dante in his Paradiso. Over the altar in the third chapel from the main door (along the left aisle) is a fresco of St Anthony of Padua (c1449) by Benozzo Gozzoli.

Il Vittoriano

Piazza Venezia/via di San Pietro in Carcere/piazza Aracoeli (06 699 1718). Buses to piazza Venezia. **Open** *Monument* 9.30am-4pm daily. *Lift* 9.30am-6.30pm Mon-Thur; 9.30am-7.30pm Fri-Sun. *Sacrario delle Bandiere* 9.30am-3pm Tue-Sun. *Museo del Risorgimento* 9.30am-6pm daily. *Complesso del Vittoriano* (06 678 0664; open during exhibitions only; last entry 1hr before closing) 9.30am-7.30pm Mon-Thur; 9.30am-11.30pm Fri, Sat; 9.30am-8.30pm Sun. **Admission** *Monument, Sacrario, Museo del Risorgimento* free. *Lift* €7; €3.50 reductions. *Complesso del Vittoriano* depends on exhibition. **Credit** AmEx, DC, MC, V. **Map** p342 E1/2.

It's worth climbing to the top of this monument, not only to appreciate the enormity of the thing, but also to see the kitsch art nouveau propaganda mosaics in the colonnade and – most importantly – to enjoy the view from the only place where you can see the whole city centre without the panorama being disturbed by the bulk of the Vittoriano itself.

In the bowels of the building are various spaces: the **Museo Centrale del Risorgimento** (entrance from via San Pietro in Carcere) has all kinds of exhibits on the 19th-century struggle to unify Italy, including the rather fancy boot worn by Giuseppe Garibaldi when he was shot in the foot in 1862, and panels (in English) explaining the key figures and events of the period. It's worth researching what's on here as some of the exhibitions held at the Vittoriano give access from the entrance in piazza Aracoeli to a maze of Roman and medieval tunnels extending deep beneath the monument.

The **Sagrario delle Bandiere** (entrance in via dei Fori Imperiali) contains standards from many Italian navy vessels. It also has a couple of torpedo boats, including a manned *Maiale* (Pig) torpedo. On the south-east side of the monument (entrance on via San Pietro in Carcere) is a building whose sign reads 'Museo Centrale del Risorgimento'; the spaces here are used for special exhibitions of mostly modern art. (Any exhibition advertised as held at the Complesso del Vittoriano will be here.) *Photo p57.* ▶ *Halfway up the terraces on the east side is the very pleasant (though expensive) outdoor Caffè Aracoeli.*

THE ZONA ARCHEOLOGICA

South from the Capitoline hill lies what is arguably the world's most extraordinary concentration of archaeological riches.

The oldest of Rome's fora, the **Foro romano** (Roman Forum; *see p62*), started life as a swampy valley that was used for burials. According to tradition, it was drained in the late seventh century BC by Rome's Etruscan king, Tarquinius Priscus, after which the Forum was to become the centre of state ceremony, commerce, law and bureaucracy.

SIGHTS

SIGHTS

As the Empire grew, and this Forum became too small to cope with the legal, social and economic life of the city, emperors combined philanthropy with propaganda and created new ones of their own: the **Fori imperiali** (Imperial Fora; *see p65*). Clearly visible on either side of via dei Fori Imperiali, there are five separate fora, each built by a different emperor. Mussolini saw fit to slice the road straight through them (propaganda for empire-building of his own) to connect his balcony at **Palazzo Venezia** (*see p57*) with the Colosseum, demolishing the medieval and early Renaissance buildings that had grown up out of the Roman ruins. Since the 1990s work has been under way to recover tens of thousands of square metres of the ancient remains. Part of Vespasian's forum is incorporated into the church of **Santi Cosma e Damiano** (*see p66*). The **Torre delle Milizie**, behind the **Mercati di Traiano** (Trajan's Markets; *see p65*), is a picturesque memento of what the area once looked like.

To reach the Roman and Imperial fora from piazza del Campidoglio, skirt Palazzo dei Senatori to the left. At the bottom of the stairs, on the left, is the entrance to the **Carcere Mamertino** (Mamertine Prison; *see right*); beyond, to the right, stretches the Foro romano; further on to the left, the Fori imperiali extend along both sides of via dei Fori Imperiali.

At the end of this wide avenue towers the **Colosseum** (*see right*) with the **Arco di Costantino** beside it. There monuments were hemmed in by the Palatine, Celian and Oppian hills, as well as the Velia, the saddle of land which joined the Oppio to the Palatine. (What was left of the Velia was bulldozed by Mussolini when he made his via dell'Impero – now via dei Fori Imperiali.

Above the Colosseum to the west (and able to be visited on a cumulative ticket with the Roman Forum and the Colosseum) is Rome's birthplace, the Palatine.

The basket holding infant twins Romulus and Remus was found, legend says, in the swampy area near the Tiber where **San Giorgio in Velabro** (*see p111*) now stands. Later – on 21 April 753 BC, the uncannily precise story continues, the luckier/fratricidal brother Romulus climbed the Palatine hill and founded Rome.

In fact, proto-Romans had already settled on the Palatine hill over a century before that, and maybe much earlier. The presence of Rome's earliest temples on the Palatine hill made the area into illustrious real estate; commerce and bureaucracy were pushed down into the Foro romano as the Palatine became increasingly residential. When Augustus had his house built here he was seeking credibility as the founder of the Empire through a link with the founder of the city.

Once he'd set the pattern, many subsequent emperors followed suit.

To the south of the Palatine, the **Circo Massimo** is believed to have opened for races in the sixth century BC.

Carcere Mamertino (Carcer Tullianum)

Clivio Argentario 1 (06 698 961). Buses to piazza Venezia. **Open** 9am-7pm daily. **Admission** €10; €7 reductions. **Map** p344 A2.

Just off the steps leading from the Capitoline hill down to the Roman Forum is the Mamertine Prison (aka Carcer Tullianum). Into this prison went anyone thought to pose a threat to the security of the ancient Roman state. A dank, dark, tiny underground dungeon, its lower level (built in the fourth century BC) was once only accessible through a hole in the floor. Innumerable prisoners starved to death here, or drowned when the water table rose and flooded the cell. The most famous of the prison's residents, according to legend, were Saints Peter and Paul. Peter caused a miraculous well to bubble up downstairs in order to baptise his prison guards, whom he converted. You can pay €7 if you're prepared to do without the audioguide.

FREE Circo Massimo (Circus Maximus)

Via del Circo Massimo. Metro Circo Massimo/ bus 60Exp, 75, 81, 118, 175, 628, 673/tram 3. **Map** p345 A/B4.

The oldest and largest of Rome's ancient arenas, the Circus Maximus hosted chariot races from at least the fourth century BC. It was rebuilt by Julius Caesar to hold as many as 300,000 people. Races involved up to 12 rigs of four horses each; the first charioteer to complete the seven treacherous, sabotage-ridden laps around the *spina* (ridge in the centre) won a hefty prize and the adoration of the populace. The circus was also used for mock sea battles (with the arena flooded with millions of gallons of water), ever-popular fights with wild animals and the occasional large-scale execution. Perhaps not accidentally, the furious, competitive flow of modern traffic around the circus goes in the same direction that the ancient chariots did. An on-going restoration project at the arena's south-eastern end should be finished by 2011.

★ Colosseo (Colosseum)

Piazza del Colosseo (06 700 5469/06 3996 7700). Metro Colosseo/bus 60Exp, 75, 81, 85, 87, 117, 175, 673, 810, 850/tram 3. **Open** 8.30am-sunset daily. **Admission** (incl Forum & Palatine) €9; €4.50 reductions. Extra charge for exhibitions. **No credit cards**. **Map** p344 B/C3.

Vespasian began building the Colosseum in AD 72 on the site of a newly drained lake in the grounds of Nero's Domus Aurea (*see p135*). Restoration carried out in 2001 opened up much larger areas of the arena to the public, including a reconstructed section of the

Cooling Systems

2,000 years of air-conditioning.

In the bustling urban centres of the Roman Empire, the summer meant unbearable heat, dehydration and epidemics. Of course, an ancient city had places in which to escape the heat: porticoes (such as the **Portico d'Ottavia**, *see p111*) and public fountains were popular antidotes.

Then there were the monumental bath complexes – among the most notable features of Roman cities throughout the Empire – shells of which are still visible in Rome (*see p120* **Terme di Caracalla**; *p141* **Terme di Diocleziano**). Most reasonable-sized urban centres would have had two large-ish baths, plus an array of smaller-scale facilities. In Timgad, in what is now Algeria, archaeologists have identified no fewer than 14 bathhouses of varying sizes, despite the fact that the population is unlikely to have ever exceeded 10,000.

If the middle and lower classes had to go out to escape the heat, the wealthy stayed at home. An area in larger houses – such as the one on view and digitally recreated beneath **Palazzo Valentini** (*see p58*) – would often be set aside for a miniature replica of a grand public bath. Another advantage in the homes of the rich and famous was the central colonnaded courtyard – the peristylium – which often contained a garden where more fortunate Romans would bask among shade and greenery, a world away from the bustle of city life... unless, of course, they had a fashionable seaside villa to escape to.

For even greater respite, some ancients would dig a cryptoporticus: a vaulted, covered gallery which provided a shady retreat on many a warm day, not to mention a cool storage space for food during the summer. (There are examples on the **Palatine**, *see p62*, and at **Villa Adriana**, *see p298*.) At times the climate was so oppressive that even more radical solutions were called for: in the African colony of Bulla Regia, for example, inhabitants developed a unique housing design with ground-floor winter quarters and subterranean summer ones.

Few, however, could hope to imitate the sumptuous style of the canopus in Villa Adriana. Here guests could recline and enjoy meals in a large, cave-like room while the water from fountains and channels played around them, and made a watery curtain cascading from the rockface above.

---

sand-covered wood floor that allows visitors to walk across a platform and look down into the elevator shafts through which animals emerged, via trap-doors, into the arena. In late 2010, the newly restored top floor of the amphitheatre and the underground pits were opened to the public.

Properly called the Amphitheatrum Flavium (Flavian amphitheatre), the building was later known as the Colosseum not because it was big, but because of a gold-plated colossal statue, now lost, that stood alongside. The arena was about 500 metres (a third of a mile) in circumference, could seat over 50,000 people – some scholars estimate capacity crowds numbered as many as 87,000 – and could be filled or emptied in ten minutes through a network of *vomitoria* (exits) that remains the basic model for stadium design today.

Nowhere in the world was there a larger or more glorious setting for mass slaughter. If costly, highly trained professional gladiators were often spared at the end of their bloody bouts, not so the slaves, crim-inals and assorted unfortunates roped in to do battle against them. And just to make sure there was no cheating, when the combat was over, corpses were prodded with red-hot pokers to ensure no one tried to elude fate by playing dead.

It was not only human life that was sacrificed to Roman blood-lust: wildlife, too, was legitimate fod-der. Animals fought animals; people fought animals. In the 100 days of carnage held to inaugurate the amphitheatre in AD 80, some 5,000 beasts perished. By the time wild animal shows were finally banned in AD 523, the animal population of North Africa and Arabia was severely depleted. On occasion, however, the tables turned and the animals got to kill the people: a common sentence in the Roman criminal justice system was *damnatio ad bestias*, when thieves and other miscreants were turned loose, unarmed, into the arena, where hungry beasts would be waiting for them.

Entrance to the Colosseum was free for all, although a membership card was necessary, and a rigid seating plan kept the sexes and social classes in their rightful places. The emperor and senators occupied marble seats in the front rows; on benches higher up were the priests and magistrates, then above them the foreign diplomats. Women were con-fined to the upper reaches – all of them, that is, except the pampered Vestal Virgins, who had privileged seats right near the emperor.

By the sixth century, with the fall of the Roman Empire, bloodsports in the Colosseum were less impressive: chickens pecked each other to death here. The Roman authorities discontinued the games and the Colosseum became little more than a quarry for the stone and marble used to build and decorate Roman *palazzi*. The pockmarks all over the Colosseum's masonry date back to the ninth century, when Lombards pillaged the iron and lead clamps that until then had held the blocks together. This irreverence toward the Colosseum was not halted until the mid 18th century, when Pope Benedict XIV consecrated it as a church. For another century it was left to its own devices, becoming home to hundreds of species of flowers and plants, as well as to a fair number of Roman homeless. After Unification in 1870 the flora was yanked up and the squatters kicked out, in what 19th-century English writer Augustus Hare described as 'aimless excavations'. 'In dragging out the roots of its shrubs,' he moaned in his *Walks in Rome* (1883), 'more of the building was destroyed than would have fallen naturally in five centuries.'

Standing beside the Colosseum, Constantine's triumphal arch was one of the last great Roman monuments, erected in AD 315, and is the best preserved of Rome's triumphal arches.

In front of the arch, the round foundation sunk in the grass is all that remains of an ancient fountain called the *Meta sudans* ('sweating cone'). More of this implausibly phallic object – almost all of it, in fact – would have been visible today if it hadn't been for Mussolini's bulldozing in the 1930s. *Photo p58.*

▶ *If the queue outside the Colosseum is daunting, save yourself the wait and buy tickets at the Forum & Palatine (see p62) and make straight for the turnstiles.*

★ Foro romano & Palatino (Roman Forum & Palatine)

Via di San Gregorio 30/largo della Salaria Vecchia 5/6 (06 3996 7700). **Open** 8.30am-1hr before sunset daily. **Admission** (includes Colosseum) €9; €4.50 reductions. Extra charge for exhibitions. **No credit cards. Map** p344 A2/3.

Numbers (❶) refer to the map on p56.

The Forum and Palatine, separate but adjoining sites, are visited on the same ticket, which also allows entrance to the Colosseum. We recommend entering from the quieter via di San Gregorio entrance, visiting the Palatine first, then making your way down to the Forum.

However, guided tours (€3, in Italian) of parts of the Forum that are generally off-limits to visitors depart from the largo della Salaria Vecchia ticket office (formerly largo Remo e Romolo, off via dei Fori Imperiali); if you wish to join these, you should book your tour and enter from there. If you want to arrange a visit (free) to Augustus' house on the Palatine, you will need to organise a time at this entrance too.

While you may not believe the story that Romulus killed his twin brother Remus for crossing the property line he had staked out on the Palatine, archaeological evidence shows that this spot was probably the site of the settlement that would become Rome. Remains have been found of a wall near the Forum area and of primitive huts on the top of the hill dating from the eighth century BC; tradition says one of these latter was Romulus' home.

Later, the Palatine became the home of the movers and shakers of both the Republic and the Empire as sumptuous palaces were built. The choice of location was understandable: the Palatine overlooks the Foro romano, yet is a comfortable distance from the disturbances and riff-raff down in the valley. But the area really came into its own after Augustus built his new home next to the house of Rome's founder; successive emperors constructed massive palaces until the Palatine became virtually one massive Imperial dwelling and government seat. With Rome's decline it became a rural backwater, home to monasteries and their vegetable gardens, its precious marble and statuary toted off by looters.

In the 1540s much of the area was bought by Cardinal Alessandro Farnese, who turned it into a pleasure villa and garden.

Wending your way uphill from the Palatine from the via di San Gregorio entrance, you pass the remains of the comparatively small **palace and baths of Septimius Severus (❶)** to the left. They are some of the best-preserved buildings in the area.

Next come the remains of the Imperial palaces built by Domitian in the late first century AD, which became the main residence of the emperors for the next three centuries. The nearest, oval, section (❷) may have been a garden or a miniature stadium for Domitian's private entertainment. It was surrounded by a portico, visible at the southern end. Next to it stands the emperor's private residence, the **Domus Augustana (❸)**, whose name derives from *augustus* ('favoured by the gods' – nothing to do with Emperor Augustus). Next door is the **Domus Flavia (❹)**, which contained the public rooms. According to Suetonius, Domitian was so terrified of assassination that he had the walls faced with shiny black selenite so he could see anybody creeping up behind him. It didn't work. The strange-looking room with what appears to be a maze in the middle was the courtyard; next to this was the dining room, where part of the marble floor has survived, although it's usually covered for protection. The brick oval in the middle was probably a fountain.

Sandwiched between the Domus Flavia and Domus Augustana is a tall grey building that houses the **Museo Palatino (❺)**. Downstairs are human remains and artefacts from the earliest communities of Rome, founded in the Forum and Palatine areas from the ninth century BC. Room 2 has a model of an eighth-century BC wattle-and-daub hut village. Emerging from the floor are the foundations of Domitian's dwelling. Upstairs are busts, gods and some fascinating eave-edgings from the first to the fourth centuries AD.

Foro romano.

North-west of here are the 'huts of Romulus', the **Domus Augusti** (⑥) and the **Domus Livia** (⑦). Restored and opened to the public in 2008, the four spectacularly frescoed rooms of the former are not to be missed: book a viewing time at the ticket office on your way in. In the house of Augustus' wife Livia – now beneath a modern brick protective covering – wall paintings dating from the late Republic were found; they include trompe l'oeil marble panels and scenes from mythology.

North of here are the **Horti farnesiani** (⑧) – originally the Domus Tiberiana – on the right. These gardens – a shady haven full of orange and olive trees but sadly in need of a makeover – were originally laid out in the 16th century, making them one of the oldest botanical gardens in Europe; what you see now is an 'interpretative recreation' from the early 20th century. Head to the 17th-century pavilion at the top of the hill, which offers a good view over the Forum. Passing beneath the gardens is the **Cryptoporticus** (⑨), a long semi-subterranean tunnel built by Nero either for hot-weather promenades or as a secret route between the Palatine buildings and his palace, the Domus Aurea (*see p135*). Lit only by slits in the walls, the Cryptoporticus is welcomingly cool in summer. At one end there are remnants of a stucco ceiling frieze and floor mosaics. Continue on your route and you'll end up at the Roman Forum.

After its period of glory, the Forum was relentlessly attacked for centuries by barbarians, after which it was gradually dismantled by anyone – from popes to paupers – who needed building materials.

There is, clearly, a lot missing; but if you bear in mind that for a thousand-plus years this was treated as little more than a quarry, what's really incredible is how much has survived. With a bit of patience (and a lot of imagination), it's possible to reconstruct what was once the heart of the Western world.

During the early years of the Republic an open space with shops and a few temples sufficed, but from the second century BC, ever spreading, ever conquering Rome needed to give an impression of authority and wealth and so expressed its political ambitions through its architecture. Out went the food stalls; in came law courts, offices and immense public buildings with grandiose decorations to proclaim the power of Rome. Space soon ran out, and emperors began to build the new Imperial Fora (*see p65*). But the Foro romano remained the symbolic heart of the Empire, and emperors continued to renovate and embellish it until the fourth century AD. After taking the brunt of barbarian violence, the low-lying land of the Forum was gradually buried by centuries of flood sediment which rose unchecked in a city dramatically depopulated by plague, pestilence and war. The ancient heart of *caput mundi* came to be known as the *campo vaccino* (cow field). Major excavation didn't begin until the 18th century, when digging for antiquities became the hobby of choice for aristocrats from across Europe.

Framing the Forum is the **arco di Tito** (arch of Titus; (⑩) built in AD 81 to celebrate the sack of Jerusalem by the Emperor Vespasian and his son Titus ten years earlier. One of the bas reliefs shows

Mercati di Traiano.

SIGHTS

Roman soldiers with their plundered prize from the Temple of Herod: the menorah and the sacred silver trumpets. The triumphal procession is shown on the east interior wall, with Titus himself accompanied by a winged Victory driving a four-horse chariot. In the centre of the vault there's a square panel that shows Titus riding to the heavens on the back of an eagle, an allusion to his apotheosis.

From here, the cobbled **via Sacra** – the Sacred Way, which ran past the Forum's most important buildings – descends east towards the Colosseum, climbing past the towering columns (left) of the Temple of Venus and Roma (⑪), the two goddesses who protected the city; this area was reopened to the public late in 2010 after a 26-year restoration.

After the arch pass the church of Santa Francesca Romana (generally closed to the public, but *see p241* **Festa di Santa Francesca Romana**) and continue on to the towering brick ruins of the **basilica di Massenzio** (⑫), begun in 306 by Maxentius but completed in 312 by Constantine. Probably the last really magnificent building constructed before Rome began her decline, its marble-clad walls occupied three times the space now covered. The great vaults are considered to have inspired Bramante when he was designing St Peter's.

From here, retrace your steps to the via Sacra. Passing the brick remains of a medieval porticus you come to a building with a set of bronze doors: this is the so-called **temple of Romulus** (⑬), built in the fourth century and named after the Emperor Maxentius' son, to whom it may or may not have been dedicated – nobody is quite sure. The interior

of the temple is visible from the church of Santi Cosma e Damiano (*see p66*).

Also on the right are the great columns of the **temple of Antoninus and Faustina** (⑭) honouring Hadrian's successor, Antoninus Pius, and his wife Faustina, who pre-deceased him. In the seventh or eighth century it became part of the church of San Lorenzo in Miranda, which was heavily remodelled in the 17th century. The distance between the level you're standing on and the bottom of the church's (now-redundant) door is an example of the difference between the ancient ground level and that of the 17th century when the new façade was added.

Continuing towards the Capitoline, what's left of the giant **basilica Aemilia** (⑮) takes up nearly a whole block. Finished in 34 BC by Lucius Aemilius Lepidus Paullus with cash he got from Julius Caesar in exchange for his support, it was once a bustling place for administration, courts and business. A large chunk of a dedicatory inscription can be seen on the via Sacra corner. Beyond is the **Curia** (⑯). The home of the Senate, it was begun in 45 BC by Julius Caesar and finished in 29 BC by Augustus. (Still under construction on the Ides of March 44 BC, it wasn't here that Julius Caesar was assassinated but at the Curia of Pompey.) It was rebuilt after the fire that heavily damaged the Forum in AD 283; in the seventh century AD it became the church of St Hadrian, almost all trace of which was removed during Mussolini's restoration of 1935-8, although some fresco fragments still cling on inside. The floor is a fabulous example of fourth-century *opus sectile*. The doors aren't the originals, though – they found their way to San Giovanni in Laterano (*see p131*) in 1660.

Opposite, directly in front of the arch of Septimius Severus, is a fenced-off, irregular patch of greyish limestone: this is the *lapis niger* (black stone) that was believed to mark the tomb of Romulus.

The **arch of Septimius Severus** (⑰) was built in AD 203 to celebrate a victory in Parthia (modern-day Iran). The reliefs of military exploits are now blurred, but some of those at the base of the columns are better preserved, having been buried until the 19th century. These show Roman soldiers (no head-gear and in shoes) leading away their Parthian prisoners (with downcast faces and floppy Smurf hats).

Just to the left after you pass through the arch is a circular brick structure believed to be the *umbilicus urbis* (the navel of the city). Next to it, the curved white steps are all that remains of the **rostra of Julius Caesar** (⑱), a platform for the declamation of speeches. Towards the Capitoline hill, the eight massive columns of the **temple of Saturn** (⑲) bear an inscription that says it was rebuilt after a fire (probably around AD 360). The cult of Saturn was an ancient one: the first temple to him was built here around 497 BC. The feast dedicated to Saturn, the *Saturnalia*, was celebrated for three days beginning on December 17 and turned the social order on its head, with slaves and servants being served by their masters. With your back to the temple of Saturn, the solitary **column of Phocas** (⑳) is clearly visible. The last monument erected in the Forum before the area became a quarry for Christian structures, it was dedicated to the murderous emperor of Byzantium, Phocas. The inscription on the pedestal records a gold statue erected on top in 608 by Smaragdus, Exarch of Ravenna (although the column itself is recycled, probably dating from the second century).

On the far side of the via Sacra stand the foundations of the **basilica Julia** (㉑) built by Julius Caesar in 55 BC and once a major – and by all accounts very noisy – law court. Following the basilica to the right, you come across an opening to the Cloaca Maxima. At the end of this path is the church of **Santa Maria Antiqua** (㉒); enquire at the ticket office about guided visits to the beautiful seventh- and eighth-century frescoes. Rising beside the basilica Julia are three elegant columns that formed part of the **temple of Castor** (㉓), one of the twin sons of Jupiter who, according to legend, appeared to Roman troops in 499 BC, helping the Republic to victory over the Latins.

Back towards the centre of the Forum is the **temple of Divus Julius** (㉔). A nondescript mass of concrete masonry beneath a low-pitched green roof is all that remains of the temple dedicated to the memory of the deified Julius by Augustus in 29 BC.

INSIDE TRACK XMAS EVE MASS

Rome's gypsy community heads to **Santa Maria in Aracoeli** (*see p59*) at midnight.

It's popularly held to be the place of Caesar's cremation (though in fact this took place at the other end of the Forum, across the via Sacra from the temple of Antoninus and Faustina), and flowers are still left here on March 15 (the Ides) each year.

Between the temples of Castor and Divus Julius are the scant remains of the arch of Augustus, believed to be the arch built in 29 BC to commemorate his victories, including that at Actium over Antony and Cleopatra in 31 BC. Just beyond, three small columns arranged in a curve mark the round **temple of Vesta** (㉕) where the vestal virgins tended the sacred fire. Within its garden, the rectangular **house of the Vestal Virgins** (㉖) was where they lived chastely: if not they could expect to be buried alive in the 'field of wickedness' (*campus scleratus*) by the Quirinale. *Photo p63.*

★ Mercati di Traiano & Museo dei Fori Imperiali (Trajan's Markets & Imperial Fora Museum)
Via IV Novembre 94 (06 6992 3521, www.mercatiditraiano.it). **Open** 9am-7pm Tue-Sun. **Admission** €7.50; €5.50 reductions. Extra charge for exhibitions. **Credit** AmEx, DC, MC, V. **Map** p344 A1.
Excavations carried out in the Imperial Fora in the 1990s opened up massive amounts of archaeological space to the public: the via dei Fori Imperiali offers a good view over all of the fora. A recent restoration of Trajan's Markets has made this site even more splendid than before; an excellent permanent display explains the development and structure of the whole imperial complex, different areas are dedicated to finds from the various fora, and one-off shows are often staged here.

Foro di Cesare (Caesar's Forum)
The earliest of the Fori imperiali, the Forum of Caesar lies on the south-west side of via dei Fori Imperiali, closest to the Foro romano. Begun by Julius Caesar in 51 BC after the Gallic wars, the forum contained the temple of Venus Genetrix (three columns of which have been reconstructed) and the *basilica argentaria*, hall of the money-changers.

Foro & Mercati di Traiano (Trajan's Forum & Markets)
On the north-east side of via dei Fori Imperiali are the extensive remains of Trajan's forum, the last of the fora, laid out in the early second century AD. At the northern extremity of this forum rises the white marble **colonna traiana** (Trajan's column), an amazingly well-preserved work of Roman sculpture, dedicated in AD 113 to celebrate the triumph over the Dacians. The spiral reliefs, containing over 2,500 figures, depict the campaigns against Dacia (more or less modern-day Romania) in marvellous detail, from the building of forts to the launching of catapults. The higher sections of the column are difficult to discern today, but would have been easily viewed by the ancients from galleries that used to stand nearby. (Plaster casts of the reliefs are now on

SIGHTS

display at the Museo della Civiltà Romana in EUR; *see p161*). At the top of the column is a bronze statue of St Peter, added in 1587 by Pope Sixtus V to replace the original one of Trajan (now lost). So beloved by the Roman people was Trajan that, when he died in AD 117, his funerary urn was placed in a chamber at the column base; this made him and his wife, Plotina, the only Romans whose remains were allowed to be placed inside the city's boundary. The height of the column, 38m (125ft), is believed to mark the elevation of that part of the Quirinal hill that extended into this area before it was cleared away to make room for Trajan's forum.

The Temple of Trajan, mentioned by ancient sources, was also around here, although the exact location is unknown. The rectangular foundation to the south of Trajan's column, where several imposing granite columns still stand, was the basilica Ulpia, an administrative building. Part of the floor of the basilica is now visible at the gallery space recently acquired and restored by Alda Fendi, of fashion fame (Foro Traiano 1, 06 679 2597, www.fondazionealdafendi.it, open for exhibitions only). To the west, under the walls that support via dei Fori Imperiali, are the remains of one of the libraries that also formed part of Trajan's forum.

The most distinctive feature of the forum complex is the multistorey brick crescent to the south-east of the basilica Ulpia. This great hemicycle, forming part of the **Mercati di Traiano** (Trajan's Markets), was built in AD 107, in part to shore up the slope of the Quirinal hill. Some scholars now argue that it was more of an administrative than a commercial space.

Entering from via IV Novembre, the first room is the Great Hall, a large space possibly used for the corn dole in antiquity. To the south of the Great Hall are the open-air terraces at the top of the great hemicycle, offering spectacular views across to the Capitoline and Foro romano. To the east of the Great Hall, stairs lead down to the so-called via Biberatica, an ancient street flanked by well-preserved shops. The shops here were probably *tabernae* (bars), hence the name 'Biberatica' (*bibere* is Latin for 'to drink'). More stairs lead down through the various layers of the great hemicycle, where most of the 150 shops or offices are still in perfect condition, many with door-jambs still showing the grooves where shutters slid into place when the working day was over. South of the hemicycle, the structure with a loggia with five large arches is the 15th-century **Casa dei Cavalieri di Rodi** (House of the Knights of Rhodes); its somewhat Venetian look is due to having been built by Venetian Pope Paul II. The tower beyond the hemicycle is the 13th-century **Torre delle Milizie**.

Foro di Augusto (Augustus' Forum)

To the south of the House of the Knights of Rhodes is the Forum of Augustus, the second of the Imperial Fora chronologically (inaugurated in 2 BC). The dominant feature here was the Temple of Mars Ultor

('the avenger'), built to commemorate the Battle of Philippi in 42 BC, in which Augustus (then called Octavian) avenged Caesar's death. Three marble columns of the temple are visible on the right side, as is the towering tufa firewall behind it, built to protect the Imperial space from the Suburra slum district just beyond.

Foro di Nerva (Nerva's Forum)

The next forum to the south, which is bisected by via dei Fori Imperiali, is the Forum of Nerva (or *Forum transitorium* because of its connective function from the sprawling Suburra slum to the Foro romano). It was dedicated by Nerva in AD 97. Vestiges of a podium are all that remain of the Temple of Minerva that once stood at the east end of the elongated space, although the frieze around two marble columns of the portico (visible just before via Cavour) depicts Minerva, goddess of household skills, weaving and spinning.

Foro di Vespasiano (Vespasian's Forum)

The *Templum pacis*, third of the Fori imperiali to be built but the last to be unearthed (on the west side of via dei Fori Imperiali), was dedicated by Vespasian in AD 75 but devastated by a fire in 192. On display inside this 'Temple of Peace' were the spoils of various wars, including treasures looted from the Temple of Herod during the Sack of Jerusalem in AD 70. The temple's library is now part of the church of Santi Cosma e Damiano. The immense *Forma urbis*, a marble map of the city made in 193 by Septimius Severus, once adorned the brick wall to the left of the church's façade. Taking his cue (as always) from the ancient emperors, Mussolini made some maps of his own: four white-and-black marble maps are still visible against the brick wall on the west side of the road. They show an area that includes Europe, North Africa and the Near East, charting the growth of the Roman Empire through antiquity. There used to be a fifth map too, which showed Mussolini's Fascist 'empire', but it was removed after the war.

FREE Santi Cosma e Damiano

Via dei Fori Imperiali 1 (06 692 0441). Metro Colosseo/bus 60Exp, 75, 85, 87, 117, 175, 571, 810, 850. **Open** 9am-1pm, 3-7pm daily. **Map** p344 B2.

This small church on the fringe of the Forum incorporates the library of Vespasian's temple of Peace (*see p92*) and the temple of Romulus (visible through the glass panel that forms the front wall; the drop in level is a reminder of the centuries of sediment and muck that swallowed up the Forum). It has a wonderful sixth-century mosaic in the apse: Saints Peter and Paul stand one on each side of the vast figure of Christ descending from the clouds, presenting Saints Cosma and Damian (the patron saints of doctors) to Jesus. On the far left, Pope Felix IV holds a model of the church; on the far right stands St Theodore in memory of Theodoric the Great, who donated the temple of Romulus to the Pope.

The Trevi Fountain & the Quirinale

A famous fountain, an ex-papal palace and art aplenty draw crowds here.

The roaring waters of the *acqua vergine* were fundamental to the development of this area: they supplied the popes' Palazzo del Quirinale, and fed the towering Trevi Fountain in the valley below. On those mornings when workmen turn the water off to clean the fountain, the quarter turns eerily silent. Water continues to be a key feature of the area: in addition to the fountain, you can hear the rush beneath the ruins of a Roman street at the **Città dell'acqua**, while a miraculous well inside the ancient church of **Santa Maria in Via** (for both, *see p70* **Extra Time**) still provides healing cupfuls for sick parishioners.

But this area is also home to art aplenty, notably in the *gallerie* Barberini and Colonna, and at the Accademia di San Luca. And there are two small but superb churches – San Carlino and Sant'Andrea – by the geniuses of Baroque Rome, Bernini and Borromini.

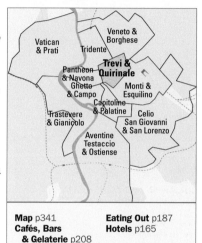

Map p341
Cafés, Bars & Gelaterie p208

Eating Out p187
Hotels p165

AROUND THE TREVI FOUNTAIN

The high walls of the presidential **Palazzo del Quirinale** loom over a tangle of medieval streets, all of which seem in the end to lead to the **Trevi Fountain**. The *acqua vergine* that feeds it is said to be the best water in Rome: Grand Tourists used it to brew their tea. Nowadays you'd be hard pressed to get your kettle anywhere near for the coin-tossing hordes elbowing their way through serried ranks of tacky souvenir vendors.

Names like via della Dataria (Ecclesiastical Benefits Office Street) and via della Stamperia (Printing Works Street) recall the era when the whole of the Trevi district acted as a service area for the palace: here were the bureaucratic departments, presses and service industries that oiled the machinery of the Papal States. To keep close to the hub of power, aristocratic

families like the Odescalchis, Grimaldis and Barberinis built their palaces close by, as did the Colonna, whose art collection can be seen at the **Galleria Colonna**.

The **Galleria dell'Accademia di San Luca** (*see p69*), keeper of the flame of artistic orthodoxy, was closed for *restauro* as this guide went to press.

FREE Fontana di Trevi (Trevi Fountain)

Piazza di Trevi. Bus 52, 53, 61, 62, 71, 80Exp, 95, 116, 119, 175, 492, 630, 850. **Map** p341 A5.

For recent generations, it was Anita Ekberg who made this fountain famous when she plunged in wearing a strapless black evening dress (and a pair of waders… but you don't notice those) in Federico Fellini's classic *La Dolce Vita*. Don't even think about trying it yourself – wading, washing and splashing in fountains are strictly against local

SIGHTS

Trevi Fountain. *See p67*.

bylaws. And unlike the Grand Tourists, you don't want to drink from it either: the sparkling waters – so called for their purity and low levels of calcium, although legend says their source was indicated to the troops of Agrippa by a virgin – is full of chlorine (though there's a chlorine-free spout hidden in a bird-bath-shaped affair at the back of the fountain to the right).

It was an altogether different affair in 19 BC, when spring water – 100,000 cubic metres of the stuff daily – was transported here by an aqueduct from the eighth mile of the via Collatina, to the east of Rome. The only aqueduct to pass underground along its whole route into the city, it was the sole survivor of barbarian destruction and other horrors of the early Middle Ages. In 1570 Pius V restored the conduit but it wasn't until 1732 that Pope Clement XII called for designs for a new *mostra* – a magnificent fountain to mark the end of the aqueduct. Completed decades later to a design by Nicolò Salvi, the *mostra* – the Trevi Fountain – immediately became a draw for tourists who drank the prized waters to ensure a return to Rome.

Tucked away in a tiny piazza and almost always surrounded by jostling crowds, the fountain's stark travertine gleams beneath powerful torrents of water and constant camera flashes. It's a magnificent rococo extravaganza of rearing sea horses, conch-blowing tritons, craggy rocks and flimsy trees, erupting in front of the wall of Palazzo Poli. Nobody can quite remember when the custom started of tossing coins in to the waters (as celebrated in *Three Coins in a Fountain*, with its Oscar-winning ditty). The money goes to charity.

▶ *For more film locations, see p251* **Walk**.

FREE Galleria dell'Accademia di San Luca

Piazza dell'Accademia 77 (06 679 8850, www. accademiasanluca.it). Bus 52, 53, 61, 62, 71, 80Exp, 95, 116, 119, 175, 492, 630, 850. **Open** *9.30am-1pm Mon-Fri.* **Map** *p341 A5.*
The illustrious Accademia di San Luca (patron saint of artists; St Luke was said to have painted the Virgin and Child from life), housed in Palazzo Carpegna, was founded in 1577 to train artists in the grand Renaissance style. From the courtyard, Borromini's beautiful staircase is clever and very practical (at least for sedan chairs and mules): the elliptical brickwork ramp to the upper floors of the palace was inspired by the winding ramp inside Hadrian's mausoleum within Castel Sant'Angelo. Access to the ramp is behind a virtuoso piece of stucco work: cornucopiae of overblown buttercups and daisies denote the riches of the earth, while crowns, mitres and chains symbolise what can be achieved by hard work in the course of a long and fortunate career. But without progeny, the allegory continues (the offspring is symbolised by a small child peering out of the herbiage), it is all worthless endeavour; it's not on record whether the few women members of the Academy, such as artistic prodigies Lavinia Fontana (1551-1614) and Angelica Kauffman (1741-1807), agreed with these sentiments. Recently reopened after a long restoration, the gallery displays a charming collection of paintings and sculptures by former students and visitors to the Accademia, including Canova and Thorwaldson. But the real charm lies in the exquisite scenes of 17th- and 18th-century Roman life.

Galleria Colonna

Via della Pilotta 17 (06 678 4350, www.galleriacolonna.it). Bus 40Exp, 60Exp, 64, 70, 117, 170, H. **Open** *9am-1pm Sat, or by appointment. Closed Aug.* **Admission** *€10; €8 reductions.* **No credit cards. Map** *p341 A6.*
Saturday mornings are your only chance to see this splendid gallery, completed in 1703 by Prince Filippo II Colonna whose descendants still live in the palace. (Among others, the Colonnas produced a pope, a saint, an excommunicated cardinal and Vittoria Colonna, the poetess who befriended Michelangelo.) The entrance leads to the Room of the Column, originally the throne room of Prince Filippo and his successors, who would have sat in state by the ancient column, back-lit by light shining through the window behind, and with a view across to a triumphal arch dedicated to Marcantonio Colonna, the family hero. (Audrey Hepburn behaved regally here too, in *Roman Holiday*.) The cannonball embedded in the stairs down to the Great Hall lies where it landed during the French siege of Rome on 24 June 1849. The mirrored hall may be the work of Gian Lorenzo Bernini, inspired by his visit to Versailles in 1665, while the immense frescoed ceiling pays tribute to Marcantonio, who led the papal fleet to victory against the Turks in the great naval battle of Lepanto in 1571. There are more Turks carved in the legs of the furniture in the next room. The gallery's most famous and much-reproduced picture is Annibale Caracci's earthy peasant *Bean Eater*. Groups of ten or more can arrange tours of the gallery as well as the private apartments at other times during the week.

PIAZZA BARBERINI & THE QUATTRO FONTANE

Art-packed **Palazzo Barberini** towers above piazza Barberini – once a semi-rural idyll and now a woeful example of the sledgehammer

INSIDE TRACK
MUSIC AT THE PALACE

When parts of it are open to the public, the **Palazzo del Quirinale** (*see p72*) occasionally hosts concerts in its chapel at noon on Sundays.

SIGHTS

school of city planning. Traffic hurtles north into via Veneto or south-east towards the Quattro Fontane, while marooned in the midst of the belching fumes is the last commission Gian Lorenzo Bernini received from the Barberini Pope Urban VIII: the **Fontana del Tritone**. The fountain is covered with the bees of the Barberini family emblem, and shows four dolphins supporting a huge open shell on their tails. On the shell sits a Triton blowing into a conch shell to tame the flooding seas, as in a tale recounted by Ovid in his *Metamorphoses*.

North-east of the piazza, charmless *vie* Barberini and Bissolati were redeveloped under Mussolini and now contain airline offices.

Ringing with the noise of life-threatening *motorini*, narrow via Barberini climbs past the Palazzo Barberini gallery to the crossroads, which – for very obvious reasons – are known as the **Quattro Fontane** (four fountains). Four delightful Baroque fountains have stood here since 1593. It's a life-threatening task trying to see them through the traffic, but they clearly represent four river gods: the one accompanied by the she-wolf is the Tiber; the females are probably Juno (the one with the duck) and Diana. But it's anybody's guess who the fourth figure is: some claim it's an allegory of the Nile while others make a case for the Florentine Arno. From here, the staggering

Extra Time

● First day of the month? Rush over to the **Casino dell'Aurora** (via XXIV Maggio 43, 06 481 4344, open 10am-noon, 3-5pm, first of each month except Jan, free) to gawp like Grand Tourists at *Aurora scattering flowers before the chariot of the sun*. The Victorian's darling Guido Reni painted it in 1614 on the ceiling of the summer house of the 17th-century Palazzo Pallavicini Rospigliosi. The rest of the Pallavicini picture collection is off-limits.

● A stone's throw from the Trevi fountain are the excavations that came to light during the remodelling of the Cinema Trevi. Called the **Vicus Caprarius** (vicolo del Puttarello 25, 06 6574 4547, open 4-7.30pm Mon, 11am-5pm Thur-Sun, admission €3, €1 reductions), it incorporates the remains of an Imperial-age apartment building, part of a Roman street and a holding tank for the waters of the *acqua vergine*, which can be heard rushing by underneath.

● Join well-heeled ladies on a break from shopping, bronzed youth rendezvous-ing and snazzily dressed denizens of the nearby parliament buildings for tea-time tunes or cocktail-hour blues played on a concert grand piano in the belle époque splendour of the air-conditioned, marble-clad, shop-filled **Galleria Alberto Sordi** (off piazza Colonna, open 10am-10pm daily).

● Stand in the presence of papal innards in **Santi Anastasio e Vincenzo** (piazza di Trevi, open 7.30am-noon, 4-7pm daily): the liver, spleen and pancreas of every pope from Sixtus V (1585-90) to Leo XIII (1878-1903) was preserved and interred in this church, before the rest of the body was buried somewhere grander. The papal offal

is not on view, but there's an inventory on a plaque by the altar.

● Perk yourself up with a cupful of miraculous water in the church of **Santa Maria in Via** (via Mortaro 24, 06 697 6741, www.santamariainvia.it, open 7.15am-12.45pm, 4-8pm Mon-Sat, 8.30am-1pm, 4-10pm Sun). In 1286 a stone bearing an image of the Virgin's face floated to the surface of a well, over which this church was later built.

Fontana del Triton.

view down both sides of the hill takes in three Egyptian obelisks – part of the city's remodelling under obelisk-mad Sixtus V. On one corner stands the little church of **San Carlo alle Quattro Fontane**, one of the great masterpieces of tortured genius Carlo Borromini.

★ Palazzo Barberini – Galleria Nazionale d'Arte Antica

Via delle Quattro Fontane 13 (06 481 4591, bookings 06 32 810, www.galleriaborghese.it). Metro Barberini/bus 52, 53, 61, 62, 63, 80Exp, 95, 116, 119, 175, 492, 630. **Open** 9am-7pm Tue-Sun. **Admission** €5; €2.50 reductions. **No credit cards. Map** p341 B5.

Top architects like Maderno, Bernini and Borromini queued up to work on this vast pile, which, despite its size and attention to detail, was completed in just five years, shortly after Maffeo Barberini became Pope Urban VIII in back in 1623. Bernini did the main staircase, a grand rectangular affair now marred by an ill-placed lift. Borromini, whose uncle Carlo Maderno drew up the original palace plans, added the graceful oval staircase. After lengthy restoration and extension of the gallery into newly acquired parts of the palace, the entrance is now through the splendid reception room containing Pietro da Cortona's ceiling work *Allegory of Divine Providence* (1629), reputedly Europe's largest painting. Highlights of the main first-floor 16th- and 17th-century collection are Raphael's *Fornarina* (said, probably wrongly, to be a portrait of the baker's daughter he may have been engaged to at the time of his death in 1520), Holbein's pompous *Henry VIII*,

Caravaggio's *Judith and Holofernes* and Titian's *Venus and Adonis*.

🆓 San Carlo alle Quattro Fontane

Via del Quirinale 23 (06 488 3261, www.sancarlino-borromini.it). Metro Barberini/bus 40Exp, 52, 53, 61, 62, 63, 64, 70, 71, 80Exp, 95, 116, 119, 170, 175, 492, 630, H. **Open** 10am-1pm, 3-6pm Mon-Fri; 10am-1pm Sat; noon-1pm Sun. **Map** p341 C5.

Carlo Borromini's first solo composition (1631-41), and the one of which he was most proud, San Carlo (often called Carlino, due to its diminuitive scale) is one of the star pieces of the Roman Baroque. The most remarkable feature is the dizzying oval dome: its geometrical coffers decrease in size towards the lantern to give the illusion of additional height – Borromini is all about illusion – and the subtle illumination, through hidden windows, makes the dome appear to float in mid-air. There is also an austere adjoining courtyard and a simply beautiful library that opens occasionally at the whim of the monastery's residents.

FROM THE QUIRINALE TO VIA NAZIONALE

The origins of the name 'Quirinale' are lost in the mists of time; it may refer to a temple of Quirinus which stood here, or perhaps it comes from Cures, a Sabine town north-east of Rome from where, legend relates, the Sabines under King Tatius came to settle on the hill. Throughout the Republican era, the hill was covered in gardens and villas where the great and the good could escape from the malarial heat of the marshy valleys. In the 16th century the pope thought it would be a good idea to do the same thing and the summer **Palazzo del Quirinale** (*see right*) was begun in 1574 for Gregory XIII (of Gregorian calendar and chant fame). After the collapse of the Papal States in 1870, Pope Pius IX, who was holed up inside the palace, refused to hand over his keys to the troops of King Victor Emanuel; they had to force their way in. Just 76 years later the reigning Savoia family were forced to quit the palace following a referendum in which the monarchy, disgraced by association with the inter-war Fascist regime, was despatched into exile. Today a constant stream of motorcades swishing across the cobbles serves as a reminder that the Quirinale – now the official residence of the Italian president – is still very much at the decision-making hub of 21st-century Italy.

The space in front of the palace is officially piazza del Quirinale, though it's generally referred to by locals as piazza di Monte Cavallo – Horse Hill Square – on account of the two towering Imperial-era equestrian statues. The giant horses rear up beside the five-metre-high (16 feet) heavenly twins Castor and Pollux. The statues, which had been lying in the nearby ruins of the Baths of Constantine, were artistically arranged by Domenico Fontana, the favourite architect of the city-planner Pope Sixtus V, in the 1580s. It was Pius VI who dragged the obelisk now standing here from outside Augustus' mausoleum (*see p92*) in 1786; Pius VII added the big granite basin that had been a cattle trough in the Forum. On the far side of the square are the papal stables, now an elegant exhibition space, the **Scuderie del Quirinale** (*see right*).

Across the road from the palace's long wing stands the splendid church of **Sant' Andrea al Quirinale** (*see right*), by Bernini.

Palazzo del Quirinale

Piazza del Quirinale (06 46 991, www.quirinale.it). Bus 40Exp, 64, 70, 71, 170, H. **Open** 8.30am-noon Sun. Closed late June-early Sept; occasionally in Apr & Dec: check website for details. **Admission** €5. **No credit cards**. **Map** p341 B6.

The new St Peter's still wasn't finished when Pope Gregory XIII started building this pontifical summer palace on the highest of Rome's seven hills; begun in 1573, the Quirinale was not completed until over 200 years later. The risk that a pontiff (not, on the whole, renowned for youthful vigour) might keel over during the holidays was such that it was decided to build somewhere suitable to hold a conclave to elect a successor. The Quirinale's Cappella

Palazzo del Quirinale.

Marks Men

Keep your eyes peeled for these papal emblems.

Noble, pope-producing families liked to make their presence felt by stamping their family crests on monuments around the city.

● Eagles and dragons, emblems of the Borghese family (Paul V, 1605-21), are the silent sentinels of Villa Borghese.

● The dragon of the Boncompagni family (Gregory XIII, 1572-85) can be spied on the façade of Palazzo Margherita, now the US embassy. The family later sold the building to Italy's royal Savoia family, whose crest can also be seen on the building's exterior, along with that of the US armouries.

● The bees of Bernini's patron Maffeo Barberini (Urban VIII, 1623-44) decorate the sculptor's Fontana delle Api at the lower end of via Veneto. The original inscription read that the pope built it 'in the XXII year of his papacy', though it was in fact completed two months before the date inscribed. A stone-cutter was hastily dispatched to remove an 'I', an action which was judged a curse on the pope… who duly popped his clogs eight days before reaching his 22nd year.

● Michelangelo placed the emblem of the Medici family (Pius IV, 1499-1565) – balls on a shield – on the façade of the Porta Pia. The emblem is variously thought to represent pawnbrokers' coins, a dented

(but unyielding) shield or, most likely considering the family's origins as apothecaries, medicinal pills.

Paolina (named after Paul V) was designed by Carlo Maderno and finished in 1617; it is a faithful replica of the Vatican's Sistine Chapel, minus the Michelangelos. Accommodation for the cardinals was provided in the *Manica lunga*, the immensely long wing that runs the length of via del Quirinale to the rear of the palace. Bernini added the main entrance door in 1638.

The presidential guard changes with a flourish each afternoon outside on the square at any time between 3pm and 6pm, depending on the season.

FREE Sant'Andrea al Quirinale

Via del Quirinale 29 (06 474 4872). Bus 40Exp, 64, 70, 71, 170, H. **Open** 8.30am-noon, 3-7pm Mon-Fri; 9am-noon, 3.30-7pm Sat, Sun. **Map** p341 B5.

With funding from Cardinal Camillo Pamphili, the Jesuits commissioned Gian Lorenzo Bernini to build a church for novices living on the Quirinale. The site was small and awkward, but Bernini solved the problem by designing an oval church (1658) with the entrance and the high altar very unusually on the short axis. Above the door, a section of the wall

seems to have swung down on to the columns, creating an entrance porch. Inside, the church is richly decorated with the figure of St Andrew (by Antonio Raggi, Bernini's star pupil) floating heavenwards through a broken pediment above the high altar.

Scuderie Papali al Quirinale

Via XXIV Maggio 16 (06 696 270, www. scuderiequirinale.it). Bus 40Exp, 64, 70, 71, 170, H. **Open** during exhibitions only. **Admission** varies. **Credit** DC, MC, V. **Map** p341 B6.

The former stables of the Palazzo del Quirinale, this large space for major exhibitions retains original features such as the brickwork ramp to the upper floors, plus acres of chic marble flooring and space-age lighting. There is a good art bookshop and a café and – best of all – a breathtaking view of Rome's skyline from the rear staircase as you leave. It's worth finding out what's on here as exhibitions are generally fascinating, though it's advisable to book in advance, as they are often very over-subscribed.

▶ *Art in Rome (see pp43-50) offers an in-depth look at Rome's tremendous art history.*

Via Veneto & Villa Borghese

Acres of green, splendid views and one of the city's greatest galleries.

Historically, the area surrounding the city's most central public park, **Villa Borghese**, was always green: ancient aristocrats built sprawling villas here, and noble families and monastic orders continued the tradition right up until the 1800s. Nowadays, Villa Borghese is all that is left, but it contains splendid sights: a great art repository – the superb **Galleria Borghese** – along with one of Rome's greatest vistas from the **Pincio**, over **piazza del Popolo** to the dome of St Peter's. South from the park, **via Vittorio Veneto** (known simply as via Veneto) was the haunt of the glamorous famous in the *dolce vita* years of the 1950s and '60s. These days, it's home to insurance companies, luxury hotels and visitors wondering where the stars and paparazzi have gone.

Map p338 &
pp340-341
Hotels p167

Eating Out p187
Cafés, Bars &
Gelaterie p208

SIGHTS

VILLA BORGHESE & THE PINCIO

In the first century BC, Rome's most extensive gardens, the **Horti Sallustiani**, spread over the valley between the Quirinal hill and the Pincio. During the Renaissance, the area was colonised by aristocratic Roman families such as the Borghese and Boncompagni-Ludovisi, who attempted to out do one another with the lavishness of their vast suburban estates. In fact, up until the building boom in Rome during the late 1800s, only the odd villa or decorative pavilion interrupted the tranquil and leafy parkland that stretched from the Pincio to Porta Pia.

When Rome was made capital of Italy in 1871, this green idyll was seen as prime building land, to be dug up and replaced by street after street of grandiose *palazzi*; of the estates, only the Villa Borghese was saved from

the property vultures; it is now the city's most central public park.

Shortly after Camillo Borghese became Pope Paul V in 1605, his favourite nephew, 26-year-old Scipione Caffarelli Borghese, was made a cardinal. An obsessive love of the arts led Scipione to embark upon the creation of a pleasure park: the Villa Borghese. What began as a family vineyard was transformed, with the acquisition of surrounding lands, into one of the most extensive gardens in Rome since antiquity. A 'Theatre of the Universe', Scipione's vision was a place where sculpture, painting and music could be enjoyed alongside fossil specimens and technological oddities of the day such as orreries, special clocks and lenses. The harmoniously proportioned *Casino*

About the author
Julia Crosse read Italian at the University of London and has lived in Italy for 15 years.

Villa Borghese.

nobile (now the Galleria Borghese; *see p78*) was designed to showcase these gems. Begun in 1608, the building was modelled on ancient Roman villas and Renaissance predecessors such as the Villa Farnesina (*see p75*).

An impressive aviary (beautifully restored, to the left as you look at the façade of the Galleria Borghese) acted as a backdrop to the land surrounding the *Casino*, which alternated formal gardens dotted with exotic plants, fountains and statues with wilder stretches of landscape used for hunting. The villa soon became *the* place to be seen in 17th-century Rome, and the magnificent gardens were further embellished until Scipione's death in 1633. The result was a Baroque amusement park, complete with trick fountains that sprayed unwitting passers-by, automata and erotic paintings, menageries of wild beasts, and an alfresco dining room where the cardinal entertained with due magnificence on summer evenings. Successive generations of the Borghese family altered the park according to changing fashions, though Scipione's descendants proved themselves to be less artistically inclined than their keen-eyed predecessor, selling off a good deal of his priceless collection; one of the worst culprits was Napoleon's notorious sister Pauline, who married into the Borghese family in 1807.

When Rome became capital of a unified Italy, the clan looked set to sell off the estate to property speculators. In a rare example of civic far-sightedness, the state stepped in, in 1901, wresting possession of the villa from the family in a bitter court battle and turning it into a public park.

Today, the Borghese family's pleasure grounds are a popular spot for jogging, dog-walking, picnicking and cruising. The entire park has been spruced up in recent years, and a spate of arty projects, such as the opening in 2006 of the **Museo Carlo Bilotti** (*see p81*), cemented its status as a 'park of the arts', of which its founder would have been proud. A wander around Villa Borghese is a great way to recuperate from an overdose of carbon monoxide. Sporty types will find bicycles and in-line skates for hire, and the park is one big wireless hotspot (see www.romawireless.com for details). Culture vultures head straight to three of Rome's greatest art repositories: the Galleria Borghese itself, the Etruscan museum at **Villa Giulia** (*see p83*) and the **Galleria Nazionale d'Arte Moderna** (*see p81*). The park also houses the **Casa del Cinema**, the **Dei Piccoli** children's cinema, the **Bioparco-Zoo** and the **Museo Civico di Zoologia** (*see p83*). Viale delle Belle Arti and via Omero are crammed with academies and cultural institutes that put on occasional

Extra Time

● Ogle the cavalry (dressed in their designer uniforms) at their **Villa Umberto** HQ, on the corner of via Raimondi and via Pinciana.

● The home of sculptor **Pietro Canonica** (viale Pietro Canonica 2, open 9am-7pm Tue-Sun, €3, €2 reductions), tucked away in Villa Borghese, is spookily unaltered since his death in 1959. It contains 19th-century paintings and furniture, Flemish tapestries and the artist's own work.

● Shakespeare buffs can catch a play at the open-air **Silvano Toti Globe Theatre**, in Villa Borghese (largo Acqua Felix, near piazza di Siena, 06 0608, www.globetheatreroma.com, open June-Sept, tickets €5.50-€18), for the novelty value of seeing the bard performed in Italian. Opened in 2005, it's a replica of London's Globe theatre.

exhibitions and concerts. The **British School at Rome** (www.bsr.ac.uk), in an imposing Lutyens-designed pavilion, hosts contemporary art exhibitions, events and lectures.

Other sights worth looking out for include the **piazza di Siena**, an elegantly shaped grassy hippodrome that is used for glitzy showjumping events, and, nearby, the pretty **Giardino del Lago**, which has a small lake with rowing boats for hire and faux-ancient temples. There is also a good view of the Muro Torto section of the **Aurelian Wall** from the bridge between the Pincio and Villa Borghese.

Overlooking piazza del Popolo, and now an integral part of the Villa Borghese, is one of the oldest gardens in Rome: the **Pincio**. The Pinci family commissioned the first gardens here in the fourth century. The present layout was designed by Giuseppe Valadier in 1814. The garden is best known for its view of the Vatican at sunset, with the dome of St Peter's silhouetted in gold. The paved area behind the viewpoint is popular with cyclists (bikes can be hired nearby) and skaters.

To the south-east is the **Casino Valadier**, now a pricey restaurant with a to-die-for view. In the manicured green to the south-east sits the **Villa Medici**, since 1804 the French academy in Rome, where many French artists, from Ingres and David to Balthus, found inspiration. The academy hosts occasional art exhibitions (phone 06 67 611 or consult www.villamedici.it for programme information) and opens its lovely gardens and some galleries of its art collection in daily guided tours

SIGHTS

Capuchins and Cappuccino

The Franciscan coffee connection.

In 1520 Franciscan friar Matteo da Bascio decided that his order was no longer sticking faithfully to the penurious lifestyle ordained by their founder St Francis, and broke away to found the Friars Minor. The Franciscans didn't like this criticism, clearly, and hounded the rebels who took refuge with the reclusive Camaldolese monks, adopting their distinctive hood and habit of never shaving.

When the brown-clad Friars Minor took to the streets again – hirsute, discalzed (shoe-less), begging bowls in hand and hoods drawn up over their penitent heads – it was the hoods (*cappucci*) which earned them their popular moniker: *cappuccini* – Capuchins.

Fast-forward 400 years to Milan, where Luigi Bezzera has just come up with a marvellous invention: the espresso machine. The initially simple gadget is honed and whittled throughout the early 20th century, and, by the 1950s, has been transformed – in the iconic Gaggia machine – into a high-pressure boiler fitted with a little spout to let the steam out – handy, *baristi* find, for heating water or whipping

milk into a creamy micro-foam-filled addition to the basic coffee: but what to name this concoction?

History does not relate which lateral-thinking wit first equated this brown-coloured beverage with froth on top to the brown-clad monks with long frothy beards whose main Roman church of Santa Maria della Concezione is on worldly, jet-setting via Veneto. But the name stuck. In the space of just a few decades, cappuccino has become not only an Italian icon but an international drink, tainted and corrupted by global chains who insist on taking a perfect recipe – good strong coffee and steamed milk – and adding unnecessary extras.

In Roman bars, the variations are *cappuccino bollente* (with really really hot milk rather than the lukewarm stuff some bars insist on using), *chiaro* (with less coffee and more milk), *scuro* (with less milk) and *al vetro* (in a glass rather than a cup). *E basta.* And it's a breakfast thing: anyone drinking cappuccino after 11am or – heaven help us! – after a meal has 'clueless tourist' written all over them.

(11.45am tours are in English, €8, €6 reductions, booking advisable).

Between Villa Borghese and the river are two more museums: a striking art nouveau villa houses the **Museo Hendrik Christian Andersen** (*see p81*); the children's museum, **Explora – Museo dei Bambini di Roma** (*see p248*), is in a former bus depot.

★ Galleria Borghese

Piazzale del Museo Borghese 5 (info & bookings 06 32 810, www.galleriaborghese.it). Bus 52, 53, 95, 116, 910. **Open** 9am-7pm Tue-Sun. **Admission** €8.50; €2-€5.25 reductions. **Credit** MC, V. **Map** p340 C2.

Note: numbers are limited and booking at least a day in advance – essential in high season – `is always advisable.

Begun in 1608 by Flaminio Ponzio and continued by Jan van Santen (Italianised to Giovanni Vasanzio) upon his death, the Casino Borghese was designed to house Cardinal Scipione Borghese's art collection. One of Bernini's greatest patrons, the cardinal had as good an eye for a bargain as for a masterpiece: he picked up many works – including the odd Caravaggio – at knock-down prices after they were rejected by the disappointed or shocked patrons who

had commissioned them. The building's imposing façade was originally adorned with sculptures and ancient reliefs, which, along with many of the gallery's priceless gems, were sold to Napoleon in 1807 and are now conserved in the Louvre. The interior decoration – which was carried out in 1775-90 by Antonio Asprucci and Christopher Unterberger for Marcantonio IV Borghese – was fully restored during the 1990s.

A curved double staircase leads to the imposing entrance salon, with fourth-century AD floor mosaics showing gladiators fighting wild animals; the spectacular trompe l'oeil ceiling fresco (Mariano Rossi, 1775-78) shows Romulus received as a god on Olympus by Jupiter and other tales of Roman glory. Also here is the statue of Marcus Curtius throwing himself into a chasm. (According to legend, when a massive crack appeared in the Roman Forum, threatening to swallow up Rome, the only way to stop it was to sacrifice the city's greatest treasure… so in leaped golden-boy Marcus.) The sculpture is an interesting palimpsest: Marcus' horse dates from the second century, whereas Marcus himself is the c1618 work of Pietro Bernini (father of the more famous Gian Lorenzo); the whole lot was stuck to the wall in 1776 as part of the villa's renovation during the 18th-century.

In Room 1 is one of the gallery's highlights: Canova's 1808 waxed marble figure of Pauline, sister of Napoleon and wife of Prince Camillo Borghese, as a topless Venus reclining languidly on a marble and wood sofa, which once contained a mechanism that slowly rotated it. Prince Camillo thought the work so provocative that he forbade even the artist from seeing it after completion. (Asked by a shocked friend how she could bear to pose naked, the irascible Pauline is said to have snapped: 'The studio was heated.')

Rooms 2 to 4 contain some spectacular sculptures by Gian Lorenzo Bernini, made early in his career and already showing flashes of his genius. His *David* (1624) merits observation from different points of view in Room 2; the tense, concentrated face on the biblical hero as he is about to launch his shot is a self-portrait of the artist. Room 3 houses perhaps Bernini's most famous piece: *Apollo and Daphne* (1625), a seminal work of Baroque sculpture. As the nymph flees the amorous sun god, her desperate plea for help is answered by her river-god father; as Apollo reaches her she morphs – fingertips first – into a laurel tree. Ovid's tale was given a moral twist by Maffeo Barberini – later Pope Urban VIII – who composed the Latin inscription on the base: 'When we pursue fleeting pleasures, we reap only bitter fruits.' Bernini's virtuosity is especially evident in the cluster of paper-thin marble leaves separating the god and the girl. In Room 4, Pluto's hand presses fiercely into Proserpine's marble thigh in *The Rape of Proserpine* (1622), as she flexes her toes in tearful struggle.

Room 5 contains important pieces of classical sculpture, many of them Roman copies of Greek originals. Among the most renowned are a Roman copy of a Greek dancing faun and a copy of sleeping Hermaphroditus, who was the offspring of Hermes and Aphrodite, displayed with his/her back to the onlooker so that the breasts and genitals are invisible. Bernini's *Aeneas and Anchises* (1620) dominates Room 6, showing the family fleeing as Troy burns, a theme reflected in the ceiling with Pecheux's painting of the gods deciding the fate of the city. Room 7 is Egyptian-themed: the ceiling paintings by Tommaso Maria Conca (1780) include an allegory of the richness of Egypt, whereas among the classical statues is a second-century Isis that is clad in black marble clothing.

The six Caravaggios in Room 8 include the *Boy with a Basket of Fruit* (c1594) and the *Sick Bacchus* (c1593), which is believed to be a self-portrait. His *David with the Head of Goliath*, also thought to be a

SIGHTS

Pincio. *See p74.*

The Legendary Harry's Bar

Legendary Harry's Bar is the unique place that evokes the "Dolce Vita" as if it were a clip from the film, creating a vivid flashback to the golden era of the Via Veneto, when Frank Sinatra sang at the piano and all the stars made their appearance in this bar/restaurant full of glamour and style. As in the roaring sixties, you can still sip an aperitif, enjoy the live piano bar every evening and dive into the magic of the Via Veneto from the exclusive and fascinating Harry's Bar. The refined cuisine recalls the freshness of Mediterranean flavours based on prime ingredients. Tradition and fantasy inspire the elegant dishes, accompanied by the most prestigious labels and a high class service.

Reservations Recommended

Via V. Veneto 150 - 00187 Roma – www.harrysbar.it - info@harrysbar.it
Tel. +39 06 48 46 43 / +39 06 47 42 103 – Fax. +39 06 48 83 117
Open from: 11:00 – to 2:00am – Piano Bar 22:00 – 2:00am (Mon - Sat)

self-portrait, was sent to Scipione Borghese as a desperate plea for pardon: since his exile for the murder of his opponent in a tennis match in 1606, the artist had been dogged by a terror of execution. The painting uses the same young model as *St John the Baptist* (1610), possibly Caravaggio's last painting. (Finally given a papal pardon in 1610, Caravaggio set sail for Rome but never made it; he was mistakenly arrested at Porto Ercole, where he became ill and died.)

Upstairs, the picture gallery is packed with one masterpiece after another. Look out in particular for: Raphael's *Deposition*, Pinturicchio's *Crucifixion with Saints Jerome and Christopher* and Perugino's *Madonna and Child* (Room 9); Correggio's *Danaë*, commissioned as 16th-century soft porn for Charles V of Spain (as told in Ovid's *Metamorphoses*, Jupiter – disguised as a 'golden shower' – attempted to seduce the reclining, half-naked maiden) and Lucas Cranach's *Venus and Cupid with Honeycomb* (Room 10); a dark, brooding *Pietà* by Raphael's follower Sodoma (Room 12); two self-portraits and two sculpted busts of Cardinal Scipione Borghese by Bernini (Room 14); Jacopo Bassano's *Last Supper* (Room 15); and Rubens' spectacular *Pietà* and *Susanna and the Elders* (Room 18). Titian's *Venus Blindfolding Cupid* and *Sacred and Profane Love*, the work that originally put the gallery on the map, are the centrepieces of Room 20. In 1899, the Rothschilds offered to buy the latter work at a price that exceeded the estimated value of the entire gallery and all its works put together; the offer was turned down. Other highlights of Room 20 include Renaissance paintings by Veronese, Giorgione and Carpaccio, and Antonello da Messina's *Portrait of a Man*.

Galleria Nazionale d'Arte Moderna e Contemporanea

Viale delle Belle Arti 131 (06 3229 8221, www. gnam.beniculturali.it). Bus 52, 95/tram 3, 19. **Open** 8.30am-7.30pm Tue-Sun. *Ticket office* 9am-2pm Mon-Fri. **Admission** *Gallery* €8; €4 reductions. *Extra charge for exhibitions.* **No credit cards. Map** p340 A2.

Several of the villas dotted around the park are the remains of a world exposition held here in 1911, and this neo-classical palace, dedicated to 19th- and 20th-century art, is one of the most eye-pleasing. The permanent collection begins with the 19th century, when big was beautiful: an enormous statue of *Hercules* by Canova dominates Room 4 of the left wing; Ettore Ferrari's plaster model for the bronze of Giordano Bruno in Campo de' Fiori stands opposite, in Room 4 of the right wing.

In the Palizzi Room (Room 5, left wing) are smaller pieces, including romantic views of the Neapolitan hinterland and views of Rome before the dramatic changes wreaked upon the urban landscape in the late 19th century. The 20th-century component (upper right and left wings) includes works by De Chirico, Modigliani, Morandi and Marini, and a powerful altarpiece to Fascism by Gerardo Dottori.

International stars include *The Three Ages* by Klimt and *The Gardener* and *Madame Ginoux* by Van Gogh. Cézanne, Braque, Rodin and Henry Moore are also represented here. *Photo p82.*

Museo Carlo Bilotti

Viale Fiorello La Guardia (06 0608, www. museocarlobilotti.it). Bus 52, 53, 95, 910. **Open** 9am-7pm Tue-Sun. **Admission** €4.50; €2.50 reductions. **No credit cards. Map** p340 A3.

This contemporary art museum is housed in a palazzo that was bought by Scipione Borghese in 1616 and used as a resting place during hunts. Damaged by French cannon fire in 1849, it was then variously used as a storehouse for oranges, a religious institute and city offices; it opened as a gallery in 2006 to house the superlative collection of billionaire tycoon Carlo Bilotti. The De Chirico paintings and sculptures that form the nucleus of the 22 works in the permanent collection (first floor) perhaps influenced Bilotti to choose Rome as the city in which to display them (De Chirico spent much of his life in Rome, and died here in 1978). Also on the first floor, an entire room is devoted to the Bilotti family: the highlights are a Larry Rivers portrait of Mr Bilotti posing before a Dubuffet canvas and a poignant 1981 Warhol portrait of Bilotti's wife and daughter. A wall of photographs capture the family schmoozing with various high-profile figures on the contemporary art scene. The ground floor hosts temporary art exhibitions. *Photo p83.*

FREE Museo Hendrik Christian Andersen

Via PS Mancini 20 (06 321 9089, www.museo andersen.beniculturali.it). Metro Flaminio/bus 95, 490, 495, 628/tram 2, 19. **Open** 9.30am-7pm Tue-Sun. **Admission** free. **Map** p338 D2.

This offshoot of the Galleria Nazionale d'Arte Moderna occupies an art nouveau villa between the river and viale Flaminia. This was the studio-home of Hendrik Christian Andersen, a Norwegian-American whose artistic ambitions were monumental but whose fans were few. Andersen favoured the bombastic homoerotic style of which Mussolini was so fond. His massive bronze and plaster figures stride manfully across the studio; more interesting, perhaps, is his megalomaniacal plan for a 'world city' (1913). Temporary exhibitions in the upper rooms are rather hit-and-miss.

▶ *The terrace of the top-floor café (open 9am-4pm Mon-Fri) is a pleasant spot to while away some time on a sunny day.*

Museo Nazionale Etrusco di Villa Giulia

Piazzale di Villa Giulia 9 (06 322 6571). Tram 2, 3, 19. **Open** 8.30am-7.30pm Tue-Sun. **Admission** €8; €4 reductions. **No credit cards. Map** p338 E1.

SIGHTS

Galleria Nazionale d'Arte Moderna e Contemporanea. *See p81.*

Founded in 1889 in the splendid Villa Giulia, this collection charts the development of the sophisticated, mysterious Etruscans. The villa was originally constructed in the mid-16th century as a sumptuous summer residence for Pope Julius III; Michelangelo gave his friend Vignola a hand with the design. The rustic façade leads into an elegantly frescoed loggia. Across the courtyard, stairs go down to the nymphaeum. Restored in 2004, the sixth-century BC *Apollo of Veio*, in coloured terracotta, is in a separate room by the nymphaeum.

In the main body of the museum, a number of rooms are dedicated to objects that were unearthed at the Etruscan necropolis at Cerveteri; the centre-piece is the almost life-size sarcophagus, from the sixth century BC, of a married couple; they have been carved as if they are reclining at a dinner party. The Etruscan fondness for eating and drinking is apparent from the vast number of bronze cooking utensils, as well as ceramic cups and amphorae (often decorated with scenes from imported Greek myths). The Room of the Seven Hills (a frescoed frieze names them) contains the Castellani collection of extraordinarily delicate jewellery from the eighth century BC right up to the 19th century. Next door is the Room of Venus, with pieces unearthed at the fifth-century BC temples of Pyrgi. The Etruscans went well prepared to their graves, and the majority of the collection comes from excavations of tombs: hundreds of vases, pieces of furniture and models of buildings made to accompany the dead. Detailed notes in English explain the excavation sites and provide information on how gold, bronze and clay were worked in times gone by. In the gardens there is a reconstruction of an Etruscan temple and a pleasant café. As this guide went to press, part of the collection (not including pieces mentioned here) was closed for restoration.

Museo Civico di Zoologia

Via U Aldrovandi 18 (06 6710 9270, www.museodizoologia.it). Bus 217, 910/ tram 3, 19. **Open** 9am-7pm Tue-Sun. **Admission** €6; €3.50 reductions. **No credit cards. Map** p340 B1.

On the north-east side of the Bioparco-Zoo (*see p248*) you'll find the Museo di Zoologia, which has a room that is dedicated to the wetlands of Lazio and has sections on animal reproduction, biodiversity and extreme habitats. A vast collection of dusty and moth-eaten stuffed animals lingers in its old wing. Access is from via Aldrovandi, or through the zoo for ticket-holders.

VIA VENETO & THE QUARTIERE LUDOVISI

Via Vittorio Veneto (VEH-neto) struggles to live up to its *dolce vita* glory days, when Fellini made it Rome's most glamorous hangout. A 2006 'restoration project' – largely financed

by restaurant owners nostalgic for the days when Burton, Taylor and pals used to run up astronomical bills in their establishments – involved widening pavements, improving street lighting and giving some of the older *palazzi* a facelift… but sadly did nothing for the lack of atmosphere. The modern-day Taylors and Burtons, when they're in town, do their hell-raising elsewhere. This tree-lined slalom curve still manages to rake in the euros, however, mainly thanks to its vast luxury hotels groaning under the weight of their own chandeliers, and its cripplingly expensive, glass-enclosed pavement cafes, aimed entirely at expense-account travellers and unwitting tourists.

This area is known as the **Quartiere Ludovisi**, after the 17th-century Villa Ludovisi, the palace and gardens of which stood here until the 1870s. Following the Unification of Italy, the Ludovisi family, like other aristocratic landowners of the day, sold their property off to building speculators; what had once been a slope of verdant tranquillity was swiftly gobbled up by pompous Piedmontese *palazzi* (nearby Villa Borghese only narrowly escaped the same fate).

Museo Carlo Bilotti. *See p81.*

Prince Boncompagni-Ludovisi (whose surnames have been given to two local streets) put the proceeds of the sale of his glorious estate towards building a huge palace on part of his former grounds. Crippled by running costs and the capital gains bill on the sale of his land, he was forced to sell his new abode to Margherita, widow of King Umberto I, who was to give her name to the classic pizza, as well as to this monument to the prince's lack of financial acumen. Halfway along via Veneto, Villa Margherita is now part of the massively barricaded US embassy.

As the new *palazzi* sprang up, the area began to acquire the reputation for luxury that it retained throughout the mid-20th century. Its fame in the 1950s was due mostly to the enormous American presence at Cinecittà (*see p249*). Fellini's 1960 film *La dolce vita*, starring Marcello Mastroianni, consecrated the scene and coined the term 'paparazzo', the surname of a character in the film modelled on legendary photographer Tazio Secchiaroli who made his name snapping away in this glam neighbourhood.

Porta Pia.

The lower reaches of via Veneto are home to the eerie **Santa Maria della Concezione** (*see below*) and to the Fontana delle Api (Bee Fountain) by Bernini.

FREE Santa Maria della Concezione

Via Veneto 27 (06 487 1185). Metro Barberini, bus 52, 62, 95, 116, 119. **Open** *Church* 7am-noon, 3-7pm daily. *Crypt* 9am-noon, 3-6pm Mon-Sat; 9am-noon, 3-7pm Sun. **Admission** *Crypt* donation expected. **Map** p341 B5.

Commonly known as *i Cappuccini* (the Capuchins) after the long-bearded, brown-clad Franciscan sub-order to which it belongs, this Baroque church has a *St Michael* (1635) by Guido Reni (first chapel on the right), which was a major hit with English Grand Tourists, and a fine *St Paul's Sight Being Restored* (1631) by Pietro da Cortona (first chapel on the left). Monks may try to tell you that the St Francis in Meditation is by Caravaggio, but this is probably wishful thinking. The real draw, though, is the crypt, which holds Rome's most macabre sight: the skeletons of thousands of monks, meticulously dismantled and arranged in swirls, sunbursts and curlicues through four subterranean chapels. Delicate ribs hang from the ceiling in the form of chandeliers, and inverted pelvic bones make the shape of hourglasses – a reminder (as a notice states) that 'you will be what we now are'.

▶ *See p78* **Capuchins and Cappuccino**.

PIAZZA SALLUSTIO & PORTA PIA

East of Villa Borghese, you'll find street after street of imposing, late 19th-century *palazzi* that cover what was once ancient Rome's greatest garden: the Horti Sallustiani. The garden was built on land that that passed from Julius Caesar to the historian and politician Gaius Crispus Sallustius around 40 BC. Ruins are still visible in the hexagonal piazza Sallustio: but, it's not what it once was and you will need a good imagination to get an idea of the lost grandeur by peering at the masonry in the hole in the middle of the piazza.

A couple of streets north-east is **Porta Pia**, its city-facing façade designed by Michelangelo for the Medici pope Pius IV in 1561. It was by this monumental entrance gate that a hole was blown on 20 September 1871, allowing Unification troops to march along what is now via XX Settembre and evict the pope from his last stronghold in the Quirinal palace. Next to the gate is the British embassy. Completed in 1971, the travertine-clad structure designed by architect Sir Basil Spence replaced a 19th-century villa demolished after a bomb explosion in 1946. It has a Henry Moore sculpture in its decorative pool.

The Tridente

Over 200 years of shopping, sightseeing and sitting around in cafés.

The Tridente has a long history of welcoming visitors: it was a home-from-home for the Grand Tourists of the 18th and 19th centuries, when English '*Milords*' took up lodgings around **piazza di Spagna**. And today it's as popular as ever – there are still people who visit Rome without ever straying out of the Tridente.

But resist the allure of the area's Fendis and Armanis and there is plenty to admire, from modern-day Roman romance on the **Spanish Steps**, to Romanticism at the **Keats-Shelley Museum**. More attractions can be found, too, in the shape of Augustus' **mausoleum**, the **Ara Pacis** and Marcus Aurelius' column in **piazza Colonna**.

Map pp338-339	**Eating Out** p188
& 341	**Cafés, Bars**
Hotels p171	**& Gelaterie** p209

SIGHTS

CINEMATIC CHARM

Presumably hoping to keep his favoured haunts to himself, Federico Fellini set his film *La dolce vita* on via Veneto (*see p74*), where gawpers from the provinces then flocked in droves for a glimpse of the glam and famous. The A-class, however, favoured the Tridente, the triangle enclosed by the three prongs – *vie* Ripetta (where Fellini lived), del Corso and Babuino – emanating from piazza del Popolo.

The super-smart grid of streets at the foot of the Spanish Steps was no stranger to jet-set attention: as long ago as the 18th century it had a *dolce vita* all of its own when this was the little St James' of the Grand Tourists, who met for coffee at the (long gone) Caffè degli Inglesi (with its daring interior decor by Piranesi, all pyramids, obelisks and sphinxes) on the corner where via delle Carozze meets the piazza.

VIA DEL BABUINO & PIAZZA DI SPAGNA

Piazza di Spagna is where everybody meets, congregating in the summer on whichever side

of the grand staircase is in the shade. In spring the loafers, couples, exhausted tourists and those whose dates are seriously late are temporarily turfed off the steps while an army of gardeners arranges a display of azaleas.

Despite being busy it's a lovely spot, but while here, spare a thought for the coughing, consumptive 25-year-old Keats, who spent a few wretched months in the winter of 1820-1 in the Casina Rossa, now the **Keats-Shelley Memorial House** (*see p87*), at the foot of the Spanish Steps.

Though the Spanish have a magnificent embassy in the square, it is the French who should be thanked for creating this sophisticated urban landscape with its grand **Spanish Steps** (*see p89*), which lead down from the French preserve of **Villa Medici** – the glorious Renaissance villa that hosts *Prix de Rome* winners – and the **Trinità dei Monti** church and convent at the top. Don't be daunted by the steep climb – though one of the best-kept secrets of the area is the passenger lift, concealed on the left just inside the main entrance to the Spagna metro station. (This is also the easiest way up to the **Villa Borghese**; *see p74*.)

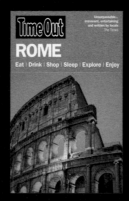

Extra Time

● Bernini and Borromini had a hand in the design of Palazzo Propaganda Fide (via Propaganda 1, 06 6907 9299, open 2-6pm Mon, Wed, Fri, €8), the Vatican-owned pile facing piazza di Spagna, recently opened to the public after a controversial restoration into which suspiciously huge – depending on who you ask – amounts of state money were poured. Art works include a previously unshown painting by sculptor Canova. And of course there's a chance to peek into the halls and offices of what was once the Inquisition.

● Gian Lorenzo Bernini lived in a fine house (now Palazzo Bernini, with commemorative plaque) in via della Mercede. From out of his window he saw – and helped rebuild – **Sant'Andrea delle Fratte** (via Sant'Andrea delle Fratte 1), the church of the Scots in Rome until 1585. Inside, in front of the main altar, are two stunning marble angels carved by the great man.

● A whole dynasty of sculptors worked in the **Museo-Atelier Canova-Tadolini** at via del Babuino 150. The studio, now an extraordinary café (*see p209*), originally belonged to 18th-century sculptor Antonio Canova; he bequeathed it (together with his sketches, models and tools) to his student and assistant Adamo Tadolini, from whom it passed to two more generations of Tadolini sculptors. You can take tea or coffee here, surrounded by those perfect forms preferred by the genius who created the *Three Graces*.

● Famed for his bleakly metaphysical paintings, De Chirico is celebrated at the **Casa-Museo Giorgio De Chirico** (piazza di Spagna 31, www.fondazione dechirico.it). Here you can nose around his attic-studio – complete with the artist's last colours dried on to palettes and brushes, favourite reading material open on his bedside table and crowded on to library shelves, and well-worn props (including some frightful plastic fruit).

● After the seven veils business, Salome convinced King Herod to cut off John the Baptist's head and present it to her on a silver tray. By tortuous routes the relic ended up in a side chapel of **San Silvestro** in piazza San Silvestro, where the blackened skull is still on display.

● The Lombard community in Rome built the vast church of **San Carlo** (via del Corso 437) to celebrate the canonisation of Milanese archbishop Carlo Borromeo in 1610.

● The German poet Johann Wolfgang von Goethe, who breezed into town from Weimar in 1786, had a jolly time in the house on via del Corso that he shared with the painter Hans Tischbein. The **Casa di Goethe** (via del Corso 18, www.casadigoethe.it) preserves many of his diaries and letters, and hosts concerts, films and cultural events. There are free guided tours on Sundays at 11am.

From the top of the steps you can get the lie of the land: just beyond the *barcaccia*, a charming fountain in the shape of a half-sunken boat, is via Condotti with its high-fashion boutiques, the Gucci and Prada emporia immediately recognisable even at this distance by the neat lines of Japanese tourists clutching lengthy shopping lists for cult-status leather goods. Here too is the **Antico Caffè Greco** (*see p209*), where clientele included Casanova and mad King Ludwig of Bavaria. If it's tea you crave, try **Babington's** tea rooms – that other august institution, located on piazza di Spagna – which has been serving reviving beverages and English-style snacks for 110 years.

To the north-west the incongruously neo-Gothic spire of All Saints' English church pokes up above the rooftops along **via del Babuino**. The origin of this oddly named street lies in the ugly statue draped over an old drinking trough, which reminded inhabitants of a member of the monkey family – another incongruity in the street to which all Rome's most beautiful people flock for their shopping.

Parallel to via del Babuino is **via Margutta**, focus of the 1960s art scene. Fellini lived here until his death in 1993. This was always an artists' quarter: models would ply for trade on the Spanish Steps. Once a year artists who still live here open their studios to the public.

Keats-Shelley Memorial House

Piazza di Spagna 26 (06 678 4235, www.keats-shelley-house.org). Metro Spagna/bus 52, 53, 61, 71, 80Exp, 85, 95, 116, 160, 850. **Open** 10am-1pm, 2-6pm Mon-Fri; 11am-2pm, 3-6pm Sat. Closed 1wk Dec. **Admission** €4; €3 reductions. **Credit** MC, V (for payments over €15). **Map** p341 A4.

The house at the bottom of the Spanish Steps where the 25-year-old John Keats died of tuberculosis in 1821 is crammed with mementos. A lock of Keats' hair and his death mask, a minuscule urn holding tiny pieces of Shelley's charred skeleton, copies of

SIGHTS

dal 1898

Ristorante

An old tale from the mid-1800 created Vitt [ ]inging passion and love for the art of ice-cream making across 5 generations.

To taste this Italian exclusivity, with all its unique flavours come to the most elegant and sophisticated Piazza in Rome, Piazza San Lorenzo in Lucina.

Our restaurant also reflect the typical Roman atmosphere and cuisine, with exceptional flavours, served with creativity and imagination. From the amatriciane to the saltimbocca alla romana, these dishes are a must to anyone visiting this city. The desserts are also typically Roman with original receipts and the f[ ]t ingredients. We also serve pastry from Sicily and Campania, as well as some international dishes from France, Austria, and the USA, to accommodate all the palates of ou visitors.

- Restaurant
- Gelateria
- Pastry Shop

Piazza San Lorenzo in Lucina 33

tel 06.6876304
email vitticentro@yahoo.it

documents and letters, and a massive library make this a Romantics enthusiast's paradise. Bring a box of tissues: even the hardest-hearted can be moved to tears by the sight of manuscripts written by consumptive poets with shaky hands.

▶ *Devotees should also make the pilgrimage to the Cimitero acattolico (Protestant Cemetery; see p122) where both Keats and Shelley are buried.*

★ FREE Spanish Steps

Metro Spagna/bus 52, 53, 61, 71, 80Exp, 85, 95, 116, 160, 850. **Map** p341 A4.
Piazza di Spagna takes its name from the Spanish Embassy to the Vatican, but is famous for the Spanish Steps (Scalinata di Trinità dei Monti), an elegant cascade down from the church of Trinità dei Monti. The steps (completed in 1725) could more accurately be called French: they were funded by French diplomat Etienne Gueffier, who felt the muddy slope leading up to the church – itself built with money from a French king – needed a revamp. At the foot of the stairs is a delightful boat-shaped fountain, the *barcaccia*, designed in 1627 by Gian Lorenzo Bernini and/or his less famous father Pietro; it's ingeniously sunk below ground level to compensate for the low pressure of the delicious *acqua vergine* that feeds it. *Photo p95.*

VIA DEL CORSO & PIAZZA DEL POPOLO

Via del Corso is the last urban stretch of the ancient via Flaminia, which linked Rome with the north Adriatic coast. Over the past 2,000 years it has been a processional route for Roman legions, a country lane, a track for *carnevale* races and, from the late 1800s, a principal showcase street for the capital.

The street's liveliest period began in the mid 15th century, when Pope Paul II began to fret over the debauched goings-on at the pre-Lenten *carnevale* celebrations in Testaccio (*see p119*). He decided to move the races and processions somewhere more central, where he and his troops could keep an eye on things. The obvious spot was via Flaminia – then known simply as via Lata ('wide street') – at the end of which he built his Palazzo Venezia. The pope had the stretch of the street within the city walls paved (using funds from a tax on prostitutes) and renamed il Corso. For over four centuries Romans flocked there at *carnevale* time to be entertained by such edifying spectacles as races between press-ganged Jews, hunchbacks, prostitutes and horses with hot pitch squirted up their recta to make them run faster.

These grotesqueries only stopped after Italian Unification in the 1870s, when the new national government set up shop halfway along via del Corso, setting the tone for what remains the country's political heart. The Lower House

(Camera dei deputati) is in **Palazzo di Montecitorio** (*see below*), in the piazza of the same name, and **Palazzo Chigi**, the prime minister's office, is next door in piazza Colonna, so named for the magnificent second-century AD **colonna di Marco Aurelio** (column of Marcus Aurelius; *see below*) that graces it.

North from Palazzo Chigi, imposing edifices such as **Palazzo Ruspoli** – seat of one of Rome's noble families and venue of the occasional important exhibition, *see* www.fondazionememmo.it – give way to lower-end clothing outlets, which attract a seething mass of suburban teenagers at the weekend. The pedestrianised **piazza San Lorenzo in Lucina** (*see p91*), is a welcome retreat.

Well hidden among the retail crush is the **Casa di Goethe** (*see p87* **Extra time**), the house where the German poet stayed during a visit to the Eternal City in 1786. Beyond, the symmetrically elegant **piazza del Popolo** (*see p91*) – once the papacy's favourite place for executions – is graced by the Caravaggio-packed church of **Santa Maria del Popolo** (*see p91*). The piazza has been gloriously restored and is virtually traffic-free.

FREE Colonna di Marco Aurelio (Column of Marcus Aurelius)

Piazza Colonna. Bus 52, 53, 61, 63, 71, 80Exp, 85, 95, 116, 119, 160, 850. **Map** p339 E5.
The 30m (100ft) column of Marcus Aurelius was built between AD 180 and 196 to commemorate the victories on the battlefield of that most intellectual of Roman emperors. Author of the *Meditations*, he died while campaigning in 180. The reliefs on the column, modelled on the earlier ones on Trajan's column (*see p65*) in the Imperial Fora, are vivid illustrations of Roman army life. In 1589 a statue of St Paul replaced that of Marcus Aurelius on top of the column.

FREE Palazzo di Montecitorio

Piazza di Montecitorio (06 67 601, www.camera. it). Bus 52, 53, 61, 63, 71, 80Exp, 85, 95, 116, 119, 160, 850. **Open** 10am-5pm 1st Sun of mth. **Admission** free. **Map** p339 E5.

INSIDE TRACK
LITERARY LODGINGS

What could be more romantic than staying in an old poet's house? Well, ignoring the fact that the exhibits at the **Keats-Shelley Memorial House** below it are rather sombre, the apartment (*see p183* **Landmark Trust**) on top of the museum makes for a lovely, unique place to stay. Be sure to bring your notepad.

SIGHTS

Obelisks

Finding your way around Rome's 13 obelisks.

For the Egyptians, obelisks were needles channelling the energy of the sun. For the Romans, they became a symbol both of conquest and of the Egyptian culture that was so readily embraced in *caput mundi*.

Palazzo Massimo alle Terme (*see p138*): an obelisk that came from Heliopolis and dates to the reign of Rameses II. Discovered in 1883, it probably once stood in Domitian's temple to Isis, east of the Pantheon.

Piazza della Minerva: also from the temple to Isis, this obelisk was originally erected at Sais by the Pharaoh Apries. In 1667 Bernini mounted it on an elephant.

Piazza di Montecitorio: made for King Psammetichus II, this sixth-century BC obelisk was brought from Heliopolis by Augustus in 10 BC and set up in the *Campus martius* as the gnomon for a giant sundial. It was placed in front of Palazzo di Montecitorio (*see p89*) in 1792.

Piazza Navona (*see p93*): custom-made in Egypt for Domitian, its hieroglyphs were cut in Rome. It stood at the temple to Isis, then later at the Circus of Maxentius, where it remained until being brought to piazza Navona in 1651.

Piazza del Popolo (*pictured; see right*): brought from Heliopolis to Rome in 10 BC

by Augustus, and placed at the centre of the Circus Maximus (*see p60*), this obelisk was later found in three pieces, and reassembled here in 1589.

Piazza del Quirinale (*see p72*) and **Piazza dell'Esquilino**: brought to stand at the entrance to Augustus' mausoleum (*see p92*), one was placed in piazza dell'Esquilino (behind Santa Maria Maggiore) and the other was erected in piazza del Quirinale by Pius VI in 1786.

Piazza della Rotonda: the obelisk in front of the Pantheon (*see p72*), from Heliopolis, is dedicated to Rameses the Great and dates from the 14th century BC. Domitian moved it to the temple of Isis in c AD 80. It was placed here in 1711.

Piazza San Pietro (*see p144*): erected in Alexandria by the Romans in the first century BC and dedicated to Augustus, it was brought on a vast ship to Rome; the ship was then sunk to form a new jetty at Ostia (*see p287*). Caligula placed it in his Vatican circus, where it stayed until Sixtus V had it moved (with the help of 8,000 men) to its current spot in 1586.

Piazza Trinità dei Monti (*see p85*): erected at its current site in 1789 by Pius VI, it originally stood in the splendid Horti Sallustiani (Gardens of Sallust; *see p74*).

San Giovanni in Laterano (*see p131*): the largest obelisk in the world were erected by Thutmose III in the 15th century BC in front of the Temple of Ammon at Thebes. Constantine brought it down the Nile to Alexandria; later (in AD 357), Constantius transported it to Rome. The last of the obelisks to be brought to the city, it was set up on the *spina* of Circus Maximus. In 1587 it was shifted here by Sixtus V.

Viale dell'Obelisco: inside the Villa Borghese (*see p74*) is a monolith brought to Rome by Hadrian. Dedicated to the Emperor's dead lover Antinous, it may have been erected on the site of Antinous' burial. Discovered near Santa Croce in Gerusalemme (*see p131*) in the 16th century, it was erected here in 1822.

Villa Celimontana (*see p130*): this obelisk was presented in 1582 by the Senate to the villa's owner Ciriaco Mattei, who placed it here. Previously it had been at the foot of the steps leading to Santa Maria in Aracoeli (*see p59*), but probably had been moved there from the temple to Isis.

Since 1871 this has been the Lower House of Italy's parliament, which is why police and barricades sometimes prevent you from getting near its elegantly curving façade. (It's best to check the website: open days can be cancelled for important parliamentary events.) Designed by Bernini in 1650 for Pope Innocent X, much of the building has been greatly altered, but the clock tower, columns and window sills of rough-hewn stone are his originals. In piazza di Montecitorio stands the tenth-century BC obelisk of Psammeticus. It was brought from Heliopolis by Augustus to act as the gnomon (projecting piece) for the emperor's great sundial. As part of a recent refurbishment of the square, a new sundial of sorts was set into the cobblestones.

Piazza del Popolo
Metro Flaminio/bus 88, 95, 117, 119, 490, 491, 495/tram 2. **Map** p338 D2.
For centuries, piazza del Popolo was the first glimpse most travellers got of Rome. If Grand Tourists arrived during *carnevale* time, they were likely to witness condemned criminals being tortured here for the edification and/or entertainment of the populace. The obelisk in the centre was brought from Egypt by Augustus and stood in the Circo Massimo until 1589, when it was moved to its present site by Pope Sixtus V. It appears to stand at the apex of a perfect triangle formed by via Ripetta, via del Corso and via del Babuino, although this is an illusion. The churches on either side of via del Corso – Santa Maria dei Miracoli and Santa Maria di Monte Santo – look like twins, but are actually different sizes. Carlo Rainaldi, who designed them in the 1660s,

made them and the angles of the adjacent streets appear symmetrical by giving one an oval dome and the other a round one. The immense Porta del Popolo gate was given a facelift by Bernini in 1655 to welcome Sweden's Queen Christina, who had shocked her subjects by abdicating her throne to convert to Catholicism. The plaque wishing *felice fausto ingressui* ('a happy and blessed arrival') was addressed to the Church's illustrious new signing.
► *The piazza's greatest monument is the church of Santa Maria del Popolo; see below.*

San Lorenzo in Lucina
Piazza San Lorenzo in Lucina 16A (06 687 1494). Bus 52, 53, 61, 63, 71, 80Exp, 85, 95, 116, 119, 160, 850. **Open** *Church* 8am-8pm daily. *Roman remains* guided tour 4.30pm 1st Sat of mth. **Admission** *Roman remains* €2. **No credit cards.** **Map** p339 E4.
This 12th-century church was built on the site of a titulus, which in turn is believed to stand on the site of an ancient well sacred to Juno. The church's exterior incorporates Roman columns, while the 17th-century interior contains Bernini portrait busts in the Fonseca Chapel, a kitsch 17th-century *Crucifixion* by Guido Reni and a monument to French artist Nicolas Poussin, who died in Rome in 1665. In the first chapel on the right is a grill, reputed to be the one on which the martyr St Lawrence was roasted to death.

FREE Santa Maria del Popolo
Piazza del Popolo 12 (06 361 0836). Metro Flaminio/bus 88, 95, 117, 119, 490, 491,

Spanish Steps. *See p89.*

495/tram 2. **Open** 7am-noon, 4-7pm Mon-Sat; 7.30am-1.30pm, 4.30-7.30pm Sun. **Map** p338 D2. According to legend, Santa Maria del Popolo occupies the site of a garden in which hated Emperor Nero was buried. The site was still believed to be haunted by demons 1,000 years later; in 1099 Pope Paschal II built a chapel there to dispel them. Nearly four centuries later, beginning in 1472, Pope Sixtus IV rebuilt the chapel as a church.

In the apse are, unusually for Rome, stained-glass windows, a northern touch created by French artist Guillaume de Marcillat in 1509. The apse itself was designed by Bramante, while the choir ceiling and first and third chapels in the right aisle were frescoed by Pinturicchio, the favourite artist of the Borgias. In Pinturicchio's exquisite works (1508-10), the Virgin and a host of saints keep company with some very pre-Christian sibyls. Most intriguing is the Chigi Chapel, designed by Raphael for wealthy banker Agostino Chigi. The mosaics in the dome depict God creating the sun and the seven planets, and Agostino's personal horoscope: with binoculars you can just about make out a crab, a bull, a lion and a pair of scales. The chapel was finished by Bernini, who, on the orders of Agostino's descendant Pope Alexander VII, added the statues of Daniel and Habakkuk. The church's most-gawped-at possessions, however, are the two masterpieces by Caravaggio to the left of the main altar, in the Cerasi Chapel. On a vast scale, and suffused with lashings of the *maestro's* particular light, they show the martyrdom of St Peter and the conversion of St Paul. To the left of the main door is a memorial to 17th-century notable GB Gisleni: grisly skeletons, chrysalids and butterflies remind us of our brief passage through this life before we exit the other end.

VIA RIPETTA

Halfway down the third arm of the Tridente, via Ripetta, is stark piazza Augusto Imperatore, built by Mussolini around the rather neglected **Mausoleo di Augusto** (*see right*) – the funeral

mound of the Emperor Augustus. Above is the Ara Pacis Augustae, erected by Augustus to celebrate peace after his conquest of Gaul and Spain, with its showcase, the **Museo dell'Ara Pacis** (*see below*). South of the square stand two fine churches: **San Girolamo degli Illirici**, serving Rome's Croatian community, and **San Rocco**, built for local innkeepers and Tiber boatmen by Alexander VI (1492-1503). Heading back towards via del Corso, the giant, curving walls of the **Palazzo Borghese** come into view; acquired in 1506 by Camillo Borghese, the future Pope Paul V, it was later the home of Napoleon's sister Pauline.

Mausoleo di Augusto (Mausoleum of Augustus)

Piazza Augusto Imperatore/via Ripetta. Bus 30Exp, 70, 81, 87, 186, 492, 628, 913. Not open to the public. **Map** p339 D3.

It's hard to believe that this forlorn-looking brick cylinder was one of the most important monuments of ancient Rome. The mausoleum was built in honour of Augustus, who had brought peace to the city and its Empire, and was begun in 28 BC. The first person to be buried here was Augustus' nephew, favourite son-in-law and heir apparent, Marcellus. Augustus himself was laid to rest in the central chamber in AD 14, and many more emperors went on to join him there. In the Middle Ages, the mausoleum was used as a fortress; during the Renaissance, it housed gardens. Mussolini had it restored, reportedly because he thought it a fitting place for his own illustrious corpse.

★ Museo dell'Ara Pacis

Via Ripetta/lungotevere in Augusta (06 0608, www.arapacis.it). Bus 30Exp, 70, 81, 87, 186, 492, 628, 913. **Open** 9am-7pm Tue-Sun. **Admission** €8, €6 reductions. **Map** p339 D3.

Now in a striking container, Augustus' great monument was inaugurated in 9 BC; this altar of Augustan peace celebrated the end of the civil war and strife that had characterised the last years of the Republic, and the wealth and security brought by Augustus' victories. Originally located a few hundred metres away (off via in Lucina, behind the church of San Lorenzo in Lucina; *see p91*), the *ara* was designed to overlook the urban stretch of via Flaminia (now via del Corso) by which Augustus had re-entered the city after three years' absence in Spain and Gaul. The altar as we see it now was reconstructed in the 1930s, after major excavations under the palazzo that had been built over the altar – its position known from fragments discovered during building work in the 16th century – and an equally major trawl through the world's museums looking for missing bits. Outside, the flank of the building towards piazza Augusto Imperatore has been carved with the *Res Gestae*, Augustus' testament to his 'things done'.

INSIDE TRACK
ALTAR OF PEACE?

US architect Richard Meier's 2006 building for **Ara Pacis** (*see right*) remains deeply unpopular with a lot of Romans, with many thinking it too large and too modern for its surroundings. It is so unpopular, in fact, that in 2008 mayor Gianni Alemmano said he would demolish it and in summer 2009 it was graffitied in protest. The critics, however, were slightly appeased in 2010 when plans were announced to demolish one of the outer walls, which obstructed views of two nearby churches.

The Pantheon & Piazza Navona

The city's historic centre is full of art, architecture and real Roman life.

After the fall of the Roman Empire, this area of the *campus martius* in the loop of the river north of **corso Vittorio Emanuele** became prime construction territory, with the building of great marble *palazzi*, interspersed with the modest homes of ordinary folk. Today, this picturesque section of the *centro storico* retains its historical mix of the very grand and the very humble: mink-coated *contessas* mingle with wrinkled pensioners and tradesmen, often living, or making a living, in parts of the same palazzo. It's a chic area after dark, with smart restaurants and hip bars. Next morning, however, it's back to business, with wheeling and dealing taking place against a stunning backdrop: two squares – both living links to ancient Rome – dominate the district: **piazza della Rotonda** – home to the **Pantheon** – and the magnificent **piazza Navona**.

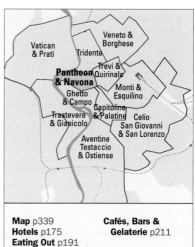

Map p339	**Cafés, Bars &**
Hotels p175	**Gelaterie** p211
Eating Out p191	

SIGHTS

INTRODUCING THE PANTHEON & PIAZZA NAVONA

Much of what is now Rome's *centro storico* flooded regularly and therefore was not properly settled in antiquity; instead it was used as a vast training ground – the *Campus martius* or Field of Mars (Mars was the god of war) – for the Roman military machine. It was not until the third century AD that the Aurelian Wall encompassed the area, which by then was fitted out with military R&R facilities such as marbled bathhouses, theatres, grand temples like the Pantheon and a 30,000-seat athletics stadium where piazza Navona stands today.

Water, and the lack of it, was a key factor in the fifth-century decline and fall of the city. Barbarians cut Rome's aqueducts, driving the remaining population of a fatally wounded city down towards its alternative water supply, the filthy Tiber. The *Campo marzio* beside the river became prime construction territory.

After Unification in the 1870s, the flooding problem was dealt with once and for all by the construction of the massive *banchine* along the river banks. Practical as they were, these embankments cut the Romans off from their river and utterly changed the topography of the city. To see to what extent, take a look at the Roman views churned out for Grand Tourists (the Museo di Roma displays some charming examples): cows graze in water meadows and rowing boats are pulled up in front of houses.

WEST OF PIAZZA NAVONA

After arriving at the northern entrance to the city at piazza del Popolo (*see p89*), pilgrims were funnelled past a succession of rosary-

Extra Time

● The curved façade of noble 16th-century Palazzo Massimo (corso Vittorio Emanuele 141), designed by Baldassare Peruzzi, follows the stands in Emperor Domitian's Odeon – a small theatre. Inside, the private church opens on 16 March each year to celebrate a young Massimo being raised from the dead by San Filippo Neri in 1583. Out back, in piazza de' Massimi, is a column from Domitian's Odeon.

● Blink and you could miss any mention of Napoleon's reign in Rome – from 1798 to 1814 – in standard accounts of the city. But dreams of empire were the Corsican's fatal fantasy; he even shipped to Pope Pius VII for his imperial coronation in Paris in 1804. Rome was mostly an opportunity for grabbing as much loot as his army could carry, hauling back cartloads of marbles and old masters. But the emperor's mother Letizia lived happily in the Palazzo Bonaparte on piazza Venezia for many years. His sister Pauline posed in the nude for sculptor Canova (see p78 Galleria Borghese) and ran up huge bills for her millionaire Roman husband, Prince Camillo Borghese.

The **Museo Napoleonico** (piazza di Ponte Umberto I, 06 6880 6286, www.museo napoleonico.it, closed Mon) contains pieces relating to the Frenchman's family.

● Urbino-born architect Donato Bramante is credited with kick-starting the Roman High Renaissance. He began with the beautiful **Chiostro del Bramante** (Arco della Pace 5, 06 6880 9036, www. chiostrodelbramante.it) in 1500-04.

● Saint Eustace is supposed to have been martyred while hunting on the very spot where the church of **Sant'Eustachio** – in the eponymous square – was (according to legend) founded by Emperor Constantine. Antlers figure on the church's 18th-century façade because, while out hunting one day, the soldier who would become the patron saint of hunters had a vision of a stag with a cross between its antlers. Most people come here for the legendary *gran caffè* across the piazza at the **Caffè Sant'Eustachio** (see p212) – its walls are covered in snaps of visiting celebrities.

makers (*coronari*) – the hard-selling souvenir touts along via de' Coronari – who vied to empty the travellers' pockets before they reached St Peter's. The faithful also paid a swingeing toll to cross the Castel Sant'Angelo bridge to reach their final destination.

Nowadays, in the golden triangle that extends south from via de' Coronari's southern tip as far as via del Governo Vecchio, humanity flows along in a continuously moving wave. Here, VIPs and movie stars parade their assets (but never before midnight) in *dolce vita*-style bars before a backdrop of dazzling Renaissance beauty, including the stunning façade of **Santa Maria della Pace** (see right).

At the south-western tip of piazza Navona, in piazza Pasquino, a severely truncated classical statue nestling against the back wall of Palazzo Braschi – now home to the **Museo di Roma** (see right) – is the most famous of Rome's 'talking' statues (see p97 **Talking Statue**); in days gone by when Vatican walls had ears and you could lose your head for an offhand irreverent remark, Romans let off steam by pinning scurrilous verse to sculptures rather than risk their lives by being vocally critical. Facts are thin on the ground but rumour had it that **Pasquino** (after whom the piece was named in 1501) was a tailor to the Vatican and that much of papal Rome's gossip emanated from his

nearby shop. The cutting witticisms came to be known as *pasquinate* (pasquinades).

Nearby, **corso Vittorio Emanuele II** (simply 'corso Vittorio' to locals) shoots north-west towards the river. When it was hacked through the medieval area after Unification in the 1870s, only the most grandiose of homes – like **Palazzo Massimo alle Colonne** (see p241) and Palazzo Braschi – were spared.

FREE Chiesa Nuova (Santa Maria in Vallicella)

Piazza della Chiesa Nuova (06 687 5289, www. vallicella.org). Bus 30Exp, 40Exp, 46, 62, 63, 64, 70, 81, 116, 492, 628, 630, 780, 916. **Open** *Apr-Oct* 8am-1pm, 4.30-7.30pm daily. *Nov-Mar* 8am-1pm, 4-7.30pm daily. **Map** p339 C5.

Filippo Neri (1515-95) was a wealthy Florentine who abandoned the cut and thrust of the business world to live and work among the poor in Rome. He experienced an 'ecstasy' of divine love at the Catacombs of San Sebastiano in 1544, after which he founded the Oratorian order. In 1575 work began on the order's headquarters, the Chiesa Nuova, on the site of Santa Maria in Vallicella (donated by Gregory XIII). Neri wanted a large, simple building; the plain walls were covered with exuberant frescoes and multicoloured marbles only after his death. Pietro da Cortona painted *Neri's Vision of the Virgin* (1665) in the vault, the *Trinity in Glory* (1647) in the cupola and the *Assumption of the Virgin* (1650) in the apse.

SIGHTS

The *Virgin and Child*, over the altar, and saints Gregory and Domitilla, to the left and right, are by Rubens (1607-08). Neri was canonised in 1622, and his body lies in an ornately decorated chapel to the left of the main altar. His rooms are open to all on 26 May (his feast day) – though you can also get in on Tuesday, Thursday and Saturday between 10am and noon by booking a 30-minute guided tour (06 6880 4695). Singing was an important part of Oratorian worship, and oratory as a musical form developed out of the order's services.

▶ *Next to the church, Borromini designed the brick Oratorio dei Filippini (1637-52).*

Museo di Roma

Palazzo Braschi, piazza San Pantaleo 10 (06 6710 8346, www.museodiroma.it). Bus 30Exp, 40Exp, 46, 62, 63, 64, 70, 81, 116, 492, 628, 630, 780, 916. **Open** *9am-7pm Tue-Sun.* **Admission** *€6.50; €4.50 reductions. Extra charge for exhibitions.* **Credit** MC, V. **Map** p339 D6.

A rotating collection displayed over two floors recounts the evolution of the Eternal City from the Middle Ages to the early 20th century. Paintings and drawings include portraits of Roman movers and shakers, and views of what the city looked like before 17th- and 19th-century building projects, such as the *banchine* flood walls along the Tiber, dramatically changed it. Sculpture, clothing, furniture and photographs help to put the city's monuments in a human context, and oddities like the Braschi family sedan chair (used by Pius VI) and the papal railway carriage (used by more recent pontiffs) round out the collection. The palazzo was built by Luigi Braschi (nephew of 18th-century Pope Pius VI) in one of the last great flurries of papal nepotism. Sold to the Italian state in 1871 and intended to house the Interior Ministry, the palazzo later became the Fascist party HQ. The bookshop is well stocked, and the reading room has a selection of Rome-oriented reference books.

FREE Santa Maria della Pace

Vicolo del Arco della Pace 5 (06 686 1156). Bus 30Exp, 40Exp, 46, 62, 63, 64, 70, 81, 116, 492, 628, 630, 780, 916. **Open** 10am-noon Mon, Wed, Sat. **Map** p339 C5.

Note: opening hours depend on the presence of the custodian, but the church is always open for mass on Saturday from 4.30pm to 6pm.

Built in 1482 for Pope Sixtus IV, Santa Maria della Pace was given its theatrical Baroque façade by Pietro da Cortona in 1656. The church's most famous artwork is just inside the door: Raphael's *Sibyls*, painted in 1514 for Agostino Chigi, the playboy banker and first owner of the Villa Farnesina (*see p136*). Even if the church is closed, you can visit the beautifully harmonious cloister by Bramante, his first work after arriving in Rome in the early 16th century.

▶ *Paying exhibitions are often held here, but no ticket is required to see the cloister itself. Walk in and climb to the upper level, where there's a pleasant bar, and a bookshop offering a tantalising glimpse of Raphael's Sibyls.*

SIGHTS

Piazza Navona.

PIAZZA NAVONA & EAST

Piazza Navona was the great theatre of Baroque Rome: at times it would be flooded in order to amuse the aristocracy with mock naval battles. Its graceful sweep – with Bernini's fountains, Borromini's church of Sant'Agnese in Agone and picturesque pavement cafés – is now frequented by more prosaic denizens, from tarot-readers, caricaturists, buskers and suburban smoothies to tourists, nuns and businessmen.

Just north of piazza Navona are **Palazzo Altemps**, with its spectacular collection of antique statuary; **Sant'Agostino** (*see p99*), with its Caravaggio masterpiece; and the **Museo Napoleonico** (*see p94* **Extra time**). Due east from the piazza are the Italian Senate, **Palazzo Madama**; the church of **San Luigi dei Francesi** (*see p98*), with yet more Caravaggios; and Borromini's breath-taking **Sant'Ivo alla Sapienza**.

★ Palazzo Altemps

Piazza Sant'Apollinare 46 (06 3996 7700). Bus 30Exp, 40Exp, 46, 70, 81, 87, 116, 492, 628. **Open** 9am-7.45pm Tue-Sun. **Admission** €7; €3 reductions. Extra charge for exhibitions. **No credit cards. Map** p339 D5.

The 15th- to 16th-century Palazzo Altemps has been beautifully restored to house part of the state-owned Museo Nazionale Romano stock of Roman treasures. Here, in perfectly lit salons, loggias and courtyards, you can admire gems of classical statuary from the formerly private Boncompagni-Ludovisi, Altemps and Mattei collections.

The Ludovisis were big on 'fixing' statues broken over the ages or which simply didn't appeal to the tastes of the day. In Room 9, for example, a stately *Athena with Serpent* was revamped in the 17th century by Alessandro Algardi, who also 'improved' the *Hermes Loghios* in Room 19 upstairs. In Room 20, the former dining room with pretty 15th-century frescoes on foody themes, is an *Ares* touched up by Bernini. Room 21 has the *Ludovisi Throne*, the museum's greatest treasure… or its greatest hoax, if you subscribe to the theory of the late, great art historian and polemicist Federico Zeri. (On what may – or, then again, may not – be a fifth-century BC work from Magna Grecia, Aphrodite is being delicately and modestly lifted out of the sea spray from which she was born; on one side of her is a serious lady burning incense, and on the other is a naked one playing the flute.) In Room 26, a Roman copy of a Greek *Gaul's Suicide* was commissioned, recent research suggests, by Julius Caesar. Also here is the Ludovisi sarcophagus, which bears some action-packed high reliefs that depict Roman soldiers trouncing barbarians.

▶ *The rest of the Museo Nazionale Romano collection is spread between the Palazzo Massimo*

alle Terme and the Terme di Diocleziano; see p138 and p141.

INSIDE TRACK TALKING STATUE

He may have a lot of influence on the media, but one place you can learn some opinions on a certain media magnate and long time prime minister is at the talking statue in **piazza Pasquino** (*see p94*). Romans vent by plastering the statue with less-than-complimentary letters about the government, their head of state, and, of course, the Vatican.

FREE Palazzo Madama

Corso Rinascimento (06 67 061, www.senato.it). Bus 30Exp, 70, 81, 87, 116, 204, 280, 492, 628. **Open** *Guided tours only* 10am-6pm 1st Sat of mth. **Admission** free. **Map** p339 D5.

Home to the Italian Senate since 1871, this palazzo was built by the Medici family in the 16th century as their Rome residence. Its rather twee façade, with a frieze of cherubs and bunches of fruit, was added a hundred years later. The 'Madama' of its name refers to Margaret of Parma (1522-86), the illegitimate daughter of Emperor Charles V, who lived here in the 1560s before moving to the Netherlands, where she instigated some of the bloodiest excesses of the religious wars.

Sant'Agostino. *See p99.*

SIGHTS

★ **FREE** **Piazza Navona**

Bus 30Exp, 40Exp, 46, 62, 63, 64, 70, 81, 87, 116, 492, 628, 630, 780, 916. **Map** p339 D5.
This tremendous theatrical space, centred on the gleaming marble composition of Bernini's Fontana dei Quattro Fiumi (Fountain of the Four Rivers), is the hub of the *centro storico*. The piazza owes its shape to an ancient athletics stadium, built in AD 86 by Emperor Domitian, which was the scene of sporting events, and at least one martyrdom. Just north of the piazza, at piazza di Tor Sanguigna 16, you can still see remains of the original arena, sunk below street level.

The piazza acquired its current form in the mid-17th century under Pope Innocent X of the Pamphili family. Its western side is dominated by Borromini's façade for the church of Sant'Agnese in Agone (*see right*) and the adjacent Palazzo Pamphili (now the Brazilian embassy), built in 1644-50. The central fountain, finished in 1651, is one of the most extravagant masterpieces designed – though only partly sculpted – by Bernini. Its main figures represent the longest rivers of the four continents known at the time: the Ganges of Asia, Nile of Africa, Danube of Europe and Plata of the Americas, surrounded by geographically appropriate flora and fauna. The figure of the Nile is veiled, because its source was unknown. For centuries, the story went that Bernini designed it that way to show the river god recoiling

Bernini Elephant. *See p100.*

in horror from the façade of Sant'Agnese, designed by his arch-rival Borromini; in fact, the church was built after the fountain was finished. The obelisk at the fountain's centre, moved here from the Circus of Maxentius on the Appian Way, was carved in Egypt under the orders of Domitian (the hieroglyphics are a Roman addition describing him as 'eternal pharaoh'). The less spectacular Fontana del Moro is at the southern end of the piazza. The central figure of the Moor was designed by Bernini in 1653, and executed by Antonio Mari.

▶ *The piazza di Tor Sanguigna remains are partially visible from the street and can be visited on guided tours on Saturdays and Sundays (10am-1pm; phone 06 0608 for bookings and information).*

FREE **San Luigi dei Francesi**

Piazza San Luigi dei Francesi (06 688 271, www.saintlouis-rome.net). Bus 30Exp, 70, 81, 87, 116, 204, 280, 492, 628. **Open** 10am-12.30pm, 3.30-7pm Mon-Wed, Fri-Sun; 8.30am-12.30pm Thur. **Map** p339 D6.
Completed in 1589, San Luigi (St Louis) is the church of Rome's French community. Most visitors ignore the gaudily lavish interior, and make a beeline for Caravaggio's spectacular scenes from the life of St Matthew in the fifth chapel on the left. Painted in 1600-02, they depict Christ singling out a very reluctant Matthew (left), Matthew being dragged to his execution (right) and an angel briefing the evangelist about what he should write in his gospel (over the altar). Don't let Caravaggio's brooding brilliance and dramatic effects of light and shade blind you to the lovely frescoes of scenes from the life of St Cecilia by Domenichino (1615-17), which are in the second chapel on the right. Take a few coins for instant meter-operated illumination.

FREE **Sant'Agnese in Agone**

Piazza Navona/via Santa Maria dell'Anima 30A (06 6819 2134, www.santagneseinagone.org). Bus 30Exp, 40Exp, 46, 62, 63, 64, 70, 81, 87, 116, 492, 628, 630, 780, 916. **Open** 9.30am-12.30pm, 4-7pm Tue-Sat; 10am-1.30pm, 4-8pm Sun. **Map** p339 D5.
Legend has it that teenage Agnes was cast naked into the stadium of Domitian around AD 304 when she refused to renounce Christ and marry some powerful local buck (possibly Romulus, the son of Emperor Maxentius), but her hair grew miraculously to save her from embarrassment. She was condemned to burn but when the fire refused to catch light, her pagan persecutors chopped her head off, supposedly on the exact spot where this church now stands. Carlo and Girolamo Rainaldi began the church for Pope Innocent X in 1652; after they quarrelled with the pope, Borromini was appointed in their place. He revised the design considerably, adding the splendidly fluid concave façade. The trompe l'oeil side chapels contain statues of St Agnes

SIGHTS

Biking It

Where's good on two wheels.

You'll need above-average derring-do and supreme confidence in your own pedalling skills, but if you're up for it, a bike is a great way to explore Rome's *centro storico* – and escape the crowds.

The municipal bike hire service is operated by the bus company ATAC. With valid ID and €10, you'll be given a smartcard with €5 credit on it (you can top up as much as you like/need subsequently); get the card in larger Metro stations. The signature green bikes can be taken from and deposited at any of the 27 racks around town, and 50c will be deducted for each half hour of use. The major drawback with the city service is the paucity of bikes – a result of high levels of theft coupled with great demand. You can check online (www.bikesharing.roma.it) to see how many bikes are available at which stands at any given time.

And remember, the ATAC bikes at the end of the train line in Ostia are a fine way of getting to the beach at Capocotta (*see p301* **Quick Dips**).

For a fascinating insight into Rome's peri-urban flora and fauna and a close-up look at the river Tiber, on the other hand, pick up one of the bikes kept at the river-side Capoprati park in the northern suburbs run by the Legambiente environmental watchdog (320 058 6050, open 9am-6pm daily, bus 32, 69, 186, 224, 271, 286 to lungotevere M Cadorna stop). Cutting through the park is a municipal cycle track which heads north out of the city, following the river for some 15km (you can also follow the track back along the embankment through the city centre for a very different perspective on Rome's glories). Ring ahead to book children's bikes, mountain bikes or bikes with kiddy-seats attached.

Altogether more bone-shaking is the Appian Way experience. When this ancient Roman road is closed to all but local traffic on Sundays, two wheels is a great way to explore the many sights along the way. But for much of the route, the huge basalt slabs used by the ancients to build their thoroughfares are still in place, and maintenance leaves much to be desired: brace yourself for a very bumpy ride.

For other bike hire outlets, *see p310.*

and another victim of a botched martyrdom, St Sebastian. The doorway in the chapel to the left of the high altar contains a reliquary with Agnes's implausibly small skull. Around the church are reliefs with cherubs holding symbols associated with the martyrdom, including the lamb most commonly used to represent her. Admire Borromini's sacristy during a Friday evening concert.

FREE Sant'Agostino
Piazza Sant'Agostino (06 6880 1962). Bus 30Exp, 70, 81, 87, 116, 204, 280, 492, 628. **Open** 7.45am-noon, 4-7.30pm daily. **Map** p339 D5.
Built over a ninth-century church that marked the burial place of St Monica, St Augustine's mother, the 15th-century church of Sant'Agostino has one of the earliest Renaissance façades in Rome, fashioned out of travertine filched from the Colosseum. Inside, the third column on the left bears a fresco of Isaiah by Raphael from 1512 (when its commissioner complained that the artist had charged him too much for the work, Michelangelo is said to have snapped: 'the knee alone is worth that'). Immediately below is a beautiful sculpture of Mary, her mother Anne and the Christ-child by Andrea Sansovino (also 1512). In the first chapel on the left is Caravaggio's depiction of the grubbiest, most threadbare pilgrims ever to present themselves at the feet of the startlingly beautiful *Madonna of the Pilgrims* (1604). So dirty were they, in fact, that the church that originally commissioned the picture refused to have it. The two highest angels of the main altar are the work of Bernini (1628); below is a Byzantine Madonna. *Photo p97.*

FREE Sant'Ivo alla Sapienza
Corso Rinascimento 40 (06 361 2562). Bus 30Exp, 70, 81, 87, 116, 204, 280, 492, 628. **Open** 9am-noon Sun. **Map** p339 D5.
You can peer, and wander, into the magnificent Renaissance courtyard of the state archives, but pick a Sunday morning to do real justice to this crowning glory of Borromini's tortured imagination. The concave façade of Sant'Ivo is countered by the convex bulk of the dome, which terminates in a bizarre corkscrew spire. The floor plan is based on a six-pointed star, but the forms of classical architecture (solid pediments, columns and logical arches, squares and circles) melt into an altogether more fluid play of convex and concave surfaces on the walls and up into the dome, in a dizzying whirl that soars up to the unknowable, intangible realm of the heavens… leaves you feeling like someone spiked your cappuccino.

SIGHTS

FROM THE PANTHEON TO VIA DEL CORSO

With the Pantheon as backdrop, all human life plays out its part in piazza della Rotonda. A 16th-century fountain is topped by an Egyptian obelisk dedicated to Rameses II. On the steps of the fountain, pierced punks with dogs on limp string hang out with hippies who forgot to go home. All seem oblivious to the bemused tour groups taking photographs and the well-heeled tourists paying through the nose for a cappuccino-with-a-view at the cafés.

South of the Pantheon, central Rome's only Gothic church, **Santa Maria sopra Minerva** (*see right*), stands in piazza della Minerva. In front is *il Pulcino della Minerva*, aka '**Bernini's elephant**' (*photo p98*). This cuddly marble animal, with wrinkled bottom and benign expression, has stood here since 1667. It was designed by Bernini as a tribute to Pope Alexander VII: elephants were both a symbol of wisdom and a model of abstinence. They were believed to be monogamous and to mate only once every five years, which, the Church felt, was the way things should be. Bernini perched a 12th-century BC Egyptian obelisk on its back; like its neighbour in piazza della Rotonda, this obelisk came from a temple to the Egyptian goddess Isis that stood nearby.

Further east, piazza del Collegio Romano contains one of Rome's finest art collections in the **Galleria Doria Pamphilj**. The charmingly rococo piazza Sant'Ignazio looks just like a stage set despite its severe Jesuit church, **Sant'Ignazio di Loyola**. In neighbouring piazza di Pietra, the columns of the Temple of Hadrian can be seen embedded in the walls of Rome's ex-stock exchange, where the occasional exhibition is now held. The quieter lanes close to via del Corso contain outposts of the parliament; journalists, MPs and assorted hangers-on haunt the area's bars. On the lower reaches of via del Corso is the privately owned **Museo del Corso**.

★ Galleria Doria Pamphilj
Via del Corso 305 (06 679 7323, www.doria pamphilj.it). Bus 62, 63, 81, 85, 95, 117, 119, 160, 175, 492, 628, 630, 850. **Open** 10am-5pm daily. **Admission** (incl audio guide) €10; €7 reductions. **No credit cards.** **Map** p339 E5.
The collection of one of the great families of Rome's aristocracy (spelled either Pamphili or Pamphilj), now headed by two half-British siblings, is a very personal one: hung according to an inventory of 1760, some extraordinarily good paintings are packed in with the occasional bad copy to give a unique view of the tastes of late 18th-century Rome. The entrance is through the state apartments

planned by Camillo Pamphili in the mid-16th century. The nephew of Pope Innocent X, Camillo escaped the College of Cardinals to marry fabulously wealthy Olimpia Aldobrandini, to whom the oldest part of the palace belonged, and who had already been left a widow by a member of the Borghese family. The family chapel was designed in 1689 by Carlo Fontana but heavily altered in the 18th and 19th centuries when the trompe l'oeil ceiling was added. The star turns are the corpses of two martyrs: St Justin, under the altar, and St Theodora, visible to the right of the door. The main galleries are on all four sides of the central courtyard. Hard-nosed Olimpia is shown in Algardi's stylised portrait bust by the windows in the first gallery. Velázquez's portrait of a no-nonsense Pope Innocent X is the highlight of the collection. With Bernini's splendid bust next to it, it's difficult to see how the vital presence of Innocent X could be bettered. At the end of the Galleria degli Specchi (Gallery of Mirrors) are four small rooms ordered by century. In the 17th-century room, Caravaggio is represented by *Rest on the Flight into Egypt* and *Penitent Magdalene*. The 16th-century room includes Titian's shameless *Salome*, and a *Portrait of Two Men* by Raphael. In the 15th-century room is a beautifully tragic *Deposition* by Hans Memling. At the end of the third gallery, steps lead to the Salone Aldobrandini, where ancient sculpture is on display (much of it damaged when snow brought down the ceiling in the 1950s). On the way, keep an eye out for Guercino's *St Agnes* failing to catch fire and Pieter Breugel the Elder's northern view of an imaginary sea battle in the bay of Naples.

Museo del Corso
Via del Corso 320 (06 678 6209, www. museodelcorso.it). Bus 62, 63, 81, 85, 95, 117, 119, 160, 175, 492, 628, 630, 850. **Open** 10am-8pm, days vary with exhibition. **Admission** varies with exhibition. **Credit** MC, V. **Map** p339 D5.
This privately owned space stages exhibitions on artistic, historical and literary themes.

★ FREE Pantheon
Piazza della Rotonda (06 6830 0230). Bus 30Exp, 40Exp, 46, 62, 63, 64, 70, 81, 85, 87, 95, 117, 119, 160, 175, 492, 628, 630, 780, 850, 916/tram 8. **Open** 8.30am-7.30pm Mon-Sat; 9am-6pm Sun; 9am-1pm public hols. **Admission** free. **Map** p339 D5.
The Pantheon is the best-preserved ancient building in Rome. It was built (and possibly designed) by Hadrian in AD 119-128 as a temple to the 12 most important classical deities; the inscription on the pediment records an earlier Pantheon built a hundred years earlier by Augustus' general Marcus Agrippa (which confused historians for centuries). Its fine state of preservation is due to the building's conversion to a Christian church in 608, when it was presented to the pope by the Byzantine Emperor

SIGHTS

Pantheon.

the heavens. The building is still officially a church, and contains the tombs of eminent Italians, including the artist Raphael and united Italy's first king, Vittorio Emanuele II. Until the 18th century the portico was used as a market: supports for the stalls were inserted into the notches still visible in the columns.

FREE Santa Maria sopra Minerva

Piazza della Minerva 42 (06 679 3926, www.basilicaminerva.it). Bus 30Exp, 40Exp, 46, 62, 63, 64, 70, 81, 87, 492, 628, 630, 780, 916/tram 8. **Open** 7am-1pm, 3-7pm daily. **Map** p339 E5.

Central Rome's only Gothic church was built on the site of an ancient temple of Minerva in 1280 and modelled on Santa Maria Novella in Florence. It was (over-) restored in the 'Gothick' style in the mid-19th century. The best of its works of art are Renaissance: on the right of the transept is the superb Carafa chapel, with late 15th-century frescoes by Filippino Lippi (1457-1504), commissioned by Cardinal Oliviero Carafa in honour of St Thomas Aquinas. Carafa took Renaissance self-assurance to extremes: the altar painting shows him being presented to a patient Virgin, right at the moment when Gabriel informs her she has conceived. The tomb of the Carafa Pope Paul IV (reigned 1555-59) is also in the chapel. He was one of the prime movers of the Counter-Reformation, chiefly remembered for the institution of the Jewish Ghetto and ordering Daniele da Volterra to paint loincloths on the nudes of Michelangelo's *Last Judgment*. A bronze loincloth was also ordered to cover Christ's genitals on a work by Michelangelo here: the statue was finished by Pietro Urbano (1514-21) and depicts a heroic Christ holding up a cross. An early Renaissance work is the *Madonna and Child*, believed by some to be by Fra Angelico, in the chapel to the left of the altar, close to the artistic monk's own tomb. On either side of the altar are the tombs of Medici popes: corpulent Leo X and Clement VII.

▶ *The father of modern astronomy, Galileo Galilei, was tried for heresy in the adjoining monastery in 1633.*

FREE Sant'Ignazio di Loyola

Piazza Sant'Ignazio (06 679 4406). Bus 62, 63, 81, 85, 95, 117, 119, 160, 175, 492, 628, 630, 850. **Open** 7.30am-7pm Mon-Sat; 9am-7pm Sun. **Map** p339 E5.

Sant'Ignazio was begun in 1626 to commemorate the canonisation of St Ignatius, founder of the Jesuit order. Trompe l'oeil columns soar above the nave, and architraves by Andrea Pozzo open to a cloudy heaven. Trickery was also involved in creating the dome: the monks next door claimed that a real dome would rob them of light, so Pozzo simply painted a dome on the inside of the roof. The illusion is fairly convincing if you stand on the disc set in the floor of the nave. Walk away, however, and it dissolves.

Phocas. The Pantheon has nevertheless suffered over the years – notably when bronze cladding was stripped from the roof in 667, and when Pope Urban VIII allowed Bernini to remove the remaining bronze from the beams in the portico to melt down for his *baldacchino* in St Peter's in 1628. The simplicity of the building's exterior remains largely unchanged, and it retains its original Roman bronze doors. Inside, the Pantheon's real glory lies in the dimensions, which follow the rules set down by top Roman architect Vitruvius. The diameter of the hemispherical dome is exactly equal to the height of the whole building; it could potentially accommodate a perfect sphere. At the exact centre of the dome is the oculus, a circular hole 9m (30ft) in diameter, the only source of light and a symbolic link between the temple and

SIGHTS

The Ghetto & Campo de' Fiori

Medieval Rome meets Jewish Rome.

Campo de' Fiori forms the heart of medieval Rome. Within this web of cobbled alleys, life is characterised by markets and washing-lines draping courtyards, just as it always has been (bar the odd satellite dish). Yet despite the fact that daily rituals have changed little over the years, this is an area of striking contrasts. Campo de' Fiori – with its lively morning market and partying crowds at night – stands alongside the solemn, dignified **piazza Farnese**.

Meanwhile, in the south-east, **largo Argentina** takes the shape of a polluted transport hub with a chunk of ancient Rome occupying the centre. South of **campo de' Fiori** lies the pretty **Ghetto**, home to Europe's oldest Jewish community.

Map p339 & p342	Cafés, Bars &
Hotels p177	Gelaterie p213
Restaurants p194	

INTRODUCING CAMPO DE' FIORI

In the ancient world, the *Campus martius* (field of war) occupied much of this low-lying area along the River Tiber: here Roman males did physical jerks to stay fighting fit for battle. However, with theatrical entertainment banned in the serious city centre itself, this was also where locals would have headed to enjoy a bit of low-brow fun.

The Teatro di Pompeo – Rome's first permanent theatre, built in the mid first century – occupied much of the swathe of land between largo Argentina and campo de' Fiori. The theatres of Marcellus and Balbus also played host to theatrical performances in barbaric times.

East of via Arenula, a warren of narrow winding streets and colossal ancient monuments make the Ghetto (*see p108*) a picturesque haven to explore during your stay. But the charm that it exudes hides a sad past of prejudice, isolation and deportation.

FROM LARGO ARGENTINA TO CAMPO DE' FIORI

Largo Argentina today is a polluted transport hub and rendezvous point for milling teenagers, who rarely give a second thought to the expanse of ancient ruins that fill the hole in the centre of the square. It's officially called largo di Torre Argentina. The name has nothing to do with the Latin American country; it refers to a tower – *torre* – in a nearby street, which was the home of Johannes Burckhardt, the powerful master of ceremonies of the Borgia papacy; Burckhardt's home town was Strasbourg, the diocesan name of which was Argentinensis. His house and tower are now occupied by a theatre museum, the Biblioteca e Raccolta Teatrale del Burcardo (via del Sudario 44, 06 681 9471, www.burcardo. org, 9am-1.30pm Mon-Fri, closed Aug).

Visible when you peer over the railings in largo Argentina are columns, altars and foundations from one round and three rectangular temples dating from the mid third century BC to c100 BC. The frescoes on the taller brickwork are from the 12th-century church of San Nicola de' Cesarini, which was built into one of the temples. If you want to take a closer look, you'll have to cosy up to the ladies of the **Rifugio Felino di Torre Argentina** cat sanctuary (06 4542 5240, www.romancats.com, open noon-6pm daily). They look after about 250 abandoned and wild cats each year among the ruins, and offer guided tours of the site and its feline residents (3pm Mon-Wed & Sat, 4pm Thur & Fri, donation appreciated) – though only when volunteers can be found, so ring ahead to check.

To the east of the square, in via delle Botteghe Oscure, is the **Crypta Balbi** (*see p104*), a tribute to Rome's architectural accretions over the ages; in via del Plebiscito, on the other hand, is **Il Gesù** (*see p105*), chief church of the Jesuit order.

West along corso Vittorio Emanuele II (universally known as corso Vittorio) is the church of **Sant'Andrea della Valle** (*see p106*), topped by Rome's second-tallest dome; the first act of *Tosca* is set here. Further on are the **Museo Barracco** (*see p105*), with its collection of ancient sculpture, and the Vatican-owned Renaissance gem, the **Palazzo della Cancelleria** (*see p106*). To escape the unbreathable air and decibels, take any left off corso Vittorio where café tables occupy cobbled pavements.

The streets converge on lively **campo de' Fiori**. The campo area has for centuries been a fascinating mix of the very smart and the very rough. The powerful Farnese clan – which spawned Pope Paul III – staked its claim

in **piazza Farnese**, a stately square with a pair of fountains made with giant Roman tubs from the baths of Caracalla. The Renaissance **Palazzo Farnese** (*see p106*) – now the French embassy – sits solidly as the undisputed elder statesman of the square. To the north and west are streets packed with antique stores and eateries. Gold and jewellery shops cluster to the south, near the old Monte di Pietà, the state-run pawn shop. Via dei Giubbonari (jacket-makers' street) seethes with clothing stores, while the **Galleria Spada** (*see p105*) is in a pretty palazzo in parallel via Capo di Ferro.

★ **FREE** **Campo de' Fiori**
Bus 30Exp, 40Exp, 62, 63, 64, 70, 81, 87, 116, 492, 571, 628, 630, 780, 916/tram 8.
Map p342 C1.
Campo de' Fiori has been a hub of Roman life since the 15th century, when the pope moved his chief residence to the Vatican; noble families flocked to this area and built palaces, just across the river from the centre of power. Tradesmen and craftsmen set up shop in via del Pellegrino and via Giulia. And innkeepers and food-purveyors clustered in the campo.

Despite galloping gentrification and a substantial population of foreign students and professionals seeking to soak up *romanitas*, the campo has retained some neighbourhood spirit; its friendly, chaotic energy remains magnetic. By day the picturesque but costly food and flower market bustles from about 6am to 2pm (Mon-Sat). Restaurant tables ringing the square fill up every lunchtime. Afternoons here are slow and quiet, except for a perpetual group of alternative types with flea-bitten

SIGHTS

Campo de' Fiori.

Extra Time

● You don't need much imagination to picture the ancient temple to Aesculapius (the god of medicine) that lies beneath the church of **San Bartolomeo** on the Tiber Island: the precious marble columns in the nave are the very ones that adorned the original temple, which was inaugurated in 293 BC. But if you need help to imagine how things were when Otto III built this church in 998, then check out the massive bronze vessel (protected by an iron grille on the right-hand wall of the nave, by the altar) in which the 18-year-old German-born Holy Roman Emperor brought relics of the apostle Bartholomew from Benevento.

● It was in the once-marshy area now known as the **Velabro** (derived from *velum*, Etruscan for marsh) that the twins Romulus and Remus were reportedly found in their basket. Close to Rome's main river port, the marsh was too tempting a real-estate opportunity and was soon drained by means of the **Cloaca Maxima** sewer system. Chunks of this Etruscan-built infrastructure can be seen (with prior permission) beneath what is popularly known as the **Arco di Giano** (Arch of Janus), the touchingly depleted gateway that marked the eastern entrance to the *forum boarium* (cattle market) in what is now via del Velabro. The niches lost their statues long ago but reliefs of four goddesses – probably Juno, Minerva, Ceres and Roma – can still be seen.

● Exuberant *latinisti* like to hold toga parties on the Ides (15th) of March, when Julius Caesar was knifed by Brutus & Co in the **Teatro di Pompeo** – Rome's first permanent theatre structure, constructed in the mid first century BC – where the Senate was meeting after its building in the Forum was destroyed by fire. Several establishments surrounding the campo de' Fiori area – restaurants Da Costanzo (in piazza del Paradiso) and Da Pancrazio (in piazza del Biscione),

and the Hotel Teatro di Pompeo (in largo del Pallaro) – all conceal chunks of the ancient walls, or at least keep their wine in hugely deep cellars, which were the ground floor of the theatre. Nearby, via di Grottapinta clearly follows the curve of the *cavea* (semicircular seating area), while via dei Chiavari and piazza dei Satiri mark where the stage stood.

● The ghastly story of Beatrice Cenci has inspired generations of artists and writers, from Guido Reni to Shelley, Stendhal and Moravia. It's a 16th-century tale of child abuse, incest, violence and murder, which ended with a sensational mass public execution of the entire family – including beautiful, aristocratic 22-year-old Beatrice – in front of Castel Sant'Angelo. Hidden deep in the Ghetto, the unassuming **Palazzo Cenci**, in vicolo dei Cenci, was the house of horrors.

● Since 1361, a pilgrim hostel has stood on the site where the **Venerable English College** (via Monserrato 45, 06 686 5808, www.englishcollegerome.org) has been training Catholic priests since 1579. During persecutions in turbulent 16th-century England, 41 priests who had trained at the college were martyred for their faith the moment they set foot in that popery-hating country. Visit the college and its church – dedicated to the Holy Trinity and St Thomas of Canterbury – by appointment, or catch mass at 10am daily from late September to late May.

● To serve the spiritual needs of the Florentine merchants who lived close to the river, near where their ships came in, Michelangelo made detailed architectural plans to build a huge church dedicated to **San Giovanni dei Fiorentini** in via Giulia/piazza dell'Oro. However, he lost the commission; it was instead entrusted to architect Antonio Sangallo, whose style better reflected the new austerity imposed by the Council of Trent.

dogs, bongos and an anarchic approach to hair-styling. At sunset the square fills up again, first with sedate wine-quaffers then later on with over-indulging Anglo students.

★ Crypta Balbi

Via delle Botteghe Oscure 31 (06 678 0167). Bus 46, 62, 70, 87, 186, 492, 571, 810, 916/tram 8. **Open** 9am-7pm Tue-Sun. **Admission** €7; €3 reductions. **No credit cards. Map** p342 D2.

Part of the Museo Nazionale Romana, the Crypta Balbi displays one of Rome's more interesting recent archaeological finds, and is packed with displays, maps and models that explain (in English) Rome's evolution from its bellicose pre-Imperial era, to early Christian times and on through the dim Middle Ages. The underground ruins themselves – visible occasionally through the day in a tour with no commentary, or on Sundays at 3pm with a guided tour – show the foundations of the gigantic *crypta*, or theatre lobby, constructed by Cornelius Balbus, a Spaniard much in favour at the court of Augustus. Excavations continue, while upstairs is a display of the minutiae of everyday life in ancient Rome: plates, bowls, glasses, amphorae, oil lamps and artisans tools. The upper levels provide a fantastic view of Roman rooftops.

★ Galleria Spada

Piazza Capo di Ferro 3 (06 687 4896, www.galleriaborghese.it/spada/it). Bus 23, 30Exp, 40Exp, 46, 62, 63, 64, 70, 81, 116, 280, 492, 630, 780, 916, H/tram 8. **Open** 8.30am-7.30pm Tue-Sun. **Admission** €5; €2.50 reductions. **Tickets. No credit cards. Map** p342 C2.

Staff here are lovely but the four dusty, hard-to-find rooms are no longer bewitching enough to make you forget that most of the contents are second-division 17th-century leftovers. Spada was an avid art collector. The walls of the four small upstairs *saloni* are crammed and old-style, but notes (in English) in each room help you to make sense of them all. There are some big names here: Domenichino, Guercino and Guido Reni – see his *San Girolamo* and *Slave of Ripa Grande* – plus the father-daughter Gentileschi duo, Orazio and Artemisia. The main attraction, however, is the Borromini perspective, which shows that the manic-depressive architect had a sense, if not of humour, at least of irony. If you're lucky to get there at the right moment (there appears to be no timetable) you'll be taken to a courtyard and misled into believing a 9m-long (30ft) colonnade is much longer by perspective trickery.

▶ *In theory, an art historian conducts guided tours around the impressive art works in the Consiglio di Stato spaces on the first Sunday of each month; phone for details and to book.*

★ FREE Il Gesù

Piazza del Gesù (06 697 001, Loyola's rooms 06 6920 5800, www.chiesadelgesu.org). Bus 30Exp, 40Exp, 46, 62, 63, 64, 70, 81, 87, 492, 630, 780, 916, H. **Open** *Church* 7.30am-12.30pm, 4-7.30pm daily. *Loyola's rooms* 4-6pm Mon-Sat; 10am-noon Sun. **Admission** free. **Map** p342 D1.

The huge Gesù is the flagship church of the Jesuits, the order founded by Basque soldier Ignatius Loyola in the 1530s. The Gesù (built 1568-84) was designed to involve the congregation as closely as possible in the proceedings, with a nave unobstructed by aisles, offering a clear view of the main altar. Giacomo della Porta added a façade that would be repeated *ad nauseam* on Jesuit churches across Italy (and the world) for decades afterwards. A large, bright fresco, *Triumph in the Name of Jesus*, by Il Baciccia (1676-79) – one of Rome's great Baroque masterpieces – decorates the gilded ceiling of the nave, which seems to dissolve on either side as stucco figures (by Antonio Raggi) and other painted images are sucked up into the dazzling light of the heavens.

(The figures falling back to earth are presumably Protestants.) On the left is another spectacular Baroque achievement: the chapel of Sant'Ignazio (1696-1700) by Andrea Pozzo, which is adorned with gold, silver and coloured marble; the statue of St Ignatius entering heaven is now covered the majority of the time with a canvas by Pozzo; at 5.30 every afternoon, however, the painting is winched down amid soaring music and readings from Loyola's works to reveal the statue that lies behind: a marvellous piece of baroque theatre. Towering above the altar is what was long believed to be the biggest lump of lapis lazuli in the entire world… in fact, the piece is merely covered concrete. Outside the church, at piazza del Gesù 45, you can visit the rooms of St Ignatius, which contain a wonderful painted corridor featuring trompe l'oeil special effects by Pozzo, and mementoes of the saint, including his death mask.

Museo Barracco di Scultura Antica

Corso Vittorio 166 (06 687 5657, www.museo barracco.it). Bus 40Exp, 46, 62, 64, 116, 571, 916. **Open** 9am-7pm Tue-Sun. **Admission** €4.50; €3.50 reductions. **No credit cards. Map** p342 C1.

This small collection of mostly pre-Roman art was amassed during the first half of the 20th century by Giovanni Barracco. The nobleman's artistic interests covered the whole gamut of ancient art, as seen in the collection of Assyrian reliefs, Attic vases,

Crypta Balbi.

SIGHTS

Egyptian sphinxes and Babylonian stone lions, as well as Roman and Etruscan exhibits and Greek sculptures. Don't miss the copy of the *Wounded Bitch* by the fourth-century BC sculptor Lysippus, on the second floor.

Palazzo della Cancelleria

Piazza della Cancelleria. Bus 40Exp, 46, 62, 64, 116, 571, 916. **Closed to the public.** **Map** p342 C1.

One of Rome's most refined examples of Renaissance architecture, the Palazzo della Cancelleria was built, possibly by Bramante, between 1483 and 1513, for Raffaele Riario. Even though his great-uncle, Pope Sixtus IV, made him a cardinal at the tender age of 17, Raffaele did not allow his ecclesiastic duties to cramp his style when collecting art. He is said to have raised a third of the cost of this palace with his winnings from a single night's gambling. He was involved in plotting against the powerful Florentine Medici family; and in retaliation, the palace was confiscated for the church and is still Vatican property. The palazzo incorporates the fourth-century church of San Lorenzo in Damaso and, as archaeologists discovered in the 1940s, sits atop a mithraeum and part of a canal connecting the Baths of Agrippa – located just north of largo Argentina – to the Tiber. These ruins are usually visible with permission (06 6988 7521, fax 06 6988 5518), but at the time of writing were closed for further digs.

▶ *From time to time chances arise to enter the palazzo for the occasional chamber-music concert or exhibition on religious themes mounted in the magnificently frescoed rooms.*

Palazzo Farnese

Piazza Farnese (06 6889 2818, www.france-italia.it). Bus 30Exp, 40Exp, 46, 62, 63, 64, 70, 81, 87, 116, 492, 571, 628, 630, 780, 916. **Open** (guided tours only; in Italian or French) 3pm, 4pm, 5pm Mon, Thur. Closed 6wks July-Sept. **Admission** free. **Map** p342 C2.
Note: tours *must* be pre-booked, preferably several months before.

This palazzo has housed the French embassy since the 1870s. Considered by many to be the finest Renaissance palace in Rome, the huge building – recently and dramatically restored – was begun for Cardinal Alessandro Farnese (later Pope Paul III) in 1514 by Antonio da Sangallo the Younger. Sangallo died before it was completed, and in 1546 Michelangelo took over. He was responsible for most of the upper storeys, the grand cornice along the roof, and the inner courtyard. Vignola and Giacomo della Porta completed the rear façade, which gives out to a large garden.

▶ *To best admire piazza Farnese try a drink or bite to eat at Ar Galletto; see p194* **Eating Old-style***.*

🆓 Sant'Andrea della Valle

Corso Vittorio 6 (06 686 1339). Bus 30Exp, 40Exp, 46, 62, 63, 64, 70, 81, 87, 116, 492, 571, 628, 630, 780, 916. **Open** 7.30am-12.30pm, 4.30-7.30pm daily. **Map** p342 D1.

Many architects got their hands on this church. Originally designed in 1524 by Giacomo della Porta, it was handed over to Carlo Maderno, who stretched the design upward and added the dome, which is the highest in Rome after St Peter's. He left much of the façade design to Carlo Rainaldi, who in turn

Palazzo Farnese.

Jesuit Trickery

Il Gesù's saintly spectacle.

SIGHTS

Flashing lights and piped heavenly choirs herald an eye-popping performance of religious theatricality at **Il Gesù** (*see p105*), Rome's most exuberant Baroque church. A bizarre daily *son et lumière* on the life, but mostly the death, of the Jesuits' founder Ignatius Loyola (*see p109* **Profile**), offers 15 minutes' respite from the dizzying frescoes on the vast church's ceiling and the sheer opulence of the gold, silver and precious marbles of the Gesù's fixtures and fittings. Be there at 5.30pm prompt: proceedings start with mechanical precision.

The Jesuits were the richest Catholic order, and the most energetic, sending teams of fired-up missionaries to the four corners of the (then) known world. This church is their showcase, and Loyola's final resting place.

After the recent discovery of the original 30ft altarpiece painted by Jesuit brother Andrea Pozzo, depicting the saint's apotheo-

sis, a full-scale restoration began of the complex Baroque mechanics once used to raise and lower the giant altarpiece. These were designed as a show to inspire awe and reverence in amazed onlookers. In the 16th century, manpower turned the levers; now the priest likens the motor harnessed to the antique wooden framework to the sort of thing 'which opens a garage door'.

After a bit of Baroque sacred music and lights dancing over Pozzo's massive canvas while excerpts are read (in Italian) from St Ignatius' *Spiritual Exercises*, the altarpiece begins to disappear, winched down soundlessly into the bowels of the church. Revealed in its place on the lapis lazuli and gold altar is a huge silver-plated statue of the Spanish mystic.

Baroque art is all about trickery, magic, delight and astonishment. Pozzo here (and at nearby Sant'Ignazio) showed himself to be a master.

commissioned artist Giacomo Antonio Fancelli to sculpt two angels to adorn it. When the first one (on the left) was complete, the story goes, it was criticised by Pope Alexander VII. Fancelli quit the job in a huff saying the pope could do the other one himself; it was never done. Giovanni Lanfranco nearly died while painting the dome fresco, allegedly because his rival Domenichino had sabotaged the scaffolding on which he was working. Puccini set the opening act of *Tosca* in the chapel on the left.

THE GHETTO

Rome's Jews occupy a unique place in the history of the diaspora, having maintained a presence in the city uninterrupted for more than 2,000 years. This makes them Europe's oldest Jewish community; they have enjoyed a surprising degree of security, even at times (such as the years following the Black Death) when waves of anti-Semitism were sweeping the rest of the Continent.

It may seem odd that the city that was the great centre of power for the Catholic church represented such a safe haven for Jews, but their security came at a price. The popes took on the double role of protectors (curbing popular violence against Jews) and oppressors, bringing Jews under their direct jurisdiction and making sure they paid for the privilege. The first documented tax on Roman Jews, dating back to 1310, set the pattern for the tradition of blackmail that was to characterise the Church's relations with the Jewish community until the 19th century. Payment of this tax exempted Jews from the humiliating *carnevale* games, during which they were liable to be packed into barrels and rolled from the top of Monte Testaccio (*see p121*).

In September 1943, the German occupiers demanded 50 kilograms (110 pounds) of gold from the Jewish community, to be produced in 36 hours. After an appeal – to which both Jews and non-Jews responded – the target was reached, but this time accepting blackmail did not bring security. On 16 October more than 1,000 Jews – mostly women and children – were rounded up and deported in cattle trucks to Auschwitz. A quarter of Rome's Jews died in concentration camps, a proportion that would have been higher had it not been for the help given by wide sections of Roman society, including the Catholic priesthood (though not, many would argue, the Vatican).

By the 13th century, Rome's Jews had started to cross the river from Trastevere to reach a cramped corner of the *centro storico*, immediately north of the Tiber Island. The Ghetto was walled off from the rest of the city in 1556 after the bull *Cum nimis absurdam*, issued by the anti-Semitic Pope Paul IV, ordered a physical separation between Jewish and Christian parts of the cities. Many Jews actually welcomed the protection afforded by the walls and curfews, despite the fact that they were also obliged periodically to attend mass to be lectured on their sinfulness.

However, over-crowding, the loss of property rights, and trade restrictions imposed on the community all took their toll, and the Ghetto experienced a long decline from the 16th until the 18th centuries. When Pius IX became pope in 1848, he opened up the Ghetto gates with a promise of bringing more tolerance and integration. But winds of revolution and secularisation were sweeping across Italy, and he closed them again two years later, issuing a series of race laws that prohibited Jews not only from owning property but from attending secondary school or university, undertaking scientific or artistic careers and receiving treatment in public hospitals. By the time that the Italian Unification took place in 1870, conditions for the more than 5,000 people who lived in the Ghetto had become desperately squalid. The new government ordered that the walls be destroyed.

Some 15,000 Jews live in Rome now, but few of them choose to reside in the old Ghetto area. They flock there for weekends and holidays, however, and to visit its chief landmark – the imposing synagogue, begun in 1874. This incorporates the **Museo Ebraico** (*see p110*), a fascinating museum tracing the history and ritual of Roman Jewish life.

Via Portico d'Ottavia, an anarchic hotchpotch of ancient, medieval and Renaissance architecture leading to the **Portico d'Ottavia** itself (*see p111*), used to mark the boundary of the Ghetto. This street still forms the centre of Rome's Jewish life, even though many of the people that you'll see sitting around chatting in the evening or at weekends have travelled into the city from the suburbs. It's also a good place to sample the unique hybrid that is Roman Jewish cuisine. Try artichokes deep-fried Jewish-style at Sora Margherita (*see p197*) or *torta di ricotta e visciole* – ricotta and damson tart – in a tiny unmarked cornershop (the Forno del Ghetto, *see p230*).

INSIDE TRACK
CAMPO DE' GORDON

By night, **Campo de' Fiori** is dominated by the statue of a brooding, book-clutching Giordano Bruno, burned at the stake here in 1600 after a run-in with the Inquisition. A few years back, Rome-dwelling Brits named the dour, threatening figure 'Gordon Brown'.

Profile Ignatius Loyola

The story of a Spanish saint.

Born in the Spanish Basque Country, Ignatius (Iñigo) Lopez de Loyola (1491-1556) was the aristocratic founder of what was to become arguably the most powerful religious movement of the Catholic church: the Jesuits. After a dissolute youth and wartime leg injury, the reformed and pious Ignatius experienced a vision at La Storta outside Rome that laid the foundation for the success of his mission: ego vobis Romae propitius ero (basically: 'Rome's the place') was God's message. In fact it took Rome a while to see the positive side of Ignatius' teachings, which initially brought him and his band of disciples up against the Inquisition which had them imprisoned and beaten up.

But the self-flagellatory stance of Ignatius – who preached utter submission, perinde ac cadaver ('well-disciplined as a corpse'), to the Church – attracted a large following in Counter-Reformation Catholic Europe, and his Society of Jesus (from whence 'Jesuits') was given the papal seal of approval in 1540. Donations from powerful supporters who followed Loyola's 'Spiritual Exercises' mounted up. Ignatius' beatification in 1609, and canonisation in 1622, led to an extraordinary flurry of church-building; by then the Jesuits were out in force, pushing to the ends of the world in search of souls to save. The iconography of Bernini's Four Rivers fountain (*see p98* **Piazza Navona**) shows the movement's global reach.

Ignatius' canonisation coincided with the zenith of Roman Baroque architecture: the order's mother-church, the **Gesù** (*see p105*), is a jaw-dropping example of theatricality and opulence. **Sant'Ignazio** (*see p100*), the other barn-like Jesuit church, has a *trompe l'oeil* ceiling which records the ecstasies and agonies of the Spanish saint.

Tiber Embankment.

FREE Fontana delle Tartarughe

Piazza Mattei. Bus 30Exp, 40Exp, 46, 62, 63, 64, 70, 81, 87, 492, 628, 630, 780, 916/tram 8. **Map** p342 D2.

Four *ephebes* (adolescent boys) cavort around the base of one of Rome's loveliest fountains, gently hoisting tortoises up to the waters above them. Giacomo della Porta and Taddeo Landini built the fountain for the Duke of Mattei at some point in the 1580s. The duke, so the story goes, had lost all his money and hence his fiancée, and wanted to prove to her father that he could still achieve great things. He had the fountain built overnight in the square outside his family palazzo; the next morning he triumphantly displayed his accomplishment from a palace window. The wedding was on again, but he had the window walled up, and so it remains. The turtles were probably an afterthought, added by Bernini during a restoration. The ones there today are copies: three of the originals are now in the Capitoline museums; the fourth was stolen and presumably graces some private fountain.

Museo Ebraico

Lungotevere Cenci (06 6840 0661, www.museo ebraico.roma.it). Bus 23, 63, 280, 630, 780/ tram 8. **Open** *June-Sept* 10am-7pm Mon-Thur, Sun; 9am-4pm Fri. *Oct-May* 10am-5pm Mon-Thur, Sun; 9am-2pm Fri. Closed on Jewish holidays. **Admission** €7.50; €3 reductions. **Credit** AmEx, MC, V. **Map** p342 D2.

Inscriptions and carvings line the entrance passage to this fascinating museum, which holds a collection that details the history of the city's Jewish community. The recently extended and refurbished display is housed beneath the magnificent neo-Assyrian, neo-Greek Great Synagogue that was inaugurated in 1904. As well as luxurious crowns, Torah mantles and silverware, this museum presents vivid reminders of the persecution that was suffered by Rome's Jews at various times throughout the city's history. Copies of the 16th-century papal edicts that banned Jews from a progressively longer list of activities are a disturbing foretaste of the horrors forced on them by the Fascists and Nazis; the Nazi atrocities are in turn represented by stark photographs and heart-rending relics derived from the concentration camps, as well as film footage tracing developments in the post-war period. There are also a number of displays on the ancient Roman synagogue excavated at Ostia in 1964, as well as Jewish items from the city's catacombs.

FREE Portico d'Ottavia

Via Portico d'Ottavia. Bus 23, 30Exp, 44, 63, 81,
95, 160, 170, 280, 628, 715, 716, 781. **Open**
Lower area walkway 9am-6pm daily. **Admission**
free. **Map** p342 D2.

Great ancient columns and a marble frontispiece,
held together with rusting iron braces, now form
part of the church of Sant'Angelo in Pescheria. They
were originally the entrance of a massive colonnaded
square (*portico*) containing temples and libraries,
built in the first century AD by Emperor Augustus
and dedicated to his sister Octavia (this, in turn, had
been built over a first-century BC square). The
mighty structure was decorated with 34 bronzes by
Lysippus depicting bellicose events from the life of
Alexander the Great; these are long lost. The isolated
columns outside, and the inscription above, date
from a later restoration, undertaken by Septimius
Severus in AD 213. After lengthy digs and restoration work in the 1990s, a walkway has been opened
allowing you to stroll through the *forum piscarium*
– the ancient fish market, hence the name of the
church. Atmospheric (if slightly rubbish-strewn) as
the place is, there are no explanations of what you're
looking at. The walkway continues past a graveyard
of broken columns and dumped Corinthian capitals
to the Teatro di Marcello (*see p112*), passing by three
towering columns that were part of the Temple of
Apollo, dating from 433 BC.

TIBER ISLAND & THE BOCCA DELLA VERITÀ

When the last Etruscan king was driven from
Rome, the Romans uprooted the wheat from his
fields and threw it in baskets into the river.
There the baskets lay, with silt accumulating
around them until that silt formed an island.
When the Roman god of medicine, Aesculapius,
came to Rome on a boat to deal with a plague
epidemic in the third century BC, his snake
jumped out at that spot, indicating that this was
the spot for a sanctuary. That's what the legend
says, anyway, and from that moment on the
island has had a vocation for public health.
Today the busy Fatebenefratelli hospital
occupies the north end of the island simply
called *l'isola tiberina* – the Tiber island. The
church of San Bartolomeo – an apostle flayed
alive by Armenians – is built over the original
sanctuary. Remains of the ancient building can
be seen from the wide footpath around the
island, down by the muddy, rushing Tiber: a
sculpted boat-shaped outcrop of travertine is
decorated with a rod and snakes, the symbol of
the god of healing. Off the southern tip is the
Ponte Rotto (broken bridge), Rome's oldest,
and the mouth of the **Cloaca Maxima**, ancient
Rome's great sewer.

Across on the left (east) bank of the river
stood ancient Rome's cattle market (*forum*

boarium) and vegetable market (*forum*
holitorium) – a bustling place from the time
of the Etruscan kings, chunks of which can be
seen beneath the church of **San Nicola in**
Carcere. Further south are two delightful
Republican-era **temples** and **Santa Maria**
in Cosmedin (for all, *see p112*), with its '*bocca*
della verità' (mouth of truth). Skirt left around
Santa Maria in Cosmedin for the touchingly
unadorned arch of Janus and the church of
San Giorgio in Velabro.

FREE Ponte Rotto & Cloaca Maxima

Views from Ponte Palatino, Isola Tiberina &
lungotevere Pierleoni. Bus 23, 63, 280, 630,
780, H/tram 8. **Map** p342 D/E3.

The Ponte Rotto – literally, 'Broken Bridge' – stands
on the site of the Pons aemilius, Rome's first stone
bridge, built in 142 BC. It was rebuilt many times –
even Michelangelo had a go – before 1598, when
great chunks collapsed (yet again) into the river and
it was decided to give up trying. To the east of the
bridge is a tunnel in the embankment: the gaping
mouth of the Cloaca Maxima, the city's great sewer.
Built under Rome's Etruscan kings in the sixth century BC to drain the area around the Forum, it was
given its final form in the first century BC.

FREE San Giorgio in Velabro

Via del Velabro 19 (06 6979 7536, www.san
giorgioinvelabro.org). Bus 30Exp, 44, 63, 81,
95, 160, 170, 628, 715, 716, 781. **Open** 10am-
12.30pm, 4-6.30pm daily. **Map** p342 E3.

The soft light from the windows in the clerestory
gives a peaceful aura to this austere little church of
the fifth century. A swingeing restoration in 1925
did away with centuries of decoration and restored
its original Romanesque simplicity. The 16 columns,
pilfered from the Palatine and the Aventine hills, are
all different. Pieces of an eighth- or ninth-century
choir, including two slender columns, are incorporated into the walls. In the apse is a restored fresco
by the school of Pietro Cavallini showing St George
with a white horse and the Virgin on one side of the
central Christ figure, and St Peter and St Sebastian
opposite. The 12th-century altar is a rare example
of the Byzantine-inspired 'caged and architraved'
ciborium, a canopy on columns. A church was first
built here by Greeks and was dedicated to St
Sebastian, who was believed to have been martyred
in the swampy area hereabouts. It was later rededicated to St George of Cappadocia (of dragon-slaying
fame); a piece of the skull of the valorous third-century saint is kept under the altar. The portico and
bell tower are 12th-century additions. Outside, to the
left, is the *arco degli Argentari*, built in AD 204; it
was a gate on the road between the main Forum and
the *forum boarium* (cattle market), along which
moneychangers (*argenteri*) plied their trade. The
church and other monuments were damaged by a
Mafia bomb in 1993 but have since been repaired.

SIGHTS

SIGHTS

FREE San Nicola in Carcere

Via del Teatro di Marcello 46 (06 6830 7198). Bus 23, 30Exp, 44, 63, 81, 95, 160, 170, 628, 715, 716, 781. **Open** *7am-7pm daily.* **Map** *p342 E2.*
The 12th-century San Nicola was built over three Roman temples: dating from the second and third centuries BC, these were dedicated to two-faced Janus, protector of gates; to the goddess Juno Sospita, perhaps a protectress of commerce; and to Spes (Hope). An informal guided tour takes you down to these, and even deeper to see a slab from the Etruscan *forum holitorium* (vegetable market), a busy commercial exchange near the main river. On the outside of the church, six columns from the Temple of Janus can be seen on the left; the ones on the right are from the Temple of Spes. The church's façade was added by Giacomo della Porta in 1599. The name, *in carcere* (prison), probably comes from a seventh-century jail that stood nearby.

FREE Santa Maria in Cosmedin

Piazza della Bocca della Verità 18 (06 678 1419). Bus 44, 63, 81, 95, 160, 170, 628, 715, 716, 781. **Open** *Apr-Sept* 9am-6pm daily. *Oct-Mar* 9am-5pm daily. **Map** p342 E3.
Despite an over-enthusiastic restoration, this is a lovely jumble of early Christian, medieval and Romanesque church design – with a touch of kitsch. Santa Maria in Cosmedin was built in the sixth century and enlarged in the eighth. The beautiful bell-tower was a 12th-century addition. Between the 11th and 13th centuries much of the decoration was replaced with Cosmati work, including the spiralling floor, throne, choir and 13th-century *baldacchino*. In the sacristy/souvenir shop is a fragment of an eighth-century mosaic of the Holy Family, brought here from St Peter's. In the crypt are ruins of the Ara maximus, a monument to Hercules over which the church was built. The name Cosmedin comes from the Greek, meaning splendid decoration; this has always been the church of the Greek community, many of whom were expelled from Constantinople in the eighth century: Byzantine rite services are still held here at 10.30am on Sundays.

INSIDE TRACK
THE MOUTH OF TRUTH

Come in high season and you might be perplexed by the queue snaking out from the **Santa Maria in Cosmedin**. It's down to a scene in *Roman Holiday* where Gregory Peck ad-libs having his hand munched by the *bocca della verità* (the mouth of truth), eliciting a (reportedly) unscripted shriek of genuine alarm from Audrey Hepburn. If you can't stomach the queues, see the film – it's genuinely one of the most delightful moments in cinema.

The church is better known as the *bocca della verità* (the mouth of truth), as, according to legend, anyone who lies while their hand is in the mouth of the mask of the horned man on the portico wall will have that hand bitten off. It was reportedly used by Roman husbands to determine the fidelity of their wives.

FREE Teatro di Marcello

Via Teatro di Marcello. Bus 30Exp, 44, 63, 81, 95, 160, 170, 628, 715, 716, 781. **Open** by appointment only; for details, phone 06 6710 3819. **Map** p342 D/E2.
This is one of the strangest sights in Rome: a Renaissance palace – inhabited, though now divided into apartments – grafted on to an ancient, time-worn theatre. Julius Caesar began building a theatre here to rival Pompey's in the *Campus martius*, but it was finished in 11 BC by Augustus, who named it after his favourite nephew. Its 41 arches were topped with marble masks. It seated up to 20,000.
Now known as the Palazzo Orsini (little bear – stone symbols of which can be seen on gateposts) after another owner, it has been split up into luxury apartments. The shops that filled the ground-level archways were thrown out in the 1930s, leaving the structure in splendid if rather sad isolation, its travertine blocks looking like they're suffering from a wasting disease.
▶ *Get a close-up look from the walkway below the Portico d'Ottavia; see p111.*

FREE Tempii di Ercole & Portuno (Temples of Hercules & Portunus)

Piazza della Bocca della Verità. Bus 44, 63, 81, 95, 170, 628, 715, 716, 781. **Open** by appointment only; for details, phone 06 6710 3819. **Map** p342 E3.
Like the Pantheon, these diminutive Republican-era temples owe their good state of preservation to their conversion into churches in the Middle Ages. The round one, which looks like a delightful English folly, was built in the first century BC and dedicated to Hercules. Early archaeologists were confused by its shape, which is similar to the Temple of Vesta in the Roman Forum, and dubbed it the Temple of Vesta. Recently restored, it's the oldest marble building still standing in Rome (the marble blocks on the temple's bottom half are what remain of the original). The original upper section, perhaps domed, has been lost, although 19 of its 20 marble columns have survived; the roof is modern.
To its right stands the square temple dedicated to Portunus (god of harbours), as ancient Rome's river port was nearby. (Inexplicably, early archaeologists attributed this one to *Fortuna Virilis* – manly fortune.) The two temples were deconsecrated and designated ancient monuments in the 1920s.
▶ *The Triton fountain in front, by Francesco Bizzaccheri (1715), was inspired by – but definitely doesn't equal – Bernini's Triton fountain in piazza Barberini; see p70.*

Trastevere
& the Gianicolo

The Rome of your romantic dreams awaits, trans tiberim.

Trastevere is a great treat if you've spent your time diligently observing ancient ruins and admiring statuary on the other, serious side of the river. Although the district's once boisterous, communal street life and artisan feel has at least partly given way to wine bars and eateries, Trastevere still feels very Roman.

Across the Tiber (*trans tiberim*), your main tasks include rambling through narrow, cobbled streets and selecting a bar for *aperitivi* and people-watching. Up above Trastevere, the **Gianicolo** is Rome's highest hill and a park with spectacular views over the *centro storico* runs most of its length, making it a great place to get your bearings or take a breather.

Map pp342-343	**Cafés, Bars &**
Hotels p177	**Gelaterie** p214
Eating Out p197	

SIGHTS

INTRODUCING TRASTEVERE

Trastevere (pronounced Tras-TEV-ver-ray) lives up to your oh-so *pittoresco* Roman fantasy – at least partially. Its transformation has been somewhat inevitable: for centuries the area has attracted artists and writers, brawlers and hookers, drawn by its lively, langorous quality.

Notoriously proud of their identity, *trasteverini* claim descent from indigenous Etruscans as well as slave stock. Through the Imperial period, much of the *trans tiberim* area was agricultural, with farms, vineyards, country villas and gardens laid out for the pleasure of the Caesars. Later, Syrian and Jewish trading communities set up here before moving in the Middle Ages to the Ghetto. Trastevere was a working-class district in papal Rome and remained so until well after the Unification in 1870. Today, *trasteverini* boast they are the only true Romans, and celebrate their exclusive heritage in a two-week-long street festival each July called the *festa di noiantri* ('we others').

Hugging the river from Ponte Sublicio in the south almost to the Vatican in the north, the district has at least three distinct personalities.

The streets and *piazzette* to the east of thundering viale Trastevere, with their vines and creepers, are the quiet part of the neighbourhood – contemplative, rather than party-going.

A different demographic gathers to the west of viale Trastevere: by day, action centres around the food market in piazza San Cosimato; come late afternoon, a buzz begins on the small around piazza Santa Maria in Trastevere, growing in intensity as the evening progresses. Night brings an international crowd to the scores of cafés, pubs and restaurants. By the wee hours, the result can be charmingly picturesque – or can degenerate unpleasantly into a rowdy frat party, especially around piazza Trilussa.

Moving towards the Vatican, via della Lungara is flanked by stately villas once owned by some of papal Rome's most illustrious families. Here also is Rome's inner-city prison, the *Regina Coeli*.

Time Out Rome **113**

Extra Time

● To the left of the 15th-century church of San Giovanni dei Genovesi at via Anicia 12 is a wooden door that opens into a glorious flower-filled Chiostro dei Genovesi (cloister); ring the doorbell to get in Tue & Fri afternoons only), with a well, part of a 15th-century hospice for Genoese sailors designed by Baccio Pontelli. Concealed among the octagonal columns supporting the double loggia is a plaque that commemorates Rome's first palm tree, planted here in 1588.

● Just inside the Porta Settimiana at via Santa Dorotea is an unassuming house, now a restaurant, with a pretty window high on the façade and a granite column embedded in its wall. It is believed to have been the home of Margherita, known as *la fornarina*, the baker's daughter who reputedly stole the heart of Renaissance genius Raphael and whose seductive portrait hangs in the Palazzo Barberini (*see p71*).

● The **Vecchia Farmacia della Scala** (piazza della Scala 23, 06 580 6217) has been whipping up cures since the 16th century. Check out the collection of beautiful ceramic medicinal-herb containers.

● Water splashes merrily from wine cask to barrel in the charming **Fontana delle Botte** on via Cisterna. It may look venerable but it's a 20th-century tribute to the wine-loving spirit of the locals. In 1927, Rome authorities got architect Pietro Lombardi to design a series of fountains to define various neighbourhoods: these also include the Fontana delle Anfore (amphorae) in Testaccio and the Fontana dei Libri (books) near Palazzo Madama (*see p97*), as well as many others.

WEST OF VIALE TRASTEVERE

Ponte Sisto, an elegant footbridge that was constructed by Pope Sixtus IV, links Trastevere to Rome 'proper'. Alternatively, you can cross the heavily trafficked Ponte Garibaldi and take via della Lungaretta to the heart of Trastevere and Santa Maria in Trastevere (*see right*). Nearby, the market square of piazza San Cosimato attracts children, elderly residents and football-playing youngsters day and night.

On the other (northern) side of piazza Santa Maria in Trastevere, **piazza Sant'Egidio** is the site of the unassuming **Museo di Roma in Trastevere** (*see below*) and home to lively open-air stalls where geegaws of varying quality from faraway places are peddled.

Further north still, the backstreets nestled against the Gianicolo (Janiculum hill, *see p118*) allow you a glimpse of the less commercial side of Trastevere. Smoggy via della Lungara leads to the lovely **Orto Botanico** (botanical gardens; *see right*), the **Villa Farnesina**, with its frescoes by Raffaele, and **Palazzo Corsini** (*see right*), which now houses part of the national art collection. Near the start of via della Lungara, by the imposing Porta Settimiana – a third-century gate rebuilt in the 15th century – the humble **Casa della Fornarina** (*see above* **Extra Time**) is where the artist Raphael's mistress is said to have lived.

Museo di Roma in Trastevere
Piazza Sant'Egidio 1B (06 589 7123, www.museodiromaintrastevere.it). Bus 23, 44, 75, 280, 780/tram 3, 8. **Open** 10am-8pm Tue-Sun. **Admission** €3; €1.50 reductions. Extra charge for exhibitions. **No credit cards**. **Map** p342 C3.

If you happen to be in Trastevere with nothing much to do, you could take in this modest museum and be pleasantly surprised, especially if you have children to bring along. A small collection of watercolours by Ettore Roesler Franz illustrates scenes of everyday 19th-century Roman life; a series of rooms with wax-work tableaux shows humble folks drinking in the osteria, dancing the *saltarello* or playing the *zampogne* (bagpipes). There are also occasional photographic exhibitions.

Ponte Sisto.

Piazza Sant'Egido.

Orto Botanico

Largo Cristina di Svezia 24 (06 4991 7135).
Bus 23, 280, 780, H/tram 3, 8. **Open** *Apr-Oct*
9.30am-6pm Mon-Sat. *Nov-Mar* 9.30am-5.30pm
Mon-Sat. **Admission** €4; €2 reductions.
No credit cards. **Map** p342 B2.

Rome's Botanical Gardens were established in 1833,
within the gardens of the Palazzo Corsini (*see below*).
But this verdant area at the foot of the Gianicolo had
first been planted in the 13th century, by order of
Pope Nicholas III, and was devoted to simples (medicinal plants) and citrus groves. Today the Orto
Botanico is a delicious haven from the rigours of a
hot, dusty day, with its Baroque stairs flanked by
cascading waterfalls, formal tableaux around fountains and statues, its bamboo grove, and varieties of
exotic plants and flowers. Check out the cactus garden, the orchids and the touching and smelling collection for the vision-impaired. One of Rome's most
under-appreciated gems.

Palazzo Corsini – Galleria Nazionale d'Arte Antica

Via della Lungara 10 (06 6880 2323, www.
galleriaborghese.it). Bus 23, 280, 780, H/tram
3, 8. **Open** 8.30am-7.30pm Tue-Sun. **Admission**
€4; €2 reductions. **No credit cards**.
Map p342 B2.

In the 1933 film *Queen Christina*, Greta Garbo
played the former owner of this palace as a graceful
tussler with existential angst; in real life, the stout
17th-century Swedish monarch smoked a pipe, wore
trousers and entertained female – and a fair number
of (ordained) male – lovers. 'Queen without a Realm,
Christian without a faith, and woman without
shame' ran one of the contemporary epithets on

Christina. But, in addition to being brilliantly scan-
dalous, Christina was also one of the most
cultured and influential women of her age. The
century's highest-profile convert to Catholicism, she
abdicated her throne and established her glittering
court here in 1662, filling what was then Palazzo
Riario with her fabled library and an ever-expanding
collection of fabulous old masters. She threw the best
parties in Rome and commissioned many of Scarlatti
and Corelli's hit tunes before dying here in 1689.

Today the palace – later redesigned by Ferdinand
Fuga for the Corsini family – houses part of the
national art collection. The galleries have beautiful
frescoes and trompe l'oeil effects, and contain paintings of the Madonna by Van Dyck, Filippo Lippi and
Orazio Gentileschi, two St Sebastians (one by
Rubens and one by Annibale Carracci) and a pair of
Annunciations by Guercino. Among the works by
Caravaggio is an unadorned *Narcissus*. There's also
a triptych by Fra Angelico and a melancholy *Salome*
by Guido Reni.

★ FREE Santa Maria in Trastevere

Piazza Santa Maria in Trastevere (06 581 4802,
www.santamariaintrastevere.org). Bus 23, 280,
780, H/tram 3, 8. **Open** 7.30am-9pm daily.
Map p342 C3.

This stunning church, with its welcoming portico
and façade with shimmering 13th-century mosaics,
overlooks the traffic-free piazza of the same name.
Santa Maria is the heart and soul of Trastevere.
According to legend, a well of oil sprang miraculously from the ground where the church now stands
the moment Christ was born, and flowed to the Tiber
all day. A small street leading out of the piazza, via
della Fonte dell'Olio, commemorates this.

SIGHTS

Santa Maria in Trastevere. *See p115.*

▶ *The 22 granite columns with Ionic and Corinthian capitals that line the nave here are thought to have come from the Termi di Caracalla; see p120.*

Villa Farnesina
Via della Lungara 230 (06 6802 7268, www.lincei.it). Bus 23, 280, 780, H/tram 3, 8. **Open** 9am-1pm Mon-Sat & 2nd Sun of month. **Admission** €5; €3 reductions. **No credit cards.** **Map** p342 B2.
Villa Farnesina was built between 1508 and 1511 to a design by Baldassare Peruzzi as a pleasure palace and holiday home for the fabulously rich papal banker Agostino Chigi. Treasurer to Pope Julius II, Chigi was one of Raphael's principal patrons. In its day the villa was stuffed to the rafters with great works of art, although many were later sold to pay off debts. Chigi was known for his extravagant parties, where guests had the run of the palace and the magnificent gardens. Just to make sure his guests knew that money was no object, he would have his servants toss the silver and gold plates on which they dined into the Tiber – into underwater nets, to be fished out later and used again. The powerful Farnese family bought the villa and renamed it in 1577 after the Chigis went bankrupt.

The stunning frescoes are homages to the pagan and classical world; the works on the ground-floor Loggia of Psyche were designed by Raphael but executed by his friends and followers, including Giulio Romano; according to local lore, the master himself was too busy dallying with his mistress, *la fornarina* (baker's girl) to apply any more paint than was strictly necessary. The Grace with her back turned, to the right of the door, is attributed to him though. Around the corner in the Loggia of Galatea, Raphael took brush in hand to create the victorious goddess in her seashell chariot. Upstairs, the Salone delle Prospettive was decorated by Peruzzi with views of 16th-century Rome. Next to it is Agostino Chigi's bedroom, with a fresco of the *Marriage of Alexander the Great and Roxanne* by Raphael's follower Sodoma. Like most of his paintings, this is a rather sordid number showing the couple being undressed by vicious cherubs.

The façade we see today was designed by Carlo Fontana in 1692, but the mosaics pre-date it by four centuries: they show Mary breastfeeding Christ on a solid gold background.

The present 12th-century Romanesque church, built for Pope Innocent II, replaced a basilica from the late third or early fourth century (though legend has it that it was founded by Pope Callistus I, who died in 222) – one of the city's oldest and the first dedicated to the Virgin. That in turn probably topped the site of a titulus – a place of worship in the house of an early Christian. The apse is made magnificent by a 12th-century mosaic of Jesus and the Virgin Mary; the figure on the far left is Pope Innocent. Further down, between the windows, are mosaics of the Virgin from the 13th century, attributed to Pietro Cavallini, whose relaxed, realistic figures represent the re-emergence of a Roman style after long years of the hegemony of stiff Byzantine models. The Madonna and Child with rainbow overhead is also by Cavallini. Through the wooden door on the left, just before entering the transept, there are two tiny, exquisite fragments of first-century AD mosaics, and in the Altemps chapel to the left of the high altar is a very rare seventh-century painting on wood of the Virgin, known as the Madonna of Clemency. Still on the left side is the 17th-century Avila chapel with its elaborate cupola by Antonio Gherardi. The wood-carved ceiling and centrepiece painting of the *Assumption* is by Domenichino. Throughout the nave, fine marble mosaic style graces the floor, but the original 12th-century work was almost totally replaced in the late 18th century.

EAST OF VIALE TRASTEVERE

In this achingly charming part of Trastevere, you won't have to battle crowds or hawkers as you wander between pretty *piazze* and washing-festooned streets. Nowhere near as showy as some of Rome's districts, it's easy, here, to imagine Roman life as it was two or three centuries ago. The area is dominated by the basilica of Santa Cecilia (*see right*) with its underground treasures and Cavallini frescoes, but look out for unexpected gems, too, which can be found at the church of San Francesco a Ripa (*see right*).

This was a busy commercial area from the 15th century through to Unification in the late 19th century, due to its proximity to the busy Ripa Grande port. The port is commemorated in a statue on the riverside façade of the huge structure of San Michele, a former hospice, orphanage and reform school, now housing offices of the cultural heritage ministry.

FREE San Francesco a Ripa

Piazza San Francesco d'Assisi 88 (06 581 9020). Bus 23, 44, 75, 115, 280, 630, 753, 780, H/tram 8. **Open** *7am-noon, 4-7.30pm Mon-Sat; 7am-1pm, 4-7.30pm Sun.* **Map** *p343 C4.*
Rebuilt in the 1680s, this church took the place of a 13th-century one that held now-lost frescoes by Pietro Cavallino chronicling the life of St Francis of Assisi. The saint stayed in the adjoining convent when he visited Rome in 1229: if you ask the sacristan, he may show you the cell where St Francis lived and the rock on which he placed his head to sleep. An orange tree in the garden was supposedly planted by the saint.

FREE Santa Cecilia in Trastevere

Piazza Santa Cecilia (064549 2739). Bus 2, 23, 75, 115, 280, 780, H/tram 8. **Open** *Church* 9.30am-1pm, 4-8pm daily. *Cavallini frescoes* 10.15am-12.30pm Mon-Sat; 11.30am-12.30pm Sun. *Archaeological site* 7am-12.30pm, 4-6.30pm daily. **Admission** *Frescoes* €2.50. *Archaeological site* €2.50. **No credit cards. Map** p342 D3.
The current 16th-century church of this magnificent religious complex was built above a fifth-century basilica, which in turn incorporated a titulus, or house where early Christians met. In this case, gruesome legend relates, that house belonged to Roman patrician Valerio, who lived at the time of Emperor Marcus Aurelius. So impressed was Valerio by his wife Cecilia's vow of chastity that he too converted to Christianity. Valerio was murdered for his pains, and Cecilia was arrested while she tried to bury him. Doing away with the saintly Cecilia proved a difficult job for the Romans. After a failed attempt to suffocate her in the house's hot baths they tried to behead her. But only three strokes of the axe were permitted by law, and after the third failed to do the

Bernini's Babes

All hail the master of racy religious art.

One hand clutches her breast, her body writhes and her face looks heavenwards in rapturous agony. Is she in the throes of death or in the midst of an erotic encounter with the Holy Spirit?

Beata Ludovica Albertoni (1671), who graces the church of **San Francesco a Ripa** (*see above*), is just one of many sexually and spiritually charged marble women scattered around Rome by Baroque genius Gian Lorenzo Bernini. An equal in celestial swooning, *L'estasi di Santa Teresa* (1647-52), draws crowds to the church of **Santa Maria della Vittoria** (*see p140*).

Lusty Bernini – father of 11 – was a highly religious individual for whom the distinction between the sensual and the sublime was blurred. Sculptor, architect and darling of a string of popes, Bernini (1598-1680) attended Mass every morning, took communion twice a week, and on the way home from work stopped by regularly at the church of the **Gesù** (*see p105*) where he reportedly underwent the rigorous Spiritual Exercises of the Jesuits.

Evidently, though, that didn't preclude a first-hand understanding of female joys and fears. Just look at the terror on the face of Proserpine as Pluto grabs her fleshy thigh in *The Rape of Proserpine* (1621-22); the woeful desperation of Daphne as she turns

into a laurel tree to escape Apollo's embrace in *Apollo and Daphne* (1622-25); or the come-hither look of the laid-back *Truth Unveiled by Time* (1646-52), all of which can be admired in the **Galleria Borghese** (*see p78*).

Bernini designed – though his workshop may have carved – the *Four Virtues* group in **Sant'Isidoro** (via degli Artisti 41, 06 488 5359, by appointment only), in which *Charity* offers her ample naked bosom with an encouraging smile – an outright solicitation that Bernini's patrons in 1662 didn't seem to find out of place in a church. (It was too much for 19th-century sensibilities though: the bronze tunics that were added to cover her and one of her buxom sisters were not removed until 2002).

Energetic and disciplined, an indefatigable worker who was at home with popes and princes, Bernini lost his head just once, for Costanza Bonarelli, the wife of a fellow artist. So steamy was the affair that Urban VIII had to step in to put out the fire. Bernini subsequently married, had his numerous brood and lived happily until the age of 82. But not before completing, for himself, an exquisite bust of his beloved Costanza (1635, in the Bargello museum in Florence), with an intelligent face and loose blouse.

SIGHTS

job, as she was slowing dying she sang, securing her place as the patron saint of music. When her tomb was reopened in 1599, her body was uncorrupted. Sculptor Stefano Maderno portrays her with her head turned away in an exquisite marble rendering beneath the altar. Her sarcophagus is in the crypt.

The excavations below the church provide extensive evidence of early Roman and palaeo-Christian buildings; here too is the pretty decorated crypt where Cecilia's body lies.

On the first floor, on the other hand, is a choir from where nuns from the adjoining convent could look down over the interior of the basilica from behind a grill. On one wall is what remains of what was possibly Rome's greatest 13th-century fresco – a *Last Judgment* by little-known genius Pietro Cavallini. With its rainbow-winged angels of all ranks and desperate sinners writhing hellwards, the once-monumental fresco shows Cavallini breaking away from the Byzantine style and giving new light and humanity to the figures.

THE GIANICOLO

This luxuriously verdant hilltop neighbourhood is one of Rome's most beautiful. A couple of winding roads lead up from Trastevere past decidedly patrician villas, many of which are now embassies and cultural institutions.

Up via Garibaldi is Bramante's lovely **Tempietto** (*see right*), in the courtyard of the church of San Pietro in Montorio (which is part of a complex that also includes the Spanish cultural centre). It contrasts oddly with the squat Fascist-era monument across the road: the Ossario Garibaldino (open 9am-1pm Tue-Sun). Inscribed with the words *Roma o morte* (Rome or death) – the rallying cry of Unification hero Giuseppe Garibaldi – the monument contains the remains of Risorgimento heroes, including Goffredo Mameli, composer of Italy's stirring national anthem.

A grand belvedere at the **Fontana Paola** (*see right*) is one of the best places to gaze down over the Eternal City.

At the top of the hill, the imposing bronze **statue of Giuseppe Garibaldi** on his dashing steed is a reminder of his role in the creation of

Italy as a nation – in 1849 this breathtaking lookout spot was the scene of one of the fiercest battles in the struggle for Italian unity (the Risorgimento; *see p29*). Freedom fighter Garibaldi and his makeshift army of red-shirted *garibaldini* – a hotchpotch of former papal troops and starry-eyed young enthusiasts – tried valiantly (but ultimately failed) to defend the short-lived Roman Republic against French troops sent to restore papal rule. From beneath this balcony a cannon fires one shot each day at noon. To the north, Garibaldi's South American wife Anita sits astride her own bronze horse, baby in one hand and pistol in the other. The busts that line the road depict Risorgimento martyrs. A lighthouse donated by Italian emigrants to Argentina flashes its light from this promontory.

FREE Fontana Paola
Via Garibaldi. Bus 44, 75, 115, 710, 870.
Map p342 B3.
This grandiose fountain, which sends lavishly splashy cascades into an equally grand pool, is fed by water that has travelled 35km (22 miles) through a Trajan-era aqueduct from Lake Bracciano, to the north of Rome. Pope Paul V had Flamino Ponzio and Giovanni Fontana design the fountain for him in 1621, in a bid to out-do his predecessor Sixtus V, who had harnessed a third-century AD aqueduct to supply his Fontana dell'Acqua Felice 20 years earlier.
▶ *For the Fontana dell'Acqua Felice; see p138.*

FREE Tempietto di Bramante & San Pietro in Montorio
Piazza San Pietro in Montorio 2 (06 581 3940, Tempietto 06 581 2806). Bus 44, 75, 115, 710, 870. **Open** *Tempietto* Apr-Sept 9.30am-12.30pm, 4-6pm Tue-Sun; Oct-Mar 9.30am-12.30pm, 2-4pm Tue-Sat. *Church* 8am-noon, 3-4pm daily.
Map p342 B3.
Located on one of the spots where St Peter is believed to have been crucified (St Peter's is another), San Pietro in Montorio conceals one of Rome's greatest architectural jewels in its courtyard: the Tempietto, designed by Donato Bramante in 1508 for Cardinal Giuliano della Rovere, who was to become Pope Julius II (and who also got him working on St Peter's basilica). The small circular structure, with its Doric columns, has classical symmetry that was subsequently imitated by many architects. Bernini got his hands on it in 1628, adding the staircase that leads down to the crypt. The church next door, founded in the late ninth century and rebuilt in the late 15th, contains a chapel by Bernini (second on the left) and one by Vasari (fifth on the right). Paintings include Sebastiano del Piombo's *Flagellation*, and *Crucifixion of St Peter* by Guido Reni. The name Montorio, or golden hill, refers to the way the sun hit sand on the Gianicolo, turning it gold.

INSIDE TRACK
BAGGAGE TRANSFER

The traffic in the warren of alleys in Trastevere is chaotic, and you'll notice that Roman matrons venturing over from the other side of the Tiber instinctively transfer their designer bags on to the curbside shoulder, beyond the reach of Vespa-borne opportunists.

The Aventine, Testaccio & Ostiense

A high-class hill and two areas light on sights but heavy on nightlife.

The leafy, upmarket Aventine hill couldn't be more different from the busy, workaday districts of **Testaccio** and **Ostiense** that lie at its southern feet. Yet there's a grudging respect between them that runs both ways. Without the proximity of Testaccio's bars and markets, and Ostiense's burgeoning cultural and nightlife scene, the **Aventine** would be nothing but a lifeless enclave of privilege; whereas inhabitants of the hectic lower areas are grateful for a respite from the bustle and din that surrounds them with a wander up to the peaceful hill that overlooks them. Quiet attractions abound here, from the **Terme di Caracalla** (Baths of Caracalla) to the **Cimitero Acattolico**.

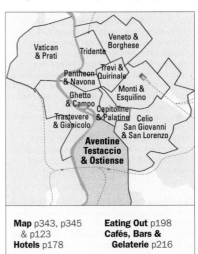

Map p343, p345 & p123	**Eating Out** p198
Hotels p178	**Cafés, Bars & Gelaterie** p216

Map p343, p345 & p123

THE AVENTINE

First settled by King Ancius Marcius in the seventh century BC, the Aventine was later colonised by sailors, merchants and other undesirables who crept inexorably up the hill from the rough-and-tumble port below.

In 456 BC the whole of the Aventine hill was earmarked for plebeians to construct homes. And there the plebs remained, organising their guilds and building their temples. As they became more successful, so their villas became gentrified. By the time the Republic gave way to the Empire, this had become an exclusive neighbourhood. By the fifth century AD there were two bath complexes here and many luxurious *palazzi*.

What the Aventine is best for nowadays is a walk: the **Parco Savello**, still surrounded by the crenellated walls of a 12th-century fortress of the Savello family, has dozens of orange trees and a spectacular view. Contemplate the beauty of the basilica of **Santa Sabina** or peek

through the keyhole of the **priory of the Knights of Malta** at nearby piazza Cavalieri di Malta 3 to enjoy the surrealistic surprise designed by Gian Battista Piranesi: a telescopic view of St Peter's dome.

Across thundering viale Aventino is the *piccolo Aventino*, aka the San Saba district (*see p120* **Extra Time**). Beyond the white cuboids of the UN's Food and Agriculture Organisation – once Mussolini's Colonies Ministry – stand the towering remains of the **Terme di Caracalla** (Baths of Caracalla).

FREE Santa Sabina

Piazza Pietro d'Illiria 1 (06 574 3573). Bus 81, 160, 175, 628, 715. **Open** 6.30am-12.45pm, 3-7pm daily. **Map** p343 E4.

Try to visit Santa Sabina on a sunny day, when the light shines softly into this magnificent, solemn basilica. It was built in the fifth century over an early Christian *titulus* believed to have belonged to a martyred Roman matron named Sabina; the only trace of this ancient place of worship is a bit of mosaic

Extra Time

● Check out the white **pyramid** that sticks out like a sore thumb in piazzale Ostiense. An obscure first-century BC magistrate and tribune named Caius Cestius took the prevailing *aegyptomania* to extremes when he decided to build himself a tomb that was fit for a pharaoh. Faint traces of fresco in the pyramid's small inner chamber can be seen by prior appointment.

● The Aventine's minor churches deserve a visit: in **Sant'Alessio** (via Sant'Alessio 23), Alexis lies in marble agony, with a bizarre wooden staircase hanging over his head, presumably for a speedy getaway to heaven; beneath **Santa Prisca** (via Santa Prisca 11) is Rome's best-preserved mithraeum; at **Sant'Anselmo**, the Rome HQ of the Benedictine order, Gregorian chant evensong is sung every day at 7.15pm.

● Cross viale Aventino for a look around the '*piccolo Aventino*' – the San Saba district – a leafy neighbourhood with a morning market in its main square, piazza Bernini, not far from the eighth-century church of **San Saba** and a series of charming detached villas with gardens, built in the early 20th century (to a design by Quadrio Pirani) as a public-housing project.

● Visible from the pavement on Lungotevere Testaccio, the **Emporio** – begun in 193 BC – was a massive riverside wharf. From here, goods were transported up steps to the Porticus Aemilius, a covered warehouse 60m (195ft) wide by 500m (1,640ft)long, and to *horreae* (grain warehouses), fragments of which can be seen dotted about Testaccio.

● Not so much a hill as a rubbish dump, 36m- (120ft) high **Monte Testaccio** is where amphorae used to transport olive oil as far as the Emporio river port were flung once they had been emptied. In the Middle Ages, Monte Testaccio and surrounding fields were the scene of such questionable Lenten revelries as rolling Jews downhill in barrels. Visit the restaurants and clubs buried into the hill's flanks for a look at the potsherds that make up this heap.

floor visible through a grate at the entrance. The church was subjected to a merciless restoration in the 1930s: what you see today is arguably the closest thing – give or take a 16th-century fresco or two – in Rome to an unadulterated ancient basilica. The late fifth-century cypress-wood doors are carved with biblical scenes, including one of the earliest renderings of the Crucifixion; ten of the original 28 panels have been lost. The high nave's elegant Corinthian columns support an arcade decorated with ninth-century marble inlay work; the *schola cantorum* (choir) dates from the same period. Selenite has been placed in the high, stone-grated arched windows, as it would have been in the ninth century. Above the entrance, the fifth-century mosaic recalls that the priest Peter of Illyria built the church while Celestine was pope; two figures on either side of the inscription represent the church members converted from paganism and Judaism. There were water additions in the church, which include Taddeo Zuccari's 16th-century fresco in the apse.

A tiny window in the entrance porch looks on to the place where St Dominic is said to have planted an orange tree that had been brought from Spain in 1220. The adjoining monastery contains a cell (which is usually closed) where the saint stayed. A peaceful 13th-century cloister is reached along a sloping corridor near the main door. Excavations here in the 19th century unearthed parts of the fourth-century BC Servian Wall; a house from the second century BC; a third-century AD bath complex; and a third-century BC temple (which can be seen by appointment only).

Terme di Caracalla (Baths of Caracalla)

Viale delle Terme di Caracalla 52 (06 3996 7700). Bus 118, 160, 628. **Open** 9am-2pm Mon; 9am-sunset Tue-Sun. **Admission** €6; €3 reductions. **No credit cards. Map** p345 B/C5.

The high-vaulted ruins of the Baths of Caracalla, surrounded by trees and grass, are pleasantly peaceful today, but were anything but tranquil in their heyday, when up to 1,600 Romans could sweat it out in the baths and gyms. You can get some idea of the original splendour of the baths – built between AD 213 and 216 – from the fragments of mosaic and statuary littering the grounds, although the more impressive finds are in the Vatican Museums (*see p142*) and the Museo Archeologico in Naples.

The two cavernous rooms down the sides were the *gymnasia*, where Romans engaged in strenuous sports like toss-the-beanbag. There was also a large open-air *natatio* (pool) for lap-swimming. After exercising, they cleansed themselves in saunas and a series of baths of varying temperatures. The baths were usually open from noon until sunset and were social centres where people came to relax after work. The complex also contained a library, a garden, shops and stalls. Underneath it all were 9.5km (six miles) of tunnels, where slaves scurried about, treading the giant wheels that pumped clean water up to bathers and tending to huge braziers that heated the chambers from below the tiles and through pipes in the walls. Caracalla's baths were in use for more than 300 years: the fun dried up in 537 when the Visigoths sacked Rome and severed the city's aqueducts.

TESTACCIO & OSTIENSE

Tucked below the quiet heights of the Aventine is bustling Testaccio, where longtime residents are stridently – even brusquely – Roman (though a more recent influx tends to be urban and professional). The produce market in **piazza Testaccio** is arguably Rome's best.

Today's Testaccio is strictly residential-commercial. Historically, though, Testaccio was a place of industry and trade. This was the site of ancient Rome's great inner-city port. With the decline of Rome as a trading power, so Testaccio became a tranquil place of vegetable gardens and vineyards belonging to the great religious orders up on the Aventine, only to be built over after Italian Unification in the 1870s: dwellings went up for the under-class who manned the municipal slaughterhouse – **il Mattatoio** – and the other noisy industries shifted here from the *centro storico*. Testaccio has no wondrous monuments, just sites that tell of its industrious past, such as the ancient port – **Emporio** – and a rubbish tip of discarded potsherds – **Monte Testaccio**.

Other noteworthy stops include the charming **Museo della Via Ostiense**; the **Cimitero Acattolico** (non-Catholic cemetery), with its illustrious company of defunct foreign artists and writers; and the totally out-of-place **pyramid**, the mausoleum of a Roman with an inflated sense of self.

Testaccio also boasts the city's best nightlife, with clubs, eateries and bars dug into the base of Monte Testaccio: you can see the broken clay pieces piled up in some of the establishments on via Galvani. If you have a strong stomach, try a typical *testaccino* meal in the vicinity of the old slaughterhouse: bits of the beast that no one else wanted go into specialities such as *rigatoni alla pajata*, *trippa alla romana* and *coratelli ai carciofi* (*see p324* **The Menu**).

Due south from Testaccio, **via Ostiense** slices through the once-run-down area of the same name, which is now destined for greater things. To the east of this ancient road is a dense concentration of nightspots, especially around **via Libetta**; the shiny, bustling new campus of the **Università Roma Tre**; and the old wholesale fruit and veg market, currently being transformed into the **Città dei Giovani**

Piazza Testaccio.

SIGHTS

Centrale Montemartini.

SIGHTS

(City of Youth) – a youth-orientated arts and entertainment hub designed by Dutch architect Rem Koolhaas. Further down the via Ostiense, the glorious classical statuary displayed against gleaming power station machinery in the **Centrale Montemartini**, is a wonderful combination and well worth the trek.

Centrale Montemartini

Via Ostiense 106 (06 5748030,www.centralemonte martini.org). Bus 23, 271, 769. **Open** 9am-7pm Tue-Sun. **Admission** €4.50; €3.50 reductions. Extra charge during exhibitions. **No credit cards. Map** p123 B3.

It may be true that the Centrale Montemartini contains merely the leftover ancient statuary from the Musei Capitolini (*see p53*) but, this being Rome, the dregs are pretty impressive; moreover, the setting itself makes this spot worth a visit. You enter through the headquarters of Rome's electricity company, beneath the skeleton of its old gasworks. Inside are fauns and Minervas, bacchic revellers and Apollos, all starkly white but oddly at home against the gleaming machinery of the decommissioned generating station. Jazz concerts with wine tastings (€8)

in the central engine hall on Friday and Saturday nights are not to be missed.

Cimitero Acattolico

Via Caio Cestio 6 (06 574 1900, www. cemeteryrome.it). Metro Piramide/bus 23, 30Exp, 75, 95, 118, 271, 280, 716, 769/ tram 3. **Open** 9am-5pm Mon-Sat; 9am-1pm Sun. **Admission** free (donation of €2 requested). **Map** p343 D/E6.

This heavenly oasis of calm in the midst of a ruckus of traffic has been Rome's final resting place for foreigners since 1784. Verdant and atmospheric, it's a mecca for modern-day travellers keen to recapture the Grand Tour ethos. Unofficially known as the Protestant Cemetery, this charmingly old-world corner of the city also hosts Buddhists, Russian Orthodox Christians and atheists: a sign points to the grave of Antonio Gramsci, founder of the Italian Communist Party. In the older sector is the grave of John Keats, who coughed his last at the age of 26, after only four months in Rome; in fine Romantic fashion his anonymous epitaph concludes: 'here lies one whose name was writ on water' (which was all the poet wanted: his executors added the rest). Next to him lies his companion, Joseph Severn. Close by is the tomb of Shelley, who died a year after Keats in a boating accident.

▶ *For the Keats-Shelley Memorial House; see p87.*

Il Mattatoio

Piazza Giustiniani/via di Monte Testaccio. Bus 23, 30Exp, 75, 95, 170, 280, 673, 716, 719, 781. Map p343 C6.

The bizarre statue of a winged hero slaughtering an ox atop the Mattatoio (slaughterhouse) leaves little doubt about its mission. Hailed as Europe's most advanced abattoir when it opened in 1891, the 24-acre complex extending from the Tiber to Monte Testaccio and the Aurelian Walls coped with an eightfold increase in the city's population, was the source of meat for the whole of central Italy and provided Testaccio's residents with work until 1975. For decades, bickering between politicians, architects and planners left the structure in picturesque abandon: now, the whole area – including the *campo boario* (cattleyards) – is gradually being reclaimed and transformed into a university architecture department, a fair-trade and organic food store, and spaces for multimedia projects and exhibitions.

▶ *For more on the centre's new food store; see p233* **Organic in the Abbatoir**. *The centre is also to contain an outpost of the MACRO gallery; see p157.*

Museo della Via Ostiense

Via R Persichetti 3 (06 574 3193). Metro Piramide/ bus 23, 30Exp, 75, 95, 118, 271, 280, 716, 769/ tram 3. **Open** 9.30am-1.30pm, 2.30-4.30pm Tue, Thur; 9.30am-1.30pm Wed, Fri Sat, 1st & 3rd Sun of mth. **Admission** free. Map p343 E6.

This humble but oddly charming museum contains artefacts and prints pertaining to via Ostiense and Ostia Antica, the ancient port that this consular road led to. There are large-scale models of Ostia and the port of Trajan, a 13th-century fresco of the Madonna and Child, and a fine view over Roman driving skills.

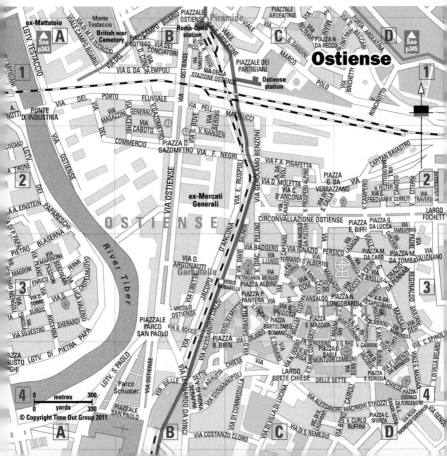

Celio, San Giovanni & San Lorenzo

Monuments galore trace Christianity's progress from cult to state religion.

SIGHTS

There are few finer places than San Giovanni and Celio to get a feel for the clash between powerful pagan Rome and early Christianity. After Emperor Constantine legalised Christianity in the fourth century, he donated land on which the basilica of **San Giovanni in Laterano** was built. This was ground breaking in that it brought the new religion out into the open, but was fence-sitting in the sense that, at the time, this neighbourhood was as far as you could get from the city's centre of power. Today, the basilica continues to attract religious visitors, while the **Celio** retains the bucolic character that made it the area of choice for wealthy Romans. Meanwhile, students and artists keep neighbouring **San Lorenzo** lively.

Map p345	**Cafés, Bars &**
Hotels p179	**Gelaterie** p217
Eating Out p200	

CELIO

Once home to Roman senators, nobility and wealthy entrepreneurs, the Caelian hill (one of the famous seven) was – like the rest of Rome – overrun in AD 410 by Alaric the Goth. Its patrician villas and shops remained largely deserted for centuries after, crumbling back to nature. Today, the hill itself retains a bucolic character; much of it is occupied by monasteries and convents, churches and nursery schools.

The greater Celio neighbourhood stretches roughly from the via delle Terme di Caracalla on the south, to the Palatine on the west, the Colosseum to the north and San Giovanni in Laterano (*see p131*) to the east. An arduous but rewarding (and crowd-free) walking tour of the area could begin at the church of **San Gregorio Magno** (*see p126*), pass under the medieval arcade to the church of **Santi Giovanni e Paolo** (*see p127*), with its fabulous Roman house underneath and on to

the lovely, leafy **Villa Celimontana** (*see p130*) park – a good place to rest your feet.

The high-walled road along the park's northern edge leads to a chunk of the **Acqua Claudia** aqueduct. At the top of the supporting arch is a blue and red Greek cross, the symbol of the Trinitarian order whose 12th-century mission was to raise money to pay the ransom of crusaders captured by the infidels.

Past that arch, and right into via della Navicella, two churches face off across the street. On the right, **Santa Maria in Domnica** (*see p127*) has pretty ninth-century mosaics and a delicate sculpture of a little Roman boat (*navicella*) in front of it. Across the road, assorted martyrdoms are depicted in the odd

About the author

Sarah Delaney has written for the Washington Post, The Times, *the* Independent, People *magazine and the Catholic News Service. She has lived in Italy since 1983.*

Santa Maria in Domnica. *See p127.*

SIGHTS

and gruesome frescoes in **Santo Stefano Rotondo** (*see p128*). Further on to the left, the monolithic **Santi Quattro Coronati** (*see p127*) complex comes into view, with its charming cloister and secret chapel. Below it is the multi-layered **San Clemente** (*see p127*).

★ FREE San Clemente
Via San Giovanni in Laterano (06 774 0021, www.basilicasanclemente.com). Metro Colosseo/ bus 60Exp, 75, 85, 87, 117, 571, 810, 850/tram 3. **Open** *9am-12.30pm, 3-6pm Mon-Sat; noon-6pm Sun.* **Admission** *Church free. Excavations* €5. **No credit cards. Map** p344 D3.

A favourite with kids for its dungeon-like underground level, this 12th-century basilica is a three-dimensional Roman time-line, a church above a church above an even older Imperial building – a full 18m (60ft) of Roman life separates the earliest structure from the one we see today.

In 1857 the Irish Dominicans – who have run the church since the 17th century – began digs that unearthed the church's fourth-century predecessor, and, beneath, an early Christian *titulus* (meeting place). The fourth-century structure was razed in the Norman sack of 1084, but the *schola cantorum* (choir), with its exquisite carving and mosaic decorations, survived and was moved upstairs to the new church, where it still stands.

Also in the upper church is the 12th-century mosaic in the apse, still in Byzantine style but with a theological complexity unusual for its period. Against a gold backdrop, cobalt blues, deep reds and multi-hued greens make up the crucified Christ. From the drops of Christ's blood springs the vine

representing the Church, which swirls around peasants at their daily tasks, Doctors of the Church spreading the divine word and a host of animals. Above the cross, the hand of God links heaven and earth, while below, sheep represent Christ and the 12 apostles. The Latin inscription above the sheep says 'I am the vine, you are the branches'. Towards the back of the church, in the chapel of St Catherine of Alexandria, a series of frescoes by Masolino (c1430), possibly with help from Masaccio, depict the life of the saint – she is shown calmly praying as her

---

INSIDE TRACKS
CULT OF MITHRAS

Just as Christianity was growing in popularity through the Roman Empire in the third century, the cult of the Persian god Mithras was also taking hold. The two religions – one all humility and the other all sacrifice and gore – appealed to very different sectors of the community. The former was big with women, the latter with the military. Yet the two also had similarities: mythology said that Mithras was born of a virgin who was called 'mother of God'... sound familiar? The sudden rise of Christianity and abrupt disappearance of Mithras in the fourth century may have been carefully orchestrated: after all, no emperor wanted hidden cultists plotting against him.

Extra Time

● On her way to be crowned in San Giovanni Laterano, legend says, **Pope Joan** gave her dark secret away when she had to pull over to have a baby. After which she was either stoned on the spot or sent into exile, depending on who you ask. A forlorn shrine at the corner of *vie* dei Querceti and dei Santi Quattro marks the spot.

● The **Museo Storico della Liberazione** (via Tasso 154, 06 700 3866, www.viatasso.eu, open 9.30am-12.30pm, 3.30-7.30pm Tue, Thur, Fri; 9.30am-12.30pm Wed, Sat, Sun) occupies the house where the Gestapo interrogated suspected Resistance fighters during the wartime occupation. From the messages carved into cell walls to the rows of photos of victims, this is a haunting place.

● Sandwiched between via San Giovanni in Laterano and via Labicana is the partially excavated first-century AD **Ludus Magnus**,

home and training ground for gladiators, just a short walk from the Colosseum where they would meet death or glory. It's particularly lovely in the spring when overrun with brilliant red poppies.

● At the eastern end of via San Paolo della Croce stands the **arco di Dolabella**, a pre-existing Roman arch incorporated by Nero into an aqueduct that carried water from the Acqua Claudia to his artificial lake on the spot where the Colosseum was subsequently built. The buildings by the arch – the church of **San Tommaso in Formis** and the Istituto Sperimentale per la Nutrizione delle Piante – were once part of a hospital for clergy and for Christian slaves who were freed by the Trinitarian order in medieval times. A 12th-century mosaic of Christ freeing a pair of slaves adorns the door of the botanical institute.

SIGHTS

torturers prepare the wheel to which she was strapped and stretched to death (and for which the firework was later named) – as well as Christ on the cross in between the two thieves.

From the sacristy, steps lead down to the fourth-century basilica, the space broken up by walls supporting the structure above. Fading frescoes show scenes from the life of St Clement, the fourth pope, exiled to the Crimea by Emperor Trajan. Even in exile, he didn't give up proselytising and so was hurled into the Black Sea, tied to an anchor. A year later, the sea receded, revealing a tomb containing Clement's body. After that, the sea would recede once a year and another miracle would occur.

Near the far end of the underground basilica is a modern shrine to St Cyril; the inventor of Cyrillic script was a great figure of the Orthodox churches and credited with bringing Clement's body to Rome.

A stairway leads down to an ancient Roman alley. On one side are the remains of a second-century Roman *insula*, or apartment building, containing a site where the Persian god Mithras was worshipped. There are three rooms devoted to the cult. In the sanctuary, a fresco depicts the god killing a bull. On the other side of the lane are the ground-floor rooms of a Roman house used by early Christians as a *titulus*. At one of the turns in this warren of antiquity, you can hear water rushing through an ancient sewer on its way down to the Tiber.

FREE San Gregorio Magno

Piazza di San Gregorio Magno 1 (church 06 700 8227, oratories 349 356 7626). Bus 60Exp, 75, 81, 175, 271, 673/tram 3. **Open** 9am-12.30pm, 3-6.30pm Mon-Fri, Sun. **Map** p345 B4.

Clivus Scauro.

This impressive Baroque church with a grandiose staircase, finished by Giovanni Battista Soria in 1633, stands on the site of the home of one of the most remarkable popes, Gregory I (the Great; 590-604). Gregory was steered by his affluent family towards a career in public administration, but instead he embraced the monastic life and converted his house into a monastery. He became Pope Pelagius II's right-hand man and was tapped for the papacy when Pelagius died. Popular lore says he fled Rome when he heard the news; dragged back, he spent his 14-year pontificate vigorously reorganising the Church.

Inside the church, in a chapel on the right, is a marble chair dating from the first century BC, said to have been used by Gregory as his papal throne. Also here is the tomb of diplomat Sir Edward Carne, who visited Rome several times to persuade the pope to annul the marriage of Henry VIII and Catherine of Aragon, so that the king would be able to marry Anne Boleyn.

Outside, across a pine-scented garden maintained by the nuns of Mother Teresa's order, stand three chapels, or *oratori* (closed Aug). The chapels of Santa Barbara and Sant'Andrea are medieval structures, heavily restored in the early 17th century and popularly believed to have been part of the house of Gregory the Great and his mother St Sylvia; Sant'Andrea has frescoes by Guido Reni and Domenichino. The chapel of St Sylvia itself dates from the 17th century. Behind the chapels are remains of shops that once lined this ancient road, the Clivus Scauri.

FREE Santa Maria in Domnica

Via della Navicella 10 (06 7720 2685).
Bus 81, 117, 673. **Open** 8.30am-12.30pm, 4.30-7pm daily. **Map** p345 C4.
Santa Maria in Domnica is known to the locals as the *navicella* (little ship), after the Roman statue that stands outside (which was the inspiration for the 16th-century *barcaccia* fountain at the Spanish Steps). A church was built here in the seventh century, over the barracks of a corps of Roman *vigiles* (firefighters). It was reconstructed in the ninth century by Pope Paschal I, who commissioned the apse mosaic – one of the most charming in Rome. The pope is portrayed sitting at the feet of the Virgin and Child with a square halo that indicates he was living when the mosaic was made. What sets this lovely design in gold and rich blues, reds and aquamarines apart is that Mary and Jesus don't show the melancholy prescience of what was to befall them as did most such depictions until then: the cherry-red daubs of blush on their cheeks give them a healthy and cheerful glow. They are surrounded by a host of angels; above, the apostles appear to be skipping through a meadow. The interior of the church is austere and peaceful, with 18 ancient marble columns supporting the graceful arches of the nave. The carved wood

ceiling and porticoed façade are the result of a 16th-century restoration. *Photo p125.*

FREE Santi Giovanni e Paolo

Piazza Santi Giovanni e Paolo 13 (church 06 700 5745, excavations 06 7045 4544, www.caseromane.it). Bus 60Exp, 75, 81, 175, 673/tram 3. **Open** *Church* 8.30am-noon, 3.30-6pm daily. *Excavations* 10am-1pm, 3-6pm Mon, Thur-Sun. **Admission** *Church* free. *Excavations* €6; €4 reductions. **No credit cards. Map** p344 C3.
In the fourth century, a church was built over the house (and probably the bones) of John and Paul, two officers at the Imperial court who were martyred in 362. The original church was hacked away, first by Goths and later by Normans, but traces of it can still be seen in the 12th-century façade on lovely piazza Santi Giovanni e Paolo, which is overlooked by a 12th-century bell tower attached to the nearby convent. Two time-worn lions flank the entrance; one seems to be gnawing on a helpless babe.

An 18th-century restoration left the church with its present lugubrious ambience inside. Better to head around the corner, beneath the medieval buttresses of **Clivus (clivio) Scauro** to locate the door leading to the labyrinthine excavations of the martyrs' house. Digs in the 19th century and others in the final years of the 20th led to the discovery of more than 20 rooms on several levels. From four different buildings, and dating from the first century AD, these rooms include some evidently used for secret Christian worship. Among these are spaces bought in the fourth century by wealthy senator Pammachius, who, after embracing Christianity, donated generously to the poor and made his home into a church. Three other Christian martyrs are said to be buried there; a well-preserved fresco from the late fourth century in the *confessio* honours them. In the nymphaeum, putti in brightly coloured boats flank a naked female divinity, perhaps Proserpine. There are several other frescoes preserved in good condition throughout the site. This is an especially good and little-visited place to time-travel through Roman history.

The sacristan may let you in through the gates at the foot of the bell tower: from there you'll get a glimpse of the massive foundations of the Temple of Claudius.

FREE Santi Quattro Coronati

Via dei Santi Quattro 20 (06 7047 5427).
Bus 85, 87, 117, 571, 810, 850/tram 3. **Open** *Church* 7am-12.30pm, 3.30-7pm daily. *Cloister* 10-11.50am, 4-5.30pm Mon-Sat; 9.30-10.30am, 4-5.50pm Sun. *Oratory* 9.30am-noon, 3.30-6pm daily. **Map** p344 D3.
The secret places in the basilica of the Four Crowned Saints make it a good candidate for dragging listless kids to. The church dates from the fourth century and was probably named after four Roman soldiers who refused to pray before the statue of Esculapius,

SIGHTS

the Roman god of healing. Another version has it dedicated to early stonemasons who refused to sculpt the aforementioned deity, making the church especially dear to present-day masons. Like San Clemente and Santi Giovanni e Paolo, it was burnt down by rampaging Normans in 1084. It was rebuilt as a fortified monastery, with the church itself reduced to half its original dimensions; the outsize apse, visible as you look uphill along via dei Santi Quattro, remains from the original church. The early basilica form is still discernible, and the columns that once ran along the aisles are embedded in the walls of the innermost courtyard. The church has a fine cosmatesque floor and an upper-level *matronium*, to which women were relegated during religious functions. There is also one of Rome's most beautiful cloisters, dating from about 1220, with lovely, slender columns supporting delicate arches and a double-cupped fountain amid its flowerbeds. The musty chapel of Santa Barbara conceals a pair of frescoes: a 12th-century *Madonna and Child* and a ninth-century unidentified saint. Just ring the bell at the door on the left side of the nave and a kind-hearted nun will probably let you have a peek.

In the oratory outside the church (ring the bell and ask for the key) is a fresco cycle depicting the *Donation of Constantine* – a false story put forward for centuries by the papacy as justification for its authority. According to the legend, an early pope, Sylvester, cured Emperor Constantine of leprosy, after which the august personage was so grateful that he granted the Bishops of Rome spiritual and worldly authority over the whole of the Western Empire (Constantine, from his capital at Constantinople, lorded it over the Eastern Empire). The frescoes, a first-class example of political propaganda, were painted in the 13th century. They show a pox-ridden Constantine being healed by Sylvester, crowning him with a tiara and giving him a cap to symbolise the pope's spiritual and – more importantly – earthly power. In one scene, Constantine's mother, Helen, indicates Christ's cross on the hill of Golgotha. Visitors should be as silent as possible: the monastery is still home to an enclosed order of Augustine nuns.

FREE Santo Stefano Rotondo

Via di Santo Stefano Rotondo 7 (06 421 191). Bus 81, 117, 673. **Open** *April-Sept* 9am-noon, 4-6pm Tue-Sat; 9.30am-12.30pm Sun. *Oct-Mar* 9.30am-12.30pm, 2-5pm Tue-Sat; 9am-12.30pm Sun. **Map** p345 C4.

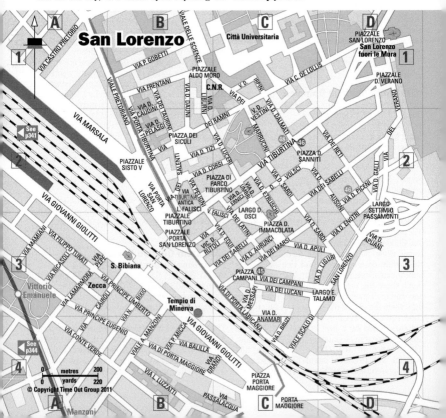

Virtual Rome

Had enough reality for one day? Check out some of Rome's more high-tech attractions.

For those who prefer their culture digitally packaged, Rome has an array of attractions: the flight-simulator **Time Elevator** (*see p248*) offers a bumpy 20-minute ride through two millennia of history – best not experienced on a full stomach. **Rewind Rome** (*see p248*) takes the latest in 3D imaging wizardry and mixes video game technology and rather cheesy virtual guides for a romp through *caput mundi*.

On a more erudite note, computers in the **Crypta Balbi** (*see p104*) offer an interactive guide to how rubbish raised Rome's street levels, while the **Terme di Diocleziano** (*see p141*) has an animated explanation (in Italian only) of how the via Flaminia would have looked when ancient Romans tramped along it, en route to the Adriatic sea port of Ariminum – modern Rimini.

In a new-for-2010 attraction, truly impressive technical wizardry is to be found in the basement of **Palazzo Valentini** (*see p58*), HQ of the Rome provincial government. During a guided tour (which – you are warned – is long and would test the sticking power of even the best behaved children) of the remains of a late Roman *domus*, computer-generated reconstructions of what this gracious dwelling, probably of a wealthy senator, would have looked like in its heyday. The effect is quite startlingly realistic.

One plan for selling a 'repackaged' Rome has – thankfully – been allowed to slip into obscurity with the onset of belt-tightening: in 2008 the city council was cock-a-hoop over plans to cover 300 hectares of countryside outside the city with an Imperial Roman theme park, predicting that the attraction would attract eight million visitors annually. More likely to materialise – though probably not by its original spring 2011 deadline – is Cinecittà World (www.cinecittaworldiginal spring 2011 deadline – is Cinecittà World (www.cinecittaworld.it), a theme park south of Rome charting the city's (www.contribcittaworld.it), a theme park south of Rome charting the city's contribution to the movie industry.

In the meantime, skeptics point out that the Appian Way is unkempt and label-less, museums complain of serious underfunding, a handful of gardeners struggle to keep parks presentable and little has been done to render the Roman Forum more 'legible'. Orlando has little else to offer besides its Disney extravaganza: Rome, well managed, is one of the world's greatest attractions in itself.

SIGHTS

Perhaps inspired by the Church of the Holy Sepulchre in Jerusalem, this unusual round church dates from the fifth century; in its measurements, some say, lies the secret of the Holy Number of God. It rests on parts of a patrician Roman villa and a mithraeum, one of many in this area of Rome. In its original form, the church must have been exceptionally beautiful, with its Byzantine-inspired simplicity – three concentric naves separated by rings of antique columns set within a Greek cross – and play of natural light. This effect was disturbed when arches were built to shore it up in the 12th century, and the portico was added. The outer ring was walled in 1450, and the atmosphere changed definitively with a 16th-century attempt at mind control: 34 horrifically graphic frescoes of martyrs being boiled, stretched and slashed were added to the interior walls for the edification of the faithful. Visit when the sun is streaming in from the upper windows and you'll catch something of the original contemplative aura.

FREE Villa Celimontana
Via della Navicella/via San Paolo della Croce (no phone). Bus 60Exp, 75, 81, 117, 175, 271, 628, 673/tram 3. **Open** dawn to dusk daily. **Map** p345 C4.
This is a pretty, leafy walled garden, with a rather pokey playground; which does not stop swarms of local kids from climbing, running and holding birthday picnics here. The pleasant lawns are dotted with pieces of marble from the collection of the Mattei family, which owned the property from 1553 until 1928, when it became a public park. The graceful family villa, now housing the Italian Geographic Society, was built in the 16th century. Forlorn and forgotten at the southern end is one of Rome's Egyptian obelisks. During the summer, the villa becomes the gorgeous venue for big-name evening jazz concerts.

FROM SAN GIOVANNI TO SANTA CROCE IN GERUSALEMME

Seat of the Bishop of Rome (ie the pope in his local role), and first and foremost of the four great Roman basilicas, **San Giovanni in Laterano** (*see right*) is high on any pilgrim's must-do list. However, many non-religious visitors write it (and the area that surrounds it) off as too far from the *centro storico*, not helped by the fact that first-class sights are thin on the ground. This is a pity because a stop at this grandiose – if rather impersonal – cathedral and nearby monuments provides a good picture of Christianity as a fledgling state religion.

San Giovanni stands on the spot donated in the third century by Emperor Constantine for the construction of the first Christian basilica: he wasn't keen to rock the boat too much – note its location inside the city walls but in a then-quiet corner far away from the centre of political power. For centuries it was to be the papal seat and residence, its importance underscored by the presence of many holy souvenirs carted here from the Holy Land by Constantine's mother Helena, an early convert to the new faith. The 28 steps of the **Scala Santa**, for example, across the road to the north of the basilica, were said to be the very ones that Christ climbed to hear Pontius Pilate's non-verdict that essentially condemned him to death. At the top is the **Sancta Sanctorum** (*see p132*), containing super-sacred relics. A few blocks north of here is the **Museo Storico della Liberazione di Roma**, a grim testament to the notorious

prison where Nazi SS officers tortured and killed suspected partisans.

On the west side of the basilica complex are the Lateran palace, now used for the administration of the Church in Italy, the Pontifical University and the octagonal baptistry. Stranded in the middle of thundering traffic in the unappealing piazza is another of Rome's Egyptian obelisks. South of the church, on the other hand, are the sunken ruins of **Porta Asinaria**, an ancient gate belonging to the third-century Aurelian Wall. The **Porta San Giovanni** is the starting-point of modern via Appia Nuova, a retail-intensive main drag that leads south out of town to the Alban Hills.

A park has been created beneath the impressive stretch of Aurelian Wall that runs from San Giovanni east towards **Santa Croce in Gerusalemme** (*see right*), a basilica that bristles with relics brought back by the redoubtable St Helena after her pilgrimage to the Holy Land at the age of 80: pieces of the cross, a nail and thorns from Christ's crown among them. A lovely vegetable garden, recently restored and lovingly tended by monks of the adjoining monastery had been closed to the public as this guide went to press. The church was built over a part of Helena's own house, known as the Sessorium, a palace that originally belonged to the Emperor Septimius Severus (193-211).

Dotted around is a panoply of minor **Roman ruins**: through the opening in the Aurelian Wall to the right of the church is the Amphitheatrum Castrense, and part of the Circus Varianus, both dating from the reign of Elagabulus; the Baths of Helena, of which only the cistern is visible; and the monumental travertine archway built by Emperor Claudius in the first century AD to mark the triumphal entrance of the aqueducts in to the city (it was later incorporated into the Aurelian Wall).

To the left of the basilica is the delightful **Museo Nazionale degli Strumenti Musicali** (museum of musical instruments).

The oven-shaped Tomb of Eurysaces (an ancient Roman baker) stands just outside the well-preserved third-century Porta Maggiore. North from here, beyond the railway tracks, is the district of San Lorenzo (*see p132*).

Museo Nazionale degli Strumenti Musicali
Piazza Santa Croce in Gerusalemme 9A (06 701 4796, www.museistumentimusicali.it). Metro San Giovanni/bus 105, 571, 649/tram 3. **Open** 8.30am-7pm Tue-Sun **Admission** €4; €2 reductions. **No credit cards.** **Map** off p345 E4.

This small museum is a treat for musicians. A recent wash-and-brush-up means that this formerly musty collection now has video loops and good explanations in English. From prehistoric to Baroque, an astonishing variety of drums, lutes, flutes and spinets showcases the evolution of instrument-making in Italy, the rest of Europe, Africa and Japan.

★ FREE San Giovanni in Laterano

Piazza San Giovanni in Laterano 4 (06 6988 6433, www.vatican.va). Metro San Giovanni/bus 16, 85, 87, 117, 186, 218, 571, 650, 665, 714, 850/tram 3. **Open** *Church 7am-6.30pm daily. Baptistry (06 6988 6452) 7.30am-noon, 4-6.30pm daily. Cloister 9am-6pm daily. Museum 9am-1pm Mon-Sat.* **Admission** *Church free. Cloister €2 (free with Vatican museum ticket). Museum €4.* **No credit cards. Map** p345 E4.

The Catholic faithful earn indulgences for visits to this major basilica. Along with the Lateran palace, it was the site of the original papal headquarters until the move across the river to St Peter's and the Vatican during the 14th century. Constantine's second wife, Fausta, gave the plot of land to Pope Melchiades to build the papal residence and church in 313. There are few traces of the original basilica, which was destroyed by fire, earthquake and barbarians. It has been heavily restored and reconstructed: the end result is a vast, impersonal, over-decorated hangar.

The façade with its 15 huge statues of Christ, the two Johns (Baptist and Evangelist) and 12 Doctors of the Church, is part of the 1735 rebuilding by Alessandro Galilei. The interior bears the stamp of Borromini, who transformed it in 1646. A few treasures from earlier times survive: a much restored 13th-century mosaic in the apse, a fragment of a fresco attributed to Giotto (hidden behind the first column on the right) showing Pope Boniface VIII announcing the first Holy Year in 1300, and the Gothic *baldacchino* over the main altar.

Off the left aisle is the 13th-century cloister, with delicate twisted columns and fine cosmatesque work by the Vassalletto family. A small museum off the cloister contains papal vestments and some original manuscripts of music by Palestrina.

The north façade was designed in 1586 by Domenico Fontana, who also placed Rome's tallest Egyptian obelisk out front. This was part of Pope Sixtus V's 16th-century urban renewal scheme. Also on this side is the octagonal baptistry that Constantine had built. The four chapels surrounding the font have mosaics from the fifth and seventh centuries, and bronze doors said to come from the Baths of Caracalla.

FREE Santa Croce in Gerusalemme

Piazza Santa Croce in Gerusalemme 12 (06 7061 3053). Bus 81, 85, 87, 105, 571, 649/tram 3, 5, 14. **Open** *7am-noon, 3.30-7.30pm daily.* **Map** off p345 E4.

Founded in 320 by St Helena, mother of Emperor Constantine (who legalised Christianity in 313), this church began as a hall in her home, the Palatium Sessorium. The church was rebuilt and extended in the 12th century, and again in 1743-44. Helena had her church constructed to house relics brought back from the Holy Land by the redoubtable lady herself. The emperor's *mamma* came back with an enviable shopping-bagful: three chunks of Christ's cross, a nail, two thorns from his crown and the finger of St Thomas – allegedly the very one that the doubting saint stuck into Christ's wound. All these are displayed in a chapel at the end of a Fascist-era hall at the left side of the nave. Apart from the wood, those venerable objects are rather hard to identify, inside their gold reliquaries. In the mosaic-ceilinged lower chapel (under the altar) is Helena's stash of soil from Jerusalem. Helena's Holy Land souvenir-collecting sparked a relic-craze exploited to the full for centuries by the wily merchants of the Holy Land; when Jesus-related bits were in short supply, scraps of saints and martyrs were fair game too.

The basilica's gorgeous vegetable garden – inside the Castrense amphitheatre – was revamped some years ago by architect Paolo Pejrone, and has been given a striking gate by sculptor Jannis Kounellis. At the time of writing, reservation-only guided tours of the garden had been suspended.

▶ *The grave of St Helena can be seen in the Ara Coeli (see p59)… though the pretty little church of Sant'Elena in Venice also claims to have the great lady's body.*

Santa Croce in Gerusalemme.

SIGHTS

FREE Scala Santa (Holy Stairs) & Sancta Sanctorum

Piazza di San Giovanni in Laterano (06 772 6641, www.scalasanta.org). Metro San Giovanni/bus 16, 85, 87, 186, 218, 571, 650, 665, 714/tram 3. **Open** *Scala Santa* Apr-Sept 6.15am-noon, 3.30-6.30pm daily; Oct-Mar 6.15am-noon, 3-6pm daily. *Sancta Sanctorum* (booking obligatory) Apr-Sept 10.30-11.30am, 3.30-4.30pm daily; Oct-Mar 10.30-11.30am, 3-6pm daily. **Admission** *Scala Santa* free. *Sancta Sanctorum* €3.50. **No credit cards**. **Map** p344 E3.

According to tradition, these steps (now covered with wooden plants) are the very ones Jesus climbed in the house of Pontius Pilate only to see the Roman governor wash his hands of the self-styled messiah. Emperor Constantine's mother St Helena brought these back in the fourth century. A crawl up the Scala Santa has been a fixture on every serious pilgrim's list ever since. In 1510 Martin Luther gave it a go, but halfway up he decided that relics were a theological irrelevance and walked back down again. Don't climb them unless you know 28 different prayers (one for each step); walking up is not allowed. Prepare for a queue on Good Friday.

At the top of the Holy Stairs (but also accessible by non-holy stairs to the left) is the Sancta Sanctorum ('Holy of Holies'), the *privatissima* chapel of the popes and one of the only monuments around here that escaped Sixtus V's revamping. Some of the best early Christian relics were kept in the crypt under the altar at one time – including the heads of saints Peter, Paul and young Agnes. Most of them have been distributed to other churches around the city, but displayed in a glass case on the left wall is a fragment of the table on which the Last Supper was supposedly served. The real treasures here, however, are the 13th-century frescoes in the lunettes and on the ceiling, attributed to Cimabue. Once, no one but the *pontifex maximus* himself was allowed to set foot in the Sancta Sanctorum.

SAN LORENZO

Colourful and hopping, the San Lorenzo neighbourhood still retains some of its original threadbare working-class character. Its proximity to Rome's **La Sapienza** university keeps it youthful and lively. A constant influx of students and artists mingles with a (diminishing) local population proud of its unswerving anti-Fascist and partisan history.

Constructed in the 1890s as a ramshackle ghetto for the poor, San Lorenzo became a hotbed of anarchist and left-wing activity. Hemmed in by urban infrastructure, such as the freight train depot and the sprawling cemetery of Il Verano, *sanlorenzini* were isolated in poverty from the rest of the city. Maria Montessori, who opened her first school here in 1907, said, 'when I first came to this quarter

where respectable people only come when they're dead, I had the impression that some huge disaster had struck.'

Unbowed by their circumstances, the locals were ready with rocks and bricks to hurl from buildings when Fascists first came calling some years later. Alas, their anti-Fascism didn't help them in World War II: on 19 July 1943, Allied planes launched a strike on the Nazi-occupied train station – in the process knocking out several buildings, including the lovely (now restored) **San Lorenzo fuori le Mura** (*see below*), and killing 3,000 civilians. The scars show, as do other vestiges of the district's history. But besides the many emporia selling tombstones, coffins and memorial lanterns, there's a happy mix of artisans, second-hand clothing shops, clubs and restaurants, plus purveyors of food and hardware to show that real people still live here. It's also home to Rome's only converted-loft artists' community.

To the north east, some 120,000 students study at La Sapienza university, a sprawling complex of Fascist-era buildings by the likes of Marcello Piacentini and Arnaldo Foschini.

FREE San Lorenzo fuori le Mura

Piazzale del Verano 3 (06 491 511). Bus 71, 492/tram 3, 19. **Open** *Apr-Sept* 8am-noon, 4-8pm daily. *Oct-Mar* 8am-noon, 4-6.30pm daily. **Map** p128 D1.

This spacious church, with its unusual chancel and ethereal light, gives an atmosphere of calm, a feature of the Romanesque tradition to which it belongs. Like most Roman places of worship, the building has been formed from a patchwork of 'improvements' over the centuries. St Lawrence, whose remains lie in a crypt beneath the church, was martyred in the mid-third century; convert-Emperor Constantine had a basilica built over his tomb during the fourth century. Several popes were subsequently laid to rest in the same underground catacombs.

In the late sixth century, Pope Pelagius II rebuilt the basilica; from this incarnation comes the broad chancel with its Corinthian columns, marble ciborium and stylised Byzantine mosaic of Pelagius and St Lawrence, with Christ seated on an orb. The nave is a 13th-century addition by Pope Honorius, even though much is a faithful restoration undertaken after it was demolished by American bombs in 1943. In the portico are 13th-century frescoes depicting the life of the saint. A lovely courtyard encloses gardens and a piece of the errant bomb that wreaked havoc on the church. A ramp on the right leads behind the chancel, to the crypt of Blessed Pope Pius IX, the last pope to rule over the Vatican States; his reportedly uncorrupted body lies with a creepy silver mask over his face.

▶ *The griddle on which St Laurence met his fiery end can be seen in the church of San Lorenzo in Lucina; see p91.*

Monti & Esquilino

Modern-day grit and ancient glamour stand side-by-side here.

The Esquilino hill, around Termini railway station (if you've come to Rome on a budget deal there's a good chance you'll find yourself staying in a hotel around here), was once where the rich and powerful had their gardens and villas. Today – despite municipal authorities trying hard to convince us that there's a 'renaissance' under way – there's no escaping the fact that Esquilino's *palazzi* are grimy and its after-dark denizens can be on the dodgy side. The area – now covered by the *rioni* (city districts) of Monti and Esquilino – has always been one of contrasts but it's a neighbourhood that definitely als has its charms – you just have to know where to look.

Map p341 & p344	**Cafés, Bars &**
Hotels p181	**Gelaterie** p217
Eating Out p203	

INTRODUCING MONTI & ESQUILINO

In ancient times the notorious Suburra – a giant slum where streets ran with effluent – was cheek by jowl with the **Imperial fora** (*see p65*) and Nero's **Domus Aurea** (*see p135*). The more salubrious Esquiline hill above was home to first-century BC magnate-impressario Maecenas and, later, to Felice Peretti (Pope Sixtus V), whose exquisite Villa Peretti spawled over the hill. Nowadays the twisting alleyways of Monti – roughly the Suburra area – are bustling, noisy, and now, also very hip.

The Esquiline hill, by contrast, was swallowed up in the 1870s by solid, soulless *palazzi*, built after Italy was unified to house the official buildings of the new state; these have seen better days, and despite claims that the whole area is undergoing a rebirth, it remains fairly grubby and gloomy. If you arrive in Rome by bus or train, your first stop will be right here, at Termini station, and first impressions may be less than favourable. But both Monti and Esquilino have their sights and charms: a little patience, and looking in the right places, will reveal them.

MONTI

The marshy ground between the Quirinal, Viminal and Esquiline hills was home to the steamy, overcrowded Suburra, which was described by Roman writers fond of excursions into the *demi-monde*. Propertius spent time here waiting for his mistress Cynthia to climb out of a first-floor window, down a rope and into his arms. Juvenal, who lived in the heart of this hottest, noisiest and most chaotic quarter of the city, reported in his *Satires* that the most common cause of death here was insomnia.

The area of Monti that was the Suburra – the enclave stretching east from the Forum between *vie* Nazionale and Cavour – is just as noisy, cosmopolitan and full of life today as it was then. Streets are cleaner, and property prices higher, but the narrow, chaotic streets full of funky clothes shops, wild bars and ethnic restaurants pulsate with the same kind of activity.

The post-Unification developers who did their worst to the Esquiline also left their mark on parts of Monti: **via Nazionale** has roaring traffic, drab carbon-copy high-street fashion emporia and rip-off tourist restaurants; via Cavour is singularly bland. The lab on undulating via Panisperna where Enrico Fermi and Ettore Majorana first split the atom in 1934 and the lumpen Bank of Italy HQ in Palazzo Koch on via Nazionale are oppressive; the bombastic, windowless **Palazzo delle Esposizioni** (*see below*), also on via Nazionale, is redeemed only by some good exhibitions. There's relief, however, in the streets south of Santa Maria Maggiore (*see p140*), where two stunning early churches dedicated to two sister saints, **Santa Prassede** and **Santa Pudenziana** (for both, *see below*), glow with extraordinary mosaics.

For a verdant break and splendid views, head for the **Villa Aldobrandini** gardens high up above the south-western end of via Nazionale (access from nearby via Mazzarino). Built in the 16th century, the garden's formal lawns and gravel paths are disturbed only by tramps snoring on benches (and the traffic noise below).

★ Palazzo delle Esposizioni

Via Nazionale 194 (06 3996 7500, www.pala expo.it). Bus 40Exp, 64, 70, 71, 170, H. **Open** 10am-8pm Tue-Thur, Sun; 10am-10.30pm Fri, Sat. **Admission** €12.50; €10 reductions. **Credit** MC, V. **Map** p341 C6.

This imposing 19th-century purpose-built exhibition space reopened, refurbished, a few years ago and continues to produce excellent shows on a host of historical, artistic and contemporary-icon themes. If the ticket price seems high, it's because it allows access to numerous exhibits running simultaneously around the 10,000 square metre space. If you're under 30, it's free from 2-7pm on the first Wednesday of the month. You don't need a ticket to access the basement bookshop and café – this latter a great place to grab a light lunch.

★ Santa Prassede

Via Santa Prassede 9A (06 488 2456). Bus 16, 70, 71, 75, 84, 360, 649, 714. **Open** 7.30am-noon, 4-7pm Mon-Sat; 8am-noon, 4-7pm Sun. **Map** p344 D1.

This church was built in the ninth century on the spot where St Praxedes is said to have harboured Christians. The saint, the story says, sponged up the blood of 23 martyrs who were discovered and killed before her, throwing the sponge into a well; its location is now marked by a porphyry disc on the floor of the nave. This tale is depicted in the 1735 altarpiece by Domenico Muratori. This church is a scale copy of the old St Peter's, a ninth-century attempt to recreate an early Christian basilica, although uneven brickwork shows that the Romans had lost the knack.

Pope Paschal I was looking for artists to decorate the chapel of San Zeno as a mausoleum dedicated to his mother, St Theodora. With the Roman Empire long dead, the pick of mosaic artists was thriving across in Byzantium, where the traditionally Roman

San Pietro in Vincoli.

art of mosaic took on a flashier and more colourful style, with coloured glass tesserae often backed with gold or silver. Undoubtedly the finest expression of Byzantine art in Rome, the chapel is topped with a vault showing a fearsome Christ supported by four angels, while around the walls are various saints, including St Theodora herself with the blue square halo that tells us she was still alive when she posed for her mausoleum mosaic. On the right the Anastasis shows Christ reaching into hell to rescue Adam, Eve and assorted Old Testament characters. In a room to the right of the chapel of St Zeno is a portion of column said to be part of the very one that Jesus was tied to for the flagellation.

In the apse, Christ riding on a cloud is being introduced to the martyr St Praxedes by St Paul on the right, while St Peter is doing the honours on the left for her sister St Pudenziana. Pope Paschal is there too, holding a model of the church.

FREE Santa Pudenziana

Via Urbana 160 (06 481 4622). Metro Cavour/bus 16, 70, 71, 75, 84, 360, 649, 714. **Open** 8.30am-noon, 3-6pm Mon-Sat; 9am-noon, 3-6pm Sun. **Map** p344 C1.

Tradition says St Pudenziana was the sister of St Praxedes; their father Pudens was a senator who harboured St Peter in a house on the spot where this church now stands. A purpose-built church was constructed in the fourth century, restored in the eighth and 11th centuries and brutally remodelled in the 16th century. Still very active, the church is now used by Rome's Filipino community. Among the glowing sacred hearts, the undoubted star is the apse mosaic.

Dating from the early fifth century (although damaged in the 16th century) this is a marvellous example of the continuity between pagan and Christian art. Christ is enthroned in majesty and the apostles on either side are depicted as wealthy Roman citizens in a Roman cityscape (albeit with the symbols of the Evangelists flying over their heads). Santa Pudenziana herself is very naturalistically depicted on the right wearing a gold cloak.

COLLE OPPIO

The serene, green Colle Oppio was the site of Nero's **Domus Aurea**, an all-too-vivid reminder of the hated emperor that was torn down, filled in and replaced with bath complexes, first by Titus (on the south-west side of today's park) and later Trajan (on the northern side). On via Terme di Traiano is a structure – closed to the public – called the *Sette sale* (seven rooms), which was in fact a nine-chamber water tank estimated to have held eight million litres of water. Nowadays the lower reaches of the Colle Oppio park, towards via Labicana, are peopled by swarms of Roman mums and their toddlers during the day. A string of unpleasant incidents involving far-right local youths, homeless immigrants and a sprinkling of the city's foolhardy cruisers has resulted in the park being firmly locked after darkness falls.

On the western slope, **San Pietro in Vincoli** (*see p136*) contains important relics and a mighty Michelangelo. Further north, on the border with Monti, the church of **Santi Silvestro e Martino ai Monti** (*see p136*) stands above a Roman house. Nearby, on via Merulana, the **Museo Nazionale d'Arte Orientale** (*see below*) provides an exotic break from ancient Rome.

Domus Aurea (Golden House)

Via della Domus Aurea (06 3996 7700). Metro Colosseo/bus 60Exp, 75, 81, 85, 87, 117, 175, 186, 204, 673, 810, 850/tram 3. **Open** closed to the public. **Map** p344 C2.
Note: Before planning a special trip here, call ahead to check the site is open as crumbling masonry has shut it down in both 2005 and early 2010 and visits have been affected. There may also be tours available of unaffected areas.

In the summer of AD 64 fire devastated a large part of central Rome. (Some blame Nero for setting the blaze intentionally – *see also p139* **Profile** – but fire was a real risk and a common occurrence.) The ashes of patrician palaces mingled with those of slums. Afterwards, anything in the area east of the Forum left unsinged was knocked down to make way for a home fit for the sun-god that Nero liked to imagine he was.

Work began on the emperor's Domus Aurea (Golden House) immediately after the fire had died down. A three-storey structure, its main façade faced south and was entirely clad in gold; inside, every inch not faced with mother-of-pearl or inlaid with gems was frescoed by Nero's pet aesthete Fabullus. Fountains squirted perfumes, and baths could be filled with sea or mineral water. In one room, Suetonius claimed, an immense ceiling painted with the sun, stars and signs of the zodiac revolved constantly, keeping time with the heavens. Lakes were dug, forests planted and a 35m-high (116ft) gilded bronze statue of Nero erected.

After Nero's death in AD 68, a *damnatio memoriae* was issued and work was begun to eradicate every vestige of the hated tyrant. Vespasian drained the lake to build his amphitheatre (the tight-fisted emperor kept Nero's colossus, simply putting a new head on it, and so the stadium became known as the Colosseum), and Trajan used the brickwork as a foundation for his baths. So thorough was the cover-up job that for decades after the house's frescoes were rediscovered in 1480, no one realised it was the Domus Aurea that they had stumbled across. The frescoed 'grottoes' became an obligatory stopover for Renaissance artists, inspiring – among other things – Raphael's weird and wonderful frescoes in the Vatican (and also giving us the word 'grotesque'). The artists' signatures can still be seen scratched into the ancient stucco.

Museo Nazionale d'Arte Orientale

Via Merulana 248 (06 469 748). Bus 16, 85, 87, 714, 810, 850/tram 3. **Open** 9am-2pm Mon, Wed, Fri; 9am-7pm Tue, Thur, Sat, Sun. **Admission** €6; €3 reductions. **No credit cards**. **Map** p344 D2.
If you've had enough of ancient and papal Rome, try this impressive collection of Oriental art, in a dusty palazzo near Santa Maria Maggiore. It's arranged geographically and roughly chronologically. First are ancient artefacts from the Near East – pottery, gold, votive offerings – some from the third millennium BC. Then come 11th- to 18th-century painted fans from Tibet, sacred sculptures, and some Chinese pottery from the 15th century. Perhaps most unusual are artefacts from the Swat culture, from Italian-funded excavations in Pakistan.

INSIDE TRACK
VILLA PERETTI

All that remains of the glorious **Villa Peretti** estate, residence of Cardinal Felice Peretti who became Pope Sixtus V in 1585, is the name of the street in front of Palazzo Massimo alle Terme.

Extra Time

● The basilica of **Santa Maria degli Angeli** (piazza della Repubblica), which Michelangelo ingeniously 'dropped' into the massive ruins of the Baths of Diocletian (*see p141*), is one of the city's grandest churches. It is also famous for Clement XI's magnificent 45-metre-long (148 feet) bronze meridian (1702), which runs across the marble floor, marking the zodiac signs of the constellations and, importantly, the exact point of the spring equinox, from which the date of Easter (first Sunday after the first full moon following the spring equinox) was calculated. Until 1870, all clocks in Rome took their cue from this sophisticated time-piece.

● The **Tempio di Minerva Medica** (via Giolitti) is one of the landmarks you see from the train as you approach Termini railway station. The much-engraved ruin owes its name to the statue of a goddess that was found here, although it has long been established that the building was never a temple at all but a third-century dining pavilion of an extensive garden complex belonging to the Licinii family, which had produced Emperor Gallienus.

As the trains hurtle by it's difficult to imagine the emperor holding summer court here.

● Just by the Tempio di Minerva Medica, and equally unexpected in this scene of urban desolation, is the little church of **Santa Bibiana** (St Vivian; via Giolitti 154), who was martyred on this spot. The fifth-century church was rebuilt in 1625 by Gian Lorenzo Bernini, who also carved the statue of the saint in the niche over the altar. Frescoes are by Agostino Ciampelli (on the right) and Pietro da Cortona (left).

● When things were at their most violent in medieval Rome, rival clans took to their towers and pulled up the ladders. By the 13th century, when anarchy had reached its peak, the city bristled with over 200 towers. Of these, about a dozen remain; half are in Monti. The **Torre dei Conti**, erected in 1203, stands skyscraper-close to the famous **Torre delle Milizie** (*see p66*). Another pair of towers – built by the Graziani and Capocci families – stands in piazza San Martino ai Monti. The **Torre dei Margani** was transformed into the belfry of the church of San Francesco di Paola (piazza San Francesco di Paola 10).

FREE San Pietro in Vincoli

Piazza di San Pietro in Vincoli 4A (06 9784 4952). Metro Cavour/bus 16, 70, 71, 75, 84, 360, 649, 714. **Open** 8am-noon, 3-6pm daily. **Map** p344 C2.

First mentioned in 431, the church was rebuilt in 439 by Sixtus III with backing from Emperor Valentian III's wife Eudoxia, and dedicated to Saints Peter and Paul. In 442 Eudoxia gave Pope Leo I the chains that had held Peter in prison in Jerusalem; he put them together with the chains that had bound the saint at the Carcere Mamertino (*see p60*), whereupon they miraculously fused. It was only in the 11th century, however, that Gregory VII changed the dedication to St Peter *ad vinculum* – in chains. The church was repaired in the 15th century, and then modified and restored in the 19th.

The chains are in a reliquary beneath the high altar and are the objective of the pilgrims who flock to the church. Secular tourists head for the funerary monument of Pope Julius II with Michelangelo's imposing *Moses* (c1513) as its central figure. Julius had wanted an enormous sepulchre with 40 life-size statues in a vast free-standing architectural framework. The proposed scale of the tomb was one of the reasons for the rebuilding of St Peter's, but it quickly became clear that neither the tomb nor the basilica would be finished before the sickly pope expired. So Julius shifted Michelangelo to work on another pet

project: redecorating the cracked ceiling in the Sistine Chapel. After the completion of the ceiling Michelangelo went back to work on the tomb, but seven months later syphilis got the better of Julius and the tomb was put on a back-burner. This considerably abbreviated version was cobbled together by Michelangelo's pupils. The magnificent *Moses* (horned, from an archaic mistranslation of an Old Testament phrase really meaning 'with light emanating from his head') dominates the composition. The master's hand can be seen in the statues of Leah and Rachel to either side of the patriarch. After a recent restoration, experts came to the conclusion that he may have carved the pope's head too, although he clearly had nothing to do with the rest of poor Julius, which is by Maso del Bosco. When completed, the monument was placed here where Julius had been titular cardinal. His body ended up in an unmarked grave across the river in the Vatican.

FREE Santi Silvestro e Martino ai Monti

Viale del Monte Oppio 28 (06 478 4701). Metro Cavour or Vittorio/bus 16, 70, 71, 75, 84, 360, 649, 714. **Open** *Church* 7.30-11.30am, 4-6.30pm Mon-Sat; 7.30am-noon, 3.30-7pm Sun. *Titulus by appointment only* 9.30-11.30am Thur. **Admission** *Church* free. *Titulus* donation expected. **Map** p344 D2.

The first church on this site was founded by St Sylvester in the fourth century. It was in that earlier church in 325 that the findings of the Council of Nicea (which established God the Father and Christ as one and the same) were presented to Constantine: the event is commemorated in the fresco on the left as you enter. The church was rebuilt in the ninth century and remodelled c1650. On the far left and right of the left-hand aisle, two frescoes show respectively San Giovanni in Laterano (*see p131*) as it was before Borromini's changes and the interior of the original St Peter's. On the wall of the right-hand aisle, the mid 17th-century frescoes by pioneering landscape artist Gaspard Dughet caught the eye of many a Roman aristocrat, sparking the fashion for landscaped rooms in grand residences such as *palazzi* Colonna (*see p69*) and Doria Pamphilj (*see p100*). Beneath the ninth-century church is a third-century *titulus* (Roman house used as a place of worship); if you're here on a Thursday morning, ask the sacristan to unlock the gate for you. It's a spooky place, littered with bits of sculpture, decaying mosaics and frescoes. But it doesn't have the usual jungle of newer foundations sunk through Roman brickwork, so it's not difficult to picture this as an ancient dwelling and/or place of worship.

▶ *In case you have some time to kill in this part of town, we have listed a selection of additional sights; see p136* **Extra Time**.

ESQUILINO

If you've come to Rome on a budget package or picked up a last-minute deal, chances are you'll end up in a hotel on the Esquilino, around Termini railway station. Despite assurances from local authorities that the area is on the up, the Esquilino's grimy *palazzi* and after-dark characters may not be what you expected of the Eternal City. But the Esquilino's charms and attractions are many.

The ancient ruins and Renaissance villas that dotted the area were swept away, and a whole new city-within-a-city built in the grid mode favoured by the Torinese planners who followed Italy's new royal family from the north after Italian Unification in the 1870s. **Piazza Vittorio Emanuele II** – the city's biggest square and always known simply as piazza Vittorio – was the new capital's showcase residential area. From optimistic beginnings the once-proud *palazzi* saw a steady decline into characterless slumhood. In the 1980s the first arrivals of a multi-ethnic community settled in the area, injecting life and colour, but no prosperity, into the run-down streets around the square. The noisy, smelly and characterful market that once occupied the pavements around the garden at the centre of the square was moved in 2002 into more salubrious covered quarters in a former army barracks

in via Lamarmora. The piazza's shady central gardens have been valiantly brought back into play. In the gardens, have a go at breaking the still-encoded recipe for changing base metal into gold on the **Porta Magica** in the northern corner; this curious door, with hermetic inscriptions dating from 1688, is all that remains of the Villa Palombara, an estate that once occupied this site. The gardens' benches are taken over by assorted down-at-heel immigrants who clearly haven't cracked the code.

North-west of the piazza, **Santa Maria Maggiore** (*see p140*) is one of the four patriarchal basilicas, and has splendid mosaics.

Due north of piazza Vittorio is **Termini railway station**. The railway reached Termini (the name comes from the nearby Terme di Diocleziano, and has nothing to do with its being a terminus) in the 1860s. The first station (1864-71) was demolished to make way for what is one of Italy's most remarkable modern buildings, a triumph of undulating horizontal geometry. Architect Angiolo Mazzoni designed the lateral wings, complete with tubular towers of metaphysical grace straight out of a De Chirico painting; building began in 1937 as a key part of feverish preparations for the Fascist Universal Expo planned for 1942 (World War II stymied the Expo). In 1947 a judging commission hedged its bets by selecting two projects in a competition for

Piazza Vittorio Emanuele II.

SIGHTS

the design for a new main station building. Despite the compromise, the result is staggering. The great reinforced concrete 'wave' was completed in time for the 1950 Holy Year. In the late '90s the station – and piazza del Cinquecento with its bus terminus – underwent a major facelift but the whole area remains less than charming. Pass through piazza del Cinquecento as dusk approaches and you'll see swirling clouds of starlings driven to insanity by the constant light and diesel fumes: the nitrogen-rich stench whenever it rains is a clue to watch your head.

Proximity to the railway terminus made the surrounding area particularly interesting to developers. Architect Gaetano Koch designed a ministerial and administrative district, focusing on the semicircular arcaded **piazza della Repubblica** (1888), once the exedra (anteroom) of the massive **Terme di Diocleziano** bath complex (*see p141*) and still frequently referred to as piazza Esedra by locals.

This heavily trafficked roundabout is the traditional starting point for many major demonstrations. The **Fontana delle naiadi** at its centre was due for unveiling in 1901, but the nudity of the art nouveau nymphs cavorting seductively with sea monsters so shocked the authorities that it was boarded up again for years. Locals, fed up with the eyesore, eventually tore the planks down – a rather undignified inauguration. Sculptor Mario

Rutelli is said to have returned to Rome once a year for the rest of his life to take his buxom models out to dinner.

The extraordinary Museo Nazionale Romano collection of ancient artefacts, which used to be confined to the Terme di Diocleziano, has spilled over into the **Palazzo Massimo alle Terme** (*see below*) on the south-east fringe of the square. To the north-west is the church of **Santa Maria della Vittoria** (*see p140*), containing one of Bernini's most extraordinary sculptures, and the **Fontana dell'Acqua Felice** (*photo p141*). Designed by Domenico Fontana in the form of a triumphal arch, this fountain was completed in 1589. It was one of many urban improvements that were commissioned in Rome by Pope Sixtus V, and provided this district with clean water from an ancient aqueduct. The statue of Moses in the central niche of the fountain, by Leonardo Sormani, has been condemned as an atrocity against taste ever since it was unveiled in 1586.

To the south-west of piazza della Repubblica, via Nazionale descends to the old centre, passing the American church of **San Paolo entro le Mura** (via Napoli 58, 06 488 3339, www.stpaulsrome.it, open 9am-4.30pm Mon-Fri), with its Arts and Crafts movement mosaics, along the way. If you've had your fill of the picturesque and need a shot of the Kafkaesque, take a look at such monolithic examples of Italian public architecture as the Interior Ministry in piazza del Viminale or the Teatro dell'Opera (*see p266*) along via Firenze.

★ Palazzo Massimo alle Terme

Largo di Villa Peretti 1 (06 480 201). Metro Repubblica/bus 16, 36, 38, 40Exp, 64, 86, 90Exp, 92, 105, 157, 170, 175, 204, 217, 310, 360, 492, 590, 649, 714, 910, C, H. **Open** 9am-7.30pm Tue-Sun. **Admission** €7; €3.50 reductions. Extra charge for exhibitions. **No credit cards.** **Map** p341 D5.

Part of the Museo Nazionale Romano collection, Palazzo Massimo has a basement diplay of coins from Roman times to the euro. On the ground and first floors are busts of emperors, their families and lesser mortals, in chronological order (allowing you to track changing fashions in Roman hairstyles). The ground floor covers the period up to the end of the Julio-Claudian line. In Room 5 is a magnificent statue of Augustus as *pontifex maximus*. Room 7 houses the undoubted stars of the ground floor, two bronzes found on the Quirinale showing a Hellenistic hero in the triumphant pose of Hercules and an exhausted boxer.

The first floor begins with the age of Emperor Vespasian (AD 69-79); portrait busts in Room 1 show the gritty no-nonsense soldier. Room 5 has decorations from Imperial villas – statues of *Apollo* and of a young girl holding a tray of religious objects are

Terme di Diocleziano. *See p141.*

Profile Nero

Has the infamous emperor been treated unjustly?

Modern historians like to make out that Nero was a victim of bad PR: they cite the emperor's advanced views on urban planning after half of Rome burned down, his public works schemes designed to boost the deflating Roman economy, his considerable education and culture, his athleticism even.

Ancient historians – Suetonius, Tacitus and Pliny included – remember him rather differently as the megalomaniac emperor who fiddled while his city burned, and whose hobbies – other than arson – included incest, matricide and torture.

In fact, Nero didn't need PR. He was the darling of the *populus romanus*, the emperor of spin who provided first-century punters with just what they wanted: *X Factor*-style talent and poetry shows, gruesome games in the circus and breakneck Grand Prix chariot-racing. He took part in everything, and always won of course. By fair means or foul. But foul was generally Nero's way.

Infamy, infamy? Did the ancient writers just have it in for Nero? Or was he a fully fledged tyrant with a talent for grasping the zeitgeist? Hard to overlook the way he kicked his pregnant wife Poppaea until she aborted and died – but modern apologists say the poor empress probably died in childbirth. Hard too, to dismiss the cack-handed attempts to murder his ghastly mother: Agrippina managed to survive a theatrically staged shipwreck but not her own equally staged 'suicide'.

In the general run of emperors, Nero wasn't much worse than Caligula or Tiberius, Commodus or Domitian, and he was a perfect saint compared to Elagabalus. But what about his treatment of the Christians? As Romans surveyed the

smouldering ruins of their city, Nero 'spun' for all he was worth and strung the inflammatory fundamentalists up, or rather nailed them to crucifixes as human floodlights to illuminate his post-blaze *son et lumières*. The idea that Nero might have razed his own city and blamed the Christians in order to build the vastest palace of the ancient world (*see p135* **Domus Aurea**) was actually an idea that occurred later.

Suetonius says the emperor was of average height, his hair was light blond, his eyes dullish blue, his neck was squat, his belly protuberant, his legs spindly and his body pustular and malodorous. The account of Nero's imperial antics makes for grim reading, yet this hatchet job must contain a kernel of truth, and any one of the biographer's horrifying anecdotes would surely be enough to consign his subject to a well deserved Hades.

Spin? No. Black by name, black by nature. You can't rehabilitate a monster on the grounds of a bit of thoughtful urban planning.

SIGHTS

both from Nero's coastal villa at Anzio, and a gracefully crouching *Aphrodite* taking her bath is from Hadrian's Villa (*see p298*) at Tivoli. Room 6 has two discus throwers, second-century marble copies of a Greek bronze original from the fifth century BC. In Room 7 is a peacefully sleeping hermaphrodite, another second-century AD copy of a Greek original.

The real highlight of the Palazzo Massimo, though, lies on the second floor, where rare wall paintings from assorted villas have been reassembled. The spectacular fresco from the *triclinium* (dining room) of the villa of Livia shows a fruit-filled garden bustling with animal life and displays a use of perspective that was rarely seen again until the Renaissance. Another, from the *triclinium* of the Roman Villa Farnesina (in Room 3), has delicate white sketches on a black background, surmounted by scenes of courts handing down sentences that have baffled experts for centuries. Also in Room 3 is a lively naval battle, from a frescoed corridor in the same villa. The three *cubicoli* (bedrooms) in Room 5 all have decorative stuccoed ceilings.

FREE Santa Maria della Vittoria

Via XX Settembre 17 (06 4274 0571). Metro Repubblica/bus 16, 36, 38, 60Exp, 61, 62, 84, 86, 90Exp, 92, 217, 360, 910. **Open** 8.30am-noon, 3.30-6pm Mon-Sat; 3.30-6pm Sun.
Map p341 C5.

This modest-looking Baroque church, its interior cosily candlelit and adorned with marble and gilt, holds one of Bernini's most famous works. The *Ecstasy of St Teresa*, in the Cornaro chapel (the fourth on the left), shows the Spanish mystic floating on a cloud in a supposedly spiritual trance after a teasing, androgynous angel has pierced her with a burning arrow; the result is more than a little ambiguous. (Writing of the angel incident in her *Life*, Teresa recalled: 'so intense was the pain I uttered several moans; so great was the sweetness caused by the pain that I never wanted to lose it.') When the chapel is seen as a whole, with the heavens painted in the dome, the light filters through a hidden window reflecting gilded rays and bathing Teresa in a

Santa Maria della Vittoria.

heavenly glow. She is surrounded by members of the Cornaro family.
▶ *There's another of Bernini's dubiously ecstatic women in San Francesco a Ripa; see p117.*

FREE Santa Maria Maggiore

Piazza Santa Maria Maggiore (06 6988 6800/museum 06 6988 6802). Bus 16, 70, 71, 75, 84, 105, 204, 360, 590, 649, 714/tram 5, 14. **Open** *Church* 7am-7pm daily. *Museum* 9am-6pm daily. *Loggia* (booking essential, groups only) usually 9am & 1pm daily; book by phone or at the ticket office. **Admission** *Church* free. *Museum* €4; €2 reductions. *Loggia* €5. **No credit cards.**
Map p341 D6.

Behind this blowsy Baroque façade is one of the most striking basilica-form churches in Rome. Local tradition says a church was built on this spot in c366; documents place it almost 100 years later. The fifth-century church was first extended in the 13th century, then again prior to the 1750 Holy Year, when Ferdinando Fuga redid the interior and attached the façade that we see today. Inside, a flat-roofed nave shoots between two aisles to a triumphal arch and

---

INSIDE TRACK
THE OTHER JULIUS' LEGACY

Julius' unfinished monumental tomb may have been stashed away in a small church far from the seats of power, but this pope – known as 'il papa terribile' (the fearsome pope) – left his mark on the Vatican in other ways. It was Julius who commissioned Michelangelo to decorate the ceiling of the Sistine Chapel (*see p148*), and who founded the Swiss Guard to protect the pope's person.

apse. Above the columns of the nave, heavily restored fifth-century mosaics show scenes from the Old Testament. There ar also thirteenth-century mosaics in the apse by Jacopo Torriti, which show Mary, dressed as a Byzantine empress, being crowned Queen of Heaven by Christ.

The Virgin theme continues in fifth-century mosaics on the triumphal arch. The ceiling in the main nave is said to have been made from the first shipment of gold extracted from the Americas by Ferdinand and Isabella of Spain, and was presented to the church by the Borgia Pope Alexander VI. The Borgias' heraldic device of a bull is very much in evidence. In the 16th and 17th centuries two incredibly flamboyant chapels were added. The first was the Cappella Sistina (last chapel on the right of the nave), designed by Domenico Fontana for Sixtus V (1585-90), and decorated with multicoloured marble, gilt and precious stones. Directly opposite is the Cappella Paolina, an even gaudier Greek-cross chapel, designed in 1611 by Flaminio Ponzio for Paul V to house an icon of the Madonna (dating from the ninth, or possibly the 12th, century) on its altar.

To the right of the main altar a plaque marks the burial place of Rome's great Baroque genius, Gian Lorenzo Bernini. In the loggia, high up on the front of the church (book tours in advance; notes are provided in English), are glorious 13th-century mosaics that decorated the façade of the old basilica, showing the legend of the foundation of the church. The lower row shows Mary appearing to Giovanni the Patrician, who, with Pope Liberius, then sketches the plan for the basilica. The legend goes that the Virgin told Giovanni to build a church on the spot where snow would fall the next morning. The snow fell on 5 August 352, a miracle that is commemorated on that day every year, when thousands of flower petals are released from the roof of the church in the Festa della Madonna delle Neve (*see p243*). The Cappella Paolina also contains a relief (1612) by Stefano Maderno showing Liberius tracing the plan of the basilica in the snow.

Terme di Diocleziano

Via Enrico De Nicola 79 (06 3996 7700).
Metro Repubblica/bus 36, 38, 40Exp, 64, 86,
90Exp, 92, 105, 157, 170, 175, 217, 310, 714,
910. **Open** 9am-7.30pm Tue-Sun. **Admission** €7; €3.50 reductions. **No credit cards**. **Map** p341 D5.

Part of the Museo Nazionale Romano, Diocletian's baths were the largest in Rome when they were built in AD 298-306, able to accommodate 3,000 people at a time. For an idea of the immense size of the structure, tour the remaining fragments: the tepidarium and part of the central hall are in Santa Maria degli Angeli (*see p136* **Extra Time**); a circular hall can be seen in San Bernardo alle Terme (piazza San Bernardo); and the Aula Ottagona (octagonal hall) – which used to house Rome's planetarium and now is occasionally used for exhibitions – is in via Romita.

A convent complex was built around the largest surviving chunk of the baths by Michelangelo in the 1560s: it now contains inscriptions and other items from the Museo Nazionale Romano ancient artefacts collection, including some of the hut-shaped funerary urns found in Lazio, which give an idea of what eighth-century BC houses looked like.

Fontana dell'Acqua Felice. *See p138.*

The Vatican & Prati

Home to the Pope.

SIGHTS

It goes without saying that no visit to Rome is complete without a trip to the Vatican City – the world's smallest state – home to St Peter's and the Vatican Museums. Once part of an area of marshland (stretching from the Gianicolo to modern-day Monte Mario), the Vatican now attracts huge crowds of worshippers to St Peter's square when the Pope is in Rome (see below for tourist information, useful visiting info and dress codes). Its half a square kilometre area also contains one of the world's finest collections of art and antiquities, including the largest array of pagan and non-Christian works.

The bourgeois district of Prati (meaning meadows) offers a pleasing antidote to all that history and culture with its excellent shopping and pleasantly quiet streets.

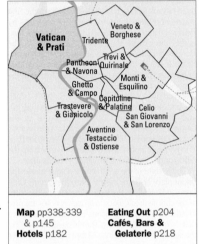

Map pp338-339 & p145	Eating Out p204
	Cafés, Bars &
Hotels p182	Gelaterie p218

HISTORY

Once the *Ager* or *Campus vaticanus* was marshland lying between the Monti Vaticani and the Tiber, across the river from the city centre and known mainly for its poor-quality wine. Then, in the first century AD, the mad, bad Emperor Caligula decided it would be a good spot for a circus and a practice-ground for the most glamorous of sports, chariot-racing.

Nero completed Caligula's circus in AD 54 and built a bridge, the Pons Neronianus, to connect it with the centre. In the summer of AD 64, a fire destroyed half of the city. When people starting muttering that Nero was the fire-setter, he in turn blamed the Christians – and the persecution of this pesky new cult began in earnest. Nero's circus was the main venue for Christian-baiting: legend says they were covered in tar and burned alive here. Top apostle Peter is traditionally believed to have been crucified in the circus then buried close by on the spot where, 250 years later, in AD 326, Constantine built the first church of St Peter.

Not all of the following 264 popes resided here – they began in the Lateran (*see p131* **San Giovanni in Laterano**), in fact, before history drove them to many other places, including Viterbo (*see p293* **Historic Viterbo**), Anagni (south of Rome) and Avignon, France – but throughout the Christian era, pilgrims have continued to flock to the tomb of the founder of the Roman Church.

All around, the **Borgo** grew up to service the burgeoning Dark Age tourist industry. Pope Leo IV (847-55) enclosed the Borgo with the 12-metre-high (40 feet) Leonine Wall, following a series of Saracen and Lombard raids. Pope Nicholas III (1277-80) extended the walls and provided a papal escape route, linking the Vatican to the impregnable Castel Sant'Angelo by way of a long *passetto* (covered walkway). He never used his getaway, but Clement VII did, in 1527, during fierce fighting with the troops of Emperor Charles V. The nine-month siege and Sack of Rome was a watershed: things in the papal stronghold were never the same again. Almost the whole papal army was slaughtered, the city was burned and looted, and the Sistine Chapel was used as a stables by the Protestant mercenaries – their graffiti in the Papal Suite (*see p149* **Stanze di Raffaello**) is still visible.

Basilica

After Paul III got Michelangelo in to build bigger, better walls, the popes withdrew back across town to the old Lateran palace, and then to the grand new Quirinal palace (*see p72*), where they stayed until the troubles of 1870 forced them back across the Tiber once more.

THE VATICAN

In 1870, when Italian troops breached Rome's walls at Porta Pia, centuries of rule by the occupant of the throne of St Peter were put to an end. Over the years, foreign despots had been either seen off or paid off but in 1870 it all went wrong: the pope lost control of a vast part of central Italy and was ignominiously forced back into the Vatican palace behind the hefty walls. Between 1870 and 1929 the pope pronounced the Italian state to be sacrilegious and national elections to be illegal. Something had to be done, and on 11 February 1929 Pius XII and Mussolini signed the Lateran Pacts, a treaty designed to sort out the status of the Vatican once and for all. The terms of the reconciliation treaty (*La Conciliazione*) awarded the Church a huge cash payment, tax-free status and a constitutional role that led to an important continuing moral influence over future legislation on social issues such as education and divorce. To commemorate the historic agreement, Mussolini decided to demolish a particularly picturesque part of the medieval Borgo, replacing it with a short but 'modern' approach road to St Peter's: via della Conciliazione.

The Vatican City occupies an area of less than half a square kilometre, making it the smallest state in the world. Despite having fewer than 800 residents, it has its own diplomatic service, postal service, army (the Swiss Guard), heliport, railway station, supermarket, and radio and TV stations. It has observer status at the UN, and issues its own stamps and currency (Vatican euros have a tiny circulation; the Holy See keeps a few collectors happy with occasional issues of coins that increase exponentially in value).

PAPAL AUDIENCES

The pope plays an active role in Rome's religious life. When he is in town, crowds gather in St Peter's square at noon on Sunday to hear him address pilgrims from the window of his study in the Apostolic Palace. On Wednesday mornings he holds a general audience in St Peter's square, if the weather

SIGHTS

INSIDE TRACK
THE DAN BROWN EFFECT

Queues have always been part and parcel of a visit to the **Vatican Museums** (*see p148*), but these days, it's worse than ever. Avoid Saturdays, Mondays and days after public and religious holidays and instead try Wednesdays at 10.30am – when many have piled into St Peter's square for the papal audience.

Vatican Essentials

It pays to be prepared.

Remember

● Entrances to St Peter's basilica and to the Vatican Museums are in separate places and involve two lengthy queues, as well as a ten-minute hike around the outside of the Vatican walls to get from one to the other. You can significantly cut your waiting times by booking a ticket and/or a tour of the museums online (mv.vatican.va) up to 60 days before your visit.

● Since the post-9/11 introduction of security checks at St Peter's, the queue to enter the basilica is almost always daunting, sometimes wrapping itself most of the way around Bernini's colonnade. Take comfort in the fact that the queue moves reasonably swiftly. But before you join it, (1) make sure you're not going to be turned away once you get there because you're unsuitably dressed (no shorts, very short skirts, or bare midriffs or shoulders)

and (2) bear in mind that the doors close at the advertised times, no matter how many people are waiting outside.

Must-haves

● Sensible shoes: absolutely essential if you are to attempt the ascent of the dome, as the 320 marble stairs after you emerge from the lift are very slippery.

● Water: only the Galleria degli Arazzi and the Sistine Chapel are air-conditioned and people have been known to keel over in the summer. There's also a shortage of toilets.

● Binoculars: a good idea for looking at the details of frescoes in the Sistine Chapel, as well as for appreciating the view if you're planning an ascent of the dome.

● A museum guide book or audio guide (€7 from the desk after the ticket barrier): these are possibly the worst labelled museums anywhere.

is fine; if the weather isn't good, it's in the modern Sala Nervi audience hall.

Outside, you can join the back of the crowd and watch the goings-on on a big screen. If you want to be close up to the pope, or attend an audience in the Sala Nervi, apply well in advance to the Prefettura della Casa Pontificia for tickets (06 6988 3114, 06 6988 3273, fax 06 6988 5863, open 9am-1.30pm Mon-Sat), which are free and can be picked up on the morning of the audience. Entry is through the bronze door, just to the left of the basilica.

VATICAN GARDENS

The Vatican walls surround splendid formal gardens, which can be glimpsed from some windows in the Vatican Museums or visited on guided tours (€31, €25 reductions; includes admission to Vatican Museums) which must be booked at least one week in advance either at the Vatican tourist office (*see p318*) or through the biglietteriamusei.vatican.va website .

TOURIST INFORMATION

The Vatican's tourist information office (06 6988 1662, open 8.30am-6.30pm Mon-Sat), situated on the left of St Peter's square as you face the basilica, dispenses information, organises guided tours, has a bureau de change, offers postal and philatelic services, and sells souvenirs and publications. The number of the Vatican switchboard is 06 6982; the general Vatican website, with information on papal

activities, church business and museums and so on is www.vatican.va; www.vaticanstate.va has information about the Holy See in general.

DRESS CODE

The Vatican enforces its dress code strictly, both in St Peter's and in the Vatican Museums. Anyone wearing shorts or a short skirt, or with bare shoulders or midriff, will be turned away.

★ St Peter's

Piazza San Pietro (06 6988 1662). Metro Ottaviano/ bus 23, 40Exp, 62, 64. **No credit cards.** **Map** p145 & off p339 A4/5.

Basilica: **Open** *Apr-Sept* 7am-7pm daily. *Oct-Mar* 7am-6.30pm daily. **Admission** free. Audio guide (€4) available at cloakroom after the security check.

Dome: **Open** *Apr-Sept* 8am-6pm daily. *Oct-Mar* 8am-5pm daily. **Admission** €5. *With lift* €7. **Note:** there are 320 steps to climb after the lift has taken you to the first level.

Grottoes: **Open** *Apr-Sept* 7am-6pm daily. *Oct-Mar* 7am-5pm daily. **Admission** free.

Necropolis: Apply at the *Ufficio degli Scavi (06 6988 5318, fax 06 6987 3017, scavi@fsp.va).* **Open** *Guided tours* 9am-5pm Mon-Sat. **Admission** €12. English-language tours must be booked at least 25 days in advance, though if you're in Rome without a reservation it's always worth asking at the *Ufficio* *degli Scavi* (beyond the Swiss Guard post on the left of St Peter's as you face the basilica) for any spaces. Under-12s are not admitted; 12- to 15-year-olds must be accompanied by an adult.

Treasury Museum: **Open** *Apr-Sept* 9am-6.15pm daily. *Oct-Mar* 9am-5.15pm daily. **Admission** €6; €4 children.

After 120 years as a building site, the current St Peter's was consecrated on 18 November 1626 by Urban VIII – exactly 1,300 years after the consecration of the first basilica on the site.

The earlier building was a five-aisled classical basilica, fronted by a large courtyard and four porticoes. Enlarged and enriched, it became the finest church in Christendom. By the mid 15th century, however, its south wall was collapsing. Pope Nicholas V had 2,500 wagonloads of masonry from the Colosseum carted across the Tiber, just for running repairs. No one wanted to take responsibility for demolishing Christianity's most sacred church. It took the arrogance of Pope Julius II and his pet architect Donato Bramante to get things moving. In 1506 some 2,500 workers tore down the 1,000-year-old basilica, and Julius laid the foundation stone for its replacement.

Following Bramante's death in 1514, Raphael took over the work and scrapped his predecessor's design for a basilica with a Greek-cross plan, opting for an elongated Latin cross. In 1547 Michelangelo took command and reverted to a Greek cross. He died in 1564, aged 87, but not before coming up with a plan for a massive dome and supporting drum. This was completed in 1590, the largest brick dome ever constructed, and still the tallest point of any building in Rome. In 1607 Carlo Maderno won the consent of Pope Paul V to demolish the remaining fragments of the old basilica and put up a new façade, crowned by enormous statues of Christ and the apostles.

After Maderno's death Bernini took over and, despite nearly destroying both the façade and his reputation by erecting towers on either end (one of which fell down), he became the hero of the hour with his sumptuous *baldacchino* and elliptical piazza. This latter was built between 1656 and 1667, its colonnaded arms reaching out towards the Catholic world in a symbolic embrace. The oval measures 340 by 240 metres (1,115 by 787 feet), and is punctuated by the central Egyptian obelisk (erected by a workforce of 800 in 1586) and two symmetrical fountains by Maderno and Bernini. The 284-column, 88-pillar colonnade is topped by 140 statues of saints.

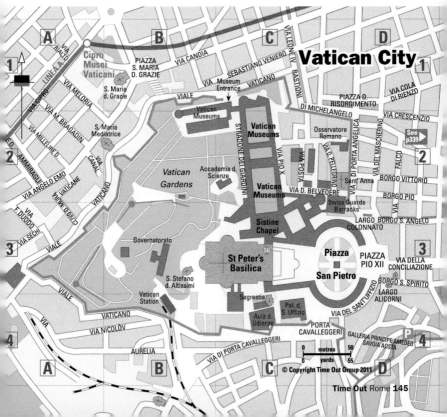

In the portico (1612), opposite the main portal, is a mosaic by Giotto (c1298) from the original basilica. Five doors lead into the basilica: the central ones come from the earlier church, while the others are all 20th-century. The last door on the right is opened only in Holy Years by the pope himself (and, as seen from the inside, is firmly cemented shut).

Inside, the basilica's size is emphasised on the marble floor, where a boastful series of brass lines measure the lengths of other churches around the world that haven't made the grade (second longest is St Paul's, London). But it is Bernini's vast *baldacchino* (1633), hovering over the high altar, that is the real focal point. Cast from bronze purloined from the Pantheon by Bernini's patron, Pope Urban VIII, of the Barberini family, it prompted local wits to quip *'quod non fecerunt barbari, fecerunt Barberini'* ('what the barbarians didn't do, the Barberini did'). An extraordinary piece of Baroque design, it takes its form from a Mesopotamian tradition in which woven silken cloth was draped over a framework to mark a sacred spot. In Bernini's hands it became a hundred feet of gilded bronze. The canopy stands over the high altar officially reserved for the Pope; below, two flights of stairs lead beneath the altar to the *confessio*, where a niche contains a ninth-century mosaic of Christ, the only thing from old St Peter's that stayed in the same place when the new church was built. Far below lies the site of what is believed to be St Peter's tomb, discovered in 1951.

Pilgrims head straight for the last pilaster on the right before the main altar, to kiss the big toe of

Vatican Museums. See p148.

Arnolfo da Cambio's brass statue of St Peter (c1296), worn down by centuries of pious lips, or to say a prayer before the crystal casket containing the mummified remains of much-loved Pope John XXIII, who was beatified in 2002. Tourists, on the other hand, make a beeline for the first chapel on the right, where Michelangelo's first major work, the *Pietà* (1499), is found. He signed his name on the thin sash across the Virgin's chest in response to cynics who claimed that he was too young at 25 to have produced the piece himself. The statue's position behind bullet-proof glass means the signature is only visible with strong binoculars or on postcards. Proceeding around the basilica in an anti-clockwise direction, notice Carlo Fontana's highly flattering monument to the unprepossessing Queen Christina of Sweden, a convert to Catholicism in 1655, to the left of the *Pietà* chapel. The third chapel has a tabernacle and two angels by Bernini, plus St Peter's only remaining painting: a *Trinity* by Pietro da Cortona (the others have been replaced by mosaic copies). In the first chapel beyond the right transept is a tear-jerker of a neo-classical tomb (1792), the last resting place of Pope Clement XIII, by Antonio Canova.

Bernini's Throne of St Peter (1665), flanked by papal tombs, stands at the far end of the nave beyond the high altar, under a stained-glass window. Encased within Bernini's creation is a wood and ivory chair, probably dating from the ninth century but for many years believed to have belonged to Peter himself. To the right of the throne is Bernini's 1644 monument to his patron Urban VIII, who commissioned the bronze portrait (between statues of *Charity* and *Justice*) before his death. On the pillars supporting the main dome are much-venerated relics, including a chip off the True Cross above the statue of St Helena bearing the cross she is said to have brought back from the Holy Land.

In the left aisle, beyond the pilaster with St Veronica holding the cloth with which she wiped Christ's face, Bernini's tomb for Pope Alexander VII (another of his patrons) shows the pope seated above a doorway shrouded with a cloth of reddish marble, from beneath which struggles a skeleton clutching an hour-glass: a grim reminder of the fleeting nature of life.

Near the portico end of the left aisle is a group of monuments to the Old Pretender James Edward Stuart (the 18th-century claimant to the throne of England and Scotland, here called King James III), his wife Maria Clementina Sobieski and their sons Charles Edward (Bonnie Prince Charlie) and Henry Benedict. They are buried in the grottoes below.

Beneath the basilica are the Vatican Grottoes – Renaissance crypts containing papal tombs. The Necropolis, where St Peter is said to be buried, lies under the grottoes. The small treasury museum off the left nave of the basilica contains some stunning liturgical relics. The dome, reached via hundreds of stairs (there's a cramped lift as far as the basilica roof), offers fabulous views of the Vatican gardens.

Profile BXVI

The real Ratzinger.

The election of Joseph Aloisius Ratzinger as Pope Benedict XVI in April 2005 was not greeted with unmitigated delight. While traditionalists were pleased to see this bastion of orthodoxy elevated to the throne of St Peter's, the forward-looking Catholic masses bridled at the snub: at 78, and with a long record as the champion of ridigity as head of the Congregation for the Doctrine of the Faith (the ex-Inquisition), Ratzinger was definitely not the man who would pilot an updated Church into the 21st century.

Neither camp, however, has had their expectations wholly fulfilled.

This small, scholarly man – an intellectual power-house and one of the greatest living theologians – suffered from day one from comparisons with his telegenic, media-manipulating predecessor, John Paul II. Even five years into his papacy, Benedict had failed to understand the impact of the sound-bite, remaining incredulous that an unappreciative international press could possibly fail to read and digest the pope's long, complex arguments to their theologically perfect conclusions.

His (or his PR minders') handling of such issues as priestly child abuse has also been breathtakingly insensitive at times. And his come-hither welcome to Anglican clergy willing to defect over the ordination of women bishops has hardly helped ecumenism.

Yet the image of Benedict in Istanbul's Blue Mosque in 2006, praying alongside Muslim clerics, remains a milestone in inter-faith tolerance. And his 2010 crack – a tiny one, but there nonetheless – in the unyielding Catholic ban on the use of contraception was a true shocker for his more hide-bound supporters.

The real Ratzinger, papal fans say, is anything but the icy ivory-tower intellectual. His relationship with parishioners as cardinal in his titular parish in the Rome suburbs was warm and caring, locals say. The piano-playing pope's love for Mozart (whose music, Benedict has been quoted as saying 'contains the whole tragedy of human existence') is matched by his love of cats. His pontifical fashion statements – the resurrection of the ermine-lined *camauro* cap, his natty red shoes (not, Vatican officials say, by Prada but close observers have their suspicions…) and cool Gucci shades – show that his mind isn't exclusively on knotty problems of dogma.

A polyglot – he speaks six languages and understands several more – Benedict pulls the same kind of multilingual stunts in his papal audiences as JPII used to woo the crowds. Yet for solace in his rare moments of privacy he has opted for the companionship of a fellow-German, his private secretary 'gorgeous' Georg Gänswein.

A pilot, tennis player and skier, stylish Don Giorgio combines pope-pleasing intellectual rigour with the action-man image Benedict has never had – and, according to Donatella Versace, he inspired her 2008 men's fashion line.

SIGHTS

SIGHTS

INSIDE TRACK
THE POPE IN PRIVATE

For a audience with the Pope, your local bishop has to make a written request, which can take a year to be granted.

Vatican Museums (Musei vaticani)

Viale del Vaticano (06 6988 3860, mv.vatican.va). Metro Ottaviano or Cipro-Musei Vaticani/bus 23, 32, 34, 49, 81, 492/tram 19. **Open** 9am-6pm Mon-Sat; 9am-2pm last Sun of each month. Closed Catholic holidays. **Admission** €15; €8 reductions. Free on last Sun of month. **Credit** MC, V. **Map** p145.

It's a brisk ten-minute walk around the Vatican walls from St Peter's to the Vatican Museums. Note that you can reduce the wait to get into the museums by pre-booking tickets and tours through the website. The ticket office shuts two hours before closing time.

Begun by Pope Julius II in 1503, this immense collection represents the accumulated fancies and obsessions of a long line of strong, often contradictory personalities. The popes' unique position allowed them to obtain treasures on favourable terms from other collectors, and artists often had little choice as to whether they accepted papal commissions.

One-way routes cater for anything from a dash to the Sistine Chapel to a five-hour plod around the lot. There are also a number of itineraries for wheelchair users, with facilities en route. Wheelchairs can be borrowed at the museum: book them by fax (06 6988 5100) or email (accoglienza.musei@scv.va). The following are selected highlights.

Appartamento Borgia

This six-room suite, known as the Borgia Rooms, was adapted for the Borgia Pope Alexander VI (1492-1503) and decorated by Pinturicchio with a series of frescoes on biblical and classical themes.

Cappella Sistina (Sistine Chapel)

The world's most famous frescoes cover the ceiling and one immense wall of the Cappella Sistina, built for Sixtus IV in 1473-84. For centuries it has been used for papal elections. In the 1980s and '90s, the 930 sq m (10,000 sq ft) of *Creation* – on the ceiling – and the *Last Judgment* – on the wall behind the altar – were subjected to the most controversial restoration job of all time. The result is very blue.

In 1508 Michelangelo was commissioned to paint a simple decoration on the ceiling of the Sistine Chapel. Julius II may have been egged on to employ a sculptor with no experience in fresco by his architect Bramante, who was jealous of the pope's admiration for Michelangelo and desperately wanted to see him fail. Michelangelo responded by offering to do far more than mere decoration, and embarked upon his massive venture alone. He spent the next four and a half years standing (only Charlton Heston lay down)

on 18m-high (60ft) scaffolding with paint and plaster dripping into his eyes. Despite a fairly handsome payment (in four years he earned as much as a regular artist could expect to earn in 15), he complained to his brother in 1511, 'I could well say that I go naked and barefoot.'

The ceiling work was completed in 1512, just seven months before the death of Julius, and is exemplary of the confident pursuit of beauty at the High Renaissance. Beginning at the *Last Judgment* end, scenes depict the *Separation of Light from Darkness*, the *Creation of Sun, Moon and Planets*, the *Separation of Land and Sea* and the *Creation of Fishes and Birds*; the *Creation of Adam*, the *Creation of Eve*, the *Temptation* and *Expulsion from Paradise*; the *Sacrifice of Noah* (which should have appeared after the *Flood*, but for lack of space), the *Flood* and the *Drunkenness of Noah*. Michelangelo painted these scenes in reverse order, beginning with Noah's drunkenness. They are framed by monumental figures of Old Testament prophets and classical sibyls foretelling the birth of Christ.

Twenty-three years later, aged 60, Michelangelo was dragged back by Paul III in 1535. Between the completion of the ceiling and the beginning of the wall, Rome had suffered. From 1517, the Protestant Reformation threatened the power of the popes, and the sack of the city in 1527 was seen by Michelangelo as the wrath of God descending on the corrupt city. The *Last Judgment* dramatically reflects this gloomy and pessimistic atmosphere. Hidden among the larger-than-life figures that stare, leer and cry out from their brilliant ultramarine background, Michelangelo painted his own frowning, miserable face on the wrinkled human skin held by St Bartholomew, below and to the right of the powerful figure of Christ the Judge.

Before Michelangelo set foot in the chapel, the stars of the 1480s had created the paintings along the walls. On the left-hand wall (as you look at the *Last Judgment*) are: the *Journey of Moses* by Perugino; *Events from the Life of Moses* by Botticelli; *Crossing the Red Sea* and *Moses Receives the Tablets of the Law* by Cosimo Rosselli; *The Testament of Moses* by Luca Signorelli; and *The Dispute over Moses' Body* by Matteo da Lecce. On the right-hand wall are *The Baptism of Christ* by Perugino; *The Temptations of Christ* by Botticelli; *The Calling of the Apostles* by Ghirlandaio; *Handing over the Keys* by Perugino; *The Sermon on the Mount* and *The Last Supper* by Cosimo Rosselli; and *The Resurrection* by Hendrik van den Broeck. The portraits are by the same masters.

Galleria Chiaramonte

Founded by Pius VII in the early 19th century and laid out by the sculptor Canova, this is an eclectic collection of Roman statues, reliefs and busts. Don't miss the replica of a Greek statue by Polyeuctos of stuttering orator Demosthenes or the copy of a *Resting Satyr* by the Greek sculptor Praxiteles.

Gallerie dei Candelabri & degli Arazzi

The long gallery studded with candelabra contains Roman marble statues, while the next gallery has ten huge tapestries (*arazzi*), woven by Flemish master Pieter van Aelst from the cartoons by Raphael that are now in London's Victoria & Albert Museum.

Galleria delle Carte Geografiche

Pope Gregory XIII (who was responsible for introducing the Gregorian calendar) had a craze for astronomy, and built this 120m-long (394ft) gallery, with its Tower of the Winds observation point. Ignazio Danti of Perugia drew the maps, which were then frescoed (1580-83), and show each Italian region, city and island with extraordinary precision.

Museo Egiziano

Founded by Gregory XVI in 1839, in rooms that are partly decorated in Egyptian style, this is a representative selection of ancient Egyptian art from 3000 BC to 600 BC. It includes statues of a baboon god, painted mummy cases and a marble statue of Antinous, Emperor Hadrian's lover, who drowned in Egypt and was declared divine by the emperor. There are a couple of mummies too.

Museo Etrusco

Founded in 1837 by Gregory XVI, this collection contains Greek and Roman art as well as Etruscan masterpieces, including the contents of the Regolini-Galassi Tomb (c650 BC), the Greek-inspired fourth-century BC *Mars*, and the fifth-century BC *Young Man and Small Slave*.

Museo Paolino

This collection of Roman and neo-Attic sculpture includes the beautifully draped statue of Sophocles from Terracina, as well as a trompe l'oeil mosaic of an unswept floor and the wonderfully elaborate Altar of Vicomagistri.

Museo Pio-Clementino

In the late 18th century Pope Clement XIV and his successor Pius VI began the world's largest collection of classical statues; it now fills 16 rooms. Don't miss the first-century BC *Belvedere Torso* by Apollonius of Athens; the *Apollo Sauroctonos*, a Roman copy of the bronze *Lizard Killer* by Praxiteles; and, in the octagonal Belvedere Courtyard, the exquisite *Belvedere Apollo* and *Laocoön*, the latter being throttled by the sea serpents Athena had sent as punishment for warning the Trojans to beware of the wooden horse.

Pinacoteca

Founded by Pius VI in the late 18th century, the Pinacoteca (picture gallery) includes many of the pictures that the Vatican hierarchy managed to recover from Napoleon after their forced sojourn in France in the early 19th century. The collection ranges from early paintings of the Byzantine School and Italian primitives to 18th-century Dutch and French old masters, and includes Giotto's *Stefaneschi Triptych*; a *Pietà* by Lucas Cranach the Elder; several delicate Madonnas by Fra Filippo Lippi, Fra Angelico, Raphael and Titian; Raphael's very last work, *The Transfiguration*; Caravaggio's *Entombment*; and a chiaroscuro *St Jerome* by Leonardo da Vinci.

Pio Cristiano Museum

The upper floor of the Museo Paolino is devoted to a collection of early Christian antiquities, mostly sarcophagi carved with reliefs of biblical scenes.

Stanze di Raffaello & Cappella di Niccolò V

The Raphael Rooms were part of Nicholas V's palace, and were originally decorated by Piero della Francesca. Julius II then let Perugino and other Renaissance masters loose on them. He later discovered Raphael, and gave the 26-year-old *carte blanche* to redesign four rooms of the Papal Suite. The order of the visit changes from time to time; if possible, try to see the rooms in the order in which they were painted. The Study (Stanza della Segnatura) was the first one Raphael tackled (1508-11), and features philosophical and spiritual themes – the triumph of Truth, Good and Beauty. Best known is the star-packed *School of Athens* fresco, with contemporary artists as classical figures: Plato is Leonardo; glum Heraclitus with the big knees on the steps at the front is Michelangelo; Euclid is Bramante (note the letters RUSM, Raphael's signature, on his gold collar); and Raphael himself is on the far right-hand side just behind a man in white, believed to be his pupil Sodoma. Raphael next turned his hand to the Stanza di Eliodoro (1512-14), frescoed with *The Expulsion of Heliodorus*. The portrayal of God saving the temple in Jerusalem from the thieving Heliodorus was intended to highlight the divine protection that was enjoyed by Julius himself (the pope's portrait is shown twice: both as the priest of the temple in the centre wearing blue and gold, and as the red-capped figure carried on a bier on the left).

The Dining Room (Stanza dell'Incendio, 1514-17), painted after Julius' death, is dedicated to his successor, Leo X (the most obese of the Popes, he died from gout aged 38), and shows other Pope Leos with the face of Leo X. The room is named for the Fire in the Borgo, which Leo IV apparently stopped with the sign of the cross. (Note that the first church of St Peter's is in the background.)

The Reception Room (Sala di Constantino, 1517-24) was completed by Giulio Romano after Raphael's death in 1520, but was originally based on Raphael's sketches of the Church's triumph over paganism, and tells the legend of Constantine's miraculous conversion.

The long Loggia di Raffaello (almost never open to the public) has a beautiful view over Rome. Started by Bramante in 1513, and finished by Raphael and his assistants, it features 52 small paintings on biblical themes, and leads into the Sala dei Chiaroscuri (Gregory XIII obliterated Raphael's frescoes here, but the magnificent ceiling remains). The adjacent Cappella di Niccolò V (Chapel of Nicholas V, usually open), has outstanding frescoes of scenes from the lives of saints Lawrence and Stephen by Fra Angelico (1448-50).

The Vatican Library

Founded by Pope Nicholas V in 1450, this is one of the world's most extraordinary libraries, containing 100,000 medieval manuscripts and books, and over a million other volumes. It is open to students and specialists on application to the Admissions office (06 6987 9403, www.vaticanlibrary.va). *See also p315.*

BORGO & PRATI

In the 1930s Mussolini's broad avenue, via della Conciliazione, was bulldozed through much of the medieval Borgo. A few of the streets remain, however, and salt-of-the-earth Romans mingle here with off-duty Swiss Guards and immaculately robed priests from the Vatican *Curia* (administration). Before his elevation, Josef Ratzinger lived above souvenir tat in a gloomy Fascist-era building just outside Bernini's colonnade and near the raised, covered *passetto*, the 13th-century escape route to Castel Sant'Angelo (*see right*). In Medieval Rome's Anglo-Saxon enclave, to the south of via della Conciliazione, you'll find the Museo Storico Nazionale dell'Arte Sanitaria (*see right*).

After Rome became capital of the unified Italian state in 1871, the meadows (*prati*) around the Renaissance ramparts north of the Borgo were suddenly required for housing for the staff of the new ministries and parliament across the Tiber. The largest of the *piazze* by the Vatican walls was provocatively named after the Risorgimento, the movement that had destroyed the papacy's hold over the whole of central Italy. Broad avenues were laid out and named after anti-papal figures such as 14th-century 'freedom fighter' Cola di Rienzo, and decidedly pre-Christian (ie pagan) leaders such as Octavian and Julius Caesar.

Still a solidly bourgeois district, Prati's main drag, via Cola di Rienzo, provides ample opportunities for retail therapy – a good antidote to a surfeit of culture. Endless imposing military barracks line viale delle Milizie; quiet, tree-lined streets lead towards the river; and the massive Palazzo di Giustizia (known as *il palazzaccio*, 'the big ugly building') is between piazza Cavour and the Tiber. On the riverbank is one of Catholic Rome's truly weird experiences: the Museo delle Anime del Purgatorio (*see below*).

Castel Sant'Angelo

Lungotevere Castello 50 (06 689 6003, http://castelsantangelo.beniculturali.it). Bus 23, 40Exp, 49, 87, 280, 926. **Open** 9am-7.30pm Tue-Sun. **Admission** €5; €3 concessions. *Extra charge during exhibitions.* **No credit cards. Map** p339 B4.
Begun by Emperor Hadrian in AD 135 as his own mausoleum, Castel Sant'Angelo has variously been a fortress, prison and papal residence. Puccini had Tosca hurl herself to her death from the upper terraces, from which there are excellent views. There is much to see here: lavish Renaissance salons, decorated with spectacular frescoes and trompe l'oeil; the glorious chapel in the Cortile d'Onore, designed by Michelangelo; and, halfway up an easily missed staircase, Clement VII's tiny personal bathroom, painted by Giulio Romano. In the summer the *passetto* – linking the castle to the Vatican – is occasionally open (to the halfway point) and worth a visit.

FREE Museo delle Anime del Purgatorio

Lungotevere Prati 12 (06 6880 6517). Bus 23, 30Exp, 34, 40Exp, 49, 70, 80Exp, 81, 87, 280, 492, 913, 926. **Open** 7.30-11am, 4.30-7pm daily. **Map** p339 D4.
This macabre collection, attached to the neo-Gothic church of Sacro Cuore di Gesù in Prati, contains hand- and fingerprints left on the prayer books and clothes of the living by dead loved ones, to request masses to release their souls from purgatory. Begun just over a century ago, the collection includes a handprint supposedly left by Sister Clara Scholers on the habit of a fellow-nun in Westphalia in 1696, and scorched bank notes left by a dead soul outside a church where he wanted a mass said.

Museo Storico dell'Arte Sanitaria

Lungotevere in Sassia 3 (06 689 3051). Bus 23, 40Exp, 62, 280. **Open** by appointment only. **Map** p339 B4.
This hostel and church was established around 726 by King Ine of Wessex to cater for weary and sick pilgrims who descended from the north. Known as the *burgus saxonum* or *in Sassia*, this district became the nucleus of the world's first purpose-built hospital. The name *in Sassia* persists although British funds for the hostel were cut off with the Norman invasion of England in 1066, after which it passed into papal hands and thence to the Templar knight Guy de Montpellier, who founded the Order of the Holy Spirit (Santo Spirito). A few rooms of the modern hospital of Santo Spirito house a gruesome collection of medical artefacts, dating from ancient times to the 19th century. The two massive 15th-century frescoed wards, the gloriously elegant fruit of a rebuilding programme in Renaissance times, were only recently emptied of their beds to provide space for itinerant exhibitions. If they are open, any opportunity to visit them should be seized.

The Appian Way

The original super-highway.

Appius Claudius Caecus, censor of 312 BC, had the inspired idea of building a road (taking advantage of a lava stream from a volanic eruption 270,000 years earlier in the Alban Hills to the south) to move troops and materials as efficiently as possible from Rome to the second city of the Republic, Capua. Soon after, the road was extended to Brindisi, opening up *caput mundi* towards the East. Officially named after its creator, the Appia became known as the *regina viarium*, 'queen of roads' and – along with ancient Rome's other great consular roads – carried men and weapons and goods and travellers to all corners of the Empire. Grim thoroughfare, this ain't: today this is undoubtedly the most picturesque of the ancient Roman *vie consolari* (consular roads).

TRAIL OF THE DEAD

In ancient times the Appian Way was a prime spot for the real estate of the after-life; the remains of the dead – whether cremated or buried – had to be kept outside the *pomerium* (a sacred city boundary), and well-to-do Roman families set up family mausoleums alongside the major road into the city. It was once lined with tombs, vaults, sarcophagi and every kind of magnificent decoration imaginable – an exquisitely picturesque gallery of the pagan departed, of which fragments remain.

Christians, too, began burying their dead here, initially in common necropoli. Later, as land became too expensive, they laid them to rest underground, creating the estimated 300-kilometre (200-mile) network of underground cemeteries known as the **catacombs**. This system wasn't used for secret worship in times of persecution as once thought: Roman authorities were aware of its existence. But for pagans, death and its rituals were sacred whatever the religion. Besides, having the cemetery close by meant that they could keep an eye on those pesky cultists. Jews also used the catacomb method for their burials; a Jewish catacomb can still be visited at Vigna Rondanini, via Appia Antica 119.

Via Appia Antica suffered at the hands of marauding Goths and Normans, although pilgrims continued to use it as the first leg of their long trip to the Holy Land. Successive popes did as much damage as barbarians had,

grabbing any good pieces of statuary or marble that remained. Miraculously, there are still things to see: the mausoleum of Priscilla, where via Appia Antica meets via Ardeatina, the tomb of Cecilia Metella and, further down the road, the Casal Rotondo and the mausoleums of the Orazi and Curiazi, maintain more or less their original shape.

With all these reminders of antiquity, this is a wonderful area to spend a day, preferably a Sunday or holiday when all but local traffic is banned. Explore more extensively by renting a bike at the **Punto Informativo** (*see p318*).

BUSES ON THE WAY

You can take the **Archeobus** (*see p309*) from Termini station, which stops by most major sights. The following regular bus services each cover some portion of the Appian Way as well.

118 Viale Aventino (outside Circo Massimo metro station) – Terme di Caracalla – Porta San Sebastiano – along via Appia Antica to Domine Quo Vadis? and the catacombs of San Callisto and San Sebastiano – Via Appia Pignatelli.

218 Piazza San Giovanni – Porta San Sebastiano – along via Appia Antica to Domine Quo Vadis? – along via Ardeatina to Fosse Ardeatine and, with a bit of a hike, the Catacombe di Domitilla.

660 Colli Albani metro station – along via Appia Antica, from Circo di Massenzio to Tomba di Cecilia Metella.

664 Colli Albani metro station – along via Appia Nuova to Villa dei Quintili.

Museo delle Mura

Porta San Sebastiano

Centro Visite Parco dell'Appia Antica

Via Latina

Catacombe di S. Callisto

Domine Quo Vadis?

Fortified Farmhouse

Fosse Ardeatine

Catacombe Ebraiche

Catacombe di Domitilla

Via

Mausoleo di Romolo

Basilica e Catacombe di S. Sebastiano

Circo di Massenzio

Sacro Bosco

Tomba di Cecilia Metella

Via Appia Nuova

Via Ardeatina

Via Appia Antica

Appia Pignatelli

Villa dei Quintili

0 metres 300
0 yards 330

© Copyright Time Out Group 2011

ALONG THE APPIAN WAY

Although it once started at the south-eastern end of the Circo Massimo, the beginning of the Appia Antica is now considered to be the **Porta San Sebastiano**, the best-preserved of the gates that were built by Aurelian when he walled the city in AD 270. Inside the gate is the little **Museo delle Mura** (*see p155*), which sometimes allows access to the Aurelian Walls to the west. On the right, ten minutes' walk beyond the gate, is the **Parco Appia Antica Punto Informativo** (via Appia Antica 58-60, 06 513 5316, www.parcoappiaantica.org, open Apr-Sept 9.30am-5.30pm daily, Oct-Mar 9.30am-4.30pm, where you can rent a bicycle (book ahead, €10 a day). The bar at via Appia 175 has bikes for rent Tue-Sun (€12 for four hours); call ahead on 338 346 5440.

Further out on the left is the tiny, austere church of **Domine Quo Vadis?** (open 8am-6pm daily). Inside the door on a raised tablet are the imprints of two long, flat feet that are said to have been left by Christ when he appeared to St Peter, who was running away from Rome

and crucifixion. Christ told Peter he was going to Rome to be crucified again himself, thus shaming Peter into returning too. These prints are a copy; the real ones are at the church of **San Sebastiano** (*see p155*).

A right fork outside the church along via Ardeatina leads to the **Catacombe di Domitilla** (access from via delle Sette Chiese; *see below*) and the **Fosse Ardeatine** (via Ardeatina 174, 06 513 6742, open 8.15am-3pm Mon-Fri; 8.15am-5pm Sat & Sun, free), this latter a moving memorial to the 355 Italians shot by the occupying Nazis in 1944 in retaliation for a Resistance ambush.

From the centre of the fork, a drive leads up to the **Catacombe di San Callisto** (*see p154*). The left fork past Domine Quo Vadis?, on the other hand, opens up two options: straight along via Appia Antica, or left again into via della Caffarella.

The latter choice takes you past sumptuous private villas and clubs before opening up to the vast **Parco della Caffarella**. Follow the main path to what's commonly known as the temple of the god Redicolo; historians say it is in fact a second-century AD tomb, perhaps of a Roman woman named Annia Regilla. It owes its good state of preservation to local farmers who guarded it jealously through the ages… as a useful barn for hay storage.

On the Appia Antica, Renaissance walls surround private villas along the road to the church (*see p155*) and **catacombs of San Sebastiano** (*see p154*). Beyond here, the Appian Way is as it was… almost. The original volcanic paving stones that lie exposed beneath a canopy of pines and cypresses are those trod by the Roman infantry. All Roman roads were built to handle five soldiers or two carriages abreast, measuring 14 Roman feet (4.2 metres/ 13.7 feet) across. On either side of the road are remains of funerary ornaments. On this stretch are the **Mausoleo di Romolo** and the vast **Circo di Massenzio** (*see p154*). The rise towards the cylindrical **tomb of Cecilia Metella** (*see p155*) marks the end of the lava flow that was used to build the road. Further south, the villas thin out and the funerary monuments are more prominent. At the fifth Roman mile is the second-century **Villa dei Quintili** (access from via Appia Nuova only; *see p155*). Beyond this point the road is quieter and landscape wilder, with occasional sheep.

Catacombe di Domitilla

Via delle Sette Chiese 282 (06 513 3956, www.domitilla.info). Open 9am-noon, 2-5pm Mon, Wed-Sun. Closed late Dec-mid Jan. Admission €8; €5 reductions. **No credit cards.** These catacombs are found on land once belonging to Flavia Domitilla, wife of a first-century consul,

Appian Way.

SIGHTS

SIGHTS

Villa dei Quintili.

banished to the island of Ponza for her faith. The guided visit starts with the fourth-century basilica of Saints Nerius and Achilleus, Roman soldiers martyred for proselytising, probably under Christian-hating Emperor Diocletian. The tomb of the martyrs is in the apse; throughout the church, inscriptions mark the tombs of early Christians who wanted their final resting place to be near these two fearless military men. On a column is a representation of the martyrdom of St Achilleus with his hands tied behind his back. The ensuing galleries of burial places in the soft volcanic rock cover some 12km (7.5 miles), though you won't see all of these monuments. The oldest part is the so-called *hypogeum* of the Flavi, a pagan burial ground taken over by Christians. Frescoes in varying states of preservation are found throughout.

Catacombe di San Callisto
Via Appia Antica 78, 110 & 126 (06 513 0151, www.catacombe.roma.it). **Open** 9am-noon, 2-5pm Mon, Tue, Thur-Sun. Closed late Jan-late Feb. **Admission** €8; €5 reductions. **Credit** AmEx, DC, MC, V.
These are Rome's largest catacombs. Buried in the 29km (18 miles) of tunnels were nine popes (venerated in a chapel known as *il piccolo Vaticano*), dozens of martyrs and thousands of Christians. They are stacked down, with the oldest on the top. Named after the banker, deacon and later pope Callixtus, who was administrator of the catacombs in the early third century, the area became the first official cemetery of the Church of Rome. The crypt of St Cecilia

is the spot where this patron saint of music is believed to have been buried before she was moved to her eponymous church in Trastevere; the statue is a copy of the one in the church.
▶ *For Santa Cecilia in Trastevere, see p117.*

Catacombe di San Sebastiano
Via Appia Antica 136 (06 785 0350). **Open** 9am-noon, 2-5pm Mon-Sat. Closed mid Nov-mid Dec. **Admission** €8; €5 reductions. **Credit** AmEx, MC, V.
The name 'catacomb' originated in this spot, where a complex of underground burial sites situated near a tufa quarry was described as being *kata kymbas* – 'near the quarry'. The guided tour will take you into the crypt of St Sebastian, the martyr always depicted nastily pierced by a hail of arrows (though these were just one of several unpleasant tortures), who was buried here, probably during Diocletian's reign in the late third century; the base of the original monument to him can be seen. The Christian burials that followed his eventually formed three layers of tombs, the second of which is what's on show; this includes the *piazzolo*, where pagan mausoleums re-used by Christians were found.

Circo & Villa di Massenzio, & Mausoleo di Romolo
Via Appia Antica 153. **Open** 9am-1.30pm Tue-Sun. **Admission** €3; €2 reductions. **No credit cards.**
This large area of lovely green countryside contains one of the best preserved Roman circuses. It was

built by Emperor Maxentius for his private use, before his defeat and death at the hands of co-ruler Constantine in AD 312. Remains of the Imperial villa are perched above the track, at its northern end. Earthenware jugs (amphorae) were inserted into the upper sections of the long walls: their empty volume helped lighten the load above the vaults. Also at the north end is the mausoleum Maxentius built for his beloved son Romulus. To the left, forming a wall of a farmhouse, is a mausoleum thought to have belonged to the Servilius family. Underneath other ancient ruins next to the road lie more catacombs, largely unexcavated.

▶ *Massenzio liked to build on a massive scale: visit his basilica in the Foro Romano; see p62.*

Mausoleo di Cecilia Metella

Via Appia Antica 161 (06 780 0093).
Open 9am-4.30pm Tue-Sun. **Admission** €6; €3 reductions; includes Baths of Caracalla & Villa dei Quintili. **No credit cards**.
This colossal cylinder of travertine is the final resting place of, and unusual tribute to, a woman who linked two major families in late first century BC Rome. A large plaque beneath the frieze honours Cecilia as the daughter of Quintus Creticus (probably so-called for his triumph in Crete in 64 BC) and the wife of Crassus (a relation of the Crassus who ruled in the triumvirate with Julius Caesar). During the 14th century the powerful Caetani family, relatives of Pope Boniface VIII, incorporated the tomb into a fortress, adding the crenellations to the top; the frieze decorated with skulls gives this area its nickname Capo di bove (ox head). Inside is a roofless gallery with a row of headless, toga-clad Romans and other marble objects, including lapidary inscriptions, crematory urns and tomb decorations – all funerary statues that used to line the Appia Antica. The spot where Cecilia was buried is a fine example of brick dome-making. Downstairs, pieces of the volcanic rock used in the construction of the ancient road can be seen. Outside and across the way are what's left of the church of San Nicola, a rare example of Gothic architecture in Rome, surrounded by further walls of the fortress, which once straddled the road. From this imposing spot the Caetani filled their coffers by exacting tolls from passing travellers.

Museo delle Mura

Via di Porta San Sebastiano 18 (06 0608, www.museodellemuraroma.it). **Open** 9am-2pm Tue-Sun. **Admission** €3; €2 reductions. **No credit cards**.
Housed in the ancient Porta San Sebastiano, the Museum of the Walls has a small collection of artefacts associated with Roman walls and roads. The museum's greatest attraction used to be the access it gave visitors to a walkway on top of a substantial stretch of the Aurelian Wall, but this *passeggiata* was closed as this guide went to press. There's a fine view from the terrace of the gate, though.

San Sebastiano (church)

Via Appia Antica 136 (06 788 7035).
Open 8am-7pm daily.
Visitors usually ignore the fourth-century basilica built over the catacombs of the same name (see left), even though pilgrims taking a tour of Rome's great basilicas understand its importance. The remains of apostles Peter and Paul were hidden in the underlying catacombs in the third century, during the persecutions by Emperor Valerian, hence the original name of the church: Basilica Apostolorum. During the ninth century, it was rededicated to St Sebastian. A soldier from Gaul, Sebastian was the target of a rain of arrows when he converted. However, according to tradition, his wounds were healed by the intercession of another saint. Emperor Diocletian then had him stoned or bludgeoned to finish off the job. Two relics of the saint – an arrow, along with the column to which he was tied while the arrows were flying – stand in the first chapel on the right. Also on display is the marble slab in which Christ is believed to have left his footprints during his miraculous apparition at Domine Quo Vadis (*see p152*).

Villa dei Quintili

Via Appia Nuova 1092 (06 718 2485).
Open 9am-one hour before sunset Tue-Sun. **Admission** €6; €3 reductions. *See also p7* **Appia Antica Card**. **No credit cards**.
The wealthy, cultured and militarily brilliant Quintili brothers – consuls under Emperor Marcus Aurelius – built this splendid villa with a large bath complex and nymphaeum before Emperor Commodus became jealous and had them killed. The emperor then took over the villa for himself, and essentially ruled from here. Digs in the 18th and 19th centuries unearthed statuary and objects now in the Vatican Museums and others around the world. The vast structure is set in splendid isolation amid fields strewn with fragments of the many-coloured marble that once faced its mighty halls. A small antiquarium displays statuary and objects which have been found in the vicinity. Check for evening events in the summer.

INSIDE TRACK
SEBASTIAN'S STICKY END

Darling of Renaissance painters who loved working on his writhing male anatomy, St Sebastian, captain of the Pretorian guard annoyed authorities with his conversions of fellow officers to Christianity. As a result he was shot full of arrows but managed to survive. However, when Emperor Diocletian found he was still alive, the story goes, he had Sebastian clubbed to death and thrown into a latrine.

SIGHTS

The Suburbs

Head out of the centre for art galleries, EUR and the Stadio Olimpico.

In 1871, when Rome became the capital of united Italy, its 212,000 residents rattled around inside the Aurelian Walls, where vast swathes were still given over to vegetable gardens. By 1901 the population had almost doubled to 422,000; by 1971 it was well over two million. These new *romani* were only too happy, in the interests of having a roof over their heads, to endorse the destruction of the countryside which was swiftly gobbled up, at first by pompous turn-of-the-century *palazzi* and, later, by unauthorised – and often unplumbed – tower blocks.

Today the result mostly looks grim, with a few notable exceptions, especially in the inner suburbs. There are Liberty (art nouveau) *palazzi* along vie Salaria and Nomentana, for example, and some memorable Fascist urban planning in EUR. Elsewhere, even some of the most architecturally uninspired districts hide surprises worth travelling for.

SIGHTS

NORTH

Flaminio

For centuries the route along which most travellers entered the Eternal City, the dead-straight via Flaminia nowadays passes through affluent residential *Roma nord* as it shoots north from piazza del Popolo to a hopping new hub of art and culture at the hyper-active Auditorium-Parco della Musica (*see p266* **The Sound of Perfection**) and architect Zaha Hadid's extraordinary new **MAXXI** art gallery.

Via Flaminia crosses the Tiber at the ancient **Ponte Milvio**; now open to pedestrians only, the second-century BC bridge offers a good view of the neighbouring Ponte Flaminio designed by Architect Brasini, a glorious example of Fascist rhetorical architecture. Across the river are the **Foro Italico** sports complex and **Stadio Olimpico**.

★ Foro Italico & Stadio Olimpico

Piazza de Bosis/via del Foro Italico. Bus 32, 69, 271, 280, 910/tram 2. **Map** p337.
A marble obelisk, 36m (120ft) high, with the words 'Mussolini Dux' carved on it, greets visitors to the Foro Italico, a sports complex conceived in the late 1920s by architect Enrico Del Debbio. The avenue leading west of the obelisk is paved with black-and-

white mosaics of Fascists flying warplanes and saluting *il Duce*. It's a wonderfully camp sight today, and well preserved considering the feet that trample the tiles on their way to the Stadio Olimpico beyond (built in the 1950s but modified for the 1990 World Cup), where AS Roma and SS Lazio both play (*see p277* **Football**). Surrounding the Stadio dei Marmi track to the north – also by Del Debbio – are 60 marble statues of naked athletes, each with some kind of sports apparatus, from crossbows to *bocce* (bowling) balls. *Photo p160.*

★ MAXXI

Via Guido Reni 10 (06 321 0181, 06 3996 7350, www.fondazionemaxxi.it). Bus 53, 280, 910/tram 2. **Open** 11am-7pm Tue, Wed, Fri, Sun; 11am-10pm Thur, Sat. **Admission** €11; €7 reductions; under-14s free. **Credit** MC, V. **Map** p337. *See p41* **Profile.**

Salario

Via Salaria – the salt road – existed before Rome, when ancient tribes brought vital salt supplies from saltpans on the east coast. Today the road begins at piazza Fiume. The real treasures of the area are the delightful art nouveau Coppedè quarter – centred on piazza Mincio – and the leafy shade of the Villa Ada public gardens and the Catacombe di Priscilla.

In via della Moschea, between *vie* Salaria and Flaminia, lies Paolo Portoghesi's mosque (*see p317*), completed in 1992.

Catacombe di Priscilla
Via Salaria 430 (06 8620 6272). Bus 63, 92, 310, 630. **Open** 8.30am-noon, 2.30-5pm Tue-Sun. Closed Aug. **Admission** €8; €5 reductions. **No credit cards.**
This two-storey second-century AD burial place contains bas-reliefs and frescoes, including what is believed to be the first-ever depiction of Mary.

Nomentano

Via Nomentana leads out of Rome to the north-east, flanked on either side by another middle-class area, with some charming art nouveau buildings. Its green lung is the Villa Torlonia (again with a touch of art nouveau in the Casina delle Civette), its art fest in the MACRO gallery and perhaps the earliest Christian mosaics in **Santa Costanza**, by the catacombs and church of **Sant'Agnese fuori le Mura**. The area around via Tiburtina is more low-rent.

★ MACRO
Via Reggio Emilia 54 (06 6710 70400, www.macro.roma.museum). Bus 36, 60Exp, 62, 80Exp, 84, 90Exp. **Open** 9am-7pm Tue-Sun. **Admission** €4.50; €3.50 reductions. **No credit cards.** **Map** p340 E3.

INSIDE TRACK CATACOMBS

The catacombs at **Sant'Agnese fuori le mura** (*see below*) are among Rome's least visited and most atmospheric, but beware: they usually close in January. Also worth a look are the Jewish catacombs (accessible only by appointment) beneath the park at **Villa Torlonia** (*see p158*).

Rome's sluggish contemporary art scene was given a shot in the arm in the 1990s with the opening of a municipal modern art gallery in a stunningly converted brewery. Rechristened MACRO (Museo d'Arte Contemporaneo di Roma), this space now covers 10,000 sq m (107,500 sq ft), thanks to an extension designed by superstar architect Odile Decq. MACRO brings big international names to Rome, gives space to young artists and showcases local artists making site-specific art.
▶ *Shows and events spill over into some of the dramatic spaces inside the Mattatoio (see p121; open 4pm-midnight Tue-Sun during shows) in Testaccio.*

Sant'Agnese fuori le Mura & mausoleum of Santa Costanza
Via Nomentana 349 (06 861 0840, www.santagnese.com). Bus 36, 60Exp, 90Exp. **Open** *Church* 7.30am-noon, 4-7.45pm daily.

San Paolo fuori le Mura. *See p159.*

SIGHTS

Catacombs (guided tours) & Santa Costanza 9am-noon, 4-6pm Mon-Sat; 4-6pm Sun. **Admission** *Church & Santa Costanza* free. *Catacombs* €8; €5 reductions. **No credit cards**.

The circular fourth-century mausoleum of Santa Costanza, 2km (1.25 miles) along via Nomentana, was built for Constantine's daughters, Constance (a saint only by popular tradition) and Helen. The sarcophagus here, containing the remains of Constance, is a plaster cast of the porphyry original, now in the Vatican Museums. The barrel-vaulted ambulatory, whose arcades rest on exquisite 'pillows' of marble, is decorated with perhaps the world's earliest surviving Christian mosaics. These fourth-century works look more pagan than Christian, with simple pastoral scenes with a spiralling vine encircling figures collecting and treading grapes; but Christian historians insist the wine-making motifs represent Christ's blood, not the pastimes of Bacchus. The vast remains of a fourth-century basilica stand in wasteland nearby. In the adjoining church of Sant'Agnese, dating from the seventh century, is an original apse mosaic showing a diminutive figure of St Agnes standing on the flames of her martyrdom, flanked by two popes. St Agnes was almost certainly buried in the catacombs below this church, though her skull was later moved to the church of Sant'Agnese in Agone (*see p98*).

Villa Torlonia

Villa Torlonia, via Nomentana 70 (06 8205 9127, 06 0608, www.museivillatorlonia.it). Bus 36, 60Exp, 62, 84, 90Exp, 140. **Open** 9am-7pm Tue-Sun. **Admission** €4.50; €3.50 reductions. *With Casina delle civette* €6.50; €4.50 reductions. **No credit cards**.

The Villa Torlonia, with its verdant palm-filled park, was the elegant home of the aristocratic Torlonia family from 1797, glorified as Mussolini's suburban HQ in the 1930s and trashed by Anglo-American forces when they made it their high command base (1944-47). When Rome city council bought it in 1978, it was in a disastrous state; the house and its out-buildings disappeared for years behind scaffolding. Enough has now emerged to make this a truly worthwhile hike. The main house – the pretty Casino nobile – was revamped in 1832 by architect Giovan Battista Caretti, who commissioned the interior's frescoes and mouldings, which have now been restored to their former glory. Mussolini's bunker beneath the house can be visited by appointment. A number of structures are dotted around the park. Exhibitions are held in the Casino dei principi, which also houses the archives of the inter-war Scuola romana artistic movement. The Casina delle civette, a wacky Swiss chalet-folly, was endowed with all kinds of stupendous stained glass and boiseries in 1916-20; the art nouveau fittings have been beautifully restored and supplemented with much more stained glass from the same period. The Limonaia – where lemon trees were kept through the winter – is now a pleasant café-restaurant, and the faux-medieval villa by its side is home to Technotown (*see p248*).

EAST

Pigneto

Bordered by via Prenestina to the north and via Casilina to the south, the Pigneto district sprang up in haphazard fashion between the 1890s and 1930s as railwaymen and artisans used micro-credits from workers' co-operatives to build dwellings amid the warehouses and railway sheds. The humble industriousness of the area attracted the directors of Italian neo-realism: Rossellini's *Roma città aperta* (1945), Visconti's *Bellissima* (1951) and Pasolini's *Accattone* (1960) were largely shot here. Though fast becoming one of the city's hippest residential zones – with property prices going through the roof and a host of restaurants and bars to make the trek out here worthwhile – it retains much of its unique appeal, thanks in large part to the thronging morning food market (Mon-Sat) along pedestrianised via del Pigneto, and a massive flea market held in the same spot on the last Sunday of every month.

EUR. *See p160.*

SIGHTS

Palazzo Palazzo della Civiltà del Lavoro. *See p160.*

SOUTH
Garbatella & San Paolo

Lying south of Testaccio and Ostiense (*see pp119-123*), San Paolo is a district of mainly uninspiring 1950s-70s high-rises, while Garbatella is a fascinating area of late 19th- and early 20th-century workers' housing: many of the apartment blocks and adorable single- or two-family villas in private grounds are architecturally outstanding. A strong community feel remains. While Garbatella has no monuments (but some exciting cultural life based around the Teatro Palladium; *see p283*), San Paolo is home to one of Rome's major basilicas, San Paolo fuori le Mura.

San Paolo fuori le Mura
Via Ostiense 184 (06 541 0341, www.basilica sanpaolo.org). Metro San Paolo/bus 23, 271.

Open *Basilica* 6.45am-6.30pm daily.
Cloister 9am-1pm, 3-6pm daily. **Map** p337.
Constantine founded San Paolo to commemorate the martyrdom of St Paul at nearby Tre Fontane (*see p161*). The church is a mix of different styles having been destroyed, rebuilt and restored several times; most of the present basilica – the largest in Rome after St Peter's – is only 150 years old. The greatest damage to the building occurred in a fire in 1823, but restorers also contributed to the destruction of the older church. Features that have survived include 11th-century doors decorated with biblical scenes; a strange 12th-century Easter candlestick, featuring human-, lion- and goat-headed beasts spewing the vine of life from their mouths; and the elegant 13th-century ciborium above the altar, by Arnolfo di Cambio. In the *confessio* beneath the altar is the tomb of St Paul, topped by a stone slab pierced with two holes through which devotees stuff bits of cloth to imbue them with the apostle's holiness.

Foro Italico. *See p156.*

The cloister is a good example of cosmatesque work, its twisted columns inlaid with mosaic and supporting an arcade of sculpted reliefs. In the sacristy are the remnants of a series of papal portraits that once lined the nave. The modern church has carried on this tradition, replacing the originals with mosaic portraits of all the popes from Peter to the present incumbent. There are only eight spaces left; once they are filled, the world, apparently, will end. An archeological museum in the basilica's garden was planned as this guide went to press.

EUR

Italian Fascism managed to be simultaneously monstrous and absurd, but its delusions of grandeur helped to produce some of the most interesting European architecture and town planning of the 20th century. In the early 1930s Giuseppe Bottai, governor of Rome and the leading arbiter of Fascist taste, had the idea of expanding landbound Rome along via Ostiense towards the sea. Imperial Rome had its monuments. Fascist Rome (*la terza Roma*), Bottai thought, should have its architectural spaces as well. He combined this with the notion of a universal exhibition, pencilled in for 1942 and intended to combine cultural exhibition spaces with a monument to the regime.

Architect Marcello Piacentini was charged with co-ordinating the ambitious project but few of the original designs were ever built. The planning committee became so embroiled in argument that little had been achieved by the outbreak of World War II. After the war, work resumed with a different spirit. Still known as **EUR** (*Esposizione universale romana*), the project united some of Italy's best architects – Giovanni Muzio, Mario de Renzi, Ludovico Quaroni, Luigi Figini and Gino Pollini. With its bombastic modernism, the EUR lets you know you're not in Kansas any more.

On either side of axial via Cristoforo Colombo, Fascist-inspired buildings such as Guerrini's **Palazzo della Civiltà del Lavoro**, popularly known as *il colosseo quadrato* (the square Colosseum), and Arnaldo Foschini's church of **Santi Pietro e Paolo** (piazzale Santi Pietro e Paolo) can be seen alongside post-war *palazzi* like Adalberto Libera's **Palazzo dei Congressi** (piazza JF Kennedy) and Studio BBPR's superbly functional post office (viale Beethoven).

A slew of museums – the **Museo dell'Alto Medioevo**, **Museo della Civiltà Romana** (containing an astronomy museum), **Museo delle Arti e Tradizioni Popolari**, the **Museo Preistorico ed Etnografico L Pigorini** (*see right*) – allows a glimpse inside these striking monuments to Fascist grandeur.

The 1960 Olympics offered another stimulus for filling out the area. The masterpiece is Nervi and Piacentini's flying-saucer-like **Palazzo dello Sport** (piazza dello Sport), hovering over EUR's artificial lake and now often used for big rock concerts and political conventions. The area contains other attractions, such as the **Luneur Park** funfair and the **Piscina delle Rose** swimming pool (*see p280*).

For relief from EUR's relentless modernity, head for the leafy charm of the **Abbazia delle Tre Fontane** (*see below*).

GETTING THERE

The quickest way from the city centre to EUR is by underground (Metro line B; get off at EUR Fermi or EUR Palasport), but approaching the district from the surface, along via Cristoforo Colombo (bus 30Exp, 170, 714), is the best way to experience the emerging-from-greenery feel of EUR, which was a significant part of the original architects' design.

Abbazia delle Tre Fontane

Via Acque Salvie 1 (06 540 1655). Bus 716, 761. **Open** *Santi Vincenzo e Anastasio* 6.30am-12.30pm, 3-7.30pm daily. *San Paolo* 8am-12.30pm, 3-6pm daily. *Shop* (06 540 2309) 9am-1pm, 3.30-7pm daily.

To the east of the Tre Fontane sports facilities lies a haven of ancient, eucalyptus-scented green, with three churches commemorating the points where St Paul's head supposedly bounced after it was severed from his body in AD 67. (Being a Roman citizen, Paul was eligible for the relatively quick and painless head-chop, as opposed to the long, drawn-out crucifixion.) These are the grounds of the Trappist monastery of Tre Fontane, where water has gurgled and birds have sung since the fifth century. The church of San Paolo delle Tre Fontane is said to be built on the spot where the apostle was executed; apart from a column to which Paul is supposed to have been tied, all traces of the fifth-century church were done away with in 1599 by architect Giacomo della Porta, who was also responsible for the two other churches. Monks planted the eucalyptus trees in the 1860s, believing they would drive away the malarial mosquitoes; a liqueur is now brewed from the trees and sold in a little shop (MC, V) along with chocolate and remedies for all ills.

Museo dell'Alto Medioevo

Viale Lincoln 3 (06 5422 8199). Metro EUR Fermi/bus 30Exp, 170, 714. **Open** 9am-2pm Tue-Sun. **Admission** €2; €1 reductions. **No credit cards**.

Focusing on the decorative arts between the fall of the Roman Empire and the Renaissance, this museum has intricate gold- and silver-decorated swords, buckles and horse tackle, as well as more mundane objects: ceramic bead jewellery and the metal frames of what may be Europe's earliest folding chairs.

Museo della Civiltà Romana

Piazza G Agnelli 10 (06 5422 0919, www.museociviltaromana.it). Metro EUR Fermi/bus 30Exp, 170, 714. **Open** *Museum* 9am-2pm Tue-Sun. **Admission** €6.50; €4.50 reductions. **No credit cards**.

This museum dates from 1937, when Mussolini mounted a massive celebration to mark the second millennium of Augustus becoming the first emperor. The fact that the celebration came about 35 years too early was overlooked by *il Duce*, who was eager to draw parallels between Augustus' glory and his own. With its blank white walls and echoing corridors, the building is Fascist-classical at its most grandiloquent. There are fascinating models: a cutaway of the Colosseum, as well as casts of the intricate reliefs on Trajan's column (*see p65*), and a giant model of Rome in the fourth century AD. The palazzo also contains the new Museo Astronomico and a planetarium (*see p248*).

Museo delle Arti e Tradizioni Popolari

Piazza G Marconi 8 (06 592 6148, 06 591 2669). Metro EUR Fermi/bus 30Exp, 170, 714. **Open** 9am-6pm Tue-Sun. **Admission** €4; €2 reductions. **No credit cards**.

This enormous collection is dedicated to Italian folk art and rural tradition. Exhibits include elaborately decorated carts and horse tackle, as well as craft-related implements and a bizarre collection of votive offerings left to local saints. Malevolent-looking puppets fill one room; another has *carnevale* artefacts.

Museo Preistorico ed Etnografico L Pigorini

Piazza G Marconi 14 (06 549 521, www.pigorini.beniculturali.it). Metro EUR Fermi/bus 30Exp, 170, 714. **Open** 10am-6pm Mon-Sat. **Admission** €6; €3 reductions. **No credit cards**.

This museum displays prehistoric Italian artefacts together with material from a range of world cultures. The lobby contains a reconstruction of the prehistoric Guattari cave near Monte Circeo (*see p304*), with a genuine Neanderthal skull. On the first floor is the ethnological collection, with a range of hut-urns, arrowheads, jewellery, masks and a couple of shrunken heads. The second floor has archaeological finds from digs all over Italy, including mammoth tusks and teeth, and some human bones.

WEST

Monteverde

Climbing the steep hill behind Trastevere and the Gianicolo (*see p118*) is Monteverde Vecchio, a leafy, well-heeled suburb that is home to the vast, green, tree-filled expanse of the Villa Pamphili park (map p337). Here, children will enjoy feeding the turtles – if you can find the pond – and riding the ponies (if they're not at their other haunt, the Gianicolo). Nearby, to the south-east, is the smaller but equally lovely Villa Sciarra garden (map p343 A4), with its rose arbours, children's play area and miniature big dipper.

SIGHTS

Consume

Etabli. *See p212.*

Hotels

Cheap hotels are few, but the top end and mid-range are improving

Once a city of polar-opposite accommodation options – exorbitantly expensive, often soulless luxury hotels on the one hand; cheap *pensioni* of dubious cleanliness on the other – Rome now has the range of hotels you might expect in one of the most-visited destinations on the planet – but they are, on the whole, considerably more expensive than in other tourist meccas. For a dirt-cheap hotel bed these days – and even that concept is relative – you may have to accept a less salubrious bit of town, or even an out-of-the-way convent. On the positive side, the general standard of

accommodation has improved in recent years. The luxury hotel market, in particular, has exploded, with a raft of new five-stars opening – though struggling somewhat when recession began to bite. The mid-range market is also flourishing: competition from boutique hotels popping up around the *centro storico* means that older-style hotels and *pensioni* have been forced to upgrade amenities and decor to keep pace.

LOCATION

There are now three five-stars near Termini station, but the vast majority of hotels in the area are cheap *pensioni* swarming with budget backpackers. It's not Rome's most picturesque corner, and almost certainly not what you dreamed of for your Roman holiday. It's well worth considering looking further afield, even if it costs you a bit more.

For atmosphere and convenience, go for a room in the *centro storico*. A shower between sightseeing and dinner and a wander (rather than the bus) back to the hotel afterwards can make all the difference. The area around **campo de' Fiori** offers mid-priced hotels with lots of character, though the campo can get very rowdy at night; the area around the **Pantheon** and **piazza Navona** is generally a bit pricier. Moving distinctly up the price range, Rome's top-end hotels have traditionally clustered around **via Veneto** – though bear in mind that it's not as lively as it was in its much-hyped *dolce vita* heyday, and there's a strong whiff of expense account in the air. The **Tridente** area near the Spanish Steps, hub of designer shopping, is full of elegant hotels at the upper end of the price scale.

If you're looking for some peace, the **Celio**, just beyond the Colosseum, offers a break from the frantic activity of the *centro storico*, as does another of Rome's seven hills: the **Aventine**, an exclusive residential outpost not far at all from the *centro*.

Heading across the river, the characterful bar- and restaurant-packed district of **Trastevere** has blossomed in recent years from hotel-desert to hotel-bonanza, offering an array of price options.

STANDARDS & PRICES

Italian hotels are classified on a star system, from one to five. The more stars, the more facilities a hotel will have, but bear in mind that a higher rating is no guarantee of friendliness, cleanliness or even decent service. One- and two-star joints can be very seedy indeed. B&Bs, on the other hand, can sometimes prove to be very pleasant surprises.

Many of Rome's hotels now model their pricing policy on low-cost airlines: the same room in an empty hotel may cost you less than

❶ Red numbers given in this chapter correspond to the location of each hotel as marked on the street maps.

Villa Spalletti Trivelli.

half what it does in heavily booked high season. A double room in a one-star will set you back €65-€120; a two-star, €80-€175; a three-star, €110-€300; a four-star, €185-€450. Five-star prices start at around €350, and don't stop until your bank manager starts to weep. Consult websites for low-season deals.

BOOKING A ROOM

Always reserve a room well in advance, especially at peak times, which now means most of the year, with lulls during winter (January to March) and in the dog days of August. If you're coming at the same time as a major Christian holiday (Christmas or Easter) it's wise to book weeks, or even months, ahead.

If you arrive with nowhere to stay, the **Hotel Reservation** service will make you a booking (free by phone, €3 at the desk). Avoid the touts that hang around Termini: you're likely to end up paying more than you should for a very grotty hotel.

Hotel Reservation
Fiumicino airport, Terminals A, B & C arrivals halls (06 699 1000, fax 06 678 1469, www.hotel reservation.it). **Open** 7am-10pm daily. **Credit** AmEx, DC, MC, V.
This agency has details on the availability of numerous hotels at all prices, and runs a shuttle service to the centre from Fiumicino airport. Check out the website for bargain-basement late-booking offers. Staff speak English.
Other locations Termini station, at head of platform 24 (06 482 3952).

OUR CHOICE

The hotels listed in this guide have been chosen for their location, because they offer

value for money, or simply because they have true Roman character. In the Deluxe category the emphasis is on opulence and luxury. Those in mid- to upper-price ranges are generally smaller, often in old *palazzi*, with attractive bedrooms (although it's worth remembering that rooms in Rome may be smaller than you'd like). Our budget suggestions are fairly basic but friendly and clean.

With the exception of large and expensive hotels, disabled access and facilities are thin on the ground in Rome: although staff are generally very willing to help guests with mobility difficulties, steep stairs and no room for anything but tiny bathrooms are insurmountable problems.

Unless stated, the rates listed below include taxes and breakfast.

TREVI & QUIRINALE

Expensive

★ Villa Spalletti Trivelli
Via Piacenza 4 (06 4890 7934, www.villa spalletti.it). Bus 40, 60, 64, 70, 117, 170, H. **Rooms** 12. **Rates** €360-€627 double. **Credit** AmEx, DC, MC, V. **Map** p341 B6 **❶**

INSIDE TRACK KIDS' BEDS

If you're visiting with children, most hotels will be happy to squeeze a cot or camp bed into your room, but they will probably charge 30 to 50 per cent extra for the privilege. Renting an apartment (*see* p183) could prove to be a cheaper and more flexible alternative.

FORTY 47 SEVEN

ALBERGO IN ROMA

Fortysevenhotel
Via Petroselli 47, 00186 – Rome
Tel +39.06.6787816; Fax +39.06.69190726
contact@fortysevenhotel.com
www.fortysevenhotel.com

CIRCUS BAR

The aristocratic Spalletti Trivelli clan has turned its family home – with views across a little park to the *manica lunga* of the Quirinale palace (*see p72*) – into a sumptuously elegant 12-room hotel with such high-class extras as an historic library with a preservation order, a formal garden where breakfast or *aperitivi* can be served and a marvellous spa in the basement. Some of the large rooms can be linked together to form immense suites. Service is charmingly discrete; and there's a chef on hand to whip up special meals on request.

Concierge. Disabled-adapted rooms. Gym. Internet (free). Room service. Spa. TV.

Moderate

Daphne Trevi

Via degli Avignonesi 20 (06 8745 0087, www.daphne-rome.com). Metro Barberini/bus 52, 62, 63, 95, 116, 119, 492. **Rooms** 7 + 7. **Rates** €140-€220 double. **Credit** AmEx, DC, MC, V. **Map** p341 B5 ❷

Owned by dynamic Italo-American couple Elyssa and Alessandro, Daphne Inn sets the standard for inexpensive but stylish accommodation in Rome. The two-part hotel – located in two central venues: Trevi and Veneto (*see p169*) – is decorated in modern, earthy tones thoughout, and the tastefully furnished bedrooms have high ceilings, terracotta or parquet floors and decent-sized bathrooms. Guests are lent a mobile phone for the duration of their stay, and staff are endlessly helpful.

Concierge. Internet (free). Parking (nearby, €25-€30).

▶ *This hotel is perfectly placed if you want to get some special pampering at the scented, oriental-style Kamispa; see p280.*

Residenza Cellini

Via Modena 5 (06 4782 5204, www.residenza cellini.it). Metro Repubblica/bus 40Exp, 60Exp, 64, 90Exp, 170, 175, 492, 910. **Rooms** 11. **Rates** €145-€240 double. **Credit** AmEx, DC, MC, V. **Map** p341 C5 ❸

This delightfully luminous *residenza* has huge rooms with faux-antique wooden furniture, parquet flooring and comfy beds. The marble bathrooms have jacuzzis or showers with hydro-massage. Three rooms have balconies, and there's a terrace, too.

Concierge. Internet (free). Parking (nearby, €20-€25). Room service. TV.

VENETO & BORGHESE

Deluxe

Grand Hotel Via Veneto

Via Veneto 155 (06 487 881, www.ghvv.it). Bus 52, 53, 63, 80, 95, 116, 630. **Rooms** 122. **Rates** €290-€600 double. *Breakfast* €40 extra. **Credit** AmEx, DC, MC, V. **Map** p341 B4 ❹

Aleph. *See p169.*

CONSUME

The newest addition to the via Veneto luxe market, the GHVV is as flashy as you'd expect, with an art deco theme worked to the hilt in the striking public spaces, and given a slightly more contemporary modernist bent in bedrooms, even the smallest of which are spacious by Rome standards. The huge bathrooms are in Carrara marble. Modern lithographs and huge black and white photos of Roman scenes line the walls. Multilingual staff are remarkably charming, and the street-level bar-restaurant Time buzzes at cocktail hour with great *aperitivi*, and later when seafood specialities are served. There's a whirlpool tub in the solarium on the roof.

THE BEST SUITES

Overlooking the Spanish Steps
Junior suite at the **View at the Spanish Steps** (*see p171*).

With your own private garden
Garden suite at the **Inn at the Roman Forum** (*see p181*).

Europe's priciest
Cupola suite at the **Westin Excelsior** (*see p173* **Big and Sassy**).

Bars (2). Business centre. Concierge. Gym. Internet *(free). Parking (€50). Restaurants (3). Room service. Spa. TV.*
▶ *For a glimpse of Rome dolce vita, in a 21st-century style, saunter down the via Veneto at aperitivo hour to h club>doney (see p209) inside the Excelsior hotel.*

Hassler

Piazza Trinità dei Monti 6 (06 699 340, www.hotelhasslerroma.com). Metro Spagna/bus 52, 62, 95, 116, 119, 492. **Rooms** 98. **Rates** (plus 10% tax) €550-€810 double. *Breakfast* €33. **Credit** AmEx, DC, MC, V. **Map** p341 A4 **⑤**
Looking down from the top of the Spanish Steps, the Hassler remains the *grande dame* of the city's deluxe hotels – ageing a little, but still charming. With acres of polished marble and abundant chandeliers, the relentless luxury may make your head spin, but the attentiveness of the staff distinguishes this place from the impersonal service often to be found at Rome's top hotels.
Bars (2). Business centre. Concierge. Disabled-adapted rooms. Gym. Internet (€20). Parking (€45). Restaurants (2). Room service. Spa. TV.

Expensive

Aleph

Via di San Basilio 15 (06 422 901, www.boscolo hotels.com). Metro Barberini/bus 52, 62, 95, 116, 119, 492. **Rooms** 96. **Rates** €330-€450 double. **Credit** AmEx, DC, MC, V. **Map** p341 C4 **⑥**
This flight of fancy, which was designed by Adam Tihany, has a theme: heaven and hell. The hotel's common areas are in various intensities of devil-red, whereas the bedrooms are bright and 'heavenly'. Tihany's playful touches, such as hologrammed bookcases in the reading room and the outsize backgammon board in the interior courtyard, are a world away from the luxe-but-dull decor of many of via Veneto's mega-hotels. *Photo p167.*
Bars (2). Business centre. Concierge. Disabled-adapted rooms. Gym. Internet (€20). Parking (nearby, €35). Restaurants (2). Room service. Spa. TV.

Moderate

Daphne Veneto

Via di San Basilio 55 (06 8745 0087, www.daphne-rome.com). Metro Barberini/bus 52, 62, 63, 95, 116, 119, 492. **Rooms** 7. **Rates** €140-€220 double. **Credit** AmEx, DC, MC, V. **Map** p341 B5 **⑦**
For review, *see p167* **Daphne Trevi**.
Concierge. Internet (free) Parking (€25-€30).

Residenza A

Via Veneto 183 (06 486 700, www.hotelviaveneto. com). Metro Barberini/bus 52, 62, 95, 116, 119,

492. **Rooms** 7. **Rates** €180-€265 double. **Credit** AmEx, DC, MC, V. **Map** p341 B4 **⑧**
On the first floor of an imposing palazzo, Residenza A has splashy modern works of art enlivening a slate-grey and black colour scheme. The rooms are luxuriously finished, with great perks such as in-room computers, extra-roomy showers and Bulgari bath products. Specify that you'd like one of the four rooms overlooking the street for a (soundproofed) view of via Veneto. Guests are given keys for hours when reception is unmanned.
Internet (free). Parking (€25). TV.

Hotel Art. *See p171.*

CONSUME

Roma: al centro della città.
Firenze: una villa immersa nel verde.

CERTOSA/MEDITERRANEO/MASSIMO D'AZEGLIO/ATLANTICO/NORD/RELAIS

HB BETTOJA HOTELS
LA TRADIZIONE
DELL'OSPITALITÀ

www.bettojahotels.it - numero verde: 800.860004

Casa Montani. *See p172.*

THE TRIDENTE

Deluxe

Hotel Art
Via Margutta 56 (06 328 711, www.hotelart.it).
Metro Spagna/bus 117, 119. **Rooms** 46. **Rates**
€270-€640 double. **Credit** AmEx, DC, MC, V. **Map**
p338 E3 ❾
On a street famed for its arty, crafty studios, the
Hotel Art sticks to its theme throughout. The lobby
area – with white pods serving as check-in and
concierge desks – sets the modern tone; only the ceiling retains a touch of the classic (the building was
once a chapel). Hallways are in acidic shades of
orange, yellow, green and blue, while the rooms
themselves are decorated in a serene palette of
neutrals, with parquet floors and chunky wood
furniture. *Photo p169.*
Bar. Concierge. Disabled-adapted rooms. Gym.
Internet (€17). Room service. TV.

Expensive

The Inn at the Spanish Steps &
the View at the Spanish Steps
Via dei Condotti 85 & 91 (06 6992 5657,
www.atspanishsteps.com or www.theview
atthespanishsteps.com). Metro Spagna/bus
116, 119. **Rooms** 24 (Inn); 4 (View). **Rates**
(plus 10% tax) *Inn* €200-€820 double. *View*
€480-€780 double. **Credit** AmEx, DC, MC, V.
Map p341 A4 & p339 E4 ❿
The Inn offers luxury boutique accommodation
smack in the middle of via Condotti, one of the

world's most famous shopping streets, while the
View enjoys a slightly more tranquil position on
the top floor of a palazzo at the end of the same
street. Rooms at the Inn are an extravagant mix of
plush fabrics and antiques; some of the deluxe rooms
have 17th-century frescoes. The View's decor is
more restrained, with sober grey and blue fabrics,
dark-wood floors and black and white tiled bathrooms. The junior suite boasts a dead-ahead view of
the Spanish Steps. Breakfast is served on the bijou
terrace when weather permits.
Bar. Concierge. Internet (€10). Room service. TV.

Portrait Suites
Via Bocca di Leone 23 (06 6938 0742, 055 2726
4000 reservations, www.lungarnohotels.com).
Metro Spagna/bus 116, 119. **Rooms** 14. **Rates**
(plus 10% tax) €330-€580 double. **Credit** AmEx, DC,
MC, V. **Map** p341 A4 & p339 E4 ⓫

THE BEST
MID-PRICE WITH STYLE

Earth tones and phones
Daphne Trevi (*see p167*) and **Daphne**
Veneto (*see p169*).

Very mod in 15th-century palazzo
Relais Palazzo Taverna & Locanda degli
Antiquari (*see p175*).

Plush fabrics, breakfast in bed
Casa Montani (*see p172*).

CONSUME

Crossing Condotti.

Portrait Suites is one of the luxury boutique hotels owned by fashion designer Salvatore Ferragamo. Though black and white photos and memorabilia from the designer's archives decorate the hallways, the rooms themselves carry little clue of the hotel's fashion pedigree (though eagle-eyed fans might spot the designer's *gancino* emblem on the curtains). A black-and-slate colour scheme is offset with touches of pink and lime, with spacious marble bathrooms, walk-in wardrobes and – ta dah! – a glamorous kitchenette. Breakfast is served in the rooms or outside on the spectacular terrace.
Bar. Concierge. Internet (free). Room service. TV.
► *There's hardly a designer boutique that isn't a stone's throw from this Ferragamo-owned hotel; for our favourite fashion boutiques, see p223.*

THE BEST ROOFTOP TREATS

Solarium & whirlpool bath
Grand Hotel Via Veneto (see p167).

The colosseum at breakfast
Capo d'Africa (see p179).

Cool pool, chic bar
Radisson SAS es. Hotel (see p181).

Moderate

Casa Howard
Via Capo le Case 18 & via Sistina 149 (06 6992 4555, www.casahoward.com). Metro Spagna or Barberini/bus 52, 63, 116, 117, 119, 492.
Rooms 10. **Rates** €170-€250 double. *Breakfast* €10. **Credit** AmEx, DC, MC, V. **Map** p341 A5 **⑫**
Casa Howard offers beautifully decorated accommodation in two locations a stone's throw from the Spanish Steps, with all rooms individually designed. All of the rooms in via Sistina have en-suite bathrooms; in via Capo le Case, you may have to go along the hall to your (private) bathroom. Details such as a mini-Turkish bath, a kimono and slippers for every guest and a sumptuous breakfast served on fine porcelain make a stay here into something of a pampering experience. There is no reception: guests are given their own set of keys.
Internet (free). TV.

★ Casa Montani
Piazzale Flaminia 9 (06 3260 0421, www.casamontani.com). Metro Flaminio/bus 88, 95, 490, 495, 628, 926, tram 2. **Rooms** 5. **Rates** €160-€220 double. **Credit** AmEx, DC, MC, V. **Map** p338 D2 **⑬**
In a busy square right outside the Porta del Popolo gate, this delightful five-room townhouse (with very good double glazing) is a rarity in Rome: charming, exquisitely decorated in contemporary-classic style with lush fabrics in warm earthy tones, impeccably run… and good value. A single bed can be added in the anteroom of some suites. A delicious breakfast is served in the rooms: wireless internet is free. *Photo p171.*
Internet (free). TV.

★ Crossing Condotti
Via Mario de' Fiori 28 (06 6992 0633, www.crossingcondotti.com). Metro Spagna/bus 52, 53, 61, 71, 80, 81, 85, 117, 119, 160, 628, 850. **Rooms** 5. **Rates** €180-€280 double. **Credit** AmEx, DC, MC, V. **Map** p339 E4 **⑭**
A short stroll from Prada, Bulgari and other fashion heavyweights, this hotel is remarkably central. The owner's gorgeous antiques are set against a cool contemporary background, and attentive staff are unfailingly helpful. Crossing Condotti is more Roman hideaway than fully-fledged hotel though; public spaces are limited to a handy kitchenette with coffee-making facilities and a fridge stocked with (free) soft drinks.
Internet (free). Room service. TV.

Hotel Suisse
Via Gregoriana 54 (06 678 3649, www.hotelsuisserome.com). Metro Spagna/bus 52, 63, 116, 117, 119, 492. **Rooms** 12. **Rates** €140-€165 double. **Credit** AmEx, DC, MC, V. **Map** p341 A/B5 **⑮**

Big and Sassy

Many of Rome's legendary deluxe hotel options cluster around the via Veneto – hub of the *dolce vita* in the 1960s but now with a rather strong odour of expense account. There are options around Termini station too: not the city's most salubrious area, but when you're staying in these lavish cocoons, that's not going to worry you unduly. Most of the following classic hotels have long since been snapped up by international chains.

Formerly the Hilton, the **Rome Cavalieri** (via A Cadlolo 101, Suburbs: North 06 35 091, www.romecavalieri.com) is now part of the Waldorf Astoria Collection. Magnificent views over the city, out-and-out luxury and a stunning art collection – not to mention a vast pool and an extraordinary restaurant (*p205* **La Pergola**) – are the hallmarks of the Cavalieri experience.

The Rocco Forte group's extremely central **De Russie** (via del Babuino 9, Tridente, 06 328 881, www.hotelde russie.it) is a favourite with the movie crowd. Design is sharp, and there's a great bar (*p211* **Stravinskij Bar**) in the wonderful garden.

Starwood's **Eden** (via Ludovisi 49, Veneto, 06 478 121, www.edenroma.com), just off via Veneto, is the epitome of understated elegance. Views over the city – including those from the rooftop bar – are breathtaking.

The Boscolo group's **Exedra** (piazza della Repubblica 47, Esquilino, 06 489 381, www.boscolohotels.com; *pictured*)

is glamorously modern, and the rooftop pool is a draw. It's very handy for Termini station, as is Starwood's **St Regis Grand** (via VE Orlando 3, Esquilino, 06 47 091, www.thestregisgrandrome.com). Founded in 1894 by César Ritz, the St Regis drips gorgeous chandeliers over acres of marble.

But for real Hollywood-style opulence, there's no beating Starwood's **Westin Excelsior** (via Veneto 125, Veneto, 06 47 081, www.westinrome.com). The Villa la Cupola suite is one of Europe's most expensive.

On the third floor of a tranquil palazzo near piazza di Spagna, Hotel Suisse has been run by the same family since 1921. Rooms are bright and airy, with parquet floors, dark-wood antique furniture and a charming, old-fashioned feel. Breakfast is served in the rooms. Air-conditioning is an extra €10 per night; the two rooms without have ceiling fans. *Internet (free). Room service. TV.*

Budget

Okapi Rooms
Via della Penna (06 3260 9815, www.okapi rooms.it). Metro Flaminia/bus 81, 117, 119, 628, 926. **Rooms** 20. **Rates** €85-€120 double (breakfast not included). **Credit** AmEx, MC, V. **Map** p338 D3 ⑯
Just off piazza del Popolo, the basic but comfortable Okapi Rooms is excellently placed for seeing the sights. Breakfast is not included but the area is full of handy cafés. The spotless rooms have air-con and one has a little balcony; some, however, are reported to be noisy so specify you want a room away from the lobby if sleeping soundly is a priority. *Internet (free).*

Pensione Panda
Via della Croce 35 (06 678 0179, www.hotel panda.it). Metro Spagna/bus 117, 119. **Rooms** 28. **Rates** €98-€108 double. **Credit** AmEx, MC, V. **Map** p339 E4 ⑰
Panda's excellent location, just west of piazza di Spagna, is its main selling point. Rooms are very basic but clean; ask for one of the more recently renovated rooms, which have terracotta floors and high, wood-beamed ceilings. There's no lift and you'll have to go elsewhere for your morning cappuccino, but *centro storico* bargains are hard to come by, and Panda is usually booked solid in high season. *Internet (free).*

PANTHEON & NAVONA
Expensive

Sole al Pantheon
*Piazza della Rotonda 63 (06 678 0441, www.
hotelsolealpantheon.com). Bus 62, 64, 116, 492,
916, tram 8.* **Rooms** 32. **Rates** €245-€440 double.
Credit AmEx, DC, MC, V. **Map** p339 D5 ⑱
Dating back to the 15th century, this – management
will tell you – is the oldest hotel in Europe. Rooms
are fresh and uncluttered, with tiled floors and frescoes. All bathrooms have whirlpool baths. Ask for
one of the rooms at the front for superb views over
the Pantheon; otherwise console yourself by seeking
out the glorious roof terrace, where breakfast is
served in the warmer months.
*Bar. Internet (€10, free in rooms). Parking
(€35-€40). Room service. TV.*

Moderate

Abruzzi
*Piazza della Rotonda 69 (06 9784 1369, www.
hotelabruzzi.it). Bus 62, 64, 116, 492, 916/
tram 8.* **Rooms** 25. **Rates** €175-€220 double.
Credit AmEx, DC, MC, V. **Map** p339 D5/E5 ⑲
The splendid location is really this hotel's selling
point. Twenty of its 25 rooms have breathtaking
views of the Pantheon, and all are outfitted in rich
yellow and emerald shades, with wood furnishings.
Some rooms are a little cramped. Breakfast is taken
nearby, in a café in piazza della Rotonda.
Internet (€10). TV.

Teatro Pace
*Via del Teatro Pace 33 (06 687 9075, www.
hotelteatropace.com). Bus 40Exp, 64, 81, 492,
916/tram 8.* **Rooms** 23. **Rates** €140-€235 double.
Credit AmEx, DC, MC, V. **Map** p342 C1 & p339
C/D5 ⑳
This 17th-century former cardinal's residence lies
down a cobbled alley near piazza Navona. An impressive Baroque stone spiral staircase winds up four
floors (no lift). Rooms are spacious and elegantly decorated with wood floors, heavy drapes and marble
bathrooms. The original, wood-beamed ceilings are
intact in all rooms, but higher on the top two floors.
Breakfast is served in the rooms.
Internet (€4). Room service. TV.

Budget

Pensione Barrett
*Largo Argentina 47 (06 686 8481, www.
pensionebarrett.com). Bus 40Exp, 64, 81,
492, 916/tram 8.* **Rooms** 20. **Rates** €120
double (breakfast not included). **Credit** MC, V.
Map p339 D6 & p342 D1 ㉑
In the same family for 40 years, this *pensione* takes
its name from the poet Elizabeth Barrett Browning,

**Relais Palazzo Taverna & Locanda
degli Antiquari.**

who stayed here in 1848. A bewildering number of
antiques and curios give it a vaguely eccentric feel:
rooms are a mishmash of faux-classical columns,
dark wood furniture, original wood-beamed ceilings
and pastel walls. Breakfast (extra, à la carte) is
served in the rooms, some of which have great views
over the square. If you want air-conditioning, it will
cost an extra €10 per night.
Internet (free). TV.

Relais Palazzo Taverna &
Locanda degli Antiquari
*Via dei Gabrielli 92 (06 2039 8064, www.relais
palazzotaverna.com). Bus 30Exp, 70, 81, 87, 116,
492.* **Rooms** 11. **Rates** €100-€210 double. **Credit**
AmEx, DC, MC, V. **Map** p339 C5 ㉒
There's an interesting contrast between the sleek,
modern decor and the 15th-century building (a few

THE BEST
BOUTIQUES WITH PANACHE

Designer-land hideaway
Crossing Condotti (*see p172*).

Turkish bath & kimonos
Casa Howard (*see p172*).

Designer detailing
Portrait Suites (*see p171*).

CONSUME

steps from antiques shop-lined via dei Coronari) that these twin *residenze* occupy. The spacious, individually styled bedrooms have white-painted wood ceilings, wallpaper with bold graphics, and bedlinen in spicy tones. Breakfast is served in the rooms. *Internet (free). TV.*

GHETTO & CAMPO DE' FIORI
Expensive

Residenza in Farnese
Via del Mascherone 59 (06 6889 1388, www.residenzafarneseroma.it). Bus 23, 116, 280. **Rooms** 31. **Rates** €290-€420 double. **Credit** AmEx, MC, V. **Map** p339 C6 & p342 C2 ㉓
On a narrow ivy-lined street, this former convent has been refurbished without losing its charm. An oversized crystal chandelier in the lobby lends a sense of opulence, but details like home-made baked goods and jams for breakfast reflect the homely charm of the place. Rooms run from basic updated cells with small marble bathrooms to more comfortable pastel-hued rooms with hand-painted furnishings. Ask for a room overlooking the gardens of Palazzo Spada, or the beautiful Palazzo Farnese. There's a wonderful view from the roof terrace.
Bar. Disabled-adapted rooms. Internet (€10). Parking (€20). Room service. TV.

Moderate

Campo de' Fiori
Piazza del Biscione 6 (06 6880 6865, www.hotelcampodefiori.com). Bus 23, 116. **Rooms** 22. **Rates** €120-€260 double. **Credit** AmEx, DC, MC, V. **Map** p339 D6 & p342 C1 ㉔
Just off busy campo de' Fiori, this hotel's rooms, although not particularly spacious, are elegantly fitted out in rich colours, and the small but elegant bathrooms have bronze-effect tiles with antique mirrors. The pretty roof terrace provides some great views. The hotel also offers self-catering apartments around the Campo.
Concierge. Internet (free). Room service. TV.

Teatro di Pompeo
Largo del Pallaro 8 (06 6830 0170, www.hotel teatrodipompeo.it). Bus 23, 116. **Rooms** 13. **Rates** €180-€205 double. **Credit** AmEx, DC, MC, V. **Map** p339 D6 & p342 C1 ㉕
This small, friendly hotel occupies a palazzo built on the site of the ancient Teatro di Pompeo; its *pièce de résistance* is its cave-like breakfast room, dug out of the ancient ruins. The rooms are simply decorated in neutral tones, with terracotta floors and high, wood-beamed ceilings. Opt for one of the attractive rooms in the main hotel building rather than the more basic annexe rooms nearby.
Bar. Internet (free). TV.

TRASTEVERE & GIANICOLO
See also p263 **La Foresteria Orsa Maggiore**.

Expensive

Donna Camilla Savelli
Via Garibaldi 27 (06 588 861, http:hoteldonna camillasavelli.com). Bus 115, 125, 780, H/tram 8. **Rooms** 78. **Rates** €230-€390 double. **Credit** AmEx, DC, MC, V. **Map** p342 B3 ㉖
This former convent, designed by Borromini, has been tranformed into a plush 4-star hotel by the Alpitur chain – though there's still a slight air of nunnery around the echoing corridors. The position – in a quiet corner beneath the Gianicolo but a shop stroll from Trastevere's lively alleyways – is great, there's a pretty garden, and the view from the roof terrace is quite spectacular.
Bar. Concierge. Disabled-adapted room. Internet (€12). Parking (free). Restaurant. Room service. TV.

Moderate

Hotel Santa Maria & Residenza Santa Maria
Vicolo del Piede 2 (06 589 4626, www.htlsanta maria.com). Bus 780, H/tram 8. **Rooms** 18. **Rates** €165-€220 double. **Credit** AmEx, DC, MC, V. **Map** p342 C3 ㉗

Hotel Santa Maria.

CONSUME

Star food

You win some, you lose some.

Rome was awarded 14 Michelin stars in 2011 and, of those, five went to hotel restaurants. With one notable exception (La Pergola, which we discuss below), this indicates a fairly recent shift in the perception of what hotels should offer – from comfort food to cutting-edge gourmet. But whether the Michelin is picking the right hotels is quite another matter.

Losing its star in 2011 was **baby**, the restaurant in the Hotel Aldrovandi (not listed) helmed by sensational southern chef Alfonso Iaccarini, who has returned full-time to his excellent eaterie on the Amalfi Coast. Rome's hotel dining options are all the poorer for this.

Thank goodness, then, that we still have **La Pergola** (in the Rome Cavalieri, *see p173* **Big and Sassy**; dinner for two €400 plus wine) – a Rome classic, and the only restaurant in this city of food to boast three Michelin stars. Given the position – high up on Monte Mario – you might think people go for the view. But with food like this on your plate, the view pales. German chef Heinz Beck creates an ever-changing menu of daring perfection.

Utterly fresh, utterly flavoursome, it also has an award-winning cellarful of wine.

The French food bible has given one star each to **Imàgo** at the Hassler (*see p169*) and **Mirabelle** at the Hotel Splendide Royale (via di Porta Pinciana, Veneto, 06 4215 8838, www.mirabelle) – two choices that are, in our opinion, questionable. On the plus side, both offer fantastic views over the city. This doesn't, however, compensate for service that can be inattentive, food that can be mediocre and tabs that can leave you reeling, in both establishments.

Not (yet) a starred chef, former news photographer **Filippo La Mantia** (*see p187*) burst on to the hotel-food scene in 2009 with his irrepressible Sicilian ebullience, taking over the restaurant at the Hotel Majestic (not listed) on via Veneto and reminding competitors that hotel food can push back barriers. The dining room is an extravaganza of burnished mirrors, Empire furniture and potted palms; there's a terrace overlooking via Veneto, too. La Mantia's delicate, onion-free, citrus-perfumed touch is the keynote here.

Just off piazza Santa Maria in Trastevere, the Santa Maria stands on the site of a 16th-century convent. Each of the bedrooms has a tiled floor, slightly bland peach decor and a spacious bathroom, and they all open on to a charming, sunny central courtyard planted with orange trees. Bicycles are available for guests to use for exploring Trastevere's winding alleys. Around the corner at via dell'Arco di San Calisto 20 (06 5833 5103, www.residenzasanta maria.com) is this hotel's charming offshoot.
Bar. Disabled-adapted room. Internet (free). Parking (€15-€25). TV.

★ Residenza Arco de' Tolomei

Via dell'Arco de' Tolomei 26C (06 5832 0819, www.inrome.info). Bus 125, H/tram 8. **Rooms** 5. **Rates** €150-€210 double. **Credit** AmEx, DC, MC, V. **Map** p342 D3 ㉘

This bijou *residenza*, which was created by Marco and Gianna Paola Fe' d'Ostiani in their own home, has a cosy and welcoming feel, with beautiful wood flooring and staircase, plentiful antiques and a sunny breakfast room. Bedrooms are decorated in a whimsical, English country-house style; the three on the upper floor have terraces, but the two below are slightly larger.
Internet (free). TV.

Budget

Arco del Lauro

Via dell'Arco de' Tolomei 27 (06 9784 0350, www.arcodellauro.it). Bus 125, H/tram 8. **Rooms** 4. **Rates** €85-€145 double. **No credit cards**. **Map** p342 D3 ㉙

On a picturesque Trastevere backstreet, Arco del Lauro has four rooms, all with private bathroom, decorated in modern, fresh neutrals. Budget *residenze* are few and far between in chi-chi Trastevere, so the Arco del Lauro, with its airy and spotlessly clean rooms, is all the more of a find. Breakfast is taken in a bar in a nearby piazza.
Internet (free). TV.

AVENTINE & TESTACCIO

Moderate

Sant'Anselmo, Villa San Pio & Aventino

Piazza Sant'Anselmo 2 (06 570 057, www.aventino hotels.com). Metro Circo Massimo/bus 60Exp, 75, 81, 175, 715/tram 3. **Rooms** 34 (Sant'Anselmo); 78 (Villa San Pio); 21 (Aventino). **Rates** €120-€270 double. **Credit** AmEx, DC, MC, V. **Map** p343 E5 ㉚

Residenza Arco de' Tolomei.

The three properties of the Aventino Hotels group may not be in the thick of things – on the quiet, leafy residential Aventine – but they're not far away either, though beware: they're on the top of a steep hill. At the Sant'Anselmo rooms are imaginatively decorated with playful touches. One, on two levels, boasts its own mosaic-tiled nymphaeum; another is dominated by a vast, sumptuous four-poster bed as well as a free-standing bath. Villa San Pio (via di Santa Melania 19) consists of three separate buildings that share the same gardens and an airy breakfast room. Ask for a room with a terrace for views either of the surrounding greenery or towards Monte Testaccio. The Aventino (via di San Domenico 10) is less manicured and has yet to be refurbished.

Concierge. Disabled-adapted rooms. Internet (free). Parking (free). Room service. TV.

rooftop breakfast room has knock-out views of the Colosseum and the fourth-century basilica dei Santi Quattro Coronati.

Bar. Disabled-adapted rooms. Gym. Internet (15). Parking (€40). Room service. TV.

CELIO & SAN GIOVANNI

Expensive

Capo d'Africa

Via Capo d'Africa 54 (06 772 801, www. hotelcapodafrica.com). Metro Colosseo/bus 75, 87, 117, 810/tram 3. **Rooms** 65. **Rates** €143-€380 double. **Credit** AmEx, DC, MC, V. **Map** p344 C3 **③**

Artfully arranged bamboo? Tick. Pastel armchairs? Tick. The Capo d'Africa is perfect for the design-conscious, and the hotel's location, on a quiet street near the Colosseum, is another thing in its favour. The rooms are spacious and comfortable, and the

Lancelot. *See p181.*

Lancelot

*Via Capo d'Africa 47 (06 7045 0615, www.
lancelothotel.com). Metro Colosseo/bus 75,
87, 117, 810/tram 3.* **Rooms** 60. **Rates**
€150-€190 double. **Credit** AmEx, DC, MC, V.
Map p344 C3 ❸❷

Rooms at this family-run hotel are decorated in an
elegant mixture of linen, wood and tiles. Some of
them have terraces looking towards the Palatine and
Colosseum. Half board is provided for those staying
three nights or more, but even if you're not on half
board you can book dinner (it costs an extra €25,
with wine and coffee included). Staff are friendly and
helpful. *Photo p179.*

*Disabled-adapted rooms. Internet (free). Parking
(€10). Restaurant. TV.*

MONTI & ESQUILINO

Expensive

The Inn at the Roman Forum

*Via degli Ibernesi 30 (06 6919 0970, www.
theinnattheromanforum.com). Bus 75, 87,
175, 810.* **Rooms** 12. **Rates** (plus 10% tax)
€210-€610 double. **Credit** AmEx, DC, MC, V.
Map p344 B2 ❸❸

The location of this boutique hotel, close to the
Forum but on a picturesque street that is comfortably off the tourist trail, gives the place an exclusive
feel. The rooms are a suave combination of rich
fabrics and antiques; the spacious deluxe double
rooms – some of which are furnished with their own
fireplaces – have canopied beds and marble bathrooms. Breakfast is served on the roof terrace or in
a cosy room with open fire in the winter. An ancient
crypt has been excavated on the ground floor. Two
rooms opening on to a garden can be joined to make
a sumptuous suite.

*Bar. Concierge. Disabled-adapted room. Internet
(€10). Parking (€28). Room service. TV.*

Radisson SAS es. Hotel

*Via F Turati 171 (06 444 841, www.rome.
radissonsas.com). Metro Termini/bus 70, 71,
105/tram 5, 14.* **Rooms** 232. **Rates** €216-€316
double. *Breakfast* €26. **Credit** AmEx, DC, MC, V.
Map p344 E1 ❸❹

Built on the site of an ancient Roman plebeian
cemetery (archaeological findings are displayed in
an excavation area just by the entrance), this self-
announced 'concept' hotel today caters mainly for
business clients and diehard design fans. The
rooftop is a vast decked area, complete with trendy
bar and pool. Beds in the minimalist rooms are set
on a low platform, divided from bathrooms by a
glass screen. *Photo p182.*

*Bars (2). Business centre. Concierge. Disabled-
adapted rooms. Gym. Internet (free). Parking
(€16). Restaurants (2). Pool (outdoor). Room
service. Spa. TV.*

The Inn at the Roman Forum.

Moderate

Artemide

*Via Nazionale 22 (06 489 911, www.hotel
artemide.com). Metro Repubblica/bus 40, 60,
64, 70, 71, 116T, 170.* **Rooms** 85. **Rates**
€158-€263 double. **Credit** AmEx, DC, MC, V.
Map p341 C5 ❸❺

The Artemide is a classically stylish haven on this
busy shopping artery, with charming professional
staff (and free mini-bars) to ensure a pleasant stay.
Smaller 'no-frills' rooms without breakfast (or
mini-bars), costing significantly less than regular
rooms, are a good budget option.

*Bar. Disabled-adapted room. Gym. Internet (free).
Room service. TV.*

Nerva

*Via Tor de' Conti 3 (06 678 1835, www.hotel
nerva.com). Bus 60Exp, 87, 117, 175, 810.*
Rooms 19. **Rates** €130-€220 double. **Credit**
DC, MC, V. **Map** p344 B2 ❸❻

The family-run Nerva may be situated right next
door to the famous Forum (*see p62*), but there's not
a view to be had of it – the hotel faces a wall. (Mind
you, this isn't just any wall: it formed part of the
ancient Forum of Nerva.) Nonetheless, the Nerva is
in a very handy location, and rooms are pleasant, if
a little old-fashioned. The staff and proprietors are
a friendly bunch.

*Bar. Disabled-adapted rooms. Internet (free).
Parking (from €30). Room service. TV.*

CONSUME

CONSUME

INSIDE TRACK ID

When you book into an Italian hotel, the receptionist will ask you to present photo-ID. Your document will generally be given back to you immediately, or the first time you come back down to reception to leave your key. If it isn't (and this happens sometimes, generally in cheaper hotels) ask for it back: you are required by law to carry photo-ID with you at all times.

Budget

The Beehive
Via Marghera 8 (06 4470 4553, www.the-beehive. com). Metro Termini/bus 40Exp, 64, 492, 910, H. **Rooms** 17. **Rates** (breakfast not included*)* €20-26 per bed (dorm); €30-€35 per person (double, triple or quad in apartment). **Credit** MC, V. **Map** p341 E5 ③⑦
American owners Steve and Linda Brenner mix design-icon furnishings (Philippe Starck on the patio), with reasonable rates and basic amenities, to create a 'youth hostel meets boutique hotel' vibe. There's a sunny garden, a cosy, organic restaurant and a yoga studio. The helpful staff provides a free in-house guide-book to the city, and there's free internet access. Breakfast is available for an extra fee on request. *Internet (free).*

★ Casa Romana
Via dei Mille 41A (329 228 0626, www.myrome apartment.com). Metro Termini/bus 40Exp, 64, 492, 910, H. **Rooms** 3. **Rates** €60-€90 double. **No credit cards. Map** p341 E5 ③⑧

Simply stylish, this three-room B&B hideaway not far from Termini station offers excellent facilities for this price bracket. The welcome is friendly, the break-fast – often including produce from the owners' property in Umbria – is excellent and Fulvia's many years of experience in the travel sector make her expert advice consistently spot-on. Casa Romana is very convenient for the airport bus if you have an early flight out of Ciampino.
Internet (free).

VATICAN & PRATI
Moderate

Hotel Bramante
Vicolo delle Palline 24 (06 6880 6426, www. hotelbramante.com). Bus 23, 40Exp, 62, 280. **Rooms** 16. **Rates** €150-€220 double. **Credit** AmEx, DC, MC, V. **Map** p339 A4 ③⑨
Hidden down a cobbled street near St Peter's, the Bramante was once home to 16th-century architect Domenico Fontana, and became an inn in 1873. It has a large, pleasant reception, a little patio and fantastically friendly staff. The 16 rooms are simple but elegant; most have high-beamed ceilings, some have wrought-iron beds.
Bar. Internet (free). Room service. TV.

Budget

Colors
Via Boezio 31 (06 687 4030, www.colors hotel.com). Metro Ottaviano/bus 23, 492, 990. **Rooms** 21. **Rates** €18-€25 per person in dorm; €80-€104 double. **No credit cards. Map** p338 B3 ④⓪

Radisson SAS es. Hotel. *See p181.*

The Beehive.

A short walk from St Peter's and the Vatican Museums, Colors offers bright, clean dormitory and hotel accommodation that's well above the average quality for this price bracket. The first two floors, decorated in zingy colours, have self-catering kitchen facilities, with cornflakes and coffee provided for guests to make their own breakfast. More neutral tones have been used in the superior rooms on the third floor (all with private bathroom, flat-screen TV, air-conditioning and breakfast). There's a sunny terrace, and members of staff are multi-lingual and very friendly.
Internet (free).

Pensione Paradise

Viale Giulio Cesare 47 (06 3600 4331, www. pensioneparadise.com). Metro Lepanto/bus 23, 49, 492. **Rooms** 10. **Rates** €60-€120 double. **Credit** AmEx, DC, MC, V. **Map** p338 B2 ⑪
Rooms are on the poky side, as you might expect for this price, but friendly staff and a decent location not far from the Vatican ensure that backpackers keep on coming. There's no breakfast and no air-con (ceiling fans are provided instead), but if you're willing to rough it a little, you could do far worse.
TV.

SELF-CATERING

Consider renting an apartment if you are staying for more than a few days, particularly if there are more than two of you. **IDEC** (06 4893 0557, www.flatinrome.com) can find a flat for you, while the London-based **A Place in Rome** (+44 (0)20 8543 2283, www.aplace inrome.com) offers delightful apartments in the heart of the *centro storico.* **Palazzo Olivia** (06 6821 6986, www.palazzo-olivia.it) has lovely apartments for rent in a newly restored 17th-century palazzo near piazza Navona (minimum stay four nights).

The UK's **Landmark Trust** (+44 (0)1628 825925, www.landmarktrust.org.uk) rents an apartment in the Keats-Shelley House (*see p87*) overlooking the Spanish Steps that sleeps up to four, with a minimum stay of three nights. It costs €2,226 a week in high season, rather less in winter, but is full of lovely details including the original painted wooden ceilings.

The **Bed & Breakfast Italia** agency (06 687 8618, www.bbitalia.it) has hundreds of chic Roman options on their books, including luxury accommodation in *palazzi* – awarded four 'crowns' by the agency's vetters.

Colors.

CONSUME

Eating Out

Great restaurants, but variety still isn't the spice of Rome's culinary life.

Rome has always taken its food seriously, valuing substance over style where eating is concerned. So although plenty of design-driven restaurants open, there's a high turnover, and the survivors are those offering something more than a few dried twigs in a vase and the chance of spotting a TV starlet. Trattorias and osterias remain the stalwarts of Rome's eating scene – more and more as times get harder. Some are unreconstructed family-run operations that have been serving up the same dishes for generations – but still do them so well that they pack in the punters day after day. Others

are *nuove trattorie* – places that take the trattoria formula (informal service, unfussy cooking based on market-fresh ingredients) but give it a twist by upping the creativity quotient in the kitchen, and by offering a range of fine wines.

THE FOODIE REVOLUTION

Rome's new foodie enthusiasm has upped quality no end, the trickle-down effect meaning that even the most basic trat now generally offers a decent bottle of extra-virgin olive oil with which to dress your salad. As far as *nuove trattorie* go, **L'Arcangelo** (*see p204*), **Tuttifrutti** (*see p200*) and **Ditirambo** (*see p194*) are all, in their ways, successful examples. Rome also offers greater variety nowadays. Once the choice was between the posh restaurant, the humble trattoria, or the ultra-cheap, no-frills pizzeria. Today the range of options extends to wine bars, mozzarella bars, gastropubs, salad bars, designer restaurants and deli-diners. Even the unchanging pizzeria has been shaken up by the arrival of gourmet pizza emporia like **Dar Poeta** (*see p198*) and **00100** (*see p198*). Only the ethnic and international scene still leaves a lot to be desired.

If there is one purely Roman contribution to the Italian culinary tradition, it's creativity with **offal**. Traditional Roman restaurants rely heavily on the *quinto quarto*, or 'fifth quarter' – those parts of the beast left over after the prime cuts have been sold off. That means brain (*cervello*), spinal marrow (*schienale*), nerves (*nervetti*), stomach and intestines (*trippa* or *pajata*), hooves (*zampi*), and the thymus and pancreas glands (*animelle*). Even tails are highly thought of by Roman gourmets, as in the classic slaughterhouse worker's dish, *coda alla vaccinara*. The once working-class areas of Testaccio and Trastevere are peppered with trattorias that serve these delicacies.

GOING THE COURSE

The standard Roman running order is: *antipasto* (hors-d'oeuvre), *primo* (usually pasta, sometimes soup), *secondo* (the meat or fish course) with optional *contorno* (vegetables or salad, served separately), and *dolce* (dessert). You're under no obligation to order four courses – few locals do. It's perfectly normal, for example, to order a pasta course followed by a simple *contorno* (often the only option for vegetarians). Top-flight places sometimes offer a *menu degustazione* (taster menu) in the evening as well, but most venues offering a *menu turistico* should be avoided, especially if it is written in several languages.

DRINKS

These days, even the humblest trattorias and osterias have started to get themselves decent

---

❶ Blue numbers given in this chapter correspond to the location of each restaurant as marked on the street maps.

About the author

Lee Marshall *is a contributing editor to Condé Nast Traveller UK and Departures, and writes on cinema for Screen International. He has lived in Italy since 1984.*

CONSUME

wine lists. There are still a few places that pride themselves on their paint-stripper house wines, but they are increasingly in the minority. More and more establishments now offer a decent selection of wine by the glass (*al bicchiere* or *alla mescita*). In pizzerias, the drink of choice is *birra* (beer). Mineral water – *acqua minerale* – comes as either *gasata* (sparkling) or *naturale* (still).

PRICES, BOOKING & TIMES

The days when Romans ate out, cheaply, two or three times a week are a distant memory: this city is expensive. But central restaurants still tend to be packed on Friday and Saturday night and Sunday lunchtime, so do book ahead.

Only the humblest of trattorias don't accept credit cards, but if there is no sticker on the door, it pays to ask. By law, when you pay the bill (*il conto*) you must be given a proper receipt (*una ricevuta fiscale*): if you're not, ask for one.

Opening times can change according to time of year and the owners' whim. In the evening, few proper restaurants open before 7.30pm. Pizzerias begin serving earlier, generally by 6.30pm or 7pm.

For more on the listings, *see above* **Inside track**; for tipping, *see p197* **Inside track**.

WOMEN AND ETIQUETTE

Women dining alone rarely encounter problems, but you have to get used to the local habit of staring frankly (usually unaggressively). Single

diners of either sex can have trouble getting a table in cheaper places at busy times: few proprietors want to waste a table that could hold four diners. Very few places impose a dress code, though shorts and T-shirts go down badly in upmarket eateries. Smoking is illegal in all restaurants, except where there is a designated smoking area that meets stringent regulations.

WINE BARS

Neighbourhood *enoteche* (wine shops) and *vini e olii* (wine and oil) outlets have been around in Rome since time immemorial, complete with

Enoteca Provincia Romana. *See p187.*

their huddle of old men knocking back wine by the glass. For a selection of places in which drinking is the main point of the exercise, *see pp206-218* **Cafés, Bars & Gelaterie** chapter. The city also has upmarket, international-style wine bars, offering snacks and even full meals to go with their wines. Those included in this chapter range from places that lay out tables among the bottle-lined shelves at lunch to full-blown wine-oriented restaurants.

VEGETARIANS

Rome has few bona fide vegetarian restaurants; but even in traditional trattorias, waiters will no longer look blankly when you say *non mangio la carne* ('I don't eat meat') – though they do tend to offer as an alternative chicken or *prosciutto* (ham). Despair not: there's plenty else to try – from *penne all'arrabbiata* (pasta in a tomato and chilli sauce) through *tonnarelli cacio e pepe* (thick spaghetti with crumbly sheep's cheese and plenty of black pepper) to *carciofi alla giudia* (deep-fried artichokes, a Roman Jewish speciality).

CAPITOLINE & PALATINE

★ Enoteca Provincia Romana

Largo del Foro Traiano 84 (06 6766 2424, www.provincia.roma.it). Bus 40, 60, 84, 85, 87,175, 186, 271. **Meals served** 12.30-3pm, 7.30-11pm Mon-Sat. **Average** €30. **Credit** MC, V. **Map** p342 E1 & p344 A1 ❶
Buried round the back of the Rome provincial government offices, overlooking Trajan's column, this new wine bar and eaterie serves wines and produce exclusively from the area immediately surrounding the capital. The atmosphere is warmly cordial; the food is original and very good; the wine menu (with large by-the-glass choice) is full of pleasant surprises. In fact, it hardly seems like a PR exercise at all, and the hordes who pack the place at lunch (local office workers) and dinner (everyone) certainly seem happy to have such a valid option right here in the *centro*. There's an aperitivo hour with buffet from 5.30 to 7.30pm. Book ahead for a table. *Photo p185.*
▶ *This enoteca is located inside Palazzo Valentini, where digs beneath the building keep turning up archaeological surprises.*

San Teodoro

Via dei Fienili 49-51 (06 678 0933, www.st-teodoro.it). Bus 30Exp, 44, 81, 95, 160, 170, 628. **Meals served** 1-3.15pm, 8pm-11.30pm Mon-Sat. **Average** €65. **Credit** AmEx, MC, V. **Map** p342 E3 & p344 A3 ❷
Of a summer's evening there are few better places for an alfresco meal than this seafood-oriented restaurant around the back of the Forum. Come prepared to splash out, though. Some dishes draw their inspiration from *cucina romana*; others, like the pasta with shrimps, courgette flowers and pecorino cheese, or the baby red mullet with artichokes and spring onion, are lighter and more creative. Lighter meals and snacks are served at lunchtime round the corner at the Caffè San Teodoro.

TREVI & QUIRINALE

€ Antica Birreria Peroni

Via di San Marcello 19 (06 679 5310, www.antica birreriaperoni.net). Bus 62, 63, 81, 85, 95, 117, 119, 160, 175, 492, 628, 630, 850. **Meals served** noon-midnight Mon-Sat. Closed 2wks Aug. **Average** €25. **Credit** AmEx, DC, MC, V. **Map** p341 A6 ❸
This long-standing *centro storico* birreria is the perfect place to grab a quick lunch or dinner. Service is rough-and-Roman but friendly, and the food – a few hot pasta or rice dishes, various salads and some cold cuts – is good and relatively cheap. Sausage, though, is the main act: three different types of German-style *wurstel* are on offer. The birreria still retains its original art nouveau decor, with a chiaroscuro frieze featuring such slogans as 'drink beer and you'll live to be 100'.

VENETO & BORGHESE

See also p209 **Cinecaffè**.

Cantina Cantarini

Piazza Sallustio 12 (06 485 528, 06 474 3341). Bus 36, 60Exp, 62, 63, 80Exp, 86, 360, 630. **Meals served** 12.30-3pm, 7.30-10.30pm Mon-Sat. Closed 3wks Aug & 2wks Dec-Jan. **Average** €35. **Credit** AmEx, DC, MC, V. **Map** p341 D4 ❹
This high-quality trattoria is always packed and it's easy to see why: the cooking is simple but spot-on, and the prices are reasonable. Meat-based for the first part of the week, it turns fishy from Thursday on. The atmosphere is as *allegro* as seating is tight – though outdoor tables take off some of the pressure in summer. But the excellent *coniglio al cacciatore* (stewed rabbit), *fritto misto di pesce* (fried mixed fish) and *risotto al nero di seppia* (with squid ink) should help to override any concerns about comfort.

Filippo La Mantia

Hotel Majestic, via Veneto 50 (06 4214 4715, 331 785 8542, www.filippolamantia.com). Metro Barberini/bus 52, 62, 95, 116, 119. **Meals served** 8.30-11.30pm Mon-Sat. Closed 2wks Jan, 3wks Aug. **Average** €75. **Credit** AmEx, DC, MC, V. **Map** p341 B4 ❺
Ebulliant Sicilian photoreporter-turned-chef Filippo La Mantia brings a touch of his native island to this recently opened restaurant which, despite its lofty ceilings and burnished mirrors, is welcoming rather than daunting: La Mantia eschews butter, onions and garlic, using citrus fruits as his keynote. Brunch is served daily, and costs around €38. *See also p178* **Star food**. *Photos p188.*

CONSUME

Filippo La Mantia. *See p187.*

brick vaulted ceiling and bottle-lined walls, which offers creative trattoria cooking at competitive prices. A changing menu might have ravioli with broccoli and anchovies, while desserts are mostly playing-it-safe standards like *crema catalana*. Vegetarians will find a better than average selection here, and the worthwhile wine list includes several by-the-glass options.

▶ *A perfect place to recoup after visiting the MACRO gallery (see p157).*

THE TRIDENTE

Buccone

Via Ripetta 19-20 (06 361 2154, www.enoteca buccone.com). Bus 81, 204, 224, 628, 926. **Meals served** 12.30-3pm Mon-Thur; 12.30-3pm, 7.30-10.30pm Fri, Sat. Closed 2wks Aug. **Average** €22. **Credit** AmEx, DC, MC, V. **Map** p338 D3 ❼

For years Il Buccone operated as a takeaway *enoteca* (wine shop) with a few wines available by the glass at the marble counter; but now tables are arranged among the high wooden shelves, and in a little room at the back, for full meals. There are always three or four pasta dishes or soups, followed by a range of meaty seconds and creative salads. The cooking is more than competent, the prices extremely reasonable, and the service friendly.

Gino in vicolo Rosini

Vicolo Rosini 4 (06 687 3434). Bus 52, 53, 61, 62, 63, 71, 80Exp, 95, 116, 119, 175, 490, 630. **Meals served** 1-2.45pm, 8-10.30pm Mon-Sat. Closed Aug. **Average** €30. **No credit cards.** **Map** p339 E4 ❽

You don't seek out this hard-to-find trattoria in a lane off piazza del Parlamento for the food – though dishes like pasta with mushrooms and tomatoes, and rabbit cooked in white wine, are competently done. It's the atmosphere in the rooms with Arcadian murals that attracts: a real rustic trattoria feel hides much political wheeler-dealing by denizens of the nearby parliament building. Desserts include homemade *crostate* (jam tarts) and an excellent tiramisù. Come early, or be prepared to wait for a table.

Osteria dell'Arco

Via G Pagliari 11 (06 854 8438, www.osteria dellarco.com). Bus 36, 38, 60Exp, 61, 62, 80Exp, 84, 88, 90Exp, 490, 491, 495. **Meals served** noon-3pm, 7.30-11pm Mon-Fri; 7.30-11pm Sat. Closed lunch in Aug. **Credit** AmEx, DC, MC, V. **Map** p340 D3 ❻

The lively neighbourhood just outside Porta Pia is on the up and up, with a sprinkling of new places to eat. One of the best is this wine-oriented osteria, all

'Gusto

Piazza Augusto Imperatore 9 (06 322 6273, www.gusto.it). Bus 81, 117, 119, 628, 913, 926. **Open** *Wine bar* noon-1am daily. **Meals served** *Pizzeria* 12.30-3pm, 7.30pm-1am daily. *Restaurant* 12.30-3pm, 7.45-midnight daily. **Average** *Pizzeria* €25. *Restaurant* €55. **Credit** AmEx, DC, MC, V. **Map** p338 D3 ❾

This multipurpose, split-level pizzeria, restaurant and wine bar, with a kitchen shop and bookshop next door, is the granddaddy of the Roman design bunch (and could do with a little sprucing up). Sitting outside eating a pizza while gazing at Augustus' mausoleum is extremely pleasant, the lunch buffet is abundant and good, and the wine bar

INSIDE TRACK SNACKS

Roman snack culture lurks in unlikely places. Any *alimentari* (grocer's), for example, will fill a fresh roll with high-quality fillings. Pizza *a taglio* (takeaway pizza) is another staple, usually to be eaten on the hoof.

CONSUME

Casa Bleve. *See p193.*

World Class

Perfect places to stay, eat and explore.

out the back is buzzy. The overpriced fusion food in the upstairs restaurant is nothing special, however, and the Osteria round the corner in via della Frezza is rather hit and miss. The 'Gusto takeover of the piazza continues with black-and-white Tati al 28 bar and restaurant where the emphasis is on fish and vegetarian foods.

Maccheroni

Piazza delle Coppelle 44 (06 6830 7895, www. ristorantemaccheroni.com). Bus 52, 53, 61, 62, 63, 71, 80Exp, 95, 116, 119, 175, 490, 630. **Meals served** 1-3pm, 7.30-11pm daily. **Average** €35. **Credit** AmEx, MC, V. **Map** p339 D5 ⑩

With painted wooden wainscotting and industrial-style iron lights, this feels like a cross between a cricket pavilion and a downhome workers' trattoria. But the clientele is more rich-kid than bricklayer, and the table staff are cooler (though at times no less grumpy) than the basic decor suggests. Still, if this is an exercise in peasant chic, it's fairly successful, and the pasta dishes served from the open-to-view kitchen are perfectly decent takes on home cooking. Play safe on the *secondi*: the grilled steaks are good, the more elaborate dishes less so. In summer, there's a real *dolce vita* vibe at the outdoor tables.

Matricianella

Via del Leone 3-4 (06 683 2100, www.matricianella. it). Bus 70, 81, 117, 119. **Meals served** 12.30-3pm, 7.30-11pm Mon-Sat. **Average** €35. **Credit** AmEx, DC, MC, V. **Map** p339 E4 ⑪

This is a friendly, bustling place with fair prices. The Roman imprint is most evident in classics such as *bucatini all'amatriciana* and *abbacchio a scottadito*, but there are creative options too, including a tasty *risotto mantecato* (creamy risotto with courgette flowers) and some great *fritti* (fried dishes). The well-chosen wine list is a model of honest pricing; service is friendly but no-nonsense. It's almost always packed so be sure to book ahead. There are a few, highly sought-after tables outside.

Palatium

Via Frattina 94 (06 6920 2132, www.enoteca palatium.it). Metro Spagna/bus 52, 53, 61, 62, 63, 71, 80Exp, 95, 116, 119, 175, 490, 630. **Open** noon-11pm Mon-Sat. **Meals served** 12.30-3pm, 8-10.30pm Mon-Sat. Closed 2wks Aug. **Average** *Restaurant* €40. **Credit** AmEx, DC, MC, V. **Map** p339 E4 ⑫

Though it's backed by the regional government, this wine bar and restaurant in the fashion district is not just a PR exercise. Dedicated to the wines and pro-duce of Lazio – the region around Rome – it gives punters the chance to explore lesser-known wines like Cesanese or Aleatico. There's a bar where you can perch for a glass and a nibble – from 6.30pm to 8pm, charcuterie, cheeses and deep-fried titbits are provided free with your *aperitivo*. At mealtimes

tables in a contemporary-minimalist space upstairs kick into restaurant mode, offering creative dishes that put regional products at centre stage.

RistorArte Il Margutta

Via Margutta 118 (06 3265 0577, www.il margutta.it). Metro Spagna or Flaminio/bus 117, 119. **Meals served** 12.30-3.30pm, 7.30-11.30pm daily. Closed 3wks Aug. **Average** €40. **Credit** AmEx, DC, MC, V. **Map** p338 E3 ⑬

Il Margutta – one of Rome's very few vegetarian restaurants – occupies a prime piece of real estate on the corner of Rome's gallery alley, and the decor pays homage to the area, with plenty of modern art. Variations on the buffet brunch – 'Green' (€12) dur-ing the week, Saturday (€15) and Festivity (€25) with live music on Sundays and holidays – are pile-your-plate affairs including soup and fruit juice... a far better option than the formal evening à la carte restaurant. At the time of writing a bar, with Wi-Fi, was about to open.

€ Vic's

Vicolo della Torretta 60 (06 687 1445). Bus 52, 53, 61, 62, 63, 71, 80Exp, 95, 116, 119, 175, 490, 630. **Meals served** 12.30-3pm, 7.30-11pm Mon-Sat. **No credit cards. Map** p339 D/E4 ⑭

This new-but-old wine and salad bar offers a range of creative salads (€7.50 standard, €9 mega) such as radicchio, pine nuts, sultanas and parmesan. There are also one or two hot pasta or soup dishes, plus *crostini* (toast) with various toppings, and a good selection of crêpes. With its pared-back Roman oste-ria decor, friendly service and fairly priced wine list, this is a popular *centro storico* lunch stop.

PANTHEON & NAVONA

★ Armando al Pantheon

Salita de' Crescenzi 31 (06 6880 3034, www. armandoalpantheon.it). Bus 30Exp, 40Exp, 46, 62, 63, 64, 70, 81, 87, 116, 492, 628, 780, H/tram 8. **Meals served** 12.30-3pm, 7.15-11pm Mon-Fri; 12.30-3pm Sat. Closed lunch in July; Aug. **Average** €35. **Credit** AmEx, DC, MC, V. **Map** p339 D5 ⑮

THE BEST TABLES WITH VIEWS

Over Michelangelo-designed elegance
Ar Galletto (*see p194* **Eating Old-style**).

Over the *centro storico* movida
Da Francesco (*see p193*).

Over architectural contrasts
'Gusto (*see p188*).

Over the whole, glorious city
La Pergola (*see p205*).

Whatever your carbon footprint, we can reduce it

For over a decade we've been leading the way in carbon offsetting and carbon management.

In that time we've purchased carbon credits from over 200 projects spread across 6 continents. We work with over 300 major commercial clients and thousands of small and medium sized businesses, which rely upon our market-leading quality assurance programme, our experience and absolute commitment to deliver the right solution for each client.

Why not give us a call?

T: London (020) 7833 6000

Armando is a no-frills trattoria of the kind that is very rare to find just a few yards from an A-league attraction. But, right by the Pantheon, it has all the hallmarks of authenticity: indifferent artworks and friendly service from the family that has run it for the last couple of generations. The menu sticks with tried-and-tested classics like *fettucine all'Armando* (with mushrooms, peas and tomatoes) or *ossobuco*. The only concessions to changing times are some filling vegetarian dishes and a much-expanded wine list, which now contains interesting bottles.

▶ *The name says it all: combine this restaurant with a visit to the Pantheon (see p100) across the square.*

Casa Bleve

Via del Teatro Valle 48-49 (06 686 5970, www. casableve.it). Bus 30Exp, 40Exp, 46, 62, 63, 64, 70, 81, 87, 116, 492, 571, 628, 630, 780, 916. **Meals served** 12.30-2.30pm, 7.30-10pm Tue, Sat; 1-3pm, 7-10pm Wed-Fri. Closed 3wks Aug. **Average** €35. **Credit** AmEx, DC, MC, V. **Map** p339 D6 & p342 D1 ⑯

Wine merchants Anacleto and Tina Bleve's wine bar-restaurant is in a huge colonnaded courtyard roofed over with coloured glass: impressive, though the tables feel a little lost in all this space. The buffet the place was known for has been done away with in favour of an à la carte menu. But wine remains the star turn here, with a tremendous selection on offer, both by the bottle and by the glass. The original Bleve *enoteca* in the Ghetto (via Santa Maria del Pianto 9-11, 06 6819 2210, open 8am-8pm daily) now purveys fantastic cheeses. *Photo p189.*

Il Convivio Troiani

Vicolo dei Soldati 31 (06 686 9432, www.il conviviotroiani.com). Bus 30Exp, 70, 81, 87, 116, 492, 628. **Meals served** 8-11pm Mon-Sat. Closed 1wk Aug. **Average** €120. **Credit** AmEx, DC, MC, V. **Map** p339 D5 ⑰

The Troiani brothers run a high-class act in this temple of foodie excellence just north of piazza Navona. The creations of chef Angelo are ultra-gourmet, some tempered by his origins in the Marche region but others – like pasta with mussels, peppers, coconut milk and saffron. *Secondi* – where meat, game and seafood take equal billing – are also fine, and the desserts are spectacular (don't miss the *zabaione* ice-cream with praline almonds and balsamic vinegar). The wine list is extensive and has a few affordable bottles. For Convivio beginners, there are five ´ (€80) and seven-course (€98) taster menus.

Cul de Sac

Piazza Pasquino 73 (06 6880 1094). Bus 30Exp, 40, 62, 63, 64, 70, 81, 87, 492, 628, 780/tram 8. **Meals served** noon-4pm, 6pm-midnight daily. **Average** €20. **Credit** MC, V. **Map** p342 C1 & p339 C5/D5 ⑱

Rome's first ever wine bar, the Cul de Sac was founded in 1977. Looking very traditional nowa-

days, it's cramped inside and out, with long pine benches and tables, and decidedly no-frills. But the location – just off piazza Navona, with a ringside view of the 'talking statue' of Pasquino – coupled with reasonable prices and an encyclopaedic wine list, ensures full occupancy all the time. The food is standard wine-bar fare, with mainly cold dishes. A generous greek salad and the lentil soup stand out.

Da Francesco

Piazza del Fico 29 (06 686 4009). Bus 40Exp, 46, 62, 64, 916. **Meals served** 11.50am-3pm, 7pm-12.30am Mon, Wed-Sun. **Average** €25. **Credit** MC, V. **Map** p342 C1 & p339 C5 ⑲

Accept no imitations: Da Francesco is the genuine *centro storico* pizzeria article. The pizzas are old-school simple, the atmosphere is crushed and rushed, service is brisk and there's a range of fairly competent classic *primi* and *secondi* if pizza isn't your thing: no gourmet treat, in other words, but incredibly central in its pretty square and definitely slice of Roman life. You can try booking but your reservation is likely to be forgotten: get there well before 8pm if you don't want to queue.

Enoteca Corsi

Via del Gesù 87-88 (06 679 0821, www.enoteca corsi.com). Bus 30Exp, 40Exp, 46, 62, 63, 64, 70, 81, 87, 492, 628, 780, H. **Meals served** noon-3.30pm Mon-Sat. **Average** €25. **Credit** AmEx, DC, MC, V. **Map** p342 D1 & p339 E6 ⑳

This wine shop was the first in Rome to begin serving lunch. The daily-changing menu is written up on the board at the entrance. Dishes follow the traditional Roman order – gnocchi on Thursdays and stewed *baccalà* (salt cod) on Fridays. A slice of ricotta tart followed by a jolt of espresso makes a fitting end to a hearty meal. No bookings are taken, so get there early or be prepared to queue on workdays, as this *enoteca* is a popular venue for a filling lunch.

Grano

Piazza Rondanini 53 (06 6819 2096, www. ristorantegrano.it). Bus 52, 53, 61, 62, 63, 71, 80Exp, 95, 116, 119, 175, 490, 630. **Meals served** 12.30-3pm, 7.30pm-midnight daily.

CONSUME

Eating old-style

The best of Rome's traditional restaurants.

Many visitors look down on them as tourist traps, but some of Rome's long-running restaurants – stuck in a rather tarnished wannabe *dolce vita* time-warp – can provide an amusing dining experience and (when the going's good) hearty, old-fashioned fare.

At piazza Farnese 112, **Ar Galletto** (06 686 1714, average €40) has tables on this extraordinarily elegant square and prices rather lower than rivals just round the corner in campo de' Fiori. They do a decent *penne all'arrabbiata* and acceptable grilled lamb ribs – no prizes for the cuisine but the view over Palazzo Farnese (*see p106*) is unbeatable.

Similarly, **Da Giggetto** (via Portico d'Ottavia 21A, 06 686 1105, www.giggetto

alportico.com, average €45) produces generally competent stalwarts of Roman Jewish cooking to exuberant crowds from out of town. Locals give it a wide berth, but it's hard to object too much to a pavement table in the ancient heart of the Ghetto.

The jury's out over **Sora Lella** (ponte Quattro Capi 16, 06 686 1601, www.sora lella.com, average €70) which had, but has lost, a Michelin star: many locals couldn't quite see why. But this welcoming, old-style restaurant serves good (if heavy) comfort food in the Roman tradition and occupies a unique position on the Tiber Island (*see p111*). Not all the dishes live up to their pretensions, but there's a good cellar to help diners overlook that.

CONSUME

Average €40. **Credit** AmEx, DC, MC, V. **Map** p339 D5 ㉑
The name (it means 'wheat') suggests a concept restaurant, and indeed pasta and delicious home-made bread make their presence felt in this country-chic eaterie with southern Italian influences. But delicious iced soups, Roman specialities such as ossobuco and a range of fish and meat dishes go well beyond the theme. The deserts are excellent and the position, in a square right by the Pantheon, perfect.
▶ *Round off your meal with a superlative ice-cream from the branch of Il Gelato di San Crispino (see p208) in nearby piazza della Maddalena.*

GHETTO & CAMPO DE' FIORI

L'Angolo Divino
Via dei Balestrari 12 (06 686 4413). Bus 30Exp, 40Exp, 46, 62, 63, 64, 70, 81, 87, 116, 492, 628, 780, H/tram 8. **Open** 6pm-midnight Mon, Sun; 10am-3pm, 6pm-midnight Tue-Sat. Closed 1wk Aug. **Average** €20. **Credit** MC, V. **Map** p339 D6 & p342 C2 ㉒
Over 20 red, white and dessert wines are available by the glass, many more by the bottle, at this relaxed wine bar on a quiet street near campo de' Fiori. There's a good range of smoked fish, salami and salads, and a vast selection of cheeses, plus some hot dishes in winter. The furniture is basic and the mood laid-back – stoked by a jazz soundtrack.

€ Antico Forno Roscioli
Via dei Chiavari 34 (06 686 4045, www.antico fornoroscioli.com). Bus 23, 63, 280, 630, 780, H/tram 8. **Meals served** 11am-2.30pm Mon-Sat. **Average** €15. **Credit** AmEx, DC, MC, V. **Map** p339 D6 & p342 C2 ㉓

This bakery (open 7am-8pm Mon-Sat) is a great place to grab something quick for lunch, though you'll have to have your wits about you to get through the crowds. A few pasta dishes are served on one side (the handful of chairs and counters to perch plates are hotly fought over) while on the other staff fill excellent pizza base with the freshest of ingredients. Down the road at via dei Giubbonari 21 (06 687 5287), the dynasty's *salumeria* (charcuterie) store sets out lunch tables and serves top-notch cured meats, cheeses, soups and a selection of pasta dishes. The staff here tends to be hassled and abrupt, and the price tag rather high (€35). Try it between 6 and 7.30pm for their *aperitivo* buffet.

Ditirambo
Piazza della Cancelleria 74 (06 687 1626, www.ristoranteditirambo.it). Bus 30Exp, 40Exp, 46, 62, 63, 64, 70, 81, 87, 492, 628, 780, H/tram 8. **Meals served** 7.30-11.30pm Mon; 1-3pm, 7.30-11.30pm Tue-Sun. Closed 3wks Aug. **Average** €40. **Credit** MC, V. **Map** p339 D6 & p342 C1 ㉔
This funky trattoria located around the corner from campo de' Fiori serves up good-value food based on mainly organic ingredients. The creative menu changes monthly, offering dishes such as baby octopus and chickpea soup, and veal roulade with a truffle and porcini mushroom sauce. There's a great choice for vegetarians, and fish features heavily on the menu. Service can be slow, but it's friendly enough, and there's usually a good buzz, with a mix of young trendsters and older gourmands.

Il Forno Campo de' Fiori
Vicolo del Gallo 14 (06 6880 6662, www.forno campodefiori.com). Bus 30Exp, 40Exp, 46, 62,

63, 64, 70, 81, 87, 116, 492, 628, 780, H. **Open**
7.30am-2.30pm, 5-8pm Mon-Sat. **No credit cards.**
Map p339 C6 & p342 C1 ㉕
This little bakery does the best takeaway sliced
pizza in the campo de' Fiori area by far. Their plain
pizza bianca base, dressed with extra-virgin olive oil,
is delicious in itself, but check out the one with *fiori
di zucca* (courgette flowers) too. Next door (or
almost), at campo de Fiori 22, is the main shop,
which turns out a variety of delicious breads, biscuits and cakes.

Open Baladin

*Via degli Specchi 6 (06 683 8989, www.open
baladin.com). Bus 30Exp, 40Exp, 46, 62, 63,
64, 70, 81, 87, 116, 492, 628, 780, H/tram 8.*
Open noon-midnight daily. Closed 2wks Aug.
Average €25. **Credit** AmEx, MC, V. **Map**
p342 D2 ㉖
Dynamic northern Italian brewer Teo Musso is turning more and more of his fellow countryfolk into beer
drinkers. Open Baladin, with its 'wall of beer' – about
100 labels served bottled, displayed up one wall of
this buzzing venue – and a choice of 40 or more on
tap, is his first Roman venture. Top-notch snack
food, from mounds of chicken wings to gourmet
hamburgers, melt-in-the-mouth mozzarella and a
signature scrambled egg with bacon helps the brews
from many of Italy's smallest and most interesting
producers slip down nicely. *Photos p199.*
▶ *If the evening scene down the road in campo de'
Fiori (see p214) gets too rowdy for you, join more
civilised beer-quaffers here.*

★ Il Pagliaccio

*Via dei Banchi Vecchi 129 (06 6880 9595, www.
ristoranteilpagliaccio.it). Bus 23, 46, 62, 64, 116,
280.* **Meals served** 8-10pm Tue; 1-2.30pm,
8-10pm Wed-Sat. Closed 1wk Jan or Feb; 2wks
Aug. **Average** €130. **Credit** AmEx, DC, MC, V.
Map p339 C5 & p342 B1 ㉗
Though prices have climbed recently – pushed up,
perhaps, by a second Michelin star – chef Anthony
Genovese still offers one of the best gourmet experiences in Rome. The successful incorporation of oriental influences is clearly illustrated in an *antipasto*
of cuttlefish dim sum with grilled octopus and broad-
bean sauce. His sure touch is equally evident in a
risotto with thom cheese and persimmons, or lamb
kebab with tamarind and goat's cheese sauce.
There's an interesting wine list. Leave plenty of
space to try out one of the excellent desserts, which
are prepared by Alsatian pastry chef-genius Marion
Lichtle. Twelve-course (€155) and ten-course (€135)
taster menus can be arranged.

Le Piramidi

*Vicolo del Gallo 11 (06 687 9061, www.cucinaraba.
com). Bus 30Exp, 40Exp, 46, 62, 63, 64, 70, 81,
87, 116, 492, 628, 780, H/tram 8.* **Open** 10am-
midnight Tue-Sun. Closed Aug. **No credit cards.**
Map p339 C6 & p342 C1 ㉘
Around the corner from campo de' Fiori, Le Piramidi
makes for a welcome change from takeaway pizza.
The range of Middle Eastern takeaway fare is small,
but it's all fresh, cheap and tasty, and the falafel is
probably the best in Rome.

Grano. See p193.

CONSUME

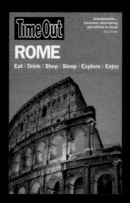

Antico Arco.

Sora Margherita

Piazza delle Cinque Scole 30 (06 687 4216).
Bus 23, 63, 280, 630, 780, H/tram 8. **Meals
served** 12.45-2.45pm, 7.30-10.30pm Mon, Wed;
12.45-2.45pm Tue, Thur; 12.45-2.45pm, 8-11.20pm
Fri, Sat. Closed July. **Average** €30. **No credit
cards. Map** p342 D2 ㉙
This spit-and-sawdust, hole-in-the-wall trat offers
one of Rome's great local dining experiences. Tables
are crammed into a couple of narrow rooms, and the
decibels generated by 20 simultaneous conversa-
tions with orders shouted over the top is literally
stunning. Sora Margherita is not for health freaks,
but no one argues with serious Roman Jewish cooking at these prices. The classic pasta and meat dishes
on offer include a great *pasta e fagioli* and *ossobuco*
washed down with rough-and-ready house wine.
Dessert consists of home-made *crostate* (jam or
ricotta tarts).

TRASTEVERE & GIANICOLO

See also p215 **Friends Art Café** and
Ombre Rosse.

Alle Fratte di Trastevere

*Via delle Fratte di Trastevere 49-50 (06 583
5775, www.allefratteditrastevere.com). Bus 23,
280, 780, H/tram 8.* **Meals served** 6-11.30pm
Mon, Tue; 12.30-3pm, 6-11.30pm Thur-Sun. Closed
2wks Aug. **Average** €35. **Credit** AmEx, DC, MC,
V. **Map** p342 C3 ㉚
This cheerful eaterie with its eye firmly on the
tourist trade does honest Roman trattoria fare with
Neapolitan influences,. The service is friendly, atten-

tive and bilingual. First courses, like *pennette alla
sorrentina* (pasta with tomatoes and runny mozzarella), are served up in generous portions. *Secondi*
include oven-roasted sea bream, veal escalopes in
marsala and a good grilled beef fillet. Desserts are
home-made; the post-prandial *digestivi* flow freely.
In summer there are a few outdoor tables.

★ Antico Arco

*Piazzale Aurelio 7 (06 581 5274, www.antico
arco.it). Bus 44, 75, 710, 870.* **Meals served**
7.30-11.30pm daily. **Average** €60. **Credit** AmEx,
DC, MC, V. **Map** p342 A3 ㉛
A recent refit gave Antico Arco a smart minimalist-
but-warm interior. Tables are spread over two floors,
and there's now a wine-bar lobby (open from 6pm)
where you can imbibe while waiting to be seated, or
just grab a glass and a snack. Chef Patrizia Mattei's
menu is strong on all fronts, from the *antipasti*, with
an outstanding onion flan with parmesan fondue, to
the *primi*, where Antico Arco classics like risotto
with castelmagno cheese are flanked by such dishes
as chickpea, porcini mushroom and rosemary soup.

INSIDE TRACK TIPPING

Service in Rome is a grey area. It's usually
safe to assume it isn't included: when in
doubt, ask. Romans tend not to tip much,
especially in family-run places. A good rule
of thumb is to leave around five per cent –
waiters have learned to expect more from
tourists than locals.

CONSUME

CONSUME

THE BEST QUICK BITES

For something exotic
Kabir Fast Food (*see p204*).

For a panino by the Vatican
Paninoteca da Guido (*see p204*).

For gourmet pizza
00100 (*see below*).

For pasta on the hoof
Antico Forno Roscioli (*see p194*).

The excellent *secondi* cover the board from meat to fish to game, and the desserts are no let-down. The wine list is extensive, and sensibly priced. Book well in advance.

▶ *Dally on the Gianicolo (see p118), which has a spectacular view over Rome, before continuing your romantic evening here.*

Bir&Fud

Via Benedetta 23 (06 589 4016, birefud. blogspot.com). Bus 23, 280, 780, H/tram 8. **Meals served** 6.30pm-midnight daily. Closed 2wks Aug. **Average** €25. **Credit** AmEx, DC, MC, V. **Map** p342 B2 ⓷

Narrow and buzzing, Bir&Fud serves exactly what the name says: interesting beers from lesser known breweries, plus food that's all super-fresh and additive-free. The pizza is excellent, with its slow-rise dough and delicious toppings overseen by Rome's pizza guru, Gabriele Bonci; there are good *bruschette* and some very Roman offal too. Bir&Fud opens at 5.30pm for *aperitivi* and stays open until 2am at weekends. Service is brisk – sometimes bordering on the brusque. Book ahead if you want to sit and eat. *Photo p202.*

Dar Poeta

Vicolo del Bologna 45 (06 588 0516, www.dar poeta.com). Bus 23, 280, 780, H/tram 8. **Meals served** noon-midnight daily. **Average** €18. **Credit** AmEx, DC, MC, V. **Map** p342 B/C3 ⓷

Dar Poeta does a better-quality pizza, based on an innovative slow-rise dough. Creative assemblages include the house pizza (with courgettes, sausage and spicy pepper). The varied *bruschette* are first-rate, and healthy salads offer a break from all those carbs. Leave room for dessert, as the sweet *calzone* stuffed with Nutella and ricotta is to die for. You can eat until late and the waiters are genuinely friendly, but do be prepared to queue, since Dar Poeta doesn't take bookings.

Glass Hostaria

Vicolo del Cinque 58 (06 5833 5903, www.glass-hostaria.it). Bus 23, 280, 780, H/tram 8. **Meals**

served 8pm-midnight Tue-Sun. **Closed** 1wk Jan-Feb; 2wks July-Aug. **Average** €45. **Credit** AmEx, DC, MC, V. **Map** p342 C3 ⓸

Despite the place being ultra-modern and vigorously kicking against the trad Trastevere dining scene, Glass Hostaria offers surprisingly warm service, an interesting wine list, a menu that is less pretentious than you might expect – and a rather lower price tag than its Michelin star might lead you to expect. It's true that chef Cristina Bowerman comes up with the occasional odd novelty number like lamb in a coffee crust with spicy cherries, but her other dishes – such as ravioli served with extra-aged parmesan and asparagus – are more persuasive. On the whole, there's little here for vegetarians.

★ Le Mani in Pasta

Via de' Genovesi 37 (06 581 6017, www.le maniinpasta.com). Bus 23, 280, 780, H/tram 8. **Meals served** 12.30-2.30pm, 7.30-11pm Tue-Sun. Closed 3 wks Aug & 1wk late Dec. **Average** €35. **Credit** AmEx, DC, MC, V. **Map** p342 D3 ⓸

This little trat offers decent, creative home cooking in large portions, friendly informal service and great value for money. On our last visit we started off with some nicely chargrilled vegetables and a *sauté* of clams and mussels, followed up by giant mounds of spaghetti with *seppioline* (baby cuttlefish) and *car-ciofi* (artichokes). The *secondi*, if you get that far, include a good fillet steak with green peppercorns. The ground-floor room has a ringside view of the kitchen action. Unusually for Rome, there's a *sala fumatori* (smoking area) though it's in the basement. Be sure to book ahead.

AVENTINE, TESTACCIO & OSTIENSE

See also p217 **L'Oasi della Birra.**

00100

Via G Branca 88 (06 4341 9624, www.00100 pizza.com). Bus 95, 170, 280, 781. **Open** noon-11pm daily. Closed 3wks Aug. **No credit cards.** **Map** p343 C5 ⓸

Elbow your way through the crowds squashed into this tiny takeaway pizza joint in Testaccio and you'll soon understand what they're doing there. Delicious slow-rise pizza – following the dictates of Rome's pizza guru Gabriele Bonci – has toppings such as stilton cheese with reduction of port, broccoli and fontina cheese or tomato, wild fennel, capers, anchovies and olives. The same dough goes into the pizzeria's trademark 'trapizzini': pizza pockets opened out and filled with anything from stewed tripe to cuttlefish and peas.

Checchino dal 1887

Via di Monte Testaccio 30 (06 574 6318, www. checchino-dal-1887.com). Bus 95, 673, 719.

Open Baladin. *See p195.*

Meals served 12.30-3pm, 8pm-midnight Tue-Sat. Closed Aug and 1wk Dec. **Average** €60. **Credit** AmEx, DC, MC, V. **Map** p343 C/D6 ❸

Nestling among the trendy bars and clubs opposite Testaccio's former slaughterhouse (Il Mattatoio; *see p121*), the Mariani family's historic restaurant is Rome's leading temple of authentic *cucina romana*. Imagine a pie shop rising to become one of London's leading restaurants, and the odd mix of humble decor, elegant service, hearty food and one of the most extensive wine cellars in Rome falls into place. Vegetarians should give this place a wide berth:specialities include tripe and oxtail. Desserts feature a delicious *stracciatella* cake with ricotta, almonds and chocolate chips.

Da Felice

Via Mastro Giorgio 29 (06 574 6800, www.felice atestaccio.com). Bus 23, 30Exp, 75, 95, 170, 280, 716, 781/tram 3. **Meals served** 12.30-2.45pm, 8-11pm daily. Closed 1wk Aug. **Average** €35. **Credit** MC, V. **Map** p343 D5 ❸

This trattoria in the heart of trendy Testaccio was once rather basic, but it has had a makeover that turned it into a stylishly *moderne* neo-osteria. The quality of the cooking has not changed. Now there are a few lighter and more creative dishes alongside the Roman classics – *tonnarelli cacio e pepe, abbacchio al forno con patate* – which first made the name of this Testaccio institution. The desserts are excellent – especially the *tiramisù*, and the wine list has improved since the days when it was cloudy *Castelli romani* or nothing.

Piccolo Alpino

Via Orazio Antinori 5 (06 574 1386). Bus 23, 75, 95, 170, 280, 716, 781/tram 3. **Meals served** 12.30-2.30pm, 6-11pm Tue-Sun. Closed 1wk Aug. **Average** €22. **No credit cards.** **Map** p343 C5 ❸

This no-frills trattoria-pizzeria in a Testaccio side-street is as far as you can get from the tourist herd. There's a telly (with live football on Sunday evenings), beer on tap and rough wine in the fridge; but the pizzas are good, and the pasta too, as long as you stick to the house specialities: *spaghetti con le vongole* (with clams) or *penne all'arrabbiata*; for restaurant fare, expect to pay a little more – say €28. In summer tables invade the road and it all feels like a scene from Fellini's *Roma*.

€ Remo

Piazza Santa Maria Liberatrice 44 (06 574 6270). Bus 23, 75, 95, 170, 280, 716, 781/tram 3. **Meals served** 7pm-1am Mon-Sat. Closed 3wks Aug. **Average** €18. **No credit cards.** **Map** p343 D5 ❹

The best place in town for authentic *pizza romana*, Remo is a Testaccio institution, with a prime location on the district's main piazza. You can sit at wonky tables balanced on the pavement, or in the cavernous

interior, overseen by Lazio team photos. The *bruschette al pomodoro* are the finest in Rome. A park with swings right across the road makes this a great place to eat with kids. *Photo p203.*

Il Seme e la Foglia

Via Galvani 18 (06 574 3008). Bus 95, 170, 673, 781/tram 3. **Open** 7.30am-2am Mon-Sat; 6pm-2am Sun. Closed 3wks Aug. **No credit cards.** **Map** p343 D6 ❹

Right-on and alternative, this lively daytime snack bar and evening pre-club stop is always packed with students and teachers from the Scuola Popolare di Musica across the road. At midday there's generally a pasta dish, plus large salads (€5-€7) and creative filled rolls.

★ Tuttifrutti

Via Luca della Robbia 3A (06 575 7902). Bus 23, 30Exp, 75, 95, 170, 280, 716, 781/tram 3. **Meals served** 7.30-11.30pm Mon-Sat. Closed 2wks Aug. **Average** €30. **Credit** AmEx, MC, V. **Map** p343 D5 ❹

Behind a frosted-glass door, this friendly, artsy trattoria is Testaccio's best-value dining experience. Host Michele guides you through a changing menu of creative pan-Italian fare, determined by whatever is in season, and which might include an *antipasto* of *pizzelle* (fried pizza balls with tomato and basil) followed by *fusilli* with sun-dried tomatoes, pecorino, bacon and pine nuts and then baked lamb with potatoes and rosemary. There are always a few options for vegetarians. The wine list is excellently priced. Finish up your meal with good desserts or chunks of chocolate and sweet wine.

▶ *A great place for refuelling before your night of clubbing at nearby Monte Testaccio (see p269).*

CELIO, SAN GIOVANNI & SAN LORENZO

See also p217 **Café Café** *and* **Said**.

Il Bocconcino

Via Ostilia 23 (06 7707 9175, www.ilbocconcino .com). Bus 60Exp, 75, 85, 87, 117, 571, 810, 850/tram 3. **Meals served** 12.30-3.30pm, 7.30-11.30pm Mon, Tue, Thur-Sun. Closed 3wks Aug. **Average** €30. **Credit** AmEx, DC, MC, V. **Map** p344 C3 ❹

With its red-check tablecloths and brick vaulted ceilings, this trattoria within a slingshot's range of the Colosseum looks like it's been around forever: in fact it opened only in 2006. The welcome is ultra-friendly, the menu mixes Roman classics like *tonnarelli cacio e pepe* or *abbacchio brodettato* (braised lamb) with more adventurous, Slow-Food-style dishes. On Tuesdays and Fridays, fish dominates the menu. The wine list is limited but honestly priced, while the desserts. Service, though affable, can be excruciatingly slow.

Profile Pigneto

Pasolini's scouting ground has become home to Rome's foodies.

Formerly happening San Lorenzo has seen some of its most interesting eating options close down, but the next stop out into the suburbs – Pigneto, east of Porta Maggiore – has stepped into the foodie breach.

Squeezed between via Casilina and via Prenestina, this funky neighbourhood mixes charming semi-rural houses and low-rise 1960s condominiums. Due to its proximity to the San Lorenzo stockyards, it suffered heavy wartime bombing. When development came it was piecemeal and barely regulated. The anarchic, bohemian feel of the place attracted artsy types like Pier Paolo Pasolini, who came scouting for locations (much of *Accattone* was shot here) and pretty young boys.

Today, partly pedestrianised via del Pigneto – the central thoroughfare, home to a morning market Mon-Sat – is lined with cool bars like **Pigneto 41** (yes, at no.41; closed Sun), though the neighbourhood feel is preserved by a sprinkling of grocers, artisan shops and multi-ethnic call centres. Pick of the restaurants is bustling, Slow Food-inspired **Primo** (*pictured; see p205*). Round the corner, book-lined wine bar **Il Tiaso** (via Perugia 20, 333 284 5283) is deliciously laid-back: like many Pigneto watering holes, a refreshing contrast to similar *centro storico* bars, which can be snooty and overpriced.

Via del Pigneto is sliced in two by a rail cutting. The area to the east of the pedestrian bridge has more modern *palazzi* than the cutesy western triangle. It's here that one of the area's more interesting new restaurants lies. Before its 2007 makeover, **Bar Necci** (*see p205*) was an old blokes' bar, and Pasolini's main casting office for *Accattone*; now it's a shabby-chic brunch, lunch, *aperitivo* and dinner hangout, with creative Italian cooking from personable English chef Ben Hirst. Ben's **Tiger Tandoori** (via del Pigneto 193, 06 9761 0172, www.tigertandoori.com, open daily), round the corner, is good for a quick non-Italian bite.

CONSUME

Bir&Fud. *See p198.*

Luzzi

*Via Celimontana 1 (06 709 6332). Bus 60Exp,
75, 85, 87, 117, 571, 810, 850/tram 3.* **Meals
served** noon-midnight Mon, Tue, Thur-Sun.
Closed 2wks Aug. **Average** €25. **Credit** AmEx,
DC, MC, V. **Map** p344 C3 ⓸

When it's busy (and it almost always is), this heavy neighbourhood trattoria is the loudest and most crowded 40 square metres in the whole of Rome. It isn't the place for a romantic tête-à-tête, then, nor for gourmet dining, but it is cheap, lively and handy for the Colosseum. And the menu's range of Roman staples and pizzas is competently done. The outdoor tables operate all year round.

INSIDE TRACK PIZZA

The city's *pizzaioli* have always been proud of their thinner, flatter *pizza romana*, but the fickle public has started to defect to the puffier Neapolitan variety. So orthodox is the range of Roman toppings, that it's worth learning the main varieties by heart. For these, and various gap-fillers to order while you're waiting for your pizza to come out of the oven, *see p324* **The Menu**. Note that pizza is an evening thing – there are very few places that serve it at lunchtime.

Marcello

*Via dei Campani 12 (06 446 3311). Bus 71,
492/tram 3, 19.* **Meals served** 7.30-11.30pm
Mon-Fri. Closed 3wks Aug. **Average** €20. **No
credit cards**. **Map** p128 C3 ⓸

From outside, this San Lorenzo eaterie looks like one of those spit-and-sawdust places that Romans refer to as *un buco* – a hole in the wall. Inside, hordes of students from the nearby university occupy the old wooden tables. Alongside Roman offal specialities like tripe and *pajata* (calf intestines) are lighter dishes such as *straccetti ai carciofi* (strips of veal with artichokes). Besides reliable traditional recipes (*spaghetti alla carbonara, all'amatriciana* or *alla gricia*), you can try home-made *ravioloni* filled with fresh cheese, ricotta and walnuts. There's a surprisingly extensive wine list, strong on big reds.

Pastificio San Lorenzo

Via Tiburtina 196 (06 9727 3519, www.pastificio-cerere.com). Bus 71, 492/tram 3, 19. **Meals
served** 12.30-3pm, 8pm-11.30am Tue-Fri, Sun;
7pm-2am Sat. Closed 3wks Aug. **Average** €45.
Credit AmEx, DC, MC, V. **Map** p128 C2 ⓸

The Cerere pasta factory stopped production in 1960, after which it was occupied by artists who transformed its loft spaces into studios: exhibitions here are first-rate. Late 2009 saw the opening of a restaurant inside the splendid building, helmed by up-and-coming young chef Stefano Preli. The menu is firmly

CONSUME

but creatively rooted in local tradition and when Preli gets it right, standards are high. Prices are somewhat on the high side, but that's to be expected in this minimal-industrial-chic venue. Try it at lunchtime for a warmer, chattier vibe… and a lower bill. The place stays open until 2am for drinks, snacks and chat.

MONTI & ESQUILINO

See also p218 **Al Vino al Vino** *and p276* **Oppio Caffè**.

Agata e Romeo

Via Carlo Alberto 45 (06 446 6115, www.agata eromeo.it). Metro Vittorio/bus 16, 70, 71, 75, 84, 360/tram 5, 14. **Meals served** 12.30-2.30pm, 7.30-10.30pm Mon-Fri. Closed 2wks Jan, 2wks Aug. **Average** €150. **Credit** AmEx, DC, MC, V. **Map** p344 D1 ⑰

A Michelin star can have different effects on different chefs, and here it hasn't been all positive. There's no doubt that Agata Parisella can cook – magnificently, if you get the right evening – nor that her contribution to the refinement of Rome's rough-and-ready traditional fare has been all-important. Service, with husband Romeo Carccio presiding, continues to be charming and the wine cellar is legendary. But the experience nowadays doesn't always seem to justify these eye-watering prices – except, as we say, on a good night when it might feel and taste like the best meal of your life.

Cavour 313

Via Cavour 313 (06 678 5496, www.cavour 313.it). Metro Cavour/bus 75, 84, 117. **Meals served** 12.30-2.45pm, 7.30pm-midnight daily. Closed Aug. **Average** €30. **Credit** AmEx, MC, V. **Map** p344 B2 ㊽

A friendly atmosphere, a serious cellar and good wine bar food explain the enduring popularity of this wood-panelled, bottle-lined place near the Forum. Prices are reasonable, and there's a selection of hot and cold snacks; in winter, soups are a strong point. With over 500 bottles on the wine list, choosing is the only problem.

Doozo

Via Palermo 51 (06 481 5655, www.doozo.it). Metro Repubblica/bus 40Exp, 60Exp, 64, 70, 71, 116, 117, 170, H. **Meals served** 12.30-3pm, 8-11pm Tue-Sat; 8-11pm Sun. **Average** €40. **Credit** DC, MC, V. **Map** p344 B1 & p341 C6 ㊾

Defining itself as an 'art books & sushi' gallery, this Japanese restaurant (the name means 'welcome') is an oasis of quality in an area dominated by tourist-oriented eateries. The interior is spacious and cultured (tables spill over into the bookshop and gallery, where art and photography exhibitions are held), but we especially like the small Zen garden out back. A Japanese chef produces genuine dishes, rather than watered-down Italo-Nipponic, with good sushi, sashimi, tempura and *karaage* chicken served in wooden bento boxes. Doozo is also open in the afternoon for tea. *Photo p204.*

CONSUME

Remo. *See p200.*

Doozo. See p203.

Aug. **Average** €38. **Credit** DC, MC, V. **Map** p344 D1 ⓼

This upmarket trattoria is more difficult to get into than many top restaurants – so book well in advance. The reasons for its popularity are simple: friendly service and ambience, excellent food and a huge wine list with reasonable mark-ups. The cuisine, like the family that runs the place, is from the Marches – so meat, fish and game all feature on the menu. Vegetarians are well served by a range of *tortini* (pastry-less pies); pasta-hounds can enjoy such treats as *tagliolini* with anchovies, pine nuts and pecorino cheese.

VATICAN & PRATI

See also p218 **Enoteca Nuvolari**.

L'Arcangelo
Via GG Belli 59-61 (06 321 0992). Metro Lepanto/bus 23, 70, 87, 492. **Meals served** 1-2.30pm, 8-11.30pm Mon-Fri; 8-11pm Sat. Closed Aug. **Average** €50. **Credit** AmEx, DC, MC, V. **Map** p338 C3 ⓽

Wood panelling, tobacco-coloured walls and a soft jazz soundtrack set the mood in this gourmet trattoria, but it's what's on the plate that really impresses: a tartlet of octopus and potato is simple but delicious, and the fresh pasta *chitarrini* with marinated anchovies and fried artichokes a worthy follow-up. *Secondi*, like steamed *baccalà* with puréed broccoli, ricotta and cocoa beans, are clever variations on Roman tradition. Service is cordial, though Arcangelo and his wife Stefania turn vague when things get busy. There's a six-course taster menu (€55). The wine list includes some real discoveries from small Italian producers.

Isola della Pizza
Via degli Scipioni 43-47 (06 3973 3483, www. isoladellapizza.com). Metro Ottaviano/bus 23, 70, 492, 913/tram 2, 19. **Meals served** 12.30-3pm, 7.30-midnight Mon, Tue, Thur-Sun. Closed 3wks Aug. **Average** €25. **Credit** AmEx, DC, MC, V. **Map** p338 A3 ⓾

A short walk from St Peter's and the Vatican Museums, the ever-popular Isola della Pizza is one throbbing eating factory with noisy hordes digging into great big pizzas that – unusually for Rome – are served at lunch too. There's a good range of pasta dishes too, and great hunks of meat are thrown on to an open fire. Book ahead, especially to secure one of the pavement tables in fine weather.

Paninoteca da Guido
Borgo Pio 13 (06 687 5491). Bus 23, 34, 40Exp, 62, 64, 280. **Open** 8am-5pm Mon-Sat. **No credit cards**. **Map** p339 B4 ⓾

This hole-in-the-wall in pedestrianised Borgo Pio is one of the best places to grab a quick daytime snack in the Vatican area. Guido does filled rolls, made up

Hang Zhou
Via Principe Eugenio 82 (06 487 2732). Metro Vittorio/bus 70, 71, 105/tram 5, 14. **Meals served** noon-3pm, 7pm-midnight daily. Closed Aug. **Average** €25. **Credit** AmEx, MC, V. **Map** p344 E2 ⓾

A 2010 move to new, larger premises left some afficionados hoping that a perceived dip in quality was just a temporary glitch, but despite this, Hang Zhou remains arguably the best among (an admittedly somewhat mediocre selection of) Chinese restaurants in the Eternal City. Certainly, it's the verve of its media-savvy owner, Sonia, that really sets that place apart, but the food is also a cut above the Roman average, with an interesting range of daily specials. It's colourful, friendly, theatrical and good value.

Kabir Fast Food
Via Mamiani 11 (06 446 0792). Metro Vittorio/ bus 70, 71, 360, 649/tram 5, 14. **Open** 11am-4pm, 5.30-10pm daily. **No credit cards**. **Map** p344 E1 ⓾

This recently refurbished Indian joint is just off piazza Vittorio. You can take away or eat in – just as well as in the capital's more upmarket Indian restaurants – accompanied by gloriously kitsch Indian music videos.

★ Trattoria Monti
Via di San Vito 13A (06 446 6573). Metro Vittorio/bus 16, 70, 71, 75, 84, 360/tram 5, 14. **Meals served** 12.45-2.45pm, 7.45-11pm Tue-Sat; 12.45-2.45pm Sun. Closed 1 wk Dec;

while you wait, from the selection of ingredients behind the counter: ham, mozzarella, olive paste, rocket. They also do a few pasta dishes at lunchtime.

▶ *You'll have to compete against off-duty Swiss Guards from St Peter's (see p144) down the road to get one of the few tables.*

Settembrini

Via Luigi Settembrini 25 (06 323 2617, www. ristorantesettembrini.it). Metro Lepanto/bus 30Exp, 70, 280, 913. **Meals served** 12.30-4pm, 8-11.30pm Mon-Fri; 8-11.30pm Sat. Closed 2wks Aug. **Average** €40. **Credit** AmEx, MC, V. **Map** p338 C2 ⑤⑥

Settembrini mixes design and tradition, both in its warmly minimalist decor and in its menu. Chef Luigi Nastri takes a pan-Med approach in creative offerings like red mullet, sea urchins and sea and land lettuce; there's a fusion element, too, in suckling pig with vegetable sushi and tomato jam. Lunch offerings are mainly cold plates and quick snacks (around €15), while the choice of wine, champagnes and spirits is encyclopaedic. The place is open all day from 11am on, with *aperitivi* served from 7pm to 8pm. Next door at number 19-23, the very urbane Café Settembrini is under the same management.

THE SUBURBS

Bar Necci dal 1924

Via Fanfulla da Lodi 68, Pigneto (06 9760 1552, www.necci1924.com). Bus 81, 810/tram 5, 14, 19. **Meals served** 12.30-3pm, 7.30-11pm Mon-Sat; 7-11pm Sun. **Average** €40. **Credit** AmEx, DC, MC, V.

This former old-blokes' bar – used by Pasolini as his HQ when filming his classic *Accattone* nearby – is now a shabby-chic brunch/lunch/dinner place (Necci is open 8am-1am daily) with great 1960s-style decor. British co-owner and chef Ben Hirst is responsible for the high quality of the mod-Med fare, which is particularly strong on fish. The 'aperidinner' on Sunday comes in at €10 a head. There are tables outside on a delightful terrace.

★ La Pergola

Via Cadlolo 101, North (06 3509 2154, www. romecavalieri.com). Bus 907, 913, 991, 999. **Meals served** 7.30-11pm Tue-Sat. Closed 3wks Jan & 2wks Aug. **Average** €175. **Credit** AmEx, DC, MC, V.

Heinz Beck is, without a doubt, the most talented chef in Rome, with three – merited – Michelin stars. His technical dexterity and unerring instinct for taste and texture combinations never fail to impress. The setting, on the top floor of the Cavalieri hotel with its panoramic view over the city, is simply breath-taking. But what emerges from Beck's kitchen – every dish dictated by season availability – is equally so: amberjack tartare with tomato mousse and olives, potato gnocchi with caviar and

INSIDE TRACK
HOTEL RESTAURANTS

Most Romans would never dream of going to a hotel restaurant for a meal, but there are one or two exceptions for very special occasions; see p178 **Star food**.

chives or seabass with olive oil-marinated vegetables are infinitely more sophisticated than they sound. Markups on wine are very steep. But around €350 for two with a good bottle still compares favourably with restaurants at the top of the gourmet ladder in other capitals. There are six- (€175) and nine-course (€198) taster menus.

Primo

Via del Pigneto 46, Pigneto (06 701 3827, www. primoalpigneto.it). Bus Bus 81, 105, 810/tram 5, 14, 19. **Meals served** 10am-1.30am daily. Closed 1wk Aug. **Average** €45. **Credit** AmEx, DC, MC, V.

Slow Food-inspired Primo is industrial-chic-cool in design and eclectic in its culinary offerings, which are usually (though not consistently) very good. The vibe is laid-back, with staff clad in matching T-shirts and an endless stream of keen customers from this hipster district and further afield coming for chef Marco Gallotta's Roman classics or dishes with a creative twist. Primo is open 10am-1.30am daily for snacks and drinks. *Photos p201.*

Settembrini.

Cafés, Bars & Gelaterie

Where to start and end your day.

If you want to provoke withering disdain from a Roman barman, demand 'a *latte, por favor.* And a *panini.*' Latte means milk, and it comes cold; panini are plural, so how many do you want? And you added insult to injury with that Spanish 'please'. The subtext to his indignation is that if you're a habitual orderer and consumer of filthy industrial lattes and iced blended coffees at home, then it's hardly worth serving you on holiday with what is undoubtedly the finest hot beverage in the world. In Italy, you'll find, coffee is an extremely serious matter. Ice-cream isn't to be scoffed at either, what with Rome's crop of serious ice-cream makers. Then there are the city's *pasticcerie*, cake shops, and its *enoteche*, unmissable neighbourhood bars.

WHERE TO ORDER, WHAT TO ORDER

Everyone's day starts with a coffee in their local café or bar (in Italy these amount to the same thing since alcohol and coffee are served all day long in both). Visits may be in order at other times of the day, too. There'll invariably be a newspaper that you can read on the counter, a public phone, snacks, maybe cigarettes and bus tickets, a clean loo, the hottest gossip and fabulous coffee: it is the heart of the *quartiere* and a backdrop to your social life.

Once you are on the tourist track in the *centro storico*, things change slightly. For example, you should think twice before sitting down. Standing at the counter like the locals to knock back your tiny cup of miraculously cheap black nectar is one thing. But take the weight off your feet at a table or, worse, at a pavement table, and watch the bill double or even treble. Of course, there are moments when nothing in the whole world is more beguiling than sitting in a piazza with your *aperitivo*, or

> ❶ Green numbers given in this chapter correspond to the location of each café, bar or *gelaterie* as marked on the street maps.

a *digestivo*, drinking in the afternoon sunshine and the incomparable vista, and you are quite prepared to pay extra for the pleasure; just be aware that this luxury costs.

Besides serving coffee, which comes in many different and delicious forms (*see p208* **Caffè Culture**), most bars have *cornetti* (croissants), which vary widely in quality, *tramezzini* (sandwiches; good when fresh, but usually to be avoided by the afternoon), *pizza romana* (a slab of pizza base that is brushed with olive oil, sliced through the middle and filled) and *panini* (filled rolls, plural; one is a *panino*). All of these snacks can be toasted (simply ask, *me lo può scaldare, per favore?*).

To accompany your snack, bars generally offer *spremute* (freshly squeezed juices) and some have *frullati* (fruit shakes) and *centrifughe* (juiced fruit) as well. All offer a range of sodas, juices and mineral waters. Tap water (*acqua semplice, acqua dal rubinetto*) is free; a small bottle of still or sparkling mineral water (*acqua minerale naturale* or *gassata*) costs around €1. Wine, beer and some liqueurs are also generally on offer. *Digestivi* like *amari* (bitters, infused aromatic liqueurs) and *limoncello* (lemon liqueur) will help you digest your meal; they should be sipped, rather than downed like shots.

CONSUME

By law, all bars must have a *bagno* (lavatory), which can be used by anyone, whether or not they buy anything in the bar. The *bagno* may be locked; ask the cashier for the key (*la chiave per il bagno*).

PUBS AND ENOTECHE

Rome's *enoteche* and *vini e olii* (bottle shops) have historically been meeting places for residents of the neighbourhood. Many of these places have recently become, at the very least, charming places to grab a drink and a slice of the *vita romana* .At best, they are chic wine bars or bars with a *dopo cena* (after-dinner) scene, offering a wide variety of drinks – from a glass of Falanghina or Chianti to caipirinhas, caipiroskas and mojitos – and a beautiful crowd for people-watching. Some *enoteche* have developed into fully fledged eateries: for these, *see pp184-205* **Eating Out**. The ones we list below have remained predominantly watering holes. Rome's pubs are divided between a handful of long-standing UK-style institutions and a host of newer casual joints. The best pubs of both categories have been listed in this chapter.

PASTICCERIE AND GELATERIE

Every *zona* of Rome has its *pasticcerie* (cake shops); most of these are bars where freshly baked goodies can be consumed *in situ* with a coffee or some other drink. The range of items on offer rarely varies: choux pastry *bignè* with creamy fillings, *semifreddi* ice-cream cakes, fruit tarts and a large assortment of biscuits. There can be huge variations, however, in the quality and freshness of the goods which are on offer: the *pasticcerie* listed below are always reliable.

THE BEST TANNING SPOTS

For morning sun
Gran Caffè Esperia. *See p218.*

For afternoon sun
Canova. *See p210.*

For all-day rays
Vitti. *See p211.*

Many *gelaterie* (ice-cream bars) in Rome boast a well-stocked freezer cabinet with a sign promising *produzione artigianale* (home-made). This is often a con: it may mean industrial ice-cream mix whipped up on the premises. While this doesn't necessarily mean the ice-cream will be bad – indeed, in some cases this not-so-genuine article can be very good – you will need to be selective when seeking a truly unique *gelato* experience. Look at the fruit *gelati*: if the colours seem too bright to be real, they probably aren't. Banana should be cream-coloured with a tinge of grey, not electric yellow… you get the picture.

Ice-cream is served in a *cono* (cone) or *coppetta* (tub) of varying sizes, usually costing from €2 to €4. As well as the two main categories, *frutta* or *crema* (fruit- or cream-based ice-cream), there's also *sorbetto* or the rougher *granita* (water ice).

When you have exhausted the *gelato,* you should sample a *grattachecca*. This is the Roman version of water ice, and consists of grated ice with flavoured syrup poured over the top. The city was once full of kiosks selling this treat, but now only a handful of outlets remain.

CONSUME

Cinecaffé. *See p209.*

Caffè Culture

Negotiating Italian coffee customs.

Whether neighbourhood bar or smart café, the etiquette is always the same: non-regulars are expected to pay at the *cassa* (cash desk) before consuming. Identify what you want, then hand over the cash and take your *scontrino* (receipt). When you order at the bar, placing a 10¢ or 20¢ coin on your *scontrino* will grab the bartender's attention. If you sit down, you will be served by a waiter and charged at least double for the privilege. It is considered very bad form to order at the counter and take your food and drink to a table yourself.

To get a short, strong espresso, ask for *un caffè*. A cappuccino is an espresso with. Cappuccino is rarely consumed after 11am; Romans wouldn't be caught dead drinking it after a meal, so don't make that faux pas.

Note that the list below covers more or less the full gamut of coffee options in any self-respecting Roman bar; the kind of novelty variations (or even skimmed milk) found in international coffee chains are beneath any local bar staff's dignity.

Variations on the espresso

caffè americano very diluted in a large cup.
caffè corretto with a dash of liqueur or spirits (indicate which).
caffè freddo iced espresso; comes sugared unless you ask for *caffè freddo amaro*, which, however, is not always available.
caffè Hag/decaffeinato espresso decaf.
caffè lungo a bit more water than usual.
caffè macchiato with a dash of milk.
caffè monichella with whipped cream.
caffè ristretto coffee essence lining the bottom of the cup – a tooth-enamel remover.
caffè al vetro in a glass.

Variations on the cappuccino

caffè latte more hot milk and less coffee.
cappuccino freddo iced coffee with cold milk; will come sugared unless you specifically ask for *cappuccino freddo amaro*.
cappuccino senza schiuma without froth.
latte macchiato hot milk with just a dash of coffee for flavour.

Such kiosks are almost always on street corners, and close in winter; in summer their opening hours are erratic.

CAPITOLINE & PALATINE
Cafés & bars

See p187 **San Teodoro**.

Pubs & enoteche

See p187 **Enoteca Provincia Romana**.

TREVI & QUIRINALE
Cafés & bars

Pan di Zucchero
Via del Lavatore 29 (06 679 3214). Bus 52, 53, 61, 62, 63, 71, 80Exp, 95, 116, 119, 175, 492, 630. **Open** 7am-8pm daily. **Credit** MC, V. **Map** p341 A5 ➊
This tiny bar/*pasticceria* is a genuine, old-school bar that caters to real Italians in a heavily touristed area by the Trevi Fountain. It offers a basic selection of Italian favourites to workers from shops, offices and ministry outposts nearby. The *bombe calde* (warm doughnut-like pastries) are legendary.

Pubs & enoteche

See p187 **Antica Birreria Peroni**.

Pasticcerie & gelaterie

★ **Il Gelato di San Crispino**
Via della Panetteria 42 (06 679 3924, www.il gelatodisancrispino.it). Bus 52, 53, 61, 62, 63, 71, 80Exp, 95, 116, 119, 175, 490, 630. **Open** noon-12.30am Mon-Thur, Sun; noon-1.30am Fri, Sat. **No credit cards. Map** p341 A5 ➋
Il Gelato di San Crispino serves what many punters consider to be the best ice-cream in Rome – some say the best in the world. The secret lies in the manufacturers' obsessive control over the whole making process. If you need one last lick, there's a branch in the domestic terminal departure lounge at Fiumicino airport. *See also p213* **Gelato Wizards**.
Other locations piazza della Maddalena 5, Pantheon (06 9760 1190); via Acaia 56, Suburbs: south (06 7045 0412); Fiumicino airport, Terminal A.

VENETO & BORGHESE
Cafés & bars

For the Eden's bar, see p173 **Big and Sassy**.

Cinecaffè

*Largo Marcello Mastroianni 1 (06 4201 6224,
www.cinecaffe.it). Bus 88, 95, 116, 490, 491, 495,
C3, M.* **Open** 9am-7pm daily. **Credit** AmEx, DC,
MC, V. **Map** p340 B3 ❸

Via Veneto is a desert if you're looking for a coffee
or a light lunch that won't break the bank. Strike off
instead into the Borghese gardens, to the ultra-
civilised Casa del Cinema (*see p252*). Here, delicious
alfresco lunches and weekend brunches, as well as
coffee, snacks and drinks, are served to cineastes,
enthusiasts and tourists.

h club>doney

*Via Veneto 141 (06 4708 2805, www.westin
rome.com). Bus 52, 53, 63, 80Exp, 95, 116,
119, 630.* **Open** 8am-1am daily. **Credit** AmEx,
DC, MC, V. **Map** p341 B4 ❹

The glamorous street-level bar of the Excelsior hotel
(*see p173* **Big and Sassy**) goes some way towards
recapturing the long-gone razzmatazz of via Veneto.
A haunt of the perma-tanned and designer-clad, it
nonetheless produces great breakfast coffee, good
(though pricey) lunchtime snacks and great *aperitivi*
accompanied on Thursdays by a buffet from 7pm.

THE TRIDENTE

Cafés & bars

Antico Caffè Greco

*Via Condotti 86 (06 679 1700, www.antico
caffegreco.eu). Metro Spagna/bus 52, 53, 61,
71, 80Exp, 85, 95, 116, 119, 160, 850.* **Open**
9am-8pm daily. **Credit** AmEx, DC, MC, V.
Map p339 E4 & p341 A4 ❺

INSIDE TRACK FESTIVE FOOD

Try Rome's feast-day seasonal delicacies:
panettoni – sponge cakes with raisins
and candied fruit – are ubiquitous around
Christmas. The Easter variation is vaguely
bird-shaped and called a *colomba* (dove).
Around the feast of San Giuseppe
(19 March), *pasticcerie* make fried
batter-balls filled with custard. During
carnevale (the run-up to Lent) you'll find
compact balls of fried dough called
castagnole and crispy fried pastry strips
dusted with icing sugar called *frappe*.

Founded in 1760, this venerable café – recently
restored and looking splendid – was once the hangout of Casanova, Goethe, Wagner, Stendhal,
Baudelaire, Shelley and Byron. Opposition to the
French Occupation of 1849-70 was planned here.
Today it has its sofas packed with tourists, while
locals cram the foyer.

★ Caffè Canova-Tadolini

*Via del Babuino 150A (06 3211 0702, www.
canovatadolini.com). Metro Spagna/bus 117, 119.*
Open 8pm-midnight daily. Closed 2wks Aug.
Credit AmEx, DC, MC, V. **Map** p338 E3 ❻

Sculptor Antonio Canova signed a contract in 1818
to ensure that this property, in the heart of the old
artists' quarter, would remain an atelier for sculpture. The master's wishes were respected until 1967:
the workshop passed through many generations of
the Tadolini family, descendants of Canova's

CONSUME

Caffè Canova-Tadolini.

THE BEST LUNCHES

After viewing the Colosseum
Café Café. *See p217.*

For a tasty salad
Vic's. *See p191.*

For a snack in the park
Cinecaffè. *See p209.*

favourite pupil and heir, Adamo Tadolini. Now refurbished as a museum-atelier, Canova's workshop has café tables among its sculpture models and a refined and elegant old-world feel: dark hardwood floors, wood-beamed ceilings, chandeliers and mustard-yellow leather banquettes and chairs. Lunch is served, and the small bar offers cocktails and assorted drinks, as well as tasty titbits, from canapés to cookies and pastries. *See also p87* **Extra Time**.

Canova
Piazza del Popolo 16 (06 361 2231).
Metro Flaminio/bus 95, 117, 119, 491.
Open 7am-midnight daily. **Credit** AmEx, DC,
MC, V. **Map** p338 D/E3 **7**

A refurbishment some years ago did away with any remains of the charmingly shabby place beloved of Federico Fellini, who lived just round the corner. Canova is now vaguely design-y, rather impersonal, but still a reasonable place to grab a quick lunch, especially if you manage to bag a table in the pretty garden out back. A charming collection of Fellini memorabilia will take your mind off the general pan-European blandness.

Ciampini al Café du Jardin *Fabulous, 4/13*
*Viale Trinità dei Monti (06 678 5678, www.
caffeciampini.com). Metro Spagna/bus 52,
53, 61, 71, 80Exp, 85, 95, 116, 119, 160,
850.* **Open** *Apr-mid May, mid Sept-mid Oct*
8am-8pm daily. *Mid May-mid Sept* 8am-1am
Mon, Tue, Thur-Sun. Closed mid Oct-Mar.
Credit AmEx, DC, MC, V. **Map** p341 A4 **8**
This open-air café near the top of the Spanish Steps is an oasis surrounded by creeper-curtained trellises, with a pond in the centre. There's a selection of sandwiches, salads, pastas, cocktails and ices, and it also serves a good breakfast. The view is stunning, especially at sunset, so whet your appetite by sipping an *aperitivo* in style.

Dolci e Doni
*Via delle Carrozze 85B (06 6992 5001). Metro
Spagna/bus 52, 53, 61, 71, 80Exp, 85, 95, 116,
119, 160, 850.* **Open** 11am-11pm daily. **Credit**
AmEx, DC, MC, V. **Map** p339 E4 **9**
This bijou tearoom, renowned for its cakes and chocolates, also specialises in breakfasts, brunches

and quick quiche-and-salad lunches (though you'll find that the takeaway options and cakes are more impressive – and less expensive – than what turns up at your table).

GiNa
*Via San Sebastianello 7A (06 678 0251, www.
ginaroma.com). Metro Spagna/bus 52, 53, 61, 71,
80Exp, 85, 95, 116, 119, 160, 850.* **Open** 11am-
8pm daily. Closed 2wks Aug. **Credit** AmEx, MC,
V. **Map** p338 E3 & p341 A4 **10**
This modern *locale* is a relief from the area's posh tearooms and over-decorated cafés. The decor is clean and white, with delicate touches like votive candles and single roses in miniature jars. It's an all-day kind of place – from late breakfast to light lunch, from evening *aperitivi* to snacky dinner, soups, salads and some pasta, plus a selection of great ice-cream. Prices are on the high side. They also do a summer picnic-hamper service for those who like the idea of a *déjeuner sur l'herbe* in nearby Villa Borghese.

Rosati *– expensive but lovely 4/13*
*Piazza del Popolo 5 (06 322 5859, www.rosati
bar.it). Metro Flaminio/bus 95, 117, 119, 491.*
Open 7am-11pm daily. **Credit** AmEx, DC,
MC, V. **Map** p338 D3 **11**
Rosati is the traditional haunt of Rome's intellectual left: Calvino, Moravia and Pasolini were regulars. The art nouveau interior has remained unchanged since its opening in 1922. The coffee and *pasticceria*

GiNa.

are excellent; splash out on a pavement table with ringside view of stately piazza del Popolo to enjoy them at. Or try the *Sogni romani* cocktail: orange juice with four kinds of liqueur in red and yellow – the colours of the city (and the Roma football team).

★ Stravinskij Bar

Via del Babuino 9 (06 328 881, www.hotelde russie.it). Metro Spagna or Flaminia/bus 117, 119. **Open** 9am-1am daily. **Credit** AmEx, DC, MC, V. **Map** p338 E3

Inside the swanky De Russie hotel (*see p173* **Big and Sassy**), this bar is divided into three sections: the small bar, a larger lounge area with sofas, and the outdoor patio. The first two are filled in cooler months with international business people, the hotel's celebrity guests and a gaggle of deep-pocketed regulars. But the real draw here is the fabulous patio, a sunken area of shady tables surrounded by orange trees. The drinks menu is interesting, the cocktails well executed – although on the patio beneath the Roman sun, the beverage the courteous staff serves most of is simply the finest spumante.

Vitti

Piazza San Lorenzo in Lucina 33 (06 687 6304). Bus 62, 63, 81, 95, 117, 119, 160, 492, 628, 630. **Open** 8am-11pm daily. **Credit** AmEx, DC, MC, V. **Map** p339 E4

Occupying a table in lovely, pedestrianised piazza San Lorenzo in Lucina is a true pleasure, and the excellent coffee, home-made cakes and pastries enhance the experience. Stand-out treats at this classic Roman café include exquisite sweet Neapolitan specialities – canolo, cassatina and rum babà are all divine. But the simple lunchtime fare is good, too. If the mark-up for consuming at a pavement table seems too steep, join the throng at the counter and consume standing up.

Pubs & enoteche

See also p188 **Buccone**, *p188* **'Gusto** and *p191* **Palatium**.

Antica Enoteca di Via della Croce

Via della Croce 76B (06 679 0896). Metro Spagna/bus 52, 53, 61, 71, 80Exp, 85, 95, 116, 119, 160, 628, 850. **Open** 11am-midnight daily. **Credit** AmEx, DC, MC, V. **Map** p338 E3

When this place opened in 1842 it was the favourite haunt of the Scandinavian painters who lived on nearby via Margutta. A revamp has retained most of the original fittings, including the marble wine vats and a venerable wooden cash desk, which makes it a great place to sip one of the many wines that are offered by the glass here. There's a cold *antipasto* buffet at the bar, and a restaurant with tables in the long back room offering a full range of hot dishes at mealtimes – even though the cuisine is generally uninspiring.

Sant'Eustachio. *See p212.*

PANTHEON & NAVONA
Cafés & bars

For a bar in the cloisters of **Santa Maria della Pace** *(Chiostro del Bramante), see p95.*

Caffè Bernini

Piazza Navona 44 (06 6819 2998, www. caffebernini.com). Bus 30Exp, 40Exp, 46, 62, 64, 70, 81, 87, 116, 492, 628. **Open** 9am-12.30am daily. **Credit** AmEx, DC, MC, V. **Map** p339 D5

Splendid piazza Navona is somewhere you'll want to linger at, but the majority of the cafés with enticing tables out on the square are substandard (but not sub-priced) tourist traps. The Caffè Bernini, on the other hand, tries to raise the stakes. The coffee is good, the *aperitivi* are fine and the pan-Med food is not *too* expensive for the glorious location.

Caffè della Pace

Via della Pace 3-7 (06 686 1216, www.caffedellapace.it). Bus 30Exp, 40Exp, 46, 62, 64, 70, 81, 87, 116, 492, 628. **Open** 4pm-3am Mon; 8.30am-2am Tue-Sun. **Credit** AmEx, MC, V. **Map** p339 C5

Rome's Antico Caffè della Pace (which is known to all and sundry as Bar della Pace) is eternally *à la mode*. In cooler months, the antiques and flower-filled rooms exude a sense of warmth, and the proximity of the tables gives ample space for cosying up

Freni e Frizion
See p216.

CONSUME

to your neighbours. Outdoors, it continues to be a great place, albeit a pricey location, from which to survey passers-by.

★ Salotto 42
Piazza di Pietra 42 (06 678 5804, www.salotto42.it). Bus 62, 63, 81, 95, 117, 119, 160, 492, 628, 630. **Open** 10am-midnight Mon, Sun. 10am-2am Tue-Sat. Closed Aug. **Credit** AmEx, DC, MC, V. **Map** p339 E5 ⑰
This spot on lovely piazza di Pietra is open morning till late. The bar's Roman/Swedish/New York pedigree is seen in little touches throughout. Incredibly comfortable chairs and sofas provide a cosy feel during the day, when a smörgåsbord of nibbles is available. By night, the sleek room becomes a gorgeous cocktail bar with a great soundtrack, excellent

---

**THE BEST
SERIOUS CAFFEINE FIX**

For scrumptious froth
Sant' Eustachio. *See above.*

For the real Neapolitan thing
La Caffettiera. *See right.*

For bags and bags of the stuff
Tazza d'Oro. *See above.*

---

drinks and local sophisticates. All this plus a selection of books on fashion, art and design.

Sant'Eustachio
Piazza Sant'Eustachio 82 (06 6880 2048, www.santeustachioilcaffe.it). Bus 30Exp, 40Exp, 46, 62, 63, 64, 70, 81, 87, 492, 628, 630, 780, H. **Open** 8.30am-1am Mon-Thur, Sun; 8.30am-1.20am Fri, Sat. **No credit cards.** **Map** p342 D1 & p339 D5 ⑱
This is one of the city's most famous coffee bars, and its walls are plastered with celebrity testimonials. The coffee is quite extraordinary, if pricier than elsewhere; the barmen turn their backs while whipping up a cup so as not to let their secret out (though a pinch of bicarbonate of soda is rumoured to give it its froth). Try the *gran caffè*: the *schiuma* (froth) can be slurped out afterwards. Unless you specify (*amaro* means 'no sugar'; *poco zucchero* means 'a little sugar'), it comes very sweet. *Photo p211.*

Tazza d'Oro
Via degli Orfani 84 (06 678 9792, www.tazzadorocoffeeshop.com). Bus 30Exp, 40Exp, 46, 62, 63, 64, 70, 81, 87, 492, 628, 630. **Open** 7am-8pm Mon-Sat. Closed 1wk Aug. **Credit** AmEx, DC, MC, V. **Map** p339 E5 ⑲
The powerful aroma wafting from this ancient *torrefazione* (coffee-roaster's) overlooking the Pantheon is a siren call to coffee-lovers. The place is packed with coffee sacks, tourists and regulars, who flock for *granita di caffè* (coffee sorbet) in summer, and *cioccolata calda con panna* (hot chocolate with whipped cream) in winter.

Pubs & enoteche

See also p271 **Bar del Fico**, *p193* **Cul de Sac** and *p271* **Etabli**.

Société Lutèce
Piazza di Montevecchio 17 (06 6830 1472, www.societe-lutece.it). Bus 30Exp, 40Exp, 46, 70, 81, 87, 116, 492, 628. **Open** 6.30pm-2am Tue-Sun. Closed 2wks Aug. **No credit cards.** **Map** p339 C5 ⑳
Despite being fiendishly difficult to find, this shabby-chic bar attracts eclectic Roman hipstersom droves. The cramped quarters often cause a spillover into the small piazza, which annoys the neighbours. Still, the a*peritivo* snacks (6.30-10.30pm – unless the food runs out earlier) are plentiful in number, the employees are as playful as the customers and the vibe is decidedly laid-back.

Trinity College
Via del Collegio Romano 6 (06 678 6472, www.trinity-rome.com). Bus 62, 63, 81, 85, 95, 117, 119, 160, 175, 492, 628, 630, 850. **Open** noon-2.30am daily. **Credit** AmEx, DC, MC, V. **Map** p341 A6, p342 E1 & p339 E5 ㉑

This is a city-centre pub that is much frequented by thirsty employees of the Cultural Heritage Ministry opposite. The venue has a more authentic feel than many of the capital's 'Irish' pubs, even though the thirsty packs of American college students prove that it's all an illusion.

Pasticcerie & gelaterie

★ La Caffettiera

Piazza di Pietra 65 (06 679 8147, www.grancaffelacaffettiera.com). Bus 62, 63, 81, 85, 95, 117, 119, 160, 175, 492, 628, 630, 850. **Open** *Oct-May* 7am-10pm daily. *June-Sept* 7am-10pm Mon-Sat. **Credit** AmEx, DC, MC, V. **Map** p339 E5 ㉒

Politicians and mandarins from the parliament buildings nearby lounge in the sumptuous tearoom of this temple to Neapolitan goodies, while lesser mortals bolt coffees at the counter. The *rum babà* reigns supreme, but ricotta-lovers rave over the crunchy *sfogliatella*, which is flavoured with cinnamon and orange peel.

★ Gelateria del Teatro

Via di San Simone 70 (06 4547 4880). Bus 30Exp, 40Exp, 46, 70, 81, 87, 116, 492, 628. **Open** 10.30pm daily. **No credit cards.** **Map** p339 C5 ㉓

See below **Gelato Wizards**.

GHETTO & CAMPO DE' FIORI

Cafés & bars

Bernasconi

Piazza Cairoli 16 (06 6880 6264). Bus 63, 630, 780, H/tram 8. **Open** 7am-8.30pm Tue-Sun. Closed Aug. **No credit cards.** **Map** p342 D2 ㉓

Cramped and inconspicuous – like so many of Rome's best bars – this venue is well worth fighting your way inside for excellent coffee and *lieviti* (breakfast yeast buns). Bernasconi's chewy, yeasty *cornetti* are unbeatable: the real vintage variety, difficult to find elsewhere. Close to the synagogue, this spot straddles Rome's Jewish and Catholic worlds, with kosher sweets and Lenten *quaresimale* cookies.

Gelato Wizards

The gourmet ice-cream revolution.

In the beginning was **Il Gelato di San Crispino** (*see p208*). In 1992, the Alongi brothers – fanatical ice-cream purists – began whipping up something completely new in their first outlet in the southern suburbs: ice-cream made from scratch (even good *gelatai* resort to industrially made ice-cream bases), with flavours provided by the finest pistacchios from Bronte in Sicily, 20-year-old marsala (*zabaione*) and seasonal fruit so fresh it's like tasting the original, whipped up and frozen.

This sudden eruption on to a Roman scene where *gelato* was good but never truly great forced others to pull themselves up by their bootstraps and unleashed a new wave of copycat gourmet *gelaterie*, some of which were not bad at all but none of which truly rivalled the original.

The past few years, though, have seen more aggressive competitors for the Alongi's unofficial title of manufacturers of some of the best ice-cream, anywhere.

Applying the same strict standards to their methods, the new generation has allowed its imagination to run free with experimental flavours and textures.

At **Gelateria del Teatro** (*see p213*), Stefano and his wife Silvia draw from a past as pastry chefs to create surprises

such as *cannolo*- and *panettone*-flavoured *gelato*. Their chocolate – 80 per cent pure cocoa – is exquisite, as is the caramel and pear with sesame.

Claudio Torcè began his ice-cream career with a suburban outlet – called, simply, **Il Gelato** (*see p217*) – which became a word-of-mouth mecca for gelato-lovers. Nowadays, you can experience his product in the Aventine district. Torcè's flavours are even more outlandish, with cream of capsicum, ricotta cheese with orange peel, and tomato with rice on the menu of around 100 varieties. His peanut ice-cream is superb, as is the wide range of chocolate flavours: 80 per cent cocoa with ginger is sublime.

CONSUME

THE BEST CAFES WITH VIEWS

The whole of Rome, laid out
at your feet
Il Ristoro. See *p218.*

Glorious Piazza Navona
Caffè Bernini. See *p211.*

Non-stop market action
La Vineria. *See below.*

Pubs & enoteche

See also p195 **Open Baladin.**

Antica Vineria
*Via Monte della Farina 37 (06 6880 6989).
Bus 30Exp, 40Exp, 46, 62, 64, 70, 81, 87,
492, 628, 630, 780, H/tram 8.* **Open** 10.30am-
3pm, 6.30-10.30pm Mon-Sat. **No credit cards.**
Map p339 D6 ㉕
First and foremost a carry-out bottle shop, this long-
running establishment near campo de' Fiori of an
evening becomes a laid-back bohemian-chic stop
with standing-only customers spilling out into the
picturesque street to sip wine by the glass at very
reasonable prices.

Bartaruga
*Piazza Mattei 7 (06 689 2299,
www.bartaruga.com). Bus 30Exp, 40Exp, 46, 62,
64, 70, 81, 87, 492, 628, 630, 780, H/tram 8.*
Open 6pm-midnight Tue-Thur; 6pm-2am Fri, Sat;
6pm-1am Sun. **No credit cards. Map** p342 D2 ㉖
This baroque *locale* – in peach and midnight blue,
with divans, candelabra and a grand piano – overlooks one of the most exquisite fountains in Rome.
A crowd of beautiful, eccentric people make the most
of the backdrop (while trying hard to ignore the
rather surly bar staff).

Il Goccetto
*Via dei Banchi Vecchi 14 (06 686 4268). Bus
40Exp, 46, 62, 64, 916.* **Open** 6.30pm-midnight
Tue-Sat. Closed 1wk Jan & 3wks Aug. **Credit**
AmEx, MC, V. **Map** p339 C6 & p342 B1 ㉗
One of the more serious *centro storico* wine bars,
occupying part of a medieval bishop's house, Il
Goccetto has original painted ceilings, dark wood-
clad walls and a cosy, private-club feel. Wine is the
main point here, with a satisfying range by the glass
from €2.50, but if you're peckish, there's a choice of
cheeses, salamis and salads too. It closes early afternoon on Saturdays in July.

La Vineria
*Campo de' Fiori 15 (06 6880 3268). Bus 40Exp,
46, 62, 64, 116, 916.* **Open** 8.30am-2am Mon-Sat.

Closed 3wks Aug. **Credit** AmEx, DC, MC, V. **Map**
p339 C/D6 & p342 C1 ㉘
Known as the Vineria Reggio or just plain Vineria,
this long-running wine bar on the Campo is the real
thing, where Romans flock to chat and plan the
evening ahead over good wines by the glass starting
at a remarkably cheap €2 (albeit in tiny glasses).
By *aperitivo* time, it's a dog-eat-dog battle to grab a
table for dinner.

Pasticcerie & gelaterie

See also p213 **Bernasconi,** *p230* **Dolceroma**
and *p230* **Forno del Ghetto.**

Alberto Pica
*Via della Seggiola 12 (06 686 8405). Bus 23, 63,
280, 630, 780, H/tram 8.* **Open** *Jan-Mar, Oct,
Nov* 8.30am-2am Mon-Sat. *Apr-Sept, Dec* 8.30am-
2am Mon-Sat; 4.30pm-2am Sun. Closed 10 days
Aug. **No credit cards. Map** p342 D2 ㉙
Horrendous neon lighting, surly staff… and some of
Rome's most delicious ice-cream: these are the hallmarks of this long-running bar close to the justice
ministry. The rice specialities stand out: imagine eating frozen, partially cooked rice pudding and you'll
get the picture. *Riso alla cannella* (cinnamon rice) is
particularly wonderful.

TRASTEVERE & GIANICOLO
Cafés & bars

Bar Gianicolo
Piazzale Aurelio 5 (06 580 6275). Bus 870.
Open 6am-1am Tue-Sat; 6am-9pm Sun. Closed
2wks Aug. **No credit cards. Map** p342 A3 ㉚
If you've slogged up here to visit Villa Pamphili (*see
p161*) or the site of Garibaldi's doomed battle with
the French on the Gianicolo (*see p118*), rest your
weary bones on the wooden benches of this tiny bar
with an intimate, chatty feel. Carrots and apples are
juiced on the spot and there's a good range of interesting sandwiches and light meals.

Bar San Calisto
Piazza San Calisto (no phone). Bus 780, H/tram 8.
Open 5.30am-2am Mon-Sat. **No credit cards.**
Map p342 C3 ㉛
Green tourists get their coffee or beer on piazza
Santa Maria in Trastevere; locals who know better
go to this bar. The place's harsh lighting would
make Sophia Loren look wan, and the dingy space
– inside and out – is no picture postcard. But it's
cheap and as such it has always been the haunt of
arty and fringe types (plus many questionable characters after sundown). The bohemian crowd will be
here downing beers or an *affogato* (ice-cream
swamped with liqueur), or savouring some of the
best hot chocolate in Rome: deliciously thick with
fresh whipped cream.

La Libreria del Cinema. *See p216.*

Friends Art Café

*Piazza Trilussa 34 (06 581 6111, www.cafe
friends.it). Bus 23, 280, 780, H/tram 8.* **Open**
7.30am-2am Mon-Sat; 6.30pm-2am Sun. Closed
1wk Aug. **Credit** AmEx, DC, MC, V.
Map p342 C2 ㉝
This lively, modern bar is a popular place where
habitués meet for everything from a morning
cornetto and cappuccino to after-dinner cocktails.
The chrome detailing, brilliantly coloured plastic
chairs and constant sound of fashion television
buzzing in the background, lend the place a retro-
'80s funhouse atmosphere. Lunch and dinner menus
offer *bruschette*, salads and pastas at reasonable
prices. There's a free wireless connection, should you
wish to bring your laptop along.
Other locations Via della Scrofa 60, Tridente
(06 686 1416).

Ombre Rosse

*Piazza Sant'Egidio 12 (06 588 4155, www.
ombrerossecaffe.it). Bus 780, H/tram 8.* **Open**
7am-2am Mon-Sat; 10am-2am Sun. **Credit** AmEx,
MC, V. **Map** p342 C3 ㉟
Located right in the heart of Trastevere, this café is
the perfect place for a morning coffee, a late lunch
or a light bite of dinner (the chicken salad and fresh
soups are great options). The Ombre Rosse fills up
to bursting point before and after dinner, when bag-
ging one of the outdoor tables can be a real coup.
Service is slow but friendly: while the bartender
hand-crushes the ice for your next caipiroska, you
will have plenty of time to watch the Trastevere
menagerie go by on the street outside.

Pubs & enoteche

See also p198 **Bir&Fud**.

Artù

*Largo MD Fumasoni Biondi 5 (06 588 0398). Bus
23, 280, 870.* **Open** 6pm-2am daily. Closed 3wks
Aug. **Credit** MC, V. **Map** p342 C3 ㉞
This friendly place, off piazza Sant' Egidio, hovers
between English pub and Italian bar. The selection of
high-quality brews suggests UK pub; the wine list,
fashion TV and *aperitivo* buffet (6.30-9pm) remind you
you're in *bella Italia*. There's also a full menu of 'pub'
fare, with sandwiches, pasta and meat courses.

Cioccolata e Vino

*Vicolo del Cinque 11 (06 5830 1868). Bus 23, 280,
780, H/tram 8.* **Open** 6.30pm-2am Mon-Fri; 2pm-
2am Sun. **No credit cards. Map** p342 C2 ㉟
Half-shop, half-bar, this tiny emporium is a joy to
visit at almost any hour: for hot chocolate, a delicious
espresso with chocolate in the bottom of your cup, a
chocolate tasting or a glass of wine from a small but
interesting selection. There are second-hand books
down in the cellars if indulging isn't your thing.

INSIDE TRACK TAP WATER

Bars must provide dehydrated passers-by
with a glass of tap water on request, with
no obligation to buy. Ask for '*un bicchiere
d'acqua dal rubinetto*'.

CONSUME

Enoteca Ferrara

*Piazza Trilussa 41 (06 580 3769,
www.enotecaferrara.it). Bus 780, H/tram 8.*
Open 6pm-midnight daily. **Credit** AmEx,
MC, V. **Map** p342 C2 ③⑥

Ignore the rather expensive restaurant in this
Trastevere stalwart and stick with the wine bar by
the entrance, with its good choice of wines by the
glass and an encyclopaedic bottle menu – with big
mark-ups. You can pick at the range of snacks on
the counter for €7-€10.

★ Freni e Frizioni

*Via del Politeama 4-6 (06 4549 7499, www.freni
efrizioni.com). Bus 23, 280.* **Open** 6pm-2am daily.
Credit DC, MC, V. **Map** p342 C2 ③⑦

Unlikely ex-garage surroundings – the name means
'brakes and clutches' – for one of Rome's hippest
early evening spot, frequented by arty types and a
creative, studenty crowd. A grand buffet is laid out
from 7pm to 10pm on a snowy white tablecloth: baskets of focaccia, ceramic bowls of couscous and
pasta, guacamole and raw vegetables. Help yourself
while you sip a cocktail, a beer, or a glass of well-
priced wine in the crowded interior or the equally
crowded square. *Photo p212.*

La Libreria del Cinema

*Via dei Fienaroli 31 (06 581 7724, www.libreria
delcinema.roma.it). Bus 780, H/tram 8.* **Open**
5pm-11pm daily. Closed 2wks Aug. **Credit** MC, V.
Map p342 C3 ③⑧

Movie buffs will love this café-bookshop with its
vast stock of cinema-related material and its busy
programme of events. In the charming café, aficiona-
dos exchange cinema stories over coffee, light
lunches and *aperitivi.*

Pasticcerie & gelaterie

See also p214 **Bar San Calisto**.

Checco er Carettiere

*Via Benedetta 7 (06 581 1413, www.checco
ercarettiere.it). Bus 23, 280, 780, H/tram 8.*
Open 6.30am-1am daily. **No credit cards.**
Map p342 C2 ③⑨

Located behind piazza Trilussa, this small bar,
annexed to one of Trastevere's oldest restaurants,
has outstanding cakes and pastries, plus fresh
quiches, crisp *crocchette* and, usually, tasty baked
pasta. There's a savvy selection of malt whiskies too,
and some of the best *gelato* this side of the Tiber.

Sora Mirella

*Lungotevere degli Anguillara, corner of Ponte
Cestio (no phone). Bus 23, 280, 780, H/tram 8.*
Open 10am-3am daily. Closed Oct-Feb. **No credit
cards. Map** p342 D3 ④⓪

Mirella styles herself as *la regina della grattachecca*
(the Queen of Water Ices), and there appears to be

Andreotti.

no reason to disagree. The place gives you an opportunity to sit on the Tiber embankment wall as you
tuck into the *speciale superfrutta* – fresh melon, kiwi
fruit and strawberry (or whatever fruit happens to
be in season) with syrups served in a specially
designed glass.

AVENTINE, TESTACCIO & OSTIENSE

Cafés & bars

See also p234 **Città dell'Altra Economia**
and *p200* **Il Seme e la Foglia**.

Andreotti

*Via Ostiense 54B (06 575 0773, www.andreotti
roma.com). Bus 23, 769.* **Open** 7.30am-9.30pm
daily. Closed 1wk Aug. **Credit** AmEx, MC, V.
Map p123 B2 ④①

The Andreotti family claims to serve up to 700 cups
of its excellent coffee every day – and that was
before a refit that doubled the space, lengthened the
counter and gave this bustling neighbourhood bar
a cool retro atmosphere. All of which provided more
space for sampling excellent breakfast *cornetti*,
cakes, light lunchtime snacks and evening *aperitivi*
with delicious nibbles.

Caffè Letterario

*Via Ostiense 83-95 (06 5730 2842, www.caffe
letterarioroma.it). Bus 23, 769.* **Open** 10am-2am

Tue-Sun. Closed 6wks mid July-Sept. **No credit cards**. **Map** p123 B2 ④
In an area swarming with students from the Terza Università campus, Caffè Letterario is a style temple showcasing not only the latest books but also the contemporary arts in general. Enjoy your morning coffee, light lunch or *aperitivo* perusing new titles, exhibitions and design-related happenings of many and various descriptions.

Pubs & enoteche

L'Oasi della Birra
Piazza Testaccio 41 (06 574 6122, www.oasidellabirra.com). Bus 23, 30Exp, 75, 95, 170, 280, 716, 781/tram 3. **Open** 4.30pm-12.30am daily. Closed 2wks Aug. **Credit** AmEx, MC, V. **Map** p343 D5 ④
In the basement of an *enoteca* on Testaccio's market square, this 'Oasis of Beer' has more than 500 brews on offer – or so it claims to serve. In fact, the wine collection upstairs (where an off-licence is open all day) is more impressive and can be enjoyed by the glass from 4.30pm to 8pm. Here you can order a plate from the very generous *aperitivo* buffet to accompany your glass of wine. An à la carte menu includes snacks and dishes with a Teutonic slant. The outdoor tables operate year round, but of course on a weather permitting basis.

Pasticcerie & gelaterie

Chiosco Testaccio
Via G Branca, corner of via Beniamino Franklin (no phone). Bus 95, 170, 781/tram 3. **Open** noon-1.30am daily. Closed mid Sept-Apr. **No credit cards**. **Map** p343 C5 ④
Still going strong after more than 80 years in this working-class neighbourhood, the Chiosco Testaccio has the unusual selling point of being painted in a different colour each year. Even though you have to push past the lounging local youth to order a hand-grated ice, the unusual flavours are worth the jostling. The selection is as varied as the outside paint job is colourful; tamarind and *limoncocco* (lemon-coconut) are among the specialities that you will find at this unique place.

**THE BEST
APERITIVI WITH SNACKS**

Laid-back and boho chic
Freni e Frizioni. *See left*.

Neighbourhood charm
Oasi della Birra. *See above*.

Dolce vita style
h club>doney. *See p209*.

Il Gelato
Viale Aventino 59 (338 446 3434). Bus 60, 75, 118, 673/tram 3. **Open** 11am-11pm Mon-Sat. Closed 3wks Jan. **No credit cards**. **Map** p345 A5 ④
See p213 **Gelato Wizards**.

CELIO, SAN GIOVANNI & SAN LORENZO

Cafés & bars

Bar à Book
Via dei Piceni 23 (06 9604 3014, www.barabook.it). Bus 71, 492/tram 3, 19. **Open** 5pm-1am Tue, Wed; 5pm-2am Thur-Sat. Closed Aug. **Credit** AmEx, DC, MC, V. **Map** p128 D2 ④
Sixties decor, shelves packed with books and magazines, and a huge central wooden table surrounded by chatting drinkers give this cosy venue in San Lorenzo the feel of a college bar... in a good sense. Closes on Saturday from mid-June to end of September.

Café Café
Via dei Santi Quattro 44 (06 700 8743, www.cafecafebistrot.it). Metro Colosseo/bus 85, 87, 117, 810, 850/tram 3. **Open** 11am-1.30am daily. **Credit** MC, V. **Map** p344 C3 ④
This attractive place offers smoothies, teas, wines, salads and sandwiches for travellers weary after a romp around the Colosseum. There's a brunch buffet from 11.30am to 4pm on Sundays.

Said
Via Tiburtina 135 (06 446 9204, www.said.it). Bus 71, 492. **Open** 12.30pm-midnight Mon-Sat. Closed 2wks Aug. **Credit** MC, V. **Map** p128 C2 ④
This chocolate factory – operative since 1923, and open as a shop from 10am – is enveloped in the glorious scent of its exquisite core product. But scattered among the antique chocolate-making equipment are tables and chairs at which to enjoy a warming hot chocolate in winter, a coffee any time, an *aperitivo* with buffet snacks (in which chocolate pops up in odd places) or – if you wish – a meal at the (rather overpriced) restaurant... though we recommend you stick to simpler pleasures.

MONTI & ESQUILINO

Cafés & bars

See also p276 **Oppio Caffè**.

La Bottega del Caffè
Piazza Madonna dei Monti 5 (06 474 1578). Bus 75, 84, 117. **Open** 8am-2am daily. **Credit** MC, V. **Map** p344 B1/B2 ④
With its tables outside on the pretty square (patio heaters keep them warm through winter) this café

draws locals – and weary sightseers from the nearby Roman and Imperial Fora – for breakfast, lunch and *aperitivi*. Friendly staff serve morning coffee or afternoon tea with tiny *cornetti* or biscuits. There's generally a cooked option alongside the usual range of sandwiches and filled rolls at lunch.

Pubs & enoteche

Al Vino al Vino
Via dei Serpenti 19 (06 485 803). Bus 40Exp, 64, 70, 117, 170, H. **Open** 10.30am-2.30pm, 5.30pm-1am daily. Closed 2wks Aug. **Credit** MC, V. **Map** p344 B1 ⑤⓪
This hostelry on lively via dei Serpenti has a range of over 500 wines, with more than 25 available by the glass. But its speciality is *distillati*: dozens of fine grappas, whiskies and other strong spirits. The food is so-so but light snacks are fine for soaking up the alcohol. Shame the staff can be less than charming.

The Druid's Den
Via San Martino ai Monti 28 (06 4890 4781, www.druidspubrome.com). Metro Cavour/bus 16, 75, 84, 360, 649. **Open** 5pm-2am daily. **Credit** MC, V. **Map** p344 D1 ⑤①
This pub was already well established before the 1990s craze for all things Irish developed in Rome. It serves a decent pint of Liffey water, as well as beaming in football from the British Isles. Happy hour lasts from 5pm to 8pm daily. The Druid's Rock outpost has live music at weekends.
Other locations Druid's Rock, piazza Esquilino 1, Esquiline (06 474 1326).

The Fiddler's Elbow
Via dell'Olmata 43 (06 487 2110, www.thefiddlers elbow.com). Metro Cavour/bus 16, 75, 84, 360, 649. **Open** 4pm-1.30am daily. **Credit** MC, V. **Map** p344 C/D1 ⑤②
One of the oldest, best-known pubs in Rome, the Fiddler's Elbow has a basic wooden-benched interior that hasn't changed for years. Though Italy's smoking ban means it's no longer a fume-filled dive, it still succeeds in giving the impression of being one.

Pasticcerie & gelaterie

★ Dagnino
Galleria Esedra, via VE Orlando 75 (06 481 8660, www.pasticceriadagnino.com). Metro Repubblica/bus 40Exp, 64, 70, 170, H. **Open** 7am-11pm daily. **Credit** AmEx, MC, V. **Map** p341 C5 ⑤③
Stunning 1950s decor sets the scene for this corner of Sicily in the heart of Rome. If it's Sicilian and edible, it's here: from ice-cream in buns to lifelike marzipan fruits. Regulars come for crisp *cannoli siciliani* filled with salty, chocolate-chip ricotta and the shiny green-iced *cassata*, uniting all the flavours of the south: the perfume of citrus, almond paste and fresh ricotta.

Il Palazzo del Freddo di Giovanni Fassi
Via Principe Eugenio 65-67 (06 446 4740, www.palazzodelfreddo.it). Metro Vittorio/bus 70, 71, 105/tram 5, 14. **Open** noon-midnight Tue-Sun. **No credit cards. Map** p344 E2 ⑤④
With its breathtakingly kitsch interior and splendid ices, Fassi is a Roman institution. Established in 1880, its walls are adorned with Edwardian adverts and Fascist-era posters, which extol the virtues of the shop's wares. Service is often irascible, and the crowds can be daunting, but the ices are never less than sublime: best of all are *riso* – the English translation, 'rice pudding', hardly does it justice – and the Palazzo's own invention, *la caterinetta*, a mysterious concoction of whipped honey and vanilla.

VATICAN & PRATI

Cafés & bars

See also p205 **Settembrini**.

Gran Caffè Esperia
Lungotevere dei Mellini 1 (06 3211 0016). Bus 30Exp, 70, 280, 492, 913. **Open** 7am-9.30pm daily. **Credit** MC, V. **Map** p339 D4 ⑤⑤
Locals vie to conquer pavement tables in the morning sun at this freshly restored *belle époque* café. Join them for a breakfast of wonderful coffee and *cornetti*; alternatively, forget about the cappuccino and go straight for a glass of *prosecco* and a smoked salmon *tramezzino*.

Il Ristoro
Basilica di San Pietro (06 6988 3376). Metro Ottaviano/bus 23, 40Exp, 62, 64. **Open** *Apr-Sept* 8.30am-6pm daily. *Oct-Mar* 8.30am-5pm daily. **No credit cards. Map** p145 C3 ⑤⑥
You're not going to bump into the Pope up here, but it's still worth paying the price of the St Peter's cupola lift to sip your coffee on the roof of the basilica. There's precious little on the menu except coffee, soft drinks and mineral water but there's a wondrous view over the city, through the row of giant saints crowning the façade.

Pubs & enoteche

Enoteca Nuvolari
Via degli Ombrellari 10 (06 6880 3018). Bus 23, 40Exp, 62, 280. **Open** 11.30am-2pm Mon-Sat. Closed Aug. **No credit cards. Map** p339 A4 ⑤⑦
Named after the legendary Italian racing driver Tazio Nuvolari, this *enoteca* is where the younger denizens of staid Borgo hang out. A lunch menu of competently prepared traditional fare is followed by a lively cocktail hour (6.30-8.30pm) accompanied by a free buffet. Home-made soups and pâtés sustain tardier wine enthusiasts in the candlelit supper room next door (meals served 8pm-1am). Music, plus regular art shows on the walls, make this a fun place.

CONSUME

Shops & Services

The Eternal City's shopping scene has an eternally vintage feel.

Shopping in central Rome can be rather a refreshing, old-fashioned experience for out-of-towners. There are no huge department stores here; no shopping malls; few of the ubiquitous chains (give or take a Benetton or two) that make every British high street, for example, a carbon copy of all the others. Instead, there are corner grocery shops, dark and dusty bottle-lined wine shops, one-off boutiques catering to every imaginable taste... and, of course, the opulent outlets of Italy's fashion aristocracy. As a fashion centre, Rome has long been overshadowed by the

moda empire that is Milan, but the past few years have seen a blossoming in the capital, which now looks set to give her foggy northern sister a run for her money. Whether you want to spend serious sums on big labels, rummage through the city's flea markets or stock up at its delis, Rome's shopping scene is a gem.

WHERE TO GO

To some extent, Rome's commercial old-worldliness is simply an illusion: the corner shop is being driven out by big-name mini-markets; shopping malls would be here were it not for the fact that space restrictions and exorbitant rents keep them away, or at least out of the centre, in the outer suburbs. There are also a number of clothing retail chains, but they simply have different names over here.

International brands such as the Spanish retail giant Zara, which has occupied the palazzo where the quintessential Italian department store Rinascente held sway over via del Corso) are creeping slowly but inexorably on to the Roman high street. Traditionalists just have to draw consolation from the fact that the tiny boutique and the family-run store still maintain a strong presence in Rome's retail sector.

The major Italian names in high fashion are huddled around piazza di Spagna and **via Condotti** (*see p220* **The A-list**). To avoid the masses, wend your way around the side streets of the area, where smaller boutiques and cafés make for a peaceful and pretty stroll. For great independent designers and the city's best vintage, on the other hand, make for via del Governo Vecchio (map p339 C5).

Via del Corso – stretching from piazza del Popolo to piazza Venezia – is home to mid-range outlets for everything from books and music to clothing and shoes. Many of the same clothing retailers can be found along via Nazionale (map p341), and while the street itself is no charmer, the nearby Monti district packs unique boutiques and hip originals along its narrow, hilly streets. Across the river in the Prati area, via Cola di Rienzo (map p338) is a less crowded version of via del Corso, with major retail chains, and some great food shopping at **Castroni** and divine deli **Franchi** (for both, *see p232*).

OPENING TIMES

Opening hours aren't as traditional as they once were here and now most central-Rome shops operate '*no-stop*' opening hours, from 9.30-10am to 7.30am-8pm, Monday to Saturday. The occasional independent still clings to the traditional 1-4pm shutdown. In the centre, stores also increasingly open on Sundays.

Times given in this chapter are winter opening hours; the timetable for shops tends to change in summer (approximately June to September) to account for the heat. In general, shops that opt for long lunches tend to reopen later, at 5pm or 5.30pm, staying open until 8-8.30pm. Most food stores close on Thursday afternoons in winter, and on Saturday afternoons in summer. The majority of non-food shops are closed Monday mornings. Some smaller shops shut down for at least two weeks each summer (generally in August) and almost all are shut for two or three days around the 15 August public holiday. If you're coming for a with something particular in mind and you want to avoid finding a particular shop *chiuso per ferie* (closed for holidays), be sure to ring ahead.

MARKETS

Though prices at Rome's many flea markets have crept up, bargain-hunters needn't despair: since the trend for all things vintage has yet to take the city by storm, there's many a find to be unearthed by those with the patience for some serious rummaging. At the larger markets, such as the legendary **Porta Portese** and **via Sannio**, haggling is expected; ignore the

---

The A-list

Italian über-labels.

Jostling for space in window-shopping heaven in the grid of streets at the bottom of the Spanish Steps in Tridente, the emporia of the big guns of Italian fashion can be reached from the Spagna metro station or by any bus going to piazza San Silvestro. (Only Davide Cenci is out of the area.) They all take major credit cards.

Roberto Cavalli
Via Borgognona 25 (06 6992 5469).
Open 10am-7.30pm Mon-Sat; 11am-7.30pm Sun. **Map** p339 E4.
Other locations Just Cavalli, via Belsiana 57 (06 6920 0415).

Costume National
Via del Babuino 106 (06 6920 0686).
Open 10am-7pm Mon-Sat. **Map** p338 E3.

Davide Cenci
Via Campo Marzio 1-7, Pantheon & Navona (06 699 0681). Bus 62, 63, 81, 85, 95, 117, 119, 160, 175, 492, 628, 630, 850. **Open** 4-7.30pm Mon; 9.30am-1.30pm, 3.30-7.30pm Tue-Fri; 10am-7.30pm Sat. Closed 1wk Aug.
Map p339 D5.

Dolce e Gabbana
Via Condotti 51-52 (06 6992 4999).
Open 10am-7.30pm Mon-Sat; 11am-1.30pm, 2.30-7pm Sun. **Map** p339 E4.
Other locations D&G, piazza di Spagna 93 (06 6938 0870).

Fendi
Largo Goldoni *420 (06 334 501).* **Open** 10am-7.30pm Mon-Sat; 11am-2pm, 3-7pm Sun. **Map** p339 E4.

Gianfranco Ferrè
Piazza di Spagna 70 (06 679 1451).
Open 10am-7.30pm Mon-Sat; 11am-2pm,

3-7pm Sun. Closed Sun in Aug.
Map p341 A4.

Gianni Versace
Via Bocca di Leone 26 (06 678 0521).
Open 10am-7pm Mon-Sat; 2-7pm Sun.
Map p341 A4.

Giorgio Armani
Via Condotti 77 (06 699 1460).
Open 10am-2pm, 3-7pm daily.
Closed Sun in Aug. **Map** p339 E4.
Other locations Emporio Armani, via del Babuino 140 (06 322 1581); Armani Jeans, via del Babuino 70A (06 3600 1848); Armani Jeans, via Tomacelli 138 (06 6819 3040).

Gucci
Via Condotti 8 (06 679 0405).
Open 10am-7pm Mon-Sat; 11am-7pm Sun. **Map** p341 A4.
Other locations via Borgognona 7D (06 6919 0661).

Max Mara
Via Condotti 17-19A (06 6992 2104).
Open 10am-7.30pm Mon-Sat; 11am-2pm, 3-7pm Sun. Closed Sun in Aug.
Map p339 E4.
Other locations via Frattina 28 (06 679 3638); via Nazionale 28-31 (06 488 5870).

Prada
Via Condotti 90 (06 679 0897).
Open 10am-7pm daily. **Map** p341 A4.

Valentino
Via Condotti 15 (06 679 5862). **Open** 10am-7pm Mon-Sat. **Map** p339 E4.
Other locations via del Babuino 61 (06 3600 1906); via Bocca di Leone 15 (06 678 3656).

Via Condotti. *See p219.*

CONSUME

dealer's well-practised air of offended disbelief when you reject his initial price. No credit cards.

Borghetto Flaminio
Piazza della Marina 32, Suburbs: north (06 588 0517, www.creativitalia.com). Bus 88, 204, 231, 490, 495, 628/tram 2, 19. **Open** *Market mid Sept-mid July 10am-7pm Sun. Office 10am-1.30pm, 2.30-5.30pm Mon-Fri.* **Admission** €1.60. **Map** p338 D1.
A huge garage sale in a former bus depot, with stalls selling bric-a-brac, costume jewellery and clothes.

La Soffitta Sotto i Portici
Piazza Augusto Imperatore, Tridente (no phone). Bus 81, 116, 117, 204, 590, 628, 913, 926. **Open** 9am-sunset 1st & 3rd Sun of mth. Closed Aug. **Map** p339 E4.
Peruse collectibles of all kinds, from magazines to ceramics, at non-bargain prices.

★ Porta Portese
Via Portuense, from Porta Portese to via Ettore Rolli, Trastevere (no phone). Bus 23, 44, 170, 280, 781, H/tram 3, 8/train to Trastevere. **Open** 5am-2pm Sun. **Map** p343 C1/2.
Rome's biggest and most famous flea market grew out of the city's thriving black market after the end of World War II. A lingering air of illegality still persists, so watch out for pickpockets. Dealers peddle bootleg CDs, furniture, clothes, fake designer gear and car stereos of dubious origin. *Photo p223.*

Via Sannio
Via Sannio, Suburbs: south (no phone). Metro San Giovanni/bus 16, 81, 85, 87, 186, 218, 650, 850. **Open** 8.30am-1.30pm Mon-Fri; 8.30am-6pm Sat. **Map** p345 E4.
Long corridors of stalls piled high with new, low-priced clothes, and a large second-hand section behind. Those prepared to sort through the slagheap of cut-price day- and eveningwear, bags and shoes, will be rewarded with rare gems.

BOOKS & MAGAZINES

See also p235 Arte5.

Al Ferro di Cavallo
Via Ripetta 67, Tridente (06 322 7303). Bus 81, 116, 119, 204, 224, 590, 628, 926. **Open** 9.30am-7.30pm Mon-Sat. Closed Aug. **Credit** AmEx, MC, V. **Map** p338 D3.
Located opposite Rome's Art Academy, this is not only the city's best bookshop for art, architecture and graphic design tomes, but it's also a gallery promoting the work of emerging artists.
▶ *Read our take on Rome's art and architecture, from p43 and p36 respectively.*

Amore e Psiche
Via Santa Caterina da Siena 61, Pantheon & Navona (06 678 3908). Bus 30Exp, 40Exp, 46, 62, 63, 64, 70, 81, 87, 186, 492, 628, 810, 916/tram 8. **Open** 3-8pm Mon; 10am-8pm Tue-

INSIDE TRACK TAX REBATES

Non-EU residents are entitled to a sales tax (IVA) rebate on purchases of goods over €155, providing they are exported unused and bought from a shop with the 'Europe Tax Free' sticker. The shop will give you a receipt and a 'Tax Free Shopping Cheque', which should be stamped by customs before departing Italy.

Sun. Closed 2wks Aug. **Credit** AmEx, DC, MC, V. **Map** p339 E6.

This cosy, wood-beamed bookshop specialises in selling psychology textbooks, but also stocks a decent selection of art and poetry titles. There are readings for children on Sundays and occasional book launches.

Bibli

Via dei Fienaroli 28, Trastevere (06 581 4534, www.bibli.it). Bus 23, 280, 780, H/tram 8. **Open** 5pm-midnight Mon; 11am-midnight Tue-Sun. **Credit** AmEx, DC, MC, V. **Map** p342 C3.

A bookshop-cum-cultural-centre, this warren-like space stocks over 30,000 titles (some in English) and hosts concerts, readings and children's events in the conference room. All this, and a café too.

Feltrinelli

Largo Argentina 5A, Ghetto & Campo (06 6866 3001). Bus 30Exp, 40Exp, 46, 62, 63, 64, 70, 81, 87, 186, 492, 628, 810, 916/tram 8. **Open** 9am-9pm Mon-Fri; 9am-10pm Sat; 10am-9pm Sun. **Credit** AmEx, DC, MC, V. **Map** p342 D1.

This spacious store has a wide range of art, history, literature, philosophy and politics books, as well as videos, DVDs and stationery. There's a selection of titles in English.

Other locations Galleria Colonna/Galleria Alberto Sordi, Trevi & Quirinale (06 6975 5511); via del Babuino 39-41, Tridente (06 3600 1842); via VE Orlando 78-81, Esquilino (06 487 0171); viale Giulio Cesare 88, Prati (06 377 2411).

Mel Giannino Stoppani

Piazza Santissimi Apostoli 59A-62, Trevi & Quirinale (06 6994 1045). Bus 40Exp, 60Exp, 64, 70, 117, 170. **Open** 9.30am-7.30pm Mon-Sat; 10.30am-1.30pm, 4-7.30pm Sun. **Credit** AmEx, DC, MC, V. **Map** p341 A6.

This bookshop sells wares only for children, stocking more than 20,000 books (including a selection in English), as well as DVDs, videos and creative toys. An array of kids' activities is organised in this colourful shop.

▶ For more ideas for keeping your kids entertained in Rome see Children chapter; see p245.

Mondadori Multicenter

Via di San Vincenzo 10, Trevi & Quirinale (06 697 6501, www.negozimondadori.it). Bus 52, 53, 62, 63, 81, 85, 95, 117, 119, 160, 175, 492, 630. **Open** 10am-8pm daily. **Credit** AmEx, DC, MC, V. **Map** p341 A5.

This well-stocked bookshop right by the Trevi fountain – with a small selection of titles in English – is also handy for all your electronic needs.

Other locations via del Corso, Tridente 472 (06 684 401).

English-language

★ The Almost Corner Bookshop

Via del Moro 45, Trastevere (06 583 6942). Bus 23, 280, 780, H/tram 8. **Open** 10am-1.30pm, 3.30-8pm Mon-Sat; 11am-1.30pm, 3.30-8pm Sun. **Credit** AmEx, MC, V. **Map** p342 C2.

Not an inch of space is wasted here: a good selection of fiction, as well as history, art, archaeology and more, is displayed on every surface. Check the noticeboard if you're seeking work, lodgings or Italian lessons. Closed Sundays in August.

Anglo-American Book Co

Via della Vite 102, Tridente (06 679 5222, www.aab.it). Bus 52, 53, 61, 62, 63, 71, 80Exp, 85, 116, 117, 119, 160, 850. **Open** 3.30-7.30pm Mon; 10.30am-7.30pm Tue-Sat. Closed 2wks Aug. **Credit** AmEx, DC, MC, V. **Map** p341 A5.

A good selection of books in English; what isn't in stock, staff will order. There's a vast selection of scientific and technical texts for students at the branch down the road. In summer (June-Sept) the shop is open on Monday mornings and closed on Saturday mornings.

Other locations via della Vite 27 (06 678 9657).

Feltrinelli International

Via VE Orlando 84, Esquilino (06 482 7878). Metro Repubblica/bus 36, 60Exp, 61, 62, 84, 175, 492, 590, 910. **Open** 9am-8pm Mon-Sat; 10.30am-1.30pm, 4-8pm Sun. **Credit** AmEx, DC, MC, V. **Map** p341 C5.

An excellent range of fiction, non-fiction, magazines and guidebooks in English and other languages.

The Lion Bookshop

Via dei Greci 36, Tridente (06 3265 4007, www.thelionbookshop.com). Metro Spagna/bus 52, 53, 61, 62, 63, 71, 80Exp, 85, 116, 117, 119, 160, 850. **Open** 3.30-7.30pm Mon; 10am-7pm Tue-Sat. **Credit** AmEx, DC, MC, V. **Map** p338 E3.

This friendly shop is great for contemporary fiction and children's books. Closed on Sundays from mid June to mid September.

FASHION

See also p220 **The A-list**; *p227* **Madò**;
p230 **NuYorica**.

★ Abito – Le Gallinelle

*Via Panisperna 61, Monti (06 488
1017/http://abito61.blogspot.com). Metro
Cavour/bus 60, 64, 70, 117, 170.*
Open 3.30-7.30pm Mon; 10am-1pm, 3.30-
7.30pm Tue-Sat. Closed 2wks Aug. **Credit**
AmEx, MC, V. **Map** p344 B1.
In this new outlet – a former convent – Wilma
Silvestri and her daughter Giorgio sell gorgeous,
reworked vintage and ethnic garments. For those
who shun the outlandish, there are classic linen suits
for men and women. At their former premises,
around the corner at via del Boschetto 76, garments
by up and coming designers are sold.

Angelo di Nepi

*Via dei Giubbonari 28, Ghetto & Campo
(06 689 3006). Bus 30Exp, 40Exp, 46, 62, 64,
70, 81, 87, 116, 186, 204, 491, 628, 916.*
Open noon-7.30pm Mon; 10am-7.30pm Tue-Sat.
Credit AmEx, DC, MC, V. **Map** p342 C2.
This Roman designer's clothes for women are
inspired by the exotic; colours and fabrics are rich,
with occasional beaded details.
Other locations via Frattina 2 (06 678 6568).

Arsenale

*Via del Governo Vecchio 64, Pantheon & Navona
(06 686 1380). Bus 30Exp, 40Exp, 46, 62, 64,
70, 81, 87, 116, 186, 204, 491, 628, 916.*

Open 3.30-7.30pm Mon; 10am-7.30pm Tue-Sat.
Closed 2wks Aug. **Credit** AmEx, DC, MC, V.
Map p339 C5.
A great place to pick something up to wear back
home, Patrizia Pieroni's wonderful designs make for
great window displays – not to mention successful
party conversation pieces – and have been going
down well with the Roman boho-chic luvvy crowd
for a fair few years.

(Ethic)

*Piazza Cairoli 11-12, Ghetto & Campo (06
6830 1063, www.ethic.it). Bus 30Exp, 40Exp,
46, 62, 63, 64, 70, 81, 87, 186, 492, 628,
810, 916/tram 8.* **Open** noon-7.30pm Mon,
Sun; 10am-8pm Tue-Sat. Closed 1wk Aug.
Credit AmEx, DC, MC, V. **Map** p342 D2.
Come here for creative clothes in bright and/or
natural colours; evening dresses are complemented
by lovely shoes and bags. It also has the added –
somewhat rare for Rome – bonus of being really
very affordable.
Other locations via del Corso 85, Tridente (06
3600 2191); via del Babuino 152, Tridente (06 3600
2676); via del Pantheon 46-47 (06 6880 3167).

Iron G

*Via Cola di Rienzo 50, Prati (06 321 6798).
Bus 30Exp, 70, 81, 186, 224, 280, 590, 913.*
Open 10.30am-7.30pm Mon-Sat. Closed 1wk
Aug. **Credit** AmEx, DC, MC, V. **Map** p341 B3.
This warehousey boutique with trashy chandeliers
supplies clubwear to the fashion victims of this well-
heeled neighbourhood. The hippest labels mix with
ethnic and local handmade accessories.

CONSUME

Porta Portese. *See p221.*

Life's Essentials

Super-convenience stores.

Your two points of reference for all life's essentials – including bus tickets, phone cards and the like – are *edicole* (newsstands) and *tabacchi* (tobacconists).

Scattered across the city, *edicole* are a testament to a generally warm and relatively dry climate. These cute kiosks have just about every journal, magazine and newspaper available in Italy, from national dailies to sports publications (which usually run out first). Stands in major tourist hubs also carry international papers and glossies in English. They also dispense bus tickets, phone cards and maps. They're your best bet for directions, getting small change for large notes, and will generally dispense sound city advice.

Identifiable by a large T, *tabacchi* deal not only in tobacco products, but are also the place to top up your Italian mobile phone SIM card (if you've got one), and purchase phone cards, bus tickets and stamps for all those postcards you've been writing. Many *tabacchi* also have a postbox out front. Some double up as stationery shops; others specialise in smoking equipment or playing cards and games. Strangely, all sell salt.

Most *edicole* open early in the morning and close around 9pm. *Tabacchi* generally follow shop hours, so it's not unusual to find them closed between 1pm and 4pm. Those located in central areas usually open around 8am, and stay open late.

Maga Morgana

Via del Governo Vecchio 27, Pantheon & Navona (06 687 9995). Bus 30Exp, 40Exp, 46, 62, 64, 70, 81, 87, 116, 186, 204, 491, 628, 916. **Open** 10am-8pm Mon-Sat. **Credit** AmEx, DC, MC, V. **Map** p339 C5.
Designer Luciana Iannace's quirky one-of-a-kind creations – including dresses, skirts and stunning hand-knitted sweaters – will provide a talking point at any party. The shop down the road at No.98 (06 687 8095, open 3-8pm Mon, 10am-8pm Tue-Sat) has more knitted and woollen items. Frequent Sunday openings too.

Momento

Piazza Cairoli 9/via dei Giubbonari, Ghetto & Campo (06 6880 8157). Bus 30Exp, 40Exp, 46, 62, 64, 70, 81, 87, 116, 186, 204, 491, 628, 916. **Open** 10am-7.30pm Mon-Fri; 10am-1.30pm, 3.30-7.30pm Sat. **Credit** AmEx, DC, MC, V. **Map** p342 D2.
The poshest of princesses and her boho cousin will be equally awed over the collection of clothes and accessories at this treasure trove. Definitely for the fearless and colourful, all pieces from jumpers to evening gowns are flirty, feminine and fun. Also a fabulous spot for knock-'em-dead shoes and handbags in colour combos you've got to see to believe. From Oct-May opens Sunday pm too.
Other locations via Nazionale 88F, Esquilino (06 474 4723).

★ Le Tartarughe

Via Pie' di Marmo 17, Pantheon & Navona (06 679 2240). Bus 30Exp, 40Exp, 46, 62, 63, 64, 70, 81, 87, 492, 628. **Open** noon-7.30pm Mon; 10am-7.30pm Tue-Sat. Closed 2wks Aug. **Credit** AmEx, DC, MC, V. **Map** p339 E6.
Susanna Liso's sumptuous designs fill this chic boutique near the church of Santa Maria sopra Minerva. The lines of these eminently wearable garments – ranging from cocktail dresses to elegant workwear – are classic with a twist; the colours are eye-catching but never garish. For her gorgeous accessories, head across the road to No.33.

Tina Sondergaard

Via del Boschetto 1D, Monti (334 385 0799). Bus 40Exp, 60, 64, 70, 71, 170. **Open** 3-7.30pm Mon; 10.30am-1pm, 1.30-7.30am Tue-Sat. Closed 3wks Aug. **Credit** MC, V. **Map** p344 B1.
This Danish designer and her team whip up delightfully stylish one-off 1960s-inspired women's clothes on the premises in this compact pared-back space on trendy via del Boschetto. Fabrics are eye-catching and Tina will do on-the-spot alterations to make sure that your purchases fit perfectly. Space is tight here, so last season's leftovers are sold off at extremely interesting prices.

weTAD

Via del Babuino 155A, Tridente (06 9684 2086, www.wetad.it). Metro Spagna or Flaminio/bus 117, 119, 590. **Open** noon-7.30pm Mon, Sun; 10.30am-7.30pm Tue-Fri; 10.30am-8pm Sat. Closed 2wks Aug and Sun from June to Sept. **Credit** AmEx, DC, MC, V. **Map** p338 E3.
The concept behind this 'concept store' is that you can shop for clothes, shoes, flowers, household accessories, CDs, magazines and perfumes, get your hair styled and eat fusion Thai-Italian and drink – all in one super-cool place. Labels include McQueen

Bulgari. *See p226.*

and Chloé, along with a selection of occasional home-grown talent.

FASHION ACCESSORIES & SERVICES

Cleaning & repairs

The city is bristling with *tintorie monoprezzo* (one-price dry-cleaners) which, despite the name, don't charge the same for all their items: tariffs generally start from around €5. Most laundries do the washing for you (charging by the kilo).

Calzolaio

Via della Lungaretta 26, Trastevere (340 762 5463). Bus 23, 280, H/tram 8. **Open** 5.30am-6pm Mon-Fri. **Map** p342 C3.
Reliable shoe repairs are available at from this old-fashioned cobbler.

F Pratesi (Clinica della Borsa)

Piazza Firenze 22, Tridente (06 6880 3720). Bus 52, 53, 61, 62, 63, 71, 80Exp, 85, 116, 117, 119, 160, 850. **Open** 9.30am-1pm, 3.30-7.30pm Mon-Fri; 9.30am-1pm Sat. Closed Aug. **No credit cards**. **Map** p339 D4.
Specialises in bag repairs… which generally means the patching up of bags slit by thieves – be warned! Repairs take up to three days.

Sartoria Paola e Fabio

Via dei Banchi Vecchi 17, Ghetto & Campo (06 6830 7180). Bus 40Exp, 46, 62, 64, 916.

Open 8.30am-1pm, 2-6.30pm Mon-Fri; 8.30am-1pm Sat. Closed 2wks Aug. **No credit cards**. **Map** p339 C6.
Run by a skilled traditional tailor and a seamstress. Clothing repairs are performed quickly.

Speedy Shoes

Via Conte Verde 29, Esquilino (328 829 3527). Metro Vittorio/bus 360, 590, 649/tram 5, 14. **Open** 8am-1.30pm, 2.30-7pm Mon-Fri. Closed Aug. **Map** p339 C5.
A handily central place at which to get heels replaced and running repairs carried out on shoes and boots.

Wash & Dry

Via della Pelliccia 35, Trastevere (800 231 172, www.washedry.it). Bus 780, H/tram 8. **Open** 8am-10pm (last wash 9pm) daily. **No credit cards**. **Map** p342 C3.
This self-service launderette is just behind piazza Santa Maria in Trastevere.
Other locations via della Chiesa Nuova 15, Pantheon & Navona (800 231 172).

Jewellery & watches

The big names in glitter production, like **Bulgari** (via Condotti 10, 06 679 3876, www.bulgari.com; *photo p225*) and **Federico Buccellati** (via Condotti 31, 06 679 0329, www.federicobuccellati.it), cluster around piazza di Spagna. Even if you don't plan to purchase, it's worth straying along diamond lane for a look at enviable and original baubles.

Ai Monasteri. *See p231.*

CONSUME

Campo de' Fiori. *See p232.*

Damiani

Via Condotti 84, Tridente (06 6920 0477, www.damiani.it). Metro Spagna/bus 52, 53, 61, 62, 63, 71, 80Exp, 85, 116, 117, 119, 160, 850. **Open** 11.30am-7pm Mon-Sat. Closed 1wk Aug. **Credit** AmEx, DC, MC, V. **Map** p341 A4.

Exquisite gems with that celebrity seal of approval: the (former) Aniston-Pitts have designed a range, and Gwyneth Paltrow has been in the ads.

Giokeb

Via della Lungaretta 79, Trastevere (06 589 6891). Bus 23, 280, 780, H/tram 8. **Open** 10am-8pm daily. Closed 1wk Aug. **Credit** AmEx, MC, V. **Map** p342 D3.

A sparkling array of silver settings adorned with natural stones. Giokeb stands out not just because its pieces are surprisingly original but also because they won't clean out your wallet.

Laboratorio Marco Aurelio

Via dei Cappellari 21, Ghetto & Campo (348 276 2842, www.marcoaurelio.it). Bus 30Exp, 40Exp, 46, 62, 64, 70, 81, 87, 116, 491, 628, 916. **Open** 11am-1.30pm, 4.30-9.30pm Tue-Sat. Closed Aug. **Credit** AmEx, DC, MC, V. **Map** p339 C6.

Designer Marco Aurelio creates stunning and often unconventional pieces in hammered and wrought silver, on site. Sizeable stones and intricate patterns vaguely recall ancient Roman styles.

Madò

Via del Governo Vecchio 89A, Pantheon & Navona (06 687 5028). Bus 30Exp, 40Exp, 46, 62, 64, 70, 81, 87, 116, 186, 204, 491, 628, 916. **Open** 11am-7.30pm Mon-Sat. Closed 1wk Aug. **Credit** AmEx, MC, V. **Map** p339 C5.

Housing a glittering collection of oriental-inspired clothing and accessories, this shop feels like an exotic (and wealthy) aunt's closet. There's a fabulous range of ethnic jewellery and pieces from the 1920s.

Tempi Moderni

Via del Governo Vecchio 108, Pantheon & Navona (06 687 7007). Bus 30Exp, 70, 81, 87, 116, 186, 204, 491, 628. **Open** 10am-7.30pm Mon-Sat. Closed 2wks Aug. **Credit** AmEx, DC, MC, V. **Map** p339 C5.

There's an eclectic assortment of 20th-century pieces in this boudoir-like shop: elegant art deco necklaces are displayed alongside 1950s Bakelite brooches and

INSIDE TRACK RETURNS

The rules on taking purchases back are infuriatingly vague. Faulty goods, obviously, must be refunded or replaced. Most shops will also accept unwanted goods that are returned unused with a receipt within seven days of purchase, though this is not obligatory.

De-Mobbed

Godfather goods.

Your chances of getting caught in crossfire in some *Cosa Nostra* shoot-out in central Rome are pretty remote. However, over the years, 10,000 Italians have been victims of gun-toting clan members, according to Roberto Saviano, fearless bestselling author of 'Gomorrah', a devastating exposé of Italy's flourishing organized crime scene.

But all is not bleak in Italy's battle with its bloodthirsty mob. A change in the law in 1996 allowed the forces of justice to confiscate organised crime-owned assets, and that includes agricultural land. The Bottega dei Sapori e dei Saperi della Legalità (see p232) is the remarkable Rome outlet for organic produce grown on land liberated from the Mafia, under the aegis of an organisation called Libera.

Father Luigi Ciotti, a frontier priest, founded Libera in 1995. He now has the satisfaction of seeing some 450 hectares (that's over 1,000 acres) of ex-Mafia land, in Sicily and the south – but also, more alarmingly, in the Lazio area around Rome – farmed by volunteer members of local groups, youth organisations and co-operatives.

Now in a new venue not far from the parliament building, the Bottega dei Sapori provides an excellent souvenir alternative to plaster casts of the Colosseum and industrially produced limoncello liqueur. In this little treasure trove, you'll find wholly legal jars of sun-dried tomatoes and packs of untainted organic rigatoni and tagliatelle pasta. There's honey, too, from hives once

buzzing with bees belonging to the Mob. They'll send you a case or two of fine green virgin olive oil; their wine is good too.

The T-shirts and handy reusable cotton bags both, disappointingly, bear restrained Libera slogans rather than Mobs Out, or Down with the Don, which few locals would dare to wear in public.

The state's asset-grabbing record is impressive and isn't restricted to farm land. Some 4,500 flats and villas have been confiscated, including Rome's fabulous Casa del Jazz (see *p182*). Once the chic pad of Rome's 'Magliana Gang' mobster Enrico Nicoletti, for the last five years the palatial villa has been a leafy haven for sophisticated swing sessions and cutting edge contemporary jazz. Try weekend jazz brunches in their excellent restaurant, or just turn up for one of their many free events.

---

chunky retro bangles. A selection of jewel-bright kimonos adds to the effect.

Lingerie & underwear

Lingerie chains like **Intimissimi** (at via del Corso 167 and many other places, www.intimissimi.com) and **Yamamay** (at via Frattina 86 and all over town, www.yamamay.it) cater for men and women looking for cheap-and-cheerful undies. Upmarket lingerie shops cluster around the Tridente.

Demoiselle
Via Frattina 93, Tridente (06 679 3752). Metro Spagna/bus 52, 53, 61, 62, 63, 71, 80, 85, 116, 117, 119, 160, 850. **Open** 10am-8pm Mon-Sat.

Closed 1wk Aug. **Credit** AmEx, DC, MC, V. **Map** p341 A5.
Luscious, sexy and classy lingerie is the temptation here. But if your planning on spending any time poolside or at the beach, head here for its selection of fab swimwear from Missoni, Pucci and hip Roman label Delfina.

Gallo
Via Frattina 122, Tridente (06 6920 2198, www.gallospa.it). Metro Spagna/bus 52, 53, 61, 62, 63, 71, 80Exp, 85, 116, 117, 119, 160, 850. **Open** 10am-7.30pm daily. Closed 3wks Aug. **Credit** AmEx, MC, V. **Map** p338 E3.
Gallo's splendid socks and tights come in cotton, wool or cashmere. The trademark stripes feature on scarves in winter and lovely bikinis in summer.

La Perla
Via dei Condotti 79, Tridente (06 6994 1934, www.laperla.com). Metro Spagna/bus 52, 53, 61, 62, 63, 71, 80Exp, 85, 116, 117, 119, 160, 850. **Open** 3-7pm Mon; 10am-7pm Tue-Sat. **Credit** AmEx, DC, MC, V. **Map** p341 A4.

From the lace and silk that have made La Perla a favourite for 50 years, to some slightly more affordable lines, this is knicker heaven.

Shoes & bags

See also p224 **Le Tartarughe** *and p121* **Testaccio Market**.

AVC by Adriana V Campanile
Piazza di Spagna 88, Tridente (06 6992 2355, www.avcbyadrianacampanile.com). Metro Spagna/bus 52, 53, 61, 62, 63, 71, 80Exp, 85, 116, 117, 119, 160, 850. **Open** 10.30am-2.30pm, 3.30-7.30pm Mon-Fri; 10.30am-7.30pm Sat; 11am-2.30pm, 3.30-7.30pm Sun. **Credit** AmEx, MC, V. **Map** p341 A4.

A vast selection of women's shoes from Roman designer Adriana Campanile at offered here, at the best prices you'll find this close to the Spanish Steps. Upstairs in the piazza di Spagna store, there are lovely kids' shoes.

Other locations via Frattina 141, Tridente (06 679 0891). **Outlets** largo del Pallaro 1, Ghetto & Campo (06 682 10670); via Mastro Giorgio 66-68, Testacccio (06 5725 0493).

Borini
Via dei Pettinari 86, Ghetto & Campo (06 687 5670). Bus 23, 40Exp, 46, 62, 64, 280, 916. **Open** 3.30-7.30pm Mon; 9.30am-1pm, 3.30-7.30pm Tue-Sat. Closed 3wks Aug. **Credit** AmEx, MC, V. **Map** p342 C2.

Franco Borini's shop is busily chaotic, packed with clued-in shoe-lovers. His elegant but durable shoes follow fashion trends religiously and prices are fair.

Creje
Via del Boschetto 5A (06 4890 5227, www.creje. com). Bus 40Exp, 60, 64, 70, 71, 170. **Open** 10am-2.30pm, 3pm-8pm Mon-Sat. Closed 3wks Aug. **Credit** AmEx, MC, V. **Map** p344 B1.

The Roman offshoot of a fashion mecca on the island of Procida, near Naples, Creje is mostly about the chic-est of handmade leather bags and belts, in splendid colours created using natural dyes. However, there's a line of accessories too, and some gorgeously eye-catching jewellery in bronze, brass and silver.

Furla
Piazza di Spagna 22, Tridente (06 6920 0363, www.furla.com). Metro Spagna/bus 52, 53, 61, 62, 63, 71, 80Exp, 85, 116, 117, 119, 160, 850. **Open** 10am-8pm Mon-Sat; 10.30am-8pm Sun. **Credit** AmEx, MC, V. **Map** p341 A4.

In eye-popping colours or as elegantly subdued classics, Furla's bags are spreading like wildfire all over the city. Prices won't reduce you to tears, and

CONSUME

Moriondo & Gariglio. *See p233.*

INSIDE TRACK THE MALL

In a city where restricted space means malls are an out-of-town phenomenon, the 19th-century Galleria Colonna – now known as **Galleria Alberto Sordi** (*map p339 E5*), in memory of the Roman cinema legend – off via del Corso is a pleasant exception. There are more than 20 shops, including bookstore Feltrinelli (with a few novels and guidebooks in English on the ground floor; *see p222*) and a couple of bars – all under one beautifully coloured glass roof.

the line extends to shoes, sunglasses and wallets as well as watches.

Other locations via Condotti 55-56 (06 679 1973); via Nazionale 54-55 (06 487 0127); via Cola di Rienzo 226 (06 687 4505).

★ Ibiz

Via dei Chiavari 39, Ghetto & Campo (06 6830 7297). Bus 30Exp, 40Exp, 46, 62, 64, 70, 81, 87, 116, 186, 204, 491, 628, 916. **Open** 9.30am-7.30pm Mon-Sat. Closed 2wks Aug. **Credit** AmEx, DC, MC, V. **Map** p342 D2.

Ibiz bags are made by hand in the on-site workshop: look on as you mull over which of the handbags, briefcases, and leather accessories you must have.

Loco

Via dei Baullari 22, Ghetto & Campo (06 6880 8216). Bus 30Exp, 40Exp, 46, 62, 64, 70, 81, 87, 116, 186, 204, 491, 628, 916. **Open** 3.30-8pm Mon; 10.30am-8.30pm Tue-Sat. Closed 2wks Aug. **Credit** AmEx, DC, MC, V. **Map** p342 C1.

If you like your shoes avant-garde, this is the place. From classy to wild and eccentric, its pieces are always one step ahead of the flock.

NuYorica

Piazza Pollarola 36-37, Ghetto & Campo (06 6889 1243, www.nuyorica.it). Bus 30Exp, 40Exp, 46, 62, 64, 70, 81, 87, 116, 186, 204, 491, 628, 916. **Open** 10am-7.30pm Mon-Sat. Closed 2wks Aug. **Credit** AmEx, DC, MC, V. **Map** p342 C1.

This is the place for extravagant but stylish shoes and clothes by the hippest designers. Owners Cristiano Giovangnoli and Emanuele Frumenti keep the collection fresh. Of course, none of this is cheap.

Silvano Lattanzi

Via Bocca di Leone 59, Tridente (06 678 6119, www.zintala.it). Metro Spagna/bus 52, 53, 61, 62, 63, 71, 80Exp, 85, 116, 117, 119, 160, 850. **Open** 3-7pm Mon; 10am-1pm, 3-7pm

Tue-Sat. Closed 3wks Aug. **Credit** AmEx, DC, MC, V. **Map** p338 E3.

The man that the Japanese *cognoscenti* call the 'poet of shoes', Silvano Lattanzi, flies to Washington DC to measure presidents' feet. The only drawback? The made-to-measure service starts at €3,000. Ready-to-wear shoes for men and women are slightly more affordable.

FOOD & DRINK

For fresh (as opposed to long-life) milk or cream, look for any bar labelled *latteria*; otherwise try chiller cabinets in *alimentari* or supermarkets. Food is sold by the *etto* (100g): ask for *un etto*, *due etti* and so on. *Enoteche* (off-licences; *see p207*) often have counter bars for downing a glass or two.

Bakeries

Pasticcerie (cake shops) attached to cafés are listed by neighbourhood in the **Cafés, Bars & Gelaterie** chapter (*see p206*).

Dolceroma

Via Portico d'Ottavia 20B, Ghetto & Campo (06 689 2196). Bus 63, 630, 780, H/tram 8. **Open** *May-June, Sept* 8am-8pm Tue-Sat; 10am-1.30pm Sun. *Oct-Apr* 10am-6pmTue-Sat; 10am-1.30pm Sun. Closed July & Aug. **No credit cards. Map** p342 D2.

Even though it specialises in Viennese cakes, Dolceroma is also the place to order American-style carrot cake and chocolate-chip cookies. Although it serves good, it's not cheap.

★ Forno del Ghetto

Via Portico d'Ottavia 1, Ghetto & Campo (06 687 8637). Bus 63, 630, 780, H/tram 8. **Open** 7am-2pm, 3.30-7.30pm Mon-Thur; 7am-2pm Fri; 7.30am-5pm Sun. Closed 3wks Aug & Jewish holidays. **No credit cards. Map** p342 D2.

A local institution run run by three dour ladies, this tiny shop has no signpost but is immediately recognisable by the queue of slavering regulars you'll find outside. Among countless other goodies, people come in to taste the unforgettable damson and ricotta (and chocolate and ricotta) pies. During the summer months, the lunchtime closing is suspended.

▶ *For more on Rome's Ghetto, see p102.*

Josephine's Bakery

Piazza del Paradiso 56-57, Ghetto & Campo (06 687 1065). Bus 30Exp, 40Exp, 46, 62, 63, 64, 70, 81, 87, 186, 492, 628, 810, 916/tram 8. **Open** 3.30-8pm Mon; 10am-2pm, 3.30-8pm Tue-Sat; 11am-5pm Sun. Closed Aug. **Credit** AmEx, DC, MC, V. **Map** p342 C1.

This former London model-turned-pastry-goddess bakes up sumptuous portions of cheesecake, chocolate fudge cake, carrot cake, cupcakes and cookies to enjoy. The food is dangerously rich and almost too beautiful to eat.

Valzani

Via del Moro 37B, Trastevere (06 580 3792). Bus 23, 280, 780, H/tram 8. **Open** 2-8pm Mon, Tue; 10am-8pm Wed-Sun. Closed Aug. **Credit** AmEx, DC, MC, V. **Map** p342 C3.

A Trastevere institution and rightly so. Come here for sachertorte and spicy, nutty *pangiallo*, which are the specialities. But they are just the tip of an iceberg of chocolatey delights, including the must-try chocolate with chilli.

Drink

For wine bars, where the focus rests more on sitting down to drink rather than buying to take away, see the **Eating Out** (*see pp184-205*) and **Cafés, Bars & Gelaterie** (*see pp206-218*). *See also p188* **Buccone**.

Costantini

Piazza Cavour 16, Prati (06 321 3210, www.pierocostantini.it). Bus 30Exp, 34, 49, 87, 280, 492, 926, 990. **Open** *Shop* 4.30-8pm Mon; 9am-1pm, 4.30-8pm Tue-Sat. *Wine bar* 11am-3pm, 6.30pm-midnight Mon-Fri; 6.30pm-midnight Sat. Closed Aug. **Credit** AmEx, DC, MC, V. **Map** p339 C4.

This cavernous cellar has a seriously comprehensive collection of wines as well as some gourmet extras such as chocolate, olive oil and pasta.

Enoteca al Parlamento

Via dei Prefetti 15, Tridente (06 687 3446, www.enotecaalparlamento.it). Bus 81, 116, 117, 204, 590, 628, 913, 926. **Open** 4-9pm Mon; 9am-midnight Tue-Sat. Closed 2wks Aug. **Credit** AmEx, MC, V. **Map** p339 D4.

Hundreds of bottles of spirits and the best Italian wines fill the wooden shelves of this warm shop. There's also delectable honey, balsamic vinegar and regional specialities.

Trimani

Via Goito 20, Esquilino (06 446 9661). Metro Termini/bus 75, 86, 92, 217, 360. **Open** 9am-8pm Mon-Sat. Closed 1wk Aug. **Credit** AmEx, DC, MC, V. **Map** p341 E4.

In the family since 1821, Trimani is Rome's oldest and best wine shop. Purchases can be shipped anywhere in the world.

General

The *centro storico* is now awash with mini-supermarkets belonging to big chains.

Ai Monasteri

Corso Rinascimento 72, Pantheon & Navona (06 6880 2783, www.aimonasteri.it). Bus 30Exp, 70, 81, 87, 116, 186, 204, 491, 628. **Open** 10am-

CONSUME

Cartoleria Pantheon. *See p234.*

1pm, 5-7.30pm Mon-Wed, Fri, Sat; 9am-1pm Thur. Closed 2wks Aug. **Credit** MC, V. **Map** p339 D5. This shop sells honey, preserves, liqueurs and other interesting foodie oddities – including an elixir for long life – made in monasteries across Italy. *Photo p226.*

Bottega dei Sapori della Legalità
Via dei Prefetti 23, Pantheon & Navona (06 6992 5262), www.liberaterra.it). Bus 70, 81, 87, 116, 628. **Open** 10am-1pm, 3-6.30pm Mon-Fri. Closed Aug. **Credit** AmEx, DC, MC, V. **Map** p339 D4 *See p228* **De-Mobbed.**

★ Castroni
Via Cola di Rienzo 196, Prati (06 687 4383, www.castroni.com). Metro Ottaviano/bus 23, 32, 49, 81, 492, 590, 982/tram 19. **Open** 8am-8pm Mon-Sat. **Credit** AmEx, MC, V. **Map** p338 D3.
This wonderful shop roasts its own espresso beans and has lots of Italian regional specialities and imported foodstuffs: it's the place for expats hankering after anything from Chinese noodles to HP Sauce. Online shopping available.

Franchi
Via Cola di Rienzo, Prati (06 687 4651). Bus 23, 32, 49, 81, 492, 590, 982/tram 19. **Open** 8am-9pm Mon-Sat. **Credit** AmEx, DC, MC, V. **Map** p338 D3.
A dream of a deli, for just about anything you could ever want to eat: cheeses from everywhere, cured meats and ready-to-eat meat and seafood dishes are freshly prepared.

Innocenzi
Via Natale del Grande 31, Trastevere (06 581 2725). Bus 780, H/tram 8. **Open** 8am-1.30pm, 4.30-8pm Mon-Wed, Fri, Sat; 8am-1.30pm Thur. Closed 2wks Aug. **No credit cards**. **Map** p342 C3.
Pulses spill from great sacks stacked around this treasure trove of foodie specialities that come from all over the world.

★ Volpetti
Via Marmorata 47, Testaccio (06 574 2352, www.volpetti.com, www.fooditaly.com). Bus 23, 30Exp, 75, 280, 716/tram 3. **Open** 8am-2pm, 5-8.15pm Mon-Sat. **Credit** AmEx, DC, MC, V. **Map** p343 D5.

INSIDE TRACK PAYING

Whether buying a banana or a bikini, you'll notice that Rome isn't cheap, and *centro storico* shops in particular are tough on the wallet. Bargaining belongs firmly at the flea-market: in shops, prices are fixed.

One of the best delis in Rome, with exceptional cheese, hams and salamis. It's hard to get away without one of the jolly assistants loading you up with samples of their wares – pleasant, but painful on the wallet. If you can't get to Testaccio, at least check the website: they ship all over the world.

Produce markets

Most neighbourhoods in Rome still have a market, opening Monday to Saturday from around 6am until 2pm. The *centro storico* ones tend to be pricey and bear in mind that none accept credit cards.

Apart from the bigger ones listed below, there are a few tiny central(ish) street markets. They can be found in **via dei Santi Quattro** (map p344 D3), a stone's throw from the Colosseum; **via Milazzo** (map p341 E5), near Termini station; and **piazza Bernini**, on the San Saba side of the Aventine hill (map p345 A5).

Campo de' Fiori
Campo de' Fiori (no phone). Bus 30Exp, 40Exp, 46, 62, 64, 70, 81, 87, 116, 186, 204, 491, 628, 916. **Map** p342 C1.
Despite exorbitant prices and swarms of tourists, this historic market – the biggest in the *centro storico* – retains oodles of charm. *Photo p227.*
▶ *Where Giordano Bruno burnt and students revel; see also p108.*

Ex-Piazza Vittorio
Via Lamarmora, Esquilino (no phone). Metro Vittorio/bus 105, 360, 590, 649/ tram 5, 14. **Map** p344 E2.
This market used to fill piazza Vittorio Emanuele and be absolute chaos. Now in a revamped former barracks, an abundance of stalls stock the usual Italian fresh produce, cheese and meats, supplemented by pulses, halal meat, spices, African fruits and Asian food, as well as some exotic fabrics and household goods in the building across the central piazza.

San Cosimato
Piazza San Cosimato, Trastevere (no phone). Bus 780, H/tram 3, 8. **Map** p342 C3.
This market in heavily touristed Trastevere manages to retain its local feel, particularly first thing in the morning.

Testaccio
Piazza Testaccio, Testaccio (no phone). Bus 23, 30Exp, 75, 95, 170, 280, 716, 781/tram 3. **Map** p343 D5.
A glimpse into the true heart of Rome; prices are considerably lower than at more central markets, too. The whole northern aisle is dedicated to cut-price shoes, with some real bargains to be had.

CONSUME

Organic in the Abbatoir

Meat factory finally gets a makeover.

For decades after it was decommissioned in 1975, Rome's immense abbatoir – *Il Mattatoio* (*see p123*) – crumbled as bureaucrats squabbled over its future. Finally this prime piece of real estate on the Testaccio riverfront is clawing its way back to life. But its organic and fair-trade retail opportunities go sadly unpublicised.

Perhaps the sheer size of the place – more than 46,000 square metres of built space in total grounds of 90,000 square metres – made a major bells-and-whistles redevelopment job prohibitively expensive. For whatever reason, the ex-*mattatoio* has been subjected to a jigsaw of partial makeovers, its various splendid pavilions – completed in 1891 when it was the envy of Europe's town planners – gradually being assigned to lucky users.

Part of the complex is occupied by the architecture department of a Roman university, part by a music school. Some is being refurbished for the city's Fine Arts Academy and in keeping with the artistic bent. a branch of the MACRO gallery (*see p157*) occupies two enormous refrigeration units, where works are displayed amid the machinery of butchery.

And in hard-to-find largo Dino Frisullo – the former holding pens for the abbatoir – a fair trade/organic food mart called the Città dell'Altra Economia (*see p234*) – complete with a delightfully wholesome café-snack bar and restaurant – has slowly built up a faithful clientele.

Foodstuffs in the organic store come almost exclusively from Lazio, the region that surrounds Rome, and many hail from within the limits of the city itself. Weekends bring the whole place alive, with farmers' markets in the vast piazza in front of the low abbatoir pavilions, opportunities for swapping goods and produce, seminars, displays and child-friendly events such as juggling and face-painting (ask in the shop or check online for events).

Chocolatiers

See also p217 **Said**.

★ Moriondo & Gariglio

Via del Piè di Marmo 21, Pantheon & Navona (06 699 0856). Bus 30Exp, 40Exp, 44, 46, 60Exp, 62, 63, 64, 70, 81, 84, 85, 87, 95, 117, 119, 160, 170, 175, 492, 628, 630, 715, 716, 780, 781, 810, 850, 916, H. **Open** 9am-7.30pm Mon-Sat. Closed Aug. **Credit** AmEx, MC, V. **Map** p339 E6.

This fairytale chocolate shop with beautiful gift-boxes is especially lovely at Christmas, when you'll have to fight to get your hands on the excellent marron glacé. It usually closes on Saturday afternoons in summer. *Photo p229.*

Organic & health foods

Il Canestro

Via Luca della Robbia 12, Testaccio (06 574 6287, www.ilcanestro.com). Bus 23, 30Exp, 75, 280, 716/tram 3. **Open** 9am-7.30pm Mon-Sat. **No credit cards. Map** p343 D5.

Il Canestro offers a huge range of natural health foods, cosmetics and medicines, including some organic versions of Italian regional specialities. Prices tend to be steep and the staff is surly and

offhand. The branch on via San Francesco a Ripa offers nutrition-related courses as well as a variety of alternative medicine.
Other locations via San Francesco a Ripa 106, Trastevere (06 581 2621); viale Gorizia 51, Suburbs: north (06 854 1991).

Città dell'Altra Economia
Largo Dino Frisullo, Testaccio (06 5730 0419, www.cittadellaltraeconomia.org).
Open *Shop* 10am-1.30pm, 2.30-8pm Tue-Sat, 10.30am-1.30pm, 2.30-7pm Sun. *Bar* 10am-8pm Tue-Thur; 10am-10.30pm Fri, Sat; 10am-7pm Sun. *Restaurant* 1-3pm Sun and by appointment. *Bus 23, 30Exp, 75, 280, 716/tram 3.*
Credit (shop) MC, V; (bar & restaurant) **no credit cards.** **Map** p343 D6.
See p233 **Organic in the Abbatoir.**
▶ *Also located inside the ex-Mattatoio (former slaughterhouse) is a branch of the MACRO art gallery; see p157.*

Imported foods

The best place for Indian, Korean, Chinese and African foodstuffs is the area around piazza Vittorio Emanuele, now home to a large slice of Rome's recent-immigrant population. The market there (*see p137*) has stalls selling halal and kosher meat, along with many other products, spices and vegetables that don't make an appearance anywhere else in the city. There are also kosher shops in the Ghetto (*see p102*). Delis Innocenzi (*p232*) and Castroni (*p232*) also carry a good selection of imports.

GIFTS & SOUVENIRS
Artists' supplies & stationery

Cartoleria Pantheon
Via della Rotonda 15, Pantheon & Navona (06 687 5313). Bus 30Exp, 40Exp, 46, 62, 63, 64, 70, 81, 87, 186, 492, 628, 810, 916/tram 8. **Open** 10.30am-8pm Mon-Sat; 1-7.30pm Sun. Closed 1wk Aug. **Credit** AmEx, DC, MC, V. **Map** p339 D5.
Bring out your literary soul with leather-bound notebooks, hand-painted Florentine stationery and rare paper from Amalfi. Nearly everything for sale has been handcrafted. *Photo p231.*
Other locations via della Maddalena 41, Pantheon & Navona (06 679 5633).

Ditta G Poggi
Via del Gesù 74-75, Pantheon & Navona (06 678 4477, www.poggi1825.it). Bus 30Exp, 40Exp, 46, 62, 63, 64, 70, 81, 87, 186, 492, 628, 810, 916/tram 8. **Open** 9am-1pm, 4-7.30pm Mon-Sat. Closed 2wks Aug. **Credit** AmEx, MC, V. **Map** p339 E6.

This wonderfully old-fashioned shop has been selling paints, brushes, canvases and artists' supplies of every description since 1825. The via Pie' di Marmo shop closes on Saturday afternoons. The main shop stays open through the day on Thursday.
Other locations via Cardinale Merry del Val 18-19, Trastevere (06 581 2531).

Officina della Carta
Via Benedetta 26B, Trastevere (06 589 5557). Bus 23, 280, 780, H/tram 3. **Open** 10am-1pm, 3.30-7.30pm Mon-Sat. Closed 2wks Aug. **Credit** AmEx, DC, MC, V. **Map** p342 C3.
A tiny shop crammed with handmade notebooks, leather-bound albums and paper-covered gift boxes.

Il Papiro
Via del Pantheon 50, Pantheon & Navona (06 679 5597, www.ilpapirofirenze.it). Bus 30Exp, 40Exp, 46, 62, 63, 64, 70, 81, 87, 186, 492, 628, 810, 916/tram 8. **Open** 10am-8pm Mon-Fri; 11am-8pm Sun. **Credit** AmEx, DC, MC, V. **Map** p339 D4.
A great place to buy something for the writer in your life, at Il Papiro Florentine paper is incorporated into albums, notebooks and more. Don't ruin the effect

L'Olfattorio – Bar à Parfums.
See p236.

with a biro: the shop also stocks quill pens and ink in a range of jazzy colours.
Other locations salita de' Crescenzi 28, Pantheon & Navona (06 686 8463).

Marble

Bottega del Marmoraro
Via Margutta 53B, Tridente (06 320 7660).
Metro Spagna/bus 81, 116, 117, 204, 590, 628, 913, 926. **Open** 8am-1pm, 3.30-7.30pm Mon-Sat.
No credit cards. Map p338 E3.
Stepping into this hole-in-the-wall shop, you'd be forgiven for thinking you'd been teleported back to the workroom of an ancient Roman craftsman: the tiny space is crammed with pseudo-classical inscriptions, headless statues and busts. The jolly *marmoraro* Enrico Fiorentini can make to order.

Studio Massoni
Via Antonio Canova 23, Tridente (no phone).
Bus 81, 117, 119, 628, 926. **Open** 9am-1pm, 3-7pm Mon-Fri. Closed Aug. **No credit cards.**
Map off p338 A2.
A selection of classical busts in *gesso* (plaster) are for sale, while copies of just about any statue or object can be made to order. They're certainly a lot lighter to carry home than the real thing.

Miscellaneous

Arte5
Corso Vittorio Emanuele 5, Pantheon & Navona (06 6992 1298). Bus 30Exp, 40Exp, 46, 62, 63, 64, 70, 81, 87, 186, 492, 628, 810, 916/tram 8.
Open 10.30am-8pm daily. **Credit** AmEx, MC, V.
Map p339 D6.
Two floors of postcards, posters, books and arty souvenirs from Rome's major museums and others in Milan, Venice, Florence and around the world. There's a selection of children's books, in a variety of languages.

Eclectica
Via in Aquiro 70, Pantheon & Navona (06 678 4228, www.eclecticaroma.com). Bus 52, 53, 61, 62, 63, 80Exp, 85, 116, 117, 119, 850. **Open** 1-7.30pm Mon; 10.30am-7.30pm Tue-Sat. Closed Aug. **Credit** AmEx, DC, MC, V. **Map** p339 E5.
An assortment of talking-point collectibles and antique toys jostles for space with a vast selection of militaria. Magic fans take note: the shop also stocks an array of tricks and hats for the professional magician. Pricey.

Too Much
Via Santa Maria dell'Anima 29, Pantheon & Navona (06 6830 1187, www.toomuch.it). Bus 30Exp, 70, 81, 87, 116, 186, 204, 628, 491.
Open noon-midnight Mon-Wed, Sun; noon-1am Thur-Sat. **Credit** AmEx, MC, V. **Map** p339 D5.

Lovers of kitsch need look no further: two storeys crammed floor-to-ceiling with gimmicky design and household objects, from retro T-shirts and badges to fuzzy dice, furry handcuffs and lava lamps.

HEALTH & BEAUTY
Cosmetics & perfumes

Beauty superstores **Sephora** (in Forum Termini, the underground mall at Termini railway station, 06 4782 3445) and **Beauty Point** (piazza di Spagna 12, 06 6992 4534; other branches across the city) stock big-name ranges plus basic toiletries at non-rip-off prices. The former's own-brand cosmetics line is excellent value. For a more refined experience, follow your nose to one of the city's elegant *profumerie*.

Antica Erboristeria Romana
Via di Torre Argentina 15, Pantheon & Navona (06 687 9493, www.anticaerboristeria romana.com). Bus 30Exp, 40Exp, 46, 62, 63, 64, 70, 81, 87, 186, 492, 628, 810, 916/tram 8.
Open 8.30am-7.30pm Mon-Fri; 9am-7.30pm Sat. Closed 1wk Aug. **Credit** AmEx, DC, MC, V.
Map p342 D1.
Visit this charming 18th-century apothecary-style shop if only to admire the carved wood ceilings and banks of tiny wooden drawers – some etched with skull and crossbones – in which herbal remedies are hidden safely away.

Officina Profumo-Farmaceutica di Santa Maria Novella
Corso Rinascimento 47, Pantheon & Navona (06 687 9608, www.smnovella.it). Bus 70, 81, 87, 116, 186, 492, 629. **Open** 9.30am-7.30pm Mon-Sat. Closed 1wk Aug. **Credit** DC, MC, V.
Map p339 D5.
From quiet beginnings – it was founded in Florence in 1612 by a group of enterprising Dominican monks – the chic Officina's all-natural products have gained themselves a global following. The handcrafted potions are exquisite; prices, needless to say, don't reflect the products' humble origins.

CONSUME

L'Olfattorio – Bar à Parfums

*Via Ripetta 34, Tridente (bookings 06 361 2325/
information 800 631 123, www.olfattorio.it).
Metro Flaminio/bus 81, 117, 119, 204, 224, 628,
926.* **Open** 11am-7.30pm Mon-Sat. Closed 1wk
Aug. **Credit** MC, V. **Map** p338 D3.

It's strictly personal shopping at this innovative per-
fumery. A 'bartender' will awaken your olfactory
organs and guide you expertly towards your perfect
scent. Once determined, exclusive lines of handmade
English and French fragrances are available on site.
Paradise for perfume-lovers. *Photo p234.*

Pro Fumum Durante

*Via della Colonna Antonina 27, Pantheon &
Navona (06 679 5982, www.profumum.com). Bus
52, 53, 61, 62, 63, 71, 80Exp, 85, 116, 117, 119,
160, 850.* **Open** 3.30-7.30pm Mon; 10am-7.30pm
Tue-Fri; 10am-1.30pm, 2.30-7.30pm Sat.
Closed 3wks Aug. **Credit** AmEx, DC, MC, V.
Map p339 E4.

The rare-brand creams, lotions and perfumes you
will find in this sophisticated shop are highly tempting... but such high-class pampering certainly
doesn't come cheap.
Other locations via di Ripetta 10, Tridente (06
320 0306); viale Angelico 87-89, Prati (06 372 5791).

Roma – Store

*Via della Lungaretta 63, Trastevere (06 581
8789). Bus 23, 280, 780, H/tram 8.* **Open**
10am-8pm daily. **Credit** AmEx, DC, MC, V.
Map p342 C3.

This blissful sanctuary of lotions and potions stocks
an array of gorgeous scents: old-school Floris, Creed
and Penhaligon's rub shoulders with modern classics such as home-grown Acqua di Parma and
Lorenzo Villoresi. Staff can be very abrupt.

Hairdressers & beauticians

Rome's hairdressers shut up shop on Mondays.
Appointments are not usually necessary, but be
prepared to wait if you haven't booked.

Centro Estetico Malò

*Piazza Tavani Arquati 120, Trastevere
(06 589 8950). Bus 23, 271, 280, H/tram 8.*
Open 10am-8pm Tue-Sat. Closed 2wks Aug.
Credit MC, V. **Map** p342 C3.

INSIDE TRACK SHOP TALK

The essential lines *mi può aiutare, per
favore?* ('Can you help me please?') and
volevo solo dare un' occhiata ('I'm just
looking') will stand you in good stead
when dealing with reticent or over-insistent
shop assistants.

This friendly Trastevere beautician offers great
deals on waxing, manicures and pedicures. It also
features a whole range of face and body treatments
for relaxation and glowing skin.

Concept Hair & Make-Up

*Via Cimarra 60, Monti (06 4554 0594). Metro
Cavour/bus 40Exp, 60Exp, 64, 70, 116T, 170,
H.* **Open** 10am-7.30pm Tue-Sat. Closed 3wks
Aug. **Credit** AmEx, DC, MC, V. **Map** p344 B1.

Forget hectic Rome in this little light-wood heaven
with a charming back garden. Bianca and Neil (both
speak English) will take care of you with trendy hair-
cuts, make-up and a refreshing cup of herbal tea.

★ Femme Sistina

*Via Sistina 75A, Tridente (06 678 0260,
www.femmesistina-rome.com). Metro Spagna/
bus 52, 53, 61, 62, 63, 71, 80Exp, 85, 116,
117, 119, 160, 850.* **Open** 10am-7pm Mon-
Sat; 11am-7pm Sun. **Credit** AmEx, DC,
MC, V. **Map** p341 B5.

Going strong since 1959, Femme Sistina was the
beauty parlour of the glam and famous during the
dolce vita era and continues to look like a glorious
time warp. But its services – facials, leg-waxing, eye-
lash tinting, hairdressing – are as up-to-the-minute
as you could wish... Nicole Kidman certainly values
them, and the old-style care taken of customers by
proprietor Lisette Lenzi.

Opticians

Replacement lenses can usually be fitted
overnight, and most opticians will replace a
missing screw on the spot. If you're having
prescription lenses fitted, it's normal to get a
discount on frame prices; if it isn't offered, ask
for one. See also *Ottica* in the Yellow Pages.

Mondello Ottica

*Via del Pellegrino 97-98, Ghetto & Campo
(06 686 1955). Bus 40Exp, 46, 62, 64, 916.*
Open 10am-1.30pm, 4-7.30pm Tue-Sat.
Closed 3wks Aug. **Credit** AmEx, DC, MC, V.
Map p342 C1.

Giancarlo and Rosaria will frame your face with
international designer eyewear. It's worth visiting
this gallery-like store just to goggle at the window
installations by local artists. Lenses can often be
replaced on the spot; and adjustments and repairs
are done for free – and executed with a smile.

Optissimo

*Forum Termini, Stazione Termini, Esquilino (06
4890 5630). Metro Termini/buses to
Termini/tram 5, 14.* **Open** 8am-10pm daily.
Credit AmEx, DC, MC, V. **Map** p341 E5.

This bright and shiny chain store in the shopping
centre beneath Termini station is open unusually
long hours; they do contact lenses too.

CONSUME

Leone Limentani.

Spas

See pp279-280.

HOUSE & HOME

Antiques

Among the best areas for antiques are via del Babuino, via Giulia and via de' Coronari; the latter stages antiques fairs in May and October. Dealers/restorers thronging via del Pellegrino may be cheaper, but quality dips too. Bargains can be picked up at flea markets (*see p220*).

Design & household

The area around via delle Botteghe Oscure and via Arenula (map p342 D2) is full of shops that sell linen, fabric, laces, curtain ribbons. *See also p188* **'Gusto**.

Celsa

Via d'Aracoeli 7, Ghetto & Campo (06 6994 0872). Bus 30Exp, 40Exp, 46, 62, 63, 64, 70, 87, 186, 204, 492, 630, 780, 810, 916. **Open** 9am-1pm, 3.30-7.30pm Mon-Sat. **Credit** AmEx, DC, MC, V. **Map** p339 E6.
This reliable shop stocks an extensive range of fabrics and tailoring odds and ends. Remnants of textiles are sold off cheaply.

C.U.C.I.N.A

Via Mario de' Fiori 65, Tridente (06 679 1275, www.cucinastore.com). Metro Spagna/bus 52, 53, 61, 62, 63, 71, 80Exp, 85, 116, 117, 119, 160, 850. **Open** 3.30-7.30pm Mon; 10.30am-7.30pm Tue-Sat. **Credit** AmEx, DC, MC, V. **Map** p338 E3.
Even the most adventurous cooks will find a utensil their kitchen lacks at this culinary gadgetry shop. It sells a vast range of kitchenware, from bamboo rice steamers to a fine selection of jelly moulds.

Leone Limentani
Via del Portico d'Ottavia 47, Ghetto & Campo (06 6880 6686). Bus 30Exp, 40Exp, 46, 62, 63, 64, 70, 81, 87, 186, 492, 628, 810, 916/tram 8. **Open** 9am-1pm, 3.30-7.30pm Mon-Fri; 10am-7.30pm Sat. Closed 2wks Aug. **Credit** AmEx, DC, MC, V. **Map** p342 D2.
A treasure-trove of high-piled crockery and kitchenware is on display here – at bargain-basement prices. Many big brand names are reduced by up to 20%.

Spazio Sette
Via dei Barbieri 7, Pantheon & Navona (06 686 9747, www.spaziosette.com). Bus 30Exp, 40Exp, 46, 62, 63, 64, 70, 81, 87, 119, 492, 571, 628, 916/tram 8. **Open** 3.30-7.30pm Mon; 9.30am-1pm, 3.30-7.30pm Tue-Sat. Closed 3wks Aug. **Map** p342 D1.
A stalwart of the Roman design circuit since it opened in the 1970s, Spazio Sette is a coolly chic treasure trove of kitchenware and furniture occupying three floors of a delightful 17th-century palazzo.

MUSIC & ENTERTAINMENT

For larger outlets, head to **Mondadori Multicenter** (via del Corso 472, 06 684 401) or **Ricordi** (branches at via del Corso 506, 06 361 2370; and inside Feltrinelli bookshop, *see p222*). The via del Corso branch of Ricordi also sells musical instruments, scores and concert tickets, and offers sound equipment for sale or hire.

CDs & records

Radiation
Circonvallazione Casilina 44, Suburbs: east (06 90 28 6578/06 70302868). Bus 81, 412, 810/tram 5, 14, 19. **Open** 4.30-7.30pm Mon; 10am-7.30pm Tue-Sat. Closed 1wk Aug. **Credit** MC, V.
This is the freshest of Rome's alternative and indie music shops. The reggae and punk sections are excellent, as is the rare-label and used vinyl.

Soul Food
Via San Giovanni in Laterano 192-194, San Giovanni (06 7045 2025, www.haterecords.com). Metro Colosseo/bus 85, 117, 650, 850. **Open** 10.30am-1.30pm, 3.30-8pm Tue-Sat. Closed 2wks Aug. **Credit** AmEx, MC, V. **Map** p344 D3.

CONSUME

A cool vintage record shop, stocking indie, punk, beat, exotica, lounge, rockabilly and more. Heaven.

DVD rental

You can rent English DVDs across the city, but check the box – not all have English soundtracks.

Hollywood
Via Monserrato 107, Ghetto & Campo (06 686 9197, www.hollywood-video.it). Bus 40Exp, 46, 62, 64, 916/tram 8. **Open** 10am-7.30pm Mon-Sat. Closed Aug. **Credit** MC, V. **Map** p342 C1.
A wide selection of auteur cinema and about 400 original-language films. Lots of film stills and original posters are for sale. Lifetime membership costs €25 and a two-day rental is €3.50.

TICKETS
Ticket agencies

Expect to pay *diritti di prevendita* (booking fees) on tickets bought anywhere except at the venue on the night. **Ricordi** (*see p237*) sells tickets for classical concerts and for many rock, jazz and other events.

Hello Ticket
Viale Manzoni 53, Celio (06 4782 5710, www.helloticket.it). Metro Manzoni/bus 85, 87, 360, 590/tram 3. **Open** 9.30am-4.30pm Mon-Fri. **Credit** (phone & online bookings) AmEx, DC, MC, V. **Map** p344 E3.
Tickets for most concerts, plays and sporting events.
▶ *For useful venue websites and more information on tickets, see p264 **Music** and p270 **Nightlife**.*

Travel agencies

Centro Turistico Studentesco (CTS Student Travel Centre)
Via Solferino 6, Esquilino (06 462 0431, www.cts.it). Buses to Termini. **Open** 9.30am-1pm, 2-6.30pm Mon-Fri; 10am-1pm Sat. **Credit** MC, V. **Map** p341 C6.
This agency offers discounts on air, rail and coach tickets for all those in full-time education. CTS services can also be used by non-students.
Other locations corso Vittorio Emanuele 297, Pantheon & Navona (06 687 2672/3/4); via degli Ausoni 5, San Lorenzo (06 445 0141).

Turicam Viaggi
Via di Torre Argentina 80, Ghetto & Campo (06 6819 3343, www.turicam.it). Bus 30Exp, 40Exp, 46, 62, 64, 70, 81, 87, 810/tram 8. **Open** 9.30am-7pm Mon-Sat. **Credit** AmEx, DC, MC, V. **Map** p339 D6.
Planes, trains, boats and the like are all bookable through this friendly centrally located agency.

TRAVELLERS' NEEDS
For newsstands and tobacconists, *see p224* **Life's Essentials**; for travel agents, *see left.*

Photocopying

If you're in town and don't have access to an office or hotel photocopier – many of the larger ones will have one – in addition to specialised shops, some *tabacchi* (tobacconists; *see p224* **Life's Essentials**) and *cartolerie* (stationers) do photocopies. Though, as a rule, give them a miss if you need crisp, clear copies. Around the university (*see p317*), many copy centres are happy to offer discounts to students.

B&M
Via Marmorata 79, Testaccio (06 5728 7289, www.bmcopie.net). Bus 30Exp, 75, 95, 170, 280, 781/tram 3. **Open** 9am-1pm, 2.30-7pm Mon-Fri; 9am-1pm Sat. **Credit** AmEx, MC, V. **Map** p343 D5.
B&M provides excellent photocopying, plus plotter and CAD services for architects. You can also send faxes from here.

Digital Service Xeromania
Viale Trastevere 119, Trastevere (06 581 4433). Bus 780, H/tram 8. **Open** 9am-2pm, 3-7.30pm Mon-Fri; 9am-1pm Sat. Closed 2wks Aug. **No credit cards.** **Map** p343 C4.
A general photocopy shop, which also has a reliable fax-sending and -receiving service.

Photo developers & cameras

Film can be bought in specialist camera shops, opticians and most tobacconists.

CocaColor
Via di Porta Angelica 41, Vatican & Prati (06 687 9498). Metro Ottaviano/bus 23, 32, 49, 81, 492, 907, 982, 990/tram 19. **Open** 9am-6pm daily. **Credit** DC, MC, V. **Map** p339 A4.
This reliable photo shop develops film as well as printing digital photos.
▶ *Sidle up to a Swiss Guard next door at St Peter's (see p144) then have your snap printed up here.*

Foto-Cine di Pennetta
Via Dandolo 2, Trastevere (06 589 6648). Bus 780, H/tram 8. **Open** 8.30am-8pm Mon-Fri; 9am-1pm, 4-7.30pm Sat. Closed 2wks Aug. **Credit** DC, MC, V. **Map** p343 C4.
High-quality photo shop with fast developing and digital processing; camera repairs too.

Arts & Entertainment

Goa. *See p274.*

Discover the city from your back pocket

Essential for your weekend break, over 30 top cities available.

**TIME OUT GUIDES
WRITTEN BY
LOCAL EXPERTS**
visit timeout.com/shop

Calendar

Rome has always known how to put on a party.

The Romans, perennial fun-seekers, have never needed much of an excuse for a knees-up; in ancient times a whopping 150 days were set aside every year for R&R. Though modern-day Romans must make do with a paltry ten annual public holidays, the final total is usually quite a bit more: any holiday that falls midweek is invariably taken as an invitation to *fare il ponte* ('do a bridge') – take an extra day or two off between the official holiday and the weekend.

Important religious holidays have different effects on the city (the Assumption on 15 August shuts it down; Easter brings hordes of pilgrims). Districts of Rome hold smaller-scale celebrations of their own patron saints in their own way, from calorific blowouts to extravagant fireworks displays. Occasional large-scale city-run events make ample use of Rome's endless supply of photogenic venues.

For precise dates of events, check www.turismoroma.it or www.060608.it.

SPRING

Festa di Santa Francesca Romana

Monastero Oblate di Santa Francesca Romana, via Teatro di Marcello 32 & 40 (06 679 3565). Bus 30Exp, 63, 95, 628. **Date** 9 Mar. **Map** p342 E2.
In 1433 Santa Francesca Romana founded the Oblate di Maria, an order of nuns who never took final vows. She was believed to possess the gift of dislocation (being in different places at once) a quality that so endeared her to Italy's pioneer motorists that they made her their patron saint. Devout Roman drivers get their motors blessed at her church in the Foro Romano (*see p62*) on 9 March.

Palazzo Massimo alle Colonne

Corso Vittorio Emanuele 141 (06 6880 1545). Bus 30Exp, 40Exp, 46, 62, 63, 64, 70, 81, 116, 492, 628, 630, 780, 916. **Date** 16 Mar (8am-1pm). **Map** p339 C6.
San Filippo Neri performed one of his most famous miracles in the *palazzo* of the Massimo family. Called to give last rites to Paolo Massimo, the saint found the boy already dead; undaunted, he revived Paolo, chatted for a while, then – when the boy was ready to meet his maker – commended him to God. On the anniversary, a procession of family, servants and altar boys escorts the cardinal or archbishop to a private room for a slap-up buffet. Turn up near 11.30am to witness the spectacle in all its Felliniesque glory.

Festa di San Giuseppe

Around via Trionfale. Metro Ottaviano/bus 23, 32, 81, 492/tram 19. **Date** 19 Mar. **Map** p338 A2.
Though no longer an official public holiday, the feast of St Joseph remains popular, especially in the Trionfale district of northern Rome. In the run-up to the feast, the city's *pasticcerie* are piled high with deep-fried batter-balls called *bignè di San Giuseppe*.

Settimana della Cultura

Information (toll-free) 800 991 199, www.beniculturali.it. **Date** one week in Spring.
For Cultural Heritage Week, state-owned museums and monuments open to the public without charge.

Maratona della Città di Roma

Information 06 406 5064, www.maratonadiroma.it. **Date** 3rd or 4th Sun in Mar.
Rome's annual marathon attracts big-name runners. The serious race begins and ends in via dei Fori Imperiali; sign up online (the sooner you register, the lower the fee). The Stracittadina fun-run is a 5km (3-mile) jog through the *centro storico*; sign up at the Marathon Village (venue varies – check online) up to a day before the event.

Festa di Primavera – Mostra delle Azalee

Piazza di Spagna (see p85). **Date** end Mar, early Apr. **Map** p341 A4.

Spring arrives early in Rome, bringing masses of blooms. When the azaleas come out, some 3,000 vases of them are arranged on the Spanish Steps.

Settimana Santa & Pasqua (Holy Week & Easter)
Vatican (see p142). **Map** p339 A45.
Colosseum (see p60). **Date** Mar/Apr.
Map p344 B/C3.
Tourists and pilgrims flood into the city on the Saturday before Palm Sunday, cramming inside St Peter's square for the open-air mass. The non-stop services of Holy Week peak in the pope's Stations of the Cross (*Via Crucis*) and mass at the Colosseum late on the evening of Good Friday. On *Pasquetta* (Easter Monday), tradition coaxes Romans *fuori porta* (outside the city gates) to feast upon lavish picnics of such specialities as *torta pasqualina* (cheesy bread, with salami and hard-boiled eggs) and *fave e pecorino* (broad beans and cheese).

Natale di Roma
Campidoglio (see pp52-59). **Date** 21 Apr.
Map p342 E2.
Not all cities celebrate their birthday... but Rome, 'born' in 753 BC, is no ordinary city. The bulk of the festivities take place at the Campidoglio. The city hall and the other *palazzi* on the hill are illuminated, and enormous quantities of fireworks are set off.

Festa della Liberazione
Date 25 Apr.
This public holiday commemorates the liberation of Italy by Allied forces at the end of World War II.

Giornate FAI
Various locations (information 06 689 6752, www.fondoambiente.it). **Date** varies (see website).
For one weekend each spring, the Fondo per l'Ambiente Italiano (FAI) persuades institutional and private owners of historic properties to reveal their spectacular interiors, usually off-limits to the public; see the website for information.

Primo Maggio
Piazza San Giovanni. Metro San Giovanni/ bus 16, 81, 87, 117, 850/tram 3. **Date** 1 May.
Map p345 E4.
On May Day, trade unions organise a huge, free rock concert, which is traditionally held in front of the basilica of San Giovanni in Laterano (*see p131*). Performers – mainly Italian, with a smattering of international has-beens – belt out crowd-pleasers from mid afternoon into the small hours.
▶ *For more spring and summer outdoors musical happenings, see p270* **Sounds of Summer**.

Campionato Internazionale di Tennis
Foro Italico, viale dei Gladiatori 31 (06 3685 4122, www.internazionalibnlditalia.it). Bus 32, 280/tram 2. **Date** 2wks early May.

Every May, Rome hosts the Italian Open tennis tournament, one of the most important European clay-court challenges outside the Grand Slam, and a warm-up event for the French Open.

Concorso Ippico Internazionale di Piazza di Siena
Piazza di Siena, Villa Borghese (information 06 326 9011, bookings 06 638 3818, www. piazzadisiena.com). Metro Spagna/bus 88, 95, 116. **Date** 2nd half of May. **Map** p340 B2.
Rome's jetset flock along to this international show-jumping event in leafy Villa Borghese.

SUMMER

Estate Romana
Various locations (www.estateromana.comune. roma.it). **Date** June-Sept.
During the event-packed Estate Romana (Roman Summer) festival, *piazze, palazzi*, parks and courtyards come alive with music from local bands, films are shown on outdoor screens late into the night, and cultural events such as readings and gastronomic events take place in venues around town. Many events are free; check local press for details.

Festival delle Letterature
Basilica of Maxentius, via dei Fori Imperiali (06 3996 7850, www.festivaldelleletterature.it). **Date** June.
The floodlit basilica of Maxentius in the Roman Forum provides a theatrical backdrop to readings by some of the most important names in contemporary literature; past guests have included Paul Auster, Hanif Kureishi and Zadie Smith.

Festa di San Giovanni
Piazza di San Giovanni in Laterano. Metro San Giovanni/bus 16, 85, 87, 117, 850/ tram 3. **Date** 23-24 June. **Map** p344 E4.

FotoGrafia. *See p244.*

Country Knees-ups

Festivals are observed with gusto in villages around Rome. Whether events are in honour of an obscure saint or the year's crop of *porcini* mushrooms, merrymaking is guaranteed.

Infiorata
Genzano, see p303 (www.infiorata.it). **Date** mid June.
For over two centuries locals have decorated Genzano's town centre with some 5,000kg (11,000lbs) of petals, in a carpet of pictorial representations from the church of Santa Maria della Cima to the main square. Once artists have sketched their designs on the paving stones, petals are placed on top to create stunning tableaux... until the town's children run rampant the following day.

Festa dell'Inchinata
Tivoli, see p297. **Date** 14, 15 Aug.
Dating back to 1524, this festival marks the assumption of the Virgin Mary's soul into heaven. On 14 August two processions of the faithful – one from the church of Santa Maria Maggiore bearing the image of the Madonna, the other from the cathedral with the image of Christ – meet in piazza Trento, where the effigies bow to each other three times under arches of greenery

before being carried into the church. The following day, after a final bow, they part company for another year.

Palio del Lago
Trevignano Romano, see p292 (www. trevignanoromano.it). **Date** 15 Aug.
The volcanic lake at Trevignano Romano is the picturesque setting for a boat procession to mark the Feast of the Assumption, but what really draws the crowds is the *Palio* – a dragon-boat regatta during which the three lakeside towns of Trevignano, Anguillara and Bracciano battle it out for victory.

I Facchini di Santa Rosa
Viterbo, see p293 **Historic Viterbo** *(www. facchinidisantarosa.it).* **Date** 3 Sept.
When the parents of a Viterbo girl, Rosa, born in 1233, thwarted her dreams of becoming a nun, she took to the streets, lugging a crucifix around with her and preaching. Her piety did not save her, however, from an early death – aged 18. Credited with saving Viterbo from plague, she was proclaimed a saint in 1457. Every 3 September, an ornately decorated 28m (92ft) column is borne through the streets on the shoulders of white-robed men with knotted handkerchiefs on their heads.

In the San Giovanni district, locals observe this saint's day by guzzling *lumache in umido* (stewed snails) and *porchetta* (roast suckling pig). The main religious highlight is a candlelit procession, usually led by the pope, to San Giovanni in Laterano.

Santi Pietro e Paolo
San Paolo fuori le Mura (see p159). **Date** 29 June.
The two founders of Catholicism are, naturally, also the twin patron saints of Rome, and each of them is honoured in his own basilica. At St Peter's, a solemn mass is the highlight of the festivities; celebrations at San Paolo fuori le Mura focus around an all-night street fair on via Ostiense.

Festa de' Noantri
Piazza Santa Maria in Trastevere & piazza Mastai. Bus 23, 280, 780, H/tram 8. **Date** mid-end July. **Map** p342 C3.
Though few traces of Trastevere's working-class roots remain today, the area's residents celebrate its humble origins with gusto during the Festa de' Noantri. Festivities kick off with a procession held in honour of the Madonna del Carmine, to whom the whole shebang is theoretically dedicated. Two

weeks of arts events and street performances follow, and fireworks round off the closing night.

Festa delle Catene
San Pietro in Vincoli (see p136). **Date** 1 Aug. **Map** p344 C2.
The chains that allegedly bound St Peter in prison in Jerusalem, and those with which he was shackled in Rome, are displayed in a special mass at the church of San Pietro in Vincoli.

Festa della Madonna della Neve
Santa Maria Maggiore (see p140). **Date** 5 Aug. **Map** p341 D6.
There was an unseasonal snowfall on the Esquiline Hill on 5 August 352, an event that is still remembered at the basilica of Santa Maria Maggiore. The day is marked with a special mass, culminating in a blizzard of rose petals, which flutter down from the roof on to the congregation.

Notte di San Lorenzo
San Lorenzo in Panisperna, via Panisperna 90 (06 483 667). Metro Cavour/bus 71, 117. **Date** 10 Aug. **Map** p344 B1.

ARTS & ENTERTAINMENT

On the night of 10 August, Roman eyes turn towards the heavens, hoping to catch a glimpse of one of the night's shooting stars. Some explain the phenomenon as the fall-out of a meteor entering orbit, while the more poetic attribute the falling stars to the tears shed by St Lawrence, martyred in Rome on this day in 258.

Ferragosto (Feast of the Assumption)
Date 15 Aug.
Those who haven't scarpered to the coast for the whole of August take a long weekend for the Feast of the Assumption, and most of the city closes down.

AUTUMN

RomaEuropa Festival
Various locations (06 4555 30050, www.roma europa.net). **Date** Sept-Nov.
Rome's cutting-edge performing arts festival offers music, dance and theatre, with an eclectic mix of international acts and emerging young talent. Buy tickets at the venues themselves or by phone or online; book well in advance for big-name acts.

FotoGrafia
Various locations (information 06 0608, www. fotografiafestival.it). **Date** Sept-Oct.
Rome's annual photography festival puts on a wide range of exhibitions (including work by photographers such as Ilkka Halso, *photo p242*) in a pleasing variety of venues across the city. You'll find shows everywhere from historic museums to avant-garde backstreet galleries. *Photo p242.*

Festival Internazionale del Film di Roma
Auditorium-Parco della Musica (www.romacinema fest.it). **Date** 10 days Oct-Nov.
Rome's new-ish film festival is firmly in the serie B of international movie meets, but generous allocations of tickets for the cinema-loving Roman public and all the usual red-carpet glamour ensures plenty of non-professional audience participation and a great atmosphere.

Ognissanti/Giornata dei Defunti
Cimitero del Verano, piazzale del Verano. Bus 71, 163, 492/tram 3, 19. **Date** 1, 2 Nov. **Map** p128 D1.
Otherwise known as *Tutti santi*, All Saints' Day (*Ognissanti*) is followed by *La commemorazioni dei defunti* (or *Tutti i morti*), when the pope celebrates mass at Verano Cemetery. Romans travel en masse to visit family graves.

WINTER

Immacolata Concezione
Piazza di Spagna (see p85). **Date** 8 Dec. **Map** p341 A4.

The statue of the Madonna in piazza di Spagna is the focus of the Feast of the Immaculate Conception. With the pope looking on, the fire brigade runs a ladder up Mary's column and one lucky fireman gets to place a wreath over her outstretched arm. At the base of the column, the locals deposit their own elaborate floral tributes.

Natale & Santo Stefano (Christmas & Boxing Day)
Date 25, 26 Dec.
Tickets for the papal midnight mass at St Peter's can be obtained from the Prefettura (*see p144*); you'll have to put your request in months in advance. Cribs can be found in most churches, but the most impressive are halfway up the Spanish Steps and in piazza San Pietro. The Roman Christmas Day is a gluttonous affair: locals feast upon *fritti* (calorific fried offerings), followed by *panettone* (currant sponge) and *torrone* (slabs of nutty chocolate or nougat). The pope says a special mass and gives his '*Urbi et orbis*' blessing in St Peter's.

San Silvestro & Capodanno (New Year's Eve & New Year's Day)
Date 31 Dec, 1 Jan.
Hordes of Romans flock to piazza del Popolo to see in the new year with a free concert and fireworks display; check the city council website (www. comune.roma.it) for a full list of events. Some people add to the fun with home-grown pyrotechnics and flying *spumante* corks, turning the *centro storico* into something resembling a war zone.

Epifania – La Befana (Epiphany)
Piazza Navona (see p98). **Date** 6 Jan.
From mid December all the way to Epiphany itself, piazza Navona hosts a Christmas fair, with market stalls peddling sweets and cheap tat. The fair is dedicated to *La Befana* – the present-bearing old witch. The climax of the fair comes late on 5 January, when *La Befana* herself touches down in the piazza.

Festa di Sant'Antonio Abate
Sant'Eusebio, piazza Vittorio Emanuele II 12A. Metro Vittorio/bus 70, 71, 105, 360/tram 5, 14. **Date** 17 Jan. **Map** p344 E1.
Romans commemorate the protector of animals, Sant'Antonio Abate, in the church of Sant'Eusebio on 17 January. Anyone who is keen to ensure their pet gets a place in heaven can bring it along to the church for a blessing.

Carnevale
Date week before Ash Wednesday (Feb/early Mar).
In the Middle Ages this riotous last fling before the rigours of Lent was celebrated with wild abandon on Monte Testaccio (*see p121*). Nowadays young Roman tykes dressed up in their finery are paraded about by their proud parents.

Children

Rome, the world's biggest theme park?

Rome, it's true, has no rollercoaster-filled amusement parks, IMAX cinemas or giant, blaring arcades. But approached with the right attitude, Rome itself is one fascinating, city-wide theme park. Moreover, Italian culture is traditionally family-oriented, so much so, in fact, that you're much more likely to be sold the juiciest fruit and veg at the market, offered a seat on a crowded bus or given priority treatment in the pizzeria if you have several small ones in tow. Most junior schools include some ancient history on their curriculum, but to guarantee a successful family holiday in Rome it's usually best to brush up on your emperors, popes, gladiators and gods in advance, so you can bring dusty places to life with some colourful characters.

PRACTICALITIES

Since there's not much in the way of baby-changing or feeding facilities, don't be afraid to corner the friendliest looking face in a café, bookshop or children's clothes store: more often than not they'll find you a quiet corner where you can do both.

If you're visiting in the heat and humidity of the summer months, you'll have to slog far from the centre to find **public pools** (*see p280*) or **beaches** (*see pp286-304* **Escapes & Excursions**). Take advantage of the drinking fountains located on street corners and in *piazze* all over the city: unless they say *non potabile*, they all have excellent quality drinking water.

Food, of course, is part and parcel of the Rome experience: here, after all, kids can sample some of the world's best *gelato*. Rather than heading for the ubiquitous fast-food chains, let your children pick out their favourite pizza topping on a takeaway slice to revive their spirits, or choose different flavoured scoops on an ice-cream cone – sure to delight even the fussiest child. Though you won't find any special children's menus, waiters tend to be kid-friendly and most restaurants are more than happy to provide you with a plate of pasta with tomato sauce, or simply with parmesan and oil. And you needn't fret if your little terror runs riot around the restaurant while you try to figure out the menu: chances are the Italians will find your bored and noisy offspring utterly charming.

The parks and gardens (*see p248*) dotted around the city centre have in recent years had some decent swings and slides added to their fountains and statues.

GETTING AROUND

Children travel free on Rome's city transport until their tenth birthday; older children pay the full price for single-journey and one- or three-day bus passes. If you're here longer term, invest in a travel pass (€18 per calendar month) for school-age children. A bus tour (*see p309*) with English commentary is a good way to whisk your family past the major sights.

Though much of Rome suffers from chronic traffic congestion, some central squares and streets (piazza Navona, piazza di Pietra, piazza di Spagna) are pedestrian zones with plenty of pigeons for toddlers to chase. Negotiating cars parked on pavements and avoiding mad moped drivers can be a problem, so a sling or backpack is often better than a buggy for babies.

SIGHTSEEING

If you're travelling with offspring, don't expect too much from most of the city's museums and galleries: they're not renowned for being user-

About the author

Vatican Radio journalist **Philippa Hitchen** *also contributes to the BBC World Service and to the cultural pages of* La Repubblica. *She has lived in Italy since the mid-1980s.*

Piazza San Cosimato.

friendly. Much better to take the family on a bus tour (or get them walking) and challenge them to spot a pyramid, an elephant with an obelisk on its back, an angel on top of a castle – the possibilities are endless. And with a few facts at your fingertips, you can keep the kids entertained and informed with tales of popes fleeing invading armies, great artists competing for their patron's favours and emperors worshipping the stars and the sun.

If you've neglected to visit the history section of your local library – or this book – you could begin your sightseeing with a whirlwind trip through the past three millennia of Roman history at the **Time Elevator** (*see p248*) or **Rewind Rome** (*see p248*). They're both pricey, and not recommended for under-fives, but they should grab your children's attention. Older kids might appreciate the use of computer wizardry in **Palazzo Valentini** (*see p58*).

After the virtual tour, it's time to tackle ancient Rome for real, starting a stroll away at the **Foro romano** (*see p62*). As there's a high risk of the kids refusing point-blank to waste time looking at heaps of old stones, you could do worse than invest in one of the 'then and now' guidebooks on sale from the many souvenir stalls around the area: they may seem tacky to you, but they could help to bring the place to life for younger visitors. The **Colosseum** (*see p60*) is a little further down the via dei Fori Imperiali. (Beat the lengthy queues by buying your ticket en route at the entrance to the Palatine.) Make

sure you immortalise your Roman holiday by posing with some of the ersatz gladiators and centurions in full regalia.

Remember *Ben-Hur*? The **Circo Massimo** (*see p60*) – once a grandiose track for chariot races – is now an elongated expanse of patchy grass. But it's a perfect (if unshaded) place to let your kids work off excess energy while re-enacting the Hollywood epic. A short walk away at the Tiber end of the track, you'll find queues of tourists waiting in the front porch of the church of **Santa Maria in Cosmedin** (*see p112*), home to the *bocca della verità* ('mouth of truth'), an ancient drain cover that is supposed to chomp off the hand of anyone unwise enough to tell a fib.

St Peter's (*see p144*) may seem like 'just another church' to your kids but, again, you can tickle their imagination with a few stories of murder and intrigue that have accompanied the long history of papal Rome. Younger kids may be more impressed by the Swiss Guards' brightly coloured costumes or the flocks of pigeons in St Peter's square. While you

---

INSIDE TRACK MAKING A WISH

Last but not least, join the crowds around the sides of the **Trevi Fountain** (*see p67*) and dig out your small change so that the kids can chuck coins over their shoulders, ensuring a return visit to the city some day.

admire Bernini's magnificent piazza, keep the children busy by telling them to find and stand on the small round plaques embedded in the pavement in front of each 'arm' of the colonnade: they'll be amazed to see the three tiers of columns perfectly aligned to form a single row. Once inside the church, challenge them to find the foot on the statue of St Peter that has been worn away by the lips of devout pilgrims or the boastful brass markers set into the floor that show how much bigger this basilica is than any other church. A trip up to the dome is always a favourite (don't try this with babes in arms or with a bulky pushchair), with wonderful views both down into the church and out across Rome. There's a café (Il Ristoro; *see p218*) halfway up.

In the vast **Vatican Museums** (*see p148*) you'll have to decide what might catch their attention: the well-preserved mummies in the Egyptian section, or the grisly, tormented faces of Michelangelo's figures descending into hell on the altar wall of the Sistine Chapel. If you're looking for a bribe or some extra energy as you trudge the 15-minute walk along the Vatican walls from St Peter's to the museum entrance, stop in at the Old Bridge ice-cream shop, just past piazza Risorgimento. Nearby **Castel Sant'Angelo** (*see p150*) has handy swings and slides in the gardens outside (not to mention some spectacular frescoes and trompe l'oeil effects inside).

If it's art you're after, then take heart: both **Palazzo Barberini** (*see p71*) and **Galleria Borghese** (*see p78*) are well situated for a picnic in **Villa Borghese** (*see p74*), where you can recover from cultural overload by hiring individual or family-size bikes or taking a rowing boat out on the artificial lake. On the northern side of Villa Borghese is the **Bioparco** – formerly the plain old Zoo – with snazzy, well-stocked reptile house.

Not far from Villa Borghese is **Explora – Museo dei Bambini di Roma** (Rome Children's Museum), while **Technotown** is within the precincts of the verdant Villa Torlonia in the suburbs to the north (*see p248*).

Other museums that may entertain your kids include **Crypta Balbi** (*see p104*), which supplements its fascinating displays on Rome in the Dark Ages with computer games to show how the ancient city was gradually incorporated into the modern; and **Palazzo Valentini** (*see p58*) where the latest technology is used to recreate the rooms of an ancient home.

The **Museo della Civiltà Romana** (*see p161*) is a hike out into the southern suburb of EUR, but rewarding for its huge plaster models of how ancient Rome looked before the rot set in. Within this enormous building there is now a new **Planetario** with a varied programme of star-gazing shows for both adults and children. The museum is also

Rewind Rome. *See p248.*

ARTS & ENTERTAINMENT

ARTS & ENTERTAINMENT

conveniently close to the **Piscina delle Rose** swimming pool (*see p280*).

Bioparco-Zoo
Piazzale del Giardino Zoologico 1, Veneto & Borghese (06 360 8211, www.bioparco.it). Bus 217, 910/tram 3, 19. **Open** *Jan-Mar, Oct-Dec* 9.30am-5pm (last entry 4pm) daily; *Apr-Sept* 9.30am-5pm (last entry 4pm) Mon-Fri, 9.30am-7pm Sat, Sun.* **Admission** €12.50; €10.50 reductions. *Reptile house* €1.50 extra.
Credit MC, V. **Map** p340 B1/2.
For guided tours (in English) call 06 361 4015 from 9.30am to 1pm.

Explora – Museo dei Bambini di Roma
Via Flaminia 82, Veneto & Borghese (06 361 3776, www.mdbr.it). Metro Flaminia/bus 88, 95, 204, 490, 491, 495/tram 2, 19. **Open** (1hr 45min sessions) 10am, noon, 3pm, 5pm daily. **Admission** €7; €6 on Thur afternoon; free under-3s. **Credit** MC, V. **Map** p338 D2.
Booking is essential at weekends and strongly advised on other days.

Planetario & Museo Astronomico
Piazza G Agnelli 10, Suburbs: EUR (06 0608, www.planetarioroma.it). Metro EUR Fermi/bus 30Exp, 170. **Open** 9am-2pm Tue-Fri; 9am-7pm Sat, Sun. **Admission** €6.50; €4.50 6-18s; free under-6s. **No credit cards**. **Map** p337.
Booking is essential for Planetarium shows.

★ Rewind Rome
Via Capo d'Africa 5, Celio (06 7707 6627, www.3drewind.com). Bus 60, 75, 85, 87, 117, 175, 271/tram 3. **Open** 9am-7pm daily. **Admission** €15; €8 reductions; under-6s free. **Credit** AmEx, DC, MC, V. **Map** p337. *Photo p247.*

Technotown
Villa Torlonia, via Spallanzani 1A, Suburbs: north (06 0608, www.technotown.it). Bus 36, 60Exp, 62, 84, 90Exp, 140. **Open** 4-7pm Tue-Fri; 2-7pm Sat; 9am-7pm Sun. **Admission** €6. **No credit cards**. **Map** p337.

★ Time Elevator
Via dei Santissimi Apostoli 20, Trevi & Quirinale (06 992 1823, www.timeelevator.it). Bus 62, 63, 81, 85, 95, 117, 119, 160, 175, 492, 628, 630.

INSIDE TRACK FOUNTAIN FUN

Though officially forbidden, there are few better ways to revive kids than letting them climb into a fountain to cool off, splash around and fill up water bottles from a spout – while you plan the rest of your tour.

Open 10.30am-7.30pm daily. **Admission** €11; €8 reductions. **Credit** MC, V. **Map** p342 E1.

PARKS & GARDENS

Besides the large, central expanse of Villa Borghese (*see p74*), with its bikes, skates and rowing boats for hire, other parks with children's attractions include:
● **Villa Celimontana** (*see p130*) has swings, a cycle/skating track for tinies and a fishpond in lush green shade dotted with fragments of classical marble statuary.
● **Villa Pamphili** (*see p161*), sprawling out to the west, is Rome's biggest park, with swings, lakes, woods, pony rides: you name it, they've got it. Finding the bit you want is not always an easy task in 1.5 square kilometres (one square mile) of parkland.
● **Villa Sciarra** (*see p161*) has swings and climbing frames, a mini-big dipper, rides, fountains, manicured lawns and an aviary.
● **Villa Ada** (*see p156*), on the north side of the city, has swings, rides, ponies and basic exercise equipment.

PUPPETS, THEATRE & MUSIC

Italy's puppet tradition centres on Sicily and Naples, but Rome also offers some good productions. One of the best-known *burattinai* (puppeteers) operates on the Gianicolo (*see p118*) and is identifiable by the sign *Non Tirate Sassi!* (Don't throw stones!). It serves up Pulcinella, just as violent and misogynistic as his English descendant Mr Punch; and don't worry about the language barrier – it's delivered in an accent so thick that most local kids understand it no better than foreigners do: it's the whacks on the head that count, anyway.
Rome's best-known children's theatre, **Teatro Verde** (circonvallazione Gianicolense 10, 06 588 2034, www.teatroverde.it, closed Aug & Sept), offers puppet shows and plays, mostly in Italian. Visit the costume and prop workshop half an hour before the curtain goes up.

BABYSITTERS & CRÈCHES

If you're staying any length of time with little ones, check out the Ladybirds mums-and-toddlers group that meets on Wednesday and Friday mornings in All Saints' English church (06 3600 1881, www.allsaintsrome.org; *see p317*). The church also runs a Sunday school and crèche during the 10.30am service and has a good selection of children's books, cards and videos on sale at the end of the service. Higher-range hotels often have their own babysitting services, and all but the most basic hotels will arrange a babysitter for you.

Film

There's plenty of action in Rome's movie scene.

Since Cinecittà opened with Fascist pomp in 1937, on 99 acres of former farmland south-east of the city, Rome has basked in its own cinematic legend. The reality was very different for many decades, with Cinecittà churning out TV variety shows and commercials, but the introduction of a film festival (*see p244*) in 2006 led Romans once more to think of their city in cinematic terms. Though that festival remains in the second division of international movie meets, the enthusiasm it creates locally is palpable. In any case, Italians are keen filmgoers, so there's no shortage of movie houses in Rome.

CINEMA THEN & NOW

Cinecittà began to make a name for itself after World War II, when US producers discovered how cheap it was to film here and the great era of 'Hollywood-on-the-Tiber' began. The Christians-to-the-lions romp *Quo Vadis?* (1951) opened the floodgates to *gli americani*, much to the delight of the post-war public and nascent paparazzi. *Roman Holiday* (1953) brought Gregory Peck and Audrey Hepburn; *The Barefoot Contessa* (1954) drew Ava Gardner and Humphrey Bogart; and Charles Vidor's *Farewell to Arms* (1957) brought Rock Hudson and Jennifer Jones. Meanwhile, Fellini was consecrating his elaborate visions in Teatro 5, the largest of Cinecittà's studio sheds, sandwiching *La Dolce Vita* between two US sword-and-sandal blockbusters, *Ben-Hur* (1959) and *Cleopatra* (1963). Spaghetti Westerns and Viscontian epics kept the place riding high through to the mid '60s, but thereafter its decline was rapid.

The 1990s saw something of a revival, with the return of big Hollywood productions, from Sylvester Stallone vehicles *Cliffhanger* and *Daylight* to Anthony Minghella's *The Talented Mr Ripley*. There was even a reprise of the over-budget glory days when Martin Scorsese's *Gangs of New York* roadshow rolled into town with Leonardo DiCaprio and Cameron Diaz. Since then Mel Gibson's *The Passion* and Wes Anderson's *The Life Aquatic* have kept the studios' costume-makers, carpenters, post-production technicians and stuntmen busy, while all-star crime caper *Ocean's Twelve* used the studios' production and office facilities. But

the biggest production of recent years has been an HBO-BBC TV series, *Rome* – television yes, but on a truly cinematic scale.

It's not just foreign directors whose cameras are rolling in Rome. Italians are still making around a hundred films a year. True, Italian cinema ain't what it used to be. Masterpieces have been thin on the ground in the last couple of decades or so, but there are some stirrings of talent among the younger generations of Italian director.

Matteo Garrone's bleak but adrenalin-fuelled Neapolitan mafia drama *Gomorra* (*Gomorrah*, 2008), Paolo Sorrentino's original Giulio Andreotti biopic-operetta *Il Divo* (2008) and Michele Frammartino's remarkable *Le Quattro Volte* (2010) – a metaphysical drama set in rural Calabria – prove that there's life in the old dog yet. Meanwhile, some directors from an older generation are still going strong, including intense maverick Marco Bellocchio and politicised comedian Nanni Moretti.

MOVIEGOING IN ROME

Italians are enthusiastic moviegoers. A rash of inner-city miniplexes and vast suburban

> ### INSIDE TRACK
> ### SHOW TIMES
>
> For a standard 90-minute film, the four daily screenings are usually at 4.30pm, 6.30pm, 8.30pm and 10.30pm. In summer, there are many opportunities to view films outdoors in Rome.

multiplexes sprung up in the 1990s, to be greeted with a leap in audience figures. Arthouse fans are well served by the Circuito Cinema chain, which controls 14 first-run outlets (including the **Metropolitan** – though beware: this cinema is regularly threatened with closure – and **Nuovo Olimpia**), and the first-run independent **Nuovo Sacher**, owned by cult director Nanni Moretti. **Filmstudio** is a two-screen reincarnation of the club that launched a thousand earnest film buffs in the 1960s and '70s; **Sala Trevi** is a *centro storico* single-screen space dedicated to retrospectives.

Housed in a former pleasure pavilion in the Villa Borghese gardens, and sponsored by Rome city council, **Casa del Cinema** ('house of cinema') hosts film-related exhibitions, press conferences and presentations. But it also has an eclectic screening programme.

The downside is the dubbing. Films in the original language (*lingua originale* or *versione originale* – VO in newspaper listings) with

subtitles are rare. But the two-screen **Nuovo Olimpia**, just off via del Corso, and the **Metropolitan** have regular VO programming. The **Alcazar** and **Nuovo Sacher** often show their current attraction in *lingua originale* on Monday and/or Tuesday.

The best source of information for what's on, including summer venues, is the local section of daily newspaper *La Repubblica*, while the paper's website hosts www.trovacinema.it with programme details for first-run cinemas all over Italy. Programmes generally change on Fridays.

FIRST-RUN CINEMAS

Alcazar
Via Cardinale Merry del Val 14, Trastevere (06 588 0099). Bus 780, H/tram 8. **Tickets** €7.50; €5.50 reductions. **No credit cards.** **Map** p342 C3.

All red and plush, this was one of the first major Rome cinemas to screen VO films on Mondays.

Students at the **Sala Trevi** film school.

Walk Many Locations, Two Ice-creams

Every corner in Rome can seem strangely familiar: you'll be wondering which iconic movie featured its peeling stucco or picturesque fountain. Italian cinema's finest hour was post-war Neo-Realism when an astonishing number of grainy, black and white movies of searing psychological intensity were shot on shoestrings in the streets of 'Hollywood-on-the-Tiber'. If you know your Italian movies, you'll feel you know Rome already.

Start your film walk on via Veneto, perusing the historic snapshots of the stars displayed outside the expensive establishments that line this leafy boulevard, but don't linger too long: the *dolce vita* went elsewhere long ago. If you need lunch, make for the alfresco **Cinecaffè** (*see p209*) in the Casa del Cinema, but save dessert for later: this itinerary includes the two best ice-cream shops in Rome (some would argue the world). The first – the legendary **San Crispino** (*see p208*) in via della Panetteria was, it seems, the inspiration behind the Julia Roberts vehicle *Eat Pray Love* (2010), the latest Hollywood blockbuster to be filmed in Rome.

Take your tub – with creole lemon sorbet, or ginger and cinnamon ice-cream – to the **Trevi Fountain** (*see p67*), backdrop to one of the most famous embraces in movie history, in Fellini's *La Dolce Vita* (1960; *pictured*). Instead of emulating Anita

Ekberg or heart-throb Marcello Mastroianni in their clinch, root about for some loose change. Throwing *Three Coins in a Fountain* (1954) may bring you back to Rome… and the money goes to charity.

Cross busy via del Tritone where key scenes of Vittorio De Sica's *Bicycle Thieves* (1948) were filmed, and head for the grand sweep of the **Spanish Steps** (*see p89*) to pose for the cameras like Audrey Hepburn and Gregory Peck in William Wyler's charming 1953 hit *Roman Holiday*.

Swing by **piazza Navona** (*see p98*) and gaze up at the far northern end for the rooftop apartment where Sophia Loren performs a memorably hilarious striptease for a languid Marcello Mastroianni in another De Sica classic, *Yesterday, Today and Tomorrow* (1963).

Via dei Coronari leads to via del Panico and ivy-covered palazzo Taverna, which housed Nicole Kidman in aristocratic splendour in Jane Campion's 1996 *Portrait of a Lady*. Just off via dei Coronari, the **Gelateria del Teatro** (*see p213*) serves such flavours as Sicilian almond or divine chocolate combos. Take your treat along to the river and enjoy it on the bridge leading to **Castel Sant'Angelo** (*see p150*), where Pier Paolo Pasolini's delinquent *Accattone* (1961) made the sign of the cross before plunging into the Tiber for a dare.

Roman locations feature in many other films too (*see p325*).

Metropolitan

*Via del Corso 7, Tridente (06 320 0933, www.
circuitocinema.com). Metro Flaminio/bus 95, 117,
119, 495, 628, 926/tram 2.* **Tickets** €7.50; €5.50
reductions. **No credit cards. Map** p338 D2.
Don't schlep across town to this four-screener without checking it still exists: closure is threatened regularly. If it's open, anything from blockbusters to
films from the artier edge of Hollywood often run in
the *lingua originale* on one of the four screens.

Nuovo Olimpia

*Via in Lucina 16G, Tridente (06 686 1068, www.
circuitocinema.com). Bus 52, 53, 61, 62, 63, 71, 80,
85, 116, 117, 119, 160, 850.* **Tickets** €7.50; €5.50
reductions. **No credit cards. Map** p339 E4.
Hidden away just off via del Corso, this two-screener
belongs to the arthouse-oriented Circuito Cinema
group; one or both screens now usually show films
in the *lingua originale*.

Nuovo Sacher

*Largo Ascianghi 1, Trastevere (06 581 8116,
www.sacherfilm.eu). Bus 44, 75, 780, H/tram 3,
8.* **Tickets** €7.50; €5.50 reductions. **No credit
cards. Map** p343 C4.
The Nuovo Sacher is owned and run by veteran
director Nanni Moretti, and is a meeting place for
local cinematic talent. VO films are usually shown
on Mondays or Tuesdays.

CINEMA D'ESSAI & CINECLUBS

Generally small and cheap, *cinema d'essai*
mainly feature classics or contemporary arthouse cinema, occasionally in *versione originale*.
In these, and even smaller cineclubs, the best of
Italy's cinema heritage can be seen. A *tessera*
(membership card) is required by many clubs,
but these are free or carry a minimal charge.

Azzurro Scipioni

*Via degli Scipioni 82, Prati (06 3973 7161,
www.azzurroscipioni.com). Metro Lepanto/bus
30, 70, 81, 280, 913.* **Tickets** (with annual
€2 membership) €6; €4 reductions. **No credit
cards. Map** p338 B3.

Azzurro Scipioni is run by director Silvio Agosti. It
has two screens showing art-house successes, world
cinema classics and themed seasons.

Casa del Cinema

*Largo Marcello Mastroianni 1, Veneto & Borghese
(06 423 601, www.casadelcinema.it). Bus 95, 116,
490, 495.* **No credit cards. Map** p340 B3.
In the Villa Borghese park, the Casa is used for
film-related presentations and screenings.
▶ *Even if you're not there to see a film,
the Cinecaffè (see p209) inside the Casa del
Cinema is a great place for a coffee or lunch.*

Filmstudio

*Via degli Orti di Alibert 1C, Trastevere (334 178
0632, www.filmstudioroma.com). Bus 23, 280.*
Tickets €5; €4 reductions. **No credit cards.
Map** p342 A1.
This historic Rome film club alternates first-run arthouse films with more *recherché* treats and themed
seasons, which include the occasional film in the
lingua originale.

Sala Trevi

*Vicolo del Puttarello 25, Trevi & Quirinale
(06 678 1206, www.snc.it). Bus 52, 53, 61,
63, 71, 80, 85, 95, 116, 119, 160, 850.*
Tickets €4; €3 reductions. **No credit
cards. Map** p341 A6.
This 100-seater cinema belongs to Italy's national
film archive. It shares its basement location with a
400sq m (4,300sq ft) archaeological site based
around two ancient Roman *insulae* (apartment
blocks), which can be seen through the glass panels
at the side of the main screening room.

FESTIVALS & SUMMER PROGRAMMES

Around the beginning of July, a raft of
second-run or arthouse open-air cinema
feasts is launched as part of the **Estate
Romana** festivities (*see p242*), many of
them in breathtaking settings. Scour the
local press for details or check the www.
060608.it website.

In addition, several *arene* (open-air
screens) – including one behind the **Nuovo
Sacher** (*see above*) – provide a chance to
catch that blockbuster you missed or to take
in an underground classic.

Two regular mini-festivals – **Cannes a Roma**
and **Venezia a Roma** – show a selection of
original-language films from the Cannes and
Venice film festivals a few days after the festivals
themselves close (in May and September
respectively). The **Festival Internazionale
del Film di Roma** (*see p244*) in October/
November is also a great time to catch some
new and up-coming releases.

Galleries

Contemporary art hits its stride.

As much a key part of an aspiring artist's education as it ever was, Rome's contribution to the art world could never be overestimated. In terms of quality and range (never mind the fact that almost all of Rome's greats were actually produced here too), the city is one giant art history lesson. But it's not just chapel ceilings and stunning ancient architecture and magnificent monuments – thanks to some impressive recent openings, it is now also a good time for modern and contemporary art in Rome. **MAXXI** and **MACRO**, in particular, have given this traditionally lacklustre sector a healthy shot in

the arm – and some seriously impressive exhibition space to show off about. The Eternal City is no longer resting on its laurels and has begun to truly embrace the contemporary.

THE SCENE

If Larry Gagosian's bells and whistles inauguration of his first Italian gallery in 2007 is now a distant memory, the arrival of the extraordinary **MAXXI** in 2010 and the slow-but-steady expansion of **MACRO** mean that finally the contemporary is no longer relegated to small galleries in tucked-away locations. The challenge now will be finding sufficient high-quality product to fill the new spaces.

These are far from being the only large public spaces where the modern and the contemporary are (fairly) regular attractions. The immense **Palazzo delle Esposizioni** reopened in 2008 after lengthy refurbishment and has resumed its role as container for high-class shows on themes from the very ancient to the very contemporary. Macro's offshoot in the Testaccio district – housed in stunning spaces inside the former municipal slaughterhouse – tends to showcase the young and the upcoming, local and international.

Other spaces dedicated to modern and contemporary art include **Cinecittà Due Arte Contemporanea** (viale Palmiro Togliatti 2, 06 722 0910) inside the slick Cinecittà Due shopping mall in the eastern suburbs; the harmonious rooms dedicated to art in Renzo Piano's **Auditorium-Parco della Musica** (*see p266* **The Sound of Perfection**); and the archaeological area inside the **Mercati di Traiano** (Trajan's markets, *see p65*), where monumental ruins provide a dramatic setting

for installations and photography. The **Centrale Montemartini** (*see p122*) sometimes displays photographs among its classical statuary. The **GATE** gallery (via Giolitti 34) inside Termini railway station had put its exhibition programme on hold as this guide went to press.

Major shows of modern and contemporary art and photography are held inside the **Vittoriano** complex (*see p59*). Other large central venues include the **Scuderie del Quirinale** (*see p73*), **Palazzo Ruspoli** (*see p89*), the **Museo del Corso** (*see p100*) and the **Chiostro del Bramante** in Santa Maria della Pace (*see p95*). Or if you just want to take it easy, head to via Margutta in Tridente (*photo p254*), which is full of small galleries and antique shops and makes for a pleasant art stroll.

Held of late in autumn as often as in its habitual spring slot, the **FotoGrafia Festival Internazionale di Roma** (*see also p244; photo p255*, shows Cedric Delsaux's *The Dark Lens* from the 2010 festival) encompasses photographic exhibitions in museums and galleries as well as less mainstream venues.

To find out what's going on at any given time, pick up the *Art Guide* (www.artguide.it), a free handout available in most galleries. It provides listings of exhibitions and information about openings. The www.merzbau.it site is informative and constantly updated. The 'Trovaroma' supplement of Thursday's *La Repubblica* has a comprehensive arts section with reliable reviews; you'll find an English-language summary at the back. *Wanted in*

Via Margutta. *See p253.*

Rome, an English-language fortnightly magazine, has an exhaustive section with venue details and exhibition reviews.

Only the most renowned or reliable galleries are listed. Even so, opening times and summer closures vary from year to year: many close Saturday and open Monday from mid-June.

THE TRIDENTE

Il Gabbiano

Via della Frezza 51 (06 322 7049, www.galleria ilgabbiano.com). Metro Flaminio/bus 117, 119, 628. **Open** 11am-1.30pm, 4-7.30pm Tue-Sat. Closed Aug. **No credit cards. Map** p338 D3.

This classic gallery has been showing the work of well-known artists since 1967.

▶ *Il Gabbiano is ideally situated for enjoying the lunch buffet at 'Gusto (see p188).*

Gagosian Gallery

Via Francesco Crispi 16 (06 4208 6498, www.gagosian.com). Metro Spagna/bus 117, 119, 628. **Open** 10.30am-7pm Tue-Sat. Closed 2wks Aug. **No credit cards. Map** p341 B4.

This international art dealer displays the biggest names of the art world in a startling white space. *Photos p256.*

Magazzino d'Arte Moderna

Via dei Prefetti 17 (06 687 5951, www.magazzinoartemoderna.com). Bus 62, 63, 81, 85, 95, 116, 117, 119, 160, 175, 492, 628, 630, 850. **Open** 11am-3pm, 4-8pm Tue-Fri; 11am-1pm, 4-8pm Sat. Closed Aug. **No credit cards. Map** p339 D4.

Strong on installations, videos and photography, this gallery works very closely with the artists that it promotes.

La Nuova Pesa

Via del Corso 530 (06 361 0892, www.nuovapesa.it). Metro Flaminio/bus 117, 119. **Open** 10.30am-1pm, 3-7pm Mon-Fri. Closed Aug. **No credit cards. Map** p339 E4.

In the 1950s, La Nuova Pesa organised the first postwar Italian shows of Picasso, Gris and Léger. The gallery now works with upcoming Roman artists and big international names alike.

Valentina Moncada Arte Contemporanea
Via Margutta 54 (06 320 7956, www.valentinamoncada.com). Metro Spagna/ bus 117, 119. **Open** 2-7pm Mon-Fri. Closed mid July-early Sept. **No credit cards.** **Map** p338 E3.
Federico Fellini lived on this street, fashionable in the 1950s and now filled with small galleries and antique dealers. Hidden away in a picturesque garden among a series of purpose-built 19th-century artists' studios, this gallery focuses on photography, alternating between 20th-century masters and emerging artists.

PANTHEON & NAVONA

Monitor
Via Sforza Cesarini 43A (06 3937 8024, www.monitoronline.org). Bus 40Exp, 46, 62, 64, 916. **Open** 1-7pm Tue-Sat. Closed Aug. **No credit cards. Map** p339 C5.
This gallery is dedicated to young, up-and-coming artists working mainly in video.

Studio Trisorio Roma
Vicolo delle Vacche 12 (06 6813 6189, www.studiotrisorio.com). Bus 30Exp, 40Exp, 46, 62, 64, 87, 628, 916. **Open** 4-8pm Tue-Sat. Closed Aug. **No credit cards.** **Map** p339 C5.
Run by mother-and-daughter team Lucia and Laura Trisorio, this branch of a Naples gallery shows the work of important artists such as Rebecca Horn, Tom Wesselman and Enzo Cucchi.

VM21 Arte Contemporanea
Via della Vetrina 21 (06 6889 1365, www.vm21contemporanea.com). Bus 30Exp, 40Exp, 46, 62, 64, 87, 628, 916. **Open** 11am-7.30pm Mon-Fri; 4.30-7.30pm Sat. Closed mid July-Aug. **No credit cards. Map** p339 C5.
This spacious, attractive gallery collaborates with notable Italian and foreign artists working in a representative selection of media.

GHETTO & CAMPO DE' FIORI

Galleria Alessandra Bonomo
Via del Gesù 62 (06 6992 5858, www.bonomogallery.com). Bus 30Exp, 40Exp, 46, 62, 63, 64, 70, 81/tram 8. **Open** 3-7pm Mon-Sat. Closed Aug. **No credit cards. Map** p342 D1.

FotoGrafia Festival. *See p253.*

Alexander Calder (above) and Takashi Murakami (below) at the **Gagosian**. *See p254*.

Tucked away in a peaceful palazzo courtyard, with light streaming through its beautiful, huge windows, this gallery, run by a member of the Bonomo dynasty, shows a mix of established Italian and emerging foreign artists.

Lipanje Puntin Arte Contemporanea
Via di Montoro 10 (06 6830 7780, www. lipanjepuntin.com). Bus 40Exp, 46, 62, 64, 116, 916. **Open** 2-8pm Tue-Sat. Closed Aug. **No credit cards. Map** p339 C6.
This branch of a Trieste gallery shows a roster of successful artists, whose bold work is often focused on the pop genre or photography.

Il Ponte Contemporanea
Via di Monserrato 23 (06 6880 1351, www.ilpontecontemporanea.com). Bus 23, 40Exp, 46, 62, 64, 116, 280, 916. **Open** noon-8pm Tue-Sat. Closed Aug. **No credit cards. Map** p339 C6.
This stylish gallery focuses mostly on photography and installation art. Pierre & Gilles and Tracey Moffat had their first Italian shows here.

Valentina Bonomo Arte Contemporanea
Via del Portico d'Ottavia 13 (06 683 2766, www.galleriabonomo.com). Bus 23, 30Exp, 63, 280, 780, H/tram 8. **Open** 11am-1pm, 3-7pm

Tue-Sat. Closed Aug-mid Sept.
No credit cards. Map p342 D2.
This space exhibits work by both established international artists and young photographers.

TRASTEVERE & GIANICOLO

Galleria Lorcan O'Neill
Via Orti d'Alibert 1E (06 6889 2980, www.lorcanoneill.com). Bus 23, 280. **Open** noon-8pm Mon-Fri; 2-8pm Sat. Closed 3wks Aug. **No credit cards. Map** p342 A1.
Headed by the former director of a major London gallery, Lorcan O'Neill is a glitzy space that is perhaps Rome's most fashionable private gallery. Inaugurations of blue-chip exhibitions invariably turn into social events in which the jet set mixes with artists.

Studio Stefania Miscetti
Via delle Mantellate 14 (06 6880 5880, www.studiostefaniamiscetti.com). Bus 23, 280. **Open** 4-8pm Tue-Sat; Mon by appointment. Closed July-Sept. **No credit cards. Map** p342 B1.
One of the more established of Trastevere's commercial art galleries, Miscetti holds unusual shows of sculpture and installations.

Volume!
Via di San Francesco di Sales 86 (06 689 2431, www.fondazionevolume.com). Bus 23, 280. **Open** 5-7.30pm Tue-Fri. Closed Aug. **Map** p339 B2.
A meeting place for those who are passionate about experimental art, the Volume! space shows almost exclusively site-specific installations, which make the most of the setting.

CELIO & SAN GIOVANNI

Galleria Sala 1
Piazza di Porta San Giovanni 10 (06 700 8691, www.salauno.com). Metro San Giovanni/bus 81, 85, 87, 186, 571, 850/tram 3. **Open** 4.30-7.30pm Tue-Sat. Closed mid July-late Aug. **No credit cards. Map** p344 E3.
For 40 years Sala 1 has been a pioneer in Rome's art world, hosting premières of young artists and groundbreaking international exhibitions.

Galleria SALES
Via dei Querceti 4-5 (06 7759 1122, www.galleriasales.it). Metro Colosseo/bus 60Exp, 85, 87, 117, 850/tram 3. **Open** 3.30-7.30pm Tue-Sat. Closed Aug. **No credit cards. Map** p344 D3.
Located in the Celio district, SALES continues to show rising young international artists.

Gay & Lesbian

Two steps forward, one back – it's a challenging time for the gay scene.

A country in which a philandering prime minister (Silvio Berlusconi) can state 'it's better to like pretty girls than to be gay' with a minimum of outrage and protest as a result is, clearly, a country in which things aren't too hot for the gay community. And after a heady period in the early 21st century of growing tolerance and expansion of a lively scene, Rome – now with a centre-right (with the emphasis on right) administration – is suffering more than most Italian cities from a degree of anti-gay backlash. Acts of aggression and arson attacks on gay venues have actually been on the rise for several years. But it's not all doom and gloom, despite the current climate, Rome's gay and lesbian community still manages to get out and have a good time.

THE SCENE

Spearheading activities in the city are the historic **Mario Mieli** group and the newer, hyperactive **Di'Gay Project** (for both, *see p262*). A diverse gay market continues to cater for distinct clienteles, with restaurants, pubs, clubs and bars attracting punters of all ages. Mixed one-nighters allow men and women to have fun under the same roof – and, for that matter, in the open air: one of the successes in the Roman calendar is the summer **Gay Village** (*see below*) which soldiers bravely on despite city hall's best efforts to put spokes in the wheels of recent editions. With its concerts, various dancefloors and bars, it's now worth staying in town for the traditionally becalmed months of July and August.

BARS, CLUBS & RESTAURANTS

Admission prices to Rome's bars and clubs can be confusing. Some places may charge no entrance fee, but will instead oblige you to buy a drink, while others include the first of your drinks in the admission price. Many venues also ask for an Arcigay card, which costs €15 for annual membership. The card can be bought at any venue that requires it and is valid throughout Italy, rather than just in Rome. In most bars you're given a printed slip on which the bar staff tick off what you consume; you pay the total amount on leaving

the venue. Where we have not specified an admission price, entry is free.

Rome now has a few rainbow-flagged restaurants. At the **Asinocotto** (via dei Vascellari 48, 06 589 8985, www.asinocotto. com, closed Mon dinner, Sat & Sun lunch, average €45), cook Giuliano Brenna impresses as much with his right-on political stance as with his culinary skills, while **Edoardo II** (vicolo Margana 14, 06 6994 2419, www.edoardo secondo.com, closed Tue, average €35) serves up double-entendre specialities like their chocolate *orgasmo* dessert.

★ Gay Village
Venue changes from year to year (no phone, www.gayvillage.it). **Open** *Late June-early Sept* 7pm-3am daily. **Admission** approx €15/wk. **No credit cards**.
A ten-week open-air bonanza that makes summer the pinkest season of the year: bars, restaurants, live acts, discos, cinema – a great event for boys and girls alike. Venue and contact details change from year to year, so check the website as the date approaches.

Aventine & Testaccio

L'Alibi
Via di Monte Testaccio 40-44 (06 574 3448, www.lalibi.it). Metro Piramide/bus 23, 95, 716,

---

About the author
Peter Douglas *is a teacher, translator and travel writer. He has lived in Rome most of his adult life.*

92N/tram 3. **Open** 11.30pm-5am Thur-Sun.
Admission €10-€20 (incl 1 drink). **Credit** MC, V.
Map p343 D6.

The Alibi paved the way for Testaccio's boom as a
nightlife quarter with an alternative feel. An increasingly straight-friendly approach, and the fact that
it's showing its age rather, has diluted its success
with punters. It's still a good place to bop the night
away, however, with a well-oiled sound system covering two floors in winter and three in summer, when
the roof garden comes into its own. If you can get
yourself on to the guest list, admission costs €10.

Frutta e Verdura
*Via di Monte Testaccio 94 (347 879 7063,
www.fruttaeverdura.roma.it). Metro Piramide/
bus 23, 95, 716, 92N/tram 3.* **Open** 4.30-10.30am
Sun. **Admission** (with Arcigay card; incl 1 drink)
€15. **No credit cards**.

This after-hours club moved here recently from the
eastern suburbs and not all its fans are happy about
the new, smaller venue. But it's central at least for
into-the-morning cruisin' and dancin'.

▶ *For nearby clubs to frequent until this after-
hours venue opens, see pp268-276* **Nightlife**.

Celio & San Giovanni

Coming Out
*Via San Giovanni in Laterano 8 (06 700 9871,
www.comingout.it). Metro Colosseo/bus 85, 850,
55N.* **Open** 10am-2am daily. **Credit** MC, V. **Map**
p344 C3.

Victim of a nasty arson attack a few years back, this
popular pub offers quick lunches, evening snacks,
beers and cocktails to a predominantly youthful
crowd of men and women. A useful address if you
need a place to meet before heading off in search of
something a bit more frantic. There's a 6.30-8.30pm
happy hour; plus a DJ set from 11pm on Wed, Thur
and Sun. *Photo p260.*

Skyline
*Via Pontremoli 36 (06 700 9431, www.skyline
club.it). Metro San Giovanni/bus 360, 55N/tram 3.*
Open 10.30pm-3am Mon-Thur, Sun; 10.30pm-4am
Fri, Sat. **Admission** (with Arcigay card) free
(Tue-Fri, Sun), €5 (Mon, Sat) with compulsory
drink. **No credit cards**. **Map** off p345 E4.

The relaxed mixed crowd at Skyline ensures there's
constant movement between the bar areas, the video
parlour and the cruisy cubicle and dark areas. Hosts
naked parties on Mondays. *Photo p260.*

ARTS & ENTERTAINMENT

Gay Village.

Coming Out. See p259.

Monti & Esquilino

Hangar

Via in Selci 69A (06 488 1397, www.hangar online.it). Metro Cavour/bus 75, 84, 40N. **Open** 10.30pm-2.30am Mon, Wed-Sun. Closed 3wks Aug. **Admission** (with Arcigay card) free. **No credit cards**. **Map** p344 C2.

American John Moss has been at the helm of Rome's oldest gay bar since it opened over two decades ago. Hangar maintains its friendly but sexy atmosphere whether half full (occasionally midweek) or packed (at weekends and for porn-video Monday and striptease Thursday). Two bar zones are linked by a long, dark passage, designed for cruising before consuming. Much to the delight of visiting tourists, and the twenty- and thirtysomething clientele, the venue also has a small dark area.

ONE-NIGHTERS

Gorgeous I Am

Alpheus, via del Commercio 36, Testaccio (340 753 8396, www.gorgeousroma.it). Metro Piramide/bus 23, 271, 769, N2, N3, N9. **Open** 11pm-4am Sat. **Admission** €10. **No credit cards**. **Map** p123 A2.

This one-nighter at the cavernous Alpheus club is a rather glamorous affair, featuring drag shows and programming a host of good-quality guest and resident DJs. There's a women-only room too, hosted by the Venus Rising crew.

★ Muccassassina

Qube, via di Portonaccio 212, Suburbs: east (06 541 3985, www.muccassassina.com). Metro Tiburtina/bus 409. **Open** 11pm-4am Fri. **Admission** (incl 1 drink) €15. **No credit cards**.

The Mario Mieli crew (*see right*) were trail-blazers of the gay one-nighter – and their Friday-night fest at the Qube still packs them in. Three floors of pop and house create a great atmosphere throughout. Members get in for €10. *Photo p263*.

Omogenic

Circolo degli Artisti (for listing, see p276). **Open** 11pm-late Fri. **Admission** €6. **No credit cards**.

Di'Gay Project's Friday rival to the Muccassassina always attracts an eclectic crowd of young boppers. If you're a member of the Di'Gay Project (*see p262*), you get in for €5.

SAUNAS

Europa Multiclub

Via Aureliana 40, Veneto & Borghese (06 482 3650, www.europamulticlub.com). Metro Repubblica/bus 36, 60Exp, 60N. **Open** 1pm-midnight Mon-Thur; 1pm Fri until midnight Sun. **Admission** (with Arcigay card) €17; €15 after 11pm Fri, Sat. **Credit** MC, V. **Map** p341 D4.

Skyline. See p259.

Cruising the Casilina

Sex and the suburbs.

All roads may lead to Rome, but many also lead straight out again to a plethora of cruising clubs that have sprung up on the eastern outskirts of the city. Sex in the suburbs is flourishing – though be warned: there are still some nasty characters out there, and recently they've been feeling empowered.

The working-class via Casilina, much loved by Pasolini, was the first to set the trend with **K Men's Club**, the first venue in the capital wholly devoted to the joy of the dark encounter.

Moving to the via Prenestina area, **Il Diavolo Dentro** is a stark, candle-lit basement that opens its doors to weekend thirtysomething hedonists, whose inner devils are tempted at the club's theme nights. Anyone for an orgy or a black mass (hoods free of charge)?

Further south, along via Appia Nuova, is **Frequency**, an unassuming sex club with a large bar area, which indulges its young regulars with an 'extreme naked Thursday', a 'black' candle-lit Friday and a fine choice of underwear or the all-together for its Sunday evening meets.

Some additional words of warning: the harder-core and further-flung the club, the greater chance there is for sudden closure – so ring ahead. As well as the 105 bus, the Casilina area is served by the Termini–Pantano tram service. Night buses back to the centre can be irregular so take your chances or ask the doorman to call you a taxi.

Il Diavolo Dentro

Largo Itri 23, Suburbs: east (392 490 7271, www.ildiavolodentro.com). Bus 20, 12N/tram 5, 14. **Open** 3-7pm Tue; 11pm-5am Fri, Sat; 6pm-3am Sun. **Admission** (with Arcigay card; incl 1 drink) free Tue; €10 Fri; €8 Sat; €6 (undressed), €10 (dressed) Sun. **No credit cards.**

Frequency

Via Enea 34, Suburbs: east (06 785 1504, 340 693 9719, www.thefrequency. it). Metro Furio Camillo/bus 628, 55N. **Open** 10pm-3am Mon-Thur, Sun; 10pm-4am Fri, Sat. **Admission** (with Arcigay card) free Mon, Wed; €5 Tue, Thur-Sun. **No credit cards.**

K Men's Club

Via A Amati 6-8, Suburbs: east (06 2170 1268, www.sexclub.it). Bus 105, 50N/tram Termini-Pantano (Filarete stop). **Open** 10.30pm-3am Tue-Thur, Sun; 10.30pm-4am Fri, Sat. **Admission** (with Arcigay card) €5-€6. **No credit cards.**

Europa has 1,300 sq m (4,300sq ft) of gym facilities and pools, complete with waterfalls. Leave your togs in multicoloured lockers and cruise down to the steam and sweat rooms and romantically star-lit booths. It's a mixed crowd, but with young, muscled tendencies. Open 24 hours over the weekend.

Mediterraneo

Via P Villari 3, Esquilino (06 7720 5934, www. saunamediterraneo.it). Metro Manzoni/bus 85, 87/tram 3. **Open** 1-11pm daily. **Admission** (with Arcigay card) €15. **No credit cards.** **Map** p344 D3.

Tasteful decor and an emphasis on hygiene set this sauna apart from its rivals. The steam room and jacuzzi provide repose prior to exertion in the 'relax rooms'. All body types, ages and nationalities.

INFORMATION & ORGANISATIONS

There are over 70 gay activist organisations in Italy, mostly in the north. Foremost among these are the organisations belonging to the Bologna-based Arcigay network.

Arcigay Nazionale

Via Don Minzoni 18, 40121 Bologna (051 095 7241, www.arcigay.it).

Arcigay Roma

Via Zabaglia 14, Testaccio (06 6450 1102, toll-free helpline 800 713 713, www.arcigay roma.it). Metro Piramide/bus 23, 30Exp, 75, 95, 280, 719, 781/tram 3. **Map** p341 D4.

The local Arci group gets together on Tuesday 7-9pm (men and women, over 26) and Friday evenings (6-9pm 16-26 year olds).

Circolo Mario Mieli di Cultura Omosessuale

Via Efeso 2A, Suburbs: south (06 541 3985, www.mariomieli.org). Metro San Paolo/bus 23. **Open** 10.30am-6.30pm Mon-Fri.

Named after the pioneer author and thinker Mario Mieli, this is the most important gay, lesbian and trans-gender group in Rome. It provides a base for debates and events, and offers counselling and care facilities. Its Muccassassina one-nighter (*see p260*) are highly popular, and it also organises Pride events (www.romapride.it) during the summer.

Di'Gay Project
Via Costantino 82, Suburbs: south (06 513 4741, www.digayproject.org). Metro San Paolo/bus 23. **Open** *Sept-June* 10am-6pm Mon-Fri.
Hosts the summer Gay Village (*see p258*) as well as a series of other worthy events. A welcome group meets at 5pm on Sundays and general meetings are held from 5.30pm to 7pm every second Thur (check the website for details).

Epicentro Ursino Romano
Information 392 579 6357, www.epicentro ursino.com.
Rome's burgeoning bear community is well served by the enterprising EUR. Check the website for details of their Subwoofer parties, held on the last weekend of the month.

Leather Club Roma
www.lcroma.com.
The LCR, a group devoted to leather and fetish lifestyles, holds themed evenings, fetish nights and second-hand leatherwear markets.

PUBLICATIONS & OUTLETS

Edicole (newsstands) are often good for gay books and videos; the *edicole* in *piazze* dei Cinquecento (map p341 D5) and Colonna (map p339 E5) are treasure troves of porn: discreet amounts are displayed by day, but piles of it come out at night.

Aut
A monthly magazine published by the Circolo Mario Mieli (*see p261*), containing interesting articles and fairly up-to-date listings. It's available free at many gay venues.

INSIDE TRACK IN THE NUDE

Rome's nudist beach at **Capocotta** also survives as one of the gay community's alfresco glories. *Il buco* ('the hole') is a short stretch of sandy dunes located between the family-fun resorts of Ostia (*see p287*) and Torvaianica (*see p304*). Gay men and women of all ages flock to *il buco* from June to September, looking to enjoy sun, sand and (the less than crystal-clear) sea. Nudism was once the order of the day, but swimming costumes are now tolerated.

Babilonia
A lively monthly magazine (www.babilonia magazine.it) that contains a detailed listings guide for things to do across the whole of Italy.

Studio Know How
Via San Gallicano 13, Trastevere (06 5833 5692). Bus 23, 280/tram 8. **Open** 10.30am-2pm, 3-8pm Tue-Sat. Closed 2wks Aug. **Credit** AmEx, DC, MC, V. **Map** p342 C3.
This Roman branch of a sex-shop chain founded in Milan focuses exclusively on accoutrements for gays and lesbians.

Lesbian Rome

There are two identifiable factions in *Roma lesbica*: older lesbian groups, which meet at the **Buon Pastore** centre (*see right*), have their roots in 1970s feminism and continue to claim separate identity from men, gay or straight; younger lesbians, on the other hand, tend to favour the less separatist **Arci-Lesbica** association or join the lads at **Circolo Mario Mieli** (*see p261*) or the **Di'Gay Project** (*see above*). Rome has yet to host a permanent lesbian club, but joint ventures like **Gay Village**, **Muccassassina** and other one-nighters (*see p260*) get a good turnout from lesbians, and bars like **Coming Out** (*see p259*) are also popular with women. Check noticeboards at gay and women's bookshops or stop by the Buon Pastore. Try www.lista lesbica.it and www.arcilesbica.it too.

ONE-NIGHTERS

See also p260 **Gorgeous I Am**.

Venus Rising
Goa (for listing, see p274), www.venusrising.it. **Open** 11pm-late last Sun of month. **Admission** (incl 1 drink) €10. **No credit cards**.
Muccassassina and Omogenic (for both, *see p260*) attract their fair share of women, but Venus Rising is the only women-only one-nighter in the capital.

ORGANISATIONS

See also p261 **Circolo Mario Mieli di Cultura Omosessuale**.

Arci-Lesbica Roma
Via Zabaglia 14, Testaccio (06 6450 1102, toll-free helpline 800 713 713, www.arcilesbica.it/ roma). Metro Piramide/bus 23, 30Exp, 75, 95, 280, 719, 781/tram 3. **Map** p341 D4.
Arci-Lesbica organises once-monthly women-only meetings (third Tue of month 9-11pm). Phone or consult the website for other events.

ARTS & ENTERTAINMENT

Muccassassina. See p260.

Casa Internazionale delle Donne (Centro Buon Pastore)

Via della Lungara 19, Trastevere (06 6840 1720, www.casainternazionaledelledonne.org). Bus 23, 280. **Map** *p342 B2.*

Once an abandoned 17th-century convent, this vast riverside complex is still better known as the Centro Buon Pastore (Good Shepherd Centre). Over 40 women's associations now use the building. There are also various facilities for visitors, including the Luna e L'altra restaurant (*see below*).

Collegamento lesbiche italiane (CLI)

Casa Internazionale delle Donne, via San Francesco di Sales 1B, Trastevere (06 686 4201, www.clrbp.it). Bus 23, 280. **Map** *p342 B2.*

This separatist group has midweek meetings in the Buon Pastore women's centre; you don't need to be a member to take part. It also organises conferences, literary evenings, concerts and dances.

ACCOMMODATION, OUTLETS & RESTAURANTS

Area Cultura

Via San Francesco di Sales 1A, Trastevere (06 6819 3001). Bus 23, 280. **Map** *p342 B2.*

The Buon Pastore offers a range of book presentations, readings, creative writing workshops and other events for the literary-inclined. There is also wall space for art exhibitions.

La Foresteria Orsa Maggiore

Via San Francesco di Sales 1A, Trastevere (06 689 3753, www.casainternazionaledelle donne.org). Bus 23, 280. **Credit** *MC, V.* **Map** *p342 B2.*

The Orsa Maggiore (Great Bear) hostel provides out-of-towners with 13 brightly decorated rooms. All are on the second floor, and some of them have an en suite bathroom. The prices range from €26 to €75 per person per night.

Luna e L'altra

Via San Francesco di Sales 1A, Trastevere (06 6889 2465, www.casainternazionaledelle donne.org). Bus 23, 280. **Open** *1-2.30pm, 8.30-11pm Mon-Fri; 8.30-11pm Sat.* **Credit** *AmEx, DC, MC, V.* **Map** *p342 B2.*

Luna e L'altra is a restaurant within the walls of the historic Buon Pastore women's centre. Self-service catering at lunchtime gives way to an à la carte menu in the evening, with the emphasis on imaginative vegetarian dishes. Male diners are only allowed in at lunchtimes.

Zipper Travel

Via dei Gracchi 17, Prati (06 4436 2244, www. zippertravel.it). Metro Castro Ottaviano/bus 30, 70, 81, 280, 590, 913. **Open** *9.30am-6.30pm Mon-Fri.* **Credit** *DC, MC, V.* **Map** *p338 B3.*

One of only a few travel agencies in Italy to offer customised travel for gay women.

Music:
Classical & Opera

Serious music – 21st-century style.

The 21st century has been good to Rome, which is now back on the music-lover's map of Europe after more than a century of neglect. This is thanks, mainly, to the activity and eclectic programming of the **Auditorium-Parco della Musica** (*see p264* **The Sound of Perfection**), which was inaugurated in 2002.

Of course, the Auditorium is not the only venue in Rome for music. Many of the more traditional concert halls and locations have also benefited from the surge of energy its development has generated, and many boast high-quality programmes with resident and visiting artists. The number of music festivals that are organised throughout the year by a variety of institutions are another feather in Rome's cap, especially since these often take place in beautiful church settings, palazzi, or in the magnificent residences of many of the city's foreign academies.

So Rome is more or less sorted for 'serious' music – opera being the one glaring exception: notwithstanding two glorious locations, the programmes tend towards constipated and productions can be rather mediocre.

ARTS & ENTERTAINMENT

THE CLASSICAL SCENE

The **Accademia Nazionale di Santa Cecilia** (www.santacecilia.it) is Italy's national music academy, with its prestigious *conservatorio*, and choir and orchestra directed by British-born conductor Antonio Pappano. It resides in Rome and plays out its season at the much-admired Auditorium-Parco della Musica, a complex of concert and exhibition spaces, designed by internationally acclaimed architect Renzo Piano. Pappano promotes the Accademia's trend of thematic cycles, with a series of mini-festivals dedicated to single composers, artists or themes in bursts throughout the season. Meanwhile, Santa Cecilia also continues to attract some of the world's greatest conductors for its symphonic season, and renowned soloists for its chamber music programme.

Many other institutions of all sizes make their voices heard. The **Accademia Filarmonica Romana** (06 320 1752, www.

filarmonicaromana.org) – which performs at the **Teatro Olimpico** *see p264* and **Teatro Argentina**, *see p283* – was founded in 1821 and boasts an illustrious history, with such composers as Rossini, Donizetti, Paganini and Verdi among its founders. It offers a varied programme of chamber music, ancient music, ballet and chamber opera.

Another major concert provider is the **Istituzione Universitaria dei Concerti** (IUC, 06 361 0051, www.concertiiuc.it), founded after World War II to inject some life into Rome's university campus. The IUC offers a varied calendar that includes often outstanding – and frequently experimental – international and Italian recitals and chamber music at La Sapienza's main auditorium, the rather stark **Aula Magna**.

The 16th-century **Oratorio del Gonfalone** hosts a chamber music season that reflects the joyous personality of director Angelo Persichilli. Every concert and recital on the programme, which runs from December to

May, seems to have been lovingly chosen to fit the beautiful frescoed surroundings, and to show off the Oratorio's magnificent 18th-century organ. In recent years, it has been giving more to concerts and recitals with an ethnic, folk and contemporary flavour.

The **Orchestra Sinfonica di Roma** (06 4425 2303, www.artsacademy.it), directed by conductor Francesco La Vecchia, offers a somewhat traditional symphonic season at the **Auditorium Conciliazione**, where famous conductors or soloists often feature as guest artists.

The **La Stravaganza** music association (329 009 9476, www.lastravaganzamusica.it) is a tiny, privately run endeavour that organises delightful chamber music concerts or recitals inside the historic **Palazzo Doria Pamphilj** (*see p100*). During the interval or after the concert, the public is invited to wander into some of the adjacent rooms to enjoy the Doria Pamphilj art collection.

The **Quirinale** (*see p71*) for programme information visit www.quirinale.it) also opens its doors to the public, on Sunday mornings, for a cycle of chamber music concerts and recitals in the cappella Paolina.

THE OPERA

Rome's opera scene has plenty to offer for fans and newbies alike. The drab exterior of the Opera di Roma's 19th-century Teatro Costanzi gives way to a beautiful and harmonious interior with a good-sized stage and perfect acoustics. And in summer the breathtaking majesty of the **Terme di Caracalla** (*see p120*) is a unique backdrop and setting for lyrical productions. But political and financial bungling have always dogged the theatre, and as this guide went to press the opera's woes continued with *maestro* Riccardo Muti reneging on a deal to take over as director. The recently renovated Teatro Nazionale provides the stage for most of the smaller productions, including chamber opera, contemporary works and ballets. Keep an eye on cast lists to avoid second-rate substitutes after the first night.

AUDITORIA

See also p284 **Teatro Il Sistina**.

Auditorium Conciliazione

Via della Conciliazione 4, Vatican (800 904 560, www.auditoriumconciliazione.it). Metro Ottaviano/bus 62, 23, 34, 40Exp, 271, 982. **Box office** noon-6pm Mon-Fri. **No credit cards. Map** p339 B5.

This was Rome's prime serious music venue until the national academy shifted its season to the Auditorium-Parco della Musica. It has since been renovated to reveal a good-sized stage that is suitable for dance. And dance – with some star-studded events – makes up part of its varied programme, which also includes music and conferences.

★ Auditorium–Parco della Musica

Via P de Coubertin 15, Suburbs: north (06 8024 1281, box office 06 808 2058, www.auditorium.com). Bus 53, 910, M/tram 2. **Box office** *July-Sept* 11am-6pm Mon-Fri. *Oct-June* 11am-6pm daily; until interval on concert days. **Credit** MC, V.

Tickets can be booked online. Guided tours cost €9 (€5 concessions; no credit cards) and take place at intervals throughout the day: times change frequently so call ahead or check the website. Alternatively, wander in (open 10am-6pm daily, admission free) and have a look around the place for yourself. *See also p264* **The Sound of Perfection**.

Aula Magna dell'Università la Sapienza

Piazzale Aldo Moro, Esquilino (IUC: 06 361 0051, www.concertiiuc.it). Metro Policlinico/bus 61, 490, 495/tram 3, 19. **Season** Oct-Apr. **Box office** 10am-1pm, 2-5pm daily; up to 1hr before concerts. **Credit** MC, V. **Map** p128 B1.

With kitsch Fascist decor but reasonable acoustics, this is the main auditorium for the Istituzione Universitaria dei Concerti (IUC; *see p262*) season. ▶ *The box office for Aula Magna dell'Università la Sapienza is at lungotevere Flaminio 50, Suburbs: north.*

Oratorio del Gonfalone

Via del Gonfalone 32, Ghetto & Campo (06 687 5952, www.oratoriogonfalone.com). Bus 40Exp, 46, 62, 64, 116, 916. **Box office** 10am-4pm Mon-Fri. **No credit cards. Map** p339 B6.

This beautiful frescoed little auditorium is located in a 16th-century oratorio adjacent to the Baroque church of the Gonfalone. It provides a suitable home for one of the city's most precious organs.

INSIDE TRACK
RETHINKING THE ARTS

Even if classical isn't your thing, it's worth checking out what's on at the **Auditorium-Parco della Musica** (*see p266* **The Sound of Perfection**). Its programme – which ranges from symphonies to soul, and from jazz to jugglers – has cast its spell over Roman citizens, many of whom have never set foot in a classical-music venue in their lives.

The Sound of Perfection

Renzo Piano's marvellous Auditorium continues to take the Roman arts scene by storm.

Barely ten years old, Rome's stunning Auditorium-Parco della Musica (for listing, *see p263*) has taken centre stage in the city's cultural life. This architectural marvel is quite the chic-est place to be seen – once you get there. Romans who can, drive to the leafy residential area north of piazza del Popolo where the lead roofs of the three giant scarab-shaped concert halls rise. Students, tourists and impecunious music-lovers strap-hang on the rattly no.2 tram. But everybody goes because... well, there's something for everybody.

Box office figures, which leap from year to year (almost 1.2 million people attended concerts here in 2008), show that low ticket prices and eclectic programming are a winning mix. All kinds of music – especially jazz – are taken seriously here, as well as poetry and debate, contemporary art, the sciences and cinema.

Most concert halls don't put Nobel laureates and other top number-crunching boffins on the stage for sell-out annual mathematics festivals. Nor do they bring Umberto Eco to encourage the innumerate: 'you can do whatever you want with numbers,' he told a thousand fans

Teatro dell'Opera di Roma – Teatro Costanzi

Piazza B Gigli 1, Esquilino (06 4816 0255, www.opera.roma.it). Metro Repubblica/bus 40Exp, 60Exp, 64, 70, 117, 170. **Box office** 9am-5pm Tue-Sat; 9am-1.30pm Sun; until 15mins after performances begin. **Credit** AmEx, DC, MC, V. **Map** p357 D5.

The lavish late 19th-century *teatro all'italiana* interior comes as quite a surprise after the grey, angular, Mussolini-era façade. There are towering rows of boxes, and loads of stucco, frescoes and gilding. The

acoustics vary: the higher (cheaper) seats are unsatisfactory, so splash out on a box, if you can.

Teatro Olimpico

Piazza Gentile da Fabriano, Suburbs: north (06 326 599, www.teatroolimpico.it). Bus 53, 280, 910/tram 2, 19. **Season** Oct-May. **Box office** 10am-7pm daily; from 8pm on concert days. **Credit** MC, V. **Map** off p338 C/D1.

Great for all types of performances, the Olimpico has good acoustics, even for cheaper seats. When

who suddenly experienced the magic of maths. They don't gather the world's top philosophers for four days of brainstorming sessions. Or blast Tchaikovsky's 1812 Overture out of extremely well balanced speakers for the delight of Christmas ice skaters.

But then, the Auditorium is unique. It even has its own Roman villa nestling between archi-star Renzo Piano's trio of cherry-wood halls. The acoustics – and the catering, of course (this is Italy!) – are beyond reproach.

Each day's programme is packed with events. Sunday is family day and the Auditorium's genial director Antonio Pappano (when he's not conducting at Covent Garden) can often be found explaining to rapt youngsters what exactly a bassoon is.

Now the Auditorium draws on its vast treasure trove of historic recordings to stream its own lively radio station, bringing its world-class offerings to an even larger public.

If Rome's Auditorium experiment has proved one thing, it's that if you provide a constant diet of excellence you will never be short of an audience.

booking, go for the central front and second-row seats in the gallery. It's owned by the Accademia Filarmonica (*see p262*).

FESTIVALS

Most of Rome's summer festivals take place under the **Estate Romana** umbrella (*see p242*). This overwhelming event-fest runs from June to September and provides such quantities of entertainment of all descriptions that it's difficult to know where to start.

The **Accademia Nazionale di Santa Cecilia** offers a full summer programme of quality crowd-pleasers, including international orchestras and classical/popular crossovers, in the outside *cavea* of the Auditorium-Parco della Musica performing arts complex.

For the **RomaEuropa** festival, *see p244*.

Concerti del Tempietto
Various venues (06 8713 1590, fax 06 2332 26360, www.tempietto.it). **Box office** at venues from 1hr before concerts. **No credit cards.**
The Associazione Il Tempietto organises year-round concerts under the Festival Musicale delle Nazioni banner in various venues, mainly the Sala Baldini (piazza Campitelli 9), in the archaeological site around the Teatro di Marcello (*see p112*) in summer, and the art nouveau Casina delle Civette in Villa Torlonia (*see p158*). It's mostly low-level musically, but there's a concert almost every evening and the venues are enchanting. You can book online.

International Chamber Ensemble
Sant'Ivo alla Sapienza, corso Rinascimento 40, Pantheon & Navona (06 8680 0125, www.interensemble.org). Bus 30Exp, 70, 81, 87, 116, 204, 280, 492, 628. **Season** mid June-mid Aug. **Box office** 10am-7pm Mon-Fri; 10am-1pm Sat. **No credit cards. Map** p339 D5.
Chamber and symphonic music, as well as opera, takes place in a splendid example of Renaissance architecture: the courtyard of Sant'Ivo alla Sapienza, the hallowed 15th-century seat of Rome university.

★ Stagione Estiva del Teatro dell'Opera
Terme di Caracalla, viale delle Terme di Caracalla, Aventine, Testaccio & Ostiense (06 4816 0255, www.opera.roma.it). Metro Circo Massimo/bus 60Exp, 75, 81, 118, 175, 628, 714. **Season** July-Aug. **Box office** (at Teatro dell'Opera; *see p264*) 9am-5pm Tue-Sat; 9am-1.30pm Sun. **Credit** AmEx, DC, MC, V. **Map** p345 C5.
The spectacular venue for the Opera di Roma's summer season is a breathtaking archaeological site. Set designers usually exploit the unique backdrop of majestic Roman ruins with few props and dramatic lighting. Back-row seats are very far away from the stage – so don't forget binoculars. Bookings can be made online at www.chartanet.it.

INSIDE TRACK MORE MUSIC

Many churches and basilicas throughout Rome host **chamber ensembles**, choirs and soloists of differing artistic worth – keep an eye on posters and the daily press for details of events.

Nightlife
& Live Music

Hip DJs, strict door policies and hot nights rule Rome's clubs.

The turn of the millennium saw a growing cultural, artistic and musical vibrancy that began to turn the once sleepy Eternal City into a lively European capital. If things have showed signs of slowing down recently, there's still plenty out there to keep night-owls busy. Dancing to the best international DJs and hearing the latest bands is now the norm in a host of small clubs and venues. You will, however, need some inside information to avoid the Eurotrash dished out by the plethora of commercial venues playing disco at weekends.

Rome gives its best over the long summer, when the breeze makes nights fresh and almost magical. There's always action of one kind or another along the river banks, where clubs, shops and restaurants go alfresco for the hotter months. For information on the plethora of summer happenings, *see p270* **Sounds of Summer**.

NIGHTLIFE

By-laws forcing *centro storico* bars to shut at 2am are respected up to a point, though they rarely impinge on that uniquely relaxed feel of Roman nights.

Discos and live venues continue to stay open until the small hours, though, allowing locals to keep up their habit of starting the evenings late and ending them early… the next day. Concerts rarely kick off before 10.30pm and most clubs close after 4am, even on weekdays. When picking your club for the night, bear in mind that many mainstream clubs serve up commercial house or retro 1980s tunes on Fridays and Saturdays.

Established venues like **Goa** (*see p274*), **La Saponeria** (*see p274*) and **Micca Club** (*see p275*) can always be relied upon to offer quality DJ sets. For something alternative, try the Brit-pop/punk rock served up by the Beatles-lookalike DJs of **Fish & Chips** (on Fridays at Akab, *see p272*) or dance the night away at **Screamadelica** (at Circolo degli Artisti; *see p276*), where international live acts are joined by DJs playing rock, pop and indie. Otherwise,

check out what's on at places like **Locanda Atlantide** (*see p275*) or the tiny **Metaverso** (*see p274*). On Tuesdays DJ Andrea Esu and guests spin their electro-house and tech sounds at **L-Ektrica** (at Akab; *see p272*). Vintage enthusiasts will find gold at **Twiggy**, Rome's best 1960s night, where Italy's top live bands precede expert DJs Luzy L and Corry X (one Saturday a month at Metaverso; *see p274* or check out www.myspace.com/twiggy60sparty).

LIVE MUSIC

To a large extent, the recent rise in the popularity of concert-going in Rome is due to the **Auditorium-Parco della Musica** (*see p265*), a multifunctional complex hosting not only classical music, but also pop, jazz, world music and rock events. Rome's vocation for live music is also being prodded along by a string of

---

About the author

Raffaella Malaguti is a journalist at Italy's public RAI TV and freelances for Italian and British publications. She grew up Bologna, studied in the UK and moved back to Italy in 1996.

smallish live clubs, and by the daring programme of goodies on offer at the cool **Teatro Palladium** (*see p283*). Moreover, city hall continues to fund the exciting **RomaEuropa Festival** (*see p244*) and the occasional free mega-concert. Strangely, Rome still lacks a major outdoor venue for musical events.

WHERE TO GO

With a few exceptions, Rome's nightlife is concentrated in a few easily accessible areas. Testaccio is one of Rome's liveliest quarters, with nightlife action concentrated around **Monte Testaccio** (map p343): you will be spoilt for choice – just walk around until you find the vibe that you're seeking for the evening. The area that lies around **via Libetta**, off via Ostiense (map p123), teems with many trendy clubs and is poised to become even more crowded: the city council has slowly begun to develop the whole district as an arts hub based around the old fruit and vegetable market.

Fashionistas head for the *centro storico*: join them in the **triangolo della Pace** (map p339) to be part of trendy Roman life. The **campo de' Fiori** area (map p342), once a fashionista meeting spot, has become increasingly chaotic and, as the evening progresses, squalid.

The **San Lorenzo** quarter (map p128) is less pretentious: drinks are cheaper, and there's always something new going on.

Trastevere has lovely alleys packed with friendly, crowded bars. If you're longing for company but your Italian's weak, this is the place for you: English is the lingua franca. Note though that around piazza Trilussa, the scene gets seriously seedy in the small hours.

GETTING THROUGH THE DOOR

Getting into *centri sociali* or alternative, down-to-earth venues is easy enough – just join the chaotic queues at the door and use your elbows. But making it inside fashionable mainstream

Piazza dell'Immacolata.

ARTS & ENTERTAINMENT

ARTS & ENTERTAINMENT

Sounds of Summer

On long summer nights Rome really comes into its own. The city bursts with an astounding number of festivals, which are often held in such breathtaking locations as Roman ruins, Renaissance villas or ancient amphitheatres.

Besides providing for top performances, opening up these venues allows visitors to access some of the city's artistic and architectural treasures that are normally beyond the reach of tourists.

The warm season starts with the free **Labour Day concert**, which is organised by Italy's trade unions on 1 May (Primo Maggio; *see also p242*). It's traditionally held in piazza San Giovanni in Laterano and hosts Italian celebrities, along with a handful of international stars, drawing half a million people from all over Italy.

In mid June, the **Estate Romana** (*see p242*) kicks off. An umbrella for most of Rome's outdoor summer festivals sponsored by city hall, it runs to the end of September. Every year, a couple of major concerts are held in the Stadio Olimpico (*see p156*).

For an incursion into an all-Italian phenomenon, look out for festivals organised by Italy's political parties (**Festa dell'Unità** by the Democratici di sinistra, and **Festa di Liberazione** by Rifondazione comunista). At these festivals – which are popular with supporters and non-affiliates alike – there are arty crafty stalls for browsing, food, live music, theatre and, of course, political debates. Check in the local press for details. Other summer events to look out for are:

Cosmophonies – Festival Internazionale di Ostia Antica

Teatro Romano-Scavi Archeologici di Ostia Antica, viale dei Romagnoli 717 (333 200 4329, www.cosmophonies.com). **Date** June-mid Sept. **Tickets** €15-€65.
No credit cards.
Held in the breathtaking scenario of the ancient Roman theatre of Ostia Antica (*see p287*), Cosmophonies is an international festival of theatre, dance and music dishing out excellent acts such as Sonic Youth, Caetano Veloso, Morrissey and Jackson

---

clubs can be stressful, no matter how elegantly you're dressed. Intimidating bouncers will bar your way, asking 'can I help you?' while supposed VIPs are whisked through the door.

Clubs and discobars generally charge an entrance fee at weekends but not on weekdays; you often have to pay for a *tessera* (membership card) on top of, or sometimes instead of, the entrance fee. *Tessere* may be valid for a season or for a month, and in some cases they're free. Admission tickets often include a 'free' drink, but you can expect the other drinks you buy to be pricey. Another popular formula is to grant 'free' admission while forcing you to buy a drink (generally expensive). To get out again you have to hand a stamped drink card to the bouncer, so hold on to whatever piece of paper they give you or you'll be forced to pay twice.

TRIDENTE

Gregory's

Via Gregoriana 54 (06 679 6386, www.gregorysjazz.com). Metro Spagna or Barberini/bus 116, 117, 119, 590. **Open** 7pm-2am Thur-Sun. Closed Aug. **Credit** AmEx, DC, MC, V. **Map** p341 A5.
This cosy venue oozes jazz culture from every pore. On the ground floor, sip a glass of whisky from one

of Rome's widest selections while admiring old portraits of legendary jazz musicians. In the small upstairs room, you can jazz up your ears to top live acts while sitting comfortably among soft lights and lacquered tables. *Photo p269.*

PANTHEON & NAVONA

Anima

Via Santa Maria dell'Anima 57 (347 850 9256). Bus 30Exp, 40Exp, 62, 64, 70, 81, 492, 628, 916. **Open** 7pm-4am daily. **Credit** DC, MC, V. **Map** p339 D5.
The improbable baroque gilded stucco that decorates this small venue could put some off, but there's a buzzing atmosphere and good drinks, and a mixed crowd of all ages and nationalities. The musical focus is on hip hop, R&B, funk, soul and reggae.

Bloom

Via del Teatro Pace 30 (06 6880 2029). Bus 30Exp, 40Exp, 62, 64, 70, 81, 492, 628, 916. **Open** 7pm-3am Mon, Tue, Thur-Sat. Closed July & Aug. **Credit** AmEx, DC, MC, V. **Map** p339 C5.
A restaurant, cocktail bar and disco, Bloom is cooler than ice. A fashionable crowd hangs out in its designer interiors. At Bloom, you can eat, sip an *aperitivo*, dance or simply relax at the bar while you check out other people's outfits. The door policy

Browne. But no matter what's happening on stage, the unique surroundings make for a memorable night.

Fiesta

Via Appia Nuova 1245, Suburbs: east (06 6618 0136, credit card bookings 199 109 910, www.fiesta.it). Metro Colli Albani/bus 590, 650, 671. **Date** mid June-mid Aug.
This hectic Latin American-themed festival regularly attracts almost a million people over the summer months with performances by Latin American bands, plus appearances by some international rock, pop and hip hop stars. There are four dancefloors, scores of restaurants and stalls... and lots of salsa and merengue. You'd be wise to come early: transport and parking can be a nightmare.

Roma Incontra il Mondo

Villa Ada, via di Ponte Salario, Suburbs: north (06 4173 4712, 06 4173 4648, www.villaada.org). Bus 63, 92, 231, 235, 310. **Date** mid June-early Aug. **Admission** €8-€22 per event. **No credit cards.** **Map** p337.
Musicians from around the world play on a lakeside stage beneath the venerable trees of the Villa Ada park. Lights reflected in the water and cool breezes make this one of the most atmospheric and relaxing of the summer festivals. If the music palls there are bars and stalls purveying ethnic food, music and books.

Villa Celimontana Festival

Villa Celimontana, Celio (06 5833 57817, www.villacelimontanajazz.com). Metro Colosseo/bus 81, 673/tram 3. **Date** early June-Aug. **Admission** €5-€30 per event. **Credit** (online bookings only) DC, MC, V. **Map** p345 C4.
This long-running jazz festival takes place in the leafy Villa Celimontana park (*see p130*) and features acclaimed artists (from Incognito to Italian star Stefano Bollani) in an astonishingly beautiful setting. Lots of candles and torches give the place a magical aura. Wine and food stands complete the idyll.

can be strict, and booking is essential for dinner, since there are only 25 seats.

La Maison

Vicolo dei Granari 4 (06 683 3312, www.lamaisonroma.it). Bus 40Exp, 46, 62, 64, 70, 81, 97, 189, 304, 492, 628, 916. **Open** 11pm-4am Wed-Sat. Closed June-Sept. **Admission** free. **Credit** AmEx, DC, MC, V. **Map** p339 D5.
The ice-cool barmen and a VIP room almost as big as the club itself speak volumes: this is one of the clubs of choice of Rome's fashion-victims. Huge chandeliers, dark red walls and curvy sofas give La Maison an opulent, courtly feel. And yet, surprisingly, the place is not snobbish, the music on offer is not banal and the atmosphere is genuinely buzzing. A word of warning: the doormen can be very picky. In summer, La Maison shifts to an outdoor spot on the river embankment beneath Castel Sant'Angelo (*see p150*).

Late bars

See also p212 **Société Lutèce.**

Bar del Fico

Piazza del Fico 26-28 (06 6880 8413, http://bardelfico.it). Bus 30Exp, 40Exp, 46, 62, 64, 70, 81, 87, 116, 304, 492, 628, 916. **Open** 8.30am-2.30am daily. **No credit cards.** **Map** p339 C5.
After a shut-down for refurbishment that seemed like it would never end, this long-established *centro storico* fixture – named after the ancient fig tree (*fico*) outside – has reopened with a French bistro vibe. But its regulars, including the old blokes playing chess, seem to have returned, so the new look hasn't changed the wonderfully laid-back boho ambience too much. Open from breakfast until the small hours, it's the perfect *centro storico* meeting place.

Etabli

Vicolo delle Vacche 9 (06 9761 6694, www.etabli.it). Bus 30Exp, 40Exp, 62, 64, 70, 492, 628, 916. **Open** 12.30-3pm, 6pm-2am daily. Closed 2wks Aug. **Credit** AmEx, DC, MC, V. **Map** p339 C5.
Pared-back decor, twiddly chandeliers and deep armchairs around a fireplace draw some seriously hip locals to this bar and restaurant in the super-chic triangolo della pace. The welcome is suave-warm, the vibe intimate.

Fluid

Via del Governo Vecchio 46-47 (06 683 2361, www.fluideventi.com). Bus 30Exp, 40Exp, 62, 64, 70, 492, 628, 916. **Open** 6pm-2am daily. Closed 3wks Aug. **Credit** AmEx, DC, MC, V. **Map** p339 C5.

ARTS & ENTERTAINMENT

Dimmidisì. *See p275.*

Ultra-sleek, with black floors, stunning chandeliers and plasma screens, this designer bar is cool to the point of chilliness. But there are DJs spinning techno, good *aperitivi* and any number of themed events.

GHETTO & CAMPO DE' FIORI

Rialtosantambrogio
Via Sant'Ambrogio 4 (www.rialto.roma.it).
Events venues, days & times vary. Closed Aug.
Admission free or €5. **No credit cards.**
Though its historic venue deep in the Ghetto was shut down by city authorities in 2009, the people behind this long-running *centro sociale* – a crucial meeting point for Rome's radical crowd – continue to function as organisers of some of the city's most interesting alternative events. Some take place the music school inside the Mattatoio (*see p121*) in Testaccio; others happen in the Angelo Mai (www.angelomai.org) on viale delle Terme di Caracalla 55A, near the eponymous ancient Roman baths (*see p120*).

TRASTEVERE & GIANICOLO

Big Mama
Vicolo San Francesco a Ripa 18 (06 581 2551, www.bigmama.it). Bus 75, 170/tram 3, 8. **Open** 9pm-1.30am Tue-Sat. Closed mid June-mid Sept.
Admission free with membership (annual €14, monthly €8); extra charge (€8-€22) for big acts.
Credit DC, MC, V. **Map** p343 C4.
Rome's blues heart throbs in this pared-back but welcoming venue, which hosts an array of respected Italian and international artists every evening. The

blues menu is punctuated with jazz, rock and ethnic music. There are drinks and hot meals to consume while listening to the top-quality music on offer. Book if you want to get a table.

Lettere Caffè
Via San Francesco a Ripa 100-101 (06 9727 0991, www.letterecaffe.org). Bus 44, 75, 780, H/tram 3, 8. **Open** 5pm-2am daily (concerts begin 10.30pm). Closed 2wks Aug. **No credit cards. Map** p343 C4.
As well as a vocation for poetry and literature, the Lettere Caffè has a choice of concerts and DJ sets. From rockabilly to jazz, passing through 1960s beat, the Lettere is both a showcase of new talent and a place to listen to well-known DJs and bands from Rome and beyond. An excellent selection of wines and spirits that won't empty your wallet and yummy own-made cakes complete the picture.

AVENTINE, TESTACCIO & OSTIENSE

Akab
Via di Monte Testaccio 68-69 (06 5725 0585, www.akabcave.com). Metro Piramide/bus 23, 30Exp, 75, 95, 719, N3, N9/tram 3. **Open** midnight-5am Tue-Sat. Closed Aug. **Admission** (incl 1 drink) €10-€25. **Credit** AmEx, DC, MC, V. **Map** p343 D6.
Formerly a carpenter's workshop, this is now a busy, long-term fixture of the Testaccio scene. It hosts well-known international DJs, especially on Tuesdays for the L-Ektrica night. Come here for retro on Wednesdays, R&B on Thursdays and house on Fridays and Saturdays. Akab has two levels: an

underground cellar and a street-level room, as well as an outside garden.

Alpheus

Via del Commercio 36 (06 574 7826, www.alpheus.it). Metro Piramide/bus 23, 769, 770, N2, N3, N9. **Open** 10.30pm-4am Fri-Sun; other evenings vary. Closed July, Aug. **Admission** €5-€20. **Credit** AmEx. **Map** p123 A2.

An eclectic club with a hotch-potch but interesting crowd, the Alpheus has four big halls for gigs, music festivals, theatre and cabaret, which are all followed by a disco. The music changes every night and varies depending on the room you're in: rock, chart R&B, Latin, world music, retro tunes and happy trash. Alpheus also hosts the Gorgeous I Am gay one-nighter (*see p260*).

Caruso Cafe de Oriente

Via di Monte Testaccio 36 (06 574 5019, www.carusocafe.com). Metro Piramide/bus 23, 30Exp, 75, 95, 280, 716, 719, N3, N9/ tram 3. **Open** 10.30pm-3.30am Tue-Thur, Sun; 11pm-4.30am Fri, Sat. Closed July-mid Sept. **Admission** (incl 1 drink) €8 Tue-Thur; €10 Fri; €10 women, €15 men Sat; free Sun. **No credit cards. Map** p343 D6.

A must for lovers of salsa and the like, this club offers Latin American tunes every night (apart from Saturdays, when it veers towards hip hop and R&B) and live acts almost daily. Shimmy your way in between scores of dancing couples to enjoy the warm atmosphere in these three, ethnic-themed, orange-hued rooms – or head up to the roof terrace.

Caffè Latino

Via di Monte Testaccio 96 (06 5728 8556). Metro Piramide/bus 23, 30Exp, 75, 95, 280, 716, 719, N23, N9/tram 3. **Open** 10.30pm-3am Wed-Sat. Closed June-Sept. **Admission** free; €8-€15 for special events. **No credit cards. Map** p343 D6.

This is one of the oldest clubs in the Testaccio area, offering a choice of live music and DJs, ranging from jazz to ethnic, Latin American to funky. If you don't feel like dancing, you can relax on comfortable chairs.

Casa del Jazz

Viale di Porta Ardeatina 55 (06 704 731, www.casajazz.it). Bus 160. **Open** 10am-midnight on concert evenings. **Admission** €5-€15. **No credit cards. Map** p123 D1.

This city council-owned jazz venue in a plush villa confiscated from a local organised-crime boss behind the Terme di Caracalla (*see p120*) offers a packed programme of high-class Italian and international jazz performers. There's a café and restaurant too, set in the villa's beautiful grounds.

▶ *For more unusual anti-crime initiatives, see p228* **De-Mobbed**.

INSIDE TRACK
LATIN AMERICAN

Rome has hosted an energetic Latin American community since the 1970s, and Romans swarm to dance courses. *Capoeira* is one of the latest fads, and schools run by resident Brazilians have popped up all over town. As well as clubs, discobars and a few tango cafés, lovers of Latin American tunes head en masse, especially on Thursdays, to **Palacavicchi** (via RB Bandinelli 130, Suburbs: south, 06 7932 1797, 349 290 7356). **Caruso** (*see left*) offers live bands almost every night while **Fiesta** (*see p270* **Sounds of Summer**) livens up Rome's summer nights with a variety of music.

Classico Village

Via Libetta 3 (06 574 3364, www.classico.it). Metro Garbatella/bus 29, 769, 770, N2, N3, N9. **Open** 9pm-1.30am Mon-Thur; 11pm-4am Fri, Sat. **Admission** €5-€15. **Credit** DC, MC, V. **Map** p123 B3.

This former factory space in super-hip Ostiense comprises three rooms, often offering three different acts simultaneously. The whole thing faces on to a courtyard, which is heaven in the warmer months. The live bands and DJ sets veer towards the rock end of the musical spectrum.

MADS. *See p275*.

Alexanderplatz. *See p276.*

ARTS & ENTERTAINMENT

Goa

Via Libetta 13 (06 574 8277). Metro Garbatella/
bus 29, 769, 770, N2, N3, N9. **Open** midnight-
4am Wed-Sat. Closed mid May-mid Sept.
Admission (incl 1 drink) €10-€25. **Credit**
AmEx, DC, MC, V. **Map** p123 B3.

In trendy Ostiense, this is one of the best of Rome's
fashionable clubs. Goa marries iron and steel with
curvy, 1960s-style whites and the quality of the
Italian and international DJs that it books is
generally above the competition. Ultrabeat on
Thursdays brings the cream of Europe's electronic
music DJs to Rome. There are occasional Sunday
openings (6pm-4.30am), including a women-only
event on the last Sunday of the month. Note that the
doormen can be picky.

Metaverso

Via di Monte Testaccio 38A (06 574 4712,
www.metaverso.com). Metro Piramide/bus 23,
30Exp, 75, 95, 280, 716, 719,N3, N9/tram 3.
Open 10.30pm-5am Fri, Sat. Closed July, Aug.
Admission €5-€7. **No credit cards**.
Map p343 D6.

This inexpensive, friendly little club plays host to
international DJs from well-known labels, along with
several of Rome's home-grown best, pulling in an
alternative crowd. Weekends are mostly dedicated
to electronica and hip hop. It also hosts exhibitions
of works by local artists.

Rashomon

Via degli Argonauti 16 (347 340 5710,
www.myspace.com/rashomonclub). Metro
Garbatella/bus 29, 769, 770, N2, N3, N9.
Open 11pm-4am Thur-Sat. Closed July,
Aug. **Admission** free-€10. **No credit**
cards. **Map** p123 B3.

This dark-walled club in Ostiense has an authentic
underground feel – which is confirmed by the choice
of DJs and live bands on the music roster. Run by a
group of young people who have a passion for the
alternative clubs of London and Berlin, Rashomon
lets loose with a line-up of electro-rock, electronica,
indie and new wave music, plus showcases of
up-and-coming bands.

La Saponeria

Via degli Argonauti 20 (06 574 6999,
www.saponeriaclub.it). Metro Garbatella/bus 29,
769, 770, N2, N3, N9. **Open** 11.30pm-5am Fri,
Sat. Closed mid May-mid Sept. **Admission** €10-
€15. **Credit** DC, MC, V. **Map** p123 B3.

One of the liveliest clubs in Ostiense's via Libetta
area, La Saponeria is a curvilinear space with a
large bar in the centre of the establishment. Not the
place to come for a quiet drink: at least not on the
weekends, when the venue gets hopelessly packed.
Fridays revolve around hip hop and R&B music,
Saturdays are house nights with the Minima crowd.
Expect queues on popular evenings.

CELIO, SAN GIOVANNI & SAN LORENZO

Beba do Samba

Via dei Messapi 8 (339 878 5214,
www.bebadosamba.it). Bus 71, 163, 204, 443,
448, 490, 491, 492, 495, 649, N10, N11/tram
3, 19. **Open** 10pm-2am daily. Closed July, Aug.
Admission free with annual membership (€5).
No credit cards. Map p128 C3.

This popular, buzzing little venue in San Lorenzo
attracts a studenty crowd for live music – mostly
ethnic, world music and jazz – almost every night,
often followed by a DJ.

Dimmidisì
Via dei Volsci 126B (06 446 1855, www. dimmidisiroma.it). Bus 71, 163, 204, 443, 448, 490, 491, 492, 495, 649, N10, N11/ tram 3, 19. **Open** 7pm-2am Thur-Sun. Closed July-Sept. **Admission** free-€10. **No credit cards**. **Map** p128 C2.
From its *aperitivo* hour, often accompanied by bands, until into the early hours, this pared-back space in studenty San Lorenzo hosts live acts and top DJs from Italy and abroad. *Photo p272.*

Locanda Atlantide
Via dei Lucani 22B (06 4470 4540, www.locandatlantide.it). Bus 71, 163, 204, 443, 448, 490, 491, 492, 495, 649, N10, N11/tram 3, 19. **Open** 9.30pm-3am Mon, Wed-Sun. Closed mid June-Sept. **Admission** €3-€10. **No credit cards**. **Map** p128 C3.
This friendly, unpretentious venue in the buzzing San Lorenzo neighbourhood hosts an array of events ranging from concerts and DJ acts to theatrical performances. It sometimes opens earlier in the evening for book launches; there are occasional events on Mondays too. It pulls an alternative crowd and can be relied upon for a good night out.

MADS
Via dei Sabelli 2 (328 641 8983, www.mads-project.it). Bus 71, 163, 204, 443, 448, 490, 491, 492, 495, 649, N10, N11/tram 3, 19. **Open** 10pm-2am Tue-Sat. Closed July, Aug. **No credit cards**. **Admission** free-€5. **Credit** MC, V. **Map** p128 C3/D2.
The cavernous space of this laid-back locale in San Lorenzo hosts regular concerts, plus themed parties,

INSIDE TRACK WHAT'S ON

For details of upcoming events, consult listings magazines **Trovaroma**, **Roma C'è** (for both, *see p316*) or **Zero6** (a monthly, free in shops and pubs). For an alternative look at Rome's nightlife, check out http://roma.zero.eu, www.romastyle.info (especially good for techno and drum 'n' bass nights), and www.musicaroma.it for gigs. Fans of indie and punk rock music can have a look at www.pogo pop.it, while reggae addicts can browse at www.reggae.it.

women-only nights and excellent DJ sets. Some special events are held on Sundays. Check the website for outdoor events over the summer. *Photo p273.*

★ Micca Club
Via Pietro Micca 7A (06 8744 0079, www.miccaclub.com). Metro Vittorio or Manzoni/bus 71, 105, N12, N18/tram 3, 5, 14. **Open** 7pm-2am Mon-Wed; 7pm-4am Thur-Sat; 6pm-2am Sun. Closed June-Aug. **Credit** MC, V. **Admission** free-€10. **Credit** MC, V. **Map** p128 B4.
This interesting space (a cellar with red-brick vaults) is a trifle impractical with its small dancefloor and a stage inexplicably stuck at the very end of the club. Yet Micca's top-notch DJ sets and live acts, plus themed evenings and burlesque shows, ensure that it's full every night. From 1960s beat to soul, from funk to jazz and rock'n'roll, the music on offer is

ARTS & ENTERTAINMENT

The Place. *See p276.*

varied and interesting. There are *aperitivi* with a generous buffet (€10) daily from 7-10pm; after which admission is free Mon-Wed, and €10 Thur-Sat. On Sunday evenings there is a crowded flea market here as well.

MONTI & ESQUILINO
Late bars

Oppio Caffè
Via delle Terme di Tito 72 (06 747 5262, www. oppiocaffe.it). Metro Colosseo/bus 60, 75, 85, 87, 117, 571, 810, 850/tram 3. **Open** 7am-2am daily. **Credit** MC, V. **Map** p344 C2.
From the people behind Micca Club (*see p275*), this happening new venture is worth frequenting simply for its view over the Colosseum. But there's also a €10 drink plus *aperitivo* buffet, a grill-restaurant (meals served noon-3pm, 7.30-11pm), resident DJs, events… and children eat for free.

VATICAN & PRATI
Alexanderplatz
Via Ostia 9 (06 3974 2171, www.alexanderplatz. it). Metro Ottaviano/bus 32, 34, 49, 81, 492, 590, 982, N6, N11/tram 19. **Open** 8.30pm-1.30am daily. Closed June-Sept. **Admission** free with monthly (€15) or annual (€45) membership. **Credit** DC, MC, V. **Map** off p338 A3.
Jazz is becoming increasingly popular in Rome, and fresh venues pop up every year in the city. But the pioneer of them all, *the* jazz club in Rome, is still the Alexanderplatz. This venue offers nightly concerts with famous names from the Italian and foreign jazz scene. Dinner is served here from 8.30pm onwards; live music starts playing at 10.30pm. Booking is strongly advised. *Photo p274.*
▶ *Alexanderplatz organises one of the summer's most delightful alfresco music options: the jazz festival in Villa Celimontana (see p130).*

The Place
Via Alberico II 27 (06 6830 7137, www.the place.it). Bus 23, 34, 49, 80Exp, 280, 492, 990, N10, N11. **Open** 8.30pm-2.30am daily. Closed mid June-Sept. **Admission** €10-€20. **Credit** AmEx, DC, MC, V. **Map** p339 B4.
A swish, vibrant club with a stage for live acts, the Place caters for a thirty- and fortysomething crowd with an appealing menu of Italian – and a sprinkling of foreign – singer-songwriters and jazz bands. Dinner is served on a platform overlooking the stage. DJs spin commercial and house after the weekend acts have finished. *Photo p275.*

SUBURBS

See also p265 **Auditorium-Parco della Musica** and *p283* **Teatro Palladium**.

Brancaleone
Via Levanna 11, Suburbs: north (06 8200 4382, http://.new.brancaleone.eu). Bus 36, 60Exp, 90Exp, N22. **Open** 10pm-4.30am Thur-Sat. Closed June-mid Sept. **Admission** €5-€10. **No credit cards**.
Brancaleone – once one of Rome's best-run *centri sociali* – has relaunched itself after a rough patch, setting itself up once again as a key venue for international electronic musicians and DJs. The live and DJ acts on offer are top-notch. Weekends get packed but weekdays can be lively too, especially the reggae Thursdays; there are occasional events on Wednesdays. The venue also houses a cinema, a rehearsal studio and an organic products bar.

★ Circolo degli Artisti
Via Casilina Vecchia 42, Suburbs: south-east (06 7030 5684, www.circoloartisti.it). Bus 81, 105, 412, 810, N18/tram 5, 14, 19. **Open** 9.30pm-3.30am Tue-Thur; 9pm-4.30am Fri-Sun. Closed Aug. **Admission** from €6. **No credit cards**.
This is Rome's most popular venue for small- and medium-scale bands from international alternative music circuits. On Fridays it hosts a popular gay night (*see p260* **Omogenic**). On Saturdays (admission €5 after midnight) the established Screamadelica event has concerts by some of Europe's best alternative artists and emerging Italian bands, followed by a DJ spinning indie, electro and new wave. The spacious, cool garden is a great place for chatting with friends or making new ones. Often opens Monday too: check the website.

PalaLottomatica
Piazzale dello Sport, Suburbs: EUR (199 128 800, www.forumnet.it). Metro EUR Palasport/bus 30Exp, 671, 714, 780, 791. **Open** days & times vary. **Admission** varies.
The flying-saucer-shaped PalaLottomatica, which was designed by architect and engineer Pierluigi Nervi for the 1960 Rome Olympics, is Rome's leading space for large indoor concerts. Refurbishment has improved the once appalling acoustics – a little. Tickets are available from the usual outlets for large-scale events (*see p238*).

Zoobar
Via Bencivenga 1, Suburbs: north (339 272 7995, www.zoobar.roma.it). Bus 36, 60Exp, 84, 211, N4, N22. **Open** 11pm-4.30am Fri, Sat. Closed Aug. **Admission** €10 Fri; €4 Sat. **No credit cards**.
This down-to-earth club used to host live acts of up-and-coming international bands, drawing crowds to its venue in club-packed Testaccio. At the time of writing, it had just moved to the northern suburbs. There's no room in the new place for bands, making it unclear exactly what Zoobar's future holds. But the club continues to offer a steady DJ diet of pop, indie, Brit pop and 1980s retro to a studenty crowd. Fridays are open-bar nights.

Sport & Fitness

Spectating is the sport of choice in Rome.

Ever since the days when the ancient masses headed to the Colosseum in droves for their dose of gladiator-slaying, the Romans have been fanatical about sport… so long as they can enjoy it sitting down. Like their slothful forebears, today's Romans prefer to save their energy for gesticulating from the sidelines, though in recent years a general obsession with looking good has sent them scurrying to work off the pasta pounds at the *palestra* (gym). Yoga and Pilates are still regarded as exotic ways to get fit and facilities for the seriously sporty remain rather limited.

The hallowed *calcio* (football), with its all-star cast of modern-day gladiators, has long been the Romans' spectator sport of choice. Rome boasts two first-class football teams, one of which plays at home almost every weekend from September to June. To do sport as the Romans do, make the weekend pilgrimage to the Stadio Olimpico, and cheer from the stands.

ARTS & ENTERTAINMENT

CYCLING

Occasional Sunday closures to cars of the *centro storico* (see the local press for current details) provide an opportunity for exploring the city on two wheels in relative safety. It's a weekly occurrence further out: the ancient Appian Way offers especially serene (if somewhat bumpy) pedalling on traffic-free Sundays; the via Appia Antica visitors' centre (*see p152* **Punto Informativo**) has bikes for hire that day only. For other **bike hire** outlets, *see p310* and *p99* **Biking It**.

Two **cycle paths** – one beginning at Ponte Milvio and heading north, the other starting at Ponte Sublicio and heading south – follow the banks of the Tiber as far as the city's GRA ringroad; each makes for a pleasant ride, mostly on good surfaces, with an alternation of inner suburb and urban green along the route. They have – in theory, at least – been joined through the city centre on the river embankment but the going is pretty rough. There's a ramp to wheel your bike down at Ponte Sublicio, and elsewhere steps have tracks for easy pushing. You may find the odd questionable character lurking under bridges but on the whole it's safe – and a peaceful way to get around the city well below the level of the thundering traffic.

FOOTBALL

During the season, the 20 teams of Italy's Serie A (Premier League) meet at weekends under the gaze of 50 million Italians, but Romans' passion as supporters has always distinguished them. The city has two first-class football clubs – AS Roma (www.asromacalcio.it) and SS Lazio (www.sslazio.it) – that share the **Stadio Olimpico** (*see p278*). Tension is thick across the city when they play each other: derbies are an excuse for *romanisti* and *laziali* to attempt to out-do each other with the wittiest banners, the rudest chants and the most impressive displays of team-colour pyrotechnics. Lazio was founded in 1900, the younger Roma in 1927. Both teams are a solid presence in Serie A.

As part of measures to curb stadium violence, **tickets** can no longer be purchased directly from the Stadio Olimpico box office. You'll need to get them online from **www.listicket.it** or from the merchandising outlets listed below. Tickets are personal and non-transferable. You can purchase up to ten tickets at a time; to do so, you'll need to present your photo ID and provide the names and dates of birth of all the other people for whom you are buying tickets. Each must present photo ID (corresponding, obviously, with the name on the ticket) at the turnstiles when they get to the stadium.

★ Stadio Olimpico
Viale dello Stadio Olimpico, Suburbs: north (06 323 7333). Bus 32, 224, 280/tram 2. **Tickets** €10-€100. **No credit cards. Map** p337.
Important matches sell out quickly. Even the cheaper seats have a decent view.

Essential accessories

An array of unofficial team scarves, jerseys and flags can be bought outside the stadium on match days. For better quality items go to the club shops listed here. They also sell match tickets up to seven days in advance.

AS Roma Store
Piazza Colonna 360, Tridente (06 6992 4643, www.asromastore.it). Bus 52, 62, 95, 116, 175, 492. **Open** 10am-7pm Mon-Sat; 11am-7.30pm Sun. **Credit** AmEx, DC, MC, V. **Map** p339 E5.
AS Roma stores have an endless array of club merchandise, from scarves to baby booties – all of it emblazoned with the highly recognisable red-and-yellow AS Roma logo.
Other locations piazza B Cairoli 119, Campo (06 6880 9775).

Forza Lazio
Via Farini 34, Esquilino (06 482 6688). Metro Termini/bus 40Exp, 64, 70, 170, 175, 492. **Open** 9am-7pm Mon-Sat. Closed 1wk Aug. **Credit** AmEx, DC, MC, V. **Map** p341 D6.

GOLF

Golf is still an exclusive game in Italy. Most clubs will ask to see a membership card from your home club and proof of your handicap, although it's not normally necessary to be introduced by a member. Green fees, including those that we list below, are usually per day rather than per round.

Circolo del Golf Roma Acquasanta
Via Appia Nuova 716, Suburbs: east (06 780 3407, www.golfroma.it). Metro Colli Albani then bus 663 or 664. **Open** 8am-sunset (Sat, Sun to members only). **Rates** (green fees incl use of range) €100. *Driving range* €15. *Club hire* €20. *Golf cart hire* €50. **Credit** DC, MC, V.
The capital's most prestigious club, situated in the green belt east of the city.

Country Club Castelgandolfo
Via Santo Spirito 13, Castelgandolfo (06 9316 0911, www.countryclubcastelgandolfo.it). Metro Anagnina then taxi. **Open** 8.30am-7pm daily. **Rates** (green fees incl use of range) €65 Mon-Fri; €80 Sat, Sun. *Driving range* €10. *Club hire* €15. *Electric cart hire* €40 Mon-Fri; €45 Sat, Sun. *Trolley hire* €5. **Credit** AmEx, DC, MC, V.

Near the Pope's summer residence in this lakeside town, this course, designed by American golf architect Robert Trent Jones, is overlooked by a 16th-century clubhouse. The course is impossible to reach by public transport and beyond most taxis' circuits, so consider hiring a car from Rome and visiting the nearby Castelli romani (*see p302* **Escapes & Excursions**) before or after your round. Reserve tee times in advance by phone or online.

GYMS

Farnese Fitness
Vicolo delle Grotte 35, Ghetto & Campo (06 687 6931, www.farnesefitness.com). Bus 40Exp, 46, 64, 116, 492/tram 8. **Open** 9am-10pm Mon, Wed; 8am-10pm Tue, Thur; 9am-9pm Fri; 11am-7pm Sat; 10.30am-1.30pm Sun. Closed Aug. **Rates** €12/day. **Credit** DC, MC, V. **Map** p342 C2.
This friendly *centro storico* gym is handily located for a post-sightseeing workout. Classes in the downstairs aerobics studio – a 16th-century cellar – are included in the daily membership fee. The Sunday opening is suspended from June to September.

Roman Sport Center
Viale del Galoppatoio 33, Veneto & Borghese (06 320 1667, www.romansportcenter.com). Metro Spagna/bus 52, 53, 63, 116, 495, 630. **Open** 8am-10pm Mon-Sat; 9am-3pm Sun. Closed Sun from June to Aug. **Rates** €30/day; €250/mth. **Credit** AmEx, DC, MC, V. **Map** p340 A3.
'La Roman' offers aerobics studios, saunas, hydromassage pools, squash courts and two Olympic-size swimming pools.

RIDING

Cavalieri dell'Appia Antica
Via dei Cerceni 15, Appian Way (328 208 5787, www.cavalieriappia.altervista.org). Bus 118, 660. **Open** (call in advance to book excursions) 9am-1pm, 4-9pm Tue-Sun. Closed Aug. **Rates** €25/hr. **No credit cards.**
This rustic facility offers excursions along the ruin-strewn via Appia Antica for small groups. Friendly owners Sandro and Armanda speak almost no English, but their easy-tempered horses are suitable for beginners. Afternoon closing is earlier in winter. Ask about moonlight rides, and reserve well in advance for excursions at weekends.

RUGBY

Though football reigns supreme, the city also has a strong rugby subculture. Since 2000 the national side has been in the Six Nations' Championship, with home games played at the Stadio Flaminio. Rome also boasts a first-class rugby side in RDS Roma, who play their league matches at the Stadio Tre Fontane.

Jogging Along

On your marks in the park.

Maratona della Città di Roma.

Streets choked with traffic and the crowds of sightseers make a casual jog through central Rome nigh-on impossible – except during the city's annual marathon and fun-run (for details, *see p241* **Maratona della Città di Roma**). The pavements along the *lungotevere* (riverside drive) are an option, if you're prepared to hurdle tree roots, but the best jogging and strolling is to be had in the city's parks, most of which are just outside the *centro storico*.

Circo Massimo
A taste of ancient Rome while you're working up a sweat. **Map** pp344-345.

Terme di Caracalla
Serious runners congregate opposite Caracalla's ancient baths. **Map** p345.

Villa Ada
This large park has running paths around its ponds and lakes. **Map** p337.

Villa Borghese
Great for joggers, but can get crowded at weekends. **Map** p338 & p340.

Villa Pamphili
The city's largest park contains picturesque walkways with workout stations. **Map** p337.

Stadio Flaminio
Viale Tiziano, Suburbs: north (06 3685 7309, www.federugby.it). Bus 53, 910/tram 2. **Tickets** *Regular games* €22-€143. *Six Nations games* €50-€233. **No credit cards.**
Tickets can be purchased online at the address given above, or at www.listicket.com. *Photo p280.*

Stadio Tre Fontane
Via Laurentina 52, Suburbs: EUR (06 5987 1977). Metro Marconi/bus 30Exp, 671, 780. **Tickets** €5. **No credit cards.**

SPAS

Several Roman hotels have spas open to the public: **Aleph** (*see p169*), **Villa Spalletti Trivelli** (*see p165*), **De Russie** and **Rome Cavalieri** (for both, *see p173* **Big and Sassy**).

Acanto Benessere Spa
Piazza Rondanini 30, Pantheon & Navona (06 6813 6602, www.acantospa.it). Bus 40Exp, 46, 64, 70/tram 8. **Open** 10am-10pm Mon-Sat. **Credit** AmEx, DC, MC, V. **Map** p339 D5.

Sidebar: ARTS & ENTERTAINMENT

Stadio Flaminio. *See p279.*

This unisex day spa is a tranquil haven with futuristic glass treatment rooms, a great range of massages and treatments, and a Turkish bath.

Acquamadre
Via di Sant'Ambrogio 17, Ghetto (06 686 4272, www.acquamadre.it). Bus 40, 64, 70/tram 8.
Open 2-9pm Tue; 11am-9pm Wed-Sun. Closed Aug. **Credit** AmEx, DC, MC, V. **Map** p342 D2.
What better way to remove the grime of Roman traffic than to sweat it out in this glamorous modern take on the ancient Roman bath house: calm, steamy and offering an array of massages and beauty treatments. On Wednesday and Friday it's women-only.

El Spa
Via Plinio 15C/D, Vatican & Prati (06 6819 2869, www.elspa.it). Bus 30Exp, 492, 926.

INSIDE TRACK
STADIO SEATING

Once inside the **Stadio Olimpico** (*see p278*), die-hard Roma fans flock to the *curva sud* (south end), marking their territory with red and yellow, while the sky blue and white of the Lazio faithful fills the *curva nord* (north end). Team mascots (Roma's wolf, Lazio's eagle) are much in evidence. The curves have the best pyrotechnics and cheapest seats, but for a better view, opt for the more expensive Tribuna Tevere or Tribuna Monte Mario.

Open 10am-9pm Mon-Thur; 10am-10pm Fri, Sat; noon-9pm Sun. **Credit** AmEx, DC, MC, V. **Map** p338 B3.
Decorated in warm, Middle-Eastern style, this spa specialises in holistic treatments. Try the *mandi lulur*, an ancient Indonesian treatment that leaves you with blissfully silky-soft skin.

Kamispa
Via degli Avignonesi 11-12 (06 4201 0039, www.kamispa.com). Bus 62, 95, 116, 175, 492. **Open** 10am-10pm daily. **Credit** AmEx, DC, MC, V. **Map** p341 B5.
Massages, scrubs and a wide selection of beauty treatments are available in this gloriously spice-scented haven of minimalist oriental decor. There's a small swimming pool and a shop. Booking ahead is recommended here.

SWIMMING

Romans flock en masse to the coast at the first hint of warm weather (*see p301* **Quick Dips**). It's no wonder, since swimming pools are scarce in the city. With a few far-flung exceptions, those pools that do exist are privately run. The **Roman Sport Center** (*see p278*) has Olympic-size pools.

Piscina delle Rose
Viale America 20, Suburbs: EUR (06 5422 0333, www.piscinadellerose.it). Metro EUR-Palasport/bus 30Exp, 714, 780. **Open** May-June, Sept 9am-7pm daily. July-Aug 9am-10pm daily. **Admission** €16 full day; €14 half day (9am-2pm or 2-7pm); €10

1-4pm Mon-Fri; €130 Mon-Fri monthly ticket. **No credit cards**.

This Olympic-size public pool in the heart of the suburban EUR district is often crowded with Roman *bambini* on warmer days.

Hotel pools

Space is tight in central Rome, which means only the swankiest of hotels can afford to have their own pool. The following pools can be used by non-residents – at a price.

Parco dei Principi

Via Frescobaldi 5, Suburbs: north (06 854 421, www.parcodeiprincipi.com). Bus 52, 53, 217, 910/tram 3, 19. **Open** *May-Sept* 10am-6.30pm daily. **Admission** €35 Mon-Fri; €70 Sat, Sun. **Credit** AmEx, DC, MC, V.

On the edge of the Villa Borghese gardens, this pool is a favourite with locals (it can be busy at weekends). Weather permitting, it's open into October.

Rome Cavalieri

Via Cadlolo 101, Suburbs: west (06 35 091, www.romecavalieri). Bus 907, 913. **Open** *May-mid Oct* 9am-7pm daily. **Admission** €45 Mon-Fri; €75 Sat, Sun. **Credit** AmEx, DC, MC, V.

This almost-Olympic-sized pool is a draw for serious swimmers and style-conscious sun-seekers alike: it's one of the chicest poolsides in Rome, as evidenced by the array of designer swimwear modelled by lounger-bound lovelies.

▶ *This is a classy place, whether you're planning to have a swim, stay the night (see p173* **Big and Sassy***) or just eat (see p205* **La Pergola***).*

TENNIS

Circolo della Stampa

Piazza Mancini 19, Suburbs: north (06 323 2452). Bus 53, 280, 910/tram 2. **Open** 8am-10pm Mon-Fri; 8am-8pm Sat, Sun. **Rates** *Court* (50mins) €10 singles; €12 doubles. *Floodlights* (50mins) €12 singles; €14 doubles. **No credit cards**.

Owned by the Italian journalists' association, but friendly and open to non-members, the Circolo offers both clay and synthetic grass courts. There's no dress code, but studded trainers are not allowed. Booking is advised.

YOGA

Both the gyms we list (*see p278*) offer yoga classes; phone to check.

L'Albero e la Mano

Via della Pelliccia 3, Trastevere (06 581 2871, www.lalberoelamano.it). Bus 23, 280, 630, 780, H/tram 8. **Open** depends on course schedule. Closed Sat & Sun; Aug. **Rates** €12-€15/class. **No credit cards**. **Map** p342 C3.

This incense-scented studio offers classes in Ashtanga and Hatha yoga, as well as in t'ai chi chuan, belly-dancing and Shiatsu, Ayurvedic and Thai massage.

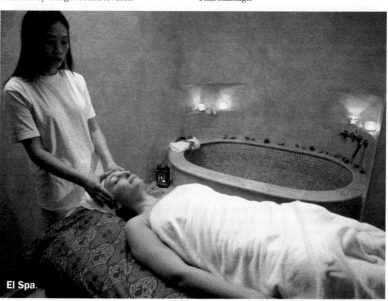

El Spa.

Theatre & Dance

Seasonal festivals are leading the way forward for Rome's theatre scene.

Rome isn't exactly renowned as the city to head to for cutting-edge contemporary theatre and dance. In fact, some would describe the scene as staid and overly focused on tradition, particularly in the arena of dance, which has lost many a talented young Italian artist to more progressive foreign companies. That said, luckily for anyone interested in dance or theatre, times are changing and some excellent seasonal festivals and events with forward-thinking programming are fast challenging Roman theatregoers to raise their expectations beyond the ordinary. Keep an ear to the ground, check local venue websites for what's on while you're here, and you might just unearth a dramatic or dance gem in the Eternal City.

THEATRE

It isn't easy for an Anglo-Saxon audience to find satisfaction in the Italian theatre scene. The school of drama, with its strong traditions and roots in the *Commedia dell'arte*, and the stiff style imposed by its dramatic arts academy, is worlds apart from what British, Irish or north American theatregoers are used to. If you are thinking of spending an evening at the theatre, don't expect the daring performances of Edinburgh's Fringe or the delightful plays of London's West End.

That said, the effects of globalisation are encroaching, and the Roman theatregoing public is becoming ever more sophisticated, its standards raised mainly thanks to some excellent seasonal festivals (in particular the **RomaEuropa** festival; *see p283* **Dance Off**) that bring the best national and international fare to the city's excitement-starved stages.

One interesting project is the **Casa dei Teatri** (*see right*). The aim of this centre is to give a multifaceted perspective to drama, integrating performances with training, workshops and research. The complex – which is located inside the **Villa Pamphili** park (*see p161*) in Monteverde – hosts a library, a space for screenings, conferences, lectures and workshops, and a permanent art collection.

Rome has no lack of performing arts venues: there are at least 80 theatres in the city. The Italian drama board ETI is responsible for the 18th-century **Teatro Argentina** (*see right*), the modern **Teatro India** (*see p284*), the

delightful **Teatro Valle** and the bleaker **Teatro Quirino**.

Alongside these, valiant private foundations and organisations offer fare of uneven quality. The **Teatro Vascello** (*see p284*) often hosts international companies and experimental productions; the **Teatro Tor Bella Monaca** (*see p284*), directed by actor Michele Placido, has mainly contemporary theatre and a handful of old favourites; the **Teatro Il Sistina** (*see p284*) hosts musicals and comic monologues; the **Teatro Olimpico** (*see p264*) holds some dance events and concerts by the **Accademia Filarmonica Romana** (*see p262*) as well as musicals; the **Teatro Ambra Jovinelli** delivers variety shows and jazz concerts; the freshly refurbished **Teatro Palladium** (*see right*) runs an innovative programme; and Rome's own version of Shakespeare's Globe Theatre, the **Silvano Toti Globe Theatre** (*see p284*) in the Villa Borghese, offers a summer programme of Shakespearean fare and Sunday matinée shows for children.

DANCE

Dance has always been the Cinderella of the arts in Italy, notwithstanding a string of influential Italian dancers and choreographers, such as Maria Taglioni and Enrico Cecchetti. An ever-inadequate arts funding package means that many excellent young Italian dancers find fame and fortune abroad, then drop in here occasionally to star as guest artists in Italian corps de ballet.

Dance fans keep an eye on the programme at the Teatro Olimpico, which hosts visiting international companies. There are some festival dance events at the Teatro Argentina, Teatro Valle and Teatro Palladium. The **Teatro Greco** (*see p284*), Teatro Vascello, the Auditorium-Parco della Musica and the **Auditorium Conciliazione** (*see p263*) are all possible venues for touring Italian and international dance companies.

The **Teatro dell'Opera** (*see p264*) and its offspring, the Teatro Nazionale, are where the Opera's corps de ballet stretches its limbs. Its seasonal programme invariably includes two or three classics and a handful of contemporary works. The standard leaves much to be desired; in fact, good soloists and sometimes brilliant stars are overshadowed by kitsch productions, mouldy old sets and costumes, and second-rate choreographers. For ticket agencies, *see p238*.

MAIN PUBLIC THEATRES

See also p265 **Auditorium Conciliazione** and *p264* **Auditorium-Parco della Musica**.

Casa dei Teatri
Villino Corsini, Villa Doria Pamphili, Suburbs: west (06 4546 0693, www.casadeiteatri.cultura roma.it). Bus 44, 75, 710, 870. **Box office**

May-Sept 10am-7pm Tue-Sun. *Oct-Apr* 10am-5pm Tue-Sun. **No credit cards**. **Map** p342 A3.
Elegant 18th-century Villa Corsini inside the Villa Pamphili park (*see p161*) is a centre for drama and drama-making, with a stage, spaces for workshops and study, and two prestigious libraries, as well as the important collection of theatrical documents donated by actor Carmelo Bene. For information on performances, call the Teatro Argot on 06 589 8111 or 06 581 4023.

Teatro Palladium
Piazza Bartolomeo Romano 8, Suburbs: south (06 5733 2768, www.teatro-palladium.it). Metro Garbatella/bus 716. **Box office** 4-8pm Tue-Sun; until 9pm on performance days. **Open** days & times vary. **Admission** varies. **Credit** AmEx, DC, MC, V. **Map** p123 C3.
This beautiful theatre dates to the 1920s. Now furnished with brightly coloured chairs, it provides a fascinating mix of electronic music, cutting-edge theatre and art performances. It is one of the venues of choice for the exciting and eclectic annual RomaEuropa Festival (*see p244*).

Teatro di Roma – Argentina
Largo Argentina 52, Ghetto & Campo (06 684 0001, www.teatrodiroma.net). Bus 30Exp, 40Exp, 46, 62, 63, 64, 70, 81, 87, 492, 628, 810, 916/tram 8. **Box office**

Dance Off

The best festivals for dance fans.

Balletomanes must rely on festivals rather than regular dance seasons to satisfy their appetites. The Auditorium-Parco della Musica (*see p265*) inaugurates its seasonal activities in mid-September with a world-class tango festival, **Buenos Aires Tango** (www.auditorium.com), featuring fantastic tango dancers and performances, as well as open classes and a *milonga*.

Malnourished dance fans especially await the delicacies that the **RomaEuropa Festival** (*see p244*) can be relied upon to serve up. This arts festival features an exciting programme of multimedia events, concerts and happenings in classic and alternative venues all over the city. Leading names of the dance world, such as Alain Platel, Sylvie Guillem and Akram Khan pace the programme of this sophisticated event, but so do many emerging artists with dance/video performances and other genre-busting events; an interesting sideline of the

programme always includes dancers and companies from far-away places like China, Thailand or Mongolia.

Next in line is **Equilibrio** (www. auditorium.com), with an interesting programme in February that includes Italian and international contemporary dance, as well as dance theatre, plus film and video projections on dance and other multimedia events. The **Teatro Vascello** (*see p284*) also kicks off its autumn and winter season with a mini-festival dedicated to dance, be it experimental, tango or folk.

In mid July the place to look for dance is Villa Pamphili (*see p161*), which hosts the annual dance feast **Invito alla Danza** (06 5831 0086, 06 3973 8323, www. invitoalladanza.it) in its beautiful gardens. The programme, which includes both classical and modern offerings, presents a performance every evening for about two weeks, and often includes international companies and stars.

10am-2pm, 3-7pm Tue-Sun. **Shows** *Oct-June*
9pm Tue, Wed, Fri, Sat; 5pm Thur, Sun.
Credit AmEx, DC, MC, V. **Map** p342 D1.
Rome's plush flagship theatre has a wide-ranging
programme, including some dance and poetry.

★ Teatro di Roma – India

Lungotevere Papareschi/via L Pierantoni
6, Suburbs: south (06 6840 00311, www.
teatrodiroma.net). Bus 170, 780, 781.
Box office 30mins before shows, or at
Teatro Argentina (*see above*). **No credit
cards**. **Map** p123 A2.
This converted industrial space, with three stages,
is used for more experimental offerings.

Teatro Tor Bella Monaca

Via Bruno Cirino/viale Duilio Cambellotti,
Suburbs: east (06 201 0579, www.teatrotorbellam-
onaca.it). Metro Anagnina then bus 20.
Box office 3.30-7.30pm Tue-Sun; from 7.30pm
on day of performance. **No credit cards**.
The city's latest theatrical initiative has found space
in the outer eastern suburbs, as part of city hall's
thrust to bring culture to peripheral areas. The
Teatro Tor Bella Monaca is a multifunctional edifice
with two theatres, rehearsal space, an open-air arena
and rooms for workshops, conferences and lectures.
At the helm is actor Michele Placido, whose varied
programme includes many free events and concerts.

Teatro Valle

Via del Teatro Valle 23A, Pantheon &
Navona (06 686 9049, www.teatrovalle.it).
Bus 30Exp, 40Exp, 46, 62, 63, 64, 70, 81,
87, 492, 628, 810, 916/tram 8. **Box office**
10am-7pm Tue-Sun. **Shows** *Oct-May* 8.45pm
Tue, Thur-Sat; 4.45pm Wed, Sun. **Credit**
AmEx, DC, MC, V. **Map** p339 D6.
This beautiful chocolate-box of a theatre hosts an
interesting range of performances plus the occa-
sional concert or ballet. Occasional Monday shows.

PRIVATE & SMALLER VENUES

See also p264 **Teatro Olimpico**.

Teatro Greco

Via R Leoncavallo 10, Suburbs: north (06 860
7513, www.teatrogreco.it). Bus 63, 135, 342, 630.
Box office 10am-1pm, 4-7pm Tue-Sun. **Shows**
9pm daily. **Credit** MC, V.
A well-designed venue that programmes some
Italian dance and has a penchant for little-tried
writers, both foreign and domestic.

Teatro Il Sistina

Via Sistina 9, Veneto & Borghese (06 420 0711,
www.ilsistina.com). Metro Barberini or Spagna/bus
52, 53, 61, 62, 63, 71, 80Exp, 95, 116, 119, 175.
Box office 10am-7pm Mon-Sat; 11am-6pm Sun.

Shows 9pm Tue-Sat; 5pm Sun. **Credit**
AmEx, DC, MC, V. **Map** p341 B5.
A tacky, overheated theatre with decent acoustics
and a lot of red velvet.

Teatro Vascello

Via G Carini 72, Suburbs: west (06 588 1021/06
589 8031, www.teatrovascello.it). Bus 44, 75, 710,
870, 871. **Box office** 10am-5pm Mon; 10am-9pm
Tue-Fri; 3-8pm Sat; 10.30am-8pm Sun. **Shows**
9pm Tue-Sat; 5pm Sun. **No credit cards**. **Map**
p343 A4.
The Teatro Vascello presents decent experimental
theatre and dance productions, along with conferences and workshops.

SUMMER VENUES

Anfiteatro della Quercia del Tasso

Passeggiata del Gianicolo, Gianicolo (06 575
0827, www.anfiteatroquerciadeltasso.com).
Bus 870. **Box office** from 7pm before shows.
Shows *July-mid Sept* 9pm daily; occasional
afternoon matinées. **No credit cards**.
Map p342 A6.
This open-air amphitheatre was built in the 17th century. It specialises in Greek and Latin theatre and
18th-century Venetian comedy.

Silvano Toti Globe Theatre

Largo Aqua Felix, Villa Borghese (06 0608,
www.globetheatreroma.com). **Box office**
June-Sept 1-9.15pm Tue-Sun. **No credit
cards**. **Map** p340 B2.
Rome's Elizabethan theatre, a reproduction of
London's Globe Theatre, can hold up to 1,250 people,
including 420 standing in the stalls. Under the direction of actor Gigi Proietti, the theatre offers a
Shakespearean menu, with a number of incursions
into Goldoni and Molière and special performances
designed for children.

Teatro Romano di Ostia Antica

Scavi di Ostia Antica, viale dei Romagnoli 117,
Ostia Antica (information 06 0608, tickets 899
500 055). Train from Ostiense to Ostia Antica.
Box office from 6pm before shows; also at
Teatro Argentina (*see above*). **Shows** *Mid July-*
mid Aug 8.30pm daily. **No credit cards**.
This superbly preserved Roman theatre fills the
summer with prestigious productions of Roman and
Greek classics, as well as a range of concerts and
ballets. It's an authentic affair, which means the
seats are made of stone – do bring a cushion. You'll
also be outside for a prolongued period of time, so
packing some mosquito repellent is a good idea, too.
For a comprehensive programme of events consult
the website www.ostiaantica.net.
▶ *For more information on the dramatic*
remains of ancient Rome's port at Ostia
Antica, see p287.

ARTS & ENTERTAINMENT

Escapes & Excursions

Bracciano. *See p292.*

Escapes & Excursions

Leave the heat behind and head to Rome's more sedate surroundings.

The economic miracle of the 1970s may have brought prosperity to Italy but it wreaked havoc on its landscape, particularly around major cities. The great magnet, Rome, suffered worst of all, with high-rise blocks striding out across what had once been glorious *campagna romana* – hailed in song and verse from antiquity – in unregulated ranks.

If you do head into the Lazio countryside, chances are you'll be travelling along a route that has been trodden for millennia. The *consolari* (the consular roads) of the Romans were well paved and well maintained. Today the *consolari* are still key traffic corridors; but along them you'll find Roman (and earlier) remains, grand *palazzi*, quaint villages, lovely countryside and some perfectly acceptable beaches.

GETTING AROUND

By car

For more information on car hire and driving while you're here, *see p308.*

The *Grande Raccordo Anulare* (GRA) ring road links with the network of *autostrade* (motorways) and *strade statali* (SS – most of which follow ancient *consolari*). Traffic on the GRA and city approach roads can be intense in rush hour, and on Friday and Sunday evenings. You can save time (but not money) at tollbooths by using a **Viacard** debit card, available from

---

INSIDE TRACK
TRANSPORT MAPS

The www.atac.roma.it site of the municipal transport company has good, downloadable maps of the railways and buses around the city. Getting to them is a problem. Don't, whatever you do, click for the English version of the site: the maps seem to disappear. Instead, from the Italian homepage click 'Biglietti', then 'Linee e mappe'. You'll find PDF files to help you on your way.

---

tabacchi (*see p224*) and most motorway service stations. Tollbooths also accept credit cards (AmEx, DC, MC, V). **Isoradio** (103.3FM; occasional English-language bulletins in summer) gives regular traffic updates for major roads; **www.autostrade.it** also details current conditions.

By train

For rail transport map, *see p352*; for mainline services, *see p307.*

The network of local railways, the Ferrovie Regionali (FR) and Ferrovie Urbane, is handy for destinations outside Rome. You can get information toll-free on 800 431 784 or from www.atac.roma.it.

By bus

The Lazio transport authority **COTRAL** (information 06 7295 7205, toll-free 800 174 471, www.cotralspa.it) covers the region efficiently; most services ply the consular roads. Buses leave from several city termini, each serving

---

About the author

Nicky Swallow *edits* Charming Small Hotel Guides: Tuscany & Umbria *and is the author of a travel guide to Naples. She has lived in Italy since 1981.*

a different direction (as indicated in the 'Getting there' listings for each section of this chapter).

Anagnina Metro Anagnina.
Cornelia Metro Cornelia.
Laurentina Metro Laurentina/bus 30Exp, 761.
Magliana Metro Magliana/bus 780.
Ponte Mammolo Metro Ponte Mammolo.
Saxa Rubra Train from Roma Nord–Flaminio (map p354 D2) to Saxa Rubra.
Termini Metro Termini/buses to Termini (map p357 E5).
Tiburtina Metro Tiburtina/bus 492, 495.

VIA OSTIENSE

If you're thinking of making the punishing trip to Pompeii during your holidays, forget it and do a comfortable day-trip to ancient Rome's port of **Ostia Antica** instead – arguably a better site for getting a feel for everyday life in a working Roman town. You could begin with a stopover at the Museo della Via Ostiense, which has a model of Ostia Antica in its heyday. If you're driving, you'll get to Ostia Antica along via Ostiense, the shortest of the *consolari*, connecting Rome with the mouth (*ostia*) of the Tiber, which in antiquity lay 30 kilometres (18 miles) from the road's origin at Porta San Paolo. The Roma–Lido railway (from the station of the same name, adjoining the Piramide metro

station) has regular services to Ostia Antica (30mins).

Legend says that Ostia was founded by Ancus Martius, the fourth king of Rome, in the second half of the seventh century BC, although the oldest remains date 'only' from c330 BC. Ostia was Rome's main port for over 600 years, until its decline in the fourth century AD. Abandoned after sackings by barbarians in the fifth century, the town was gradually buried by river mud. Visit the **Scavi di Ostia Antica** site on a sunny weekday and bring a picnic (not actually allowed, but keep a low profile and you probably won't be ejected). Purchasing a site plan is a good idea.

The *decumanus maximus* (high street) runs from the Porta Romana for almost a kilometre (half a mile), past the theatre and forum, before forking left to what used to be the seashore (now three kilometres/two miles away at Ostia). The right fork, via della Foce, leads to the Tiber. On either side of these main arteries is a network of intersecting lanes, where the best discoveries can be made.

Behind the theatre is the Forum of the Corporations. Here the various trade guilds had their offices, and mosaics on the floor of small shops that ring the open square refer to the products each guild dealt in – shipowners had ships on the floor, ivory dealers had

Ostia Antica.

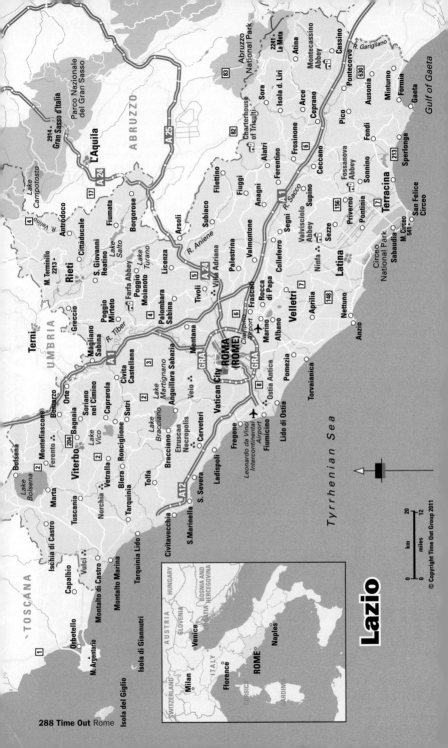

Lazio

elephants. Further along on the right is the old mill, where both the grindstones and the circular furrows ploughed by the blindfolded donkeys that turned them are still visible. In the tangle of streets between the decumanus and the museum, don't miss the *thermopolium* – an ancient Roman bar, complete with marble counter, a fresco advertising the house fare and a garden with a fountain. Located off the forum to the south-east are the forum baths – the terracotta heating pipes are still visible. Nearby is the *forica*, or ancient public latrine. In mostly residential districts off via della Foce, the House of Cupid and Psyche is an elegant fourth-century construction; the House of the Dioscuri has beautiful mosaics; the Insula of the Charioteers still has many of its frescoes. The wealthy lived in the garden apartments at the western end of the site, set back from the busy streets; recently restored, these can be visited on tours on Thursday morning, at 10.30am by booking on 06 5635 8044. The **museum** has a good collection of artefacts from the site, including statues, fresco fragments and bas-reliefs of scenes of ordinary life; there's a café and bookshop next door.

Five minutes' walk from the entrance to the excavations, the medieval village of Ostia Antica has a **castle** – built in 1483-86 for the bishop of Ostia, the future Pope Julius II – and picturesque cottages, once inhabited by the people who worked in the nearby salt pans.

If you have your own transport (and it's the right day, and you've booked…), you might consider prefacing your Ostia jaunt with a look at the port that eclipsed Ostia in the second century. As Rome's population grew to around a million at the height of the Empire, its port activities overflowed five kilometres (three miles) north from Ostia to a more sheltered section of the coast. The earliest port here, built by Emperor Claudius in the 40s AD, had a unique jetty: a ship built to transport the Egyptian obelisk now in St Peter's square was sunk in front of the harbour and a lighthouse mounted on it. Claudius' port was later absorbed by the larger and more efficient **Porto di Traiano** (AD 110), where the hexagonal harbour could cater for up to 200 ships at once. Canals were cut to link the harbours to the Tiber, along which river barges were hauled the 35 kilometres (20 miles) to Rome. Almost nothing is left of Claudius' port – what there is lies between airport runways – but in Fiumicino (ancient Portus), the ruins of the Porto di Traiano can be visited on guided tours. Or take a horse-and-carriage trip around the basin for some bird-spotting at the **Oasi di Porto**.

With private transport, it's a short hop from here to Rome's closest beach resort at the modern town of Ostia, and to its fishing port – and seafood restaurants – at **Fiumicino** (not to be confused with the airport of the same name).

FREE Castello di Giulio II (Castle of Julius II)
Piazza della Rocca, Ostia Antica (06 5635 8013). **Open** (guided tours only) 10am, noon Tue; 10am, noon, 3pm Thur. **Admission** free.
Tours can be booked at other times at the number given above.

Oasi di Porto
Via Portuense 2264, Fiumicino (06 588 0880, www.oasidiporto.it). **Open** 10am-4pm Thur, Sun. Closed June-mid Oct. **Admission** €10; €8 reductions. **No credit cards.**

FREE Porto di Traiano
06 652 9192. **Open** (guided tours only; pre-booking and own transport essential) 9.30am 1st Sat, last Sun of mth. **Admission** free.

★ Scavi di Ostia Antica
Viale dei Romagnoli 717, Ostia Antica (06 5635 2830, www.itnw.roma.it/ostia/scavi). **Open** Apr-Oct 8.30am-7.30pm Tue-Sun. Nov-Mar 8.30am-5pm Tue-Sun. **Admission** €6.50; €3.25 reductions. **No credit cards.**

Getting there

By car
Ostia Antica: via del Mare or via Ostiense. **Fiumicino, Porto di Traiano**: autostrada Roma–Fiumicino.

By train
Ostia Antica, Ostia: train from Roma–Lido station, next to Piramide metro: for downtown Ostia, get off at Lido Centro; for full-on beach umbrellas, use the Stella Polare or Cristoforo Colombo stops.
Fiumicino: FR1 to Fiumicino Aeroporto, then frequent bus services to Fiumicino town.

By bus
COTRAL services run to Fiumicino (Aeroporto, and in town at piazza Marinai d'Italia) from Cornelia. There is no direct bus to Ostia but there are connections from Fiumicino; the half-hourly service stops in front of Lido Centro station.

VIA AURELIA

Built in the third century BC, via Aurelia not only connected Rome with upper Tyrrhenian seaports, it also had the advantage of cutting the mysterious, sophisticated (and declining) Etruscans off from their port at Pyrgi, thus effectively crippling this once-powerful trading people. Along the Aurelia are a host of Etruscan places, most notably Cerveteri and Tarquinia. And if you need a break from all that antiquity, there's plenty of opportunity for swimming along the way.

From Rome's western suburbs, the road travels due west, curving north at Ladispoli to follow the coast, eventually reaching Genoa. (It can also be picked up from the A12 Rome –Civitavecchia motorway.) Despite the occasional unfortunate outbreak of modern eyesores – including the entire town of **Ladispoli** – the Aurelia today remains a pretty drive through rolling hills and by the sea, with the occasional Roman tomb or medieval watchtower along the way. Unless you're looking for a beach, ignore signposts to the seaside towns of **Maccarese**, **Fregene** and unforgivably ugly Ladispoli, and head straight for the town of Cerveteri with one of the most important sites in Etruscan Lazio.

With three ports, Etruscan Kysry – known to the Romans as Caere, now **Cerveteri** – was one of the great Mediterranean trading centres from the seventh to fifth centuries BC. The 16th-century Orsini castle here houses the small **Museo Cerite**, stocked with local finds.

Much more interesting than the town itself is the **Necropoli di Banditaccia**. This town of the dead – with streets, *piazze* and tidy little houses – is one of the most touching

archaeological sites in Italy. There's plenty of ancient atmosphere here, with a wilderness of vines, cypresses and oaks growing on and around tufa-cut tumuli (mound-shaped tombs). The most important tombs are clearly labelled in both English and Italian; the earliest date from the seventh century BC and the latest from the third, by which time there had been a progressive impoverishment of tomb size and decoration. Don't miss the well-preserved sixth-century BC Tomba dei Capitelli (with finely carved stone), the fourth-century BC Tomba dei Rilievi (with bas-reliefs of weapons and utensils), and the three parallel streets of fifth- and sixth-century BC cube-shaped tombs between via degli Inferi and via delle Serpi. Outside the main gate, the Tomba degli Scudi e delle Sedie has chairs carved out of rock and bas-reliefs of shields.

The Etruscan port of **Pyrgi** was the main sea outlet for Cerveteri. Its remains lie offshore from the squat Orsini **Castle of Santa Severa**. Pygri was the site of an important sanctuary to the Etruscan goddess Uni (whom Romans called Juno); the **Antiquarium di Pyrgi** contains finds from local excavations.

Northwards, past the family resort of **Santa Marinella** and the port of Civitavecchia, **Tarquinia** lies three kilometres (two miles) inland from the Aurelia, bristling with medieval defensive towers. Once a major Etruscan

Museo Nazionale & Necropolis.

Bracciano. *See p292.*

stronghold, Tarquinia has a **necropolis** with the art that Cerveteri's lacks: some 100 tombs, hidden beneath a grassy hill about two kilometres (1.25 miles) out of town, are vividly painted with scenes of work and social life, athletic contests, mysterious rituals and erotic encounters. The Tomba della Caccia e della Pesca has delightful fishing and hunting scenes; in the Tomba dei Leopardi, couples recline at a banquet (note the man passing his partner an egg – a recurrent symbol, though experts disagree about what it represents). There's a similar scene with dancers in the elegant Tomba delle Leonesse. The Tomba dei Tori, one of the oldest, depicts Achilles waiting to ambush Troilus. (Only a handful of the tombs are open at any one time.) Housed in the impressive, 15th-century Palazzo Vitelleschi, Tarquinia's **Museo Nazionale** has one of the best Etruscan collections outside Rome. Among some marvellous examples of carved sarcophagi and exquisite Attic vases, its chief exhibit is a pair of fourth-century BC terracotta winged horses.

Some 16 kilometres (ten miles) north of Tarquinia, just past the huge bulk of the decommissioned power station overlooking the sea at Monalto di Castro, a right turn off the Aurelia will bring you to **Vulci**, once a large and important Etruscan town. Built on a volcanic plateau on the Tuscany/Lazio border, it reached its heyday in the sixth century BC. Near the sea, it was a maritime power. It was also famous for its production of ceramics and objects in bronze, but after being conquered by

Rome in 280 BC, it rapidly declined. Although the Etruscan and Roman remains are relatively scant at the **Parco Naturalistico Archaeologico Vulci**, the extensive open site is rather lovely. Tracts of the early city walls (including two of the original city gates) can be seen, while within the walls are the remains of a fourth-century BC temple and a long stretch of Roman road. Four necropoli containing over 15,000 tombs have been found around the city, mostly dating from the eighth century BC. The Vulci tombs had statues of imaginary beasts guarding the entrances.

`FREE` Antiquarium di Pyrgi

Castello di Santa Severa (0766 570 209, www.museosantasevera.org). **Open** 9am-1pm, 3-5pm Tue-Sun. **Admission** *Antiquarium* free. *Tours of the site* €4.50. **No credit cards**.

Museo Cerite & Necropoli di Banditaccia

Museum: piazza Santa Maria, Cerveteri. Necropolis: via della Necropoli (06 994 1354). **Open** Sept-June 9am-1pm, 3-5pm Tue-Sun. *July & Aug* 9am-1pm, 5-8pm Tue-Sun. **Admission** *Museum or necropolis* €4; €2 reductions. *Both* €6.50; €3.25 reductions. **No credit cards**.

Museo Nazionale & Necropolis

Museum: Palazzo Vitelleschi, piazza Cavour, Tarquinia (0766 856 036, www.tarquinia.net). Necropolis: via Ripagretta (0766 856 308). **Open** *Museum* 8.30am-7.30pm Tue-Sun.

Necropolis Apr-Oct 8.30am-7.30pm Tue-Sun. Nov-Mar 8.30am-2pm (last entry 1hr 30mins before closing) Tue-Sun. **Admission** *Museum or necropolis* €6; €3 reductions. *Both* €8; €4 reductions. **No credit cards**. *Photo p290*.

Parco Naturalistico Archaeologico Vulci

Via della Volta Buia, Montalto di Castro (0766 879 729, www.vulci.it). **Open** *Jan-Mar, Oct-Dec* 9am-5pm Mon, Wed-Sun; 2-5pm Tue. *Apr-Sept* 10am-6pm daily. **Admission** €8; €5 reductions; €16 family ticket. **No credit cards**.

Getting there

If you're visiting the Aurelia by public transport, you'll be hard pressed to cover more than one site in a day, though combining the Pyrgi Antiquarium, or the Necropolis at Cerveteri, with a swim is perfectly feasible. Vulci cannot be reached by public transport.

By car

The A12 motorway runs parallel to via Aurelia as far as Civitavecchia.

By train

Ladispoli-Cerveteri, Santa Marinella, Civitavecchia: from Ostiense or Trastevere. A local bus connects Marina di Cerveteri station to Cerveteri.
Tarquinia: mainline services from Termini, Ostiense or Trastevere.

By bus

COTRAL services along the Aurelia from Cornelia.

VIA CASSIA

Leading north-west out of Rome and passing through the heart of ancient Etruria to Siena and Florence, via Cassia winds through Lazio's lakeland – gentle hilly countryside dotted with picturesque towns built on Etruscan or Roman foundations. It also passes by a number of glorious gardens.

Little is known of the origins of this ancient road: nobody seems sure exactly who built it or when. From the GRA ring road, the modern via Cassia Veientana, parallels it to the east. Between the old and new roads (but best reached from the former), the **Parco Regionale di Veio** – just before you reach the medieval village of Isola Farnese and across a bridge over an impressive waterfall – surrounds **Veio**, an Etruscan city founded in the eighth century BC and which until the fourth century BC was Rome's chief rival for control of the Tiber's right bank. The site

contains rare examples of Etruscan houses and temples, plus a striking sixth-century BC sanctuary of Apollo, with a canopy-covered altar area and a pool.

In the crater of an extinct volcano, pretty **Lago di Bracciano** – about 40 kilometres (24 miles) north of Rome – is Rome's emergency water supply, so it's kept reasonably clean; the best swimming spots are just north of Bracciano town on the western shore, and on the eastern side near Trevignano. Boats run around the lake from Bracciano in summer.

A handful of pretty villages overlook this body of water. **Bracciano**, the main town on the lake, is dominated by the grim-looking **Castello Orsini-Odescalchi**, built in 1470, with fine apartments decorated by Antoniazzo Romano and the Zuccari brothers.

Overshadowed by a ruined Roman *rocca* (fortress), lively **Trevignano** has a pretty medieval centre with a hotchpotch of stone houses and cobbled lanes.

Just to the south-east is tranquil **Lago di Martignano**, with a beach where you can rent sailing boats, pedalos and canoes. You'll need your own transport to reach it.

Further north on the Cassia is the town of **Sutri**, which sits on a tufa rock outcrop above its ancient amphitheatre: some say the Etruscans carved this out of the rock; others argue it dates from the first century BC. The amphitheatre is located in the lovely **Parco Urbano dell'Antica Città di Sutri**, where an itinerary leads you past ancient Sutri's remains, including a necropolis and a mithraeum.

Just past the town, a winding local road heads north off the Cassia towards medieval **Ronciglione** and on to **Lago di Vico**, which sits in the crater of the extinct Monte Cimino volcano; most of the area is a natural park. Skirt around the eastern rim of the volcano for about four kilometres (2.5 miles) and turn right for **Caprarola**, a little town dwarfed by the imposing **Palazzo Farnese**, a huge villa designed as a castle by Sangallo the Younger and Baldassare Peruzzi, but transformed into something less fortified by Vignola in the 1560s. You can visit the lavishly decorated rooms accessed by a spiral staircase. Behind the villa are two formal gardens and a steep, wooded park (*barchino*) that leads up to the fountains of the *Giardino grande* and the *Palazzina del piacere* summer house.

Six kilometres (3.5 miles) east of Viterbo (*see right* **Viterbo**), the hill town of **Bagnaia** is dominated by **Villa Lante**. The villa's two identical palaces (closed to the public except for two frescoed loggias), built by Vignola in rather forbidding dark grey stone in the 1570s

Historic Viterbo

From grand palazzi to mud baths.

Viterbo was an important Etruscan town and an insignificant Roman one. In the eighth century it was fortified by the Lombard King Desiderius as a launching pad for sacking Rome. Caught up in the medieval quarrels between the Holy Roman Empire and the Church, Viterbo played host to popes and anti-popes, several of whom relocated here when things got too hot in Rome.

Today, Viterbo's *centro storico* is a jumble of narrow streets concealing a mix of rather grand *palazzi*, medieval laundries, ancient porticoes, imposing towers and crenellated buildings, as well as the lion (the symbol of Viterbo) and many fountains. The medieval quarter of San Pellegrino lies at the city's southern edge, flanked by piazza della Morte. Across the bridge is the elegant 12th-century cathedral of **San Lorenzo**, which has been much altered and restored through the centuries. Next door is the **Palazzo Papale**, built for the popes in the 13th century and restored in the 19th. The pretty 12th-century church of **Santa Maria Nuova** (open 8am-noon, 4-7pm) has

an ancient head of Jupiter (on the façade), and a pulpit from which St Thomas Aquinas preached. Behind it are the remains of a small Lombard cloister (always open).

Piazza del Plebiscito is dominated by the early 16th-century **Palazzo Comunale**, or town hall (open to the public 10am-1pm, 3-8pm daily), whose lavishly frescoed senate rooms are still used by the town council.

Outside the walls, opposite Porta della Verità, is the 12th-century **Santa Maria della Verità** (open 8am-noon, 4-7pm). In 1469 local boy Lorenzo di Viterbo painted some of the most Tuscan frescoes outside of Tuscany in its Gothic Cappella Mazzatosta. In the old convent next door is the renovated **Museo Civico** (piazza Crispi 2, 0761 348 275, €3.10) with Etruscan finds, works of art from local churches, and two canvases by Sebastiano del Piombo.

There are several bubbling pools of sulphurous water, where local residents wallow, smeared in greeny-white clay, within a short radius of the town. At the **Bagnaccio**, four basins of varying degrees of heat allow you to admire the surrounding countryside through the steam rising off the water in which you're submerged. To get there, leave Viterbo on the Montefiascone road, and after five kilometres (three miles) turn left on to the road to Marta. After a kilometre (half a mile) an unpaved road branches off to the Bagnaccio. If you prefer to wallow in luxury, head for the **Hotel Terme dei Papi** (strada Bagni 12, 0761 3501, www.termedeipapi.it), which offers anything from a dip in a sulphurous pool to a full range of spa treatments involving mud and sulphur-rich thermal waters.

Museo Archeologico di Palestrina. *See p301.*

for Cardinal Gambara, are surrounded by a stunning formal Italian garden, punctuated by fountains, statues and pools. Water originally cascaded down five terraces, with spectacular effects. Some of it still works: the ropework cascade is impressive. The carved prawn motif you see all over the garden is the Gambara family crest (*gambero* is Italian for prawn).

Some 24 kilometres (15 miles) west of Viterbo is **Tuscania**, an Etruscan town in an eerie landscape of low hills. Tuscania was an important city around the fourth century BC and enjoyed a few glory years in the Middle Ages. Tuscania's most important buildings are the two unique Romanesque-Lombard churches of **San Pietro** and **Santa Maria Maggiore**, situated on the Colle San Pietro, a hill just outside the centre. The *colle* was the site of an Etruscan and then a Roman settlement; fragments of the pre-Christian acropolis are incorporated into the apse of San Pietro. Founded in the eighth century, the church was reworked from the 11th to the 13th centuries. The façade is startling: three-faced trifrons, snakes and dancers owe more to pagan culture than to Christian iconography. The interior has a cosmatesque pavement and 12th-century frescoes. Built at the same time, Santa Maria Maggiore (strada Santa Maria) has tamer beasts on its façade and a more harmonious interior. The main Etruscan sight here is in the small **Museo Archaeologico**, in the cloisters of the convent of Santa Maria del Riposo. Inside, four generations of the same Etrusco-Roman family gaze from the lids of their sarcophagi.

Castello Orsini-Odescalchi
Piazza Mazzini 14, Bracciano (06 9980 4348, www.odescalchi.com). **Open** *Apr-Sept* 10am-noon, 3-6pm Tue-Sat; 9am-1.30pm Sun. *Oct-Mar* 10am-noon, 2-4pm Tue-Sat; 10am-1pm, 2.30-5pm Sun. **Admission** €7; €5 reductions. **No credit cards.**

FREE Museo Archaeologico
Largo Professore Moretti, Tuscania (0761 436 209). **Open** 8.30am-7.30pm Tue-Sun. **Admission** free.

Parco Regionale di Veio – Tempio di Apollo
Isola Farnese (06 3089 0116, www.parcodiveio.it). **Open** 8.30am-1.30pm Tue, Wed, Fri, Sun; 8.30am-3.30pm Thur, Sat. **Admission** €2; €1 reductions. **No credit cards.**

FREE Parco Urbano dell'Antica Città di Sutri
Via Cassia, km49.5 (0761 609 380). **Open** 8.30am-1.30pm Tue, Wed, Fri, Sun; 8.30am-5.30pm Thur, Sat. **Admission** free.

To visit the mithraeum, ask at the ticket office: if there are any takers, tours will depart from there on the hour at 9am, 11am and 1pm.

★ Villa Farnese
Caprarola (0761 646 052, www.caprarola.com). **Open** *Villa* 8.30am-6.45pm Tue-Sun. *Gardens* tours depart 10am, 11am, noon, 3pm Tue-Fri; 10.30am, noon, 3pm Sat, Sun. **Admission** €5; €2.50 reductions. **No credit cards.**

★ Villa Lante
Bagnaia (0761 288 008). **Open** *Mar* 8.30am-5.30pm Tue-Sun. *1 Apr-mid Apr, mid Sept-Oct* 8.30am-6.30pm Tue-Sun. *Mid Apr-mid Sept* 8.30am-7.30pm Tue-Sun. *Nov-Feb* 8.30am-4.30pm Tue-Sun. **Admission** €5; €2.50 reductions. **No credit cards.** *Photo p299.*

Getting there

By car
Veio, Caprarola, Bagnaia, Sutri, Tuscania: take the Cassia (SS2).
Lago di Bracciano & around: exit the Cassia at La Storta and take via Claudia-Braccianense (SS493).
Trevignano: take the Cassia bis.

By train
Veio: to La Storta, then bus to Isola Farnese.
Lago di Bracciano & around: to Anguillara or Bracciano.
Sutri: from Ostiense or Trastevere.
Viterbo: the Roma–Viterbo train from Flaminio station.

By bus
COTRAL services from Saxa Rubra.

VIA FLAMINIA & VIA TIBERINA

Ancient via Flaminia leads north-east along the Tiber river valley to the Adriatic coast. Once it was a wide country road with the occasional hamlet or farm; now it takes a while to get to the idyllic parts. The first 25 kilometres (16 miles) beyond the GRA ring road are hideous, but concealed within the nightmarish shells of towns like Sacrofano, Riano, Morlupo and Rignano Flaminio are medieval villages and churches: keep your eyes peeled for yellow signs pointing to '*borgo medioevale*' or '*chiesa medioevale*'.

Running parallel to, and east of, the Flaminia, **via Tiberina** looks much more like an ancient road should. About five kilometres (three miles) south of Fiano Romano is **Lucus Feroniae**, an ancient religious and trading hub of the Sabine people. By the third century BC, when it was colonised

Villa Farnese. *See p295.*

by the Romans, the city was famous for ceremonies held at its sanctuary of Feronia (goddess of agriculture). Hannibal took a break from his march on Rome in 211 BC to help himself to the treasure but, despite the sacking, Lucus Feroniae continued to grow; heavily rebuilt during Augustus' reign, it flourished throughout the Imperial age and into the early Middle Ages. What remains is a fascinating microcosm of a Roman urban centre, complete with a basilica, bath complex, forum and, further to the north-west, a charming little amphitheatre.

Further north on via Tiberina, rising sharply from the low-lying undulating hills of the Tiber valley, is the silhouette of **Monte Soratte**, shaped distinctly like the scaly back of a sleeping dinosaur (though many Italians see Mussolini's profile in it).

Just off the Flaminia, **Civita Castellana** is a pretty medieval town atop a massive tufa outcrop. Originally known as Falerii Veteres, it was razed by the Romans in the third century BC. The Falisci people were forced to pack up and move west to conspicuously indefensible flatlands in the valley, creating a settlement called Falerii Novi. It was not until the 11th century, when Normans invaded, that the locals once again took advantage of their natural stronghold and hiked back up the hill. Civita Castellana has a lovely medieval centre and a solemn 15th-century castle, the **Rocca**

(aka Forte Sangallo); commissioned by the Borgia Pope Alexander VI, it was completed under Julius II by Antonio da Sangallo the Elder. Inside is the **Museo Nazionale dell'Agro Falisco** (0761 513 735, open 8am-6pm Tue-Sun). The **Duomo** (open 8.30am-noon, 4-6pm daily) is a gorgeous Romanesque church from the 12th century, with a perfectly preserved portico that was decorated in delicate gold, porphyry and green geometric mosaic motifs in the early 13th century; some of the decorative elements on the façade are from the abandoned town of Falerii Novi. Inside, the bright white, sugar-frosted extravaganza is the result of an unfortunate 18th-century makeover – thankfully, the cosmatesque floors were left unmolested.

Ten kilometres (six miles) west of Orte, is the *parco dei mostri* (monster park) at **Bomarzo**. Duke Vicino Orsini (1523-84) had the park built in his **Sacro Bosco** gardens after his wife died; but it's more Renaissance theme park than dignified retreat. It's a unique place that makes an interesting change from most typical grand Italian attractions. Using the volcanic *peperino* stone that dotted his estate, Orsini spent years filling the park with surreal, sometimes grotesque, sculptures that were completely at odds with the tastes of his day. Lurking in the undergrowth are a skewed house and enormous beasts.

FREE Lucus Feroniae

Via Tiberina, km18.5 (06 908 5173).
Open *Museum* 8.30am-7.30pm Tue-Sun.
Site 8.30am-sunset Tue-Sun **Admission** free.
Note: Times given above are the official opening
hours; in fact, severe staff shortages mean the site
generally closes at 2pm. Even in the morning, it's
best to call ahead to make sure it's open.

Sacro Bosco

Località Giardino, Bomarzo (0761 924 029).
Open 8.30am-sunset daily. **Admission**
€9; €7 4-8s. **No credit cards.**

Getting there

By car

Lucus Feroniae: A1 to Fiano Romano,
then follow signs for Capena.
Bomarzo: Flaminia, then SS315; or A1 to
Attigliano exit, then minor road to Bomarzo.

By train

Cività Castellana: frequent services
from Tiburtina, Ostiense or Flaminio.
Bomarzo: to Orte, then mainline train
to Attigliano-Bomarzo (5km/3 miles
from the park).

By bus

COTRAL services from Saxa Rubra
(for Bomarzo, change at Riello).

VIA TIBURTINA

Via Tiburtina more or less follows the
Aniene river, which wends its way from
the Monti Simbruini east of Rome to join the
Tiber north of the city centre. Far from the
most attractive way to exit the city, the early
section of this consular road contains such
sights as the Rebibbia high-security prison.
Beyond the GRA (ring road) the congested
traffic lurches through a landscape scarred
by decades of unregulated construction; to
avoid all this, take the faster Roma–L'Aquila
autostrada (A24) and head straight for
via Tiburtina's original, ancient destination,
Tibur (modern Tivoli).

Just 20 kilometres (12.5 miles) from Rome
are two UNESCO World Heritage Sites that
are worth a visit – Villa d'Este, in Tivoli itself,
and Hadrian's Villa (*see p298*), five kilometres
(three miles) down the hill.

As you approach Tivoli, the foul stink of
the sulphorous *acque albule* springs fills the
air; the curative properties of the water beloved
by the ancients can still be experienced at
the spas in **Bagni di Tivoli**. The Tiburtina
passes massive quarries of travertine, where
gaping chasms of limestone are still exploited.

Just south of the Tiburtina is the town of
Villa Adriana, site of the spectacular second-
century AD retreat designed and built by
Emperor Hadrian (*see p298*).

High on a hill five kilometres (three miles)
above, the town of **Tivoli** was founded by an
Italic tribe, and conquered by the Romans in
338 BC. The town was littered with temples,
and the surrounding territory became a popular
location for country villas. Dominating Tivoli
itself is the **Villa d'Este**, a lavish pleasure
palace built over a Benedictine monastery
in 1550 for Cardinal Ippolito d'Este, son of
Lucrezia Borgia.

Across town are a Republican, circular
Temple of Vesta, and a second-century
AD, rectangular **Temple of the Sibyl** (both
on via della Sibilla). From here you can catch
a glimpse of the **Villa Gregoriana** across
the rocky gorge: it's a wild park next to
two waterfalls.

The cathedral of **San Lorenzo** (via
Duomo), reconstructed in the Baroque style in
1635, contains a carved 13th-century *Descent
from the Cross*. At the town's highest point
(piazza delle Nazioni Unite) is **Rocca Pia**, a
15th-century castle built by Pope Pius II.

In 300 BC work began to extend via
Tiburtina from Tivoli eastwards across the
Apennines, to the Adriatic at Pescara. The
new road made conquering hostile tribes
easier, and brought the abundant mountain
springs feeding the Aniene river under
Roman control; in 272 BC work began on four
aqueducts, which routed large quantities of
fresh water to the metropolis for centuries.

The area's verdant countryside attracted
the ancient jet set; in 33 BC Maecenas invited
Rome's hottest poet, Horace, to move into
his country villa outside Licenza.

Past Roviano, the SS411 forks off to the
south towards **Subiaco** (Sublaqueum, 'under
the lakes'). Around AD 60 Emperor Nero, began
his grandiose villa here, damming the Aniene
to create a massive lake on the property which
is estimated by archaeologists to have covered
75 hectares (185 acres). The lake has since
disappeared and only traces of the villa
survive: the emperor abandoned it soon
after its completion when lightning struck
the table in front of him as he dined – a very
bad omen. Much of the land where the villa
stood is private property and little has been
excavated, but a small thermal complex (and
part of **San Clemente** – the first monastery
built by St Benedict, which is made from
villa masonry) can be seen; call ahead to
the Monastero di Santa Scolastica (*see
p298*) to visit.

In the late fifth century, Western
monasticism was born here. The isolated

area became popular with assorted ascetics, and when young nobleman Benedict of Norcia turned his back on the licentious hedonism of his contemporaries, it was at a cave above Subiaco that he did his praying. The **Monastero di San Benedetto** grew up around the *Sacro speco* – the 'Holy Cavern' where Benedict spent three long years.

After three years of solitude Benedict had attracted such a flock of disciples that he founded the first of 13 monasteries inside the ruins of Nero's villa. Only one is still going: the **Monastero di Santa Scolastica**, named after Benedict's twin sister, whose dedication to her sacred sibling earned her a place among the saints too.

Between the tenth and 11th centuries, the Church and nobility constructed fortresses on the hills along the strategic Aniene valley. The feudal castles still dominate the landscape as you roll along via Tiburtina.

Not only is Subiaco the birthplace of Western monasticism, but it was also a cradle of Italian printing. In 1464 two Germans set up a Gutenberg press at the St Scholastica monastery. They printed three titles, using the unique *sublacensi* characters. Only one work printed here remains at the monastery, a copy of Lactantius' *De divinis institutionibus*. Behind the monastery lies the extraordinary **Biblioteca Nazionale Santa Scolastica**.

FREE Monastero di San Benedetto & Sacro Speco
Via dei Monasteri (0774 85 039, www.benedettini-subiaco.org). **Open** 9am-noon, 3-5.30pm daily. **Admission** free.
Note: during Sunday mass (9.30am & 11am) the upper part of the monastery is closed to visits.
The Monstery of St Benedict is a mountain-hugging complex of twisting corridors and stairways. The Upper Church (*Chiesa superiore*) is covered in early 15th-century frescoes of the Sienese school, while the Lower Church (*Chiesa inferiore*) dates from the second half of the 13th century. On the right of the staircase is the *Sacro speco* – the cave where Benedict spent three years pondering his vocation – with a 17th-century marble statue of the young hermit by Bernini's pupil, Antonio Raggi, and one of the

life-saving food hampers that were lowered regularly into the cave by a friendly local. The *Scala santa* (Holy Staircase) leads further down, its undulating walls decorated with frescoes; on your left there is a simplistic identification of the processes of decomposition, on your right a horse-riding Death wields his scythe. Part-way down the staircase, the Cappella della Madonna was decorated by the same Sienese artists as the Upper Church. At the bottom of the *Scala santa*, the *Grotta dei pastori* (Shepherds' Grotto) is where Benedict first taught in the sixth century; on the right, fragments of an eighth-century Byzantine Madonna and child remain.

Up the spiral staircase beside the *Grotta dei pastori* is the Chapel of St Gregory. Decoration dates from the first half of the 13th century and includes a fresco of St Francis of Assisi (behind glass). The portrait of St Francis – shown pre-halo and stigmata – was probably done soon after he visited the monastery in 1218.

Monastero di Santa Scolastica

Via dei Monasteri (0774 82 421, www.benedettini-subiaco.org). **Open** 9am-12.30pm, 3.30-6.30pm Mon-Sat; 11.30am-12.30pm, 3.30-6.30pm Sun. **Admission** donation expected.
The sixth-century chapel of St Silvester is the oldest remaining bit of the monastery; the church dedicated to Scholastica was erected in 981. Most of the rest is the result of a late 18th-century makeover – with the exception of the beautiful campanile, built in 1053. A shop near the main entrance sells monk-made 'curative' spirits, thick liqueurs, chocolate, chunky fruit jams and herbal products.

★ Villa Adriana (Hadrian's Villa)

Via di Villa Adriana, Villa Adriana (0774 382 733). **Open** 9am-one hr before sunset daily. **Admission** €6.50; €3.25 reductions. *Extra charge for exhibitions.* **No credit cards**.
Strewn across a gentle slope, the Villa Adriana (Hadrian's Villa) was built from 118 to 134 and has some fascinating architectural spaces and water features. Hadrian was an amateur architect and is believed to have designed many of the unique elements in his villa himself. He drew on inspiration from his travels in Greece and Egypt. In the centuries following the fall of the Empire it became a luxury quarry for treasure-hunters. At least 500 pieces of statuary in collections around the world have been identified as coming from this site, and marble and mosaic finds from the villa now make up a significant portion of the collections of Roman art at the Capitoline and Vatican museums. The restored remains are still impressive; the model in the pavilion near the entrance gives an idea of the villa's original size. The layout of the complex is seemingly haphazard: it's easy to get lost and just as easy to stumble upon charming surprises.

Where the original entrance to the villa lay is uncertain; today the first space you'll encounter after

---

INSIDE TRACK SKI TRIP

Monte Livata, 15km (24 miles) from Subiaco, is where Romans desperate for a quick buzz down a piste head in winter: the closest bit of (fairly) reliable snow to the capital. For snow reports, ski pass prices and information on skiing gear hire, see www.livata.it.

Villa Lante. *See p295.*

climbing the road from the ticket office is the *pecile* (or *poikile*), a large pool that was once surrounded by a portico with high walls, of which only one remains. As it was constructed on land that originally sloped dramatically (the eastern end was 15 metres/47ft higher than the western), a massive complex of sub-structures (the 'hundred chambers') was built to level things off. The *poikile* was probably used for post-prandial strolling: seven laps around the perimeter of the space constitute two Roman miles, the distance that ancient doctors recommended walking after meals.

Directly east of the *poikile*, the *Teatro marittimo* (Maritime Theatre) is one of the most delightful inventions in the whole villa, and one of the parts generally attributed to Hadrian himself. A circular brick wall encloses a moat, at the centre of which is an island of columns and brickwork; it was a self-sufficient *domus* (mini-villa) – complete with its own baths, bedrooms and gardens. Today a cement bridge crosses the moat, but originally there were wooden bridges, which could be removed to give the impression of absolute isolation. South of the Maritime Theatre is a three-storey building known simply as the 'building with a fish pond' (*peschiera*), or the Winter Palace (*Quartiere invernale*). The highest of the structure's levels, where traces of a heating system are preserved, may have been the emperor's private residence, with a large banquet hall overlooking the Nymphaeum-Stadium and the plains towards Rome. The 'fish pond' is a now-empty rectangular basin in the east side of the structure, beneath which visitors can walk along the *cryptoporticus*. Continuing south, locate the *Piccole terme* (Small Baths), where intricate plaster mouldings are amazingly intact on some of the vaulted ceilings, giving an idea of the grandeur of the entire villa's decoration.

In the valley below is the lovely *Canopus*. Built to recall the canal that connected Alexandria to the city of Canopus – famous for its temple of Serapis – on the Nile delta, this is a long, narrow pool, framed on three sides by columns and statues, including a marble crocodile. At the far (southern) end of the pool is a structure called the *Serapeum*, used for lavish entertaining, where sculpture once embellished the apse; despite its Egyptian inspiration, the architectural style couldn't be more Roman. Summer guests enjoyed an innovative form of air-conditioning – a sheet of water poured from the roof over the open face of the building, enclosing diners. The villa also included extensive guest and staff apartments, dining rooms, assembly halls and libraries, a stadium and theatres. The whole complex was connected by underground passages, so that servants were invisible whenever possible.

★ Villa d'Este

Piazza Trento 1, Tivoli (0774 332 920, www.villadestetivoli.info). **Open** (Tue-Sun) *Feb* 9am-5.30pm. *Mar* 9am-6.15pm. *Apr* 9am-7.30pm. *May-Aug* 8.30am-7.45pm. *Sept* 9am-7.15pm. *Oct* 9am-6.30pm. *Nov-Jan* 9am-6pm. **Admission** €6.50; €3.25 reductions. Extra charge for exhibitions. **Credit** (online bookings) AmEx, DC, MC, V.

Mannerist architect Pirro Ligorio made detailed studies of Hadrian's Villa (*see p298* **Villa Adriana**), and he drew on these in his plans for the Villa d'Este and its gardens. Inside the villa there are frescoes and paintings by artists such as Correggio, Da Volterra and Perin Del Vaga (including, in the Hall of the Fountain, views of the villa shortly after its construction). The gardens are the main attraction, drawing busloads of day-trippers to admire their ingenious fountains.

Ligorio developed a complex 'hydraulic machine' that channelled water from the Aniene river (still the source today) through a series of canals under the garden. Using know-how borrowed from the Romans, he created a homage to the natural springs on the hillsides of Tivoli in the 51 fountains spread around the terraced gardens. The sibyls (pagan high priestesses) are a recurring theme and the grottoes of the sibyls behind the vast fountain of Neptune echo with thundering artificial waterfalls.

Technological gimmickry was another big feature; the Owl Fountain imitated an owl's song using a hydraulic mechanism, while the *Fontana dell'organo idraulico* (restored in 2004 and now fully functioning) used water pressure to compress air and play tunes. There is a programme of summer evening openings and events at the villa. Electric carts are provided for disabled visitors to tour the gardens; booking essential.

Getting there

By car

A24 (exit Tivoli) or via Tiburtina (SS5).

By bus

Tivoli: COTRAL services from Ponte Mammolo. Note that the bus marked *autostrada* is a quicker (although less frequent) service; the regular service is marked 'via Tiburtina' and takes about 45mins. Get off at the main square (piazza Garibaldi) for Villa d'Este.

Villa Adriana: Most Rome–Tivoli services also stop at Villa Adriana. As well, frequent local buses connect Tivoli town to Villa Adriana (10mins). The site is not very well signposted: ask where to get off.

Subiaco: Some buses continue on from Tivoli. There are infrequent local services from Subiaco town centre to the monasteries.

VIA PRENESTINA

For a totally unexpected (and very rewarding) taste of the ancient world, head to the unassuming town of Palestrina, the chief

Quick Dips

Nice and easy beach breaks.

The dog days of summer in the Eternal City can be very, very hot, and unless you're staying in a seriously swanky hotel such as the Rome Cavalieri, the Exedra or the Radisson ES (*see p173* **Big and Sassy**), you're going to find getting into a swimming pool a little difficult. In fact, if you're desperate to cool off, or just escape the frenzy, your best bet is to hop on a train and head for the coast: in an hour or less you can be basking on the sand.

The stretch of beach closest to Rome is at **Ostia** – the modern town, not the *antica* one, *see p287* – where the sand isn't exactly golden and the seafront is wrapped up by *stabilimenti* renting umbrellas and deck chairs, but efforts have been made to clean up the sea. A little.

Just north of here but as easily accessible from the city by train or coach, **Fregene** (*see p290*) is a town of holiday homes, where spouses and offspring are parked for the summer while the bread-earner languishes back in the city heat – so if summer weekends are busy here, summer weekdays are almost equally so. Still, the beach is long and the water wet.

Go just a little further, though, to **Santa Severa** (*see p290*), and during the week at least, you may find a corner of the pretty beach where your towel isn't actually touching your neighbours'. It's a quarter-hour walk from the station to the coast, where a castle squats comfortably on the sea front. The little museum is a lovingly curated gem dedicated to the coast around, from the Etruscans on up, and navigation in general.

Immediately south of Ostia, on the other hand, lies a long, long stretch of sand called Capocotta. The coast road separates the dunes and beach from the presidential hunting reserve of Castel Porziano (see www.riservalitoraleromano.it for guided tours of the estate): there's no built-up area, in other words to impinge and pollute. What goes on on the beach depends on which kilometers marker you access it from: there's a naturist bit around km9, which merges into a gay stretch in one direction and a (clothed) family-fun bit towards the town of Torvaianica. To get there, take the metro to the last stop in Ostia, then bus 07 along the coast road.

'modern' claim to fame of which is as birthplace of the 16th-century motet and madrigal composer Giovanni Palestrina (c1525-94).

Nowadays it's an uninspiring little town. In antiquity, however, Praeneste was an important Etruscan settlement, which battled long and hard against Rome until capitulating around 338 BC. The town was known for its huge temple and the shrine of an oracle. Parts of the temple, dedicated to the goddess Fortuna Primigenia, date from the sixth century BC. Under Roman control the temple complex was rebuilt on a grander scale on a series of mountainside terraces, and Praeneste became a fashionable holiday resort (Pliny the Younger had a villa here). The oracle shut up shop in the fourth century AD, the temple fell into disuse, and a medieval town – Palestrina – was built on top. It wasn't until World War II that air raids devastated the town but unearthed the lower part of the temple. The sprawling complex was a semicircular affair crowned by a statue of the goddess Fortuna where the 17th-century **Palazzo Colonna-Barberini** now stands: the **Museo Archeologico** (*see right*), housed in the palazzo, really markes Palestrina worth a stopover.

Museo Archeologico di Palestrina

Piazza della Cortina (06 953 8100). **Open** *Museum* 9am-8pm daily. *Archaeological site* 9am-1hr before sunset daily. **Admission** *Museum & site* €5; €2.50 reductions. **No credit cards**.

This fascinating museum is located inside the Palazzo Colonna-Barberini, which was built on the highest terrace of the temple to Fortuna. Today the palazzo-museum incorporates some remains of the ancient construction (Plexiglas floor tiles show where the columns once stood), while a model on the top floor shows how the temple complex might have been. There's a selection of Republican and Imperial Roman artefacts: art, instruments and objects either found in the area or associated with the worship of Fortuna. But the star exhibit is the second-century BC Nile mosaic, a work admired by Pliny, which came from the most sacred part of the temple (where the cathedral now stands). It is an intricately detailed, bird's-eye representation of the flora and fauna of the flooded banks of the Nile from Ethiopia to Alexandria. Gallant warriors hunt exotic animals, and diners recline while pipers pipe and goddesses preach. If your Greek is good, you'll be able to identify the labelled beasts.

In a niche off the ground-floor entrance hall, look out for the *Capitoline Triad*, a second-century AD sculpture of Minerva, Jupiter and Juno sitting together on one throne – the only known portrayal of Rome's three tutelary gods together. This sculpture was stolen in 1992, but subsequently salvaged from the murky underworld of stolen artefacts.

Getting there

By car
Via Prenestina (SS155) or via Casilina. Also reached from the A1 (exit San Cesareo or Valmontone) or the A24 (exit Tivoli) motorways, then local roads.

By bus
COTRAL services run from Anagnina or Ponte Mammolo.

VIA TUSCOLANA

Via Tuscolana forks off via Latina (an ancient alternative route to via Appia, *see p151*), passes the centre of Italian filmmaking at Cinecittà (*see p249*), heads out through the rolling Alban hills and the Castelli romani and ends at the ruined city of Tusculum.

Frascati is the closest to Rome of the Castelli romani – a group of towns so-called for the grand abodes erected here by Rome's papal and patrician glitterati. Twentieth-century additions have tarnished the gloss, but the towns still have a certain charm.

There are Renaissance villas sprinkled over the hillside behind the town, but only the garden of the 17th-century **Villa Aldobrandini**, built 1598-1603 by Giacomo della Porta for Cardinal Pietro Aldobrandini, is open to the public. In nearby **Villa Torlonia** – a public park – Carlo Maderno's 16th-century *Teatro delle acque* fountain has been gloriously restored; there's an elegant smaller fountain here too, by Gianlorenzo Bernini.

Four kilometres (2.5 miles) down the road, but a world away from Frascati's summer crowds, ancient **Tusculum** (always open) is part pastoral green and part archaeological treasure trove. The remnants of a volcano that last blew its top 70,000 years ago are now grassy slopes covered by oaks and umbrella pines, fanned by cool breezes. From the picnic ground, the ancient via dei Sepolcri winds up to a Roman cistern and tomb. Or start from the main parking lot at the top of the hill and head west to find the spectacular remains of the **Villa di Tibero** – presumed to have been one of the many villas of Emperor Tiberius. To the east is a second-century BC theatre and forum. Ignore the hideous cross and enjoy more great

Sabaudia. *See p304.*

views from the summit; if you search among the twisted oaks and blackberry bushes here, you'll come across more ruins of the acropolis.

FREE Villa Aldobrandini

Via CG Massaia, Frascati (06 942 0331). **Open** (gardens only) *May-Sept* 9am-1pm, 3-6.30pm Mon-Fri. *Oct-Apr* 9am-1pm, 3-5pm Mon-Fri. **Admission** free, but call first to arrange a visit.

Getting there

By car

Frascati: best reached using via Appia (*see below*) and minor roads.
Tusculum: take via Tuscolo from Frascati.

By train

Frequent trains leave from Termini for the 20min ride to Frascati (and Castelgandolfo, *see below*). Check destinations carefully: the route divides and not all stops are covered.

By bus

COTRAL services run from Anagnina every 30mins.

VIA APPIA

(For the stretch of via Appia that is nearer to Rome, *see pp151-155*.)

While a trip down the ancient *regina viarum* – or Queen of Roads, as **via Appia Antica** was known – is today an enchanting experience thick with antiquity, you're unlikely to be captivated by modern **via Appia Nuova** (SS7), which is thick only with traffic fumes. Persevere, though, and the SS7 leads to the lake-dotted countryside south of Rome, along via dei Laghi (SS217) and to the southern side of the Castelli romani and the Alban hills.

Perched on the lip of the **Lago Albano** crater, **Castelgandolfo** is best known as the town where the pontiff spends his summer hols. (Pope Clement VII began the tradition in the 1500s.) The papal palace and pretty, cobbled piazza della Libertà – with its enchanting view of the lake – were completed by Bernini. Enjoy the same breezes the pope does by taking a stroll around the lakeshore; indulge in pleasures that are off-limits to the pontiff by renting a pedalo or lakeside deckchair.

A few kilometres to the south, **Albano Laziale** was the site of a huge army base built by Septimus Severus for the Second Legion, and its remains – such as the main gate and a third-century cistern – can be seen all over the town. The church of **Santa Maria della Rotonda** (which looks a bit like the Pantheon in miniature) was once the nymphaeum of a huge Roman baths complex; you can still see mosaic fragments depicting sea monsters.

Overlooking **Lago di Nemi**, **Genzano** is home to the **Museo delle Navi** (Roman Ship Museum). When the lake was partially drained in 1929, two massive (formerly) floating temples emerged. Followers of Isis worshipped the Egyptian goddess on sacred vessels on lakes at the full moon. Emperor Caligula – an Isis devotee – had two fabulously decorated vessels built on Lake Nemi; after his demise, the disapproving Roman Senate had them sunk. The museum built for the 70-metre (230-foot) ships was destroyed during World War II, but today there are scale models and reproductions of artefacts found on board.

Of all the Castelli romani villages, **Nemi** is the most picturesque, perched on the edge of a tree-covered crater overlooking the lake. The name comes from the Latin word *nemus* (forest); the surrounding woods were once the haunt of worshippers of Diana, goddess of the hunt. Avoid visiting on Sundays, when Nemi fills up with Roman strollers.

Situated on the plain south-east of the Castelli romani, **Ninfa** was named – local legend says – after a nymph who was so devastated by the loss of her lover that she cried herself a river. Today a stream flows though some of Italy's most beautiful gardens, which ramble around the ruins of a medieval town. The origins of Ninfa are obscure, but in the 12th century it made the mistake of supporting a rival to the pope and was sacked. It rallied, and by the early 1380s had 150 large *palazzi*. Afterwards, however, the town came to grief in clan warfare, followed by outbreaks of malaria. The Caetani family acquired Ninfa in the 14th century, but showed little interest in their ghost estate until the 1920s, when Don Gelasio Caetani decided to plant his vast collection of exotic species here. The result of his botanical dabbling – the **Oasi di Ninfa** – is pure magic.

Museo delle Navi

Via Diana 15, Genzano (06 939 8040/06 3996 7900). **Open** 9am-6.30pm daily. **Admission** €3. **No credit cards.**

★ Oasi di Ninfa

Doganella di Ninfa (0773 633 935/06 687 3056, www.fondazionecaetani.org). **Open** *Apr-June* 1st Sat, 1st Sun & 3rd Sun of mth 9am-noon, 2.30-6pm. *July-Oct* 1st Sat & 1st Sun of mth 9am-noon, 3-6.30pm. **Admission** €10; under-11s free. **No credit cards.**
Obligatory guided tours must be booked in advance. Any extra openings are posted on the website. Groups can arrange private visits at other times.

Getting there

By car
For all destinations, take the Appia (SS7).
Nemi: exit after Ciampino and take via dei Laghi.
Ninfa: exit at Tor Tre Ponti, then follow signs to
Latina Scalo and Ninfa.

By train
Ninfa: take mainline services from Termini
to Latina Scalo, then haggle with waiting taxi
drivers for the 9km (5-mile) ride to the gardens.
Castelgandolfo: hourly from Termini.

By bus
COTRAL services run from Anagnina to Genzano
and Castelgandolfo. For Nemi, change at Genzano.
There are also services from Frascati (*see p302*) to
Genzano and Nemi.

VIA PONTINA

Slicing south from the city, via Pontina (SS148)
can make no claim to antiquity. It was built in
the 1930s to connect Mussolini's capital to the
Pontine marshes – which had been recently
reclaimed from brackish water and malarial
mosquitoes – and 'ideal' Fascist settlements
like Littorio (now Latina, a dingy centre of
provincial life) and the smart beach
resort of Sabaudia.

Pick the Pontina up just outside EUR (*see
p160*) and head through the soulless, high-rise
dormitory suburbs. Before the industrial town
of Pomezia, signs point off to the right (west)
for beaches around **Torvaianica**, a miasma
of roasting human flesh in high season.

At Aprilia the SS207 forks right to **Anzio**,
where the Allies landed in 1944 to launch their
victorious march on Rome, and **Nettuno**, with
its serried rows of heart-rending white crosses
in the British and American military cemeteries.

The first cleanish sea south of Rome is at
Sabaudia. With its striking 1930s architecture,
the town is a favourite with Italy's holidaying
intelligentsia. It owes its miles of unspoilt
sandy beaches to the fact that it is inside the
Parco Nazionale del Circeo. Forget the
dusty exhibits in the park's museum and
visitors' centre; hire bikes or set out on foot
for walks and picnics instead (note that
mosquito repellent is as important as
water and sandwiches).

Looming to the south is **Monte Circeo**,
where Odysseus was waylaid by the
enchantress Circe, who turned his ship's crew
into pigs. A hike to the top through cork- and
holm-oak forests on the western, seaward side
is spectacular. Or drive most of the way up
from the landward side to explore the ancient
ruins along the ridge. East of the outcrop, a

road winds up to **San Felice Circeo**, a pretty
little town and a poseurs' paradise in summer.

The Pontina merges with the Appia
(becoming the SS213) at **Terracina**, which
is a port town with two centres. The pleasant
modern part is down by the sea, while the
medieval town above lies on top of the forum
of the Roman port of Anxur. Its cathedral
was built in a Roman temple to Augustus;
above the portico is a 12th-century mosaic
frieze, and below it is a big basin that was
reputedly used for boiling Christians. The
paving slabs in the piazza are from the
forum. World War II bombing uncovered
the ancient remains and made space for
the modern town hall and **Museo Civico
di Terracina**. Standing above the town
is the first-century BC Tempio di Giove
(Temple of Jupiter).

Sperlonga is a pretty seaside resort.
The whitewashed medieval town on the
spur above the two beaches – its narrow
lanes lined with potted geraniums, boutiques
and restaurants – fills with well-heeled Romans
in the summer. The **Museo Archeologico
di Sperlonga**, at the end of the southerly
beach, contains important second-century
BC sculptures of scenes from the *Odyssey*;
the ticket includes a tour of **Tiberius'
Villa and Grotto**.

Museo Archeologico di Sperlonga & Villa di Tiberio
Via Flacca km 16.3, Sperlonga (0771 548 028).
Open 8.30am-7.30pm daily. **Admission** €5;
€2.50 reductions. **No credit cards**.

Museo Civico di Terracina
Piazza Municipio 1, Terracina (0773 707 313).
Open *July, Aug* 9am-2pm Mon; 9am-2pm, 3-9pm
Tue-Sat; 10am-1pm, 5-9pm Sun. *Sept-June* 9.30am-
2pm Mon; 9am-8pm Tue-Sat; 9am-1pm, 3-6pm
Sun. **Admission** *Museum* €1.55. *Museum
& site* €2.50. **No credit cards**.

Getting there

By car
Head south out of Rome, and pick up the Pontina
(SS148) in EUR. For minor destinations, your own
transport is essential.

By train
Sabaudia, Terracina, Sperlonga: mainline
train to Priverno (for buses to Sabaudia and
buses/trains to Terracina) and Fondi (for buses
to Sperlonga).

By bus
Sabaudia, Terracina, Sperlonga:
COTRAL services run from Laurentina.

Directory

© Elan Fleisher

timeout.com/travel
Get the local experience

Spectacular interior in the Hotel Diagonal lobby, **Barcelona**

Getting Around

ARRIVING & LEAVING

By air

Rome has two major airports: Fiumicino, about 30km (18 miles) west of the city, handles scheduled flights; Ciampino, 15km (nine miles) south-east of the city, is for low-cost airlines and for charter flights.

Aeroporto Leonardo Da Vinci, Fiumicino

Via dell'Aeroporto di Fiumicino 320 (06 65 951, information 06 6595 3640, www.adr.it). **Open** 24hrs daily.

There's an **express rail service** between Fiumicino airport and Termini railway station. It takes 31mins and runs every 30mins from 6.36am until 11.36pm daily (5.52am-10.52pm to Fiumicino). Tickets in either direction cost €14. Note that at the Termini end, the airport train departs from platform 27 or 28, a good ten-minute walk from the main concourse; tickets bought at the departure platforms cost €15.

The **regular service** from Fiumicino takes 25-40mins, and stops at Trastevere, Ostiense, Tuscolana and Tiburtina stations. Trains leave about every 20mins (less often on Sun) from 5.57am and 11.27pm (5.05am-10.33pm to Fiumicino). Tickets cost €8.

You can buy tickets for both these services with cash or credit card from automatic machines in the airport lobby and rail stations, and at the airport rail station ticket office and the airport *tabacchi*. Some carriages have wheelchair access (*see also p311*). You must stamp your ticket in the machines on the platform before boarding.

SIT (06 591 6826, www.sitbus shuttle.it) runs frequent buses from Fiumicino to Termini railway station (in front of the Hotel Royal Santina on via Marsala, 8.30am-12.30am) and vice versa (5am-8.30pm). Tickets cost €8 single, €15 return.

During the night, a Cotral **bus service** runs between Fiumicino (Terminal C) and Termini and Tiburtina railway stations in Rome. Tickets cost €4.50 from newsstands or €7 on the bus. Buses leave Tiburtina at 12.30am, 1.15am, 2.30am and 3.45am, stopping at Termini railway station 10mins later. Departures from Fiumicino

are at 1.15am, 2.15am, 3.30am and 5am. Neither Termini nor Tiburtina are attractive places at night, so it's advisable to get a taxi from there to your final destination.

Aeroporto GB Pastine, Ciampino

Via Appia Nuova 1650 (06 65 951, www.adr.it). **Open** 24hrs daily.
The most hassle-free way to get into town from Ciampino is to take the Terravision **coach service** (06 488 0086, 06 9761 0632, www. terravision.eu) to Termini station (journey time: 45mins). Buses leave from outside the arrivals hall after each arrival. Buses from Termini to Ciampino leave from via Marsala. This is a dedicated service for the low-cost airlines, so you will need to show your ticket or boarding pass. Bus tickets (€4 single, €8 return) can be booked online, or bought (cash only) in the arrivals hall at Ciampino or at the Terravision office in the Termini forecourt (next to Benetton) or on the bus.

A rival company, SIT Bus Shuttle (06 591 6826, www.sit busshuttle.it), has recently begun a frequent service from Termini (via Marsala) to Ciampino (€6, 4.30am-9.30pm), and Ciampino to Termini (€5, 8.45am-11.45m). Tickets can be purchased on the bus or online.

Alternatively, Schiaffini **buses** (800 700 805, www.schiaffini.it) runs a service between Ciampino and Anagnina metro station every 30-40mins between 6am and 10.40pm daily and to Ciampino station (where frequent trains depart for Termini) between 5.45am and 11.25pm daily; both cost €1.20. They also run a direct service between the airport and Termini station (€3.90). Buy tickets on board the bus, which leaves from in front of the arrivals hall; at Termini, it departs from via Giolitti, by the station's side entrance.

Cotral (www.cotralspa.it) buses run regularly between the airport and Anagnina metro station, and between the airport and Ciampino town's railway station (both €1.20).

After the last bus has departed, getting into the city is well-nigh impossible, as taxis don't bother to pass by. If you are arriving late, phone ahead and organise a taxi before your arrival (*see p309*).

Major airlines

Alitalia *06 22 22, www.alitalia.it.*
British Airways *reservations 199 712 266, www.ba.com.*
Easyjet *899 234 589, www. easyjet.com.*
Ryanair *899 018 880, www. ryanair.com.*

By bus

There is no central long-distance bus station in Rome. Most services terminate outside these (metro) stations: Saxa Rubra (routes north); Cornelia, Ponte Mammolo and Tiburtina (north and east); Anagnina and Laurentina (routes south). For more details, *see pp286-287*.

By train

Mainline trains are operated by Ferrovie dello Stato (FS)/Trenitalia (www.trenitalia.it). Most long-distance trains arrive at Termini, the hub of Rome's transport network – and pickpockets, so beware. Night trains arrive at Tiburtina or Ostiense, both some way from the *centro storico*. If you arrive after midnight, take a taxi.

Some daytime trains bypass Termini, while others stop at more than one station in Rome:

Stazione Ostiense *Piazzale dei Partigiani, Testaccio. Metro Piramide/bus 60Exp, 95, 175, 280, 719, 91N.* **Map** p123 C1.
Stazione Piazzale Flaminio (Roma Nord) *Piazzale Flaminio, Suburbs: north. Metro Flaminio/ bus 88, 95, 204, 490, 491, 25N, 55N/tram 2.* **Map** p338 D2.
Stazione Termini *Piazza dei Cinquecento, Esquilino (06 4730 6599). Metro Termini/bus 16, 36, 38, 40Exp, 64, 70, 75, 84, 86, 90Exp, 92, 105, 170, 175, 204, 217, 310, 360, 590, 649, 714, 910, C, H, 6N, 12N, 40N, 45N, 50N, 55N, 78N, 91N/tram 5, 14.* **Map** p341 E5.
Stazione Tiburtina *Circonvallazione Nomentana, Suburbs: south. Metro Tiburtina/bus 71, 111, 163, 168, 204, 211, 309, 409, 443, 448, 490, 491, 492, 495, 545, 649, C, 40N.* **Map** p337.
Stazione Trastevere *Piazzale Biondo. Bus 170, 228, 719, 766, 773, 774, 780, 781, 786, 871, H, 72N, 96N/tram 3, 8.* **Map** p337.

Trains and tickets

For bookings and information on Italian rail services, phone the Trenitalia call centre (24hrs daily) on 892 021 – 199 166 177 from mobile phones, +39 066847 5475 from abroad – or consult the useful official website (www.trenitalia.it).

Tickets can be bought at stations (over the counter or from machines; both accept credit cards), from travel agents with an FS sign, or online; ticketless travel is also available (*see below*). Under-12s pay half fare; under-4s travel free. For wheelchair access, *see p311*.

Train timetables can be purchased at any *edicola* (newsstand) or can be checked online. Slower trains (*diretti, espressi, regionali* and *interregionali*) are cheap; faster services – InterCity (IC), EuroCity (EC), Eurostar Italia (ES) and the new super-fast Alta Velocità (AV) – are closer to European norms. Advance seat reservation is automatic on most faster services; check and obtain reservations at peak times to avoid standing in packed corridors. If your plans change, partial refunds are given (phone Trenitalia).

Queues at Termini ticket desks can be lengthy; speed things up by using one of the many automatic ticket machines (most accept credit cards). You'll often find an unofficial 'helper' by the machines, keen to show you how it's done for a euro or so; if they seem threatening, report them to the station police.

Trenitalia's **Ticketless** service allows you to book tickets with a credit card online (www.trenitalia.it) or by phone up to 10mins before the train's departure time. Either way, you'll be provided with a carriage and seat number, and a booking code, checked by ticket inspectors on board. The service is available on all AV, ES and some IC trains. Seat reservation is obligatory for all passengers using this service.

Note: with paper tickets, you *must* stamp your ticket and supplements in the yellow machines at the head of the platform, before boarding. You risk being fined if you don't.

PUBLIC TRANSPORT

For train and bus transport maps, *see pp350-352*.

Rome's transport is co-ordinated by **ATAC** (06 57 003, toll-free 800 431 784, www.atac.roma.it). The city centre and inner suburbs are served by the buses and trams of the Trambus transport authority. The system is relatively easy to use and as efficient as the traffic-choked streets allow. Pickpocketing is a problem on buses and metros, particularly major tourist routes, notably the 64 and 40 Express between Termini and the Vatican.

Tickets

The same tickets are valid on all city bus, tram and metro lines, whether operated by Trambus, MetRo (for both, *see below*) or regional transport authority COTRAL (*see pp286-287*), but not on airport services (*see p307*). Tickets must be bought before boarding, and are available from ATAC ticket machines, information centres, some newsstands and bars, and all *tabacchi* (*see p224*). Newer buses have ticket dispensers on board; these require exact change.

BIT (*biglietto integrato a tempo*) is valid for **75mins**, during which you can take an unlimited number of city buses, plus a metro trip; €1. **BIG** (*biglietto integrato giornaliero*) is valid for **one day**, until midnight, and covers the urban network; €4. **BTI** (*biglietto turistico integrato*) is a **three-day** pass, covering all bus and metro routes, and local mainline trains (second class) to Ostia; €11. (Before purchasing a BTI, consider whether the three-day **Roma Pass** might not be better value; *see p6*.) **BIRG** (*biglietto integrato regionale giornaliero*) is valid for **one day** on rail journeys in the Lazio region. Depending on the zones covered, it costs from €2.50 to €10.50, and is valid on metro, buses and local mainline trains (second class), but not Fiumicino airport lines. **CIS** (*carta integrata settimanale*) is valid for **seven days**; it covers all

bus routes and the metro system, including the lines to Ostia; €16. **Abbonamento mensile** Valid for unlimited travel on the entire metropolitan transport system during the **calendar month** in which the ticket was bought; €30 (€18 for under-20s and over-65s who should, theoretically, be Roman residents but it isn't very likely that inspectors would ask).

Note: when you get on, you *must* stamp tickets in the machines on board.

Under-10s travel free; older kids have to pay the adult fare, as must pensioners. Discounts for students, the disabled and pensioners are only available for residents. Fare-dodging is common, but if caught without a validated ticket, you'll be fined €51 on the spot, or €101 if you pay later at a post office.

Metro

Part of the ATAC-Metro-Trambus consortium, MetRo (06 57 531, www.metroroma.it – there's also information at www.atac.roma.it) is responsible for Rome's two metro lines, which cross beneath Termini mainline train station. Line A runs from south-east to north-west; line B from EUR to the north-eastern suburbs. Both are open 5.30am-11.30pm (until 1.30am Sat & Sun). From 11.30pm (1.30am weekends) to 5am, buses N1 and N2 ply the same routes.

Buses

Trambus routes are added or suspended and numbers change with some regularity: regularly updated bus maps can be bought at news kiosks. The ATAC website, www.atac.roma.it, has a journey planner and maps to download.

Regular Trambus services run 5.30am-midnight daily, every 10-45mins, depending on the route. The doors for boarding (usually front and rear) and alighting (usually centre) are clearly marked. A sign at each bus stop displays the lines and routes they take.

Note that the 'Express' buses make few stops along their route: check before boarding so you don't get whisked past your destination.

A small fleet of electric mini-buses also serves the centre, navigating *centro storico* alleys too narrow to accommodate regular buses. The 116, 116T, 117 and 119 connect places such as piazza di Spagna, campo de' Fiori and piazza Venezia with via Veneto and Termini.

BUSES TO TERMINI

For convenience, we have indicated '**buses to Termini**' in the listings in this guide, as all of the following bus routes pass by (or terminate at) Termini rail station: 16, 36, 38, 40Exp, 64, 70, 75, 84, 86, 90Exp, 92, 105, 150, 170, 175, 217, 310, 360, 590, 649, 714, 910, C2, C3, H, M; and night buses 5N, 6N, 12N, 40N, 45N, 50N, 55N, 78N, 91N. (Trams 5 and 14 terminate at Termini as well).

Trams

Tram routes mainly serve suburban areas. An express tram service – No.8 – links largo Argentina to Trastevere and the western suburbs.

Suburban transport

For transport maps, *see pp350-352.*

MetRo (*see left*) operates suburban railway lines, which are integrated with local lines of the **Ferrovie dello Stato** (FS; state railway). Regular bus, tram and metro tickets are valid on trains as far as the stations in red on the map. **COTRAL** coaches cover more distant destinations.

For more on travel to destinations in the vicinity of Rome, *see pp286-287.* For tickets, stations and rail information, *see p307.*

TOUR BUSES

Trambus' city-tour bus, the 110 (06 684 0901, toll-free 800 281 281, www. trambusopen.com), leaves Termini station every 10min (8.30am-8.30pm). It makes 11 stops on a two-hour circuit, including the Colosseum, Circus Maximus, piazza Venezia, St Peter's and the Trevi Fountain. Tours include commentary (in six languages). An all-day stop-and-go ticket costs €15. Buy tickets on board, online or at the booth in front of Termini train station.

The **Roma Cristiana** service (toll-free 800 917 430) departs from Termini and St Peter's every 30mins (8.30am-7.30pm daily), taking in the major basilicas and pilgrim sites. Tickets can be bought on board, at Termini, San Giovanni in Laterano or at piazza Pia near St Peter's. A 24hr stop-and-go ticket costs €17.

The **Archeobus** passes by the Baths of Caracalla and along via Appia Antica (the Appian Way; *see p151*) to the Catacombs, Cecilia Metella tomb, Villa dei Quintili and the Parco degli Acquedotti, leaving Termini station about every 40mins (9am-4pm daily). Stop-and-go tickets cost €10; without stops, the trip takes two and a half hours.

A ticket that combines the 110 and Archeobus tours costs €20 and is valid for two days. Tickets that combine the tours with museum entry are also available, including those listed below. Tickets for these can be purchased at the booth in front of Termini station, on board or online (www.trambusopen.com).

Trambus Open tickets allow you to purchase admission tickets at a reduced rate for many museums and galleries that are administered by Rome city council.

TAXIS

Licensed taxis are painted white and have a meter. Touts are rife at Termini and other major tourist magnets; ignore them if you don't want to risk an extortionate fare.

Fares & surcharges

When you pick up a taxi at a rank or hail one in the street, the meter should read zero. As you set off, it will initiate the minimum fare – currently €2.80 (€4 on Sundays and public holidays; €5.80 between 10pm and 7am).

Each kilometre after that is 92c. The first piece of luggage put in the boot is free, then it's €1 per piece. Tariffs outside the GRA, Rome's major ring road, are much higher. There's a ten per cent discount for trips to hospitals, and for women travelling alone 9pm-1am, and a €2 surcharge for any trip starting at Termini station.

Fixed airport tariffs from anywhere inside the Aurelian walls (ie most of the *centro storico*) are €45 to/from Fiumicino; €35 to/from Ciampino. This is for up to four people and includes luggage: don't let taxi drivers tell you otherwise.

Most of Rome's taxi drivers are honest; if you do suspect you're being fleeced, take down the driver's name and number from the metal plaque inside the car's rear door. The more ostentatiously you do this, the more likely you are to find the fare returning to its proper level. Report complaints to the drivers' co-operative (phone number on the outside of each car) or, in serious cases, the police (*see p316*).

Taxi ranks

Ranks are indicated by a blue sign with 'Taxi' written on it in white. In the centre, there are ranks at largo Argentina, the Pantheon, piazza Venezia, piazza San Silvestro, piazza Sonnino (Trastevere), piazza di Spagna and Termini station.

Phone cabs

When you phone for a taxi, you'll be given the taxi code-name (always a location followed by a number) and a time, as in *Bahama 69, in tre minuti* ('Bahamas 69, in three minutes'). Radio taxis start the meter from the moment your phone call is answered.

Cooperativa Samarcanda *06 5551, www.samarcanda.it.* **Credit** AmEx, DC, MC, V.
Cosmos Radio Taxi *06 88 177, 06 8822.* **Credit** AmEx, DC, MC, V.
Società Cooperativa Autoradio Taxi Roma *06 3570, www.3570.it.* **Credit** AmEx, DC, MC, V.
Società la Capitale Radio Taxi *06 49 94.* **Credit** AmEx, DC.

DRIVING

If you plan to drive a car here, brace yourself for Roman driving. To the uninitiated it seems like every-man-for-himself, but it's really a high-speed conversation, with its own language of glances, light-flashing and ostentatious acceleration.

Short-term visitors should have no trouble driving with their home licence, but if it is in a less common language an international licence can be useful. All EU citizens are obliged to get an Italian licence after being resident for one year.

● You are required by law to wear a seat belt at all times, in both front and back, and have a reflective jacket and warning triangle in the car.
● Outside urban areas, you must drive with headlights on at all times.
● You must keep your driving licence, vehicle registration and personal ID on you at all times.
● Do not leave anything of value in your car. Take all luggage into your hotel when you park.
● Flashing your lights in Italy means that you will not slow down (contrary to British practice).
● Traffic lights flashing amber mean stop and give way to the right.
● Beware death-defying mopeds and pedestrians. Pedestrians assume they have the right of way in the older, quieter streets without clearly designated pavements.

Restricted areas

Large sections of the city centre (marked ZTL – *Zona a Traffico Limitato*) are closed to non-resident traffic during business hours, sometimes in the evening. Municipal police and video cameras guard these areas; any vehicle without the required pass will be fined €70 if it enters at restricted times.

If your accommodation is in a restricted area, make arrangements with your hotel before arrival.

Petrol

Petrol stations sell unleaded petrol (*Senza Piombo* or *Verde*) and diesel (*Gasolio*). Liquid propane gas is *GPL*.

DIRECTORY

Most stations offer full service on weekdays; pump attendants don't expect tips. At night and on Sundays many stations have self-service pumps that accept €5, €10, €20 and €50 notes, in good condition; some also accept credit cards. Unofficial 'assistants' may offer to do the job for you for a small tip (€1).

Breakdown services

Before taking a car to Italy it's advisable to join a national motoring organisation, like the AA or RAC in Britain or the AAA in the US. They have reciprocal arrangements with the Automobile Club d'Italia (ACI), offering breakdown assistance and giving general information. Even non-members will do best to call ACI if you have any kind of breakdown.

If you require major repairs, pay a bit more to use the manufacturer's official dealer: the reliability of any garage depends on having built up a good client–mechanic relationship. Dealers are listed in the Yellow Pages under *auto*, along with specialist repairs such as *gommista* (tyres), *marmitte* (exhausts) and *carrozzerie* (bodywork). The *English Yellow Pages* has a list of garages at which English is spoken.

Automobile Club d'Italia (ACI)
Toll-free 800 116, www.aci.it.
The ACI has English-speaking staff and provides services for all foreign drivers. Members of associated organisations get basic repairs for free, and other services at lower rates; non-members will be charged, but prices are reasonable.

Parking

A system in which residents park for free and visitors pay is in place in many areas of the city. It's efficiently policed, so watch out for the telltale blue lines. Buy parking tickets (€1-€1.20 per hour) at pay-and-display ticket dispensers or *tabacchi*. In some areas parking is free after a certain time (usually 8pm or 11pm) or on Sundays – check instructions on the machine.

Your vehicle may be clamped if it's improperly or illegally parked: you will have to pay a fine, plus a charge to have the clamp removed. If your car's in a dangerous position or blocking trams and buses, it will be towed (*see below* **Car pounds**).

In zones with no blue lines, anything resembling a parking place is up for grabs, but with some exceptions: watch out for signs saying *Passo carrabile* ('access at all

times') or *Sosta vietata* ('no parking'), and disabled parking spaces (yellow stripes on the road). The sign *Zona rimozione* ('tow-away area') means no parking, and is valid for the length of the street or until the sign is repeated with a red line through it. If a street or square has no cars parked in it, assume it's a strictly enforced no-parking zone. In some areas, self-appointed *parcheggiatori* will 'look after' your car for a small fee; it may be illegal and an absurd imposition, but it's probably worth paying up to preserve your tyres.

Cars are fairly safe in most central areas, but you may prefer the hefty rates for underground car parks to keep your vehicle off the street. Central locations include:

ParkSì Villa Borghese *Viale del Galoppatoio 33, Veneto & Borghese (06 322 5934/7972, www.sabait.it). Metro Spagna/bus 88, 95, 116, 204, 490, 491, 495.* **Open** 24hrs daily. **Rates** *Cars* €1.60/hr for up to 3hrs; €1/hr for 4-15hrs; €20 for 16-24hrs. *Scooters & motorbikes* €1.20/hr. **Credit** AmEx, DC, MC, V. **Map** p340 A3.
Vehicle entrances are on via del Muro Torto (both sides of the road). The car park is linked to the Spagna metro station, with 24hr pedestrian access to piazza di Spagna.
Valentino *Via Sistina 75E, Veneto & Borghese (06 678 2597). Metro Spagna/bus 590.* **Open** 7am-1am Mon-Sat; 7am-12.30pm, 6pm-1am Sun. **Rates** €4/hr for up to six hours; €30-€33 for 24hrs. **Credit** AmEx, MC, V. **Map** p341 B5.

Car pounds

If your car is not where you left it, it may have been towed. Phone the municipal police (*Vigili urbani*) on 06 67 691 and quote your number plate to find out which pound it's in.

Car hire

To hire a car you must be over 21 – in some cases 23 – and have held a licence for at least a year. You will be required to leave a credit card number or substantial cash deposit. It's advisable to take out collision damage waiver (CDW) and personal accident insurance (PAI) on top of basic third-party cover. Companies not offering CDW are best avoided.

Avis *06 481 4373, 06 4521 08391, www.avisautonoleggio.it.*
Europcar *199 307 030, 06 488 2854, www.europcar.it.*

Maggiore *06 2245 6060, 06 488 0049, 199 151 120, www.maggiore.it.*

CYCLES, SCOOTERS & MOPEDS FOR HIRE

To hire a scooter or moped (*motorino*) you need a driving licence, photo ID, credit card and/or a cash deposit. Helmets are required on all motorbikes, scooters or mopeds (the police are very strict about this). For hiring bicycles, you can usually leave ID rather than pay a deposit.

Rome's bus company ATAC runs a city-wide cycle hire scheme called **ATAC-Bikesharing**. You'll need photo-ID to sign up at the larger central bus ticket booths. A swipe card costs €10, including €5 of credit which can be recharged at the same booths. Each half hour of bike use costs 50c. You'll often find the most central bike racks empty.

Bici & Baci *Via del Viminale 5, Monti (06 482 8443, www.bicibaci. com). Metro Repubblica/bus 40Exp, 60Exp, 64, 70, 84, 86, 90Exp, 170, 175, 492, 910, H.* **Open** 8am-7pm daily. **Rates** (per day) €11 bicycles; €32 mopeds (50cc); from €50 scooters (125cc). **Credit** MC, V. **Map** p341 C6.
This friendly outlet also offers hourly and weekly rates.
Romarent *Vicolo dei Bovari 7A, Ghetto & Campo (phone/fax 06 689 6555). Bus 46, 62, 64, 116, 116T, 916.* **Open** 9.30am-7pm daily. **Rates** (per day) €12 bicycles; €40 mopeds (50cc); €50-€70 scooters (125cc); €80 scooters (250cc). **Credit** AmEx, MC, V. **Map** p342 C1.
Scoot a Long *Via Cavour 302, Monti (06 678 0206). Metro Cavour/bus 75, 84, 117.* **Open** 9.30am-7.30pm daily. **Rates** (24hrs) from €35 mopeds; €45 scooters (125cc); €80 motorbikes. **Credit** AmEx, MC, V. **Map** p344 B2.
A credit card or deposit of €350 (125cc)/€200 (50cc) required. This company offers student discounts.
Scooters for Rent *Via della Purificazione 84, Veneto & Borghese (06 488 5485, www. rentscooter.it). Metro Barberini/ bus 52, 53, 61, 62, 63, 80Exp, 95, 116, 119, 175, 492, 590, 630.* **Open** *May-Sept* 9am-7pm daily. *Oct-Apr* 9am-6pm daily. **Rates** (per day) €40 mopeds; €50-€60 scooters (125cc); €80-€100 scooters (250cc) **Credit** AmEx, DC, MC, V. **Map** p341 B5.
Weekly rates are available. Deposit of €155 or credit card required.

DIRECTORY

Resources A-Z

ADDRESSES

Rome addresses follow the standard Italian format with the street name coming before the number on the first line, and the postcode preceding the name of the town or city on the second; two-letter code in brackets after the city name indicates the province.

AGE RESTRICTIONS

Cigarettes and alcohol cannot be sold to under-16s (for hard liquor or alcopops you must be 18). Over-14s can ride a moped or scooter of 50cc, but 14-18s are required to pass a practical test and obtain a pre-licence first (*see also p309* **Driving**). The age of heterosexual and homosexual consent is 16.

BUSINESS

If you are doing business in Rome, visit your embassy's (*see p312*) commercial section. You'll find trade publications and databases of fairs, buyers, sellers and distributors. Use any personal recommendations you have shamelessly: in Italy these will always smooth your way immensely.

Conventions & conferences

Rome offers superb facilities for conferences in magnificent *palazzi* and castles. Most major hotels cater for events of all sizes. A number of agencies can help handle the details.

Studio Ega
06 328 121, www.ega.it
Tecnoconference Europe
06 7835 9617, www.tecno conference-europe.com

Couriers & shippers

International couriers include:

DHL *199 199 345, www.dhl.it*
Federal Express *199 151 119, www.fedex.com*
TNT *199 803 868, www.tntitaly.it*
UPS – United Parcel Service *02 3030 3039, www.ups.com*
For local deliveries:
Easy Rider *06 5823 7506, www.easyrider2.it*
Speedy Boys *06 39 888, www.speedyboys.it*

Interpreters & translators

CRIC
Via S Alberto Magno 9, Aventine (06 574 5323, www.cric-interpreti. com). Metro Circo Massimo/bus 3, 60Exp, 75, 118, 271, 673/tram 3. **Map** p345 A5.
Rome At Your Service
Via VE Orlando 75, Esquilino (06 484 583, 06 482 5589, www.rome atyourservice.it). Metro Repubblica/bus 36, 60Exp, 61, 62, 84, 175, 492, 590, 910. **Map** p341 C5.

CONSUMER

Rome city council's general help-line 060606 is the best place to go in the first instance for advice. In serious cases, ring the Carabinieri police on 112 where you should find English-speaking switchboard staff. The city council's Ufficio Tutela del Consumatore (Consumer Protection Office) at via dei Cerchi 6 (06 6710 4282, open 9am-1pm, 2-4.30pm Tue, Wed; 9am-1pm Thur) advise on shoppers' rights.

CUSTOMS

People travelling between EU countries are not required to declare goods imported into or exported from Italy if they are for personal use. For those arriving from non-EU countries, these limits apply:

● 200 cigarettes or 100 cigarillos or 50 cigars or 250g of tobacco;
● one litre of spirits (over 22% alcohol) or two litres of wine.
● One bottle of perfume (50 ml), 250 ml eau de toilette;
● Gift items not exceeding €175 (€95 for children under 15).

Anything above that will be subject to taxation at the port of entry.
For further information, visit www.agenziadogane.it. For tax refunds, *see p222* **Inside Track**.

DISABLED

Rome isn't the easiest city for disabled people, especially wheelchair-users. You'll almost certainly have to depend on other people more than you would at home. Narrow streets make life awkward for those who can't flatten themselves against a wall to let vehicles by. Cobble-stones turn wheelchairs with excellent suspension into bone-rattlers and getting on to pavements is well-nigh impossible due to bumper-to-bumper parked cars. Off the streets, old buildings tend to have narrow corridors and the lifts (if any), are usually too small.

Blind and partially sighted people often find there's no kerb between the road proper and the bit of street pedestrians are entitled to walk on (the one exception is a smooth brick walkway laid into the cobbles leading from the Trevi Fountain to piazza Navona, with Braille notes about landmarks on bronze plaques along the way).

DIRECTORY

Wheelchair-accessible public toilets are found in many central areas... but there's no guarantee they'll be in working order or open.

Information

Information for disabled people is available from PIT information booths (*see p318*) and the following organisations:

CO.IN
06 5717 7001, www.coinsociale.it.
Contact CO.IN for information on disabled facilities at museums, restaurants, shops, theatres, stations and hotels. The group also organises transport for disabled people (up to eight places), which must be booked several days in advance but can cover airport journeys as well as travel within Rome. Its phone service, in Italian and English, offers up-to-date information (toll-free 800 271 027; operates 9am-5pm Mon-Fri, 9am-1pm Sat, only from within Italy). The website is in Italian only.

Roma per Tutti
06 5717 7094, www.romapertutti. it. **Open** 9am-5pm Mon-Fri.
An information line run by CO.IN (*see above*) and the city council. English-speaking staff answer questions on accessibility in hotels, buildings and monuments.

Sightseeing

Well-designed ramps, lifts and toilets have been installed in many attractions; Roma per Tutti (*see above*) has up-to-date information.

Museum
06 513 9855, 338 148 5361, www.assmuseum.it
This volunteer group offers tours of some galleries and catacombs for individuals or groups with mobility or, especially, sight problems. Their museum guides – some speak English; if not, an interpreter can be arranged – have Braille notes, copies of paintings in relief, and permission to touch artefacts. Guides also make works of art comprehensible to the non-sighted with music cassettes and recorded text. A voluntary donation to cover costs is requested.

Transport

Rome's buses and trams have been made more accessible, with most buses plying central routes able to accommodate wheelchairs.

On the metro, most of the central stations on line A are no-go areas. All stations on line B have lifts, disabled WCs and special parking spaces, though work on the third metro line means that access at some stations is being closed off for long periods. The www.atac. roma.it website lists wheelchair-accessible stations.

Most taxi drivers will carry (folded) wheelchairs; when you can, phone for a cab rather than hailing one (*see p309*).

To ascertain which trains have wheelchair facilities, call 06 3000 (when prompted, press 7 for information) or 199 892 021 (06 488 1726 for international trips), or consult timetables on the Trenitalia website (www. trenitalia.it): there's a wheelchair symbol next to accessible trains. To secure assistance, you must phone the numbers given above or make a request by email (assistenzaclientidisabili.rm@ trenitalia.it) 24hrs prior to departure. Reserve a seat when buying your ticket, and make sure you arrive at least 45mins early.

This also applies to trains to and from Fiumicino airport; in theory, you must call or fax your airline to arrange assistance the day before arrival; in practice, you'll be helped on the train anyway.

Both Rome's airports have adapted toilets and waiting rooms. Inform your airline of your needs so that it can contact the office at Fiumicino or Ciampino airport.

Wheelchair hire

Ortopedia Colosseo
Viale Carlo Felice 91-3, San Giovanni (06 7720 9393, www. ortopediamazzotta.it). Metro San Giovanni/bus 571/tram 3. **Open** 8.30am-1pm, 3.30-7pm Mon-Fri; 8.30am-1pm Sat. **Credit** MC, V. **Map** p344 C3.
Rents all kinds of wheelchairs (from €8 per day). These can be delivered by taxi: you pay the fare unless you are in one of the larger hotels with which the shop has an agreement. **Other locations** via Carlo Felice 91-3 (06 7720 9393).

Where to stay & eat

There may be a greater number of accessible hotels – CO.IN (*see above*) has details – but cheaper hotels and *pensioni*, often housed on upper floors of *palazzi*, can be a problem. If you have special needs, make them known when you book.

Local by-laws require restaurants to have disabled access and toilets; in practice, many have not made the necessary alterations. If you phone ahead and ask for an appropriate table, most will try to help. In summer the range of outdoor restaurants makes things easier, but getting to toilets can be almost impossible.

Most bars open on to the street at ground level, and/or have tables outside. Again, most bar toilets are tiny dark holes down long staircases.

DRUGS

Anyone caught in possession of narcotics of any kind must be taken before a magistrate. The severity of the punishment – which can extend to years in prison – depends upon the quantity of drugs, and whether they are deemed *leggera* (light) or *pesante* (heavy).

Sniffer dogs are a fixture at most ports of entry into Italy; customs police are likely to allow visitors entering with even negligible quantities of narcotics to stay no longer than it takes a magistrate to expel them from the country.

ELECTRICITY

Most wiring systems work on 220V – compatible with UK-bought appliances (with a plug adaptor); US 110V equipment requires a current transformer. Adaptors can be bought at any electrical or hardware shop (*elettricità* or *ferramenta*).

EMBASSIES & CONSULATES

For a full list of embassies, see *Ambasciate* in the phone book.

Except where indicated, consular offices (which provide the majority of services of use to tourists) share the same address as these embassies.

Australia *Via Antonio Bosio 5, Suburbs: north (06 852 721, www.italy.embassy.gov.au). Bus 36, 60Exp, 62, 84, 90Exp.*
Britain *Via XX Settembre 80A, Esquilino (06 4220 0001, fax 06 4220 2334, www.britain.it). Bus 36, 60Exp, 61, 62, 84, 90Exp, 490, 491.* **Map** p341 E4.
Canada Embassy: *via Salaria 243, Suburbs: north (06 854 441, 06 8544 43937, www.canada.it). Bus 53, 63, 86, 92, 168, 630/tram 3, 19.* Consulate: *via Zara 30, Suburbs: north. Bus 36, 60Exp, 62, 84, 90Exp.*

Ireland *Piazza Campitelli 3, Ghetto (06 697 9121, www.ambasciata-irlanda.it). Bus 30Exp, 44, 63, 81, 95, 160, 170, 628, 630, 715, 716, 780, 781, H.* **Map** p342 E2.

New Zealand *Via Clitunno 44, Suburbs: north (06 853 7501, www.nzembassy.com). Bus 63, 86, 92, 630.*

South Africa *Via Tanaro 14, Suburbs: north (06 852 541, www.sudafrica.it). Tram 3, 19.* **Map** p340 E1.

US *Via Vittorio Veneto 119, Veneto & Borghese (06 46 741, www.us embassy.it). Metro Barberini/bus 52, 53, 61, 62, 63, 80Exp, 95, 116, 116T, 119, 175, 204, 590, 630.* **Map** p341 C4.

EMERGENCIES

See also below **Health**; *p317*
Safety & security; *p316*
Police; *p316* **Money**.

Thefts or losses should be reported immediately at the nearest police station. Report the loss of credit cards immediately to your credit card company (*see p316*), and of passports to your consulate/embassy (*see above*).

National emergency numbers

Police *Carabinieri* (English-speaking helpline) 112; *Polizia di Stato* 113
Fire service *Vigili del fuoco* 115
Ambulance *Ambulanza* 118
Car breakdown *see p310*.

Domestic emergencies

Report a malfunction in any of the main services to these 24hr emergency lines.

Electricity *ACEA 06 57 991, toll-free 800 130 336 (8am-7pm)*
Gas *Italgas toll-free 800 900 999, toll-free 800 900 700*
Telephone Telecom Italia *187*
Water *ACEA toll-free 800 130 335*

GAY & LESBIAN

For information, *see pp258-263*.

HEALTH

Emergency health care is available through the Italian national health system; hospital accident and emergency departments (*see below*) treat all emergency cases for free. If you are an EU citizen, the EHIC (European Health Insurance Card; *see p314*) entitles you to free

consultation with any doctor. Non-EU citizens are advised to obtain private health insurance (*see p314*).

Accident & emergency

If you need urgent medical care, go to the *pronto soccorso* (casualty department). All the hospitals listed here offer 24hr casualty services. If your child needs emergency treatment, head straight for the excellent Ospedale Bambino Gesù.

Ospedale Fatebenefratelli *Isola Tiberina, Ghetto (06 68 371, www.fatebenefratelli-isolatiberina. it). Bus 23, 63, 271, 280, 630, 780, H/tram 8.* **Map** p342 D2.
Ospedale Pediatrico Bambino Gesù *Piazza Sant'Onofrio 4, Gianicolo (06 68 591, www.ospedale bambinogesu.it). Bus 23, 115, 116, 280, 870.* **Map** p339 A6.
Ospedale San Camillo-Forlanini *Via Portuense 332, Suburbs: west (06 55 551, 06 58 701, www. scamilloforlanini.rm.it). Bus 228, 710, 719, 773, 774, 786, 791, H/tram 8.*
Ospedale San Giovanni *Via Amba Aradam 8, San Giovanni (06 77 051, 06 7705 6605, www. hsangiovanni.roma.it). Metro San Giovanni/bus 81, 117, 650, 673, 714.* **Map** p344 E3.
Policlinico Umberto I *Viale Policlinico 155, Suburbs: north (06 49 971, www.policlinicoumberto1. it). Metro Policlinico/bus 61, 310, 490, 491, 495, 649/tram 3, 19.*

Contraception & abortion

Condoms (*preservativi*) are relatively inexpensive and on sale near checkouts in supermarkets or over the counter in pharmacies; the pill is available on prescription. Abortion, available on financial hardship or health grounds, is legal only when performed in public hospitals.

Most districts have a local health authority *consultorio familiare* (family planning clinic). EU citizens with an EHIC (*see p314*) form pay the same low charges as locals. Phone first to make an appointment. The most centrally located is:

Via San Martino della Battaglia 16, Esquilino (06 7730 5505, appointments 803 333). Metro Castro Pretorio/bus to Termini station. **Open** 8.30am-1pm, 2.30-5pm Mon; 8.30am-1pm Tue-Fri. **Map** p341 E4.

These private gynaecological clinics are also recommended:

AIED
Via Toscana 30, Veneto & Borghese (06 4282 5314). Metro Barberini/bus 52, 53, 63, 80Exp, 95, 630. **Open** 9am-1pm, 2-7pm Mon-Fri; 9am-1pm Sat. **Credit** MC, V. **Map** p340 C3.
Offers check-ups, contraceptive advice, menopause counselling and smear tests. You buy a membership card (*tessera*) for €5, then check-ups cost €45. Smear tests are €18.

Artemide
Via Sannio 61, San Giovanni (06 7047 6220). Metro San Giovanni/bus 87, 360. **Open** 10am-7pm Mon-Fri; 10am-1pm Sat. **No credit cards**. **Map** p345 E4.
Gynaecological check-ups here are €70, smear tests are €25, and there's a wide range of other services. Appointments should be made a few days in advance, but emergencies are invariably dealt with immediately.

Dentists

For serious dental emergencies, head to a hospital casualty department (*see above*).

Most dentists (see *Dentisti* in the Yellow Pages) in Italy work privately; treatmentis not cheap and may not be covered by your health insurance, but you can wait months for a dental appointment in a national health service hospital (children are somewhat better served at the out-patients department of the Ospedale Bambino Gesù; *see above*).

Doctors

EU nationals with an EHIC (*see p314*) can consult a national health service doctor free of charge, and buy drugs at prices set by the Health Ministry. Tests and out-patient treatment are charged at fixed rates too. Non-EU nationals who consult a health service doctor will be charged a small fee at the doctor's discretion.

Helplines & agencies

Alcoholics Anonymous
06 474 2913, www.aarome.info
An English-speaking support group holds meetings at the church of St Paul's Within the Walls at via Napoli 56. Phone for meeting times.

DIRECTORY

Associazione Differenza Donna

Viale Villa Pamphili 100,
Suburbs: west (06 581 0926).
Bus 44, 710, 871.
A helpline for victims of
sexual violence. The women-
only volunteers (some English-
speaking) can offer support and
legal assistance.

Samaritans

Toll-free 800 860 022.
Open 24hrs daily.
Staffed by native English speakers.

Telefono Azzurro

19 696. **Open** 24hrs daily.
A toll-free helpline for children
and young people suffering abuse
(normally Italian-speaking only).

Telefono Rosa

06 3751 8261. **Open** 10am-1pm,
4-7pm Mon-Fri.
Offers counselling and legal advice
for women who have been victims
of sexual abuse or sexual
harassment.

Hospitals

See p313 **Accident**
& Emergency.

Opticians

See p236.

Pharmacies

Farmacie (identified by a green
cross) give informal medical advice,
as well as making up prescriptions.
Most also sell homeopathic and
veterinary medicines, and all will
check your height/weight/blood
pressure on request. Make sure
you know the generic as well as
the brand name of your regular
medicines: they may be sold under
a different name here. The best-
stocked pharmacy in the city is
in the Vatican: it has a whole
range of medicines not found
elsewhere in Italy.

Normal pharmacy opening
hours are 8.30am-1pm, 4-8pm
Mon-Sat. Outside these hours,
a duty rota system operates. A
list displayed by the door of any
pharmacy (and in local papers)
indicates the nearest ones open
at any time. A surcharge of €3.87
per client (not per item) applies
when only the special duty
counter is open.

Farmacia della Stazione

Piazza dei Cinquecento 49-51,
Esquilino (06 488 0019). Metro
Termini/buses to Termini/tram
5, 14. **Open** 24hrs daily. **Credit**
AmEx, DC, MC, V. **Map** p341 E5.

Farmacia del Vaticano

Porta Sant'Anna entrance, Vatican
(06 6988 3422). Metro Ottaviano/
bus 23, 32, 49, 62, 81, 492, 590,
982, 990/tram 19. **Open** 8.30am-
6pm Mon-Fri; 8.30am-1pm Sat.
Credit MC, V. **Map** p339 A4.

Piram Via Nazionale

228 Esquilino (06 488 0754).
Metro Repubblica/bus 40Exp,
60Exp, 64, 70, 71, 170, H, 78N,
91N. **Open** 24hrs daily. **Credit**
DC, MC, V. **Map** p341 C5.

ID

You are required by law to carry
photo ID with you at all times.
You must produce it if stopped
by traffic police (along with your
driving licence, which you must
carry when you're in charge of
a motor vehicle) and when you
check into a hotel. Smaller hotels
may try to hold on to your
passport/ID card for the length
of your stay; you are within
your rights to ask for it back.

INSURANCE

See also p313 **Health** and
p316 **Police**.
    EU citizens are entitled to
reciprocal medical care in Italy
provided they leave their own
country with an **EHIC** (European
Health Insurance Card), which
has replaced the old form E111.
In the UK, you can apply for an
EHIC online (www.ehic.org.uk)
or by post using forms available
at any post office. If you use it
for anything but emergencies
(which are treated free anyway
in casualty departments; *see*
p313), you'll need to deal with
the intricacies of the Italian state
health system. For short-term
visits, it is advisable to take out
private travel/health insurance.
Non-EU citizens should take out
private medical insurance before
setting off.
    Visitors should also take out
adequate insurance against loss or
theft. If you rent a car, motorcycle
or moped, make sure you pay the
extra for full insurance cover and,
for a car, sign the collision damage
waiver (CDW).

INTERNET & EMAIL

Most hotels offer internet access,
either cable or wireless. In some
places it's offered free; elsewhere –
including most high-end hotels –
you will have to pay. Many cafés
offer free wireless access.

Much of central Rome, plus the
major parks – *ville* Ada, Borghese,
Pamphili, Torlonia – and the
Auditorium-Parco della Musica
zone, is covered by wireless
hotspots sponsored by the city
council. As soon as you open your
browser, you'll be asked to log on;
initially you'll need to register,
giving a mobile phone number
when you do so. Access is free.
For further information, including
a map of the hotspots, see
www.romawireless.com.
    A number of Italian ISPs
offer free access, including
Libero (www.libero.it), Tiscali
(www.tiscali.it), Kataweb
(www.kataweb.com) and
Telecom Italia (www.tin.it).

LEFT LUGGAGE

The left-luggage office by platform
24 in Termini station (06 474 4777)
is open 6am-11.50pm daily. A
suitcase costs €4/hr (for up to
5hrs); 60¢/hr from the sixth to
the 12th hour; thereafter, 20¢/hr.
At Fiumicino airport, left luggage
in Terminal C is open 7am-11pm
daily. Each item costs €2 for 7hrs;
thereafter €3.50 per day. Hotels
will generally look after your
luggage during the day, even
after you've checked out.

LEGAL HELP

Legal advice should first be sought
at your embassy or consulate (for
listings, *see p313*).

LIBRARIES

Rome's libraries are dogged by
red tape, restricted hours and
patchy organisation. All libraries
listed are open to the public; other
specialist libraries can be found
under *Biblioteche* in the phone
book. Always take some ID
along; in some cases, a letter
from your college stating the
purpose of your research will
be required.

Archivio Centrale dello Stato
(State Archives)

Piazzale Archivi 27, Suburbs: EUR
(06 545 481, fax 06 541 3620,
www.archivi.beniculturali.it/ACS).
Metro EUR Fermi/bus 703, 707,
765, 767. **Open** 9am-7pm Mon-Fri;
9am-1pm Sat. Closed 1wk Aug.
The original documents, historical
correspondence and many other
items at this efficiently run archive
have to be consulted *in situ* (but
most can be photocopied).

Biblioteca Alessandrina
Piazzale Aldo Moro 5, Esquilino (06 447 4021, www.alessandrina. librari.beniculturali.it). Metro Policlinico/bus 71, 310, 492, C. **Open** 8.30am-7.30pm Mon-Fri; 8.30am-1pm Sat. Closed 2wks Aug. **Map** p128 C1.
This library is grossly inefficient for the needs of La Sapienza (*see p317*), Europe's largest university.

Biblioteca Nazionale
Viale Castro Pretorio 105, Esquilino (06 49 891, www.bncrm.librari. beniculturali.it). Metro Castro Pretorio/bus 310, 492, 649, C. **Open** 8.30am-7pm Mon-Fri; 8.30am-1.30pm Sat. Closed 2wks Aug. **Map** off p341 E5.
The national library holds a large proportion of all that's in print in Italy, plus books in other languages.

Biblioteca dell'Università Gregoriana
Piazza della Pilotta 4, Trevi & Quirinale (06 6701 5131, www. unigre.it/newbiblio). Bus 40Exp, 60Exp, 62, 63, 64, 70, 81, 85, 95, 160, 170, 175, 204, 492, 628, 630, 850, H. **Open** 8.30am-6.30pm Mon-Fri; 8.30am-12.30pm Sat. Closed mid July-Aug; 2wks Dec-Jan. **Map** p341 A6.
Better organised than Biblioteca Alessandrina (*see above*), but books here are not allowed off the premises.

Biblioteca Vaticana
Via di Porta Angelica, Vatican (06 6987 9411, www.vatican.va). Metro Ottaviano/bus 23, 32, 49, 62, 81, 492, 982, 990/tram 19. **Open** (postgrads only) 8.45am-5.15pm Mon-Fri. Closed mid July-mid Sept. **Map** p339 A4.
To obtain an entrance card, students need a letter on headed paper, signed by a professor, stating their research purpose. Go between 8.45am-noon to get a membership card.

The British School at Rome
Via Gramsci 61, Veneto & Borghese (06 326 4931, www.bsr.ac.uk). Bus 52, 926/tram 19. **Open** *Library* 9am-6.45pm Mon-Fri. Closed mid July-Aug. **Map** p338 E1.
The library has 60,000 English and Italian books on all aspects of Rome, especially art history, archaeology and topography. Annual membership costs €30, monthly €10; you must present a photo, a valid document and a letter of introduction from a museum or university. No lending facilities.

LOST PROPERTY

For anything lost on Rome's buses, call ATAC's toll-free number (*see*

p308) and they'll search for it for you, after which you can pick it up at their offices.

Ufficio oggetti smarriti
Circonvallazione Ostiense 191, Suburbs: south (06 6769 3214). Metro Garbatella/bus 23, 271, 770. **Open** 8.30-1pm Mon, Wed, Fri; 8.30am-5pm Thur.
Anything lost on Metro lines A and B, on FS trains or at Termini station may turn up at this council-run lost property office.

MEDIA

National dailies

Long, indigestible political stories with little in the way of background predominate in Italian newspapers. On the plus side, dailies are refreshingly unsnobbish and happily blend news, leaders by internationally recognised commentators, and well-written, often quite bizarre, human-interest stories. Sports coverage is extensive; and there are always the mass-circulation sports papers *Corriere dello Sport*, *La Gazzetta dello Sport* and *Tuttosport*.

Free papers are distributed each weekday in the metro and bus stations.

Corriere della Sera
www.corriere.it
To the centre of centre-left, this solid, serious but often dull Milan-based paper is good for foreign news.

La Repubblica
www.repubblica.it
Rome-based, centre-ish, left-ish, and providing a good selection of supplementary inserts.

La Stampa
www.lastampa.it
Part of the massive empire of Turin's Agnelli family; it offers good (albeit pro-Agnelli) business reporting.

Il Sole-24 Ore
www.ilsole24ore.it
This business, finance and economics daily has a great arts supplemtn on Sunday.

Local dailies

La Repubblica and *Corriere della Sera* (*see above*) have large daily Rome sections.

Il Messaggero
www.ilmessaggero.it
The Roman daily *per eccellenza*. Particularly useful classified ads – with many flat rents – on Saturdays.

L'Osservatore Romano
www.vatican.va
The Vatican's official newspaper reflects the conservative orthodoxies issuing from the top. Weekly English edition on Wednesdays.

Foreign press

The *Financial Times*, *Wall Street Journal*, *USA Today*, *International Herald Tribune* and most foreign dailies can be found on the day of issue at central newsstands.

Magazines

For details of English-language publications, *see below* **Listings & small ads**.

Panorama and *L'Espresso* each provide a generally high-standard round-up of the week's news, while *Magazine* and *Venerdì* – the colour supplements of *Corriere della Sera* (Thur) and *La Repubblica* (Fri) respectively – have nice photos but are textually rather weak; *La Repubblica*'s rather glossy Saturday supplement *D* is the best of the lot. For tabloid-style scandal, try the weird mix of sex, glamour and religion in *Gente* and *Oggi*, or even the compulsively awful *Eva 3000* and *Cronaca Vera*. Far more highbrow, *Internazionale* (www.internazionale.it) provides a readable digest of articles gleaned from the world's press over the previous week. *Diario della Settimana* (www.diario.it) offers informed investigative journalism. But the biggest-seller is *Famiglia Cristiana* – readily available from newsstands and in most churches – which alternates between Vatican line-toeing and Vatican-baiting, based on the current state of relations between the Holy See and the idiosyncratic Paoline monks who produce it.

Listings & small ads

The American Magazine
www.theamericanmag.com
A monthly online English-language magazine that covers cultural and political life in Italy, and runs useful classified ads.

Porta Portese
www.porta-portese.it
Essential reading for flat-hunters in Rome (whether you're planning to rent or to buy). Published Tuesday and Friday, it also has sections on household goods and cars. Place ads free on 06 70 199.

DIRECTORY

Roma C'è
www.romace.it
Comprehensive listings for
theatre, music, dance, film
and nightlife every Wednesday,
with a small English-language
section as well.

Solocase
www.solocase.it
Houses for sale and rent. Comes
out on Saturdays.

Trovaroma
Comes free with *La Repubblica*
every Thursday; its English-
language section covers the
week's concerts, exhibitions
and guided tours.

Wanted in Rome
www.wantedinrome.com
Essential information and
upmarket housing ads for English-
speaking expats; out fortnightly.

Radio

These state-owned stations play
a programme of classical and
light music, interspersed with
chat shows and regular, excellent
news bulletins:

RAI 1 89.7 FM, 1332 AM
RAI 2 91.7 FM, 846 AM
RAI 3 93.7 FM, 1107 AM
www.rai.it

For UK and US chart hits, mixed
with home-grown offerings, try:

Radio Capital 95.8 FM,
www.capital.it
Radio Centro Suono 101.3 FM,
www.radiocentrosuono.it
Radio Città Futura 97.7 FM,
www.radiocittafutura.it
Italy's most PC 24hr station.
Radio Kiss Kiss Network 97.25
FM, *www.kisskissnetwork.it*
Radio 105 96.1 FM, *www.105.net*
Vatican Radio 105 FM, 585 MW,
www.vaticanradio.org
World events, as seen by the
Catholic church, and broadcast
in English.

Television

Italy has six major networks (three
are owned by the state broadcaster
RAI, three by Silvio Berlusconi's
Mediaset group), and two channels
that operate across most of the
country: La7 and MTV. Local
stations provide hours of tacky
programming, from tarot-reading
to zero-budget soaps.
TV in Rome and the Lazio region
is now digital, allowing access to
BBC World as well as French and
German language channels.

MONEY

The Italian currency is the euro,
with banknotes of €5, €10, €20,
€100, €200 and €500, and coins
worth €1 and €2, plus 1¢, 2¢, 5¢,
10¢, 20¢ and 50¢ (*centesimi*). Money
from any Eurozone country is valid
tender. Vatican euros are a highly
collectable rarity.

Banks & ATMs

Most banks have 24hr cash-point
(*Bancomat*) machines. The vast
majority accept cards with the
Maestro, Cirrus and Plus logos,
and will dispense up to a daily
limit of €250.

Banking hours

Opening hours vary, but most
banks operate 8.30am-1.30pm,
2.45-4.30pm Mon-Fri. Some central
branches now also open until 6pm
Thur and 8.30am-12.30pm Sat. All
banks close on public holidays, and
work reduced hours the day before
a holiday (many close by 11am).

Bureaux de change

Banks usually offer better exchange
rates than private bureaux de change
(*cambio*). Take a passport or other
photo ID. Commission rates vary
(from nothing to €5 per transaction).
Beware 'no commission' signs: the
rate will likely be terrible.
Many city-centre bank branches
have automatic cash-exchange
machines, which will accept
most currencies (notes in good
condition only).

American Express
*Piazza di Spagna 38, Tridente (06
67 641). Metro Spagna/bus 52, 53,
61, 71, 80Exp, 117, 119, 160, 850.*
Open 9am-5.30pm Mon-Fri; 9am-
12.30pm Sat. **Map** p341 A4.

Credit cards

Nearly all hotels of two stars and
above now accept at least some of
the major credit cards; all but the
cheapest local eateries will take
them too.
Should you lose a credit card,
phone one of the 24hr emergency
numbers below.

American Express *06 7290 0347,
06 7228 0371, US cardholders 800
874 333*
Diner's Club *800 864 064*
MasterCard *800 870 866*
Visa *800 877 232*

POLICE

The principal *Polizia di Stato*
station, the Questura Centrale,
is at via San Vitale 15 (06 46 861,
www.poliziadistato.it). Others, and
the Carabinieri's *Commissariati*, are
listed in the phone directory under
Polizia and *Carabinieri*. Incidents
can be reported to either.

POSTAL SERVICES

For postal information, call 803 160
(8am-8pm Mon-Sat; Italian only) or
visit www.poste.it.
The once-notorious Italian postal
service is now generally efficient.
If you still have any doubts, the
Vatican Post Office (*see right*) is
run in association with the Swiss
postal service.
Most postboxes are red and
have two slots, *per la città* (for
Rome) and *tutte le altre destinazioni*
(everywhere else).
On the whole, mail arrives swiftly
– up to 48hrs delivery in Italy, three
days for EU countries and between
five and nine days for other
countries (in zones 2 and 3). A
letter of 20g or less to Italy costs
60¢; to other countries in the EU
costs 65¢; to zone 2 costs 85¢; to
zone 3 costs €1.
The *Posta Celere* service costs
more (€10 for up to 3kg) and
promises (though doesn't always
achieve) 24hr delivery. You can,
however, track the progress of your
letter on the website or by phoning
(details as above).
Registered mail (ask for
raccomandata) starts at €2.80
for a letter of 20g or less.
Parcels can be sent from any
post office. It is advisable to send
any package worth more than
€50 insured.
There are local post offices
(*ufficio postale*) in each district;
opening hours can vary, but they
are generally 8.30am-6pm Mon-Fri
(8.30am-2pm Aug), 8.30am-1.30pm
Sat and any day preceding a public
holiday. They close two hours
earlier than normal on the last day
of each month. Main post offices
in the centre have longer opening
hours and offer a range of
additional services, including fax
facilities (though not at the Posta
Centrale). Several postal services
are available online; visit www.
poste.it to avoid the queues.

Posta Centrale
*Piazza San Silvestro 19, Tridente
(06 6973 7232, information 803
160). Bus 52, 53, 61, 71, 80Exp,*

85, 116, 116T, 117, 119, 160, 850. **Open** 8am-7pm Mon-Sat. **Map** p341 A5.

The hub of Rome's postal system has been treated to a facelift: shiny new internet terminals, numerous counters, an information desk… and vastly reduced queues. Letters sent poste restante/general delivery (*fermo posta*) to Rome should be addressed to Roma Centro Corrispondenza, Posta Centrale, piazza San Silvestro, 00186 Roma. You'll need your passport to collect and have to pay a small charge.

Other main offices

Via Marsala 39, Esquilino. Metro Termini/buses to Termini. **Map** p128 A2.

Piazza Bologna 3, Suburbs: east. Metro Bologna/bus 61, 62, 93, 168, 309, 310, 445, 542.
Via Marmorata 4, Testaccio. Metro Piramide/bus 23, 30Exp, 75, 280, 673, 716, 719/tram 3. **Map** p343 E5.
Viale Mazzini 101, Suburbs: north. Bus 30Exp, 88, 495. **Map** p338 B1.
Via Taranto 19, Suburbs: south. Metro San Giovanni/bus 85.
Poste Vaticane Piazza San Pietro, Vatican (06 6988 3406). Metro Ottaviano/bus 23, 49, 62, 81, 492, 590, 982, 990/tram 19. **Open** 8am-7.30pm Mon-Fri; 8.30am-6.30pm Sat. **Map** p339 A4.

RELIGION

For information about papal audiences, *see p143*.

There are over 400 Catholic churches in Rome, but few hold mass in English. The main English-speaking Catholic church is San Silvestro (piazza San Silvestro 17A, 06 697 7121); San Patrizio (via Boncompagni 31, 06 4290 3787, www.stpatricksrome.com) is the principal Irish church; the American Catholic church is Santa Susanna (via XX Settembre 15, 06 4201 4554, www.santasusanna.org).

Anglican

All Saints, via del Babuino 153B, Tridente (06 3600 1881, www.all saints.org). Metro Spagna/bus 117, 119, 590. **Services** 8am, 10.30am Sun; 8am, 10.30am, 6pm first Sun of month. **Map** p338 E3.

All Saints hosts a programme of cultural events, including regular concerts, and activities for children.

Episcopal

St Paul's Within the Walls, via Napoli 58, Esquilino (06 488 3339, www.stpaulsrome.it). Metro Repubblica/bus 40Exp, 60Exp, 64,

70, 116T, 170, H. **Services** 8.30am, 10.30am, 1pm (in Spanish) Sun. **Map** p341 C5.

Jewish

Comunità Israelitica Ebraica di Roma, lungotevere Cenci, Ghetto (06 6840 0661, www.museoebraico. roma.com). Bus 23, 63, 271, 280, 630, 780, H. **Map** p342 D2.

There are daily services, but times vary. Guided tours of the synagogue are offered from the Museo Ebraico (*see p110*).

Methodist

Ponte Sant'Angelo Church, via del Banco di Santo Spirito, Pantheon & Navona (06 686 8314). Bus 40Exp, 46, 62, 64, 98, 280, 870, 881, 916. **Services** 10.30am Sun. **Map** p339 B5.

Muslim

Moschea di Roma, viale della Moschea, Suburbs: north (06 808 2167, www.moscheadiroma.it). Train to Campi Sportivi/bus 230.

Paolo Portoghesi's masterpiece is always open to Muslims for prayer. Non-Muslims can visit 9-11.30am Wed and Sat.; €2, €1 reductions.

Presbyterian

St Andrew's, via XX Settembre 7, Veneto & Borghese (06 482 7627, www.presbyterianchurchrome.org). Bus 36, 60Exp, 61, 62, 84, 175, 492, 590, 910. **Services** 11am Sun. **Map** p341 C4.

SAFETY & SECURITY

Muggings are fairly rare in Rome, but pickpocketing is rife in the main tourist areas. Below are a few basic precautions:

● Don't carry wallets in back pockets, particularly on buses. If you have a bag or camera with a long strap, wear it across the chest.

● Keep bags closed, with your hand on them. If you stop at a pavement café or restaurant, don't leave bags or coats where you cannot see them.

● When walking down a street, hold cameras and bags on the side of you towards the wall – you're less likely to become the prey of a motorcycle thief.

● Avoid groups of ragged children brandishing pieces of cardboard, or walk by quickly keeping hold of your valuables. The cardboard is to distract you while accomplices pick your pockets or bags.

If you are the victim of crime, call the police helpline (*see left*) or go to the nearest police station and say you want to report a *furto* (theft). A *denuncia* (written statement) of the incident will be made. It's unlikely your things

will be found, but you will need the *denuncia* for insurance claims.

SMOKING

A law introduced in January 2005 prohibits smoking in all public places in Italy except for those that provide a distinct, ventilated smokers' room. This legislation is strictly enforced.

Tabacchi

Tabacchi or *tabaccherie* (identifiable by signs with a white 'T' on black or blue) are the only places you can legally buy tobacco products. They also generally sell stamps, telephone cards, tickets for public transport, lottery tickets and the stationery required for dealing with Italian bureaucracy. Most *tabacchi* keep shop hours, but some are attached to bars and so stay open into the night. *See also p224* **Life's Essentials**.

STUDY

See also p314 **Libraries**.

The state universities – La Sapienza (www.uniroma1.it), Tor Vergata (www.uniroma2.it) and Roma Tre (www.uniroma3.it) – plus the private LUISS (www. luiss.it) offer exchanges with other European universities. All EU citizens have the same right as Italians to study in Rome's universities, paying the same fees. Get your certificates translated and validated by the Italian consulate in your own country before lodging your application at the *ufficio stranieri* (foreigners' department) of the university of your choice.

Several US universities have campuses in Rome, which students attend on exchange programmes. Private Catholic universities run some of Italy's most highly respected medical faculties. Specialist bookshops are near La Sapienza in San Lorenzo, and on viale Ippocrate (north-east of the campus).

TELEPHONES

Dialling & codes

There are three main types of phone numbers in Rome:

● Land-lines have the area code 06, which must be used whether calling from within or outside the city. Numbers generally have eight digits. If you can't get through, it

DIRECTORY

may be an old number; check the directory or ring enquiries (see below). When phoning Rome from abroad, keep the initial 0.

● Numbers beginning 800 are toll-free. Numbers beginning 840 and 848 are charged at low set rates, no matter where you're calling from or how long the call lasts. These numbers can be called from within Italy only; some of them function only within a single phone district.

● Mobile numbers begin with a 3.

Mobile phones

GSM phones can be used on both 900 and 1800 bands; British, Australian and New Zealand mobiles work fine, but US mobiles are on a different frequency that doesn't work (unless it's a tri-band phone). The main mobile phone networks in Italy are Tim (www.tim.it), Vodafone (www.vodafone.it), Tre (www.tre.it) and Wind (www.wind.it). All have numerous branches located throughout the city.

Operator services

To reverse the charges (make a collect call), dial 170 for the international operator. If you are reversing the charges from a phone box, insert a 10¢ coin (refunded after your call).

The following services operate 24hrs daily:

Operator & Directory Enquiries (in Italian) 1254
(in Italian & English) 892 412
International Operator 170
International Directory Enquiries 892 412
Communication problems (national calls) 187
(international calls) 170
Wake-up calls 4114; an automatic message asks you to dial in the time you want your call (on a 24hr clock) followed by your phone number.

Public phones

Rome has no shortage of public phone boxes and many bars have payphones, most of which are readily available as locals are addicted to mobiles. Most only accept phone cards (schede telefoniche); a few also accept major credit cards. Phone cards cost €5, €15 and €30 and are available from tabacchi (see p224 **Life's Essentials**), some news-stands and some bars.

TIME

Italy is one hour ahead of London, six hours ahead of New York, eight hours behind Sydney and 12 hours behind Wellington. In all EU countries clocks are moved forward one hour in early spring and back again in late autumn.

TIPPING

Foreigners are generally expected to tip more than Italians, but the ten or more per cent that is customary in many countries is considered generous even for the richest-looking tourist in most eateries, where anything between €1 and €5 is normal; some smarter places, however, now include a 10-15% service charge. For drinks, follow the example of many locals, who leave a 10¢ or 20¢ coin on the counter when ordering at a bar. Taxi drivers will be happy if you round the fare up to the nearest whole euro.

TOILETS

If you need a toilet, the easiest thing to do is go to a bar (it won't necessarily be clean or provide toilet paper). There are modern lavatories at or near most major tourist sites, some with attendants to whom you must pay a nominal fee. Fast-food restaurants and department stores may also meet the need. For wheelchair-accessible toilets, see p311.

TOURIST INFORMATION

For tours, see p309 **Tour buses**; for the Vatican tourist office, see below.

Rome's city council operates a number of well-stocked green-painted tourist information kiosks (PIT) that are open 9.30am-7/7.30pm daily (apart from the Fiumicino airport and Termini branches, which open 8am-9pm daily).

For Rome tourist information on your mobile appliance, see http://mobile.turismoroma.it. The excellent, exhaustive www.060608.it website is the city council's one-stop shop for information on museums, galleries, events, hotels and much more besides.

The city council-affiliated APT (Azienda per il Turismo di Roma) no longer has offices open to the public, but its www.romaturismo.com website contains plenty of useful information.

PIT (Punti Informativi Turistici)
For information by phone, call 06 0608.
Piazza Pia, Vatican & Prati. Bus 23, 34, 40Exp, 62, 280, 982. **Open** 9.30am-7pm. **Map** p339 B4.
Piazza delle Cinque Lune, Pantheon & Navona. Bus 30Exp, 70, 81, 87, 116, 116T, 186, 492, 628. **Open** 9.15am-7pm. **Map** p339 D5.
Piazza del Tempio della Pace, Capitoline & Palatine. Bus 60Exp, 75, 85, 87, 117, 175, 186, 810, 850. **Open** 9.30am-7pm. **Map** p344 B2.
Via Nazionale, Trevi & Quirinale. Bus 40Exp, 60Exp, 64, 70, 71, 116, 116T, 170, H. **Open** 9.30am-7.30pm. **Map** p341 C6.
Piazza Sonnino, Trastevere. Bus 23, 280, 630, 780, H/ tram 8. **Open** 9.30am-7.30pm. **Map** p342 D3.
Via Minghetti, Tridente. Bus 62, 63, 81, 85, 95, 117, 119, 160, 175, 204, 492, 628, 630, 850. **Open** 9.15am-7pm. **Map** p341 A6.
Termini station, platform 24, Esquilino. Metro Termini/buses to Termini/tram 5, 14. **Open** 8am-9pm. **Map** p341 E5.
Fiumicino airport, terminal 3. **Open** 9am-7pm.
Piazza Santa Maria Maggiore. Metro Termini/bus 16, 70, 71, 75, 84, 105, 360, 590, 649, 714, H. **Open** 9.30am-7.30pm. **Map** p344 C1.

Ufficio Pellegrini e Turisti
Piazza San Pietro, Vatican (06 6988 1662, www.vaticano.va). Bus 23, 34, 40Exp, 62, 280, 982. **Open** 8.30am-6.15pm Mon-Sat. **Map** p339 A5.
The Vatican's tourist office.

VISAS

EU nationals and citizens of the US, Canada, Australia and New Zealand do not need visas for stays of up to three months. For EU citizens a passport or national ID card valid for travel abroad is sufficient; non-EU citizens must have full passports. In theory, all visitors must declare their presence to the local police (see p316) within eight days of arrival. If you're staying in a hotel, this will be done for you.

WATER

Most of Rome's water comes from a vast underground lake to the north of the city and is completely safe for drinking. Some areas of the centro storico still get water through the ancient aqueducts that draw from springs in the countryside: this water is so good that Romans come from the suburbs to fill up plastic containers with it.

WHEN TO GO

For annual events in the city, *see pp241-244* **Calendar**.

Climate

Spring and autumn are the best times to see Rome; the weather's pleasantly balmy and the city is bathed in a glorious, raking yellow light. To visitors arriving from chillier climes, the weather in May, June, September and October may seem like a fairly convincing approximation of summertime, but the actual Roman summer is a different matter altogether: searing, 40°C heat and energy-sapping humidity mark July and August, when the city empties as Romans scurry for the hills and sea. You may be tempted to do the same.

Between November and February the weather in Rome is very unpredictable: you might strike it lucky with a run of crisp, bright, sunny days, maybe punctuated by the odd bone-shakingly icy blast of wind buffeting in from northern Europe… or you may arrive in the midst of a torrential downpour that shows no sign of letting up, putting a dampener on your sightseeing plans. But there is some compensation: you'll find there's a relative scarcity of other tourists.

Public holidays

On public holidays (*giorni festivi*) virtually all shops, banks and businesses close, although (with the exception of May Day, 15 August and Christmas Day) bars and restaurants tend to stay open. There's only limited public transport on 1 May and Christmas afternoon.

New Year's Day (Capodanno) 1 Jan
Epiphany (La Befana) 6 Jan
Easter Monday (Pasquetta)
Liberation Day 25 Apr
May Day 1 May
Patron Saints' Day (Santi Pietro e Paolo) 29 June
Feast of the Assumption (Ferragosto) 15 Aug
All Saints (Tutti i santi) 1 Nov
Immaculate Conception (Festa dell'Immacolata) 8 Dec
Christmas Day (Natale) 25 Dec
Boxing Day (Santo Stefano) 26 Dec

WOMEN

Rome is generally a safe city for women. Stick to central areas and if you do find yourself being hassled, take comfort in the fact that Italian men are generally all mouth and no trousers. Common sense is usually enough to keep potential harassers at bay: if you're not interested, ignore them and they'll probably go away.

Young Roman blades head for major tourist magnets, like piazza Navona, piazza di Spagna and the Trevi Fountain, to pick up foreign talent. If you would rather enjoy Rome's nocturnal charm without the benefit of a self-appointed guide, stick to the areas around campo de' Fiori, Testaccio or Trastevere. The Termini station area gets seriously seedy after the sun has gone down.

Accommodation

The vast majority of Rome's hotels and *pensioni* are perfectly suitable for women.

If you're worried, avoid those near Termini station and via Nazionale (a major shopping artery that's deserted once the shops shut); stick to more populated areas in the *centro storico*. For women-only accommodation, *see p263* **La Casa Internazionale delle Donne**.

Health

See also p313 **Health**.

In case of gynaecological emergencies, head for the nearest *pronto soccorso* (accident and emergency department; *see p313*). Tampons (*assorbenti interni*) and sanitary towels (*assorbenti esterni*) are cheapest in supermarkets, but also sold at pharmacies and *tabacchi*.

WORKING & LIVING IN ROME

Foreign nationals residing in Italy are obliged to pick up a series of forms and permits. The basic set is described below. EU citizens should have no difficulty getting their documentation once they are in Italy (see the website www.portaleimmigrazione.it, or contact the toll-free number 800 309 309), but non-EU citizens are advised to enquire at an Italian consulate before travelling. There are agencies that specialise in obtaining documents for you if you can't face the procedures yourself – but at a price (see *Pratiche e certificati – agenzie* in the Yellow Pages).

Carta d'Identità (identity card)

You will need three passport photographs, the original and one photocopy of your *permesso di soggiorno* (*see p320*), your passport and a form that will be given to you at your *circoscrizione* – the local branch of the central records office, which eventually issues the ID card. You will also need to be officially resident in Rome (*see below*). There's a €5.42 charge for the card. Consult the phone book (*Comune di Roma: Circoscrizioni*) for your area's office.

Codice fiscale & Partita IVA (tax code & VAT number)

A *codice fiscale* is essential for opening a bank account or setting up utilities contracts. Take your passport and *permesso di soggiorno* (*see below*) to your local tax office (*ufficio delle entrate; see below*). Fill in a form and return a few days later to pick up the card. It can be posted on request.

AVERAGE LOCAL CLIMATE				
Month	Avg High (°C/°F)	Avg Low (°C/°F)	Rainfall (mm/in)	Sunshine (hrs/day)
Jan	12/54	4/39	71/2.8	4
Feb	14/57	4/39	62/2.4	4
Mar	15/59	6/43	57/2.2	6
Apr	18/64	8/46	51/2.0	7
May	23/73	13/55	46/1.8	8
June	26/79	16/61	37/1.5	9
July	30/86	19/66	15/0.6	11
Aug	30/86	20/68	21/0.8	10
Sept	26/79	17/63	63/2.5	8
Oct	22/72	13/55	99/3.9	6
Nov	17/63	9/48	129/5.1	4
Dec	13/55	6/43	93/3.7	4

DIRECTORY

DIRECTORY

The self-employed or anyone doing business in Italy may need a *Partita IVA*. The certificate is free. Most people pay an accountant to handle the formalities. Take your passport and *codice fiscale* to your nearest tax office. Be sure to cancel your VAT number when you no longer need it: failure to do so may result in a visit from tax inspectors years later.

Call the Finance Ministry's information line (848 800 444, www.finanze.it) for details of *uffici delle entrate* (revenue offices); addresses are also in the phone book under *Ministero delle Finanze*. The office you should visit depends on the city district (*circoscrizione*) in which you live; offices open 9am-1pm Mon, Wed, Fri; 9am-1pm, 2.50-4.50pm Tue, Thur.

Permesso/carta di soggiorno (permit to stay)

You need a *permesso di soggiorno* if you're staying in Italy for over three months; you should, in theory, apply for one within eight days of arrival in Italy. Requirements vary depending on whether or not you are an EU citizen. You'll need four passport photographs, your passport (and a photocopy), proof that you have some means of support and reason to be in Italy (preferably a letter from an employer or certificate of registration at a school or university) and a stamp (*marca da bollo* – EU citizens don't, in theory, need this) costing €14.62, available at *tabacchi*.

Both EU and non-EU citizens can now, in theory, apply for their *permesso/carta di soggiorno* at main post offices. Complicated cases may find themselves getting redirected to the *ufficio immigrazione* in via Teofilo Patini (no street number – the office is on the corner of via Salviati; open 8.30-11.30am Mon-Fri). To get to the office, take Metro B to Rebibbia, then bus 437 or 447. For information, call 06 4686 3098.

The *carta* (card) *di soggiorno* is similar to the *permesso* but allows you to stay in Italy indefinitely – though it has to be renewed every five years. EU citizens who have been resident in Italy for at least five years and who also have a renewable *permesso di soggiorno* can request a *carta*. If a foreigner already has a *carta*, their spouse can also request one.

Permesso di lavoro

Most EU citizens do not require a work permit; only those from new member states, as well as non-EU

citizens, are legally obliged to have one, though many don't. A policy introduced in January 2005 places limits on the numbers of people in the latter two categories officially allowed to work in the city. Employers are therefore required to put in a request to the *Direzione Provinciale del Lavoro* (www.lavoro. gov.it) before taking them on. Once authorisation has been granted, a passport and *permesso di soggiorno* (plus photocopies) are needed for a *permesso di lavoro*, obtained from the *Direzione*'s office at via dei Vestini 13 (06 4487 1642, open 9am-noon Mon, Wed, Fri; 9am-noon, 2.45-4.30pm Tue, Thur). The whole business is fiendishly complicated, and you may feel that it's worth leaving it in the hands of an agency (see *Pratiche e certificati – agenzie* in the Yellow Pages) or a lawyer.

Residenza (residency)

This is your registered address in Italy. It's required to buy a car, get customs clearance on goods brought here from abroad and many other transactions. You'll need your *permesso di soggiorno* (*see above*; it must be valid for at least another year), your passport and a residency request form (downloadable from the website www.comune.roma.it). Take everything to your local *circoscrizione* (*see above*), where staff will check that rubbish-collection tax (*nettezza urbana*) for your address has been paid (ask your landlord about this) before issuing the certificate.

Accommodation

Try *Porta Portese*, the *American Magazine* and/or *Wanted in Rome* (for all, *see pp315-316*) and English-language bookshops (*see p222*). Look out for *affittasi* ('for rent') notices on buildings, and check the classifieds in *Il Messaggero* (Thur, Sat). When you move into an apartment, it's normal to pay a month's rent in advance, plus two months' deposit (it should be refunded when you move out, but some landlords create problems over this). You'll probably get a year's renewable contract. Renting through an agency will cost the equivalent of two months' rent in commission.

Bank accounts

To open an account, you'll need a valid *residenza* or *permesso di*

soggiorno, proof of regular income (or a fairly substantial deposit), a *codice fiscale* and your passport.

Doctors

See also p313 **Health** and *p314* **Insurance**.

If you are officially resident in Rome and have a valid *permesso* or *carta di soggiorno* and *codice fiscale* (tax code), you are entitled to the same medical care from the national health service (*Servizio sanitario nazionale*, SSN) that Italians receive. Take the above documents and *certificato di residenza* (plus photocopies) to your nearest ASL (*Azienda sanitaria locale*, 06 7730 7215). Branches are listed in the telephone directory under *Azienda Unità Sanitaria Locale*. You will be able to choose from a list of local doctors. You are eligible for medical treatment for as long as your *permesso* is valid. Non-residents and holders of student *permessi*, although they are not entitled to free medical treatment, can still receive SSN medical care if they pay regular monthly health service contributions.

Work

Casual employment can be hard to find, so try to sort out work in advance. English-language schools and translation agencies are mobbed with applicants, so qualifications and experience count. The classified ads paper *Porta Portese* (*see p315*) has lots of job ads. Other good places to look are *Wanted in Rome* (see *p316*) and noticeboards in English-language bookshops (*see p222*). You can also place ads in any of the media above. For serious jobs, check *Il Messaggero* and *La Repubblica*, or these agencies:

Adecco

Via Ostiense 91A, Testaccio (06 571 7821, www.adecco.it). Metro Piramide/bus 23, 60Exp, 118, 271, 280, 716, 719, 769/ tram 3. **Open** 9am-1pm, 2-6pm Mon-Fri.

Manpower

Via Barberini 58, Trevi & Quirinale (06 4287 1339, www. manpower.it). Metro Barberini/ bus 52, 53, 61, 62, 63, 80Exp, 95, 116, 119, 175, 492, 590, 630. **Open** 10am-noon, 3-5pm Mon-Fri. **Map** p341 C5. **Other locations** via Molajoni Pio 70 (06 4353 5349, fax 06 4353 5357).

Vocabulary

Romans always appreciate attempts at spoken Italian, no matter how incompetent. In hotels and all but the most spit-and-sawdust restaurants, there's likely to be someone with basic English.

There are two forms of address in the second person singular: *lei* (formal, used with strangers and older people) and *tu* (informal). In practice, the personal pronoun is usually omitted.

PRONUNCIATION

a – as in ask; **e** – like a in age or e in sell; **i** – like ea in east; **o** – as in hotel or hot; **u** – as in boot.

Romans have a lot of trouble with their consonants. **C** often comes out nearer **g**; **n**, if in close proximity to an **r**, disappears. Remember: **c** and **g** both go soft in front of **e** and **i** (becoming like the initial sounds of **ch**eck and **g**iraffe respectively). An **h** after any consonant makes it hard; before a vowel, it is silent.

c before a, o and u: as in **c**at; **g** before a, o and u: as in **g**et; **gl** like lli in million; **gn** like ny in can**y**on; **qu** as in **qu**ick; **r** always rolled; **s** has two sounds, as in **s**oap or ro**s**e; **sc** like the sh in **sh**ame; **sch** like the sc in **sc**out; **z** can be **ts** or **dz**.

USEFUL PHRASES

hello/goodbye (informal) *ciao, salve;* **good morning** *buon giorno;* **good evening** *buona sera;* **good night** *buona notte;* **please** *per favore, per piacere;* **thank you** *grazie;* **you're welcome** *prego;* **excuse me, sorry** *mi scusi;* (formal), *scusa* (informal); **I'm sorry, but...** *mi dispiace...;* **I don't speak Italian (very well)** *non parlo (molto bene) l'italiano;* **do you speak English?** *parla inglese?* **can I use/where's the toilet?** *posso usare/dov'è il bagno/la toilette?* **open** *aperto;* **closed** *chiuso;* **entrance** *entrata;* **exit** *uscita*

FEMALE SELF-DEFENCE

no thank you, I can find my own way *no grazie, non ho bisogna di una guida* **can you leave me alone?** *mi vuole lasciare in pace?*

DIRECTIONS

(turn) left *(giri a) sinistra;* **(it's on the) right** *(è a/sulla) destra;* **straight on** *sempre diritto;* **where is...?** *dov'è...?* **could you show me the way to...?** *mi potrebbe indicare la strada per...?* **is it near/far?** *è vicino/lontano?*

TRANSPORT

car *macchina;* **bus** *autobus, auto;* **coach** *pullman;* **taxi** *tassi, taxi;* **train** *treno;* **tram** *tram;* **plane** *aereo;* **bus stop** *fermata (d'autobus);* **station** *stazione;* **platform** *binario;* **ticket/s** *biglietto/biglietti;* **one way** *solo andata;* **return** *andata e ritorno;* **(I'd like) a ticket for...** *(vorrei) un biglietto per...;* **where can I buy tickets?** *dove si comprono i biglietti?* **are you getting off at the next stop?** (ie get out of my way if you're not) *che, scende alla prossima?* **I'm sorry, I didn't know I had to stamp it** *mi dispiace, non sapevo che lo dovevo timbrare*

COMMUNICATIONS

phone *telefono;* **fax** *fax;* **stamp** *francobollo;* **how much is a stamp for England/Australia/ the US?** *quanto viene un francobollo per l'Inghilterra/l'Australia/ gli Stati Uniti?* **can I send a fax?** *posso mandare un fax?* **can I make a phone call?** *posso telefonare?* **letter** *lettera;* **postcard** *cartolina;* **courier** *corriere, pony*

SHOPPING

I'd like to try the blue sandals/ black shoes/brown boots *vorrei provare i sandali blu/le scarpe nere/ gli stivali marroni;* **do you have it/them in other colours?** *ce l'ha in altri colori?* **I take (shoe) size...** *porto il numero...;* **I take (dress) size...** *porto la taglia...;* **it's too loose/too tight/just right** *mi sta largo/stretto/bene;* **can you give me a little more/ less?** *mi dia un po' di più/meno?* **100 grams of...** *un etto di...* **300 grams of...** *tre etti di...* **one kilo of...** *un kilo/chilo di...* **five kilos of...** *cinque chili di...* **a litre/two litres of...** *un litro/ due litri di*

EATING, DRINKING & ACCOMMODATION

I'd like to book a table for four at eight *vorrei prenotare una tavola per quattro alle otto;* **that was poor/good/delicious** *era mediocre/buono/ottimo;* **the bill** *il conto;* **is service included?** *è incluso il servizio?* **I think there's a mistake in this bill** *credo che il conto sia sbagliato;* **a reservation** *una prenotazione;* **I'd like to book a single/twin/double room** *vorrei prenotare una camera singola/doppia/ matrimoniale;* **I'd prefer a room with a bath/shower/window over the courtyard** *preferirei una camera con vasca da bagno/doccia/ finestra sul cortile;* **can you bring me breakfast in bed?** *mi porti la colazione al letto?*

DAYS, NIGHTS & TIMES

Monday *lunedì;* **Tuesday** *martedì;* **Wednesday** *mercoledì;* **Thursday** *giovedì;* **Friday** *venerdì;* **Saturday** *sabato;* **Sunday** *domenica* **yesterday** *ieri;* **today** *oggi;* **tomorrow** *domani;* **morning** *mattina;* **afternoon** *pomeriggio;* **evening** *sera;* **night** *notte;* **weekend** *fine settimana, weekend* **could you tell me the time?** *mi sa (formal)/sai (informal) dire l'ora?* **it's ... o'clock** *sono le (number);* **it's half past...** *sono le (number) e mezza;* **when does it (re)open?** *a che ora (ri)apre?* **does it close for lunch?** *chiude per pranzo?*

NUMBERS & MONEY

0 *zero;* 1 *uno;* 2 *due;* 3 *tre;* 4 *quattro;* 5 *cinque;* 6 *sei;* 7 *sette;* 8 *otto;* 9 *nove;* 10 *dieci;* 11 *undici;* 12 *dodici;* 13 *tredici;* 14 *quattordici;* 15 *quindici;* 16 *sedici;* 17 *diciassette;* 18 *diciotto;* 19 *diciannove;* 20 *venti;* 30 *trenta;* 40 *quaranta;* 50 *cinquanta;* 60 *sessanta;* 70 *settanta;* 80 *ottanta;* 90 *novanta;* 100 *cento;* 200 *duecento;* 1,000 *mille;* 2,000 *duemila* **how much is it/does it cost?** *quanto costa/quant'è/quanto viene?* **do you take credit cards?** *si accettano le carte di credito?* **can I pay in pounds/dollars/ travellers' cheques?** *posso pagare in sterline/dollari/ con i travellers?*

Menu

ROMAN OFFAL SPECIALITIES

coda alla vaccinara oxtail braised in a celery broth; **pajata** veal/lamb intestines with the mother's milk still inside; **fagioli con le cotiche** beans with pork scratchings; **animelle** pancreas and thymus glands, generally fried; **tripa** tripe; **cervello** brain; **lingua** tongue; **guanciale** cured pig's cheek; **nervetti** strips of cartilage.

PIATTI DI CARNE – MEAT DISHES

carpaccio, bresaola thinly sliced cured beef; **ossobuco** beef shins with marrow jelly inside; **polpette** meatballs; **porchetta** roast piglet; **salsicce** sausages; **saltimbocca** veal strips and ham; **spezzatino** casseroled meat; **spiedini** on a spit; **straccetti** stir-fried beef/veal strips.

FORMAGGI – CHEESES

cacio, caciotta cow's milk cheese; **gorgonzola** strong blue cheese, in creamy (*dolce*) or crumbly (*piccante*) varieties; **parmigiano** parmesan; **pecorino romano** hard, tangy sheep's cheese; **ricotta** crumbly white soft cheese; **stracchino** creamy, soft white cheese.

PESCE – FISH

Sarago, dentice, marmora, orata, fragolino bream of various kinds; **alici, acciughe** anchovies; **baccalà** salt cod; **branzino, spigola** sea bass; **cernia** grouper; **merluzzo** cod; **pesce San Pietro** John Dory; **pesce spada** swordfish; **razza, arzilla** skate or ray; **rombo** turbot; **salmone** salmon; **sarde, sardine** sardines; **sogliola** sole; **tonno** tuna; **trota** trout.

acqua water; **olio d'oliva** olive oil; **pane** bread; **pepe** pepper; **sale** salt; **zucchero** sugar; **vino** wine.

SUGHI, CONDIMENTI E RIPIENI – SAUCES, TOPPINGS & FILLINGS

alle vongole with clams; **al pesto** with a sauce of pine nuts, pecorino and basil; **al ragù** with minced meat and tomatoes (ie 'bolognese', a term not used in Italy); **al sugo** with puréed cooked tomatoes; **all'amatriciana** with tomato, chilli, onion and sausage; **all' arrabbiata** with tomato and chilli; **alla carbonara** with bacon, egg and parmesan;

alla puttanesca with olives, capers and garlic in hot oil; **cacio e pepe** with sheep's cheese and black pepper; (ravioli) **ricotta e spinaci** (ravioli) stuffed with cottage cheese and spinach; **agnolotti, tortellini** pasta like ravioli but usually meat-filled.

CARNE – MEAT

abbacchio, agnello lamb; **capra, capretto** goat, kid; **coniglio** rabbit; **maiale** pork; **manzo** beef; **pancetta** similar to bacon; **pollo** chicken; **prosciutto cotto** ham; **prosciutto crudo** Parma ham; **tacchino** turkey; **vitello** veal

FRUTTI DI MARE – SEAFOOD

astice, aragosta lobster; **calamari** squid; **cozze** mussels; **crostacei** shellfish; **gamberi, gamberetti** shrimps, prawns; **granchio** crab; **mazzancolle** king prawns; **moscardini** baby octopus; **ostriche** oysters; **polipo, polpo** octopus; **seppie, seppioline** cuttlefish; **telline** small clams; **totani** baby flying squid; **vongole** clams.

VERDURA/IL CONTORNO – VEGETABLES/SIDES

asparagi asparagus; **basilico** basil; **broccoli siciliani** broccoli; **broccolo** green cauliflower; **broccoletti** tiny broccoli sprigs, cooked with the leaves; **carciofi** artichokes (*alla romana* steamed; *alla giudea* deep-fried); **carote** carrots; **cavolfiore** cauliflower; **cicoria** green leaf vegetable resembling dandelion; **cipolle** onions; **fagioli** haricot or borlotti beans; **fagiolini** green beans; **fave** broad beans; **funghi** mushrooms; **funghi porcini** boletus mushrooms; **insalata** salad; **lattuga** lettuce; **melanzane** aubergine; **patate** potatoes; **patatine fritte** french fries; **peperoncino** chilli; **peperoni** peppers (capsicum); **piselli** peas; **pomodori** tomatoes; **porri** leeks; **prezzemolo** parsley; **puntarelle** bitter Roman salad usually dressed with an anchovy sauce; **radicchio** bitter purple lettuce; **rughetta, rucola** rocket; **scarola** type of lettuce; **sedano** celery; **spinaci** spinach; **verza** cabbage; **zucchine** courgettes.

FRUTTA – FRUIT

albicocche apricots; **ananas** pineapple; **arance** oranges; **cachi** persimmons; **ciliege** cherries; **coccomero, anguria** watermelon; **fichi** figs; **fragole, fragoline** strawberries, wild strawberries; **frutti di bosco** woodland berries; **mele** apples; **nespole** loquats; **pere** pears;

pesche peaches; **prugne, susine** plums; **uva** grapes.

DOLCI/IL DESSERT – DESSERTS

gelato ice cream; **pannacotta** 'cooked cream', a very thick, blancmange-like cream; **sorbetto** sorbet; **tiramisù** mascarpone and coffee sponge; **torta della nonna** flan of pâtisserie cream and pine nuts; **torta di mele** apple flan; **millefoglie** flaky pastry cake.

PIZZA & PIZZA TOPPINGS

calzone a sealed pizza pie, usually filled with cheese, tomato and ham; **capricciosa** ham, hard-boiled eggs, artichokes and olives; **funghi** mushrooms; **marinara** plain tomato, sometimes with anchovies; **margherita** tomato and mozzarella; **napoli,**

napoletana tomato, anchovies and mozzarella; **quattro formaggi** four cheeses; **quattro stagioni** mozzarella, artichoke, egg and mushrooms.

PIZZERIA EXTRAS

bruschetta toast with garlic rubbed into it and oil on top, and usually diced raw tomatoes; **crochette** potato croquettes; **crostini** slices of toast, usually with a grilled cheese and anchovy topping; **filetto di baccalà** deep-fried salt cod in batter; **olive ascolane** deep-fried olives stuffed with sausage meat; **suppli** deep-fried rice balls with mozzarella inside (may contain minced meat).

GOOD VEGGIE OPTIONS

orecchiette ai broccoletti/cima di rape ear-shaped pasta with broccoli sprigs/green turnip-tops; **pasta e ceci** soup with pasta and chickpeas; **pasta e fagioli** soup with pasta and borlotti beans; **pasta alla puttanesca/alla checca** based on olives, capers and tomatoes, though anchovies (*alici*) are sometimes slipped into the former; **penne all'arrabbiata** pasta with tomato sauce and lots of chilli; **ravioli** acceptable if filled with *ricotta e spinaci* and served with *burro e salvia* (butter and sage); **spaghetti aglio, olio e peperoncino** with garlic, chilli and olive oil; **spaghetti cacio e pepe** with crumbled salty sheep's cheese and black pepper; **fagioli all'uccelletto** haricot beans with tomato, garlic and olive oil; **melanzane alla parmigiana** aubergine with mozzarella (occasionally has meat in the topping); **scamorza** grilled cheese – specify without ham (*senza prosciutto*) or without anchovies (*senza alici*).

DIRECTORY

Glossary

Amphitheatre oval open-air theatre in ancient Rome
Apse large recess at the high-altar end of a church
Atrium courtyard

Baldacchino canopy supported by columns
Baroque artistic period in the 17th-18th centuries, in which the decorative element became increasingly florid, culminating in the **rococo** (*qv*)
Basilica ancient Roman rectangular public building; rectangular Christian church

Campanile bell tower
Caryatid supporting pillar carved in the shape of a woman
Cavea step-like seating area found in an **amphitheatre** (*qv*) or **theatre** (*qv*)
Chiaroscuro from Italian *chiaro* (light) and *scuro* (dark), juxtaposition of light and shade to bring out relief and volume
Ciborio dome-shaped canopy on columns over high altar
Clivus ancient name for a street on the side of a hill
Cloister exterior courtyard surrounded on all sides by a covered walkway
Column upright architectural element that can be round, square or rectangular; usually structural, but sometimes merely decorative, and usually free-standing; conforms to one of the classical **orders** (*qv*)
Confessio crypt under raised altar
Cosmati, cosmatesque mosaic technique using coloured marble chips, usually to decorate floors and church fittings
Cryptoporticus underground corridor
Cubicolum bedroom

Decumanus main road, usually running east–west
Domus Roman city house

Entablature section above a column or row of columns that includes the frieze and cornice

Ex-voto an offering given to fulfil a vow; often a small model in silver of the limb, organ or loved one cured as a result of prayer

Fresco painting technique in which pigment is applied to wet plaster

Giallo antico yellowish marble
Gothic architectural and artistic style of the late Middle Ages (from the 12th century), of soaring, pointed arches
Greek cross (of a church) in the shape of a cross with arms of equal length
Grisaille painting in shades of grey to mimic sculpture

Insula an ancient multi-storey city apartment block
Intarsio form of mosaic made from pieces of wood of different colours; also known as intaglio

Largo square
Latin cross (of a church) in the shape of a cross with one arm longer than the others
Loggia gallery open on one side
Lunette semicircular area, usually above a door or window

Maiolica fine earthenware with coloured decoration on an opaque white glaze
Mannerism High Renaissance style of the late 16th century; characterised in painting by elongated, contorted human figures
Matronium gallery (usually screened) where women sat in early Christian and Byzantine basilicas
Mithraeum temple, usually underground, to the deity Mithras

Narthex enclosed porch in front of a church
Nave main body of a church; the longest section of a **Latin-cross** (*qv*) church
Necropolis literally, 'city of the dead'; graveyard
Nymphaeum grotto with pool and fountain dedicated to the Nymphs (female water deities)

Ogival (used of arches, windows and so on) curving in to a point at the top
Orders rules governing the proportions and decoration of columns, the most common being the very simple Doric, the curlicue Ionic, and the Corinthian, which is decorated with stylised acanthus leaves

Palazzo large and/or important building (not necessarily a palace)
Pendentives four concave triangular sections on top of piers supporting a dome
Peristyle temple or court surrounded by columns
Piazza square
Pilaster a rectangular column designed to project slightly from a wall
Pillar upright architectural element, always free-standing, but not conforming to classical **orders** (*qv*); *see also* **column**

Rococo highly decorative style of the 18th century
Romanesque architectural style of the early Middle Ages (c500-1200), drawing on Roman and Byzantine influences
Rosso antico red-coloured marble brought from Matapan, Greece, by the Romans

Sarcophagus a coffin made of stone or marble
Spandrel the near-triangular space between the top of two adjoining arches and the ceiling (or other architectural feature) resting above them

Tepidarium warm (as opposed to hot), steam-filled room in a Roman baths complex
Theatre in ancient times, a semicircular open-air theatre
Titulus an early Christian meeting place
Transept shorter arms of a **Latin-cross** (*qv*) church
Travertine cream-coloured calcareous limestone
Triclinium dining room
Triumphal arch arch in front of an **apse** (*qv*), usually over the high altar; monumental victory arch
Trompe l'oeil decorative painting effect that makes a flat surface appear three-dimensional

Further Reference

BOOKS

Classics

Catullus *The Poems* Sometimes malicious, sometimes pornographic
Juvenal *Satires* Contemporary view of ancient Rome's seedy underbelly
Ovid *The Erotic Poems* Handbook for cynical lovers that got Ovid banished from Rome
Suetonius *The Twelve Caesars* Salacious biographies of rulers from Julius Caesar to Domitian
Virgil *The Aeneid* Rome's foundation myth is a great yarn

Fiction & literature

Lyndsey Davis *The Falco series* Ancient detective romps
Michael Dibdin *Vendetta* Thriller set in contemporary Rome
George Eliot *Middlemarch* Dorothea's big honeymoon let-down takes place in 19th-century Rome
Nathaniel Hawthorn *The Marble Faun* A quaint, moralising novel about two female artists in Rome
Henry James *The Portrait of a Lady* Also try *Daisy Miller* and a couple of essays in *Italian Hours*
Elsa Morante *History* Compelling evocation of life for the very poor in wartime Rome
Shakespeare *Julius Caesar, Antony and Cleopatra, Titus Andronicus, Coriolanus*

Non-fiction

Donald Dudley *Roman Society* Culture, politics and economics from 9th century BC to 4th century AD
Paul Ginsborg *Italy and its Discontents* Fine introduction to the ups and downs of post-war Italy
Michael Grant *History of Rome* Highly readable and full of facts
Peter Hebblethwaite *In the Vatican* Opinionated insight into the inner workings of the Vatican
Christopher Hibbert *Biography of a City* Engaging account of the history of Rome
Tobias Jones *The Dark Heart of Italy* Exploration of some of the country's contemporary secrets
John Kelly *The Oxford Dictionary of Popes* Life stories of the pontiffs
Georgina Masson *Queen Christina* Biography of the Catholic Church's illustrious Protestant

convert, giving great insights into 17th-century Rome
Alexander Stille *The Sack of Rome, Excellent Cadavers* Studies of Italy under Berlusconi, and of the Mafia
Rudolf Wittkower *Art and Architecture in Italy 1600-1750* All about the Baroque

FILMS

Italian

See also pp249-257 Film.

Accattone
(Pier Paolo Pasolini, 1961)
Sub-proletarian no-hoper Franco Citti careers from bad to worse to ignominious early death in Testaccio in this devastating portrait of the lowest of Rome's low
Bellissima (Luchino Visconti, 1951)
Screen-struck mamma Anna Magnani pushes her plain, ungifted daughter through the agony of the film-studio casting circuit
Caro Diario (Dear Diary)
(Nanni Moretti, 1994)
As much a wry love letter to Moretti's home town as a diary
La Dolce Vita
(Federico Fellini, 1960)
The late, great Fellini's unforgettable portrait of the fast-lane, paparazzo-fuelled life in 1950s and '60s Rome
Fellini's Roma
(Federico Fellini, 1972)
Patchwork of cameos with visual gems that only the master could pull off
Mamma Roma (Pier Paolo Pasolini, 1962)
Anna Magnani as a mother who strives, and fails, to keep her son from a bad end in the mean streets of Rome's outskirts
Roma, Città Aperta (Roberto Rossellini, 1945)
This semi-documentary on the wartime Resistance is considered the foundation stone of neo-realism

International

The Agony and the Ecstasy
(Carol Reed, 1965)
Charlton Heston – looking much like a muscly Michelangelo statue, if not the artist himself – daubs the Sistine ceiling as Pope Rex Harrison looks on

Ben-Hur (William Wilder, 1959)
Charlton Heston pushes sexual ambivalence to its limits in this epic, with religion and a chariot race chucked in for good measure
Gladiator (Ridley Scott, 2000)
Russell Crowe's general Maximus flexes his muscles in the Colosseum, watched by Emperor Commodus
Ocean's Twelve
(Steven Soderbergh, 2004)
George, Brad, et al target a Roman art museum for their big heist
Quo Vadis?
(Mervyn Le Roy, 1951)
Blood, sand and love in the lions' den; a huge (and hugely long) epic
Roman Holiday
(William Wyler, 1953)
Endlessly endearing story of bored princess Audrey Hepburn on the lam in Rome – uniquely for its time, it was filmed on location
The Roman Spring of Mrs Stone (Jose Quintero, 1961)
Fading, widowed Vivien Leigh tries to spice up her Roman holiday with an affair with gigolo Warren Beatty
Spartacus (Stanley Kubrick, 1960)
Kirk Douglas does his best to get the slaves revolting
The Talented Mr Ripley
(Anthony Minghella, 1999)
Jude and Matt play out part of their tortuous relationship in Rome
Three Coins in the Fountain
(Jean Negulesco, 1954)
Rome looks like one big, luscious postcard, and the three American tourist lasses get their Latin lovers

WEBSITES

For information on museums, archaeological sites and events in the city, your first port of call should be the exhaustive **www.060608.it**. The Cultural Heritage Ministry's website **www.beniculturali.it** is rather more difficult to navigate.

Other informative sites include:
www.atac.roma.it
Transport in and around the city, with downloadable maps and a useful journey-planner
www.pierreci.it
Information and bookings for museums and exhibitions
www.romaturismo.com
The city council/APT (*see p318*) site: exhibitions, theatres and what to do with your kids

Content Index

DIRECTORY

Venue Index

DIRECTORY

DIRECTORY

DIRECTORY

DIRECTORY

DIRECTORY

Advertisers' Index

Please refer to the relevant pages for contact details.

INDEX

Maps

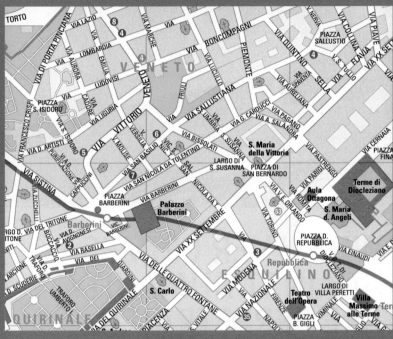

Place of interest and/or entertainment ......
Railway station ....
Parks ....
Area name .... TRIDENTE
Metro lines .... ✕
Hospital .... H
Church .... ⚲

WHEREVER CRIMES AGAINST HUMANITY ARE PERPETRATED.

Across borders and above politics.
Against the most heinous abuses
and the most dangerous oppressors.
From conduct in wartime
to economic, social, and cultural rights.
Everywhere we go,
we build an unimpeachable case
for change and advocate action
at the highest levels.

HUMAN RIGHTS WATCH TYRANNY HAS A WITNESS

WWW.HRW.ORG

HUMA
RIGHT
WATC

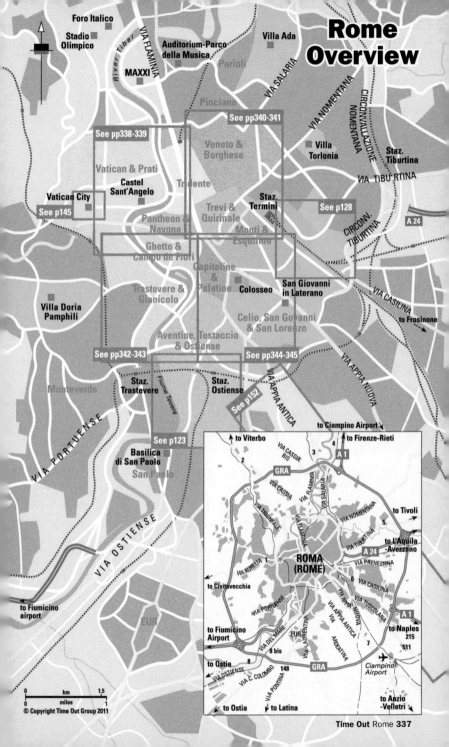

Rome Overview

Foro Italico
Stadio Olimpico
VIA FLAMINIA
River Tiber
MAXXI
Auditorium-Parco della Musica
Villa Ada
Parioli
Pinciano
VIA SALARIA
VIA NOMENTANA
CIRCONVALLAZIONE NOMENTANA

See pp338-339
Vatican & Prati
Veneto & Borghese
Villa Torlonia
See pp340-341
Staz. Tiburtina
VIA TIBURTINA

Vatican City
See p145
Castel Sant'Angelo
Tridente
Pantheon & Navona
Trevi & Quirinale
Staz. Termini
See p128
A 24

Ghetto & Campo de' Fiori
Monti & Esquilino
CIRCONV. TIBURTINA

Capitoline & Palatine
Colosseo
San Giovanni in Laterano

Trastevere & Gianicolo
VIA CASILINA
to Frosinone

Villa Doria Pamphili
Celio, San Giovanni & San Lorenzo

See pp342-343
Aventine, Testaccio & Ostense
See pp344-345
VIA APPIA NUOVA

Monteverde
Fiume Tevere
Staz. Trastevere
Staz. Ostiense
VIA APPIA ANTICA

VIA PORTUENSE
See p152

See p123
Basilica di San Paolo
San Paolo
to Ciampino Airport

VIA OSTIENSE
to Fiumicino airport
EUR

to Viterbo
VIA CASSIA BIS
A 1
to Firenze-Rieti
4
GRA
2
3
VIA CASSIA
VIA FLAMINIA
VIA SALARIA
to Tivoli
VIA NOMENTANA
VIA TIBURTINA
5
to L'Aquila -Avezzano
A 24
VIA TRIONFALE
VIA FLAMINIA
ROMA (ROME)
VIA PRENESTINA
VIA AURELIA
1
6
VIA CASILINA
to Civitavecchia
VIA TUSCOLANA
A 1
VIA PORTUENSE
VIA APPIA NUOVA
to Naples
215
to Fiumicino Airport
VIA DEL MARE
EURENTINA
VIA AURENTINA
VIA APPIA ANTICA
ARGEATINA
511
7
to Ostia
8 bis
GRA
Ciampino Airport
8
148
VIA OSTIENSE
VIA C. COLOMBO
VIA PONTINA
to Ostia
to Latina
to Anzio -Velletri

km 0 — 1.5
miles 0 — 1
© Copyright Time Out Group 2011

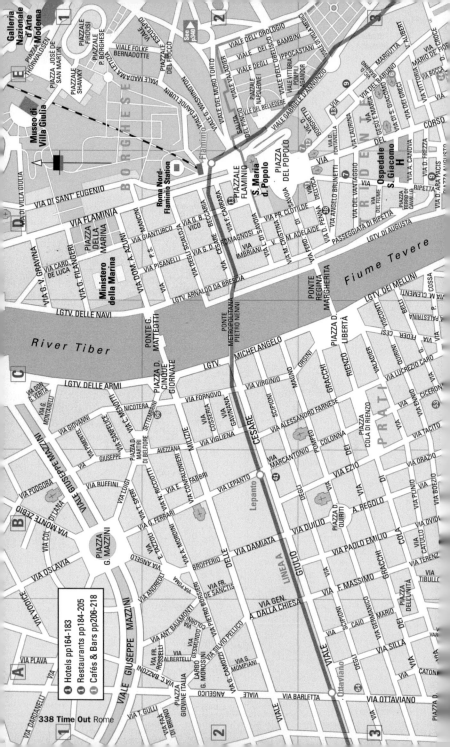

Galleria
Nazionale d'Arte
Moderna

Museo di
Villa Giulia

Roma Nord-
Flaminio Station

River Tiber

Fiume Tevere

PIAZZA
G. MAZZINI

S. Maria
d. Popolo

PIAZZA
DEL POPOLO

Ministero
della Marina

Ospedale
S. Giacomo

1 Hotels pp164-183
2 Restaurants pp184-205
3 Cafés & Bars pp206-218

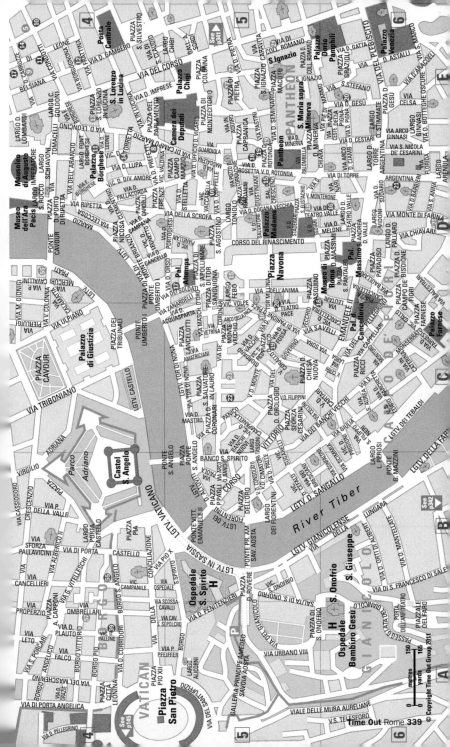

See p341

See p342

See p145

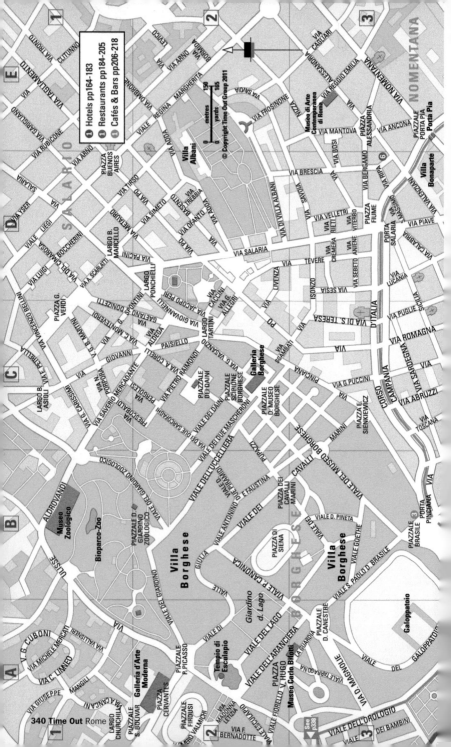

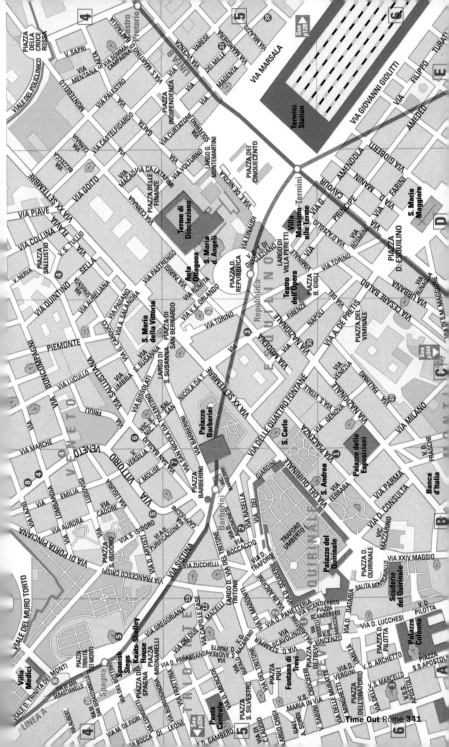

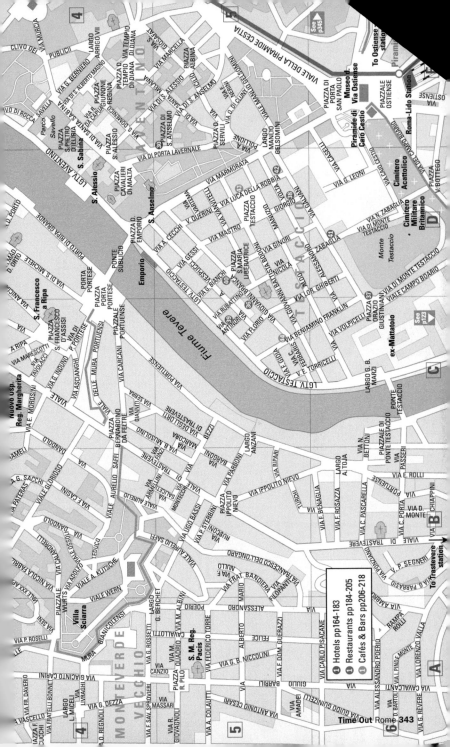

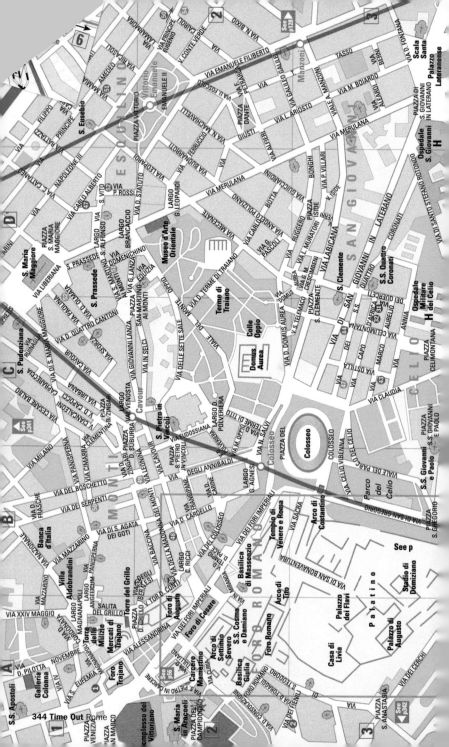

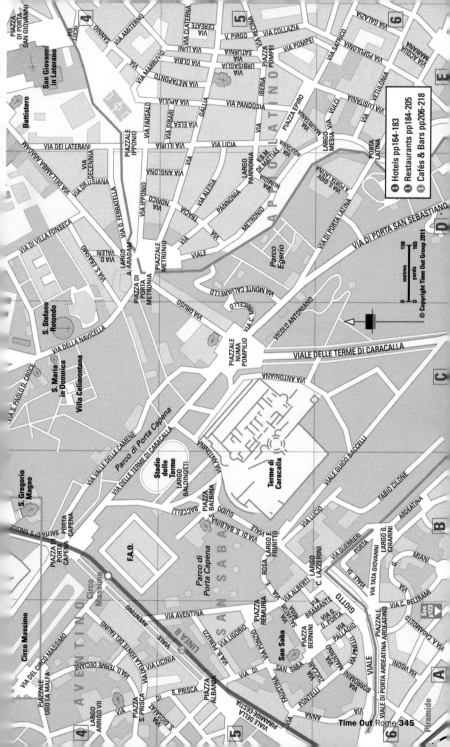

Street Index

STREET INDEX

STREET INDEX

STREET INDEX

Central Rome

Rome Metro

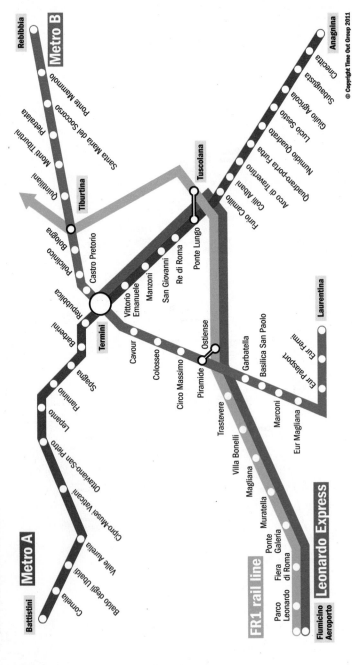

© Copyright Time Out Group 2011